Advertising theory and practice

Advertising theory and practice

C. H. SANDAGE, Ph.D.
Professor Emeritus
University of Illinois
President, Farm Research Institute

VERNON FRYBURGER, Ph.D.
Professor of Advertising and Marketing
Chairman, Department of Advertising
Northwestern University

Eighth Edition
1971

RICHARD D. IRWIN, INC., Homewood, Illinois 60430
Irwin-Dorsey International, London, England   WC2H 9NJ
Irwin-Dorsey Limited, Georgetown, Ontario   L7G 4B3

EIGHTH EDITION

First Printing, April, 1971
Second Printing, May, 1972
Third Printing, June 1973

Library of Congress Catalog Card No. 77–149904

PRINTED IN THE UNITED STATES OF AMERICA

PREFACE

THIS BOOK is intended to give the student broad perspective and penetrating understanding of advertising—its social and economic functions, its role in business, how it works, how it is planned and created, its challenges and opportunities.

Advertising is dynamic. It changes with changing markets, changing life styles, changing methods of distribution, and changing techniques of communication. Significant developments during the past few years include a growing awareness that advertising is an institution performing essential social and economic functions, a recognition that advertising must be planned in the context of total marketing strategy, a more sophisticated use of research to better understand consumer motivation and behavior, a more concerted effort to build favorable brand and corporate identities, a greater use of information bearing on media audiences, and a burgeoning concern about consumer welfare.

This eighth edition of *Advertising Theory and Practice* incorporates all of these developments. It retains the social consciousness of previous editions and emphasizes the importance of professional standards of performance. It places the consumer in the pivotal role and consistently demonstrates that serving the consumer's interest, popularly referred to in recent years as consumerism, is not only a matter of ethics, it also is good business.

Part I positions advertising as a subsystem within an economic system which in turn is part of a larger system of social values. As a form of communication, advertising is viewed as being neither good nor bad. It can, however, be used for good or bad purposes depending on the value system by which it is judged. Generalizations about advertising should distinguish between process and practice. The great diversity of practices and the uniqueness of each advertising situation make any generalizing tenuous at best.

Part II involves the student in total marketing thought. Here is set forth the basic philosophy that advertising should interpret want-satisfying qualities of products in terms of consumer wants. This becomes the unifying theme for a logical progression through all stages of advertising planning and execution.

Research is emphasized to highlight the importance of building an advertising program on a foundation of facts, to indicate the kinds of facts that should be sought, and to demonstrate how such information can be used in solving the full range of advertising problems. With a research viewpoint the student is more apt to think analytically, to probe for deeper understanding, and to develop a healthy respect for the uncertainties in the present state of the art.

Recognizing that the quality of an advertisement largely depends on the quality of the thinking that precedes the writing and designing, Part III concentrates on consumer motivation and the communication process. Chapters 12, 13, and 14 explain how advertising works in the context of prevailing behavioral science concepts. Chapters 15, 16, and 17 relate theories of verbal and visual communication to the development of advertising ideas. Chapter 18 examines modern graphic arts processes and offers a brief glimpse of television production.

Significant among recent trends is the top priority that management is assigning to measures of advertising effectiveness. With larger budgets, keener competition, greater plant capacity, and greater dependence on new products, the need for more efficient advertising is apparent. Part V evaluates current methods of measurement and indicates techniques that hold promise for the future.

The general organization of previous editions is retained. It is based on the idea that a sound theoretical approach is the most practical approach to any problem, that one should have a clear concept of advertising before he begins constructing an advertisement. Such a treatment appeals to the student's desire to learn the "whys" as well as the "hows."

To the many educators, former students, and practitioners who gave counsel and advice, a note of deep gratitude. Their number is legion. Failure to enumerate names here does not indicate lack of appreciation, but rather failure in keeping a catalog of all who have influenced our thinking.

March, 1971

C. H. SANDAGE
VERNON FRYBURGER

CONTENTS

tion. Physical standards for consumer goods. Hidden psychological qualities. The road map concept. Who should initiate communication? The protection of competition. Consumer education. The factor of persuasion.

part III
The advertising
message

part IV
Advertising media

costs. Standard rate and data service. Editorial or program content. Advertiser usage. Summary.

chapter 25

OPINION AND ATTITUDE TESTS   558

Opinion ratings. Selecting the test group. Criteria for judging. Rating techniques. Evaluation. ATTITUDE MEASUREMENT: Rating scales. Brand preferences. PROTECTIVE TECHNIQUES.

chapter 26

RECOGNITION AND RECALL   577

THE RECOGNITION METHOD: Usefulness of readership scores. Evaluation. LARORATORY TESTS OF RECOGNITION. RECALL TESTS: Gallup & Robinson's impact post-test. Dummy magazine tests. Portfolio tests. Television recall tests. Association tests. Awareness and knowledge tests.

chapter 27

CONTROLLED EXPERIMENTS IN THE FIELD   594

INQUIRY TESTS: External variables affecting inquiries. Split run. Keying the advertisement. Media tests. Evaluation. SALES TESTING: Single-variable experimental design. Selection of test and control markets. Measuring sales. Multivariable experimental design. Matched samples of exposed and nonexposed groups.

part VI
The advertising
organization

chapter 28

THE ADVERTISING AGENCY   619

History. Functions of a modern agency. Agency organization. Coordination of complete campaign. Protection of ideas. Methods of paying the agency. Qualifications for agency commission. Appraisal of the commission system. Specialized agencies. Future of the advertising agency.

chapter 29

THE ADVERTISING DEPARTMENT   642

Organization of advertising department. Relations with other departments. Functions of the advertising department. Choosing the agency. Working with the agency. Checking on work of agency. Control of advertising expenditures. Getting new ideas.

part I

Basic values and functions

chapter 1
INTRODUCTION

PERHAPS NO STUDENT will approach the reading of this book without already having formed some ideas about advertising. Nearly everybody encounters advertising every day. Nearly everybody, therefore, has some thoughts on the subject. The tendency is to judge advertising as good or bad, to single out ads that one likes or dislikes, to wonder if advertising is worth the large sums of money spent on it, to question the contribution advertising makes to social welfare. Public opinion on these matters warrants consideration. However, exposure to advertising does not reveal the thinking behind it. Hopefully, the reader of this book will discover "there is more to it than meets the eye."

Several views

Advertising is multidimensional. It can be viewed as a form of communication, as a component of an economic system, and as a means of financing the mass media.

As a *form of communication* the advertising message, or advertisement, is delivered to its intended audience through the various media including newspapers, television, magazines, radio, billboards, and direct mail. Advertising is distinguished from other forms of communication in that the advertiser pays the medium to deliver the message. For this payment the advertiser receives the opportunity to control the message. Within legal constraints designed to prevent deception and assure fair competition, and within standards of practice enforced by the media, the advertiser is free to say what he wants to say the way he wants to say it. He can select the particular issue of a newspaper or magazine in which the message will run. He can select the hour and even the minute when

3

the television or radio message will be broadcast. The style of presentation usually identifies the message as an advertisement. If it is not readily distinguishable from a medium's editorial or program content, the notation "this is an advertisement" and the name of the advertiser or sponsoring organization are included. As a form of communication advertising is used to promote the sale of a product or service, to influence public opinion, to gain political support, to advance a particular cause, or to elicit some other response desired by the advertiser.

As a form of communication, advertising is neither good nor bad. It can be used for good or bad, but in itself it is neither. Like atomic energy, advertising can be used to advance or to subvert the welfare of mankind. Judgments of good and bad, therefore, are more appropriate when confined to specific uses of advertising.

As a *component of an economic system* advertising has been most highly developed in countries having a free market system. In a free market system consumer choices determine what goods and services will be produced. A consumer's decision to buy this item instead of that in effect is telling the economic system to make more of this and less of that. The many suppliers competing for consumer favor use advertising to influence those decisions by informing consumers that a given product exists, that it is available at certain retail outlets, that it is priced at a certain amount, and that it offers certain want-satisfying qualities. The "middleman" nature of advertising should be highlighted. It serves as a specialized intermediary between business firms with goods and services to sell and individuals who might benefit from the purchase of those goods and services. Advertising thus performs the function of *interpreting the want satisfying qualities of goods and services in terms of consumer needs and wants.*

Advertising functions quickly and efficiently. A manufacturer can reach 60 to 70 percent of the nation's population in a week's time and he can do so at a cost as low as $3 per thousand people reached. There is no alternative for reaching so many people so quickly at so low a cost. Personal selling is appropriate for reaching relatively small, well-defined, highly concentrated markets such as industrial buyers, but advertising is the only feasible means for communicating with the millions of ultimate consumers. Advertising hastens the trial and acceptance of new products. It also hastens the rejection of those items that fail to live up to expectations. Advertising, therefore, helps make the economic system more sensitive to consumer needs and wants.

Advertising's contribution to economic growth derives primarily from its role in expanding consumer needs and wants. In a modern industrial society the basic wants of food, clothing, and shelter are reasonably well met for most people. For them to spend more they must want more. As Professor Frank H. Knight wrote, "The chief thing that the common-sense individual actually wants is not satisfaction for the wants which he has, but more and better wants."[1] Professor David Potter, who referred to advertising as "the institution of abundance" stated that "the only institution we have for instilling new needs, for training people to act as consumers, for altering men's values, and thus for hastening their adjustment to potential abundance is advertising."[2]

As a *means of financing the mass media* advertising provides 60 to 70 percent of the total revenue of newspapers and magazines. Commercial television and radio broadcasting are financed entirely by advertising. The notion that "he who pays the fiddler calls the tunes" underlies the suspicion that advertisers influence news coverage by suppressing and distorting the news to their own advantage. The only formal study of the matter, *A Free and Responsible Press,* which was undertaken by the Commission on Freedom of the Press, reported that "the evidence of dictation of policy by advertisers is not impressive. Such dictation seems to occur among the weaker units. As a newspaper becomes financially stable it becomes more independent and tends to resist pressure from advertisers."[3] As we shall see, perhaps the strongest deterrent to intrusion on press freedom is the advertiser's dependence on the press. He needs their circulation and audiences to advertise effectively. If advertisers influenced news coverage, the press would risk losing public confidence, which in turn would reduce circulation and jeopardize the effectiveness of the press as an advertising medium.

Advertising may also be viewed as a *social institution,* as an *art form,* as an *instrument of business management,* as a *field of employment,* and as a *profession.* Therefore, this book offers no single definition. Instead, it seeks to widen the reader's scope of observation and deepen his understanding by approaching the study of advertising from several points of view.

Classification of advertising

The layman is inclined to view all advertising as being much the same. Yet, no two advertising situations are exactly alike. Different kinds of

---

[1] Frank H. Knight, *The Ethics of Competition* (New York: Harper & Bros., 1935), p. 22.

[2] David Potter, *People of Plenty* (Chicago: University of Chicago Press, 1954), p. 175.

[3] Commission on Freedom of the Press, *A Free and Responsible Press* (Chicago: University of Chicago Press, 1947), p. 62.

businesses use advertising to motivate different kinds of markets toward different kinds of responses.

The following classification outlines the broad scope of these differences. Each class is described in terms of *who* advertises *what* to *whom* and *where* to bring about what *response.*

1. National Advertising:
   Who: Producers of consumer goods and services.
   What: Branded products or services closely identified with firm's name. (Examples: Plymouth automobile, Campbell's Soup, Ivory Soap, Allstate Insurance.)
   To whom: Ultimate consumers.
   Where: Nationwide.
   Response: "Buy my brand."

2. Retail Advertising:
   Who: Retail stores, such as department stores, grocery stores, drugstores, and clothing stores. Service institutions such as dry cleaners, laundries, and banks.
   What: The items and services available at the particular retail establishment.
   To whom: Ultimate consumers.
   Where: Within a local market area.
   Response: "Buy at my store."

3. Industrial Advertising:
   Who: Producers of industrial goods such as steel, machinery, lubricants, packaging, and office equipment.
   What: Items and services that are used in manufacturing or that facilitate operation of the business.
   To whom: Industrial buyers.
   Where: Nationwide or regionally, depending on the degree of geographic concentration of the industry involved. Practically every industrial buyer can be reached through one or more specialized business publications.
   Response: "Use my product or service in your business operation."

4. Trade Advertising:
   Who: Producers and distributors of branded and nonbranded consumer goods.
   What: Products ready for consumption that are bought by merchants for resale.

To whom: Retailers and wholesalers of consumer goods.
Where: Nationwide.
Response: "Stock and promote the sale of my product."

5. Professional Advertising:
    Who: Producers and distributors who depend on professional men to recommend, prescribe, or specify their products to buyers.
    What: Items the purchase of which is strongly influenced by a professional person. (Examples: baby foods, ethical drugs, building materials, textbooks.)
    To whom: Doctors, dentists, architects, engineers, educators.
    Where: Nationwide.
    Response: "Recommend, prescribe, or specify my product."

6. Nonproduct or "Idea" Advertising:
    Who: Churches; political parties; fraternal, trade, and social groups; and individuals.
    What: Institutions, ideologies, and social betterment. (Examples: religion, political candidates, Red Cross, Community Chest, safety, education.)
    To whom: Lay citizens, voters, community leaders.
    Where: Nationally and locally.
    Response: "Accept my idea, vote for my candidate, or contribute to my cause."

This classification is not intended to be all inclusive. However, it does demonstrate that the scope of advertising is wider than the small fraction one sees in his newspaper, in the few magazines he reads, and on his favorite television programs. This classification also demonstrates that each advertising situation is a unique set of circumstances. Therefore, any generalization is tenuous. Perhaps the only appropriate generalization is that one should not generalize.

The advertising process

The advertisements we see and hear are end products of a series of investigations, strategic plans, tactical decisions, and executions that all together comprise the total advertising process. The field is much broader than the construction of advertisements. It includes (1) researching consumers, the product or service to be advertised, and the market to be cultivated; (2) strategic planning in terms of objectives, market delineation, setting the appropriation, developing creative strategy and media plans; (3) tactical decisions in regard to budgeting expenditures, buying media and scheduling insertions and broadcasts; and (4) advertisement construction including copywriting, layout, art, and production. Figure 1–1 diagrams these various components of advertising and indicates the sequence of events.

Money spent for advertising

Something' of the importance of advertising in our economic life can be seen from an analysis of the money spent for it. The total amount spent for advertising in 1969 was more than $19 billion. This was more than double the amount spent in 1955 and three times what was spent in 1951.

Some of the increase in dollar expenditures has been the result of cheaper dollars, but the ratio of advertising expenditures to the gross national product and to total consumption expenditures also increased markedly during the 1950's. The ratio of advertising dollars to personal consumption expenditures remained fairly constant during the first half of the 1960's. However, it would appear that advertising expenditures did not keep pace with the inflation that accompanied the South Vietnam war from 1967 to 1969. A comparison of expenditures for advertising and personal consumption items for a period of 20 years is shown in Table 1–1.

The implications of this steady increase in total investment in advertising are substantial. It is, in part, an indication of our expanding economy, but more particularly a product of the changing character of the economy. We have moved rapidly from a need to a need-want economy, where an increasing amount of personal consumption expenditures are for products and services that persons do not need to meet the physical *needs* of living (food, shelter, clothing) but choose to purchase to satisfy psychological *wants*. It requires more information and stimulation to bring consumers into the market place to purchase *want* goods than it does to get them to buy *need* goods. Advertising is ideally suited to provide this information and stimulation.

Advertising is also assuming an increasingly important role in the total marketing mix. Supermarkets, self-service shopping, and discount houses tend to place more responsibility on the manufacturer of consumer goods to educate and sell consumers concerning the want-satisfying qualities of his brands than was true when retail merchants had more

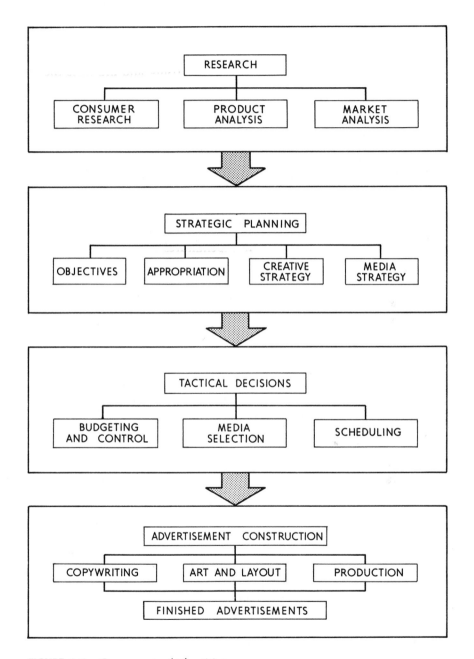

FIGURE 1–1. Components of advertising

TABLE 1–1.   Total U.S. advertising expenditures and personal consumption expenditures, 1950–69

| Year | Expenditures (in millions of dollars) | | Advertising expenditure as percent of consumption expenditure |
	For advertising	For personal consumption	
1950	$ 5,710.0	$194,026	2.94
1951	6,426.1	208,342	3.08
1952	7,156.2	218,328	3.27
1953	7,755.3	230,542	3.36
1954	8,164.1	236,557	3.45
1955	9,194.4	254,421	3.61
1956	9,904.7	267,160	3.71
1957	10,310.6	285,200	3.62
1958	10.301.8	293,200	3.51
1959	11,254.8	315,500	3.57
1960	11,931.7	328,500	3.63
1961	11,845.0	338,000	3.51
1962	12,380.8	355,057	3.48
1963	13,107.4	374,982	3.49
1964	14,155.0	401,356	3.52
1965	15,255.0	431,465	3.53
1966	16,545.0	465,000	3.56
1967	16,866.0	492,200	3.43
1968	18,127.0	536,600	3.38
1969	19,565.0	576,000	3.40

Sources: *Marketing/Communications,* February 1970; *Survey of Current Business,* April 1970.

personal contact with their customers. Advertising is thus being called on to do some of the work previously performed by personal salesmen.

The addition of a new advertising medium—television—to other media has also helped to increase the role of advertising in the marketing mix and invite the investment of additional advertising dollars. Television permits product demonstration and personal selling on a mass basis. This has resulted in some diminution of direct selling and some increase in total advertising expenditures.

Media other than television have also played their part in making investments in advertising productive, thus attracting additional advertising dollars. Table 1–2 lists each of the major media and also provides a breakdown of advertising expenditures in each for 1969.

The people who perform the advertising function

There are more than 4,500,000 business firms and service establishments in the United States. Each does some advertising at one time or another. The very small firm can seldom afford to operate with any sig-

TABLE 1–2. U.S. advertising expenditures in 1969, by media

Medium	Amount spent	
	Dollars in millions	Percent of total
Newspapers	$ 5,850	29.9
Magazines (including national farm papers)	1,375	7.0
Farm publications (regional)	33	0.2
Business papers	720	3.7
Television	3,585	18.3
Radio	1,270	6.5
Direct mail	2,680	13.7
Outdoor	206	1.0
All other	3,846	19.7
Total	$19,565	100.0

Source: *Marketing/Communications,* February 1970, p. 55.

nificant departmentalization of functions or do much in the way of specialization of labor. In the case of such firms any advertising that is done must usually be handled by the manager or proprietor.

Larger firms may establish a department of advertising with one or more employees whose sole responsibility is to plan and execute the advertising program for the firm. Common examples of such firms are department stores, large men's and women's specialty stores, furniture stores, mail-order houses, book publishers, and other large retail and service organizations.

Business firms and institutions that do not wish to do their own advertising work can secure help from outside sources. Retailers especially get much assistance from the various advertising media such as newspapers, radio and television stations, outdoor poster companies, car-card operators, and specialized direct-mail organizations. These media usually have men and women who devote their entire time to helping business firms plan their advertising operations.

The most highly specialized and perhaps most competent personnel in the field of advertising are to be found in the general advertising agencies. There were 4,800 advertising agencies in the United States in 1970. About two thirds of these were equipped to render a complete advertising service for business firms and institutions.

Personnel needs

The total number of persons engaged full time in some aspect of advertising work is not known. Estimates range all the way from 200,000 to 500,000. The 1967 Census of Business listed 212,000 employees and

Advertising people help even in the development of a product. They invent product names, design packages, suggest pricing and selling methods, advise in many other ways before the product is introduced.

When the product is finally ready for market, the agency creates advertising which best presents the product's benefits to the public. This joint effort involves writers, artists, TV producers, many others.

Meanwhile, specialists decide which media (TV, magazines, newspapers, etc.) should carry the advertiser's message—present the advertising to as many potential buyers as possible, and at the lowest cost.

SHOULD YOU GO INTO ADVERTISING?

PEOPLE often ask me what the advertising business is really like.

To begin with, it is seldom as "glamorous" as it has often been portrayed in novels, movies and TV shows.

Actually, advertising is a serious, sober business—the business of applying talent, time and money to the job of keeping sales moving and the economy alive.

Let's suppose that a great new product has been developed and it is your job to introduce it to the American people.

You don't just dream up a slogan. It takes skill, creativity, teamwork and long, patient effort on the part of dozens, perhaps hundreds, of specialists to produce effective advertising.

First, the product is pre-tested among consumers to make sure it fills a real need and is acceptable to them. Then various advertising campaigns are prepared and examined in an effort to find the single, most dramatic and convincing selling theme. Meanwhile, media specialists deliberate on how best to deliver the message. Should it appear in national magazines or local newspapers? Star-studded TV shows or radio "spots"? Should you combine these media and others to boot—outdoor posters, car cards and the like?

Month after month, you and your associates work to develop and test the campaign. Finally it is launched from coast to coast and you await the results anxiously. If the product moves according to expectations, fine. If not, it may mean going "back to the drawing board" and starting the grueling process all over again.

Interesting and Exciting

To my mind, advertising is one of the most interesting and exciting occupations in the world. Its chief product is ideas, and ideas are wonderful things to work with.

Recently a veteran of the business—a man who works long and hard at his job just because he loves it—said this: "I believe that advertising, the business of selling in the face of competition, is one of the most stimulating ways ever invented to make a living."

I agree with him one hundred percent. I wouldn't give back a minute of my forty-four years in the field. And I would willingly recommend it to young people with the right qualifications. It offers big horizons, big rewards, big dreams.

Role in the Economy

The vital role that advertising plays in our American economy has long been recognized.

Just as the assembly line makes mass production possible, so advertising gives rise to mass consumption. By holding up an image of a better, fuller life, it stimulates the demand that keeps our factories rolling.

New York City can testify to what would happen to our economy without advertising. For days and days, most of its newspapers were closed down by a strike a while ago.

The impact on business in the city was dramatic. Department stores' receipts fell twenty-five percent. The sale of used cars dwindled. So did applications for jobs. Theaters were almost empty.

When people were asked afterwards, "What did you miss most in not having your newspaper?" forty-two percent replied, "The ads."

Aids Many Public Causes

Advertising is more than a tool for selling goods and services. It is a weapon for defending our free, democratic institutions.

Take, for example, what happened during World War II. Under the aegis of the War Advertising Council, a group representing all elements in the field, over 150 campaigns were run for the government—free—to get people to buy war bonds, save fats, plant victory gardens and do other patriotic things. Every one of these campaigns was a success.

Since then, advertising has been equally effective in the public interest. The Advertising Council (as it is now known) has run successful campaigns on everything from traffic safety and mental health to the need for better schools and anti-polio inoculations.

Offers Broad Opportunities

You'd like to know what the prospects are for a young person in advertising today? To commence, let me tell you that advertising is a fine, healthy business.

It is really amazing how it has grown. In 1945, the total outlay for advertising in the United States came to $2,874,000,000. Now it is nearly $11,000,000,000. By 1965 we expect it to exceed $15,000,000,000 a year!

One hundred and fifty thousand persons are now working in the field. In another ten years the number should be 250,000.

This means that advertising will continue indefinitely to need many new people. It is estimated that a minimum of 15,000 jobs must be filled each year.

These jobs are in four areas. There are, first, the advertising agencies, 5,063 of them at last count. It is they who create the majority of advertisements we see and hear. In this they act for advertisers who have engaged them. These agencies maintain creative, research, media and marketing staffs that are at the advertisers' call.

Next are the advertisers, big and small—manufacturers, retailers, utilities and others, all over the country. They pay for and have the ultimate control over the advertising that the agencies produce. Sometimes, as in the case of most department stores, these companies prepare advertising themselves.

The third category comprises media: the magazines, newspapers, outdoor poster companies, TV and radio stations and networks who are anxious to sell space and time to the advertisers. The TV and radio people—and I'm including the special "package producers" among them—create most of the programs that go on the air.

Last are the advertising suppliers. They include printers, typographers, lithographers, engravers, photographers and others who help in the preparation of advertising materials.

Talents of All Kinds Welcome

What kinds of jobs are available in these various areas?

The greatest assortment conceivable. A young person who wants to write can have a field day in advertising. You can do magazine and newspaper ads, TV commercials, car cards, pamphlets, mailing pieces, sales letters. And lots more besides. An artist can run the gamut from oil painting to cartoons. Or you can become an art director who designs ads and has other artists illustrate them. A person with theatrical talent can develop TV and radio shows. Musicians can find places, too.

There are positions for researchers, statisticians, marketing and merchandising experts, psychologists, public relations men. For media specialists and sales experts. For layout and printing production men. For business administrators, accountants, secretaries and clerks. For smart, personable young people who can work their way up to be liaison officers between advertising agencies and their clients. Account executives we call them. And, of high priority, for young people of vision and versatility to become advertising managers.

Are the best jobs only for men?

Certainly not! Women are more than welcome in all echelons of the advertising world. I know women who are ranking copy chiefs, art directors, TV producers, research directors. Many women have risen to be top agency executives or advertising managers of multi-

FIGURE 1–2. An advertisement designed to help young men and women know more about the nature of advertising

Next step is for agency account executives to present the recommended campaign to the client for approval. Because advertising is such an important selling tool, this decision involves the client's top executives.

Before being sold nationally, most products are advertised and sold in limited areas. Specially trained researchers then interview consumers to learn their reactions to both the product and the advertising.

The product is finally offered nationally, and / the true test of advertising begins—at the point of sale. Both agency and client check sales frequently to determine how well the product is being accepted by the public.

by Paul B. West *President, Association of National Advertisers, Inc., as told to Donald Robinson*

million-dollar corporations.

Actually, the opportunities for advancement are excellent for anybody with ability. In no other business is talent recognized so quickly. A gifted young man ten years out of college can often make $20,000 a year. At age forty-five, a top-notch person may be earning $40,000. Or more.

It is difficult in a field so extensive as this to set forth a comprehensive salary scale. I can cite a few sample figures, though.

Not long ago, an authoritative trade magazine made a study of 212 advertising agencies to ascertain the salaries they were paying. It found that in agencies placing over $10 million of advertising a year, senior copywriters were paid from $10,990 to $14,200 a year. Account executives were getting from $11,000 to $14,970, supervising account executives from $19,500 to $26,500. Research directors averaged just over $18,800, directors of TV departments about $23,000. In the "command ranks," executive vice presidents were drawing up to $62,000 a year, heads of agencies as high as $110,000.

Another study showed that salaries of advertising managers in industry ranged from $7,000 to as much as $70,000 a year.

Incidentally, many advertising managers have graduated to the presidencies of their companies. Some have gone beyond that. A man I know recently rose through advertising to become President of one of the nation's leading corporations and then Secretary of Defense.

Pressures Can Be Great

The satisfactions that may be derived from a life in advertising are many. You are likely to associate with prominent men in industry, broadcasting, and the press. You face new, challenging problems every day and you can be as creative as you wish in solving them. You constantly have a chance to do a real sales job —learning what millions of people want, why they want it, and then figuring out the most persuasive means of selling its benefits to them. You continually enjoy the zest that comes from meeting and beating tough competition.

In short, advertising can be an enjoyable career—for those who are mentally and temperamentally suited for it. However, as in any other business, art or profession, there are some who, perhaps lured by false visions of making untold money at a "glamorous" career, just don't belong. And most of them are pretty unhappy.

A job in advertising is no sinecure. The hours are long, the demands many, and the pressures great.

Anonymity is the painful rule. Few people on the outside will ever know who wrote the slogan that all America repeats. Rather than public applause, ad men are more likely to hear private criticism. Everyone thinks he knows better than the professionals how a campaign should be handled.

DID YOU KNOW . . .

... advertising needs many new people— a minimum of 15,000 each year?

... it is estimated that in ten years there will be a quarter million persons working in this field?

... women are more than welcome in all echelons of the advertising world?

... the annual outlay for advertising is now nearly $11,000,000,000?

It is no occupation for the man solely concerned with finding security. Men quite often move from one job to another. However, I have known some men who have remained happily with the same organizations for thirty years and more.

Calls for Imagination

Now, I'd like to mention some of the traits that you should have to make a career in advertising. I feel that you should be imaginative, quick-thinking, and have a bent for solving problems. You should like ideas for their own sake, and all kinds of creative activity. You should have a wide range of interests. You should enjoy working hard under pressure. Above all, you should like people and be curious as to what makes them tick. "Why" should be a favorite word with you.

A college education will be a help. Most employers prefer to hire college graduates. Not that a degree is imperative. Many men have achieved success who never got closer to college than a football game. They learned by experience.

Boys and girls who do go to college would be wise to take liberal arts courses, with emphasis on English, literature, history and sociology. Plus some classes in advertising, marketing and economics.

If you are interested in advertising, remember this. It is a career you can be proud of and one that can give you the gratification of knowing that you are contributing to the growth of our economy.

---

proprietors of firms whose principal occupation was that of rendering specialized advertising service to other business enterprises.

This number would probably more than double if we added to it those persons employed by manufacturers, retailers, mail-order houses, and media who devote most or all of their time to company advertising. It is perhaps reasonable to estimate the total number of persons devoting full time to advertising practice as being somewhere between 400,000 and 450,000 in 1970.

Future manpower needs will be substantial. The need will be for both quantity and quality. Leaders in the advertising agency field estimate that agencies alone need from 2,000 to 3,000 new people each year and expect this need to increase. In terms of the quality of people needed Martin Mayer says, "Few occupations are as dependent as advertising on the quality of the incoming talent, and nowhere does the absence of talent show so plainly."[4] With such need it is important that an increasing number of young men and women undertake to prepare themselves for effective careers in advertising.

The advertisement reproduced in Figure 1–2 is one of a series published by New York Life Insurance Co. to bring information to young men and women about career opportunities in various fields. This particular advertisement is concerned with the field of advertising. The coupon at the end of the advertisement offers a booklet on any of a large number of fields.

Advertising policy

Of course, the men and women who devote their full time to the practice of advertising exert a great deal of influence in the determination of advertising policy at the executive level. Final responsibility for policy, however, must rest with the owner or executive head of the firm or department. There has been a growing tendency among large national advertisers to have a vice president in charge of advertising. This person is usually not concerned with the details of advertisement construction or media selection but is vitally interested in the overall advertising program and how it dovetails with the personal selling and merchandising activities of the company. It is important that this person understands something of advertising techniques, too, in order that he can properly appraise the work of the advertising practitioners.

---

[4] Martin Mayer, *Madison Avenue, U.S.A.* (New York: Harper & Bros., 1958), pp. 322–23.

Advertising policy should be correlated with overall business objectives. Since such objectives must be concerned with the products, services, or ideas that are to be promoted, policymakers must consider not only the seller's wares but also the buyer's interests. Here, again, the importance of research as a guide to sound policy is evident.

With this brief look at what advertising is, its functions, scope, and personnel, we are ready to examine various aspects of advertising in detail. First consideration might properly be given to reviewing the long history of advertising.

QUESTIONS AND PROBLEMS

1. In the light of what you have read in this chapter and your attitudes toward advertising before that, what do you now believe the function or functions of advertising to be?
2. Do you think it is logical to make a distinction between the words "advertising" and "advertisement"? What distinction do you make between these words?
3. Even though you are probably just beginning your study of advertising, you no doubt have some rather definite ideas about it. Prepare a 200-word statement of your ideas about advertising. Include in that statement any ideas you might have as to whether it is good or bad for (1) the nation as a whole; (2) individual consumers; (3) individual business firms; (4) organizations such as schools, churches, or political parties; and (5) yourself. You might also point out why you believe as you do.
4. Get from your library the latest issue of *Marketing/Communications* "Advertiser's Guide to Marketing" and calculate the change from 1961 in (*a*) advertising expenditures and (*b*) personal consumption expenditures.

chapter 2
HISTORY OF ADVERTISING

ADVERTISING IS ONLY one of several selling tools which businessmen have used for centuries to assist them in getting their wares into the hands of consumers. Its early use was distinctly a minor supplement to other forms of selling. Storekeepers erected signs on or in front of buildings or placed posters in public places, merely to draw the attention of prospective customers to their places of business. After customers were thus attracted, personal selling and display of merchandise were depended upon to make the sale.

Today advertising has become a major form of selling. It not only supports other forms of selling but also frequently serves as the only selling tool used to move merchandise. Whereas early advertising might have been referred to as written or printed publicity, serving wholly as an adjunct to personal selling, today it takes a position on a par with personal selling. This does not mean that the two are competitive; instead, one complements, rather than supplants, the other.

Modern advertising is closely associated with the development of mass selling. The manufacturer who sells his merchandise throughout an entire nation or in many nations finds advertising a valuable ambassador. Messages dealing with new or old products, their qualities and want-satisfying characteristics, can be sent to millions of people at low cost through newspapers, magazines, television, radio, direct mail, billboards, car cards, and motion pictures. Dealers in every market, stocked with such merchandise, find it relatively easy to meet the needs and desires of people. Thus, automobiles, refrigerators, radios, electrical equipment, and many other items can be manufactured and sold on a basis to obtain the advantages of mass production and distribution.

Modern advertising has demonstrated its power as an independent and complementary selling tool. So important has it become, that careful attention has been given to its scientific application to modern business. Thus, modern advertising covers a broad field. Its effective application requires a thorough understanding of the importance of its various component parts. An approach to such an understanding can be gained by looking backward for a brief moment to trace the evolution of advertising. This remigration will provide a contrast with the character of our present-day forms of advertising. It will also furnish a picture of the general direction toward which advertising is traveling and thus give a possible insight into its immediate future.

Broadly speaking, the history of advertising might be divided into six periods or stages, as follows:

1. Pre-printing period, prior to the 15th century.
2. Early printing period, from the 15th century to about 1840.
3. Period of expansion, from 1840 to 1900.
4. Period of consolidation, from 1900 to 1925.
5. Period of scientific development, from 1925 to 1945.
6. Period of business and social integration, from 1945 to the present.

PRE-PRINTING PERIOD

Signs

Perhaps some form of advertising has existed as long as we have had buying and selling. The nature of such advertising has depended upon the media available for carrying the message of the seller to the prospective buyer. Before the days of the newspaper and magazine, almost the only media available were signboards and town criers.

Sampson, in his *History of Advertising,* published in 1874, points out that "signs over shops and stalls seem naturally to have been the first efforts in the direction of advertisements and they go back to the remotest portions of the world's history."[1] These early signs were, for the most part, made of stone or terra cotta "and set into the pilasters at the sides of the open shop fronts."[2] Later, signs were hung over the walks and above shop entrances. Some extended entirely across the street.

---

[1] Henry Sampson, *History of Advertising* (London: Chatto & Windus, 1930), p. 19.
[2] *Ibid.,* p. 22.

The principal function of these early signs was to identify a merchant's place of business. A valuable by-product, however, was that of providing a landmark for the citizens of a town. House numbers were unknown; and directions, such as "three doors down from the sign of the Three Crowns," provided a real service.

In addition to being the first major form of advertising, signs have continued to serve as an important advertising medium. The relative importance, rather than the absolute position, of this means of advertising has been reduced by the increase in literacy, development of the printing press, growth of electronic media, and other marks of progress.

The town crier

The town crier was the first means of supplementing sign advertising. The criers had charters from the government and were often organized in a sort of union. Their numbers were usually restricted. In the province of Berry, France, in the year 1141, twelve criers organized a company and obtained a charter from Louis VII giving them the exclusive privileges of town crying in the province.[3]

The power of commercial criers grew until they were able in some instances to obtain an edict from the ruler of the land forcing shopkeepers to employ a crier. Typical of such orders was the decree issued in France by Philip Augustus in 1258:

> Whosoever is a crier in Paris may go to any tavern he likes and cry its wine, provided they sell wine from the wood and that there is no other crier employed for that tavern; and the tavern keeper cannot prohibit him.
>
> If a crier finds people drinking in a tavern, he may ask what they pay for the wine they drink; and he may go out and cry the wine at the prices they pay, whether the tavern keeper wishes it or not, provided always that there be no other crier employed for that tavern.
>
> If a tavern keeper sells wine in Paris and employs no crier, and closes his door against the criers, the crier may proclaim that tavern keeper's wine at the same price as the king's wine (the current price) that is to say, if it be a good wine year, at seven dinarii, and if it be a bad wine year, at twelve dinarii.
>
> Each crier to receive daily from the tavern for which he cries at least four dinarii and he is bound on his oath not to claim more.[4]

Some of our modern "criers" of merchants' wares would no doubt like to have a government order similar to that issued by Philip Augustus. And such an order might be of benefit to some merchants.

---

[3] Frank Presbrey, *The History and Development of Advertising* (Garden City, N.Y.: Doubleday & Co., Inc., 1929), pp. 10–11.

[4] *Ibid.,* pp. 11–12.

EARLY PRINTING PERIOD

The invention of the printing press and the revival of learning meant much to business. It, of course, made possible the production of advertisements in large quantities for wide distribution. The first printed English advertisement was a handbill or "poster" announcement written by William Caxton in 1472. That advertisement is reproduced in Figure 2–1 on the next page. Translated into modern English the advertisement would read as follows:

If anyone, cleric or layman, wants to buy some copies of two or three service books arranged according to the usage of Salisbury Cathedral, and printed in the same desirable type in which this advertisement is set, let him come to the place in the precincts of Westminster Abbey where alms are distributed, which can be recognized by a shield with a red central stripe (from top to bottom), and he shall have these books cheap.
Please don't tear down this notice.[5]

In addition to handbills, the printing press gave rise to mass media in the form of newspapers, magazines, and books. These agencies served as media to carry messages of sellers to potential buyers. Authors of pamphlets, servants seeking positions, people wanting servants, announcements of runaway slaves, slaves listed for sale, publication of articles of association of public companies, and the formation of deeds of partnership illustrate the type of advertising material run in the early newspapers.

According to Blanche B. Elliott, probably the first English Press advertisement appeared in 1622 and was by an author of a series of pamphlets who inserted a note in *The Times Handlist* to inform buyers and prospective buyers that the pamphlets would be continued and available for purchase. The text of that early advertisement follows:

If any Gentleman or other accustomed to buy the Weekely Relations of Newes, be desirous to continue the same, let them know that the Writer or Transcriber rather of this Newes hath published two former Newes, the one dated the second and the other the thirteenth of August, all of which doe carrie a like title, with the Armes of the King of *Bohemia* on the other side of the title page, and have dependance one upon another: which manner of writing and printing he doth propose to continue weekly by God's assistance, from the best and most certain intelligence.
Farewell; this twenty-third of August 1622.[6]

---

[5] This translation was made by Dr. Edward Pousland of Worcester Junior College.

[6] Blanche B. Elliott, *A History of English Advertising* (London: Business Publications Ltd., 1962), p. 22.

This "first press advertisement" was a soft, dignified announcement of a pure informative nature. Unfortunately, it did not set the tone for later advertising of the period. Instead, this early period saw the use of exaggeration in its boldest form. Beverages, cosmetics, and patent medicines held a prominent place in the early media. The famous coffee advertise-

FIGURE 2–1.   First printed English advertisement

ment printed as a handbill in 1652 is illustrative of the early beverage advertisements. It might be interesting to compare this more than three-century-old selling appeal with some of the advertising of today. The 1652 advertisement is here reprinted:

THE VIRTUE OF THE COFFEE DRINK
First made and publicly sold in England by
PASQUA ROSEE

The grain or berry called coffee groweth upon little trees only in the deserts of Arabia. It is brought from thence and drunk generally throughout all the Grand Seignour's dominions. It is a simple, innocent thing, composed into a drink, by being dried in an oven, and ground to powder, and boiled up with spring water, and about half a pint of it to be drunk fasting an hour before, and not eating an hour after, and to be taken as hot as can possibly be endured; the which will never fetch the skin of the mouth, or raise any blisters by reason of that heat.

The Turk's drink at meals and other times is usually water, and their diet consists of much fruit; the acidities whereof are very much corrected by this drink.

The quality of this drink is cold and dry; and though it be a drier; yet it neither heats nor inflames more than hot posset. It so incloseth the orifice of the stomach, and fortifies the heat within, that it is very good to help digestion; and therefore of great use to be taken about three or four o'clock afternoon, as well as in the morning. It much quickens the spirits, and makes the heart lightsome, it is good against sore eyes, and the better if you hold your head over it and take in the steam that way. It suppresseth fumes exceedingly, and therefore is good against the headache, and will very much stop any defluxion of rheums that distil from the head upon the stomach, and so prevent and help consumptions and cough of the lungs.

It is excellent to prevent and cure the dropsy, gout, and scurvy. It is known by experience to be better than any other drying drink for people in years, or children that have any running humours upon them, as the king's evil, etc. It is a most excellent remedy against the spleen, hypochondriac winds and the like. It will prevent drowsiness, and make one fit for business, if one have occasion to watch, and therefore you are not to drink of it after supper, unless you intend to be watchful, for it will hinder sleep for three or four hours.

It is observed that in Turkey, where this is generally drunk, that they are not troubled with the stone, gout, dropsy, or scurvy, and that their skins are exceedingly clear and white. It is neither laxative nor restringent.

Made and Sold in St. Michael's Alley, in Cornhill, by
Pasque Rosee, at the sign of his own Head.[7]

The quest for beauty provided a fertile field for quackery in the sale of cosmetics in the 18th century, as in the 20th century. Note the following advertisement, which appeared in the *Spectator* in 1712:

The Gentlewoman who lived 20 years in Raquet-Court, and 7 years in Crane-Court, Fleet-street, and has served most of the Quality in England, Scotland and

---

[7] Samson, *op. cit.*, pp. 68–69.

Ireland, also the East and West Indies, with the most excellent Curiosoties for preserving the Face, Hands, and Teeth, in present Beauty; for colouring red or grey Hair to a lovely brown or black, a Cosmatick that certainly takes away the Spots and Marks remaining after the Small-Pox with many other rare Secrets in Physick, is now removed to her own House the upper End of Wine-Office-Court in Gough-Square next Door to the Sun-dial on the Left hand, where you may be furnished with all things as formerly, and all prepared with her own hand. She is to be spoken with every Day from 9 to 12, and from 2 till 8 at night. . . .[8]

Or here is a "modern" one, printed in 1711:

A most incomparable Paste for the Hands, far exceeding anything ever yet in Print: It makes them delicately white, sleeke and plump; fortifies them against the scorching Heat of the Fire or Sun, and Sharpness of the Wind. A Hand cannot be so spoil'd but the Use of it will recover them. Sold only at Mr. Allcraft's Toy-shop, over-against the Royal-Exchange, at 1 s. 6 d. a Pot, with Directions: Where is sold the excellent German Powder for the Scurvy in the Gums and Teeth, which by only scouring them every Morning, whitens and fastens the Teeth to A Miracle, at 1 s. a Seale.[9]

A few examples of patent medicine advertising will serve to illustrate the dependence of the early vendors upon the credulity of afflicted persons. The following example, published in the *Spectator* in 1711, introduces the testimonial feature:

This is to certify, That my Child being almost reduced to the very Grave from the extream Agony he underwent by violent Breeding of Teeth, was thro'-God's Goodness restored to perfect Ease and Safety, upon the use of that truly Noble Medicine, prepared for those Cases, by Mr. Perronet Surgeon in Dyot-Street near Bloomsbury, Witness my Hand, S. Warburton, Raisor-maker in Grays-Inn-Passage, by Red Lyon-Square. This medicine is sold at 2 s. 7 d. the Vial, by the Author aforesaid, Mr. Alcraft at the Blew-Coat Boy Against the Royal Exchange, Cornhill, and by Mr. Watkins Tobaconist against the Market, in King-street Westminster.[10]

It it difficult to determine from the advertisement whether it was "God's Goodness" or the medicine which restored the youngster to "perfect ease and safety." The same dilemma is presented in the following example. In both cases, however, the makers of the "medicine" are willing to attribute credit to their concoction and ask a price for it.

R. Stoughton, Apothecary, in Southwak, having some Time since, by Order of a Merchant, sent 50 Dozen of his Cordial Elixir to Sweden, has lately receiv'd Advice, that Numbers of People finding it a great Preserver of Health, drink it every Morning: And further to assure it is so, hath a Certificate from thence, That

---

[8] Lawrence Lewis, *The Advertisements of the Spectator* (New York: Houghton Mifflin Co., 1909), pp. 116–17.

[9] *Ibid.,* pp. 117–18.

[10] *Ibid.,* p. 113.

(to the Person's best Knowledge and Observation) not one who took it hath had the Disease; and many are of the Opinion it hath been of great Use in stopping the Progress of it. He hath also a certificate from on board a Ship at Jamaica, That after 6 or 7 of the men died in 24 hours of a malignant Distemper, the Captain himself (fearing he should lose all his Men) gave the rest, who were seiz'd plentifully of this Elixir (which for many Years he took with him) and by God's Blessing on it saved every Man after. He is not only willing, but desirous this may be publish'd for the Good of others. Few now will go to Sea or travel without it. The certificates themselves any Gentleman may see if they please. Another large box is just now ordered again for Sweden.[11]

The center of advertising growth during the first half of the early printing period was England. It began to develop in America in significant amounts in the 1700's. Early American advertising, however, was largely devoid of the exaggeration found in English ads. James Young, in comparing patent medicine advertising in these two countries up to 1750, said, "While the English proprietor sharpened up his adjectives and reached for his vitriol, in America, with rare exceptions, advertisers were content merely to list by name their supplies of imported English remedies."[12]

An example of the mild form of American advertising in this period is the following that appeared in Benjamin Franklin's newspaper in 1735.

To Be SOLD

A Plantation containing 300 Acres of good Land, 30 cleared, 10 or 12 Meadow and in good English Grass, a house and barn &c. lying in Nantmel Township, upon French-Creek, about 30 Miles from Philadelphia. Enquire of Simon Meredith now living on the said place.

ALL Persons indebted to the Estate of Joseph Harrison, Carpenter, late of Philadelphia, deceased, are hereby required to make speedy Payment to John Harrison, or John Leech, Executors. And those that have any Accounts to settle, are desired to bring them in.

These examples give some idea of the character of the advertising of the early printing period. In general, the growth of advertising during this period in both Europe and the United States paralleled the increase in population, learning, and number of periodicals and newspapers. However, in 1712 England levied a tax on newspapers and advertising which retarded the growth of both newspapers and advertising. It caused the death of such a leading publication as Addison's *Spectator*. The first tax amounted to a halfpenny, then increased to fourpence (8 cents), and

---

[11] *Ibid.*, p. 114.

[12] James H. Young, *The Toadstool Millionaires* (Princeton, N.J.: Princeton University Press, 1961), p. 10.

reduced to a penny a paper in 1837. The tax on each advertisement, regardless of size, amounted to 84 cents at its peak. Taxes on both newspapers and advertisements were abolished in 1853.

The circulation of newspapers in the United States, where no tax was imposed, was much greater than in England during this period. Presbrey compares the two countries for 1850 as follows:[13]

	Population	Number of papers	Annual circulation
United Kingdom	27,368,736	500	91,000,000
United States	23,191,876	2,302	422,600,000*

* Estimated.

PERIOD OF EXPANSION

This period includes, roughly, the 60 years between 1840 and 1900. It was during these six decades that great changes were witnessed in the United States—changes which had a vital influence on the business of advertising.

Transportation

By 1840, railroads in the United States were recognized as an efficient means of transportation. They were rapidly piercing the West and causing businessmen to look beyond their own small communities for trade. This broadening of markets encouraged the use of advertising in magazines which served large territories, and the growth of magazines was likewise encouraged and made possible by the development of rapid and long-distance transportation.

Figures 2–2 and 2–3 give a graphic presentation of the growth of newspapers and magazines during this period. Figure 2–2 shows the parallel growth of the number of publications and railway mileage from 1840 to 1890. This parallel movement is rather striking. While it does not prove a causal relationship between the growth of long-distance transportation and advertising media, it is logical to believe that the increase of transportation facilities did have a definite influence on the rapid rise in the number of publications. Certainly a wide distribution of magazines was absolutely dependent upon an efficient method of long-distance transportation. Of course, increased revenue from the sale of advertising space encouraged a growth in the number of publications, and the wider circu-

---

[13] Presbrey, *op. cit.,* p. 75.

FIGURE 2–2. Relative changes in number of publications, railway mileage, and illiteracy in the United States from 1840 to 1890

lation, in part made possible by improved transportation facilities, attracted more advertisers.

Figure 2–3 is even more striking. It is adapted from a study made by Daniel Starch.[14] Here we see a comparison of the volume of advertising in a typical magazine and two newspapers. The volume of advertising in the *Century Magazine* increased more than elevenfold between 1860 and 1890. The best that the *Boston Transcript* could do in the same period was to double its advertising volume, while the *New York Times* had only a small percentage increase.

Since the markets opened up by railway transportation were perhaps best reached by magazines, the increase in the advertising volume of the *Century Magazine* would seem to be due, in large part, to the increase in railway mileage. It is evident that the railroad did have a tremendous influence on broadening markets and thus gave encouragement to an increase in the volume and scope of advertising.

Education

Until the advent of radio, most forms of advertising required an ability to read on the part of the prospective buyer. Today the literacy of the

---

[14] Daniel Starch, *Principles of Advertising* (New York: McGraw-Hill Book Co., 1923), p. 34.

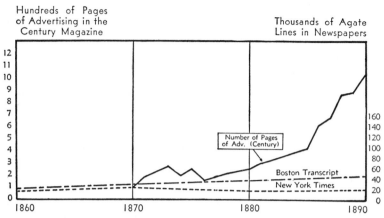

FIGURE 2–3. Growth of advertising space in the *Century Magazine* and in two newspapers from 1860 to 1890

American people is high, but such was not the case at the beginning of the period of advertising expansion. It was during this period, however, that tremendous advances were made in educational facilities for the masses. It was during this period that free schools were provided for workers' children. Some compulsory school-attendance legislation was enacted. These forces reduced the amount of illiteracy in the United States. Twenty percent of the population ten years of age and over could not read in 1870. By 1890, this had been reduced to 13 percent. An interesting comparison can be made between the decline in illiteracy and the growth in the number of magazines and newspapers by referring back to Figure 2–2.

The advertising agency

The growth of advertising during this period encouraged individuals to set themselves up as specialists in the sale of advertising space. Those who made this work their major occupation established themselves as a general advertising agency in that they would represent a number of media in the sale of space to advertisers. While there were agencies in England as early as 1800, the first agency in the United States was organized by Volney B. Palmer in 1840 or 1841. Palmer's organization served as salesman of space in magazines and newspapers, as did all subsequent agencies for many years. They received "inside" prices from publishers and made their money by selling space to advertisers at a higher rate. There was no standardization of prices, and no services were rendered by the agent such as writing copy, making layouts, or doing research work. The agent was strictly a seller of space.

Nevertheless, the growth in the number of men devoting their time to promoting the sale of space in publications tended to focus attention upon themselves, and later led to the recognition of the advertising agency as a vital factor to both the publisher and the advertiser. This specialized group of salesmen helped to increase the volume of advertising.

PERIOD OF CONSOLIDATION

By 1900 the area of the United States had been rather completely explored and settled. No longer was there a frontier to conquer. The territorial expansion of domestic markets had been halted. The job of the businessman was to cultivate the territories already existing.

New functions assumed by agency

In like fashion the business of advertising as exemplified by the agency had reached a point where continued growth depended upon changing the methods of operation. By 1890, as one writer put it, "the woods were full" of advertising agents. To consolidate their gains, new functions were assumed. These included the writing of copy, selection of media, and occasionally some analysis of the market. It was also during this period that a fairly stable method of paying the agency was developed.

Truth crusade

In 1911 a crusade against the ranker types of untruthfulness in advertising was launched. Printers' Ink, Inc., the Curtis Publishing Company, and other organizations led the fight to reduce or eliminate the use of gross exaggeration, false testimonials, and other forms of misleading and untruthful advertising. Although the motive for this crusade was perhaps an attempt to benefit the publisher rather than the consumer, the progress made reacted to the mutual benefit of all parties concerned.

The establishment of the Audit Bureau of Circulations in 1914 was another move for less untruth in the field. This Bureau served to validate the circulation statements made by publishers. The guaranteed circulation figures of members of the Bureau thus carried conviction. Again, this was a measure for self-preservation, but it served to consolidate the gains made in the heyday of publication and advertising growth.

Advertising organizations

Various advertising organizations were formed or became active during this period. A list of some of the leading groups would include the Advertising Federation of America, American Association of Advertising Agencies, Association of National Advertisers, Audit Bureau of Circulations, Direct Mail Advertising Association, Outdoor Advertising Association, and various publishers' associations.

These groups tended to give a semiprofessional character to the advertising business. They have had some influence in solidifying the business and in raising the ethics somewhat above the level of previous periods.

PERIOD OF SCIENTIFIC DEVELOPMENT

The designation of this period may be questioned by those who object to associating the word "science" with advertising. Few will deny, however, that this period saw the application of the scientific method to problems of advertising. Knowledge was systematized to a much greater degree than before; and facts were observed, recorded, and classified.

Decline of blind faith in advertising

For years advertising grew upon the success of those firms spending great sums in printed forms of sales promotion. If the question, "Are we big because we advertise, or do we advertise because we are big?" were ever asked, it was always answered in favor of advertising. The advertising agency, with its income depending upon the size of the advertising appropriation, helped to foster and perpetuate a blind faith in the efficacy of advertising. Did not St. Jacob's Oil and Pear's Soap lose out when they stopped advertising? Was not the success of Campbell's Soup due to advertising? Such questions, by inference, contained their own answer. It was absurd to be a disbeliever in the face of such "conclusive" evidence. No one stopped to ask how Hershey's Chocolate continued to be a success in the face of little or no advertising. The answer might have been found in Hershey's fine dealer organization, its early start, and its use of other sales promotional methods; but these were kept out of the discussion.

There were a few "radical" advertising men before 1920 who were so bold as to suggest that advertising be subjected to tests to prove or disprove its ability to work the wonder claimed for it. Not until the depression, starting in 1929, did these men get much of a hearing. But with advertising appropriations receiving liberal cuts, both professional advertising men and advertisers set out to test the effectiveness of advertising as a selling tool.

Market research and consumer analysis

This period witnessed a revision of advertising philosophy. It saw advertising men come to the realization that their business was only a part of the great field of selling, and that to be successful in their work a close harmony of effort with all other factors in the problem of selling must be obtained. Not merely was a consideration of the former "all-important" factors of art, copy, layout, and typography necessary; but thought must be given to the product to be advertised, the character of the prospective buyers, their purchasing power, their place of abode, etc.

Some of these factors were emphasized by the American Association of Advertising Agencies as early as 1918. In a report issued in that year, the Association laid down the following program as vital to an advertising campaign:

1. A study of the product or service in order to determine the advantages and disadvantages inherent in the product itself, and in its relation to competition
2. An analysis of the present and potential market for which the product or service is adapted:
   As to location
   As to the extent of possible sale
   As to season
   As to trade and economic conditions
   As to nature and amount of competition
3. A knowledge of the factors of distribution and sales and their methods of operation
4. A knowledge of all the available media and means which can profitably be used to carry the interpretation of the product or service to consumer, wholesaler, dealer, contractor, or other factor
   This knowledge covers:
   Character
   Influence
   Circulation.................... $\left\{ \begin{array}{l} \text{Quantity} \\ \text{Quality} \\ \text{Location} \end{array} \right.$
   Physical Requirements
   Costs

Acting on the study, analysis and knowledge as explained in the preceding paragraphs, recommendations are made and the following procedure ensues:

5. Formulation of a definite plan

6. Execution of this plan:
   a) Writing, designing, illustrating of advertisements or other appropriate forms of the message
   b) Contracting for the space or other means of advertising
   c) The proper incorporation of the message in mechanical form and forwarding it with proper instructions for the fulfillment of the contract
   d) Checking and verifying of insertions, display or other means used
   e) The auditing, billing and paying for the service, space and preparation
7. Cooperation with the sales work, to insure the greatest effect from advertising.[15]

It is interesting to note that the A.A.A.A. in 1918 placed little or no emphasis on the importance of studying the consumer, his buying habits, needs, and desires. This factor emerged as a vital element in advertising later.

By the end of this period many advertisers had established their own market- and consumer-research departments, and specialized research firms had been organized to make independent and unbiased investigations for advertisers and media. This increased the quality of advertising strategy and performance as well as the benefits rendered consumers.

Testing results

During the period of scientific development serious attention was given by many agencies and organizations to methods for testing the sales effectiveness of advertising strategy, media, and copy. This was a new philosophy in that it meant subjecting the work of the creative man, the artist, the person who depended upon his own insights and intuition to some kind of performance yardstick.

PERIOD OF BUSINESS AND SOCIAL INTEGRATION

During the decade following World War II advertising was recognized and accepted as an essential part of total business in the plentiful economy of free America. Production techniques and facilities were greatly increased during the war years, and these facilities were released after the end of armed conflict for use in producing consumer goods. There was purchasing power in the pockets of consumers to pay for all that industry could produce. However, there was not always the will to buy.

---

[15] *Report of American Association of Advertising Agencies* (New York, 1918).

Economists both inside and outside of business pointed to advertising as a necessary ingredient in the total business mix to stimulate consumption to a point where it would balance production. Economists pointed out that high-level production and full employment could be sustained only by high-level consumption. Emphasis was placed on the fact that consumers needed to learn to live better in the future in order to absorb all of the goods and services that industry could supply. Under such circumstances advertising became an integral part of the total economy, taking its place alongside production, finance, distribution, and entrepreneurship as a part of the whole.

Social integration, too

During the past two decades the institution of advertising has also been accepted as a part of the total fabric of society. It has become a common medium whereby churches, political parties, labor groups, trade associations, and lay citizens communicate their ideologies, platforms, ideas, and concepts to the many publics making up total society. Advertising has become an institution of persuasion to promote such social and economic values as safety, health, education, benevolence, liberty, democracy, free enterprise, and tolerance.

This trend has been enhanced by the Advertising Council, an outgrowth of the War Advertising Council of World War II, which donates its time to develop complete advertising campaigns to promote ideas and projects that are recognized as being in the public interest.

Along with social integration has come a deeper appreciation of social responsibilities that rest upon the institution of advertising.

New emphasis has been given to the problem of untruthful advertising. The old organizations developed to foster truth in advertising have attacked the problem with new vigor, and new agencies have supplemented the work of the old. Legislation, both state and national, has been sought and obtained to promote a greater degree of truthfulness in advertising. Machinery for self-regulation of advertising has been set up. There seems to have been a growth in the belief that advertising effectiveness will be increased by making it more truthful.

Strong leadership in the renewal of the truth crusade was again taken by various publishers and leading practitioners.

The character of modern advertising is such that it must be accorded a vital position in our total economic and social life. Its power is substantial; its responsibility even greater.

Summary

The foregoing brief history of advertising is intended to give a bird's-eye view of the evolution of this selling tool from its simple beginning to its present position. It is in no way intended as a complete history.

The important features of modern advertising will be treated at length in the chapters that follow. Emphasis will be placed upon those qualities peculiar to its modern development. Consideration will be given to the place which advertising might properly and profitably hold in our social and economic order. The problems and techniques of consumer, product, and market analysis will form an important part of our further study. Attention will be given to the preparation of advertising messages that will be effective and to the selection of media to carry such messages.

The organization of modern advertising, including the general advertising agency, special agencies, and the advertising departments of the manufacturer and retailer, will be treated in detail. Finally, attention will be given to the philosophy and techniques of testing advertising effectiveness.

Thus, the features of modern advertising which we have viewed but briefly here will be amplified in the material which follows.

QUESTIONS AND PROBLEMS

1. Contrast the advertising of the "early printing period" with that of today, and account for the factors that influenced the change.
2. "Advances in educational facilities in the period of expansion resulted in increasing not only the use but also the quality of advertising." Do you agree? Why?
3. What influence do you think World War II might have had on advertising during the war period?
4. What might have been some of the reasons for a slower expansion of advertising in England than in the United States in the early printing period?
5. Wherein do the modern beverage advertisements differ from those exemplified by the early coffee advertisement reproduced in this chapter?
6. How did the development of our transportation industry after 1840 affect advertising? Why was it that the advertising in some media was influenced more by the growth of transportation than that in other media?
7. In view of the trend of the changing character of advertising in the past, what forecast would you make as to the character of the advertising business for the future?

8. Would a law which forced present-day businessmen to employ a "town crier" or modern advertising expert be particularly detrimental to business? Explain.

9. If you can secure copies of newspapers or magazines that are ten or more years old, compare the advertisements of that period with those in current media to see if you can detect any fundamental differences in the advertisements of the two periods.

10. Do you see any evidence to suggest that we might now be entering a seventh period in the history of advertising—the period of social responsibility?

chapter 3
SOCIAL AND ECONOMIC ASPECTS OF ADVERTISING

ADVERTISING IS A SUBSYSTEM of an economic system which in turn is a subsystem of a larger system of social values and beliefs. To understand how advertising works one must first understand how the total system works.

Reflecting different values and beliefs, different political philosophies, and different stages of industrial development, different nations have devised different economic systems. Whatever the system, be it a primitive barter system or a modern price system, it is called upon to do certain things: (1) to determine what goods and services will be produced and in what quantities, (2) to allocate scarce resources (land, labor and capital) among alternative uses, and (3) to distribute goods and services among individuals and occupational groupings. Inasmuch as advertising has developed most rapidly and has reached its highest level of sophistication in one particular kind of economic system let us consider how that system works.

A FREE MARKET SYSTEM

In a free market system consumers tell the system what to produce. Their decisions to purchase this item and not that, in effect, say "make

34

more of this, less of that." Millions of these "dollar votes" are registered every hour of every day. Relayed from retailers to wholesalers to manufacturers to farmers, miners, lumbermen, oil drillers, fishermen, etc., consumer choices guide the allocation of resources. It is assumed that each consumer acting in his own self interest not only advances his own welfare, but all consumers collectively advance the welfare of society.

In a free market system there are many suppliers competing for consumer favor. Just as each consumer is free to choose, each supplier is free to enter. Competition among suppliers is counted on to provide the incentive for innovation and greater efficiency. As each supplier seeks to offer a better value—i.e., a better product at the same price or the same product at a lower price—the total supply of products increases, quality improves, and costs decrease. Prices represent a balancing of consumer satisfactions and supplier production costs. Prices are free to fluctuate in accordance with fluctuations in supplies and demands. Thus, consumers ultimately control the system, not only through the choices they make but also through the prices they pay.

This, of course, is an oversimplified version. Among other omissions it leaves out the intricate and automatic adjustments that distribute the gross national product in the form of wages, rents, interest payments and dividends, thus providing consumers with purchasing power to complete the cycle. Concentrating on the marketplace, the purpose here is simply to spotlight the pivotal role of the consumer. The system assumes that the consumer is competent, not only to maximize his own satisfactions, but in so doing to also advance the interests of society at large.

How competent is the consumer? Does he choose wisely and well? Does he function as a rational "economic man" weighing carefully the pros and cons? How independent, how reasonable, how well informed is he? Proponents of a free market system have faith in the ability of large numbers of consumers to choose well. Opponents are skeptical. They assume the consumer needs to be protected against himself. They place their faith in some form of centralized government authority. In their view, economic control should rest with the few at the top instead of the many at the bottom. However, even the proponents recognize that a free market system cannot be left entirely free. Some laws have to be passed and some regulatory agencies established to assure safety in the use of foods, drugs, cosmetics, automobiles, etc. Other laws are needed to protect the consumer against fraudulent and deceptive practices. Still others are required to foster competition. Because the system fails to directly provide schools, roads, social welfare programs and national defense, a considerable amount of consumer spending is diverted in the form of taxes to government spending. As a result, what we have in the United States is a "mixed economic system," both free and regulated. However, in the consumer goods market, in the supermarkets, department stores, discount stores and in the field of consumer services, where a wide assortment of competing goods and services are available, it can be assumed that the forces of consumer choice are relatively free.

How well has the system worked? This can only be answered in terms of a nation's larger system of values and beliefs. If a relatively high standard of living, an abundance of material goods, widely distributed purchasing power, and personal freedom are highly valued—the system in those countries where it exists has performed reasonably well. If, on the other hand, the national interest as perceived by government leaders is more highly valued than individual preferences and material well-being, then some other system probably would better serve that goal.

ADVERTISING'S ROLE IN THE SYSTEM

An economic system that depends on the choices of millions of consumers in many widely scattered markets requires a highly developed communication system. Every buyer cannot transact business directly with every seller nor can every buyer examine every product offered for sale. Both buyers and sellers depend on advertising to carry the news of available products and services, to establish them in consumers' minds, to interpret their want-satisfying qualities. Through advertising consumers are able to anticipate satisfactions, to compare values, and to do much of their shopping before they ever leave home. Consumers tend to choose products they know and trust. Advertising creates awareness and builds confidence. Consumers forget. Advertising reminds.

These communication functions are performed quickly and efficiently. The vast network of newspapers, magazines, television and radio stations, direct mail, etc. makes it possible for a single manufacturer to reach millions of consumers throughout the country in a week's time, or for a retailer to reach the hundreds or thousands of his customers every day. Such efficient communication hastens the trial and acceptance of new products. It also hastens the rejection of those items that fail to live up to their claims. In this way advertising helps make the economic system more responsive to consumer preferences. Ultimately it speeds up the process of resource allocation.

Advertising contributes to a dynamic, expanding economy. In fact,

Professor Neil H. Borden in his exhaustive study of the economic effects of advertising concluded that this was the outstanding contribution.

Advertising's outstanding contribution to consumer welfare comes from its part in promoting a dynamic, expanding economy. Advertising's chief task from a social standpoint is that of encouraging the development of new products. It offers a means whereby the enterpriser may hope to build a profitable demand for his new and differentiated merchandise which will justify investment. From growing investment has come the increasing flow of income which has raised man's material welfare to a level unknown in previous centuries.[1]

Knowing they have a quick and efficient means to introduce a new or improved product to a large market, manufacturers are willing to make substantial investments in new product research and development. The faster they can get millions of consumers to try and accept a new product the faster they can build a profitable volume of sales and the faster they can recover their investment in research and development.

Having the means to tell the consuming public about a new product is, in itself, an incentive to invention and innovation. Having the means to proclaim a product's superiority is an incentive to making it live up to its claim. Having the means to compete in advertising stimulates competitive rivalry in the laboratories and factories. Advertising enhances the opportunity to succeed. It also enhances the opportunity to fail. Even though it may not be the cause of a successful or an unsuccessful product introduction advertising accelerates both outcomes.

Expanding consumption is essential to an expanding economy. Expanding consumption involves more people spending more money for more goods and services to satisfy more wants. In a modern industrial society the basic wants of food, clothing and shelter are reasonably well met for most people. For them to spend more they must want more. As Professor Frank H. Knight wrote, "The chief thing that the common-sense individual actually wants is not satisfactions for the wants which he has, but more and better wants."[2] It might be assumed that consumer wants are automatically and infinitely expansible. Such is not the case. Once the appetite for food and drink as nourishment becomes satiated the satisfactions to be derived from menu planning from more exotic foods and serving rituals must be learned. Similarly, once the need for clothing and shelter as means of protection against the elements is met, the uses of these items for self adornment, social approval, and hedonistic pleasures

---

[1] Neil H. Borden, *The Economic Effect of Advertising* (Homewood, Ill.: Richard D. Irwin, Inc., 1942), p. 881.

[2] Frank H. Knight, *The Ethics of Competition* (New York: Harper & Bros., 1935), p. 22.

must be recognized. In our affluent society a multiplicity of services accounts for a large portion of the nation's economic activity. These have to be sold.

The view expressed in The Twentieth Century Fund study of American needs and resources highlights the importance of advertising in a luxury economy:

> In a scarcity economy the consumer needs no conditioning to make him want enough food to keep alive, sufficient clothing and shelter to keep warm. But in an economy of luxury and plenty, the consumer has to be persuaded to want, for example, an electric blanket with a separate thermostatic control for each side of the bed, or an air-conditioned automobile with power steering and a hydramatic drive. This constant "education" of consumers to desire products never heard of before is just as essential to the smooth functioning of an economy which is geared to turn out a steady flood of new and different products as are an adequate supply of electric energy and plentiful raw materials. The American standard of living is thus the cause no less than the result of American creativeness and productivity.[3]

In a sense, all marketing activity which includes advertising is designed to sell a higher standard of living.

As an individual's wants are expanded and intensified his motivation to work increases. Basically, one does not work for money, but rather for the satisfactions that money can buy. His anticipation of satisfactions to be derived from additional products, services, and financial security stimulates his incentive to work and increase his earnings. Thus, we see the circularity of the free market system. Consumer wants not only support production—they also provide the incentive to produce. In a primitive economy where only the essentials for survival are available there is much leisure time. There is little or no incentive to do more work because there is little or nothing more to have. This suggests that economic progress in the so-called underdeveloped nations rests largely on the concurrent growth of their wants, productivity, and production. Advertising can make only a modest contribution in the early stages of development. However, as discretionary spending power increases, as the distribution of income widens, and as the supply of goods and services grows advertising becomes a more important part of the system.

Some observers suggest that the power of advertising is so great that it deprives consumers of their discretion in the marketplace and makes it

---

[3] J. Frederic Dewhurst and Associates, *America's Needs and Resources* (New York: The Twentieth Century Fund, 1955).

possible for suppliers to "manage demand." John Kenneth Galbraith, one
of the more articulate of these observers, notes:

The control or management of demand is, in fact, a vast and rapidly growing
industry in itself. It embraces a huge network of communications, a great array
of merchandising and selling organizations, nearly the entire advertising industry,
numerous ancillary research, training and other related services and much more.
In everyday parlance this great machine and the demanding and varied talents that
it employs, are said to be engaged in selling goods. In less ambiguous language
it means that it is engaged in the management of those who buy goods.[4]

Mr. Galbraith overrates the power of advertising and underrates the
power of consumers. As we shall see in subsequent chapters the consumer
controls his own behavior. He is highly selective, accepting that which
serves his purpose, rejecting the rest.

VALUE ADDED

Value, in an economic sense, is not easily defined. Various terms have
been used to describe it. Various models have been devised to measure
it. The fact that different people operate from different standards of value
complicates the matter still further. Our purpose here is not to embark
on an exhaustive examination of the subject but rather to illuminate the
relationship of value and advertising.

Early explanations of value used the word utility (usefulness) and
various kinds of economic activity have been explained in terms of the
kind of utility they added. Thus, manufacturing adds *form utility* by
converting raw materials to a more useful form. Transportation adds
place utility by moving goods from places where they are abundant to
places where they are scarce. Storage adds *time utility* by holding goods
for future use. These kinds of utilities are tangible and readily understood. Any activity that increased these utilities was recognized as productive activity. The productivity of any activity that didn't fit into one
of these categories was open to question.

The term "value added" has been used to denote increases in value of
raw materials as they move through the manufacturing process. The value
of lumber is increased when it is cured, cut, and shaped into a piece of
furniture. The amount of value added at each stage is the difference in
market prices before and after that stage of processing.

---

[4] John Kenneth Galbraith, *The New Industrial State* (Boston: Houghton Mifflin Company, 1967), p. 200.

A more sophisticated view treats value as an intangible psychological phenomenon. Value exists in the mind or within the person, not in the thing. Value is what it is perceived to be. It is the sum total of all the perceived utilities, satisfactions, and rewards—either in the realm of expectations before purchase or in experiences during and after use. The image of the brand is as much a part of value as the product's utilitarian functions. Obviously, a steel razor blade has greater value than a chunk of iron ore. Also, a Gillette Platinum-Plus blade is perceived by some people as having greater value than any other brand of blade. The known and familiar brand has more value than the unknown brand. Confidence in a product or service is worth paying for. Among competing brands in some product categories, such as gasoline, there may be no discernible physical differences. However, the consumer who perceives one brand as being superior will attach greater value to it. For him it is more valuable.

Advertising modifies the consumer's perceptions of goods and services. It might be said that advertising adds *perceptual utility*. Insofar as these changes in perceptions make the product more desirable, advertising adds value. Martin Mayer, in his book *Madison Avenue, U.S.A.*, stated this concept succinctly: "Whenever a benefit is promised from the use of a product, and the promise is believed, the use of the product carries with it a value not inherent in the product itself."[5] The fact that a consumer will pay more for an advertised brand than an unadvertised brand clearly demonstrates that advertising has added value. For example, all aspirin tablets are required by the U.S. Pharmacopoeia to contain the same quantity and purity of active ingredients, yet millions of consumers pay two to three times more for Bayer than for unadvertised brands. Even though all brands of aspirin are technically identical they are perceived as being different and for the perceiver they are different. As Professor George J. Stigler has observed:

"Reputation" is a word which denotes the persistence of quality and reputation commands a price (or extracts a penalty) because it economizes on search. When economists deplore the reliance of the consumer on reputation . . . they implicitly assume that the consumer has a large laboratory, ready to deliver current information quickly and gratuitously.[6]

Reputation of the brand is largely the result of product performance and advertising.

---

[5] Martin Mayer, *Madison Avenue, U.S.A.* (New York: Harper & Row, 1958).

[6] George J. Stigler, "The Economics of Information," *The Journal of Political Economy,* June 1961, p. 224.

ADVERTISING, COMPETITION AND MONOPOLY

Underlying the classic theory of pure competition are two assumptions: (1) a large number of sellers each operating independently so that no single seller can control supply, and therefore, price; (2) a standardized product so that any seller's product is substitutable for anothers', thereby depriving every seller the opportunity to distinguish his product and command a higher price than his competitor's. Under these conditions prices move freely reflecting the counter forces of supply and demand. Such a situation is approximated in the commodity markets, but otherwise does not exist in the real world. At the other extreme is monopoly, a single seller who controls the supply, and therefore, the price. Except for so-called natural monopolies in the field of government-regulated public utilities, monopolies do not exist in the real world either. What we have in most industries are relatively few competitors each differentiating his product in an attempt to attain some degree of monopoly power. Professor Edward H. Chamberlin labelled this kind of activity "monopolistic competition."[7]

Product differentiation may be based on certain characteristics of the product itself, such as exclusive patented features, trade mark and brand name; or on the uniqueness of the package; or on any singularity in quality, design, color, or style. Patents and copyrights confer a monopoly granting "for limited times to authors and inventors, exclusive rights to their respective writings and discoveries." The inventor has the sole right to manufacture and sell his invention for seventeen years. Thus, even though a patent confers a monopoly, it also stimulates competition by encouraging initiative, invention, innovation and enterprise. Similarly, the exclusive right to use a particular trade mark or brand name stimulates competitive rivalry among brands. The advertiser seeks to differentiate his brand, to embellish it with attractions so that a large number of consumers will prefer it over all others. Whatever reputation he is able to build for the brand accrues solely to that brand. A brand monopoly depends on consumers *thinking* that the brand will give greater satisfaction per dollar spent than some other brand. Such a monopoly is dependent on a control of human attitudes rather than a control of supply.

What kind of monopoly power does a successful brand-name adver-

---

[7] Edward Hastings Chamberlin, *The Theory of Monopolistic Competition* (Cambridge, Mass.: Harvard University Press, 1947).

tiser achieve? In theoretical terms, the demand schedule shifts so that more units will be bought at the same price. Demand also becomes more inelastic which means he can raise his price while experiencing a less than proportionate decrease in unit sales. With greater stability in sales he can program production more efficiently. Instead of competing on a price basis alone, he has the option of competing on the basis of advertising and promotion. In effect, he gains some power to maximize revenue and profit by controlling volume and/or price, and/or advertising and promotion. Whatever control he gains is based on the loyalty of his customers to the brand. If the price differential becomes too great he risks losing customers to competing brands. Brand monopolies, therefore, are subject to the whims of consumers and the counter moves of competitors.

Some observers contend that advertising enhances the monopoly power already enjoyed by large corporations. Professor Jules Backman, who does not agree with this contention, refers to it in his book, *Advertising and Competition,* as "the power of the large purse:"[8]

1. The large company has the power of the large purse, which enables it to spend substantial sums on advertising, particularly to implement varying degrees of product differentiation which enables a company to pre-empt part of a market.
2. Advertising thus creates a barrier to new firms entering an industry or a product market.
3. The result is high economic concentration.
4. Because of their protected position and because of product differentiation these firms can charge monopolistic prices which are too high. Moreover, they must recover the cost of the advertising by charging higher prices.
5. High prices in turn result in excessively large profits.

The high cost of using national media such as network television on a large scale restricts the use of such media to the few advertisers who can afford them. This supports the charge that advertising gives an unfair competitive advantage to the large firms. Their ability to bear the high cost of introducing new products nationally and to outspend small competitors is assumed to discourage would-be entrants and also make it difficult for others to survive. It is further assumed that large firms gain a larger share of the market because they can afford to gain a larger share of the public mind. Undoubtedly, large firms with great financial resources can do many things that small firms cannot do—including large-scale advertising. However, the opportunity to advertise gives the small firm a chance to get started. If he has a good product or service fairly

---

[8] Jules Backman, *Advertising and Competition* (New York: New York University Press, 1967), p. 4.

priced he can advertise and build a market. He obviously can't match the giant firms on a national scale, but he might be able to outspend them in his local market area. As his business grows he can use advertising to enter new markets and expand his own competitive capabilities. Many local and regional advertisers compete successfully against large national advertisers.

Ultimately, consumers pay for the cost of all advertising in the prices they pay for goods and services. This leads to the belief that large advertisers must charge higher prices, or that prices would be lower without advertising. Such a belief overlooks the lower unit manufacturing and marketing costs that result from large scale production. To the extent that advertising builds a mass market it can be assumed that advertising facilitates mass production with its concomitant lower unit costs. A free market system counts on competition, even competition among a few giant firms referred to as an oligopoly, to pass along the benefit of such cost reductions in the form of lower prices.

In his study of the effects of advertising on competition, Professor Backman concluded:

> Practically all markets are an amalgam of elements of monopoly and of competition. The possession of the monopoly of a brand is not the totality of the market situation. National brands must meet the competition of other national brands, substitute products, private brands, local or regional brands, and products sold solely on a price basis. The dynamic, competitive nature of these markets is underlined by the marked changes in brand shares, the successes achieved by many new national brands and private brands against so-called entrenched brands, and the inability of well-known and financially strong companies successfully to establish new brands at will. These developments indicate that the degree of market power, which supposedly accompanies product differentiation identified by brand names and implemented by large-scale advertising, is much weaker than claimed and is usually outweighed by competitive pressures.[9]

ADVERTISING AND THE PRESS

The fact that the press, including television and radio, is supported financially by advertising raises some questions about the freedom of the press from advertiser control. Newspapers and magazines get 60 to 70 percent of their revenue from advertising. Commercial television and radio broadcasting are financed entirely by advertising. The notion that "he who pays the fiddler calls the tunes" underlies the suspicion that ad-

---

[9] *Ibid.*, pp. 155–56.

vertisers influence news coverage by suppressing and distorting the news to their own advantage.

In the case of labor difficulties in some industrial plants, it has been maintained that the press has built up public opinion against the demands of labor, and that only news items favorable to the employer and unfavorable to the employees have been offered to the public.

The Federal Trade Commission, in its inquiry into the publicity and propaganda activities of the electric power and gas industries of the country, has presented evidence bearing on the question of the influence of advertisers on the character of news printed. The Commission pointed out that, "when it is understood that 'the newspaper or magazine is practically a by-product of advertising,' and that advertising expenditures therefore frequently carry a certain element of goodwill response from the recipients, the large total spent by utilities for advertising is relevant...."[10]

The extent to which advertisers do or do not exercise control over the press has been studied and reported on at various times by objective scholars of the subject. In 1947 the Commission on Freedom of the Press reported that "the evidence of dictation of policy by advertisers is not impressive. Such dictation seems to occur among the weaker units. As a newspaper becomes financially stable it becomes more independent and tends to resist pressure from advertisers."[11] Theodore Peterson, in commenting on the pressures of advertisers on magazine editorial content in the first half of the twentieth century, stated, "A safe generalization perhaps is that direct advertising pressure—especially successful pressure—was much less than the average reader may guess; that most advertising pressure was subtle and just part of a greater pressure, the economic struggle for survival."[12]

Consolidation is registered by some from the fact that advertisers make possible low-priced magazines and newspapers and free radio and television entertainment. It is pointed out that the education of the masses is greatly increased by low-priced newspapers and magazines. The tremendous circulation of newspapers and magazines is made possible by the

---

[10] Federal Trade Commission, "Propaganda Activities of Utility Interests," *Public Utilities Release No. 240,* p. 1.

[11] Commission on Freedom of the Press, *A Free and Responsible Press* (Chicago: University of Chicago Press, 1947), p. 62.

[12] Theodore Peterson, *Magazines in the Twentieth Century,* 2d ed. (Urbana, Ill.: University of Illinois Press, 1964), p. 38.

subsidy rendered by advertisers. If this subsidy were eliminated, either some other means of financing the press would be necessary or a great drop in circulation would result, with many publications going out of existence entirely.

Alternative methods of financing the press perhaps hold many more dangers than the present method of major financial dependence upon advertisers. Early newspapers, both in England and America, were dependent upon the government or political parties for their economic life. With the development of advertising as an important source of revenue for newspapers, the press was able to free itself from political control. Steven Shaw, in reviewing the history of newspapers in colonial America, says, "It was during this period (1690–1750) that freedom of the press was fought for and won, and newspaper advertising was built up to the point where editors could begin to divorce themselves from dependence on political subsidy, postmasterships, job printing, and other revenues except copy sales."[13]

This point is emphasized even more strongly in the history of the *Times* (London) in this statement: "The commercial interest lies at the root of Press independence in daily journalism. . . . In the main, the commercial body is essential in journalism, and such freedom as the Press enjoys is dependent on commercial advertising."[14]

In some countries the press is financed by political parties. If that were true in America freedom in editorial and news policy would be in great danger. In general, the advertiser is not interested in news and editorial policy except as such policy tends to select the kind of audience which he wishes to reach with paid sales messages. This audience selection is left to the medium in the case of newspapers and magazines. The advertiser often influences the program content of radio and television as a means of selecting a desired audience, but such programs are primarily of an entertainment character and are recognized by the audience as sponsored by the advertiser.

There is safety, too, in the large number of advertisers. The influence that one advertiser might like to exert is directly opposite to what another would want. The large number of advertisers also means that a publisher can "afford" to lose some of them without particular financial harm. The

---

[13] Steven Shaw, "Colonial Newspaper Advertising: A Step Toward Freedom of the Press," *The Business History Review*, Vol. XXXIII, No. 3 (1959), p. 410.

[14] Blanche B. Elliott, *A History of English Advertising* (London: Business Publications, Ltd., 1962), p. xiv.

most vital factor, however, is the fact that advertisers need the press as much as the owners and managers of the press need advertisers. Advertisers need the press's circulations and audiences to advertise effectively. If they succeeded in influencing the news the press would risk losing public confidence which in turn would reduce circulation and jeopardize the effectiveness of the press as an advertising medium.

A word should also be said about the control which the press might exercise over advertisers. Since advertisers need the press as much as the press needs advertisers, it would seem that the latter should not be denied access to the various media of communications. This has not always been true. There have been times when publishers have refused to carry the advertisements of legitimate business firms. Refusal has been, not on grounds of false or exaggerated claims but rather for purposes of influencing the private business policy of the advertiser.

This control or pressure is illustrated by the case of a Loraine, Ohio, publisher who refused to accept the advertisements of any local business firms that also advertised over the local radio station. The purpose of such action was to injure a competitor of the publisher, but it also injured the advertiser. Both aspects of such action were condemned by the Federal Trade Commission.

ADVERTISING AND FREEDOM OF SPEECH

Freedom of speech has always been a cardinal principle of American life. Freedom to speak one's mind to influence others would generally not be questioned. Ability to speak freely to the masses, however, has usually been limited to those with large financial resources. Editors, columnists, and public speakers whose comments get into news reports have made up the bulk of those able to reach a mass audience. The "layman" without great wealth has been obliged to speak to only the few who can hear his voice.

Very recent developments in advertising have changed this. Today there is a rapidly growing use of the advertising pages of our newspapers and magazines to sell ideas. This development means that our mass media are becoming available as an open forum which can be used by almost any person or group wishing to speak to the masses. Large audiences can thus be reached with a very small financial outlay. For a few thousand dollars one can speak to millions. This use of advertising is expanding the meaning of free speech in a manner never before conceived as being possible.

A slightly different emphasis on advertising's contribution to free speech is given by John Dollard. He says:

Advertising is one form of free speech in a business society. As such, I see no serious threat in it. So long as we rely on persuasion, in the loose and relatively free situation of the democratic society, advertising cannot be a menace to individual integrity. Totalitarian coercion is indeed something to be feared. Only when there is a monopoly of power over life and death as well as a monopoly of influence is there a real possibility of the robotized public. In a democratic society with its freedom of thought and speech advertising may be at times a blessing and at others a nuisance but it can never be a menace to the free man.[15]

Mr. Dollard was referring primarily to the freedom to speak about one's products and commercial services. Perhaps even more basic from a social viewpoint in a democracy is the availability of advertising as a medium for distributing the thoughts and ideas of individuals and groups who wish to "speak" to the multitudes—ideas that have no direct commercial implications.

The famous "Heed Their Rising Voices" newspaper advertisement that ran in the *New York Times,* March 29, 1960, illustrates this point. Here a group of serious people wanted to get a message before a large audience and chose an advertisement as the method to do so. The message criticized public officials and brought violent reaction from some officials who sued the *Times* and the advertisers for libel.

Had this same message been delivered by a speaker from a public platform or presented as an editorial by the newspaper, it is likely that no action would have been taken. The plaintiff, however, argued that, because the message appeared as a paid advertisement, it did not have the protection of the guarantee of freedom of speech and press in the Constitution.

The U.S. Supreme Court in the *New York Times Co.* v. *Sullivan* decision (March 10, 1964) denied the plaintiff's claim. It held that "any other conclusion would discourage newspapers from carrying 'editorial advertisements' of this type, and so might shut off an important outlet for the promulgation of information and ideas by persons who do not themselves have access to publishing facilities—who wish to exercise their freedom of speech even though they are not members of the press."[16]

Additional attention to this aspect of advertising is given in Chapter

---

[15] John Dollard, "Fear of Advertising," in Sandage and Fryburger, *The Role of Advertising, op. cit.,* p. 317.

[16] *New York Times Co.* v. *Sullivan* 376 U.S. 254 (1964).

6. Certainly the development of editorial advertising has great social significance.

SOCIAL INFLUENCE

Historian David Potter in his book *People of Plenty* observed that "advertising now compares with such long-standing institutions as the school and the church in the magnitude of its social influence." He says "it dominates the media, has vast power in the shaping of popular standards and is really one of the very limited group of institutions which exercise social control."[17] Mr. Potter concludes that advertising, unlike the school and the church, makes people like what they get, diminishes the range and variety of choices and "exalts the materialistic virtues of consumption." Other observers subscribing to this "powerful force" theory claim that advertising distorts human values, that it makes people want the wrong things (too much beer, liquor and cigarettes; not enough schools, antipollution controls and urban renewals), that it promotes private luxuries at the expense of public squalor, that it creates discontent by making people dissatisfied with what they have or by making them wish for things beyond their reach, that it contributes to waste by encouraging people to discard clothing, appliances, automobiles, and the like before they are worn out.

Observers holding these views of social influence are making various assumptions about the power of advertising, about the wisdom of people, and about the importance of the individual. They assume that the power of advertising is so great it can get people to do what they don't want to do—that people are not capable of making choices in their own self-interest. They assume that individual free choice should be superseded by authoritarian control.

The power of advertising is not that great. The audience's predispositions, their attitudes, beliefs, motives and values largely determine the media they select, the advertisements they see, the messages they accept and the products they buy. Instead of forcing a response, advertising elicits responses the audience was predisposed to make. Advertising succeeds when it gives people what they want. Consumer responses in the marketplace are free and voluntary. *Caveat emptor* (let the buyer beware) has given way to *caveat venditor* (let the seller beware).

---

[17] David Potter, *People of Plenty* (Chicago: University of Chicago Press, 1954), Chapter VIII.

Evidence that consumers are competent to advance social welfare while functioning as consumers is abundant. Individual efforts to advance one's standard of living helps expand the economy which, in turn, provides the financial support for government programs. As voters in a democratic society consumers voluntarily support social welfare legislation and foreign aid programs. As taxpayers they pay the society's bills. Advertising communicates a wide range of choices and facilitates the selection process. Much as a democratic society depends on an informed electorate, a free market system depends on informed consumers.

If consumers are not competent to choose wisely, who is? Can any one person decide better than consumers themselves what best serves their interest? In view of the great diversity of tastes, preferences, life styles, means of self expression and measures of success should anyone be empowered to impose his choices on others? A free market system assumes that everybody allocates resources better than anybody.

Advertising does educe dissatisfaction, but ordinarily it does so by holding forth the benefits of superior products. Changing from less satisfying to more satisfying products should result in a net gain. Again, it should be noted that expanding consumption is essential to an expanding economy. Insofar as advertising stimulates greater consumption, or sells a higher standard of living, it contributes to social progress through industrial growth.

Advertising is now being used more frequently to meet social problems head-on, as evidenced by the Advertising Council's campaigns dealing with drug abuse, crime prevention, rehabilitation of the handicapped, continuing education, and traffic safety. The advertisers, agencies, and media who finance these campaigns recognize the potential of advertising for influencing the conscience of society as well as the spending of consumers.

QUESTIONS AND PROBLEMS

1. "Since manufacturers that advertise could sell their products for less if they did not spend so much on advertising, the consumer will usually get better value for his money in unadvertised brands of products than in advertised brands." Do you agree? Support your stand.

2. "Present-day advertising is desirable because it encourages people to want things." Do you agree? Why?

3. Advertising makes people choose the wrong things—too much beer, liquor and cigarettes; not enough schools, urban renewals and foreign aid. Do you agree or disagree? Why?

4. In a free market system the producers of goods and services allocate the nation's economic resources. Do you agree or disagree? Why?

5. Borden says: "Advertising's outstanding contribution to consumer welfare comes from its part in promoting a dynamic, expanding economy." Explain.

6. Should advertising play a different role in a country where consumer purchasing power is high and broadly distributed and where there is an abundance of both "need" and "want" goods than it should in a country where goods are relatively scarce and purchasing power is low?

7. Do you believe that the present standard of living would be at its present stage if we had had no advertising in the past? Why?

8. Assuming that a product is what it is perceived to be, how does advertising enhance a product's value?

9. Advertising gives a competitive advantage to "big business" because big advertisers can win a larger share of the public mind than smaller advertisers. Do you agree or disagree? Explain.

10. What kind of monopolies, if any, are built up by advertising? Upon what are they based?

11. Democracies point with pride to their freedom of the press. Do advertisers threaten this freedom? Explain.

12. A wholesaling firm which sells new types of household appliances does little advertising but employs twenty traveling salesmen to call on retail stores. Their sales account for most of the firm's business. Next year the company will change its policy and spend $50,000 for direct-mail advertising to the stores and in trade journals. Will the company need to raise the prices of its merchandise to cover the advertising expense?

13. Dr. Alberto Gainza Pas, exiled publisher of *La Prensa,* a Buenos Aires daily newspaper, said this about advertising's relationship with the press: "The free press has always been an unconditional ally of freedom, and I can say today through personal experience. . . . that the best ally that the free press has is in advertisements and advertising people. In my opinion, in the contemporary world it is impossible to have a free press without economic independence, and you cannot have economic independence without advertising."

14. Comment on the following statement: "Freedom of speech in modern America is largely a hollow freedom unless those who wish to speak have available modern facilities for distributing their speech to the masses."

Is advertising one of the "modern distribution facilities" for free speech?

chapter 4
ADVERTISING AS COMMUNICATION

IN A COMPLEX economy such as that in the United States it is essential to have some system of mass communication between producers and consumers. This was not so essential before our great industrial development with its concentration of production facilities and wide dispersion of consumers. It was not too many years ago that production was highly localized and producers depended largely on consumers who lived close by to take their products. Under such circumstances face-to-face and word-of-mouth communication was generally sufficient to inform consumers of what goods were available to them. Furthermore, there was a relative scarcity of production, and it was largely confined to meeting the basic physiological needs of people. The variety of choices available to consumers was minimal. With need as a motivating force consumers would exert extra effort to seek out sources of supply, thus diminishing the necessity for producer-originated information about their commodities.

Today, consumers are highly mobile. They move from one to another part of the country with significant frequency. Producers do not limit their market to people living in the immediate vicinity of their farms or factories but consider the entire nation and much of the world as their market. Also in the United States, and to an increasing degree in other countries, production is plentiful and the variety of choices available to consumers is great.

With specialization and centralization in production, with dispersion of consumers, and with great abundance of supply, it is imperative that some kind of formalized machinery be available to provide effective mass communication between producers and consumers. Advertising performs this role in modern society in both capitalist and communist countries. In speaking of advertising in Russia, D. Kurnin said, "Thanks to well-organized advertising, the consumer can more rapidly find the goods needed by him, purchase them with a smaller expenditure of time, and select the goods according to his particular taste."[1]

What to communicate

In general, the communication function of advertising should serve to assist consumers in their search for goods and services and to satisfy their needs and wants. In short, it should be a guide to buying. Communication, to be helpful to consumers in guiding them in their search for satisfaction, should be informative, educational, and persuasive. It should tell consumers of (1) the existence of want-satisfying products and services; (2) where they can be obtained; and (3) the qualities possessed, expressed in terms that will enable the consumer to make an intelligent choice. It should be educational in the sense that it not only increases consumer knowledge, but also enhances judgment in the process of reaching a buying decision. It should be sufficiently persuasive to move people to try the new and to test their inherent skepticism.

Notice of existence and where available

When we consider products in a generic sense, advertising in America has served and is now serving many of the functions of a buyer's guide. Such advertising has acquainted consumers with the existence and general utility of electric refrigerators, radios, telephones, television sets, and so on through practically every item of human consumption. The importance of such a guiding factor was admirably illustrated 40 years ago by the experience of Norman Angell, as portrayed in an article in the London *Spectator*.

Angell narrated his experiences in attempting to buy a "horse scraper"

---

[1] D. Kurnin, "Iz Opyta Sovetskoi Torgovloi Reklamy," *Sovetskaia Torgovlia,* February, 1958, p. 46.

to use for excavation work on one of his farms in England. He knew the type of product desired but did not know where it could be purchased. A persistent search among dealers and through the advertising pages of agricultural magazines brought no results, although the instrument he sought was manufactured in England.

Sometime later, Angell journeyed to Chicago. While there he located, through the advertising section of the telephone directory, the names of dealers and manufacturers of the product he had sought in England. In addition, a telephone call to a mail-order firm brought him, within 24 hours, a catalog giving an illustration, a description, and the price of a horse scraper.

Angell contrasts the situation in England and America thus:

> The point to be observed is this: horse scrapers (and many other items) may be obtainable in England at somewhere near the price for which they are obtainable in America. But the fact is very carefully hidden from the man who wants to buy them, or would want them if he knew of them. If one prospective buyer who knew that such things existed, and wanted them, could not discover where they were obtainable, what is the chance of selling them when even merchants that would be logical dealers for such items believe they do not exist? In America the manufacturer takes care to see that everything that he has for sale which can be useful to farm, house, or factory, is made known in the right quarter. If the knowledge were more readily available in Britain, it would add as much to the market of the farm as to the market of the factory.[2]

This admirable contrast emphasizes the fact that advertising in America has served the buyer by informing him of the existence of want-satisfying commodities. It has further aided him by pointing out where these items can be purchased and at what price.

The need for informing consumers of the existence of new products is especially acute in an expanding economy where a large part of the new products developed for consumption are products designed to meet wants rather than needs. Consumers cannot be expected to seek out luxury and semiluxury items that manufacturers have just made available. Each year sees the introduction of many new consumer items in the American and international markets. Out of the several hundred consumer products currently made by one of America's large manufacturers, 60 percent of them were not even in existence in 1950.

Consumers may leaf through the advertising pages of almost any

---

[2] Norman Angell, as quoted in *News Bulletin,* a publication of J. Walter Thompson & Co., March, 1928.

magazine and learn something about more products (new and old) than would generally be possible from visits to scores of manufacturing plants. Figure 4–1 is an example of one of the many ads that could be found in general magazines.

Advertisements in specialized business and professional publications are regularly checked by purchasing agents and others to note announcements of new products and pertinent information about old ones. An example of such a guiding help to prospective buyers is shown in Figure 4–2.

Advertisements in local newspapers serve consumers as guides to retail outlets and professional offices where new as well as familiar products and services can be obtained. Another type of advertising that provides a guide to consumers in this respect is the familiar classified section of the telephone book. Figure 4–3 shows this type of guide provided through advertising.

The need for some kind of guide to bring buyers and sellers together was recognized by Montaigne more than three centuries ago. He wrote:

> In every town I would like to see established an official with a great register. On one side would be inscribed all those things which their owners desired to sell: a pearl necklace, a horse, a house; on the other side of the register a list of all those things sought by those desiring to purchase: this burgher, it may be, needing a horse, that one a house. And it would be the duty of this official to make known the existence of the two parties, the one to the other. Too often it happens that the man wanting the horse does not know of the horse for sale, or vice versa, and both are the losers by this ignorance.

The nearest approach today to such a register is the want-advertisement sections of our modern newspapers. Here we do have the seller listing his wares and the buyer listing his wants.

During the time of Montaigne, the supply of goods for consumers was quite meager, and buyers often found it necessary to seek out suppliers rather than to wait until sellers came to them. The "register" or "want-ad" kind of advertising was then as now initiated by the buyer as well as by the seller (see Figure 4–4).

The general supply of goods today is such that sellers initiate most of the advertising and do so for purposes of guiding consumers toward their wares. There are still, however, many consumers who place their own ads when they want to buy a piece of furniture, an automobile, or an appliance. The same is often true for people who are seeking employment or a place to live.

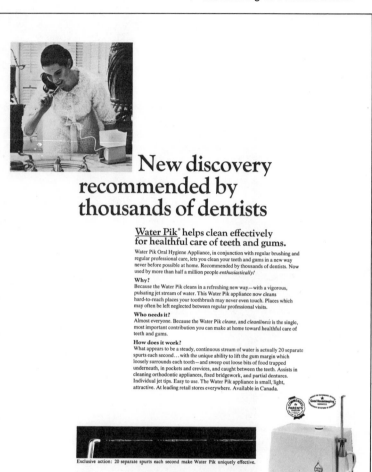

FIGURE 4–1. Consumers are informed of the new through ads like this

Keep paper rolls round and presses rolling with new Clark vacuum clamps

When your customer has to shut down a high-speed press because of creasing or ovality of newsprint rolls, you're in trouble. Clark paper handling experience keeps you out of trouble.

"Our new Clarklift® with Vacuum Newsprint Roll Handler substantially reduces paper damage and roll distortion—major causes of web tearing," says Ken Daniels, Pressroom Foreman of one of the nation's newest, most modern printing plants, the Binghamton, N.Y., Evening Press.

Here's how the Clark vacuum clamp works. Vacuum power forces the paper roll against gripper pads. Shear reducing strips, plus a vacuum seal on the outer edges of the pad, provide a secure, fast pick-up. Fail-safe indicator lights and a reserve tank provide a hold period in case of vehicle power failure.

The Vacuum Roll Handler permits rapid breakout of rolls for unloading, eliminating gouging by completely eliminating manhandling of key rolls. And since you don't have to leave room for hydraulic clamp arms, you save 15% floor space by touch stacking.

To help make sure your newsprint rolls arrive in top condition, start them on their way with a Clark Vacuum Roll Handler. For a demonstration, call your local Clark dealer listed in the Yellow Pages under "Trucks, Industrial."

Clark *is* material handling

CLARK®
EQUIPMENT

Battle Creek, Michigan 49016

FIGURE 4–2. Information helpful to industrial buyers

Air Conditioning Equipment & Systems

Aire Temperature Co 3912 N Ashlnd------472-2911
Commercial Refrgrtn Service
  24 Hour Emergency Service
  2102 N Clark------------------248-5487
Crose Co 4150 N Lincln--------------477-0600
Globe Engnrng & Eqpmnt Co 3161 N Clybn-348-2155
LAKE SHORE REFRGRTN SALES &
  SERVICE 5786 N Ridge----------LO 1-3333
YORK AIR CONDITIONING EQUIPMENT—
  RESIDENTIAL & COMMERCIAL—
  DEALERS
  MAYNARD C S CO INC
    2757 N Lincln--------------BI 8-2868

Air Conditioning Equipment & Systems—Repairing

AIR COMFORT CORP

24 HOUR SERVICE
ALL MAKES - ALL SIZES
Industrial - Commercial - Residential
CARRIER AUTHORIZED
SALES & SERVICE

816 N Kostner------------------342-3400
Nites - Sat & Sundays 342-3472

Gold Coast Refrgrtn & Air Condtg Co
  1758 N Larrabee---------------MI 2-5735
MAYNARD C S CO INC

24 HOUR SERVICE
Commercial - Industrial
AIR CONDITIONING
Refrigeration Specialists
Heating & Piping

2757 N Lincoln----------------BI 8-2868

Air Conditioning Equipment & Systems—Supplies & Parts

Gatz A Suply Co 4204 N Lincln-------BU 1-4845
Starr Walter W 2833 N Lincln----------248-8269

Air Conditioning—Room Units

Albion Div McGraw-Edison Co
  1030 W North-------------------337-2626
B&G Serv Co 1804 W Irvng Pk---------WE 5-5675
Chambers Telvsn & Appliance Co
  3546 N Ashlnd-----------------BU 1-7373
S & S TELVSN ENGNRS
  Installation-Service-Repairs
  4949 N Bway------------------LO 1-9643

Air Conditioning Systems—Cleaning

A-1 Duct Clng & Fire Protection Service
  514 W Grant-----------------EA 7-3226
Available Duct Clng Co 3116 N Cliftn----248-4482
Industrial Clng Service 3804 N Clark----WE 5-5120
Kleen Air Service Co 2611 N Halstd-----327-2658
Midwest Duct Clng Co 1905 W Wolfrm---GR 2-8387

Air Cooling & Heating Systems

See specific headings, such as—Air Conditioning
Equipment & Systems; Heating Contractors;
Ventilating Contractors; Refrigerating Equipment
—Commercial

Air Freight Service

Airline Cartage Inc 2626 N Clybn-------248-9107

Aircraft Models & Supplies

See Hobby & Construction Supplies headings

Alarm Systems—See Burglar Alarm Systems

Ale—See Beer Distributors

Ambulance Service

A AS AMERICAN AMBULANCE & OXYGEN SERVICE

AMBULANCES
Anywhere - Anytime
RADIO DISPATCH OFFICE

RA 3-4200

7831 S. Racine

A-C AMBULANCE & OXYGEN SERVICE
Since 1880
ARNTZEN-COLEMAN
24 HR. SERVICE ● CITY & SUBURBS
Long Distance Trips A Specialty

561-1885   787-0056

4611 N. Lincoln   800 N. Clark

Aaron Ambulance & Oxygen Service Inc
  1328 W Belmnt----------------327-5252
ACORN ENTERPRISES 2848 N Talmn-KE 9-9696

Listings of this classification,

AMBULANCE SERVICE

are continued on next page.

RADIO DISPATCHED

LAKE VIEW

ALL CADILLAC AMBULANCES
OXYGEN EQUIPPED

DAY | NIGHT SERVICE

COMPLETE OXYGEN RENTAL SERVICE

Call Radio Dispatch

DI 8-1838

Central AMBULANCE
SERVICE
CLARK & FULLERTON
2334 N. Geneva

FIGURE 4–3. A familiar guide for buyers

AUTO SERVICES

BATTERIES
$8.95 ANY CAR with exchange
Unconditionally Guaranteed

13 Oak St.
Monee, Ill.
563-8150

AUTO SERVICES

GENERATORS
$9.95 ANY CAR with exchange

12156 S. Halsted St.
South Chicago, Ill.
928-1623

BEAUTY SCHOOL

LEARN A
REWARDING CAREER
IN HAIR FASHIONS
Day or Part-time Classes
No age limit
Come in for Information
WITH NO OBLIGATION
BLUE ISLAND SCHOOL
OF BEAUTY CULTURE
12761-63 So. Western
Blue Island

388--4949

BEAUTY SERVICES

SPECIAL
Carol Richards Permanents
with Lanolin
Reg.
$15.00 . . . . . Now $7.50
Tues. & Weds. only with this
ad.

ANN'S BEAUTY SHOP
106 W. 154th St.
Harvey
ED 3-5070   331-8149

BEAUTY SHOPS

FREE

EMPRESS WIGLET
With a $19.00 Permanent
REG. $35.00 Value

PIERRE'S

COIFFURE SALON
Western Ave.
Park Forest, Ill.
PI 8-0800

BOWLING

OAK FOREST BOWL
32 Automatic Lanes
OPEN BOWLING
EVERY DAY
COCKTAIL LOUNGE
ALL MODERN EQUIPMENT
BANQUET HALL, PRO SHOP
INSTRUCTORS AVAILABLE
152nd and Cicero 687-2000

BUSINESS SERVICES

FOR SALE

BUSINESS CARDS
$4.45 per thousand & up. Ad
pens and pencils. Book Matches
Envelopes, Letterheads, Sales
Books, Statements, Shipping
Tags, Labels, Etc.
ASK FOR PAUL
SK 5--1581   OR SK 5--5594

CARPENTRY

PORCH & DECK WORK
General Remodeling - Repairing. Does Own Work-Free Estimates.
8 A.M. to Midnight- Mon to Fri.
8 A.M. to 6 P.M. Saturdays

CALL: 785--0810

CARPETING

CARPETING
From Model Homes
Balanced rolls
Never used.
Tremendous savings
PR 6-5950

CARPET & RUG CLEANERS

**PROFESSIONALLY
CLEANED CARPETING
& UPHOLSTRY**
Work Guaranteed!
Also - Stripping & Waxing
On All Types of Floors.
For FREE Estimates
PHONE 425--3337

ANNOUNCEMENTS

MUSIC POOL
A BAND FOR YOUR
SPECIAL NEED
Weddings   Lounges
Parties   College Dances
Teen Dances   Any Occasion
ANY TYPE OF MUSIC
CALL 424--3182

ANTENNA'S

ANTENNA'S
INSTALLED — REPAIRED
PROMPT SERVICE
TRI–STATE ANTENNA'S
238--383R

ANTIQUES

BUY — SELL — TRADE
Antiques, Antique Furniture,
Used Furniture, Glassware,
Clothing, and etc.
YOU NAME IT-WE'VE GOT IT
COLONY RE–SALE SHOP
1649 Chicago Rd.,
Chicago Heights
54--4608

**THREE BLIND MICE
ANTIQUE MART**
We buy and sell Antiques

Highway 54
Monee, Illinois
563--8871

ARTS & ANTIQUES

ANTIQUES, COLLECTA—
BLES, GLASS, CHINA,
BEAMS, FURNITURE, ETC.,
CHAIR RECANING.
MARJO COLLECTIONS
HOURS
Tues. and Fri., 10 A.M. to 2 P.M.
Wednesday 7 P.M. to 10 P.M.
Saturday, 10 A.M. to 5 P.M.
Sunday, 1 P.M. to 5 P.M.
36 E. 34TH ST.   STEGER
755--3737

AUCTIONS

**COL VAN DOREN'S
AUCTION**
Merchandise Consignments
Wanted - New & Used
Home, Farm, etc. Articles
SALE EVERY SAT. AT 7 P.M.
6415 W. 111th   Worth
PHONE 636-8131

AUTO RENTALS

RENT A CAR
$7 A WEEK AND UP

We have good used cars that
we will rent to you on a 52-
week basis. NO MILEAGE
CHARGES! After 6 months
you may apply rental payment
to purchase.

CALL: MR. THOMAS
9 a.m. to 9 p.m.

868--1115

AUTO ALARM

AUTO ALARM
2 hour service
for free estimates
call
928--8888
CREATIVE ELECTRONICS
10643 S. State St.
Chicago, Ill.

AUTO-DRIVING SCHOOL

DRIVING LESSONS.
• Bonded Instructors
• Dual Control Cars
"Your only Driving School in
the area"
UNITED DRIVING SCHOOL
522 E. 162nd-South Holland
333--6265

AUTOMOBILE REPAIRING

**CHUCK HOLE
SPECIAL**
WHEEL ALIGNMENT
$4.99
• We Correct Caster
• We Correct Camber
• We Correct Toe In
• Inspect Idler Arm
• Inspect Ball Joints
• Inspect Front Shocks
• Inspect Steering Geometry
• Adjust Steering if Required
CALL 339--9200
EXT. 254
**MONTGOMERY WARD
AUTO CENTER**
Dixie Square in Harvey
152nd & Dixie Hwy.

For the Finest Car Care-
See. . .
**ABELL BODY & FENDER
REPAIR**
AUTO & TRUCK PAINTING
16100 SUNTONE DRIVE
SOUTH HOLLAND
333--9047

AWNINGS

AWNINGS
CARPORTS — PATIO COVERS
PORCH ENCLOSURES
Permanent Aluminum Type
New Translucent Vinyl
Large Selection of Styles
FRAME WINDOWS - SIDING
STORM WINDOWS & DOORS
ROLLING PATIO DOORS
WHOLESALE & RETAIL
Free Estimates - FHA Terms
**JACOBS AWNING &
WINDOW CO.**
25 W. Sauk Trail- S. Chgo. Hts.

AWNINGS & CANOPIES

QUALITY STORM DOORS
AND CANOPIES
SPECIALLY PRICED
AWNINGS —

All Types
Prompt Service
Free Estimates

L & M HOME IMPROVEMENTS

15820 KEDZIE, MARKHAM
331--8284

CARPET & RUG CLEANERS

**CARPETS and
FURNITURE
CLEANED** in your home

the safe **DURACLEAN**
"flower-fresh"
way

JOE MATUS
SK 5--6504

**SMITH
CARPET CLEANING
and
UPHOLSTERY CLEANING**
Carpets Tacked Down or Tack-
less - Cleaned & Moth Proofed
Rooms May Be Used Im-
mediately. Furniture Legs Pro-
tected Against Rust.
Baseboard Areas Cleaned By
Hand.
For Free Estimates
ED 3-2117   849-1590

**CARPETS CLEANED IN
YOUR HOME BY
VONSCHRADER METHOD**
Ready to use in a few hours
Free Estimates   Insured

**CHAPMAN
CARPET CLEANERS**
754--7399

CAR WASH

**HOMEWOOD
CAR WASH**
IS FIRST IN SERVICE
Now . . . . SAVE 5c

PER GALLON
of gas toward purchase of your
car wash.

**HERTZ
RENT-A-CAR
SERVICE**
175th & Dixie Highway

PHONE
SY 8.9751

CERAMICS

CATHY — WARE CERAMICS
Ceramic Instruction
-Custom Firing-
Retail and Wholesale
GIFT ARTICLES ON ORDER
15704 Park Harvey 331-6895

CLOCK REPAIR

Restore, Repair &
Rebuild All Types of
Clocks - Inc. Antiques
MASTER DEGREE IN
CLOCK REPAIRING

We also Buy & Sell
Antique Clocks
FOR INFOR: CALL
389--6618

DISPOSAL SERVICE

**ALL SUBURBAN
DISPOSAL SERVICE**
TOM VOOGD, MGR.

GA 2--6029

RESIDENTIAL &
COMMERCIAL

DOG GROOMING

**OO—LA—LA
POODLE COIFFURES**

Complete Grooming on
Schnauzers & All Poodles.

SAVE $2.00 WITH THIS AD!
A.K.C. Reg. Poodle Puppies
Available.

By appointment Only
PLEASE PHONE 389-8487

DOG GROOMING

Prof. Grooming of
SCHNAUZERS
Min. -Stand. - Giants
Puppies Usually Available
Also Stud S*ervice
No Tranquilizers Used
PRIVATE
Ser. 7 days wk. & evenings
FOR APPT. CALL 448--8329

Poodle Grooming
"LA POODLE BAR"
Featuring Fluff Drying.
Styling Fur The
Pampered Poodle!!
798--9288
8 A.M. — 5 P.M. PRIVATE.

DOG TRAINING

DOG OBEDIENCE!
Group Training - Novice &
Advanced Eve. Classes
GER. SHEPHERD
ALL BREEDS
CANINE OBEDIENCE
COLLEGE
15701 S Cicero, Oak Forest
445--2616   687--3500

DRESSMAKER

EXPERIENCED
GERMAN SEAMSTRESS
Wishes to do sewing and al-
terations of all kinds.

PHONE 747--3884

THE PERSONAL TOUCH
Dresses Made for Special
Occasions. Alterations on
Dresses or Patterns
Bridal Parties Welcome!
For Infor. and Appt.
PLEASE CALL
312--448--4390

ELECTRICAL

240 VOLT 3 WIRE SERVICE
100 amp. fusion fuse box
Outside meter.
$91.
SHOCK ELECTRIC
331--7035
Any type electrical work
HAVE ELECTRICAL prob-
lems? Need new electrical
work? Call 221-7860.

ELECTRIC SHAVERS

ELECTRIC SHAVERS
• PARTS FOR ALL ELECTRIC
SHAVERS
KAUFMAN JEWELRY
3336 Chicago Road
Steger, Illinois
Phone SK 4-2298

ELECTROLYSIS

NELL MAE McCORKLE
—ELECTROLOGIST—
SPECIALIZING IN THE
PERMANENT REMOVAL OF
UNSIGHTLY HAIR.
Hours by Appointment
754 --5550
1010 Dixie Hwy., Chicago Hts.
(Executive Plaza-Suite 304)

FABRICS

CLOSE—OUT BARGAINS
Mill-ends of fabrics, plain &
quilted - suitable for wearing
apparel, bedspreads, throw
pillows, etc. 25c per yard and
up. Also some sample bed-
spreads and throw pillows at
low clearance prices.

PHONE 424--8583
Evenings Only

Guides to want-satisfying qualities

Another element in communication to guide consumers in their search for satisfaction of their needs and wants is that of telling them the qualities possessed by products and services in terms that will help them make an intelligent choice. The problem of decision making is not an easy one to solve in our highly competitive economy that offers a great variety of brands within any given generic classification of products. If only one supplier existed for each generic product, decision making would be relatively easy, but if such were the case, consumer freedom of choice would be greatly reduced.

The concept of freedom to choose from among the many brands of commodities available is a freedom that consumers generally wish to preserve—even though it involves making comparisons among vast numbers of brands. That there are vast numbers is well illustrated by data presented by the *Milwaukee Journal* for the greater Milwaukee market. In the *Journal's* consumer analysis[3] of that market is shown the great variety of brands in each of many generic classifications of products. A partial list of products and the number of brands reported for Milwaukee include: pipe tobacco 27, bottled catsup 14, regular coffee 19, canned tuna fish 11, frozen orange juice 13, canned peas 19, laundry soap 25, liquid shampoo 15, deodorant 21, hand lotion 17, television sets 19, and butter 21.

The consumer is generally benefited by having a number of producers competing for her business. But when the number of brands available becomes great, the consumer is often bewildered and confused. It is here that the advertiser needs to give maximum attention to detailed description and meaningful exposition of the want-satisfying qualities of his particular brand. The consumer wants intelligent guidance. To receive intelligent guidance through advertising, individual ads must be abundantly informative.

Complete presentation

Unless an advertisement contains statements that are true, it cannot serve as a real guide to consumer purchases. Untruthful advertisements

---

[3] *Consumer Analysis* (Milwaukee, Wis.: *Milwaukee Journal,* 1970).

would establish false direction posts to lead the consumer astray. Truth is necessary, not only for the individual advertiser, but for the great bulk of advertising. Consumers wish to compare one brand with another; hence, it is quite vital that each producer be honest in presenting the merits of his particular brand. The presence of only a few false prophets makes it practically impossible for the consumer to distinguish the true from the false.

To be an effective guide, truth must be interpreted to mean the inclusion of all quality factors that would have a bearing on the ability of the product to meet the needs and wants of consumers. This means that some characteristics of the product which might appear to be negative in character should be mentioned. If a particular brand of canned peas is grade C in quality, that might be a factor of importance to the consumer, and if so, it should be mentioned in the advertisement. That brand would undoubtedly have a lower price, too, than a brand that was grade A quality. If the consumer is told both the grade and the price, a more intelligent decision can be made than if only one factor is presented.

In considering the element of complete presentation, one must recognize that completeness usually cannot be achieved in one advertisement or commercial announcement. The concept of completeness must encompass a series of advertisements, including not only those in the mass media but also direct mail, package inserts, and dealer-distributed brochures. The significant point is that, through the institution of advertising, consumers can be helped in their understanding of products and services and the benefits to be derived from them.

Adequate information

The information in advertisements must be adequate to meet the needs of those who seek guidance in their purchasing problems. Contrast the two advertisements reproduced in Figures 4–5 and 4–6. Both are truthful, but one is full of information that should help the consumer evaluate the product and make a choice while the other tells the consumer very little that would contribute to decision making.

It is easier to provide adequate information in advertisements for consumer guidance if there is a "language" or vocabulary of terms having precise meaning applicable to the field or product being advertised. There are many areas where words do have precise meaning and aid the process of communication. Analyze, for example, the copy in the ad reproduced

5 *in one*

ONE PAINT FOR 5 EXTERIOR SURFACES

PENTAFLEX
FLAT EXTERIOR PAINT

- For shakes—wood shingles—
  clapboard and trim—
  —asbestos shingles—
  stucco, brick, cement.

SEE YOUR BENJAMIN MOORE PAINT DEALER
FOR THE BEST IN PRODUCTS AND SERVICE

FIGURE 4–5. An inadequate guide to buying

FIGURE 4–6. A helpful guide to the consumer

in Figure 4–7 to evaluate the extent to which a prospective buyer of a roll paper color printer might judge its quality and capacity on a rather exact basis. Various types of controls can be compared on the basis of power in terms of watts, and resistance in terms of ohms. Should the prospective buyer wish to compare the Allen-Bradley printer with another make, there would be no difficulty in making exact comparisons in respect to power and resistance.

In the industrial-goods field terms having exact qualitative meaning are commonly used in advertisements to describe the product and guide the buyer. A milling machine may be described as being capable of machining a bearing with a tolerance of .0005 inches. The noise level of a ballast for a flourescent light may be rated in terms of so many decibels. The pressure capacity of a compressed air tank can be given in pounds per square inch.

Such terms are not the creation of advertising persons, but their existence helps the advertiser in performing his function of interpreting the qualities of want or need satisfaction embodied in the product to be advertised. Their use helps the buyer to evaluate the product and compare it with other makes before a purchase is consummated.

Physical standards for consumer goods

In the field of consumer goods many terms with precise meaning also exist and can be used by advertisers for providing qualitative information. Many weights and measures have standard meanings. A foot is 12 inches long, and a gallon is equivalent to four quarts. A size 16 dress, however, is not always the same for all manufacturers of garments.

An advertisement for a dress manufacturer which says that his brand of dresses are cut "extra" full would not provide a particularly helpful guide to buyers. Would a size 16 dress in that brand be equivalent to a size 18 of a competing brand? Such confusion and difficulty in making qualitative comparisons make for confusion and difficulty in buying.

Terms such as "colossal" to designate size and "super quality" to describe grade do not contribute to ease of understanding or of comparison among brands. Such use complicates the problems of free exchange. That is why our commodity exchanges have established quality standards with precise meaning for such commodities as wheat, corn, lard, butter, cotton, and coffee.

FIGURE 4–7. Effective use of terms to provide measure of hidden qualities

Perhaps manufacturers themselves could make their communication task easier by giving somewhat greater attention in the future than they have in the past to the development of terminology having easily defined meaning when applied to certain characteristics of their products. Such terminology or standardization of terms would be limited to physical qualities of a product, and they should be applicable to all units within a given industry. Considerable progress has been made in this direction. Examples would include the "approved" stamps or labels on gas and electrical appliances and precise meanings attached to "mahogany" furniture and "Sanforized" garments.

Hidden psychological qualities

Not all communication about products should be devoted to giving information about their physical properties. Many items are purchased or sought to provide psychological values. It was noted in an earlier chapter that advertising can add value or utility to a product in a number of ways. One way is to extract from the product hidden psychological values that are not apparent from a consideration of its physical properties. The satisfaction many men get from wearing a Hathaway shirt is the feeling of being well dressed. They could "get by" with a brand having less prestige. They could even buy one that would wear longer and cost considerably less, but would not receive from it the psychological lift afforded by a Hathaway. This factor is emphasized in the Sears advertisement reproduced in Figure 4–8. Truly, some of the satisfaction received from many products is the feeling of self-confidence they impart.

Perfume for the lady could be advertised in terms of its chemical composition, its evaporation factor, and its low price, but these are not the basic elements for which women choose their perfume. Instead, they are seeking some hidden factor that will make them feel accepted and permit them to live on "cloud nine" even if only for a short time.

Study carefully the advertisement for Steuben Glass reproduced in Figure 4–9. Physical properties of glass are, of course, important to the buyer, but the buyer of glass for decorative purposes is more concerned with what the product will do for her "frame of mind" than with such elements as durability, specific gravity, weight or fusion point. Primary values sought are psychological, and the advertiser has a responsibility to help guide the consumer in her search for psychological satisfaction.

Many more examples could be presented to emphasize the nonphysical qualities of a product that contribute to human satisfaction. If advertising

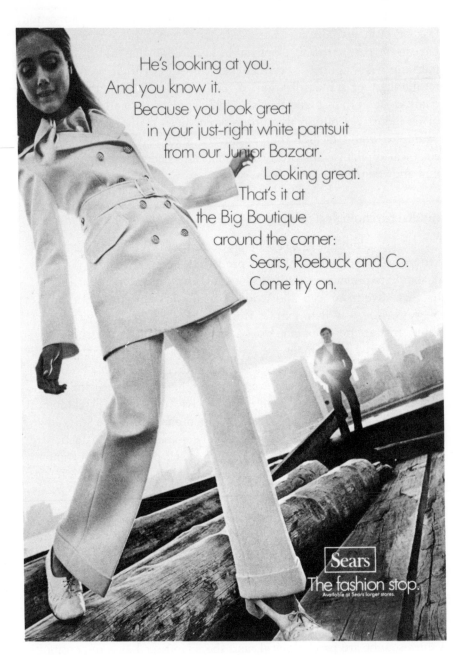

FIGURE 4–8. Satisfaction comes from both feeling and being well dressed

Sea Horse and bowl—both by Steuben

STEUBEN piques your decorative urge with this unusual centerpiece. Use it to create arrangements to your heart's content. The crystal Sea Horse can frolic in a foam of flowers, an ocean of fruit, or a sea of mints.

Or you can free the Sea Horse to go elsewhere while you use the bowl alone. Bowl, diameter 12 inches, $80. Sea Horse, 9 inches tall, $100.

Made at the Corning Glass Center, Corning, New York.

STEUBEN GLASS

FIFTH AVENUE AT 56th STREET · NEW YORK 22, N.Y.

FIGURE 4–9. Beauty Is in the Eye of the Beholder

is to serve as a guide to buying, it cannot ignore this aspect of consumer desire. It is therefore not only proper, but also vital in a consumer-oriented economy to use advertising to communicate the psychological as well as the physical properties of products to prospective buyers.

The road map concept

Advertising as a communication aid to buying is somewhat like a road map, supplemented with a tour book with perhaps minimum but significant information about places or items of interest. In the case of the traveler seeking a vacation spot, he may not know exactly where he wants to go or what specific places he would like to see. He can, however, spread his map before him and note the great variety of opportunities available to him. He will find the names and locations of cities, mountains, resort areas, lakes, deserts, and national monuments. He will find detailed guides as to roads to take and the cost in time and miles to get to the various places available to him.

Our traveler may have little interest in certain kinds of places and will quickly reject them. For those places that remain on his list more detailed information may be needed before a choice is made. For this he may turn to his tour books to learn what each of several places has to offer. He eventually makes a specific decision and sets forth on his journey confident that his map will guide him to the place of his choice.

Advertising provides service of much the same kind to persons seeking goods or services to satisfy a need or want. Newspapers and magazines, television and radio, direct mail, and outdoor posters carry the road maps that list the products that are available for purchase, give some information about each product, and directions as to where to go to get them. "Tour guides" in the form of booklets, folders, and package inserts are available from product manufacturers to those who wish more detailed information about specific products.

Who should initiate communication?

In capitalist, free enterprise countries the major responsibility for preparing product "road maps" and "tour guides" has been assumed by the manufacturer or seller. In other countries the state performs this service.

Some have questioned the wisdom of depending largely on sellers to provide consumers with product information. Sellers are obviously biased. They wish always to present their products in the best possible light. They cannot be wholly objective or impartial.

Professor Nicholas Kaldor, an English economist, has stated that "impartial and unbiased information could only be provided if the writers of 'adveriisements' were financially independent of the products advertised."[4]

As yet no independent source of product information is available on a broad scale. There are organizations such as Consumers Union ånd Consumer Research that provide independent information infrequently on a minimum of products. These organizations are financed by consumers and hence should be impartial. Some product information is also provided by the press, but this is relatively meager.

There is, however, a growing recognition that the professional advertising man is more and more assuming the role of impartial and unbiased communicator of product information. As will be seen in a later chapter, the advertising agency is now at least partially financially independent of the seller in that much of its compensation comes from the media. But even if this were not true, the truly professional advertising man will not falsify product qualities or knowingly mislead the consumer. He is more and more recognizing his responsibility to serve as a helpful guide to consumers in their quest for products and services to satisfy needs and wants.

The protection of competition

The force of competition provides consumers with significant protection against false guides. In an economy of abundance the power of the consumer becomes extremely evident and meaningful. Manufacturers vie with each other to produce goods with a maximum of want-satisfying qualities per dollar of cost. In many respects they become self-appointed employees of consumers. As such they recognize the necessity of keeping their master informed of what is available and the various qualities possessed by such products. They also feel obliged to point out directly or indirectly how their products compare with or differ from those of competitors. The famous "We Are Number Two" campaign of the Avis automobile rental company forced a mental comparison with Hertz, the number one company in that field.

There are times, too, when a given company has competing products

---

[4] Nicholas Kaldor, "The Economic Aspects of Advertising," *The Review of Economic Studies,* 1949–50, Vol. XVIII (1), No. 45, p. 6.

offered under different brand names or the same brand with different quality and prices classes. Qualitative information supplied through advertisements of such competitive items can be helpful to consumers in making their buying decisions. Figure 4–10 provides an example of differences in two models of the same basic product.

Consumer education

In many respects the communication function of advertising contributes substantially to education in consumption. This is vital in a society where consumers enjoy great freedom in choosing what to buy and where the level of discretionary buying power is high.

We have already seen how such communication provides consumers with knowledge of the existence and qualities of goods and services. Education, however, must go deeper than that—it must be concerned with the development of judgment on the part of consumers. Advertising should not be called upon to assume the full responsibility for educating consumers at the judgment level, but this is one of its significant roles.

In a free society high emphasis is placed on human dignity and the right of the individual to make his own decisions. There are, of course, people who suffer through making wrong decisions in their buying. The philosophy underlying freedom, however, is not to take freedom away from those who make errors in judgment but rather to educate them in the effective exercise of their freedom.

Perhaps this concept of the educational function of advertising can be clarified with an illustration and a comparison. There are many advertisers of many kinds of products and services competing for the patronage of consumers. Each advertiser presents his case with conviction and hopes it will be accepted. Descriptive materials and persuasive literature are made available to consumers for review and analysis. One group of advertisers provides material that extolls the merits of investing in stocks, bonds, savings and loan associations, or insurance companies. These messages emphasize the values of postponing consumption in order to have greater consumption rewards in the future.

Opposed to the idea of current saving are advertisements that present the merits of spending now for such things as a trip to Europe, a new home, a second automobile, a pleasure boat, or a new lawn mower. These opposing views will create conflicts in the minds of consumers. It is through such conflicts that consumers are forced to examine the pros and

OK, decision-maker. Decide.

This one's a toughie.

Whether you pick the economy model of the Polaroid Color Pack Camera or the deluxe job on the right, you're going to get a whole lot of camera for the money.

The under-$60 one will give you big, beautiful color prints in 60 seconds, black and white in 15. Which is what it's all about, right?

It has the same electric eye as the most expensive model. Uses the same film. Loads just as fast. Yet Polaroid has figured out a way to bring it out at this low price.

What will your something-under-$150 buy? The finest automatic camera Polaroid has ever produced. It makes black and white pictures indoors without flash, automatic time exposures up to 10 seconds. It allows you to do beautiful closeup work with the special closeup and portrait attachments. It has a sharp triplet lens, two exposure ranges for color, two for black and white, superimposed-image, coupled rangefinder. Brushed chrome finish, leather strap and a flashgun thrown in.

We told you it was tough, didn't we?

FIGURE 4–10. Comparison of two models of same brand

What's new in new ways to live?

Now you can take your pick of wonderfully comfortable, excitingly modern homes

"Hi-rise" apartments

Magnificent "hi-rise" apartment houses—like Chicago's Outer Drive East—are going up in cities across the country. The people who live in them enjoy clean, comfortable Gas heating and cooling all year round. And Gas heat is so reasonable, it's often included in the rent.

Modern villages

Today, more and more couples are enjoying the benefits of convenient modern retirement villages like Friendly Valley near Los Angeles. Their homes have comfortable, clean "Fresh-Air" Gas heating and cooling, economical Gas water heating and clothes drying, too!

City-within-a-city

There's a new kind of urban living—self-contained communities like Hartford's Constitution Plaza that are actually cities-within-a-city, offering the most modern apartments, office buildings, shops, hotels—all heated and cooled from one central plant by clean, dependable Gas.

New suburbia

America's growing young families are on the move. And Gas is the choice for heating in 8 out of 10 new homes today (where natural Gas is available). Most of America cooks with Gas, too. Visit your Gas company and see what Gas can do for you. AMERICAN GAS ASSOCIATION, INC.

For the best in modern living,
Gas makes the big difference
…costs less, too

FIGURE 4–11. Gas power encouraged

20 years from now the electric heating in your home will still be one of the brightest ideas you ever had.

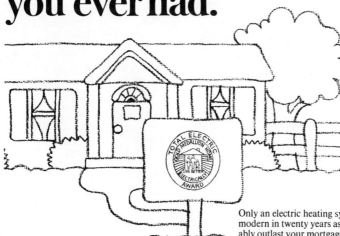

Only an electric heating system will be just as modern in twenty years as today. It will probably outlast your mortgage. (No other heating system can make that statement.)

Electric heat has other things going for it, too. Like flexibility, cleanliness, economy of installation, silence, trouble-free operation, odorlessness, and five different types of systems to choose from.

All of which adds up to keeping your home bright and modern for many years to come. And electricity is making it possible. Check into electric heat . . . the *modern* heat.

Call Electric Heat Consultant Tom Rogers at RA 6-1200.

Commonwealth Edison Company

The bright new ideas are Electric.

FIGURE 4–12. Electric power encouraged

FIGURE. 4–13. Smoking encouraged

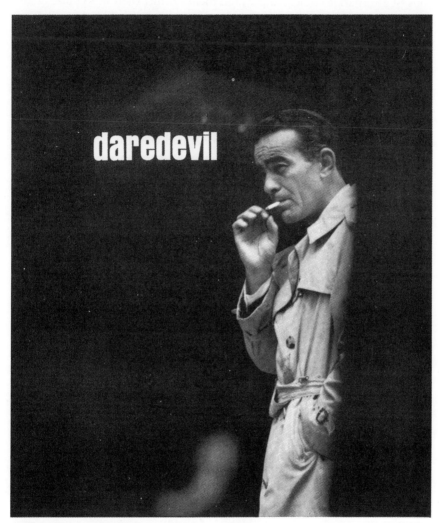

daredevil

No, he's not a free-fall parachutist. Or an X-15 test pilot. Or a stock car racer. With a wife and kids to think about, he can't afford to take chances.

But he goes on taking the *big* risk...clinging to a habit which *every day* causes 100 deaths from lung cancer and contributes to many more from coronary artery and respiratory diseases. Studies show that the death rate from lung cancer alone for cigarette smokers (one-pack-a-day or more) is 10 times higher than for nonsmokers.

Nobody says it's easy to stop. But living *that* dangerously often winds up in not living at all.

american cancer society

FIGURE 4–14. Smoking discouraged

cons of alternative choices and weigh them against their individual goals. This is, in itself, an educational process and is enhanced by the supply of advertisements made available to consumers.

Compare this with the process of education in our schools where we insist on presenting students with conflicting ideologies, hypotheses, theories, and descriptive matter with the knowledge that this will help to develop discrimination, enhance judgment, and sharpen the intellect. Universities purposely include on their staffs professors with differing beliefs so that students can become acquainted with the existence of such differences and thus strengthen their own independence of thought.

Take a look at Figures 4–11 and 4–12. One is advertising *gas* as a power source for heating, cooling, cooking, drying clothes, and the like, while the other speaks of the virtues of using *electricity* for home heating. The competition between these two products supplies suggestion and information that may enhance the quality of consumer judgment in reaching a purchase decision.

Another interesting challenge to consumers in respect to their freedom to choose is illustrated in Figures 4–13 and 4–14. To smoke or not to smoke is a proposition many consumers are facing. Each of the two advertisements shown presents a strong case for its viewpoint and though neither begins to supply all the information the consumer might desire it may influence his final decision to buy or not to buy.

The factor of persuasion

Advertising, in any form, contains within itself an element of persuasion. Advertising that is purely informative is often all that is needed to persuade a reader or listener to buy the product. In periods when some consumer goods have been very scarce, bare announcement by any local merchant that a shipment has been received is enough to produce a rush for the store. There is much persuasion in the one word "fire" when shouted with sincerity and truth to persons in a burning building.

Persuasion is not the result merely of using strong words and phrases to urge people to buy a product or accept an idea. Persuasion is a two-way process. In the case of advertising, it involves a recognition or belief on the part of the reader or listener that the advertised product will satisfy a need or desire. When a person is already clearly conscious of some need or want, and a product exists which will satisfy that need or want, it requires very little in the way of advertising to persuade the person to buy. Under such conditions, about all an advertisement needs is an announcement of the product's existence, its price, and where it can be bought. Such advertising, however, will be highly persuasive. When consumers are not conscious of specific needs or wants or when the qualities of a product are not clearly observable, it then becomes the task of advertising to interpret the hidden qualities of the product in terms of basic human desires. Such was the situation and such the task of advertising when new products such as the bathtub, toothbrushes, mechanical refrigerators, television receivers, and garden tractors were first available. Each such product was capable of meeting some fundamental human desire, but this fact was not appreciated by the consumer. The desire for cleanliness may have been recognized, but not the desire for a bathtub. Good advertising would explain the qualities of the bathtub in terms of the human desire for cleanliness and, through such explanation, would exercise persuasive powers.

Certainly there is nothing about buyer's guide advertising that would rule out the element of persuasion. In fact, persuasion is necessary to get people to enrich the range of their wants and, therefore, their lives.

QUESTIONS AND PROBLEMS

1. What comparisons would you make between a road map which directs or guides travelers to a desired destination and the advertisements in a mail-order catalog, a newspaper, or a magazine which may guide consumers in their quest for goods or services?

2. From a recent issue of a newspaper, select three advertisements which you believe are good, and three which you believe are poor guides for the consumer.

3. Is the use of advertising to build psychological values into a product socially justified? Explain.

4. Discuss the merits and shortcomings of having some agency other than the seller be responsible for communicating the characteristics and qualities of a product to potential consumers.

5. "The only real justification for advertising is to give product information; advertising should not seek to persuade people to buy products or services." Do you agree with that statement? Why or why not?

6. Compare the buyer's guide character of advertisements in the following types of media: newspapers, radio and television, mail-order catalogs, general magazines, and specialized trade or business magazines.

7. Summarize briefly the advantages of proper labeling to (a) the producer, (b) the consumer.

8. Would the establishment of quality standards by an entire industry reduce the importance or value of brand names?

9. Will buyer's guide advertising generally be less or more effective as a sales force than advertising that does not meet the requirements of buyer's guide advertising?

10. How might advertisers function to educate consumers to a higher level of buying sophistication?

chapter 5
ETHICS AND
TRUTH IN
ADVERTISING

ADVERTISING IS A POWERFUL economic and social force. Consumers look to it for information in respect to products and services that might help to meet their material needs and wants. Consumer actions are influenced by the character of advertisements that are distributed by our mass media.

Because of the power and influence of advertising, it is vital to the welfare of society that high ethical standards guide the actions of advertising practitioners.

High ethical standards are also vital to the long-run economic health of advertising itself. If advertising does not have the confidence of most consumers, it will lose its influence and surely die. If people grow to disbelieve a substantial percentage of the advertising messages that come to them, they will soon tend to reject most or all advertising.

Ethics and morality should be considered primarily at the personal level. Unethical practices are the result of unethical practitioners. If the individual is guided by high ethical and moral standards, his business or professional practice will most likely be on the same high plane.

Individual leaders of thought in the field of advertising have been striving to establish standards of practice that will, hopefully, be followed by all practitioners. Fairfax Cone, a leading advertising agency man, expresses his own credo as follows:

I believe that advertising should be done *by* us precisely as we would like it done *to* us: clearly as to its promises, honestly as to its intentions, and with sufficient substance to allow each reader or listener or viewer to make up his or her own mind with regard to the proposition that is presented. Its single appeal, whether large or small, should be to *reasonable* self-interest.[1]

Unfortunately, not all advertising follows the recommendation of Mr. Cone. There is too much that is untruthful, exaggerated, misleading, in poor taste, disparaging of competitors, and inconsiderate of the reader, listener, or viewer.

Perhaps attention here to some of the practices that are to be condemned will help reduce such practices in the future. If you are planning to enter the field of advertising practice, you can exercise direct leadership in increasing the ratio of good to bad advertising. If you are to be a "consumer" of advertising, perhaps you can learn not to be misled by the bad and to inform the unethical advertiser of your disapproval.

Untruthful advertising

Untruthfulness is practically undefinable. It is easy to pick out statements in advertisements that are definitely untrue and others that are definitely true; but the dividing line between truth and untruth is difficult, if not impossible, to determine.

From an advertising viewpoint, how far can the advertiser legitimately go in using superlatives or in exaggerating the merits of his product? The Federal Trade Commission and other government regulatory agencies have sanctioned the use of some exaggeration. This has been allowed under the phrase "trade puffing." A case prosecuted by the Bureau of Animal Husbandry of the United States Department of Agriculture illustrates the attitude of one government agency. Action was brought against the Jones Dairy Farm, Inc., for the use of false advertising. Dr. John R. Mohler, chief of the Bureau, explained the position of the government in the following words: "Our only desire is to see that the Jones advertising, or any other does not overstep that indefinite boundary which suggests to the reader a fact which cannot be proved, even with the addition of considerable poetic license. There is no objection to reasonable trade puffing. We are concerned only with what may be called extreme assertions giving definite suggestions of fact which cannot be literally proven."

The problem of defining untruthfulness in a legal sense has been of concern to both legislators and judges. During the early 1930's, when

---

[1] "The Case against Advertising," a speech before the Regent Advertising Club, London, England, April 28, 1961.

much social legislation was enacted by the federal government, legislators debated the question of what constituted untruthful advertising. There were many who held that an advertisement should be labeled as false if it were untrue in any particular sense or if, by ambiguity or inference, it created a misleading impression in the minds of consumers.

Others held that legislation that defined false advertising in terms of erroneous impressions created in the minds of consumers would make enforcement extremely difficult, if not impossible. It was argued that, if enforcement were to be effective, advertisements should be judged in terms of *material facts* rather than in terms of the *attitude of mind* of consumers.

As a result of the many debates in Congress the Wheeler-Lea Amendment to the Federal Trade Commission Act was enacted in 1938 and is still in effect. It defines false advertisement as follows:

> The term "false advertisement" means an advertisement, other than labeling, which is misleading in a material respect; and in determining whether any advertisement is misleading, there shall be taken into account (among other things) not only representations made or suggested by statement, word, design, device, sound, or any combination thereof, but also the extent to which the advertisement fails to reveal facts material in the light of such representations or material with respect to consequences which may result from the use of the commodity to which the advertisement relates under the conditions prescribed in said advertisement or under such conditions as are customary or usual [sec. 15].

Thus, the Wheeler-Lea Act focuses attention on the *material* aspects of a statement to determine whether it is true or false. This approach is tangible and makes administration easier than would be true if dependence were placed on consumer attitude. However, the Federal Trade Commission (which administers the Wheeler-Lea Act) has progressively "liberalized" its interpretation of the law by placing increasing emphasis on impressions which advertisements create in the minds of consumers. This is illustrated by the following excerpt from a Federal Trade Commission ruling: "The buying public does not weigh each word in an advertisement or a representation. It is important to ascertain the impression that is likely to be created upon the prospective purchaser."[2]

The advertiser, however, must be interested in more than the law when he is preparing his message to the consumer. He must be interested in the *attitude of mind* created by his advertisement. He must give thought to the degree to which the message offered the public is accepted

---

[2] *Aronberg et al.* v. *Federal Trade Commission,* 7 Cir., 132 F. 2d 165, 167 (65 F.T.C. 979; 3 S & D–647).

as truthful. Much of the power of the advertisement is lost if it creates in the mind of the potential buyer an impression which is not supported by results obtained from use of the product.

To test the reaction of consumers on this point, the copy in ten advertisements of well-known products was taken recently from reputable magazines. This copy was submitted to 46 potential buyers of the advertised products. They were asked to mark whether the copy *impressed* them as being true or untrue. Of the ten advertisements, only three received a majority vote for giving a truthful impression. One piece of copy had a 100 percent vote for an untruthful impression. Regardless of the nature of legislation or the attitude of the courts concerning untruthful advertising, the advertiser cannot afford to ignore the effect which his message will have on consumer attitudes. He cannot afford to write advertising that will meet the legal requirements alone; but, in addition, he must consider whether consumers will believe his message.

Testimonials

The use of testimonial advertising is based upon a fundamental human quality—namely, that people like to read about other people. It is to satisfy this human quality that a goodly portion of the small-town newspapers are devoted to news items about persons. The success of the tabloid newspapers and picture magazines is no doubt due in part to the fact that news is presented in terms of people and that photographs intensify the reality and intimacy of the personal approach. Confession magazines utilize this same human trait in their presentation of intimate gossip about ostensibly real people. The use of the first person magnifies the appeal of such magazines.

The spirit of emulation is, in part, the basis of this desire of people to read about other people. Human beings want to copy those whom they deem superior in taste or knowledge or experience. In large part this spirit of emulation gives the advertising testimonial its strength. Psychologists claim that people have an ability to excite their imagination with external objects. This enables women to become princesses, movie queens, sweethearts, or brides by using the cold cream or toilet soap recommended by their "superior."

Advertisers have recognized the value of getting the testimonials of persons acknowledged as leaders and authorities—persons whom prospective purchasers would wish to emulate or to use as their guides in consumption. Figure 5–1 illustrates a dignified, honest, and effective use of testimonials.

"I've got 300 feeder pigs on Aureo S·P 250 right now, with no trouble from scours," says Harley Doyle, Wymore, Nebraska.

"I produce 1,500 feeder pigs a year free of scours thanks to AUREO S·P® 250"

"I put my pigs on feeds with Aureo S·P® 250 as soon as they start eating ...about four to five days old. And I keep them on it, until I sell them as feeders at 40 to 45 pounds. That's usually seven to eight weeks of age," says Mr. Doyle.

"Freedom from disease is the main thing with Aureo S·P 250. But I also find pigs grow faster on less feed, and they reach selling

weights earlier on Aureo S·P 250. There was some atrophic rhinitis in the area last year, but with this feed additive I've run into no losses from the disease."

Whether you're raising feeder pigs or finishing them out, don't take chances. Start them on formula feeds with Aureo S·P 250 and finish them on Aureomycin. ®*Aureo S·P is the trademark for a premix of Aureomycin® chlortetracycline, Sulmet® sulfamethazine and penicillin.*

CYANAMID ➤ *SERVES THE MAN WHO MAKES A BUSINESS OF AGRICULTURE*

AMERICAN CYANAMID COMPANY
PRINCETON, NEW JERSEY

FIGURE 5–1. An honest and effective use of testimonials

There are times, however, when some advertisers use unethical methods in obtaining the "proper" testimonials. The term "testimonial racket" has been aptly applied to the techniques used by such advertisers. The payment of large sums of money for the testimonials of particular persons has been very common. Baseball and football players, movie stars, dentists, physicians, lawyers, the socially elite, and others with a large popular following have been richly rewarded for allowing their names to be attached to a testimonial for a given product or products.

Too often the testimonial has not been written by the person whose signature is attached. And the cases are not uncommon in which the signatory is not even a user of the product praised. There are also instances in which a testimonial of the same person has appeared on competing brands. In the case of movie stars and others under contract, the manager of the individual often has the right to endorse any product in the name of the celebrity. This leads to insincerity and misrepresentation.

Indirect and shady methods are often used to obtain the endorsement of a product by particular groups. Thus, the advertising agency representing the American Tobacco Company a number of years ago is reputed to have received by the indirect method the endorsement of some 20,000 physicians for Lucky Strikes. The Federal Trade Commission investigated the practices of the company in obtaining endorsements and the following statements are based upon the Commission's findings. The advertising agency circularized a large number of American physicians in the interest of Lucky Strike cigarettes. Each physician received a carton of a hundred cigarettes and a card carrying this question: "In your judgment is the heat treatment, or toasting process, applied to tobacco previously aged and cured likely to free the cigarette from irritation to the throat?"

The American Tobacco Company followed this canvass of physicians with an advertisement stating that, "20,679 physicians say 'Luckies are less irritating.' " To emphasize to the reader the "accuracy" of the statement, a little note,"The figures quoted have been checked and certified to by Lybrand, Ross Bros., and Montgomery, Accountants and Auditors," was placed in the advertisement.

In 1930 the Federal Trade Commission attempted to check the practice of buying testimonials. In a decision handed down on this subject, the Commission stated that when a company paid for and used a testimonial in its advertising, it must also print in the same advertisement and in equally conspicuous type, a statement that the testimonial had been paid for. This decision of the Commission was overruled in 1933 by the United States Circuit Court of Appeals. The Court held that paid testimonials need not be labeled as such so long as they were truthful.

Patent medicine manufacturers have less difficulty in obtaining testimonials than almost any other kind of company. Nature will cure most common human ailments if allowed to do so. If the medicine taken does no harm, the patient will usually get well in spite of it. But credit is almost always given to the medicine rather than to nature. Many such users are willing and anxious to sing the praises of the curative.

But producers of patent medicines offered as a cure for serious diseases, such as tuberculosis, cancer, and diabetes, often pay for testimonials. The United States Food and Drug Administration has uncovered many cases of fraudulent practice in this respect. One example offered by them concerns a product sold to the public as a cure for diabetes. Curative claims were made in the advertising, and testimonials from sufferers praising the product's curative value were included. In checking over these testimonials, government investigators were able, in many instances, to obtain the death certificates of the writers. In most cases the certificate listed diabetes as the cause of death. Yet the producers continued to use the testimonials and to deal with relatives of the deceased in paying for their use.

Misleading names and labels

The practice of using names on products and in advertising which tend to give a wrong impression as to quality or origin is to be condemned. The following cases of such use were recorded in reports of the Federal Trade Commission. The word "Havana" or "Habana" was used for a cigar made of tobacco not grown in Cuba. "Dirigold" was used to designate and describe flatware and hollow ware made from an alloy of base metals and containing no gold.

One company used the names "France" and "Paris" in cosmetic advertising when such products were not imported from or manufactured in France. Implication of foreign origin of another company's product was provided by the use of such statements as "Les Parfums des Jardine de Fioret." In all these cases the Commission issued complaints or cease and desist orders.

Names and labels are used by some companies to confuse the consumer as to the real manufacturer. This is done in an attempt to capitalize on the goodwill enjoyed by the company being imitated. Thus, the name "Uneeda" brought imitators with "Iwanta," "Ulika," "Uwanta," and "Abetta." The name "Zu Zu" was imitated with "Hoo, Hoo." The similarity of "Sparkle" and "Twinkle" causes confusion.

These practices make it difficult, if not impossible for the consumer always to duplicate previous purchases by depending on remembering a name. The deception is of such character that consumers and dealers have at times ordered company A's product from company B. This is obviously not in the best interests of the consumer or the legitimate businessman.

Exaggeration and misrepresentation

This element in advertising has been an ever-present one. From a consumer's point of view, much of advertising exaggeration is perhaps ignored. Why sellers of merchandise will continue to use such methods when it should be evident that such exaggeration does not carry conviction to most readers is hard to understand. There seems to be less use of superlatives and exaggerated statements in current advertising than was true a few years ago. And yet there can be found plenty of the exaggerated type of copy today.

For example, in a recent issue of a metropolitan newspaper the following statements were found: "Buy now! . . . The quality and beauty of the fur trimmings, the fine fabric values, the variety of styles and the careful making cannot be matched later on at anywhere near these August prices." It is difficult to see how the writer of this copy could accurately forecast the future. Another advertisement stated: "More lavishly furred models, more beautifully styled, more dollar-for-dollar value than we've ever offered before." And this one: "We are just as certain that the quality could not be better as we are that prices could not be lower." While this last statement may be true, the impression is left that quality could not be better or the price lower, whereas the writer of the copy may have been uncertain about both.

Among advertisements appearing in a well-known magazine was one for a food product which promises to curb nervousness in growing children and add weight at the rate of a pound a week. Another offers the skinny adult a "new discovery which adds solid flesh quick" by using a new double tonic. The following testimonial from a reputed user formed a part of the copy: "I was so skinny and weak that everybody laughed at me and called me a scarecrow. Finally I tried ————. In 5 weeks I gained 14 pounds. Now I go out regularly and enjoy life."

A case involving misrepresentation through outright false statements and inferences is illustrated by a New York firm that made a fire extin-

guisher and sold it under the name "Kill Flame." In its advertising the
company stated that its product was "safe" and "non-toxic." It stated that
"Kill Flame positively does not contain carbon-tetrachloride, chloro-
bromomethane (CB) or any other hazardous, toxic or possibly injurious
ingredient."

A complaint against the company was brought before the Federal
Trade Commission. The false and misleading character of claims made in
advertisements was emphasized in the following excerpt from the Commission's findings:

> Said statements and representations were and are false, misleading and decep-
> tive. In truth and in fact, said product is not safe and non-toxic when used to extin-
> guish a fire. The chemical components of "Kill Flame" are Freon 11 and Freon 12.
> These chemicals tend to and do decompose in a flame and on hot surfaces yielding
> highly toxic substances such as chlorine, phosgene, carbon monoxide, hydrochloric
> acid and hydroflouric acid. In a closed room or when no ventilation is provided,
> these decomposition products may form harmful or lethal mixtures.[3]

Creating erroneous impressions

There are also examples of advertising which make no actually false
statements but which create a definitely false impression. Thus, one company advertised three yards of pure silk in any one of six colors for 25
cents. This carried a guarantee that the advertised merchandise was pure
silk of the best quality. Those who sent in their quarter received a spool
containing three yards of silk *thread*. The answering of an advertisement
offering for 25 cents a picture of George Washington made from a steel
engraving brought a postage stamp.

The purposeful creation of erroneous impressions is also found in areas
other than advertising. Some newspapers "slant" their news, and columnists occasionally adroitly and knowingly write to lead readers to
false conclusions. In political campaigns a candidate's statements may be
quoted out of context by the opposition with the idea of misleading the
voter.

A dramatic example of the use of news pictures by a news-picture
firm to create an erroneous impression was reported by *Time* magazine.
That magazine reproduced a picture of a navy fighter plane torn in two
as it landed on the deck of a carrier. The picture had been distributed
widely to newspapers throughout the country by the news-picture firm.
Time carried the following explanation under the picture:

---

[3] Federal Trade Commission Decisions, 56 (Washington, D.C.: U.S. Government Printing Office, 1962), pp. 480–82.

A plane crack-up like this is rare. So when International News Photos and Acme Newspictures spied this shot in *Naval Aviation News,* they hastily got prints from the Pentagon, wired them to papers across the U.S. last week. Their captions said that the F6F fighter was pulled apart by arresting gear as it landed on the carrier, U.S.S. *Princeton.* More than 100 papers printed the picture. What the picture services knew, but carefully did not say, was that the crash took place eight years ago, on the old *Princeton,* later sunk at Leyte. One I.N.P. editor breezily explained: "Things were awfully slow. . . . If I had put in the date, nobody would have used the picture—and it did get a big play."[4]

Poor taste

There are also advertisements and advertising practices that are in poor taste or are inconsiderate of the reader, listener, or viewer. The blatant use of sex symbols, unrestrained references to the most personal of body functions, and excessive repetition are all too common.

In the case of radio and television commercials advertisers are too often insensitive to what the listener or viewer might be doing at the time of the commercial. For example, a manufacturer of a laxative sponsored a radio program of dinner music broadcast from 6:00 to 6:30 P.M. The program was excellent and provided an enjoyable background for gracious family dining, but the commercial messages of the most personal and biological nature broke in on the program two or three times during the half hour. A personal salesman for this company would hardly choose the dinner table as a place to sell his pills. It is equally in poor taste to broadcast commercials of this type at dinnertime.

Other examples of inconsiderateness would include the multiple spotting of commercials and increasing the sound volume of commercials over that employed for the program. These practices would probably not be employed if advertisers followed the recommendation of Mr. Cone to advertise to others as we would like others to advertise to us. Advertisements and practices that are in poor taste will, in the long run, be detrimental to the total field of advertising.

Agencies aimed at improving advertising ethics

Much progress has been made in bringing about a decline in the amount of untruthful and fraudulent advertising. It is difficult to find advertisements today in any of the reputable magazines or newspapers that begin to match the exaggeration or misrepresentation found in many advertise-

---

[4] *Time,* September 24, 1951, p. 75. Quoted by permission of *Time.* The picture itself would have been reproduced here, but the picture agency would not give permission.

ments of 20 to 30 years ago. This should not be interpreted to mean that advertising is all above criticism today, but rather that it has been going in the right direction and should continue to improve.

A number of forces have contributed to this improvement in advertising ethics. A list of the more important agencies would include the following:

1. Printers' Ink Statute
2. Better Business Bureaus
3. Publishers
4. Advertising organizations
5. Federal government
6. Self-regulation

Printers' Ink Statute

The truth-in-advertising crusade took root in 1911 when the Printers' Ink Publishing Company prepared a model statute regulating untruthful advertising. In its feature articles and in its editorials, *Printers' Ink* magazine urged the inclusion of its model statute as a part of the law of every state in the United States. The provisions of the statute were as follows:

Any person, firm, corporation, or association, who with intent to sell or in any wise dispose of merchandise, securities, service, or anything offered by such person, firm, corporation or association, directly or indirectly, to the public for sale or distribution, or with intent to increase the consumption thereof or to induce the public in any manner to enter into any obligation relating thereto, or to acquire title thereto or an interest therein, makes, publishes, disseminates, circulates, or places before the public, or causes, directly or indirectly, to be made, published, disseminated, circulated or placed before the public, in this State, in a newspaper or other publication, or in the form of a book, notice, handbill, poster, bill, circular, pamphlet, or letter, or in any other way, an advertisement of any sort regarding merchandise, securities, service, or anything so offered to the public, which advertisement contains assertions, representation, or statement of fact which is untrue, deceptive or misleading shall be guilty of a misdemeanor.

Two years after this model statute was suggested by *Printers' Ink,* it was adopted by Ohio, followed closely by Minnesota, Washington, and Nebraska. It is now a law in the District of Columbia and the following 27 states:

Alabama	Louisiana	Ohio
Colorado	Michigan	Oklahoma
Hawaii	Minnesota	Oregon
Idaho	Missouri	Rhode Island
Illinois	Nebraska	Virginia
Indiana	Nevada	Washington
Iowa	New Jersey	West Virginia
Kansas	New York	Wisconsin
Kentucky	North Dakota	Wyoming

Seventeen other states have passed laws similar to that suggested by *Printers' Ink*. In general, such laws are not so effective as those which legalized the model statute in its entirety. The Printers' Ink Statute starts off: "Any person, firm, corporation or association, who. . . ." Many of the substitute laws insert the word "knowingly" or its equivalent. Enforcement of the law is much more difficult when it must be proved that the offender *knew* he was offending.

Many cases involving violations of the model statute have been brought before the courts. The law has been upheld and violators punished. It has been helpful in checking certain types of untruthful retail advertising, particularly in those states where adequate enforcement machinery has been set up. It naturally does not touch advertising classified as interstate in character.

Suggestions are frequently made to strengthen and broaden state laws relating to the regulation of advertising practice. Typical of such suggestions is that offered by Mr. Paul Rand Dixon, Chairman of the Federal Trade Commission (1966). He urged states to adopt a general statute that:

> . . . is sufficiently broad to reach practices such as bait advertising; deceptive guarantees; fictitious pricing; referral selling, oral misrepresentation by house-to-house salesmen; misbranding; sale of used products as new; false claims as to performance of products; price fixing conspiracies; and boycotts to eliminate competition.[5]

Such a general statute would encompass more than advertising practices, but much of it would relate to advertising.

Better Business Bureaus

Printers' Ink was instrumental not only in getting legislation adopted making certain types of advertising illegal but also in promoting the establishment of agencies to watch out for infractions of the law, collect evidence, and see that the violators were brought to trial. The development of Better Business Bureaus resulted from the agitation by *Printers' Ink*. These agencies are not confined to the states having laws pertaining to false advertising.

Most large cities in the United States now have their own local Better Business Bureaus. In addition to the local organizations, there is the National Better Business Bureau, which operates on a broader scale, giving

---

[5] As quoted in *Advertising Age,* July 11, 1966, p. 8.

assistance to national as well as local advertisers. Both the national and the locals serve to curb unethical advertising and selling practices of the unscrupulous and assist the honest to stay within the bounds of law and accepted ethical practices. False comparisons, misleading statements, false claims as to quality, and "not on sale" and bait advertising are among the factors checked on by both the national and local agencies.

The support of these bureaus comes from business firms desirous of eliminating the unfair practices of unscrupulous competitors. Complaints concerning such practices are made to a bureau, which in turn investigates the charge and, if it is found to be true, tries to persuade the offender to stop such methods. If this procedure does not bring results, the facts are often published. If this does not work, legal action may be instituted.

The National Better Business Bureau carries on research into the changing tenor of public reaction to different types of advertising, as well as into state and federal legislation affecting advertising and selling methods. It also handles cases of unfair trade practices that are regional or national in scope.

This organization gives further assistance to individual business houses by furnishing suggestions of the types of advertising and selling procedure that should not be used. Its suggestions cover specific trade practices as they might apply to many different kinds of merchandise. Thus, in the case of furniture, specific rules dealing with the use of words or terms such as "veneer," "solid," "finish," and "solid walnut top" are set forth for the guidance of merchants. A *solid walnut top,* according to the Better Business Bureau, should mean a top constructed of walnut throughout and not veneered, while a *walnut top* should mean a solid walnut top or a top constructed of walnut veneer on walnut.

The work of the Better Business Bureaus has been built upon the philosophy that progressive advertisers believe in the policy of fair and truthful advertising. Bureaus generally cooperate with advertisers and advertising media "in the interest of truthful advertising by serving as a consultant to copy acceptance personnel, by providing factual information for determining the accuracy of questioned advertising claims, and by giving objective views concerning the reader effects of particular language usage."[6]

The basic principles that guide Better Business Bureaus are well stated as follows by the New York Metropolitan Bureau:

---

[6] Better Business Bureau of Metropolitan New York, *Retail Advertising Copy Standards* (New York, 1961), p. 1.

BASIC PRINCIPLES

1. The primary responsibility for truthful and nondeceptive advertising copy rests with the advertiser. Advertisers shall present substantiation for any claims or offers made, before or after publication, if requested to do so by the advertising medium or by the Better Business Bureau.

2. Advertisements which are untrue, misleading, deceptive, fraudulent, disparaging of competitors, insincere offers to sell, or unprovable as to material claims, shall not be used.

3. Advertisements are to be considered in their entirety and as they would be read by the consuming public.

4. Advertisements are not intended to be carefully dissected and analyzed by the general public, but rather to produce an impression upon prospective purchasers. They must therefore not only be truthful in all particulars but also in the general impression which they convey.

5. Advertisements as a whole may be completely misleading although every sentence separately considered is literally true. This may be because things are omitted that should be said, or because advertisements are purposely composed or printed in such a way as to mislead.

6. Advertisements which are ambiguous and capable of being understood to have two meanings, one true and the second false or misleading, will be interpreted to have the capacity to create the latter effect and, therefore, shall not be used.[7]

The Bureau's various publications can provide helpful guides to the advertiser. Particular mention should be made to the Bureau's *Do's and Don't's of Advertising Copy* and *A Guide for Retail Advertising and Selling.*

Media

Advertising media have helped materially to bring about better standards in advertising practice. Magazines and newspapers have led the way, but in recent years the broadcast industry has considerably expanded its effort. The owners of those media for which a large volume of advertising and a long life are desired appreciate the wisdom of eliminating from their pages and air waves the worst type of advertising. The position is rightly taken that one rotten apple in a basket can easily pollute the entire basket. Thus, it is felt that sound advertising will be received and continued if the rotten is kept out. One "rotten" advertisement in a medium might easily injure the selling ability of good advertisements.

Most reputable media reserve the right to refuse any advertisement

---

[7] *Ibid.*, p. 2.

offered for publication if it does not come up to certain ethical standards. Some publishers refuse to accept advertisements for certain drugs, patent medicines, stock-selling schemes, and hidden advertisements.

A number of publishers have set up "advertising acceptability standards" and distributed them to current and prospective advertisers. A good example of this is the set of standards established by *The Detroit News.* Some publishers go even further and provide a consumer protection guarantee as to the basic accuracy of claims made in advertisements appearing in their publications. The number of such publications is, however, limited.

Notable leadership has been given to the fight for high advertising ethics by such trade publications as *Advertising Age* and *Printers' Ink.* The former has waged a forthright fight, not only for a reduction in untruthful and misleading advertising, but also for the practice of good taste in all advertising. In both its editorials and in articles carried in the magazine, standards of practice have been suggested and plans for implementing them offered.

Printers' Ink spearheaded the truth crusade starting in the second decade of the 20th century. It added new vigor in 1952 to the self-regulation program of the advertising industry. Mr. C. B. Larrabee, then president and publisher of *Printers' Ink,* printed a powerful report in 1952 titled "Thunder on the Right." He prefaced his report with the following statement: "We at *Printers' Ink* are worried about the mounting criticism of advertising coming from responsible leaders of American thought. They do not question the value of advertising as an economic necessity, but they are repelled by its shortcomings. We are presenting this report because we believe that this problem demands action now, a solution from within our industry—not from government people whose well-intentioned cures might kill the patient."[8]

Again in 1960 *Printers' Ink* presented a series of articles on "Truth and Taste in Advertising" and set forth a specific program for implementation. The *Printers' Ink* recommended program is reproduced in Figure 5–2.

Federal government

Many look to the federal government as the only source capable of policing advertising. Yet it is perhaps no more possible for the government, acting alone, to police advertising than it was for the same agency

---

[8] C. B. Larrabee, "Thunder on the Right," *Printers' Ink,* March 7, 1952, p. 39.

A program for
Truth and taste in advertising—1960

Because the problem is complex and the needs are multiple, any program to rescue advertising from its deteriorating image must be comprehensive and thorough. Such a program will cost what, to some, may seem a great amount of money. But the investment would be small in relation to the losses that advertising would suffer through taxes, controls, advertiser disenchantment, consumer rejection and other threats that the program is designed to forestall. On the positive side, the investment would be small also in relation to the returns that can be expected when advertising builds a solid new foundation for the era of economic growth just starting.

A personal program

I.

It is proposed that the entire advertising industry immediately re-dedicate itself to the highest standards of truth and taste in advertising. Such dedication by each individual—and by top management in particular—could accomplish a fast improvement in advertising.

A. In advertiser companies, a forceful statement by management can make clear to all sales and advertising personnel that the company seriously insists on maintaining high standards of truth and taste in its advertising and that sales and advertising executives will be held responsible for seeing that the standards are observed.

B. In advertising agencies, a similar statement of management policy can make clear to all employees that the agency supports the highest standards of truth and taste in advertising and brooks no com-

promise with these standards in recommendations to clients or instructions from them.

C. In media, a review of standards of acceptability can make sure that the standards explicitly cover the gray areas of truth and taste as well as the black. A statement by management to its ad censors can establish that management backs them to the limit.

II.

It is proposed that every individual in advertising strongly press for adoption of the Truth in Advertising Statute in the states where no such law exists, and a revision of existing statutes to cover bait advertising and fictitious comparative prices in states where no such provisions exist. (See revised Model Statute for Truth in Advertising in December 4, 1959, issue of PRINTERS' INK.) The individual can also press for strict enforcement of these basic controls.

An industry program

I.

It is proposed that the responsible leaders of the advertising industry will immediately set up a group that will operate as an Advertising Action Committee composed of representatives from the media associations, the American Assn. of Advertising Agencies, the Advertising Federation of America, the Association of National Advertisers, the Advertising Assn. of the West, and the National Industrial Advertisers Assn.

II.

It is proposed that the Advertising Action Committee have three broad responsibilities:

1—To determine the economic and sociological influence of advertising in our present society.

2—To conduct an integrated program for raising the levels of truth and taste in advertising.

3—To direct and coordinate public relations activities on behalf of advertising's image.

This committee would also initiate a plan to appropriate the substantial funds needed to support such a program from advertisers, advertising agencies and media.

III.

It is proposed that the Action Committee support a comprehensive study by a team of leading economists and sociologists, drawn largely from universities, on the heretofore unexplored subject of *the influence of advertising in an economy of plenty.* The basic, urgent need for this study is manifest in the attacks on advertising based on old, economy-

FIGURE 5–2. The *Printer's Ink* program for self-regulation of-scarcity theories. The economists and sociologists selected to conduct this study must have no preconceived conclusions based on the old theories, but they must be free to arrive at conclusions of their own, independent of any influence from the advertising industry. The cost of this study may be as much as $350,000—or more.

IV.

It is proposed that the Action Committee support a second study to determine exactly what the image of advertising is among top business management, educators, legislators and the general public. This study will be conducted by one of the leading research firms and may cost $250,000 or more.

V.

It is proposed that the Advertising Action Committee set up a Panel for Truth and Taste in Advertising, composed of representatives from all media and advertising associations, the National Better Business Bureau, the Assn. of Better Business Bureaus, and the Federal Trade Commission. The panel will also include a prominent educator, elder statesman, economist and sociologist, who can lend the kind of thinking not colored by the expediencies of commerce or the intricacies of regulation.

A. The Truth and Taste Panel will be designed primarily to be a pervading influence insuring that all existing controls on truth and taste in advertising are made to function effectively.

B. The Truth and Taste Panel will have the freedom for public comment and criticism when any of the controls break down. By majority vote, the panel may issue public reports naming advertisers, agencies, media and associations when the basic controls won't halt a transgression of truth or taste.

C. The Truth and Taste Panel will employ a full-time staff, headed by a permanent panel chairman. The chairman will be a distinguished, prominent person, dedicated to the principle that the highest standards of truth and taste in advertising are essential to advertising's best interests as well as the public interest. The staff will assemble all pertinent information on the specific problems under analysis. The cost of employing the chairman and the staff and of maintaining the office might run as high as $200,000 or more a year.

D. The Truth and Taste Panel will find ways to insure that the basic legal controls on fraudulent advertising become more effective. It will strongly urge Congress to allocate adequate funds for prompt and effective action by the FTC. Through local advertising clubs and its direct contacts with state legislators it will advocate enactment of the PRINTERS' INK Model Statute for Truth in Advertising in the states where no such law exists and enactment of the new provisions against bait advertising and fictitious comparative pricing. It will also advocate more frequent invocation of those laws.

E. The panel will elicit an analysis from the National Better Business Bureau and the Assn. of Better Business Bureaus of the bulletins sent to media and the instances in which media chose to ignore them. It will then determine what measures are necessary in order to increase the influence of the bureaus.

F. The Truth and Taste Panel will encourage media to seek Better Business Bureau investigations of claims of doubtful truth *before* accepting an ad.

G. The panel will support, and urge that the advertising industry support, media in their efforts to maintain high standards of truth and taste in advertising—and make media aware of this support.

H. The panel will help ANA and 4As intensify their education of their members in the area of truth and taste. The panel will encourage the advertising associations to expel members who insist on violating standards of truth and taste.

I. The panel will suggest ways in which local advertising clubs can conduct their own campaigns to clean up local advertising.

VI.

It is proposed that the Advertising Action Committee, with the enlisted help of leaders in the field of public relations, set up and coordinate an over-all public relations program for advertising.

A. The Action Committee will determine, on the basis of the broad study of advertising's image, the objectives and range of public relations programs directed at the general public and at special publics—business leaders, legislators and educators. It will analyze what's being done, what's needed, who can do it.

B. The Action Committee will create a full-time public relations unit, headed by an established expert in the field, to fill the great voids in advertising's public relations efforts. The budget and the specific objectives of the public relations unit will be worked out with the enlisted help of the public relations leaders.

C. The Action Committee will analyze the piecemeal public relations activities directed at educators and students by different groups and associations and will integrate them into the over-all public relations program. It will also arrange for the immediate endowment of college lectureships and scholarships in advertising—a need that is clearly apparent now.

D. Guided by the findings of the broad research on advertising's image, the public relations arm would immediately begin efforts to improve advertising's image with top management, reinforcing ANA's work.

E. The public relations unit, with the survey findings pointing the direction, will conduct a public relations program aimed at the general public.

VII.

It is proposed that the Advertising Action Committee will release to the advertising industry semiannual or annual reports on its work and progress. It will also release to the general public semiannual analyses of the current level of truth and taste in advertising, the current offenses and offenders, and the progress of the advertising industry's program for higher standards of truth and taste.

to bring reform in the use of alcoholic beverages. The federal government, however, must be included in any thoroughgoing system of reform. Through the work of the Federal Trade Commission and the Food and Drug Administration a great deal of reform has been accomplished.

The Federal Trade Commission was established in 1914 "to prevent persons, partnerships, or corporations, except banks, and common carriers subject to the Act to Regulate Commerce, from using unfair methods of competition in commerce."[9] The Commission considered false and misleading advertising an unfair method of competition, and it brought action against a number of companies on such grounds. The position of the commission was materially weakened in 1931 by the Supreme Court decision in the Raladam case, which held that the Commission must establish that questioned advertisements must substantially injure or tend to injure the business of any competitor or competitors in general. This, of course, ignored completely the influence such advertising might have on the public.

A great advance was accomplished in 1938 with the Wheeler-Lea amendments to the Federal Trade Commission Act. These amendments eliminated the difficulties emphasized in the Raladam case by amplifying the phrase "unfair methods of competition in commerce" with the addition of "and unfair or deceptive acts or practices in commerce."[10]

This addition makes it no longer necessary for the Commission to prove injury to a competitor. If the act of advertising is proved unfair or deceptive, it is unlawful.

A new section dealing specifically with advertising was added by the 1938 amendments. This section labeled false advertising as a definite "unfair or deceptive act or practice in commerce." The new section reads in part:

a) It shall be unlawful for any person, partnership, or corporation to disseminate, or cause to be disseminated, any false advertisement—

1. By United States mails, or in commerce by any means, for the purpose of inducing, or which is likely to induce, directly or indirectly, the purchase of foods, drugs, devices, or cosmetics or

2. By any means for the purpose of inducing, or which is likely to induce, directly or indirectly the purchase in commerce of food, drugs, devices or cosmetics.[11]

---

[9] Federal Trade Commission Act, Sec. 5 (Washington, D.C.: U.S. Government Printing Office, 1914).

[10] *Ibid.,* as amended, 1938.

[11] *Ibid.,* Sec. 12.

It should be noted that these provisions apply only to the advertising of food, drugs, devices, or cosmetics. The definition of false advertising as set forth in the Wheeler-Lea amendment is reproduced in an earlier part of this chapter.

This legislation strengthened the hand of the Commission by placing the burden of proof on the offender rather than on the Commission. If a cease and desist order is issued, the alleged defender has 60 days in which to initiate action in the appropriate United States Circuit Court of Appeals. If such action is not taken, the order becomes final, and the offender is liable for monetary penalties in case of future violations.

This strengthening of the enforcement aspects of the Commission's work has not altered the general procedure followed in checking on false advertising. A special board was set up as early as 1929 to examine the advertising columns of newspapers and magazines for instances of false advertising. Radio broadcast continuities were added to the list in 1934, and television in the mid-forties. When the Commission receives information of unfair advertising practices, it turns the material over to this special board, and an investigation is initiated. A questionnaire seeking certain data may be sent to the advertiser, who is asked also to send in copies of all recent advertisements, including booklets and circulars. If the product advertised is a preparation or compound, a request is made for the quantitative formula.

After receipt of the material, the board examines it carefully; if it finds representations that appear to be false or misleading, it may, through the Commission, order the docketing of an application for complaint against the offending advertiser. The advertiser is then notified of this action and is given an opportunity to submit evidence justifying, verifying, or explaining the representations he is making to the public, or otherwise to show cause why a complaint should not be issued.

Other legislation of importance to the advertiser and consumer included the Federal Food, Drug, and Cosmetic Act. This act became operative June 25, 1939. It, like the Wheeler-Lea Act, deals with foods, drugs, devices, and cosmetics, but applies primarily to the *labeling* of such products.

The following quotation from the act defines the term "label" and sets forth the elements to be considered in a determination of whether a given label is misleading:

k) The term "label" means a display of written, printed, or graphic matter upon the immediate container of any article; and a requirement made by or under authority of this Act that any word, statement, or other information appearing on the label shall not be considered to be complied with unless such word, statement, or other information also appears on the outside container or wrapper, if any there be, of the retail package of such article, or is easily legible through the outside container or wrapper.

l)   The term "immediate container" does not include package liners.

m)   The term "labeling" means all labels and other written, printed, or graphic matter (1) upon any article or any of its containers or wrappers, or (2) accompanying such article.

n)   If an article is alleged to be misbranded because the labeling is misleading, then in determining whether the labeling is misleading there shall be taken into account (among other things) not only representations made or suggested by statement, word, design, device, or any combination thereof, but also the extent to which the labeling fails to reveal facts material in the light of such representations or material with respect to consequences which may result from the use of the article to which the labeling relates under the conditions of use prescribed in the labeling thereof or under such conditions of use as are customary or usual.[12]

The Federal Trade Commission and the Food and Drug Administration were given additional powers to regulate advertising under the *truth in labeling and packaging law* enacted in 1966. Under that law designated federal agencies were given the charge to promulgate regulations in respect to product labels and packages to insure adequate identification of the product, its producer, and the net quantity of contents. Such agencies were also authorized to develop rules to prevent consumer deception and to facilitate value comparisons.

It is significant that the 1966 legislation made a substantial move from a "thou shalt not" to a "thou shalt" approach. The new law says that government will still be concerned with preventing advertisers from deceiving the consumer but will also take more positive action to see that product labels and packages contain information that will aid consumers in making significant comparisons of product values. This law should enhance the further development of advertising as a helpful consumer's guide to buying.

Self-regulation

There is a recognition on the part of most businessmen that truthful advertising is distinctly beneficial if the great majority of members of a trade can be forced or encouraged to eliminate false and misleading ad-

---

[12] Federal Food, Drug, and Cosmetic Act, Sec. 201 (Washington, D.C.: U.S. Government Printing Office, 1938).

vertising. Because of this viewpoint, many industries are glad to accept the presence of government regulations. Some industries go a step further and set up a program of self-regulation which accepts the work of government agencies, but supplements that with a program for checking the advertising of its members against government standards and its own industry standards, which may go beyond those established by law. Such a philosophy is distinctly laudable, as well as good business practice. It will increase the public faith in advertising and make further legislation unnecessary.

The editor of a leading advertising journal, in commenting on this point, said, "Some regulation (of advertising) is necessary and useful. The best and most sensible regulation is self-regulation, imposed by advertisers and media themselves, in an effort to eliminate poor practices and bad taste. The more effective and the more sensible such self-regulation is, the less is the need for government regulation of any kind."[13]

Self-regulation has taken many forms. The work of the Better Business bureaus is essentially self-regulatory in nature in that these bureaus are financed by advertising and business institutions. Trade associations, media, and individual firms all engage to a degree in regulating their own or their members' advertising practices.

The method followed by one national advertiser is to present "the basic facts about the performance of each product to both its advertising copy section and its legal section. The copy section works with the advertising agency in the production of the copy. The advertising is then submitted to the legal section, a department completely divorced from advertising, which checks it against the known facts, using policies and rules developed over a period of time from within and without the company."[14] Other individual companies have a practice of submitting all advertising copy to a research or testing division to have claims matched against the results of product tests before approving for release to media.

Trade associations have not been too active in the field of regulation, partly because of their fear that such activity might be construed as a violation of antitrust laws. Many associations do, however, prepare and issue codes of ethics that members are supposed to follow in their advertising practices. One example of such a code is reproduced in Figure 5–3.

On the matter of self-regulation and antitrust, an editorial in *Advertising Age* had this to say:

---

[13] Editorial, *Advertising Age*, March 11, 1957, p. 12.

[14] "The Regulation of Advertising," *Columbia Law Review*, Vol. 56 (November), 1956, p. 1079.

THE
ADVERTISING CODE
OF AMERICAN BUSINESS

1. Truth ... Advertising shall tell the truth, and shall reveal significant facts, the concealment of which would mislead the public.

2. Responsibility ... Advertising agencies and advertisers shall be willing to provide substantiation of claims made.

3. Taste and Decency ... Advertising shall be free of statements, illustrations or implications which are offensive to good taste or public decency.

4. Disparagement ... Advertising shall offer merchandise or service on its merits, and refrain from attacking competitors unfairly or disparaging their products, services or methods of doing business.

5. Bait Advertising ... Advertising shall offer only merchandise or services which are readily available for purchase at the advertised price.

6. Guarantees and Warranties ... Advertising of guarantees and warranties shall be explicit. Advertising of any guarantee or warranty shall clearly and conspicuously disclose its nature and extent, the manner in which the guarantor or warrantor will perform and the identity of the guarantor or warrantor.

7. Price Claims ... Advertising shall avoid price or savings claims which are false or misleading, or which do not offer provable bargains or savings.

8. Unprovable Claims ... Advertising shall avoid the use of exaggerated or unprovable claims.

9. Testimonials ... Advertising containing testimonials shall be limited to those of competent witnesses who are reflecting a real and honest choice.

Developed and initially distributed by: Advertising Federation of America;
the Advertising Association of the West; the Association of Better Business Bureaus, Inc.
and adopted by International Newspaper Advertising Executives, 1965.

FIGURE 5–3. An example of an industry code of ethics

Viewed narrowly from an antitrust position, there undoubtedly are aspects of self regulation which could be construed as, in some sense, collusive and involving restraint. But this is not a good reason for abandoning these efforts. In most instances programs of self regulation have come into existence to deal with demonstrated needs. One example consists of the efforts of the tobacco industry, through its code authority, to withdraw from the sponsorship of television programs which appeal to young people. Self regulation developed because efforts of this kind, concerned essentially with matters of "taste," are largely beyond the reach of government—and should be. It is hard to see how "public interest" can be advanced if the concerted efforts of the antitrusters are used to inhibit the development of such programs.[15]

In 1946 the American Association of Advertising Agencies inaugurated a program to reduce to a minimum the amount of objectionable advertising. The Association of National Advertisers joined the endeavor in 1960. The plan is known as the A.N.A.-A.A.A.A. Interchange of Opinion on Objectionable Advertising. "Any agency, member or nonmember, may forward to the Interchange its criticism of any advertisement which, in its opinion, is in any way objectionable. The criticism is reviewed individually by each member of the Interchange's Committee of the Board on Improvement of Advertising Content, and the result is then forwarded to the agency originating the advertisement, along with a report of the Committee vote and remarks, if any. The Interchange promotes this system by periodically distributing brochures to remind all agencies of their affirmative duties to the industry and to the public."[16]

Figure 5–4 is a reproduction of the cover of a folder designed to urge members to help implement the Interchange. Included in the folder is the following copy code that serves as a statement of principles to guide the reporting of objectionable advertising.

COPY CODE OF A.A.A.A., A.N.A., AND A.E.A.

The advertising agency should not recommend, and should discourage any advertiser from using, any advertising of an untruthful, indecent or otherwise objectionable character, as exemplified by the following copy practices disapproved in a code jointly adopted by the American Association of Advertising Agencies and the Association of National Advertisers, and also by the Advertising Federation of America:

a. False statements or misleading exaggerations.
b. Indirect misrepresentation of a product, or service, through distortion of details, or of their true perspective, either editorially or pictorially.
c. Statements or suggestions offensive to public decency.

---

[15] *Advertising Age,* July 11, 1966, p. 20.
[16] "The Regulation of Advertising," *op. cit.,* p. 1085.

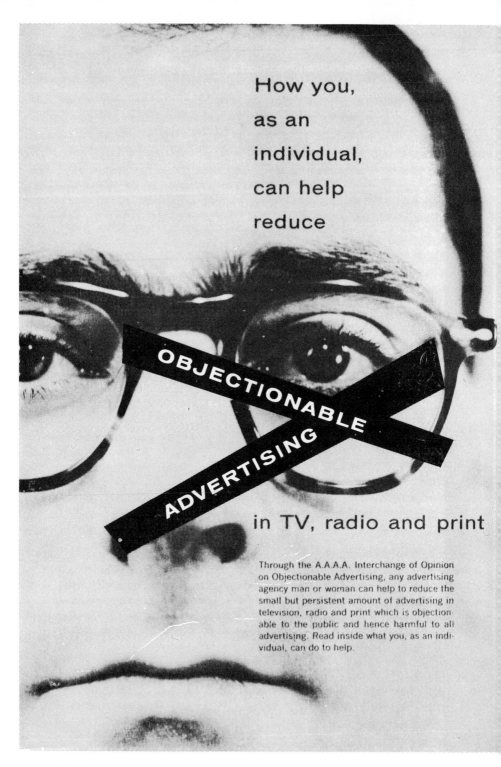

FIGURE 5–4. An invitation to assist in self-regulation

d. Statements which tend to undermine an industry by attributing to its products, generally, faults and weaknesses true only of a few.

e. Price claims that are misleading.

f. Pseudoscientific advertising, including claims insufficiently supported by accepted authority, or that distort the true meaning or practicable application of a statement made by professional or scientific authority.

g. Testimonials which do not reflect the real choice of a competent witness.[17]

Figure 5–5 illustrates a poster, mailing price, or advertisement to be distributed by an advertiser or agency to encourage professionals and laymen to report questionable advertisements.

The Cleveland Advertising Club has gone directly to consumers to help raise the ethical level of advertising. In newspaper advertisements and by other means consumers are asked to report to the Club any commercials or advertisements they find objectionable. Forms such as that reproduced in Figure 5–6 are provided to make it easy for people to report. The Cleveland Plan has also been adopted in other cities.

A type of partial self-regulation is found in the *trade practice conferences* encouraged by the Federal Trade Commission but entered into voluntarily by members of a trade. These conferences may result in the establishment of rules of fair conduct for an entire industry. Misbranding and misrepresentation in various forms, including deceptive packaging or advertising of industry products, are often covered by the rules promulgated. During recent years trade rules have been established in the following fields: in the manufacturing of popular-priced dresses, toilet brushes, cotton textiles, luggage and related products, and sun glasses, and in the rayon, fur, wholesale jewelry, and confectionery industries.

Many of the leading newspapers in the country have established their own advertising regulations, censorship, or acceptance committees. In the spring and summer of 1951, when there were exceedingly heavy inventories of television sets throughout the country, a number of manufacturers and dealers forgot their standards of truthfulness. Through the self-regulatory action of many newspapers much of the untruthful and exaggerated copy was eventually eradicated. The *Milwaukee Journal* action illustrates what was done. The paper announced to all television, appliance, and radio advertisers that advertising copy would have to "conform to a single code—clear truth." In announcing this specific regulation the advertising manager of the *Journal* said:

---

[17] American Association of Advertising Agencies, Inc., New York, December, 1959.

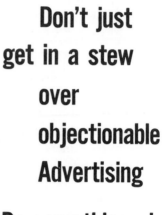

Don't just get in a stew over objectionable Advertising

Do something about it!

We are cooperating with the ANA-AAAA Interchange to reduce the small but persistent amount of advertising that embodies disparagement or is in questionable taste. Such material offends the public, and hence harms all advertising. You, personally, need only find examples, but that first step is up to *you*.

Here's what do do:

Printed Media. Give tear sheets of objectionable advertisements, with place and date of publication.

Radio and TV. Give name of advertiser, and as exact an account as you can of what was said or shown. If possible give date, time, and station or network. (Report objectionable material, though even if you don't get complete information.)

Outdoor or Car Cards. Give any description that will help to identify the copy in question.

Report examples seen or heard to:

....

(Agency Coordinator)

FIGURE 5–5. Brochure encouraging use of interchange

```
-------------------------------------------------
|                      Date                       |
|                                                 |
|   TO:   Cleveland Advertising Club              |
|         Statler-Hilton Hotel                    |
|         Cleveland 15, Ohio                       |
|                                                 |
|       I want to register my objection to the following advertising: |
|                                                 |
|   TV OR RADIO COMMERCIAL     Station . . . . . . . . . . . |
|                                                 |
|                              Date and Time . . . . . . . . |
|                                                 |
|                              Advertiser . . . . . . . . . |
|                                                 |
|   ADVERTISING IN NEWS-       Publication . . . . . . . . . |
|   PAPER OR MAGAZINE                              |
|   (Attach Ad When Possible)  Date . . . . . . . . . . . . |
|                                                 |
|   OTHER KINDS OF             Describe or Attach . . . . . . |
|   ADVERTISING                                   |
|   (Outdoor, Direct Mail, Etc.)    . . . . . . . . . . . . . . . |
|                                                 |
|   This advertising is objectionable to me because . . . . . . . . . . |
|                                                 |
|   . . . . . . . . . . . . . . . . . . . . . . . . . . . . . |
|                                                 |
|   . . . . . . . . . . . . . . . . . . . . . . . . . . . . |
|                                                 |
|   . . . . . . . . . . . . . . . . . . . . . . . . . . . . |
|                                                 |
|                     Name. . . . . . . . . . . . . |
|                                                 |
|                     Address  . . . . . . . . . . . . |
|                                                 |
|                     City . . . . . Zone . . . State . . . |
-------------------------------------------------
```

FIGURE 5–6.   How the Cleveland Plan invites consumer pressure

In the interests of honest advertising, promotional advertising copy which in any way stretches the truth and goes beyond the bounds of reasonableness and fair play, or which may mislead or confuse the reader is to be carefully censored by the *Journal* and omitted if not properly revised. We believe in imaginative, compelling, hard-selling copy. We like attractive, dramatic illustrations. We have faith in the power of words to make people want something, to convince them to buy it from the advertiser who gives him good reason. We know that advertising can sell wanted, good-brand merchandise at profitable, reasonable prices. We know, too, that there is no substitute for truth.[18]

In the words of the Federal Trade Commission "antideceptive work protects consumers and honest sellers of goods and services from the unfair competition of those few who distort truth for profit." It is important to remember that most business firms today operate on an honest basis and see to it that their advertising is honest. False advertising is usually the product of persons inclined toward falsehood. The institution of advertising is, in itself, not false, not untruthful, not misleading.

---

[18] "Milwaukee Journal's Appliance Ad Censorship Called Success," *Advertising Age,* October 1, 1951, p. 60.

Individual advertisements may, however, be any one or all of these things if the persons behind the ads choose to make them so.

Improvement in personal practice has come about partly through government regulation and partly through industry or self-imposed regulation. That such improvement has occurred is obvious from the following statement of a Federal Trade Commission official as reported by *Advertising Age:* "In recent years," he said, "lots of companies and advertising agencies have come to recognize they have a sacred trust to protect the believeability of advertising. In the recognized media, advertising as a whole is good. And considering the great increase in volume, an amazingly small percentage is questionable."[19]

Lasting improvement, however, can come only through the acceptance on the part of individuals of the efficacy and profitability of high ethical operations. For the weak and short-sighted, the pressure of external regulation of one type or another will continue to be essential. For the leader in society—be it in religion, philosophy, government, education, science, or advertising—emphasis must be placed on raising the ethical standards of all. As one of the great pioneers in the fight for truth in advertising said, "Advertising . . . by and large reflects the morals, manners, customs, habits, desires, and economic conditions of the community and generation which it serves."[20] Of course, advertising practice should be on a high ethical plane, but one should not expect it to rise too high above its source.

But let not advertising men and women hide behind this concept to justify their failure to assume leadership in building and keeping advertising to a high ethical level. Advertisers would do well to heed the admonition of Earl W. Kintner, former Chairman of the Federal Trade Commission, in a statement addressed to them. "Advertising men and women," he said, "must find within themselves a belief in their capacities to meet responsibilities and the will to discharge those responsibilities. It was John Stuart Mill who said that 'one person with a belief is equal to a force of 99 who have only interest.' Now is the time to demonstrate that you have beliefs. Now is the time to demonstrate that you are determined to be responsible citizens in a free society."[21]

Colston Warne has offered, at the policy level, a recommendation that

---

[19] "FTC Finds Ad Ethics Better," *Advertising Age,* September 10, 1956, p. 3.

[20] H. J. Kenner, *The Fight for Truth in Advertising* (New York: Round Table Press, 1936), p. xiv.

[21] Earl W. Kintner, "1961—Armageddon for Advertising?" *Printers' Ink,* June 16, 1961, p. 26.

all advertising men could well afford to consider and strive to implement. His recommendation follows:

Specifically, a policy is proposed of *caveat venditor*—let the seller beware—a policy to be enforced by our social and legal institutions. An advertisement should be a warranty to the purchaser of the price and quality of an article. Thus, the burden of proof as to an advertising claim will lie squarely upon the seller of a branded good. A claim should be accurate and complete as to all essential details, and should constitute full disclosure of both the merits and demerits of the good in its intended use. Advertising should not be poised on the slippery edge of irrelevance, misrepresentation, or deception. The obsolescent and socially destructive idea of *caveat emptor* should be approximately buried as a relic of the days of simple markets and well-understood commodities.[22]

Willard L. Thompson voices the same view when he says, "What is needed is some means of providing all persons within advertising with a renewed sense of their obligation, not to themselves but to the consumer. This is a seemingly impossible task, considering the breadth of the advertising world. And yet, it must be undertaken if advertising is to approach its fullest success in our society, and if it is to serve society as it must."[23] Thompson recommends the establishment of an industry "authority" to "police" members so that their practice would be in the interests of consumers. This might be one way of implementing the *caveat venditor* policy suggested by Mr. Warne.

QUESTIONS AND PROBLEMS

1. By referring to the library files of popular periodicals, compare three soap advertisements published before 1940 with three of those currently published. Do you note any change toward a greater degree of truthfulness?
2. Obtain from your library a recent issue of Federal Trade Commission Decisions. Study several of the cases showing action against advertisers.
3. Assume that an advertisement of a flour company reads: "Stale, rancid flour is bad for your nerves. Buy ——— dated flour and be assured of fresh, healthful flour." Assume that the advertisement goes on to state that the label of each package bears the date it was delivered to the grocer, so that when one buys ——— flour one gets fresh flour.

     Assume that the actual practice of this company was as follows: The flour was milled and packed in unlabeled containers at central plants in New York, Cleveland, Chicago, etc., and shipped to small distributing plants. Here, labels

---

[22] Colston E. Warne, "Advertising—A Critic's View," *Journal of Marketing,* Vol. 26 (October, 1962), p. 14.

[23] Willard L. Thompson, *Self-Regulation in Advertising* (Ph.D. thesis; University of Illinois, Urbana, 1958), p. 382.

were placed on the flour as fast as local demand necessitated. The flour was then delivered by truck to the grocer. Occasionally, if a retailer needed more than his usual supply, he was given flour dated several days ahead, and told not to put it on his shelves until the date printed on the label.

Could the advertising of such a company be regarded as ethical and truthful?

4. Which of the several agencies endeavoring to correct untruthful advertising is more likely to succeed? Which will be the least likely to succeed?

5. Why does the advertiser lose when his advertisement creats a *false* impression in the mind of the buyer? Is a deliberate untruth necessary?

6. Do you believe that testimonial advertising is convincing? What arguments can be advanced against it? What for it?

7. What is to be gained by advertisers and publishers from efforts at self-regulation of advertising?

8. Check the advertisements in a current issue of a metropolitan daily paper against the rules outlined in the National Better Business Bureau's *Do's and Don't's of Advertising Copy.* Comment on those advertisements which you believe fail to meet the standards of the B.B.B.

9. Which of the following degrees of control do you think the government should exercise over advertising:

    a) Establish a special board to censor *all* advertisements *before* publication to prevent objectionable advertising?

    b) Establish a special board to censor *all* advertisements *after* publication to stop further objectionable advertising?

    c) Leave to the regular law enforcement officers the task of investigating and stopping objectionable advertising which they observe or which is called to their attention?

    d) Permit interference with advertising only in cases of clear-cut dishonesty or fraud?

    e) Leave control of advertising entirely in the hands of the advertisers?

10. Assume that you have been employed by a metropolitan newspaper, such as the *New York Times* or the *Chicago Daily News*, as "advertising censor." It is your responsibility to check all advertisements submitted for inclusion in your paper, and to accept, reject, or recommend modifications before the advertisements are to be run.

    Draw up a list of factors or standards against which you would rate advertisements of home appliances before making your decision to accept, reject, or recommend modification or advertisements.

11. Discuss in some detail the implications of Mr. Warne's recommendation that *caveat venditor*—let the seller beware—guide the practice of all advertising people.

chapter 6
NONPRODUCT
ADVERTISING

THE TERM "nonproduct advertising" is used to cover the vast new field of idea advertising not related directly to products or commercial services. It would include individual company and trade association advertising of a public relations character as well as individual and group efforts to secure action on matters of public interest. It would also include the use of advertising to sell religion, political ideas, social change, and economic ideologies.

Advertorials

Advertising space and time in our mass media can provide a forum for the presentation of information and ideas related to social, economic, political, and personal issues as well as a market place for information about products available for purchase. Such space can be used to present ideas and information to readers that might not be presented if complete dependence were placed upon newspaper and magazine publishers and editors to do so on their own initiative. Furthermore, by using advertising space, the sponsoring organization or individual can present information and ideas in the form and manner desired, subject only to the general restrictions of the press.

An interesting example of this use of advertising space is the "advertorial" which was first introduced by *Atlantic Monthly* in its December, 1951 issue. The publisher of the *Atlantic* had this to say in explanation of the first advertorial carried by the magazine:

The *Atlantic* believes that there is a need for an entirely new kind of advertising, designed to transmit those compelling and often complex facts about American business which are in the public interest—and too little understood . . .

This calls for a new technique in advertising. For generations, *product advertisements* have been based upon the constant repetition of a theme, expressed in a slogan, a picture, a piece of short copy, or a jingle. Such skillful simplification will remain the most effective way to *advertise products*. But business cannot compress its problems and aspirations into a slogan or singing commercial. It cannot depend upon a reflex action; it must appeal to the reader's intelligence and let him draw his own conclusions.

The need creates the opportunity, the opportunity for a new and explicit kind of advertising. Watch the magazines and newspapers and you will see the pioneers are already reaching out for the *intelligence* of readers. These advertisers are beginning to realize that the success of these new advertisements depends upon *trading information for the reader's time. . . .*

To provide the facility for advertising to convey information, the *Atlantic* has developed a new form for the expression of business ideas. We call them advertorials. They will be paid advertisements, of course. . . . They are predicated upon the belief that the free competition of ideas has made this country great.[1]

Figure 6–1 is a reproduction of the first page of a four-page advertorial that illustrates the concept emphasized by Mr. Snyder. This use of advertising can, in fact, make anyone his own editor without the risk and cost of operating his own publishing enterprise.

Figures 6–2 and 6–3 illustrate advertisements of an advertorial nature that deal with subjects more often treated by public speakers, editors, or newspaper columnists.

Advertisements may also be used to bring before the large audiences assembled by newspapers a point of view held by the signers of the advertisement. This view may be different from that of the publishers or editors of the media used but can be presented in advertisement form without being edited by some outside or unfriendly party.

This kind of advertising can provide a forum for the presentation of opposing ideas to the public or ideas that may not be effectively presented in news or orthodox editorial material. Some may fear this use of advertising since it could lead to the presentation of highly unpopular material. For example, Russia purchased advertising space in a number of American newspapers in July, 1962, and ran the full text of then Premier Khrushchev's 13,000-word speech before the Communist-organized World Peace Congress in Moscow. One newspaper, *The Washington Post,* did not accept the Russian advertisement but wrote the Soviet

---

[1] Donald B. Snyder, "Business *Is* the Public Interest," *Atlantic Monthly,* December, 1951, p. 19.

COMPETITION IN TRANSPORTATION

by NEIL J. CURRY

Chairman, American Trucking Associations, Inc.

As early as 1904 railroads had established a speed record of 115.2 miles per hour. There it remained until 1934, thirty years later, when the Union Pacific achieved the current accepted record of 120 miles per hour for passenger trains. Between 1928 and 1936 the speed of freight trains, not as a record but on the whole, increased 22 per cent.

The significance of these figures is obvious. Not until the auto and airplane became factors in passenger transportation and motor trucks became significant in freight hauling, did the rails have the spur to compel improved performance.

One of the twin gods to which, figuratively, American business builds altars is competition. The other is maximum freedom of action, a notable national credo in all fields of activity, interpreted in business to mean dislike of all but the most essential governmental restraints.

The ideal climate in agriculture, industry and commerce, from the standpoint of the entrepreneur, would be one in which ownership operating through management would have maximum power and discretion to solve any and all problems which arise. Such, at least, would be the impulsive reaction of the entrepreneur, suddenly confronted with an opportunity to state the terms under which he would prefer to function.

Historically, the invasion of the field of management discretion by local, state and federal agencies has seldom been achieved without resistance of varying intensity, whether in the areas of health, insurance and welfare, marketing and trade practices or labor relations. Each such overlay of ordinances, rules, regulations or statutes has seemed to some segments of management a handicap which was unwarranted or costly or an impediment to full development of potential.

Transportation is "Public" Business

What I have been saying is particularly, but not exclusively, applicable to so-called "private" business. Economists recognize the essential difference between a private business, which is one whose activities reflect impact on a relatively limited number of people or a limited area of the economy and a "public" business, if I may use that term, whose operations cut across the whole economy.

An example of a "private" business might be a television manufacturer. However excellent his product, its purchase by anyone is optional, both as to his particular brand of television and as to television as a whole. An example of a "public" business would be an electric light and power company since it would be difficult if not impossible to operate our economy without that facility.

Despite the "private" nature of the great bulk of American agricultural, industrial and commercial activity there has been a steady trend toward intervention in its operation by government, based on the theory that the public interest can be and is affected by the cumulative or total result of certain practices in business or agriculture, indulged in by otherwise "private" business or farming.

In spite of the vigorous devotion which our people as citizens and as entrepreneurs pay to the

FIGURE 6–1. The first page of a four-page "advertorial"

How to retire at 35

It's easy.

Thousands of men do it every year. In all walks of life. And it sets our economy, our country, and the world back thousands of years in terms of wasted human resources. But worst of all is the personal tragedy that almost always results from "early retirement."

It usually begins with a tinge of boredom. Gradually a man's work begins to seem endlessly repetitious. The rat race hardly seems worth it any more.

It's at this point that many a 35-year-old boy-wonder retires. There are no testimonial dinners or gold watches. He still goes to work every day, puts in his forty hours, and even draws a paycheck. He's retired, but nobody knows it. Not at first, anyhow.

The lucky ones get fired in time to make a fresh start. Those less fortunate hang on for awhile—even decades —waiting and wondering. Waiting for a raise or promotion that never comes, and wondering why.

There are ways to fight back, though, and most men do. They counteract the urge to coast by running as they've never run before. They run until they get the second wind that is now known as "self-renewal."

Self-renewal is nothing more or less than doing for yourself what your parents, teachers, coaches, and bosses did for you when you seemed young enough to need it. It's the highest form of self-discipline. And it can be one of the most satisfying experiences a man can enjoy.

Self-renewal is the adult's ability to motivate himself; to reawaken his self-pride in the face of spiritual fatigue. Self-renewal is the device by which the boy-wonders become men. Leaders. Creators. Thinkers.

Self-renewal is probably the greatest test a businessman must face. It's worth the effort, though. With the life expectancy approaching the century mark, 65 years is a long time to spend in a rocking chair.

MARSTELLER INC.

ADVERTISING · PUBLIC RELATIONS · MARKETING RESEARCH

NEW YORK · CHICAGO · PITTSBURGH · TORONTO · GENEVA · BRUSSELS

FIGURE 6-2. An editorial type ad

Can a good businessman be a good American?

If your biggest single interest is your company's profit, and if you have to spend eight, ten, twelve hours a day to make it, how can you call yourself a good citizen?

Look at it this way:

Good profits enable your company to offer more jobs. And more secure jobs.

Good profits make your company an attractive investment which gives you more capital to expand to offer still more jobs. And even more secure jobs.

Good profits enable your company to design and manufacture better products. And provide better service to your customers. And make your company a better place to work.

Good profits enable your company to make meaningful bequests to community projects such as new hospitals, new schools, new recreational facilities.

And, of course, good profits make it possible for your company to pay your full share of the cost of government—at all levels. The bigger your profit, the bigger your tax contribution.

Come to think of it, maybe one type of ugly American is the businessman who constantly loses money.

MARSTELLER INC.

ADVERTISING · PUBLIC RELATIONS · MARKETING RESEARCH

NEW YORK · CHICAGO · PITTSBURGH · TORONTO · GENEVA · BRUSSELS · LONDON · PARIS · SÃO PAULO · STUTTGART

FIGURE 6–3. Use of advertising to present an idea

Embassy that "it would publish the Khrushchev text in its news columns if one of the official Russian newspapers, *Pravda* or *Izvestia*, would do the same with the text of President Kennedy's disarmament speech before the United Nations General Assembly"[2] in September, 1961.

One of the most dramatic advertorials of recent years was a two-page advertisement placed in the *New York Times*, May 23, 1966. This was an ad by Morihiro Matsuda, a citizen of Japan and operator of a small business in Tokyo. The headline and theme of the advertisement was "Idea for Peace in Vietnam."

Mr. Matsuda paid $11,184 to have this advertisement carried in the *Times*. This is a large sum for a relatively poor man to pay to have a nonbusiness message distributed to the multitudes. He was motivated by a "burning desire to share his thoughts with the rest of mankind." Such sharing is possible through the medium of advertising.

Public relations

Many definitions have been offered for "public relations." The field is too new to have a universally acceptable definition. Uncertainty is too great in respect to breadth of function, relation to other economic and social agencies, and character of application in solving particular problems to expect a standard definition at this time. Perhaps most students would agree with the statement of Harlow and Black that "public relations is an art and a science which deals with the difficult problem of how an individual or an institution can get along satisfactorily with other people and institutions."[3]

Business institutions have many groups of people to consider. Among such groups are stockholders, employees, customers, prospective customers, professional educators, legislators, and citizen voters. All these and others have some interest in and association with specific business houses. The attitudes which individuals and groups of people have toward the policies and practices of specific business institutions can have an important bearing on strikes, slowdowns, consumer patronage, education of youth, and business legislation.

Business firms should, of course, operate in the public interest, but that alone is not enough to develop favorable public opinion. Relations with

---

[2] From UPI wire story, July 27, 1962.

[3] Rex F. Harlow and Marvin M. Black, *Practical Public Relations* (New York: Harper & Row, 1947), p. 10.

various publics can be left to develop without a plan, or they can be planned. The producer of a better mousetrap can wait to have customers find out through their own desires about the better trap, or he can plan a program of education or advertising to carry the story of the better trap to would-be buyers. Planned interpretation of the merits of the institution in all its social and economic aspects is equally vital. Advertising is being used in increasing amounts to help in this interpretation.

A mounting public concern over water pollution and a growing belief that phosphates in detergents were upsetting the ecological balance of our lakes and streams led the Procter & Gamble Company to run the full page ad reproduced in Figure 6–4. In this ad, P & G seeks to explain the benefits of phosphates in detergents, to dispel the notion that this ingredient was a primary cause of pollution, and to assure the public that they were concerned about the effect of their products on the natural environment.

Some companies seek to determine the attitude of the public toward them and their business policies and practices as a means of guiding them in their efforts to explain and interpret company action properly. This approach was used recently by a large oil company to find out what people thought about the size of business profits and other aspects of the economics of business. A copy of the questionnaire used in this study is shown in Figure 6–5.

In answer to the first question, one third of all persons withheld an answer, but two fifths guessed that profits ranged anywhere from 25 to over 50 percent. Only six out of a hundred gave the correct answer—something under 10 percent. In harmony with the same attitude, a great majority of people canvassed believed that total payments to stockholders and management exceeded total payments to workers. Only 13 percent thought workers' wages constituted half or more of the total paid out in the form of dividends, top-management salaries, and workers' wages. The great majority of respondents, 79 percent, stated that company heads failed to give information to employees about profits. This survey provided the basis for an informative advertising program to raise the level of general public understanding concerning that particular company.

Although the advertisement reproduced in Figure 6–6 is designed primarily to render a public service, it also serves to create a favorable image for the New York Life Insurance Company. This advertisement

Questions and answers about phosphates in detergents

and their possible effect on our lakes and streams

WHAT ARE PHOSPHATES IN DETERGENTS?
The most commonly used phosphate in detergents is called sodium tripolyphosphate. About 25% of this material is made up of phosphorus and this is the only part which is being questioned in relation to our lakes and streams. The phosphorus content of most household laundry detergents varies between 10% and 12½%.

Phosphates, because they contain phosphorus, are a nutrient. They are essential to all life. They are in the food we eat, the water we drink, and occur abundantly in nature. They are one of the safest chemicals known to man.

WHY ARE PHOSPHATES IN DETERGENTS?
They combine with the active material in household detergents to provide the "muscle" to get dirty clothes clean. They also materially contribute to the reduction of germs in clothes, thereby reducing the danger of cross infection. They perform these two important tasks in a way that is safe for people, fabrics, and all washable surfaces, as well as for the washing machines and dishwashers in which they are used.

WHAT WOULD BE THE RESULT OF ELIMINATING PHOSPHATES FROM DETERGENTS?
If we were to eliminate all phosphates from detergents today there would be a serious reduction in cleanliness and sanitation in the homes of America as well as in our hospitals, restaurants, hotels and schools. There would also be other adverse results. For example, the soil removal from clothes and silverware in automatic dishwashers would be so poor that all automatic dishwashers would become virtually unusable.

In addition, there would be harmful results in the dairy, poultry, meat packing and other food processing industries in which detergents are required for cleanliness.

WHAT IS EUTROPHICATION?
Contrary to common belief, eutrophication is not the same as pollution. It is a natural process which is vital to sustaining the life of any lake or stream and thus provide food for fish.

What is of concern to all of us today is "excessive" or "accelerated" eutrophication. Too much plant life in lakes and streams consumes the oxygen needed by fish and thus destroys the proper ecological balance in these bodies of water.

WHAT CAUSES "EXCESSIVE" EUTROPHICATION?
It is caused by too many nutrients going into lakes and streams.

Phosphates are one such nutrient. Phosphates come into lakes and streams from human waste, chemical fertilizers, agricultural run off, as well as from detergents.

Phosphates by themselves regardless of their source — do not cause excessive eutrophication. Other nutrients such as carbon and nitrogen must also be present. It is the combination of nutrients which stimulates the growth of plant life.

WHAT IS PROCTER & GAMBLE'S POSITION IN REGARD TO PHOSPHATES IN DETERGENTS?
Procter & Gamble is engaged in an "all out" effort to reduce — and eventually to eliminate — the phosphate content of its detergents.

We have not waited for "proof" that the elimination of phosphates from our products will have any significant effect one way or the other on lakes and streams. Scientific opinions on this matter do differ. But it may take years to develop the necessary proof one way or the other.

Neither are we waiting for proper sewage treatment facilities which could answer this and other problems. Again, we recognize it may take many years to secure such facilities.

Our position is that if there is any possibility that our detergents are contributing to the excessive growth of plant life in lakes and streams, we want to correct this situation. We are working toward that end with all possible speed.

WHAT HAS PROCTER & GAMBLE DONE TO DATE?
We have tested literally hundreds of materials which might be used in place of phosphates in detergents. Out of all these materials, we have found one which can be used as a partial replacement for a material called NTA which is the abbreviation for sodium-nitrilotriacetate.

Procter & Gamble started to ship in experimental areas a product containing NTA in place of 25% of the usual phosphate content as long ago as 1966. By 1968, we were using NTA to replace 25% of the phosphates in approximately 10% of the Company's laundry detergent volume. By May of this year, we will be using NTA to replace 25% of the phosphates in approximately one-third of the Company's laundry detergent volume.

This is as fast as we can go until more NTA supplies are available. New NTA plants are being built and others are being designed and engineered. NTA will be used to make a 25% reduction in the phosphates of all our household laundry detergents just as rapidly as the necessary manufacturing facilities can be made available.

IS THERE A POSSIBILITY OF FURTHER REDUCTIONS IN PHOSPHATES — BEYOND THE 25% REDUCTION WHICH IS NOW UNDER WAY?
Yes. We are already producing detergents experimentally with a 50% reduction in phosphate content. Simultaneously, we are conducting extensive tests to confirm our belief that the materials we must use to replace this amount of phosphates in detergents will have no adverse effects in homes or on the environment.

WHAT ELSE IS PROCTER & GAMBLE DOING?
It is conducting an all-out research effort to find a way to eliminate 100% of the phosphate content of detergents. The Company has set no money limit on this program. The only limit is the number of fruitful avenues of exploration. Every productive lead is being pursued aggressively by our research organization.

WHY CAN'T PROCTER & GAMBLE MOVE FASTER TO REPLACE PHOSPHATES IN DETERGENTS?
Any time we replace any material in our detergents it means that we are putting a new material into the environment in vast quantities. This material finds its way into the ground water as well as into lakes and streams which means that it finds its way into the drinking water in many areas.

We must be certain that this new material will not, in itself, have adverse effects on the health of men, women or children or on the ecology of the nation. We must proceed carefully. Many tests have to be run. No one other than ourselves would accept the moral, ethical and financial responsibility for any damage that too hasty an action might cause.

WHAT CAN THE GOVERNMENT DO TO HELP?
We need the help of government in cooperative research endeavors. We own no lakes which can be used to study the eutrophication process and the effect of the injection of new materials into surface water systems. The study of the eutrophication process is relatively new; many of the findings to date are conflicting; and much remains to be learned about the whole subject. Procter & Gamble cannot do this part of the job by itself although its scientists are ready to cooperate with the government or with any reputable scientific organizations on such programs.

Procter & Gamble will continue to work just as fast as possible to find ways to reduce and eliminate phosphates from detergents. It will do this with the utmost care for the health of the people who use our products, with a proper respect for the job house-wives have in keeping their homes and families clean, and with a deep concern for the effect of our products on the natural environment of our country.

We hope these questions and answers give the public some understanding of this whole problem and some appreciation of what Procter & Gamble is doing about it.

The Procter & Gamble Company
Box 599, Cincinnati, Ohio 45201

FIGURE 6–4. Use of advertising to get an unrestricted message before the public

1. Just as a rough guess, what percent profit would you say the average manufacturer makes in peacetime? _____
2. After a factory or plant has paid for overhead and materials, which would you say gets the bigger share of what's left—stockholders and top management or workers?
   a) _____ Stockholders and top management
   b) _____ Workers
3. Out of every dollar paid in dividends, salaries to top management, and wages to workers how much do you think the worker gets? _____
4. In general, do you think our large corporations are paying too big a share, too small, or about the right share of what they make to their a) stockholders, b) top executives, c) office workers, d) labor?

Worker Classification	Pay is—		
	Too big	Too small	About right
a) Stockholders			
b) Top executives..........			
c) Office workers..........			
d) Labor			

5. Suppose the cost of living went up 15 percent in the next few months. Would you say that most companies could afford a 15 percent increase in wages without raising prices? _____yes; _____no.
6. Does your company make a practice of giving you information about profits? _____yes;_____no.

FIGURE 6–5. Questionnaire designed to measure public attitude toward certain business situations

was given a top award by *Saturday Review* as an example of a leading public service ad.

Association and group advertising

A significant number of professional, trade, labor, and civic associations make use of idea advertising. During periods of labor strife, both business and labor groups often purchase advertising space or time to present their side of the problem to various publics. In the early 1960's the American Medical Association used advertising extensively to present the case against socialized medicine. Various business groups regularly use advertising to inform and influence readers as to the merits of their

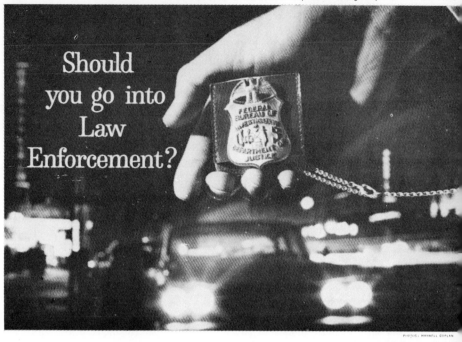

Should you go into Law Enforcement?

PHOTOS: MAXWELL COPLAN

by J. EDGAR HOOVER

Director, Federal Bureau of Investigation, United States Department of Justice, as told to Lester David

OUR COUNTRY is confronted today with the worst era of lawlessness in its history.

Consider these shocking facts: every four minutes that tick off on the clock, another human being is the victim of a murder, forcible rape or assault to kill. Every 46 seconds a burglary is committed, and each hour of the day and night 33 more automobiles are stolen from their owners. *In the time it has taken you to reach the end of this paragraph— about 20 seconds—a serious crime of some kind has occurred in the 50 states!*

The human suffering caused by lawbreakers is limitless. The financial cost— $22,000,-000,000 every year—is staggering. Thus the conclusion is clear:

Never before has there been such an urgent need for dedicated young men and women to enlist in the war against the crime colossus in America. Never before has our nation so needed the support of all its citizens to maintain and improve our standards of morality.

Right now, an army of more than 315,000 law enforcement officers is fighting that war in our federal, state and local law enforcement agencies. It is a large force but I cannot stress this too strongly: *It is not large enough.*

New recruits, well-trained and unswerving in their devotion to justice, are critically wanted. To these young people, the law enforcement profession offers a life of challeng-

ing, dedicated service to community and to country.

Enforcement is but one of the two facets of this service that awaits newcomers to the profession. The other lies in that equally broad and vital area—the prevention of crime. Officers work closely with the thousands of dedicated teachers, social workers, recreation leaders and church workers to raise standards of personal morality among our people and to keep our nation clean, decent and vigorous.

The profession offers a number of specific opportunities as well:

There is a broad field for the scientifically minded young person who wishes to specialize in ballistics, fingerprinting, communications or any of the other fascinating and diverse fields that are now an integral part of law enforcement.

The opportunity for advancement to positions of great trust and responsibility is available to qualified personnel. From today's recruits must come the law enforcement executives of tomorrow, the officials who plan, co-ordinate and administer departments of law enforcement agencies or the agencies themselves. These officials attain the respect and admiration of neighbors, friends and fellow citizens. It is unquestionably true that officers who move into high-

ranking positions are also leaders in community life.

A Specialized Profession

I hope you have noticed that I refer to this vital work as a "profession." It is exactly that! You see, law enforcement has moved into an entirely new era. Gone are the days when a recruit was sent into the streets with no more equipment and training than a badge, a stick and a list of rules. Today the field is highly specialized, calling for a keen intelligence to master and apply the complex techniques now employed in crime detection and prevention.

As a result, the nation's law enforcement agencies are attracting young persons of high caliber, many of them college graduates. Studies have actually shown that the educational background of America's police officers today is higher than at any other time in our history.

It is important to understand why a career in law enforcement now appeals strongly to the above-average person.

First, cleanliness attracts cleanliness. An aroused public conscience has rooted out, and is continuing to expunge, corruption wherever it is found infesting our police departments. While some bad apples remain, the ugly aura of scandal that made law enforcement work unsavory in the past has all but disappeared today.

Second, law enforcement now offers the same intellectual challenge as other scientific pursuits. This is true inasmuch as the profession has become far more technical. One of the police officer's most potent weapons is

FIGURE 6–6. An ad dealing with a basic public institution he scientific crime laboratory. There, the celprint, the toolmark, the altered document, the microscopic paint chip can provide the essential bit of evidence linking the criminal to his crime.

Third, the increasing emphasis on crime prevention has added a new dimension to the profession. An individual has the added satisfaction of knowing that while he helps protect his community he is also keeping other human beings from making tragic wastes of their lives.

No matter where his duties may take him, the law enforcement officer knows that his prime objective is to prevent the crime from happening at all. Indeed, special bureaus charged with crime prevention have been set up in departments all over the country. These generally work with young people to help create finer citizens and human beings.

Fourth, there is the realization that those qualified by experience, performance and academic training can win promotion to positions of command, including assignments at the very top levels.

Demands and Rewards

What, specifically, are the duties and responsibilities of a law enforcement officer?

He protects life and property. He preserves the peace. He prevents crime. He detects and apprehends violators of the law. He safeguards the rights of the individual. He enforces laws and ordinances.

These are the definitions you have heard, but the bare words hardly convey the full meaning of the task.

They do not tell you, for example, that a law enforcement officer comes into daily contact with the raw material of life itself; that he is a witness to humanity in moments of crisis; that he must match his intelligence and bravery against the cunning of criminals; that lives, including his own, can hinge on a split-second decision he may be required to make.

They do not say how long and selflessly an officer will work to establish, not only the guilt, but also the innocence of an arrested man.

They say nothing of the wonderful satisfaction of working with youngsters in the various police-sponsored juvenile programs, and helping to instill in them a life-long respect for the laws of our land.

Nor, finally, do they reveal how a person can feel, deep in his soul, when he knows that

The scientific crime laboratory plays a major part in law enforcement. There, specialists can link a criminal to his crime through the merest bit of evidence.

he is in the front line of the battle against hatemongers and subversive elements that would degrade and even destroy our country.

There are more than 40,000 law enforcement units throughout the nation where you, when properly qualified, may apply. These range from the village police force and sheriff's department on the local level, to Federal agencies such as the United States Secret Service and Federal Bureau of Investigation. In your state, you can select the State Police or Highway Patrol, among others. You can also become a probation or parole officer, or choose a career in correctional work.

Character Requirements

Are there any special personal qualifications for law enforcement work? Indeed there are:

The profession calls for sound health, physical stamina and a plentiful supply of courage.

It calls for the emotional stability to cope with crises.

It calls for the ability to work with others as a team. Despite popular belief, there are no individual stars in law enforcement work. Anyone with strong personal ambitions for the limelight would be well advised to look elsewhere.

Above all else, it calls for integrity, unimpeachable and absolute.

A young man can start preparing for a law enforcement career early in life. He can engage in sports that will keep him physically fit. He can join groups such as the Boy Scouts and Boys' Clubs of America which encourage character development. He can work with his school safety patrol.

The courses that can prove most valuable to him are American history, sociology, psychology, chemistry, physics, criminology, civics and government, English, report writing, business law, economics, public speaking, physical education, typing and shorthand.

A high school education is the minimum schooling required by most law enforcement units. Many junior colleges, colleges and universities now offer courses in the field, some leading to academic degrees.

Salary and Security

How about salaries and hours? And, to be realistic, what about the unpleasant aspects of the profession?

I often tell young people: "You will never become rich if you follow a law enforcement career except in the satisfactions that come from within." While pay has improved in recent years, it is still too low in some areas. Salaries vary from unit to unit, but generally average about $5,000 annually for patrolmen in the larger cities. Earnings are somewhat less in smaller communities. High officials can earn a great deal more, depending on their duties.

If a law enforcement officer's earnings are not high, he does have the important twin advantages of job security and pension and retirement rights because of his civil service status.

Hours of work average between 40 and 48 weekly, depending on the community, but can be much longer in emergencies. Once he accepts his badge, an officer is subject to instant call to duty any hour of the day or night.

This irregularity of hours and the consequent disruption of home life is a hard fact that must be clearly understood and accepted at the start. Another is the blunt truth that the work can be dangerous. Every year, an average of 54 police employees sacrifice their

lives in the line of duty. Still another physical hazard: an officer may be assigned to work outdoors, often for hours on end, in any extreme of weather.

Policewomen Needed

Are there opportunities for women in law enforcement? Certainly. There are many thousands of women in this field all over the country. Unquestionably, the profession has achieved recognition as an outstanding one for girls interested in a career. And for good reason: the assignment offers a girl an unparalleled chance to participate in work that is at once fascinating, adventurous and valuable to her community.

The exploits of America's policewomen are noteworthy. They have captured gunmen, helped crack narcotics rings, brought blackmailers and embezzlers to book and worked side by side with the men on difficult and dangerous cases.

A high school education is generally required of applicants for policewomen, while some law enforcement units also stipulate that women have some prior training in social work. Usually policewomen have the same hours, pay and civil service status as policemen.

I can think of no career that can offer the individual a greater sense of accomplishment than law enforcement. Certainly, there are few others as significant to the welfare of our nation in these anxious times.

Booklets Available on Many Careers

This article is one of a continuing series on career opportunities for young men and women. Each is available in booklet form. Additional help will be found in "The Cost of Four Years of College." Use the coupon to indicate booklets you wish.

"way of life." Others employ advertising in an attempt to influence legislation.

The American Home Laundry Manufacturers' Association ran, in the *Washington Post,* the advertisement which is reproduced in Figure 6–7. At the time this was run Congress was debating a new tax bill which was designed to increase taxes on many consumer goods. By using the public press to reach senators, the stand of the Association was dramatized much more effectively than would have resulted had dependence been placed on direct mail only.

Cigarette advertising has been under attack from many quarters during recent years. Congressional hearings and impending legislation to prohibit cigarette advertising on television and radio resulted in the tobacco companies' offering in 1969 to take their advertising off the air by January 1971. The *New York Times,* acting independently from other newspapers, stated they would accept cigarette ads only if they contain a caution notice along with tar and nicotine figures. The American Tobacco Company retaliated with the ad in Figure 6–8.

Some associations or groups use advertising as a means of dispelling erroneous impressions held by different segments of the population. It was for this purpose that various farm cooperatives ran a series of advertisements to emphasize the democratic character of cooperatives. Preceding these advertisements a study was made among business and professional leaders in a midwestern state to determine their attitudes toward farm retail cooperatives. In that study respondents were asked whether they believed the farm retail cooperative with which they were familiar was an asset to *their community.* Of the total answering, 51 percent said yes. When attention was focused on farm cooperatives in general and when respondents were asked whether they believed that "farm cooperatives were an asset to *a* community," only 42 percent answered yes. At best, then, only one half of the business and professional leaders thought farm retail cooperatives were worthwhile.

Even more negative was the attitude on specific aspects of cooperatives. Only 29 percent of the respondents in this study believed that cooperatives stood for or promoted the free enterprise system. Almost one third (32 percent) believed farm cooperatives stood for communism or socialism. Thus, the ad in Figure 6–9 was run to say, in effect, "Cooperatives are democratic."

In the case of a new type of business service or operation, the job of informing or educating the public as to the characteristics and merits of the new is often great. This job of education may be undertaken by indi-

It's not right, Senator!

It's not right for the Congress of the United States to deprive countless thousands of housewives all over the country of the benefits of a Washing Machine by imposing an excise tax that would add $25 to $35 to the retail price

Don't Tax Washing Machines!

Washing clothes by hand is probably the ugliest household job a woman has to perform. It is hard, back-breaking work.

In families where every penny counts, women look forward to the day when they'll be able to own a Washing Machine. These women deserve the highest consideration from the Senate of the United States.

Tax money has to be raised. The people know it ... and the people will pay it. But ... is it right to tax a woman's health and well-being by making it harder for her to replace the washboard and tub with a labor-saving Washing Machine. An excise tax on Washing Machines would do just that.

By the time this tax is pyramided from the manufacturer—to the distributor—to the retailer ... it would add a burdensome $25 to $35 to the consumer's cost.

Actually, Congress doesn't like the idea of taxing Washing Machines. It refused to do so during World War II. In the current bill, the House expressly exempted Washing Machines from the excise tax. It accepted the fact that a Washer is an essential household machine tool. Congress has never imposed an excise tax on a machine tool for a factory. Congress should not now tax the most essential machine tool in the American home.

A Washing Machine is not a luxury—it is a necessity. It is a labor-saving machine that relieves women of untold drudgery and fatigue—especially among the modest income groups. In all fairness to these women, the Senate, like the House, ought to refuse to impose an excise tax on Washing Machines.

AMERICA DOESN'T WANT THIS, SENATOR

A consumer tax on Washing Machines would delay the time when every American housewife could afford to free herself from the back-breaking toil of the washboard and tub ...

DON'T TAX WASHING MACHINES

AMERICAN HOME LAUNDRY MANUFACTURERS' ASSOCIATION, CHICAGO, ILLINOIS

FIGURE 6–7. Use of advertising to influence legislation

vidual leaders in the field or by an association of most or all of the members. Such group action is familiar procedure in the product field. Examples include group promotion of oranges, nuts, vegetables, flowers, cement, candy, and silver.

Why we're dropping The New York Times

Last week the Times said it would accept cigarette ads only if they contain (1) a health caution notice, and (2) "tar" and nicotine figures.

We don't go along with this.

We offered to take our ads off TV and radio because of the claim that those media unavoidably reach large numbers of children.

We did not take that action because we agree with anticigarette crusaders (including The New York Times) who would like to blame cigarettes for the thousand and one ills that flesh is heir to.

Sure there are statistics associating lung cancer and cigarettes. There are statistics associating lung cancer with divorce, and even with lack of sleep. But no scientist has produced clinical or biological proof that cigarettes cause the diseases they are accused of causing. After fifteen years of trying, nobody has induced lung cancer in animals with cigarette smoke.

We believe the anticigarette theory is a bum rap. And each time the Congress of the United States has held Hearings on the cigarette controversy, distinguished, independent scientists have gone to Washington to say so.

Therefore, we are not going to knuckle under to the Times or anybody else who tries to force us to accept a theory which, in the opinion of men who should know, is half-baked.

In 1884, the New York Times said:

"The decadence of Spain began when the Spaniards adopted cigarettes and if this pernicious practice obtains among adult Americans the ruin of the Republic is close at hand..."

We think the New York Times was wrong in 1884. We think it is wrong in 1969.

The American Tobacco Company
A DIVISION OF AMERICAN BRANDS, INC.

FIGURE 6–8.   Use of advertising to balance normal news and editorial material

In the nonproduct field such group action to present a business message is less extensive. In some states chambers of commerce and other local business groups jointly sponsor advertising to attract vacationists to their area. During World War II groups combined to advertise how consumers could prolong the life of scarce products. This was honest, straightfor-

"OF THE PEOPLE"

—BY THE PEOPLE—AND FOR THE PEOPLE—are the standards given a great nation — by a great man. Every school child in America learns this fundamental truth about the government of his United States.

Every American takes simple pride in being part of a government "of the people." It means freedom in the pursuit of life, liberty and happiness for our 140,000,000 citizens. It has given America the mantle of leadership for millions seeking freedom throughout a war-torn world. Democracy is the American way—

Farm cooperatives are founded on the basic principles of American democracy. They too are "of the people." And they contribute to the security and prosperity of thousands of rural communities throughout America —

In Auglaize and Shelby Counties several thousand farm families work together in a pattern of friendly and purposeful cooperation. The more than twenty cooperative enterprises have — by increasing farm purchasing power — helped farmers become the most important customers in the rural community. Cooperatives — of the people — by the people — and for the people — are helping build sound and prosperous American communities.

Cooperatives of Auglaize and Shelby Counties

AUGLAIZE COUNTY FARM BUREAU CO-OP.
AUGLAIZE COUNTY FARM BUREAU, INC.
FARMERS EQUITY UNION CREAMERY CO.
MINSTER FARMERS CO-OP. EXCHANGE
WAPAKONETA NATIONAL FARM LOAN ASS'N.
WAPAKONETA PRODUCTION CREDIT ASS'N.

WAPAKONETA PRODUCERS LIVESTOCK CO-OP.
JACKSON CENTER FARM BUREAU CO-OP.
SIDNEY FARMER EXCHANGE
MIAMI-DARKE-SHELBY-NAT'L FARM LOAN ASS'N.
PIONEER ELECTRIC CO-OP.
AUGLAIZE COUNTY POMONA GRANGE

THE BUCKLAND COOPERATIVE CO.
MIDWEST ELECTRIC INC.
MINSTER FOOD STORAGE CO-OP.
POULTRY PRODUCERS ASS'N.
WAPAKONETA FARMERS GRAIN
SHELBY COUNTY FARM BUREAU

FIGURE 6–9. "Cooperatives are democratic," says this advertising message ward advertising in the public interest, but it was also a message that had long-range business value to participants.

Figure 6–10 presents a business message by an association which represents firms dealing in mutual funds investment. It is one of a series of advertisements designed to educate people about a relatively new type of investment method and to persuade them as to the advantage and values of this type of saving.

Use in politics

Advertising is being used more and more by political parties and candidates as a means of getting their messages before vast numbers of people. In major campaigns professional advertising counselors and practitioners are employed to plan and execute advertising strategy. Various reports and studies suggest that more than $44 million was spent for broadcast and newspaper political advertising in the primary and general state and national elections in 1964.

The late Senator Richard L. Neuberger in commenting on political advertising said, "I consider the trend toward wider use of (advertising) techniques in politics significant. In fact, it is so significant that it may well revolutionize politicking in this country and could definitely turn out to be the most decisive single factor governing American politics during our generation."[4]

Martin Mayer is somewhat skeptical about the value or appropriateness of advertising in political campaigns. The following comment of Mayer is worthy of serious thought:

> The most common objection to the use of advertising to magnify political issues is that advertising oversimplifies. A good part of the technique of advertising has the single purpose of simplification, of finding from the welter of causes which make people buy a product the one or two or three which can be refined down to a "reason" and then blown up to a slogan. Applied to branded products, the technique at its worst can do little harm to society as a whole, because product purchases are trivial matters and because people do not buy even the most heavily advertised product a second time unless it has given satisfaction. Applied to political issues, however, the technique must partially misinform, create undesirable emotions, and distort the realities which, in theory, underlie the decision of the electorate.[5]

The use of advertising in political campaigns is still quite new. Experimentation with different methods of use is still in order. It may be that it

---

[4] Richard L. Neuberger, "Madison Avenue in Politics," *Esquire,* August, 1957, p. 79.

[5] Martin Mayer, *Madison Avenue, U.S.A.* (New York: Harper & Row, 1958), pp. 300–301.

Considering college costs? Consider Mutual Funds.

Consider the cost of putting your children through college. Or consider the kind of retirement you want. Or just the good things you'd like for your family. Then consider how much costs may rise in the years ahead. Today—shouldn't you consider mutual funds? Although no investment can assure the achievement of a specific objective, mutual funds do provide you with a sensible approach to your financial goals. **MUTUAL FUNDS** are professionally managed investments in which 3½ million people, concerned for the future of themselves and their families, have pooled about 35 billion dollars to share the risks and rewards of investing in a growing economy.

Why not talk to your investment dealer or mutual fund representative today. Or contact the fund of your choice. / Investment Company Institute, 61 Broadway, New York, New York

FIGURE 6–10. Use of advertising by an association to present a new investment idea will be used more in the "advertorial" sense in the future rather than as a means for merely saturating the media with slogans and some surface issue. In any event, it is perhaps good that political parties and candidates for public office have this means for "direct" communication with the electorate in an age where face-to-face communication is possible to only a limited degree. It is not that advertising can, in itself, determine the course of an election but rather that it can provide another and an important dimension in the process of informing, educating, and persuading the electorate on basic as well as surface issues.

The Advertising Council

Organized and systematic group action for idea advertising was developed during World War II. Such organized efforts were centered in the War Advertising Council. The Council was established in 1942 as a nonprofit voluntary organization financed by both business and individual sponsors. Its purpose was to marshal the talents of the advertising profession to prepare advertising campaigns which would "induce people to take desperately needed actions" in the interest of national welfare.

The War Advertising Council would select, in cooperation with government agencies, the areas needing strong public support. After selection was made, some agency in the profession would volunteer to develop strategy and prepare advertisements for use in "selling" the public on the need for action. Completed advertisements would be made available to press, radio, and other media for voluntary use.

Accomplishments. During the war period, voluntary contributions of time and space resulting from Council action approximated $300 million annually. The organized power of advertising was behind the job of telling American people what needed to be done to speed victory. A partial list of the fields covered by such cooperative support follows:

War bond drives.
Developing victory gardens.
Recruiting women for military service.
Urging early mailing for overseas Christmas gifts (95 percent of all such gifts were mailed before the deadline).
Reduction of absenteeism in factories.
Conservation of food.
Salvage of waste fats, paper, tin.
Support of Red Cross.

There was no attempt to measure the exact influence of advertising in securing public action on things advertised. However, the tremendous response that paralleled advertising effort indicated that advertising was a powerful stimulus to action. Strong advertising support, work of civic groups, and efforts of other agencies combined to produce outstanding results in many fields. In the field of conservation and salvage, such efforts induced the American people to salvage 538 million pounds of waste fat, 800 million pounds of tin, and 23 million tons of paper. Equally impressive response was accorded other drives, such as those to sell bonds, plant victory gardens, donate blood, and recruit nurses' aides.

Change from war to peace. Group action during a war crisis is a relatively easy thing to accomplish, but it is more difficult to achieve such cooperation when a crisis is less evident. However, the War Advertising Council chose to attempt such cooperation on a regular and continuing basis. It therefore changed its name immediately after the war to the Advertising Council. It has grown apace with the times and has helped to meet some of the increased social responsibilities accepted by the advertising profession.

The Council also broadened its function beyond that of its predecessor. It operates as a "nonprofit organization which marshals the forces of advertising in helping to conserve our human resources, to conserve our natural resources, to strengthen our democracy and our national economy, to build our national defense, and to strengthen freedom overseas."[6]

Advertisers and media give free advertising time and space in support of campaigns developed by the Council, and agencies prepare materials without charge. It is governed by a Board of Directors of 70 businessmen who meet monthly to plan and supervise the various projects accepted for promotion.

Projects are selected by the Board and a Public Policy Committee of 20 members. This latter group is recruited from leading citizens representing all phases of American life. Included on the Policy Committee are representatives from philanthropy, religion, education, labor, business, and foreign affairs. A chart showing the facilities and operations of the Council is presented in Figure 6–11.

An average of about 150 requests are received for advertising help each year, but only a fraction of these are accepted by the Council for promotion. During a recent 12-month period the Council conducted major campaigns for 16 public service projects. These included the promotion of ideologies, alleviation of human distress, and conservation of natural resources. Names of some of the specific projects were: people's capital-

---

[6] Advertising Council, *Fifteenth Annual Report* (New York: 1957), p. 1.

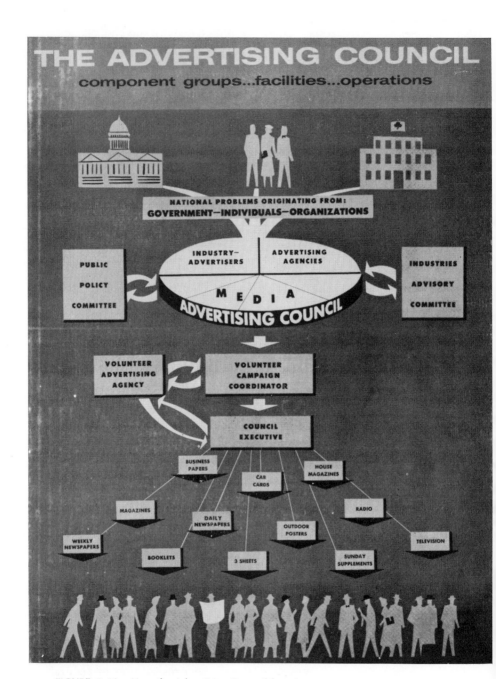

FIGURE 6–11. How the Advertising Council functions

ism, the Peace Corps, better schools, improvement of neighborhoods, accident prevention, crusade for freedom, religion in American life, U.S. Savings Bonds, and prevention of forest fires. The amount of space and time donated by media to the promotion of these and other Council campaigns in the 12-month period ending June 30, 1966 amounted to more than $236 million.[7]

Figure 6–12 shows one of the advertisements in the Council's "Keep America Beautiful" campaign.

In 1956 the Council undertook to advertise the importance of higher education and to emphasize the need for financial aid to colleges. A national campaign on "Help the College of Your Choice" was developed and has been continued annually. Figure 6–13 is an example of an advertisement from the 1962 campaign. Mr. Theodore Repplier, then president of the Council, stated that, after the campaign had been in operation for four years, "voluntary financing of colleges [had] stepped up sharply. Representative figures show that . . . nonalumni contributions increased 25%, corporation contributions 41%, and annual alumni contributions 101%."[8]

Not all of this, of course, was the result of Council advertising, but it is reasonable to assume that such advertising hastened the acceptance of an idea that had basic public values and stimulated action on the part of individuals and corporations.

Religious organizations

Various religious groups have been consistent users of idea advertising for some time. Several million dollars are spent annually for radio and television time and publication space by churches to sell a particular creed or a way of life. A number of church users of advertising solicit inquiries and follow up with additional literature in good orthodox selling fashion. Some employ advertising agencies or public relations counsel to direct their advertising efforts.[9]

One of the outstanding examples of this type of advertising is that done by the Knights of Columbus, a society of Catholic laymen. This group started some local advertising in 1944 with the avowed purpose

---

[7] Advertising Council, *Annual Report 1965–66* (New York, 1966), p. 2.

[8] Theodore Repplier, speech delivered before Association of National Advertisers, New York, May, 1962.

[9] Detailed information on church advertising may be found in James W. Carty, Jr., *Advertising the Local Church* (Minneapolis: Augsburg Publishing House, 1965).

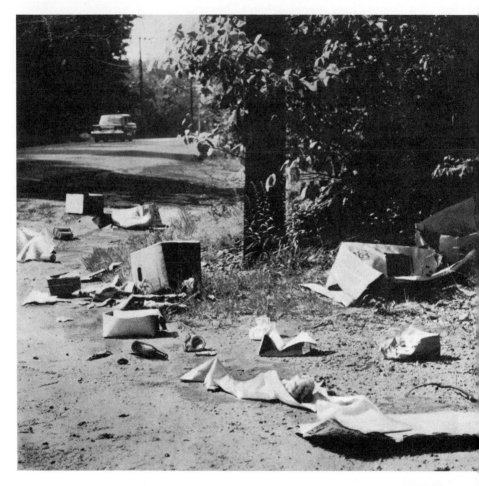

Every litter bit hurts

Trash? Litter? Empties? Don't discard them as you drive! Carry a litterbag in your car. Hold everything for the first roadside basket or take it home for proper disposal. Remember—our roads and highways belong to all of us. Litter spoils your view... menaces highway safety . . . costs tax dollars! Every litter bit hurts . . . YOU. America's beauty is your duty. Please help

KEEP AMERICA BEAUTIFUL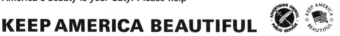

FIGURE 6–12.   One of a series of public service magazine ads prepared by the Advertising Council

WILL I WEAR ONE OF THOSE
WHEN I GROW UP?

Will you?

Of course you want to grow up and be like your big brother—go to college, become an electronics engineer, an architect, a doctor. And we hope you do, because our country is growing and we'll need many more highly trained men and women to keep America strong and free.

Of course you want to go to college!

But, will you? Well, that depends.

It depends on you, of course. You've got to be bright, ambitious, hard-working. But it depends on something else, too. For you to go to college, there has to be a college for you to go to—or room for you in the college you select. Because in ten years—maybe less—applications to colleges and universities from bright boys and girls like you are ex-

pected to double. If you and your friends are to receive a really good education, it will mean more classrooms, libraries, up-to-date laboratories—above all, thousands more top-quality professors. And all that will mean money—a great deal of money.

If grown-ups will realize the problem and do something about it, your chances of going to college will improve. Let's hope they start now to give you the gift of knowledge—by helping to support the college of your choice.

If they want to know more about what the college crisis means to you—and to them—tell them to write for a free booklet to Higher Education, Box 36, Times Square Station, New York 36, N. Y.

Good luck, son!

Sponsored in cooperation with The Advertising Council and the Council for Financial Aid to Education.

FIGURE 6–13. An ad from the Council campaign on higher education

of answering gently but effectively some of the unfavorable ideas some had about Catholicsim. The advertising program was expanded to a national and Canadian campaign in 1948. The annual expenditure for the campaign is about $500,000.

Advertisements generally carry a compelling headline, a very small illustration, and full unbroken copy. The following are some of the headlines used in past advertisements: "Is the Catholic Church a Menace to Democracy?"; "Learn the Truth about the Catholic Church by Mail . . . at No Cost!"; "The Real Secret of Successful Marriage"; "But How Can Educated People Be Catholics?" See Figure 6–14 for a reproduction of one of the advertisements.

Kelly, Zahrndt & Kelly, Inc., of St. Louis, has served as the advertising agency for the Knights of Columbus campaign. Mr. Virgil A. Kelly, president of the agency, comments as follows on the campaign:

> One of the most important things to be kept in mind in appraising this program is its positive character. It aims to present the Catholic doctrine, philosophy and history on their own merits and not by comparison with other creeds. In this respect we conform to the best product advertising by describing what we believe, without trying to point out how much better this may be than some conflicting beliefs. We realize, of course, that conflicting beliefs are inherently and necessarily controversial, whether explained from the pulpit or in paid space; but we are most careful to avoid injecting this inherent controversy into our advertisements. We tell our own story and let our readers judge it and accept or reject it on the basis of its truth and its appeal to their thinking.[10]

The results of this campaign have been substantial. The agency handling this project reported that the average number of requests for copies of the various pamphlets offered in the advertisements averaged better than one thousand per day.[11]

Another example of the use of regular advertising space to sell a religious message is illustrated by the experience of Christ Church in Cincinnati, Ohio. That church was located in the downtown section of the city and was faced with many of its members moving to the suburbs. It chose to remain in its old location and attempt to serve a downtown population. Such a population generally had a high turnover and many belonged to no church.

An advertising agency, whose president (Leonard Sive) was a member of Christ Church, headed a committee to plan and execute an advertising campaign to explain the services offered by Christ Church and to encour-

---

[10] From letter in file of author.
[11] *Ibid.*

Why The Catholic Church Says "INVESTIGATE!"

Probably not more than a handful of people hate the Catholic Church as it really is.

But many have heard anti-Catholic calumnies from sources they have been taught to respect, and have come to fear and suspect the Church as it has been falsely represented to them.

It is hardly reasonable to believe that 25 millions of Americans would remain in the Catholic Church if the rumors circulated against the Church are true. Nor would thousands of others become Catholics every year if they believed such things — without inquiring into the facts.

That is why the Catholic Church says again and again to people everywhere: "Investigate! Investigate!"

The Church makes this appeal not merely to settle an argument, nor primarily to win the good-will of the non-Catholic people, although this is a hoped-for result.

Its more important aim is to invite people to inquire into Christ's truth as taught and preserved by the Catholic Church down through the centuries. For no man, seeking the salvation of his own soul, can conscientiously discount the Catholic claim to be Christ's Church on the basis of mere rumor and slander when the truth is so readily at hand.

The Catholic Church therefore invites you to inquire into its teaching and practices ... to find out for yourself if what you believe about the Church is true or false.

Learn for yourself, for instance, if it is true that Catholics give divine worship to Mary, the Mother of Christ ... or if this is not just another calumny. If you have been led to believe that Catholics worship idols and statues ... buy and sell the divine worship of the Mass ... are opposed to the religious freedom granted all religions by our Bill of Rights, then you have been deceived and misled.

If you have harbored these or any other false beliefs about the Catholic Church and its teachings ... and if, above all, such misunderstanding has kept you from examining the Catholic claim to be the Church established by Christ Himself ... you owe it to yourself in good conscience to seek the truth.

We shall be glad to send you free on request, a booklet dealing with the points mentioned here and many others ... including the attitude of the Church toward Birth Control ... secret societies ... the salvation of non-Catholics ... why Catholic priests are called "Father" ... the Inquisition and the alleged goings-on behind convent walls. Write today ... ask for your copy of Pamphlet No. 7—KC.

SUPREME COUNCIL
KNIGHTS OF COLUMBUS
Religious Information Bureau
4422 LINDELL BLVD.   ST. LOUIS 8, MO.

FIGURE 6–14. Use of advertising by religious groups

Are you all alone in the city?

Everyone needs to "belong." The biggest crowds can be the loneliest places. No one needs to be alone; we were meant not to be. Some try to escape loneliness on a superficial level—at bars, taverns, in clubs. This can never satisfy the deepest longings. If you want to find the secret of escaping loneliness, the Church can show you the most satisfying way never to be lonely again.

There are many organizations, activities, and services of worship at Christ Church to which you would be welcomed. Phone GArfield 1-1266, or come in any time for a talk with one of our clergy.

CHRIST CHURCH
EPISCOPAL
318 East 4th Street   Phone GA 1-1266

Every Monday Evening, 7 to 9 p. m., in the parish house, the Rev. Milton Saville is available for personal counseling or to give information about the Episcopal Church. No appointment is necessary, but you may make one if you wish.

FIGURE 6–15. A newspaper ad by a Cincinnati church

age persons to make use of such services. An example of the kind of advertising run in the Cincinnati newspapers is shown in Figure 6–15. *Advertising Age* reported on this use of advertising as follows:

> Mr. Sive and his committee embarked on a "fascinating adventure"—to try to reach the populace with modern consumer-appeal advertising, in place of the conventional "religious page" sermon announcements.
>
> He began putting 200-line ads into Cincinnati papers, generally avoiding the Saturday church-listing pages and making it a point to hit readers where they live. "Is it proper to join a church to meet people?" asked one of the most potent ads.
>
> Its answer: "One of the most elementary needs of human beings is to 'belong.' We were never intended to live all alone for ourselves. If you are interested in meeting or belonging to a group of people who have learned how to overcome loneliness through a sharing of something worth while . . . you are invited to attend any of our services of worship and to join in the many activities and organizations of Christ Church."[12]

After a few months of advertising Mr. Sive estimated that the campaign had increased regular attendance at Christ Church by 40 or 50 persons and the number of confirmed members by 20.[13]

Idea advertising and national welfare

The social and economic welfare of a nation can be greatly enhanced when concerted and harmonious effort is exerted to educate citizens to an understanding of what is beneficial and to urge them to act to secure such benefits. Such efforts can reduce traffic accidents, improve health, reduce forest fires, and, in general, serve basic social and economic needs. Stuart Chase and F. J. Schlink emphasized this possibility some years ago when they wrote as follows:

> The technique of advertising is a magnificent technique. Sanely applied, it could remake the world. Think of what might be done with applied psychology in a great publicity drive for public health, for better housing, for cleaning up the slums, for honest and timely information about goods, for genuine education in a hundred fields! Many advertisers see this; a few of them try to practice it, but their hands are tied. Between the interest of the whole community in more abundant life, and the individual in his profit and loss account, there yawns a chasm which no optimism, no sophistries about "service," no pretty little talks by Dr. Frank Crane and his friends may cross.[14]

---

[12] *Advertising Age,* "Consumer-Appeal Ads Attract Members to Downtown Church Deserted by Suburbanites," December 17, 1956, p. 82.

[13] *Ibid.*

[14] Stuart Chase and F. J. Schlink, *Your Money's Worth* (New York: Macmillan Co., 1935), p. 42.

The vision expressed by Messrs. Chase and Schlink more than 30 years ago is being implemented today through the work of the Advertising Council and individual advertisers. A Council or a corporate advertising campaign on each of the areas mentioned in the above quotation could be cited. Figure 6–16 is illustrative of ads that could be selected from these areas.

It is also possible that group education or advertising, properly timed, could effectively influence such a basic economic phenomenon as the business cycle. Agencies like the Federal Reserve Board will vary the rediscount rate of commercial paper or the margin requirements for trading in securities as a means of influencing business activity. Perhaps an advertising council could channel advertising effort to check extreme optimism and extreme fear on the part of either businessmen or consumers. To the extent that optimism and fear are factors in the business cycle, such advertising effort could serve as a modifying influence.

Fear and optimism influence both businessmen and consumers. Optimism often encourages businessmen to expand operations at an unhealthy rate and to raise prices unnecessarily; they also tend to increase their advertising of commodities as a means of increasing purchases by consumers. Many economists believe that such practices soon throw out of balance the ability to produce and the ability of consumers to buy. When that occurs, both production and consumption must decline.

Advertising conceived and executed by business, labor, and consumer leaders and directed to both sellers and buyers might be effective in modifying both the inflation and deflation aspects of the business cycle. The injury to the overall economy of wage-price spiraling might be dramatized through advertising directed to labor and business management and thus help such inflationary actions. Likewise, strong group advertising, directed at consumers when business is slow and the fundamental economy is sound, might hasten a resumption of healthy and active trade.

How far advertising can go in modifying injurious business fluctuations is not known, but the possibilities are sufficiently promising that experimentation might well be encouraged. Such force can be utilized for both good and bad purposes, but the interest of the student is only in the good and in how such force can be applied to improving our economy.

Reversing the flow of idea advertising

The great majority of advertising, regardless of its type, is initiated by the few to influence the many. One retail firm will communicate with

A fifty cent test spared this baby from spending his life mentally retarded.

But only in Massachusetts, New York, Louisiana and Rhode Island is the test legally required.

There is a disorder of body chemistry called phenylketonuria, or PKU. Once, there was no way to diagnose it. Once, babies born with it were doomed to lifelong mental retardation.

But no longer. For a new test—given during the first few days of life—detects PKU *before* brain damage occurs.

A special diet corrects the trouble. A PKU baby then grows and develops as normally as any other child.

This test costs only 50¢ a baby. But a PKU victim, undiscovered, can cost $100,000 for lifetime care in an institution.

If your state doesn't require the PKU test, urge its adoption. It should be a must for all babies everywhere.

Here are six things you can do now to help prevent mental retardation and bring new hope to the 5½ million people whose minds are retarded:

1. If you expect a baby, stay under a doctor's or a hospital's care. Urge all expectant mothers to do so. Take your baby to the doctor regularly for health checkups.

2. Visit local schools and urge them to provide special teachers and special classes to identify and help mentally retarded children early in their lives.

3. Urge your community to set up workshops to train retardates who are capable of employment.

4. Select jobs in your company that the mentally retarded can fill, and hire them.

5. Accept the mentally retarded as American citizens. Give them a chance to live useful, dignified lives in your community.

6. Write for the free booklet to the President's Committee on Mental Retardation, Washington. D.C.

FIGURE 6–16. Increasing understanding by use of advertising thousands of potential customers by means of advertising. One manufacturer, church organization, political party, or professional association will use advertising to reach millions. Only in the classified or want-ad sections of the press do we find any appreciable use of advertising space by the individual consumer to communicate his needs or wants to potential sellers of goods, jobs, or services.

There are numerous examples of individual citizens and groups who have used advertising to influence the attitudes and actions of political bodies. Mr. Matsuda's ad on Peace in Vietnam was one.

Is it not, however, reasonable to think that, at some future time, consumer groups will use significant amounts of paid advertising in business media to influence business attitudes and actions? Such advertising might interpret consumer and general public attitudes and desires to management on such matters as use of quality labels on merchandise, inclusion of complete price and quality information in product advertising, public interest in labor-management peace, wage rates, price levels, high-volume operations and low margins verus low-volume operations and high margins, competitive business practices, and business ethics. It is doubtful whether such a reverse flow of advertising will materialize to any significant degree, but the thought is perhaps worth suggesting.

QUESTIONS AND PROBLEMS

1. Examine several recent issues of some newspaper or magazine to see if you can find any examples of advertorials.
2. Donald Snyder says that the new pioneers of idea advertising "realize that the success of these new advertisements depends upon trading information for the reader's time." What do you think of this concept of the relation between advertiser and consumer? Would the same concept apply equally well to product advertising?
3. "Good public relations cannot be bought, but must be earned." Does this mean that the use of advertising to help build favorable public attitudes toward a company is useless? Explain.
4. The Commission on the Freedom of the Press issued a report in 1947 which was criticized by some on the grounds that the public was excluded from hearings and investigations. Excerpts from the comments of one public relations counselor on this subject follows:

   "Thirteen intellectuals sitting for about three years as the Commission on the Freedom of the Press have reached the conclusion that press freedom is in jeopardy. Absent from the commission's table during the entire study period was one guest, whose presence might well have turned what appears to be a $215,000 folly into a powerful success. The Public, that absent guest, was not taken into the commission's confidence. . . . The Public, especially in what purports to be a democracy, does not choose to be thus treated. The Public prefers participation in the probe of any problem, and in particular one in which it happens to be the prime factor. . . .

"When a public is 'counted in' by any organization, business or social, we say that organization maintains good public relations. When an organization works 'in the dark,' behind the public's back, the reverse is true. . . ."

Should a business firm that excludes the public from its deliberations also be criticized? Explain.

5. Does public relations concern itself with one large public or with several "publics"?

6. Do you think that advertising could properly be used by an individual or by a group of people to transmit to the management of business firms the individual or group attitudes and wishes toward important business practices and policies? Explain.

7. To what extent might groups of lay citizens use advertising to get their ideas before other citizens or legislative officers at local, state, or national levels?

8. There is strong evidence that the Advertising Council has been highly effective in persuading countless American citizens to act affirmatively on many matters having social, public, and humanitarian values. In recounting some of the successes of such persuasion, Mr. Repplier, president of the Council, said:

"Results are not the real point of the story. The point is that America, alone among the democracies of the world, has a well-tested system, initiated and powered by business rather than by government, for inducing her citizens to take action to correct a crisis. . . . The point is that it relies on the lump of sugar instead of the lash . . . solves the national problem, yet preserves the dignity, decency and self-determination of the individual. I believe this is why word of this American invention has gone almost around the world, and why five of the countries in the free world are now trying to form Advertising Councils of their own."

Comment on the above statement of Mr. Repplier.

9. Someone has said that "the dignity and public service aspects of advertising have been enhanced by the fact that many religious organizations are using it to present their ideas to the millions." What is your attitude toward this use of advertising?

10. What is your attitude toward the use of advertising in political campaigns? Do you have any suggestions as to techniques that might enhance the effectiveness of political advertising?

11. Would you favor or oppose a mutual agreement among United States and Russian newspapers to accept paid advertising of an ideological nature? Would not such an agreement tend to foster the concept of democracy?

part **II**

Background for planning advertising strategy

chapter 7
THE ROLE OF
RESEARCH

THE STUDENT of advertising is often overanxious to start writing and designing advertisements. However, in building advertisements, as in building any substantial structure, much attention must first be given to establishing a solid foundation upon which the final edifice is to be erected. In the next several chapters, therefore, major attention shall be given to the foundation work involved in the development of a complete advertising program. The success of other aspects of advertising depends a great deal upon the thoroughness with which this is done.

In Chapter 1, we noted that advertising is essentially a process involving a series of decisions and that the advertisements we encounter as consumers are end-products of this process. The advertiser must decide on such matters as what he seeks to accomplish through advertising, what markets to cultivate, how to frame his messages, what media to use, when and how often to advertise, and how much to spend. He must decide which among countless alternatives will most likely lead to business success. He must make these decisions while constantly faced with the risk of making wrong decisions that could lead to business failure.

Each decision maker, whether he is deciding on matters of broad campaign strategy or the content of a specific advertisement is confronted with circumstances that increase the risk of making wrong decisions. He has no direct contact with the thousands or millions of consumers he hopes to influence with his advertising messages. He cannot converse with them as the personal salesman does to gain firsthand knowledge of their wants, their buying behavior, their opinions, their language. He isn't present to answer their questions or see their reactions when his messages arrive. He is called upon to interpret want-satisfying qualities of products to consumers whose wants and satisfactions are different from his own. The temptation to assume that "what I like everybody likes" is always present. His desire to win praise from the boss and his colleagues frequently interferes with his quest for a more substantial reward, i.e., purchase by consumers.

He must adapt advertising strategy and tactics to markets that are ever changing and to competition that is ever threatening. A campaign that succeeded last year may fail this year. He must select media to carry his messages to vast audiences he never sees. Therefore, he has no direct way of knowing how many and what kinds of people he is reaching or missing. Superimposed on all these complicating circumstances is the fact that he cannot readily determine the effects of specific decisions. His right decisions as well as his wrong ones are concealed in a maze of multiple causes and effects.

In an environment such as this, the way one makes decisions is of vital importance.

Methods of making decisions

Decisions are made in many different ways, most of them unconsciously geared to substituting something else for logical reasoning. Some people are content to follow whatever is considered standard practice in the trade. What is good for Adam is good for Eve. Others are willing to flip the coin or play the odds. The lucky few among these make out occasionally. A stopped clock is right twice every 24 hours. The so-called "self-made man" is willing to let his feelings dictate the answer. He relies on a sort of sixth sense to do his decision making. Some people in decision-making positions shift this job to the advice of experts—advice which often is given without all the necessary facts, and certainly without the necessary responsibility. Authority without responsibility is not hard to take.

The logical reasoning method involves: (1) a clear understanding of the problem to be solved; (2) recognition of various alternative solutions; (3) collection of all facts that would help in selecting a particular alternative; (4) weighing these facts and applying human judgment to them in the final selection of a course of action. The logical reasoning method is a systematic, factual approach to problem solving and therefore holds the most promise for reducing the risk of wrong decisions.

Logical reasoning is admirably illustrated by a letter that Benjamin Franklin wrote to a young man in response to a request for advice on how to solve a difficult problem. The following is a quotation from Franklin's letter:

In the affair of so much importance to you, wherein you ask my advice I can not, for want of sufficient premises, counsel you *what* to determine; but if you please, I will tell you *how*. When those difficult cases occur, they are difficult chiefly because while we have them under consideration, all the reasons *pro* and *con* are not present to the mind at the same time; but sometimes one set present themselves, and at other times another, the first being out of sight. Hence the various purposes or inclinations that alternately prevail, and the uncertainty that perplexes us.

To get over this, my way is to divide a half sheet of paper by a line into two columns; writing over the one *pro* and over the other *con;* then, during three or four days' consideration, I put down, under the different heads, short hints of the different motives that at different times occur to me *for* or *against* the measure. When I have thus got them all together in one view, I endeavor to estimate their respective weights; and when I find two (one on each side) that seem equal, I strike them both out. If I find a reason *pro* equal to *two* reasons *con,* I strike out the *three*. If I judge some two reasons *con* equal to *three* reasons *pro,* I strike out the *five;* and thus proceeding, I find where the balance lies; and if, after a day or two of further consideration, nothing new that is of importance occurs on either side I come to a determination accordingly. And though the weight of reason can not be taken with the precision of algebraic quantities, yet when each is thus considered separately and comparatively, and the whole lies before me, I think I can judge better and am less liable to take a false step. And in fact I found great advantage from this kind of equation, in what may be termed *moral* or *prudential* algebra.

Franklin's system as demonstrated in this letter depends a great deal on one's own powers of observation, which may be entirely adequate when the decision maker is primarily the person affected. However, when thousands or millions of people are involved, the decision maker needs some means of extending his scope of observation far beyond the range of his own experience. This, in brief, indicates the role of research in advertising. Through research the advertiser projects his scope of observation so that he can see more clearly the characteristics of his widely scattered consuming publics and predict more accurately the effects of his decisions upon them.

The logic of using research in solving advertising problems is now widely acclaimed. Yet, many frontiers remain unexplored and much of the work done under the guise of research is not sound research. Research is often used as a drunk uses a lamppost—for support instead of illumination. To more fully appreciate the role of this vital element in advertising one must first recognize the characteristics of sound research.

Characteristics of sound research

Research has long been the accepted tool of science. Its association with science has been so close that the term "scientific method" is often used in referring to the use of research in any field. Research in advertising, then, is basically the use of scientific method in solving advertising problems. Soundness of the research depends on the extent to which the precepts of scientific inquiry are followed.

Although there is no single, generally accepted definition of scientific method, there are several standards by which one may judge whether or not a piece of research has been conducted in a scientific way. These standards concern the researcher's attitude toward his work and the procedure he follows from inception of the project to its completion.

The researcher strives for objectivity. He recognizes that as a human being he cannot set himself apart from his own attitudes and preconceived ideas. However, as a researcher he strives to be impartial and takes every precaution to prevent his personal predispositions from coloring his findings. He is dedicated to seeking and reporting facts as he finds them, not as he or someone else would like them to be. He is ever mindful that other researchers confronted with the same evidence should come up with findings the same as his.

The researcher qualifies his measurements. While attempting to obtain the most accurate measurements possible, he is constantly aware of the lack of precision inherent in the measuring devices he uses. All studies in which he surveys samples of the population are subject to error —error stemming from the kinds of questions asked and the way the questions are asked, error in sampling procedures, and error in data processing. However, the researcher can measure the error due to sampling, and he is continuously improving his techniques for controlling other sources of error. He tests his data and qualifies his findings by indicating the probable error present in them, thereby minimizing the chance of reaching erroneous conclusions.

The researcher is creative. Noting that he subordinates intuition to objectivity and that he relies heavily on statistical concepts, many people look upon the researcher as a mechanically inclined fact-gathering robot. Nothing could be further from the truth. The researcher is primarily creative in his work. He explores the unknown. He charts new areas for investigation. He formulates new theories. He designs new techniques and experimental models. He sees relationships between seemingly isolated phenomena. He is a good researcher only to the extent that he is creative.

Too often research is thought to begin and end with the data-collection operation which actually is only part of a much broader process. Perhaps the tangibility of procedures used in gathering and recording data leads to this misconception. Less apparent but more important is the researcher's creative imagination that precedes, governs, and follows the data-collection operation.

Research is continuous. The only aspect of research that is constant is the element of change. New findings generate other new findings. The phenomena under investigation change. For example, in the environment of advertising, markets change, products change, distribution methods change, competition changes, communication techniques change. To keep abreast of these changes research must be continuous.

There are other criteria of sound research, but they pertain more specifically to techniques which are adequately treated in books and journal articles dealing with research methodology.

Research in marketing

The productivity of research has been dramatically demonstrated in the development of new products, new manufacturing processes, new machinery, new equipment, and new management systems. However, many firms that invest great sums in research and development (R & D) consider it a great achievement to develop a new product and then turn the product over to the marketing department with orders to sell it. The use of research to increase the efficiency of marketing is often overlooked. This oversight is due to many factors. The components of selling and advertising are intangible. The processes are not mechanized. The scene of action ranges far and wide. Many forces, such as competitive activity and general economic conditions, are outside of management's control. The value of marketing research cannot be readily translated into dollars and cents. Research techniques that work well in the laboratory cannot be readily applied in the marketplace.

The incentive to use research in marketing has not been as great as in production. In the past the capacity to consume has generally run ahead of the capacity to produce. Under such conditions major attention has been directed to producing goods. Any production-machinery improvements that would increase the amount of goods for sale and reduce manufacturing costs have been immediately beneficial and recognized as such.

Selling goods has been comparatively easy; hence, less attention has been given to improving marketing practices.

Now we have an economy of abundance. Manufacturers are finding that their operations and growth are no longer limited by their productive capacity, for they can now produce as much as the market will absorb. The limiting factor now is the physiological and psychological capacity of consumers to assimilate the tremendous outpouring of goods and services. Under these conditions business firms must direct more attention to the psychological needs and wants of consumers, to cultivating new sales opportunities, and to increasing the efficiency of marketing practices. Having used research effectively in production, they are now turning more and more to the same approach as an aid in solving marketing problems.

Along with an increasing use of research as a means of gathering "marketing intelligence" is a greater tendency to use research in the decision-making process itself, to use research as a means of testing alternative actions before the decision is made. Insofar as the decision maker is better able to predict the probable consequences of alternative actions, the more likely he is to choose the best course. A survey by the National Industrial Conference Board in 1969 reports:

The changing role of marketing research in recent years is to no small degree attributable to its increased acceptance by management, or to what one sales executive describes as "the change in the nature of managing." In his company, as in so many others, "problem-solving is more clearly organized than ever before. Alternative strategies to reach an objective are being more carefully weighed in advance." And he adds: "Many sectors of management now embrace marketing research information as an aid to the management process, whereas they might previously have been inclined to view it as a threat to management prerogatives."[1]

Research in advertising

In building an effective advertising program, attention must be focused upon the function of such a program. The function of advertising is to *interpret the want-satisfying qualities of products and services in terms of human needs and wants.* Successful interpretation can come only after many facts have been collected concerning consumer wants, the ability of the product to satisfy their wants, their location, and their buying potential.

---

[1] Lewis W. Forman and Earl L. Bailey, *The Role and Organization of Marketing Research* (New York: National Industrial Conference Board, 1969), pp. 23, 24.

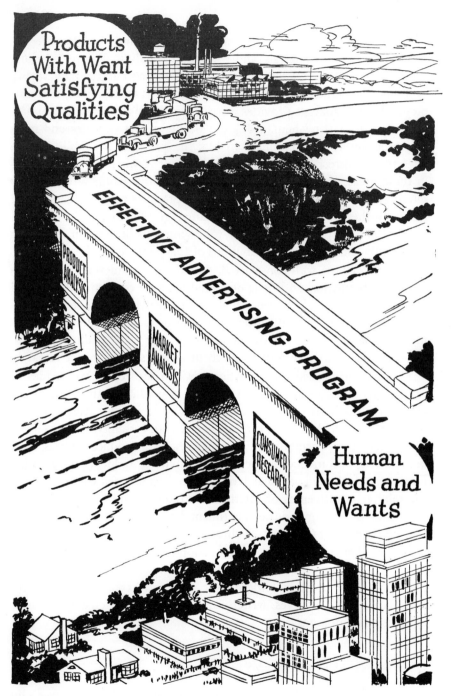

FIGURE 7–1. An effective advertising program must be supported by product analysis, market analysis, and consumer research

Three fields of advertising research, therefore, are (1) consumer research, (2) product analysis, and (3) market analysis. Figure 7–1 illustrates how these three fields of research support an effective advertising program. Consumer research uncovers human wants, motives, and attitudes. Product analysis provides a basis for shaping the product to harmonize with existing human desires. Market analysis locates and measures the ability of consumers to buy the product, thus guiding the advertiser to direct his efforts toward his most fertile markets. Research in these areas, if properly used, supports an advertising program that interprets the want-satisfying qualities of products to consumers in the language they understand best—the language of their own wants and desires. The chapters immediately following will develop in detail the philosophy and strategic contributions of this research triad.

No matter how well constructed, the advertising message cannot accomplish its mission until it is delivered to those consumers for whom it is intended. To select media that will deliver his message most efficiently to the right people, the advertiser needs factual evidence concerning the size and character of the audience that each medium reaches. Therefore, a fourth field of research in advertising is media research.

Decisions are based on predictions. When the advertiser decides to present his message in a certain way, he is predicting that among the alternative methods of presentation known the one he selects will be most effective. Although he cannot predict with certainty, he can reduce the degree of his uncertainty. Consumer research, product analysis, market analysis, and media research all contribute to reducing uncertainty. However, a fifth field of research more directly concerned with predicting the relative effectiveness of alternative strategies and tactics is testing. The value of testing and the experimental procedures used in this field will be covered in Chapters 24 through 27.

We see that research plays a major supporting role in the structure of effective advertising. Yet, it is well to remember that research supplements; it does not replace the artistic skill and experienced judgment required of the executives, writers, and designers who create successful advertising campaigns.

QUESTIONS AND PROBLEMS

1. Advertising is essentially a process involving a series of decisions. Make a list of specific decisions that would have to be made when planning and executing a national advertising campaign for a room air conditioner.

2. What factors tend to increase the risk of making wrong decisions in advertising?

3. How does research reduce the risk of making wrong decisions?

4. One does not have to be a researcher himself to distinguish good research from bad research. Do you agree or disagree? Explain.

5. Would you expect research to play a more important role in national advertising than in retail advertising? Explain.

6. Research alone does not assure effective advertising. Why not?

chapter 8

CONSUMER RESEARCH

IN A FREE market system consumer choices direct production. These choices are, presumably, independent of the producers who attempt to furnish want-satisfying commodities to consumers. This position has given rise to the statement, "The consumer is king." It means that the producer who provides goods that will most effectively satisfy consumers' needs and wants will be the one most richly rewarded; and, conversely, that the producer who fails to provide want-satisfying commodities will be forced out of business from lack of buyers.

Can the producer create wants?

Some writers question the concept of consumer sovereignty. They assume that human wants can be created or molded to fit the objectives of producers. Professor John Kenneth Galbraith holds that large corporations have the power to "manage demand" and their "key to the management of demand is effective management of the purchases of final consumers."[1] This notion is not of recent origin. Thirty-five years ago A. S. J. Baster wrote that "resources are being used to serve not the needs of the people as they are, but the needs of the people as they are distorted by the uneven pressure of skillful forcing tactics in selling . . ."[2] If this is

---

[1] John Kenneth Galbraith, *The New Industrial State* (Boston: Houghton Mifflin Company, 1967), p. 200.

[2] A. S. J. Baster, *Advertising Reconsidered* (London: P. S. King & Son, 1935), pp. 99–100.

true, then the manufacturer can "distort" consumer needs and make consumers want whatever he wants to sell.

Professor Galbraith elaborates on his point as follows:

It is true that the consumer may still imagine that his actions respond to his own view of his satisfactions. But this is superficial and proximate, the result of illusions created in connection with the management of his wants. Only those wishing to evade the reality will be satisfied with such a simplistic explanation. All others will notice that if an individual's satisfaction is less from an additional expenditure on automobiles than from one on housing, this can as well be corrected by a change in the selling strategy of General Motors as by an increased expenditure on his house.[3]

Thus, Galbraith assumes that the consumer who thinks he is freely expressing his wants in the marketplace is suffering from illusions, from "illusions created" by General Motors and other large corporations who are "managing his wants."

Those who accept Galbraith's views attribute too great a power to advertising, and too little power to the consumer. They overlook the power of basic wants that motivate all human behavior. All mankind seeks to satisfy his needs for self-expression, social approval, love, belongingness, a longer life span, and security for his loved ones. Each consumer may employ somewhat different means toward satisfying these needs, but the means should not be confused with the ends. Differences among consumer preferences for products and brands simply demonstrate that different people find different ways of satisfying the same basic needs.

Advertising has some influence in directing consumer purchase toward a given product as a means of satisfying a particular want, but that is not want creation. Even if we consider surface wants, i.e., the desire for individual products for the satisfaction of fundamental wants, we find it exceedingly difficult and often impossible to change such wants at will. Attempts to mold human wants to fit producers' desires are too costly. Nystrom states the proposition cogently: ". . . that consumer demand is wholly or even largely a result of producers' promotion is a theory which has proved exceedingly expensive to many headstrong advertisers who have put their millions of dollars as well as their faith into it."[4]

Advertising succeeds when it goes with the tide of consumer demand,

---

[3] Galbraith, *op. cit.*, pp. 214, 215.

[4] Paul H. Nystrom, *Economic Principles of Consumption* (New York: Ronald Press Co., 1929), pp. 16–17.

but is doomed to fail when in opposition. This point of view was clearly expressed by Walter Weir, a veteran copywriter, when he wrote:

> During the first five years in advertising, I developed the feeling that I was in a sort of superior profession—superior as it dealt in ways and means by which one could influence people he would never see to perform actions they had never thought of performing.
>
> I spent the next fifteen years unlearning this misconception. I found that, despite my technical proficiency in the art of persuasion, I was not half so shrewd or wise as those millions I was being paid to address. I had to unlearn the reasons for which I thought they would buy—to learn the reasons for which they actually bought. Actually, *they* were exerting *their* influence on *me*.
>
> I found the great contribution advertising makes is in reverse to what is generally thought. Instead of forcing upon people what advertising wants, it forces upon advertising *what people want.*"[5]

It seems quite apparent that basic human wants cannot be created and that even surface wants can be molded only slightly and gradually by advertising. It would, therefore, seem to be the part of wisdom for businessmen to harmonize their products to basic consumer needs and wants rather than to attempt to mold basic wants to fit their products.

Philosophy of consumer research

Consumer research is built upon the general theory that the consumer is king—that his wants form the foundation of economic endeavor and should direct production. This viewpoint is particularly important in an economy where consumers' freedom of choice is emphasized. The value producers can obtain from information concerning consumer wants is pointed out by Dr. Harry R. Tosdal in the following quotation:

> The need on the part of the producers for useful information as to consumer wants exist at every stage of industrial development; but that need is most pressing in the society which aims to give its members freedom of choice as consumers and high standards of living through the utilization of advanced techniques of large-scale production and distribution. Today a large proportion of the products which form the basis of industrial and commercial enterprise in modern states is produced or distributed by large-scale enterprises. Large-scale production requires prior judgments upon direct consumer demand or upon derived demand based upon ultimate consumption. Large-scale distribution likewise compels manufacture and purchase in advance of express demand. Administrators and executives of both large- and small-scale business enterprise must, therefore, make decisions as to the quantity, type, quality, design, style, and other characteristics of products to be offered for sale or allotted to customers. To translate these decisions into

[5] Walter Weir, "After Hours," *Printers' Ink,* October 7, 1949, p. 144.

working plans for the enterprise requires knowledge not only of the general characteristics of consumer choice but of a vast amount of detail concerning the goods the consumer wishes to buy.[6]

The problems of the modern manufacturer are thus quite different from those confronting the producer under our earlier handicraft system, where the contact between producer and consumer was direct. Under the handicraft system, it was possible for the consumer to inform the producer in detail concerning the type and character of the product desired before the product was made. With the development of a high degree of specialization and division of labor, production took place in advance of specific demand. So long as we operated in a sellers' market this reversed procedure was not fraught with the dangers of business loss that is true today in a buyers' market. With this shift to a buyers' market, manufacturers are placing increased emphasis on methods of measuring consumer demand before goods are produced. Consumer research is thus devoted to the task of approximating the old and, in many respects, highly desirable direct contact of producer and consumer. The manner in which consumer research serves as a substitute for the old direct-contact method is graphically shown in Figure 8–1.

A determination of consumer demand before goods are produced reduces the risk of making goods that are hard to sell. Under such a philosophy, "low-pressure buying" takes the place of "high-pressure selling." The difference between these two methods is made visual in a demonstration provided by General Motors Corporation. This company has a large, heavy metal ball hanging from a beam. Visitors are asked to take a 12-pound sledge hammer and to see how far they can move the ball by striking it with the hammer. The usual visitor strikes the ball with a mighty blow only to find that it hardly moves. Instead, the hammer rebounds with such force that the visitor is almost thrown from his feet. This is high-pressure selling.

The visitor is then instructed to drop the hammer and press his finger against the ball. The ball "gives" a little and then swings back. Instructions are given to pull back with the backswing of the ball and then to push again as the ball starts forward. If the visitor will work *with* the laws of nature as demonstrated by the action of the ball, he can get the ball to swing with such power that it would crash through the wall were it to break loose from its mooring. This is low-pressure buying.

---

[6] Harry R. Tosdal, chapter on "Consumer Demand" in *Business and Modern Society* (Cambridge, Mass.: Harvard University Press, 1938), p. 314.

100 YEARS AGO

Under the conditions of the one man shop, with the head of the business serving as designer, manufacturer, purchasing agent, salesman, and service expert—an intimate understanding of customer tastes and desires was automatically assured.

MODERN INDUSTRY

By the very nature of things, the bigger an institution grows, the wider becomes the gap between the customer and those responsible for directing the destiny of the institution. With producer and consumer so widely separated it becomes increasingly difficult to keep the business sensitively attuned to the requirements of the customer.

GENERAL MOTORS

There is a need for some kind of liaison which would serve as a substitute for the close personal contact which existed automatically back in the days of the small shop.

CUSTOMER RESEARCH—fills this need by providing an auxiliary and more direct line of communication between producer and consumer.

Source: Adapted by permission from General Motors.

FIGURE 8–1. Consumer research, the connecting link between the producer and consumer

Consumer research is thus built on the philosophy of ascertaining as nearly as possible the laws of human action and then operating in harmony with those laws. Advertising will be used to show the consumer that the product produced will actually satisfy his needs and wants. The producer will be pratically assured that his product will be accepted because he directed his production toward the definite goal of satisfying a known need.

General Motors Corporation illustrates the use of consumer research and, although it is by no means the only modern concern placing emphasis on this factor, it probably has done more to popularize the procedure than any other company. Its position seems to be summed up by H. G. Weaver, the company's original director of customer research. He says:

If a company can ascertain concretely and in detail just what its buyers would like to have if it can build its products in conformity with those desires and design its sales and advertising messages so that they will definitely answer the questions that are uppermost in the minds of the motorist, obviously there will be continued improvement in the merchandising processes and a broadening of the service tendered. Merchandising has been aptly defined as a problem of getting the *right product*, at the *right place*, at the *right time*, and at the *right price*. Consumer research contributes to this end.[7]

Mr. Weaver holds that service should be the basic philosophy underlying business activity, and he would use consumer research extensively and intensively to equip the manufacturer with the facts necessary to become an effective servant of the consumer. Weaver says that "the major objective of all business should be that of serving the customer in the way that the customer wants to be served,"[8] and he adopts this philosophy on a purely selfish basis. He seems to agree with that well-known philosopher who said: "He who would be greatest among you must be the servant of all." For, in explanation of General Motors' work with consumer research, Weaver says:

There is nothing altruistic about General Motors Customer Research. We expect it to broaden our good will. We expect it to sell more automobiles, and we expect these benefits to be permanently assured instead of short lived because having the facilities, the talent, and the desire to serve, coupled with the knowledge of how you want to be served, there seems no reason why we cannot serve you in line with your desires—*serve you in a manner that will merit your continued and increasing patronage.*[9]

The consumer-king philosophy does not mean that consumers are to write their own specifications for commodities. Nor does consumer research insist that this be done. The consumer is not an engineer. He cannot be expected to tell the manufacturer the length of the stroke or the cubic-inch piston displacement of an automobile engine. He can tell the manufacturer that economy of operation is more desirable than excessive

---

[7] General Motors Corporation, *The Proving Ground of Public Opinion* (Detroit), p. 9.

[8] *Ibid.*, p. 6.

[9] *Ibid.*, p. 6.

speed and then engineers can attempt to design a product which will give this result. When the manufacturer gets this broad but fundamental picture of human wants, the direction of his manufacturing efforts will be more clearly mapped out for him. His reward will be in proportion to his ability to follow this lead in manufacturing and to present his finished product convincingly to the public.

Advertising and consumer research

By placing emphasis upon the consumer and his wants, advertising will have its most glorious opportunity. Under such a philosophy, the production department of an industry will provide the sales and advertising departments with a product of real merit, a product around which an honest, straightforward, convincing selling appeal can be built.

The function of selling and advertising will thus reduce itself to the problem of *interpreting the utility of the product in terms of the customer's needs and wants.* It will necessitate a clear understanding of consumer tastes and consumer psychology. Selling will really become a teaching, rather than a forcing process. It will point out that XYZ air-conditioning equipment will provide cooler rooms, that it will provide the proper humidity and thus reduce the number of colds contracted in the winter, and that it will increase one's working efficiency.

Glenn Frank expressed this point of view when he stated that "the advertising man is a liaison officer between the materials of business and the mind of the nation. He must know both well before he can serve either wisely."[10] The validity of the social viewpoint is further expressed by Frank:

> The business order and the social order are too intimately related to the advertising man who aspires to be more than a tricky tradester to tear them apart in his thinking. . . . The really great advertising man must be as much interested in increasing the sanity of consumption as in increasing the size of consumption, for great businesses are not built upon fads that are worthless and passing, but upon appetites that are worthy and permanent.[11]

Consumer research is, therefore, charged with the responsibility of turning the searchlight of facts upon consumer tastes and desires. It is a study of the mechanics of human action. It is a philosophy of enlightened self-interest and one which should be beneficial to both producer and consumer. As illustrated in Figure 8–2, such a procedure will lead

---

[10] Glenn Frank, "The Dignity and Duties of the Advertising Profession," *Printers' Ink,* April 14, 1927, p. 81.
[11] *Ibid.*

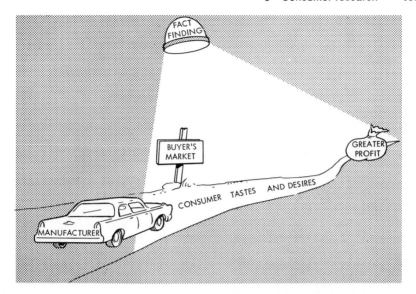

FIGURE 8–2.   Facts concerning consumer tastes and desires will lead the
manufacturer to greater profits

the manufacturer to greater profits. It provides business with an effective
tool to direct its production, selling, and advertising program with a minimum of cost and a maximum of social and individual return.

Consumer motivation

Advertisers in recent years are turning more attention to the complex
and subtle aspects of human behavior referred to as motivation. The following explanation of motivation by Frederick H. Lund gives some idea
of its nature:

To define motivation is difficult for the reason that there is no one condition
with which it can be identified. In the main, however, behavior is said to be motivated when it shows fairly definite directional trends. The motive, in such instances,
may be thought of (1) in terms of the external objective of behavior, (2) in terms
of the inner condition activating the individual, or (3) in terms of the activities
themselves. Popularly, the emphasis is usually placed upon the first of these—the
external objective. Psychologically, the emphasis has more frequently been placed
upon the second—the source of motivation. Thus, the older psychologists were
inclined to trace most behavior to the *will,* an inner agency or power which, while
in the body, was assumed to be independent of its structures. As this concept began
to lose favor, emphasis tended to shift to the *instincts.* These were conceived as
special mechanisms, hidden away within the organism and waiting only to be
released through the action of appropriate stimuli.

Today, with our better understanding of body function, we are more inclined to identify motives either with the activities themselves or with the tissue needs which prompt their action. Of these, the tissue conditions may be considered a matter of constitution, while the behavior forms in which they are expressed may be considered a matter of learning.[12]

As the most compelling inner determinants of human behavior, motives are also called drives, urges, impulses, needs, wants, tensions, and willful cravings. Whatever they are called, the assumption is that people consistently seek to satisfy these inner motivating conditions. Psychologist George Horsley Smith says:

> Motivating conditions are varied. Thus we seek sensory gratification, pleasant feelings, emotional variety, and at times even enjoy tension and turmoil rather than the quiescence of a fulfilled appetite. We look for meaning in the environment. We work hard for economic security and acceptance by our fellows and look for ways to express our individuality, satisfy our curiosity, and experience new value qualities. Sometimes we are torn by conflicting needs; for example, we want to be both masterful and submissive, to have fun and to "purge" ourselves through hard work.[13]

Psychologists tend to agree that some human motives are primary and others secondary. They generally include in any list of primary motives those that are or have a strong tendency toward being innate, biogenic, or unlearned and in a secondary list those motives that tend toward being acquired, sociogenic, or learned. There is not much agreement among students of human behavior on any detailed listing of either primary or secondary motives or desires.

The lack of agreement on primary and secondary motives has not deterred persons from providing us with ample lists. C. N. Allen[14] included the following ten motives in a list of primary wants: appetizing food, thirst-quenching drinks, comfortable surroundings, escape from pain and danger, sex companionship, welfare of loved ones, social approval, superiority over others, mastery over obstacles, and play. Allen's secondary list[15] included beauty and style, cleanliness, convenience, curiosity, dependability and quality, economy and profit, education and information, efficiency, health, and universality.

It is claimed by many that advertising appeals directed to primary desires or motives will be more effective than appeals directed to secondary motives. This point of view stems from the belief that primary motives

---

[12] Frederick H. Lund, *Psychology* (New York: Ronald Press Co., 1933), p. 231.

[13] George Horsley Smith, *Motivation Research in Advertising and Marketing* (New York: McGraw-Hill Book Co., 1954), p. 10.

[14] C. N. Allen, "A Psychology of Motivation for Advertisers," *Journal of Applied Psychology*, 1941, Vol. XXV, No. 4, p. 386.

[15] *Ibid.*, p. 388.

are largely biogenic in nature, and thus closely associated with body needs, while secondary motives are sociogenic and related to learned desires. This point of view, however, is not necessarily true. It might be true if most human consumption consisted of goods and services to meet these biogenic needs. But in an economic society where many are above the subsistence level of consumption, appeal to other motives may be more powerful in the advertising of certain products. Lund states: ". . . but the satisfaction of organic and bodily needs is surely not the only condition motivating human behavior. In addition to this there are a number of other motives, usually called *social*, which exercise an important and determining influence."[16]

Most psychologists, today, refrain from arranging any list of motives in an order of strength or potency in moving people to act. Dewey and Humber say, "When asked which motive is strongest, the answer must always be in terms of the value systems of particular persons and particular cultures. Universally, there is no strongest motive."[17]

Motivation is always multiple and complex. There is seldom just one reason for doing anything. When a person buys an automobile he may do so because he needs transportation *and* wants to extend his horizons *and* wants to keep up with the Joneses *and* surpass the Smiths *and* proclaim his solvency and status to the world *and* experience the mastery of controlling a powerful new engine, etc. While these motives are apt to have different degrees of importance to different people, they are all likely to be involved to some extent in a purchase of a new car.

Motivation patterns change. Motives that are strong today might be weak tomorrow since individual values change as circumstances are altered. The motives which caused a person to buy his first television set will not generally be effective in moving him to purchase a second or third set.

Studies to determine and measure the relative strength of motives underlying the purchase of specific products and services have become an important part of consumer research.

Other motivational variables

In addition to motives there are other variables in the psychological make-up of consumers that predispose them to buy some products and

---

[16] Lund, *op. cit.*, p. 243.

[17] Richard Dewey and W. J. Humber, *The Development of Human Behavior* (New York: Macmillan Co., 1951), p. 193.

reject others, to respond to some advertisements and ignore others. These variables are attitudes, beliefs, habits, and customs.

Attitudes are states of readiness to make value judgments in support of or against certain stimuli. Consumers are more inclined to buy products or brands toward which they hold positive attitudes. They are less inclined to buy things toward which they hold negative attitudes. Thus, an important function of research is to reveal the direction and intensity of consumer attitudes. If research shows that negative attitudes are hindering a product's sales, then it would behoove the advertiser to change his product and/or his advertising to overcome this handicap.

In a study of consumer attitudes toward tea, the National Tea Council found that tea drinking in the United States was inhibited because many people felt that tea was a weak beverage associated with effeminacy, old age, and sickness. To combat these negative attitudes the Tea Council switched advertising themes from "Nervous? Try tea" to "Make mine hefty, hot, and hearty." A declining sales trend turned sharply upward.

Beliefs are subjective concepts of truth. What people believe is not always true, and what is true is not always believed. Beliefs are based more on feelings and emotion than on reason. People believe what they want to believe. These statements about the nature of belief suggest that, of all the claims and counterclaims made in competitive advertising, what consumers believe is a matter of personal interpretation instead of a mere acceptance of facts. Such personal interpretations of advertising claims and product performance can only be made available to advertisers through consumer research.

Habits and customs are closely related. One is individual, the other social. Nystrom says: "Habit is a term that applies to practices of individuals. Customs are habits followed by masses of people."[18] Habits, both individual and social, are of great importance in human life. It has been estimated that three out of every four human acts are habitual.

Motives, attitudes, and beliefs lead to and reinforce habits. However, once they are firmly established, habits themselves become motivating forces for buying activity. Individuals get in the habit of calling for a particular brand of cigarettes. Or custom may dictate that certain members of society should not call for cigarettes at all.

Not only are habits ascertainable, but their relative strength is measurable. Such measurements serve to indicate the advisability of using advertising to break an old habit and establish a new one or to establish the old habit more firmly.

---

[18] Nystrom, *op. cit.,* p. 61.

How these motivational variables fit in to the development of advertising strategy will be treated in more detail later.

Sampling

Obviously, an advertiser whose market may number in the millions would not find it feasible to interview each and every consumer. The cost and time required for such an undertaking would be prohibitive. However, by studying a relatively small cross section he can estimate characteristics of his entire market with reasonable accuracy. This process of selecting a representative cross section is called sampling, and its widespread use in consumer research is based on the premise that information obtained from a carefully selected sample closely resembles the information that would be obtained if all consumers were questioned. Thus, sampling makes it possible for the advertiser to study wants, desires, attitudes, beliefs, and buying behavior of his vast consumer market.

Sample surveys do not yield exact measurements. They do provide approximations of what is true in an entire population; and when the laws of chance are given free play in selecting sample members, the researcher can measure the range of error arising from the sampling operation. In effect, he is able to predict the probability, or what the chances are, that sampling estimates approximate the true conditions in the total population from which the sample was drawn.

A question frequently asked is: "How can such a small fraction of people be counted upon to accurately represent the wants and desires of so many other people when we know that each person is different from another?" We can count on relatively small fractions because we can make two valid assumptions about large numbers of people. The first assumption is that suffcient similarity exists among large numbers of people to permit us to accurately predict behavior of the large group even though we can't predict the behavior of any one individual. The second assumption is that errors tend to balance out when a large enough number of people are included in the sample—some sample members who err in one direction are balanced by other sample members who err in the opposite direction.

The predictability of occurrences among large numbers of people is clearly demonstrated in insurance. To insure the life of only one person would be the rankest sort of gambling. But to insure the lives of 10,000 or 100,000 persons widely scattered and engaged in a diversity of occupations is a safe business proposition. Although they cannot predict who will die, life insurance companies can predict that fewer than ten persons in any average thousand will die within any given year. With almost the same certainty, the probability of deaths from automobile accidents, train wrecks, drownings, injuries on the Fourth of July, marriages in June, births in 1970, and suicides in 1975 can be predicted.

Another question frequently asked is: "How large should a sample be?" There is no easy answer to that one. For our purposes here it should be recognized that determining the appropriate size of a sample is a matter of judgment and requires consideration of several factors such as: How homogeneous is the population to be studied? How much error can be tolerated? How much should be spent on the study or what is the information worth? How much time can be allowed for the study? The more homogeneous the population the smaller the sample required. Theoretically, if all members of a group of consumers were identical and would respond the same way, one member of that group would be an adequate sample. The larger the error that can be tolerated the smaller the sample required. To obtain a given amount of information from a small sample is less costly and time consuming than from a large sample. Therefore, when deciding on sample size the researcher has to weigh the precision and value of the information needed against the cost and time required for the study.

Structure of consumer research

The structure of a typical consumer research project is graphically illustrated in Figure 8–3. This chart and the following brief outline indicate the major steps involved in research procedure.

The statement of objectives sets forth the specific purposes of the study and defines the scope of the investigation. To do this, a thorough understanding of the advertising problem and how the study will contribute to its solution is essential.

1. *Analysis of internal conditions.* The researcher seeks to obtain all pertinent information concerning the company's product, its marketing and advertising strategy, its competitive strengths and weaknesses, its past experience, and its future goals from company records and executive personnel.
2. *Review of secondary data.* To take advantage of readily available information bearing on the problem and to avoid unnecessary duplication, the researcher reviews data that are published by government agencies, trade associations, universities, business publications, and advertising mediums.

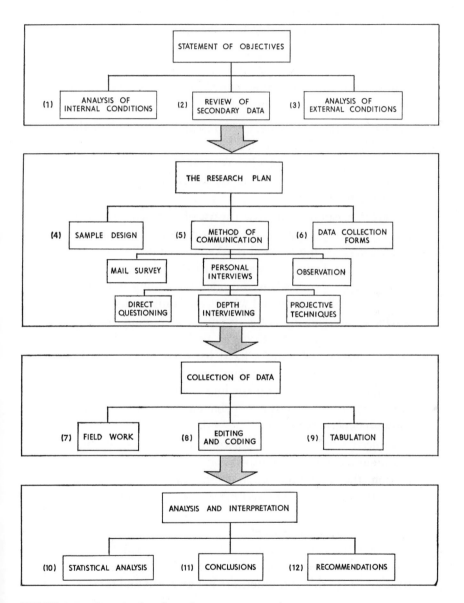

FIGURE 8–3. Organization chart of consumer research

3. *Analysis of external conditions.* The researcher talks informally with consumers, dealers, and company salesmen to appraise the competitive environment and to develop ideas or hunches about the direction the study should take.

4. *Sample design.* The researcher determines the type and size of sample that will yield the desired information within allowable limits of error at minimum cost.

5. *Method of communication.* The researcher decides whether he will gather the desired information by mail, by personal interviews, or by observing consumers' overt behavior. If he decides to use personal interviews, he selects and plans the interviewing procedure most appropriate for his study.

   Direct questioning involves the use of a predetermined list of questions that usually anticipates or allows for all alternative answers. Every consumer interviewed is asked the same questions in the same sequence, and his answers are recorded in the same way. This procedure is appropriate when consumers are willing and able to provide the desired information and when quantitative evidence is necessary.

   Depth interviewing is the technique of probing beneath the consumer's surface answers to get at underlying motives, attitudes, or beliefs. Instead of using a fixed list of questions, the interviewer improvises and asks leading questions to stimulate free discussion of the subject at hand. This procedure is appropriate for seeking ideas or hypotheses about consumer behavior that may eventually be tested through experimentation.

   Projective techniques are borrowed from clinical psychiatry. These techniques include word association, sentence completion, story completion, thematic apperception tests, and others. Their purpose is to get the consumer to project his personality, through a process that is not apparent to him, into the answer that he gives. These techniques are appropriate when seeking information about motives and attitudes that consumers are unwilling to reveal or are unable to provide. These techniques enable the researcher to get at strong motivating forces that consumers are not aware of and cannot verbalize.

6. *Data collection forms.* The researcher prepares forms for eliciting and recording the desired information. A standardized list of questions enhances consistent and accurate collection, tabulation, and analysis of data. The structured questionnaire for direct questioning in personal interviews is the most widely used form.

7. *Field work.*   This is the interviewing or data-collecting operation which includes selection, training, and supervision of interviewers.

8. *Editing and coding.*   The questionnaires are edited to eliminate errors and coded to facilitate tabulation.

9. *Tabulation.*   The data are tabulated to summarize and quantify the responses.

10. *Statistical analysis.*   Statistical techniques are used to test the significance of relationships and to determine what the relationships mean.

11. *Conclusions.*   The researcher interprets the results with direct reference to the objectives of the study.

12. *Recommendations.*   On the basis of his findings the researcher predicts the consequences of alternative solutions to the problem and recommends the course of action that he thinks should be taken.

The student of advertising should seek a more detailed understanding of research techniques through individual reading or in specialized courses in research.

Summary

The importance of the consumer in our economic society has long been recognized. Economic theorists for more than a century have emphasized the fundamental proposition that economic endeavor is built around the production of goods and services for the satisfaction of human wants. A mutuality of interest has been recognized between consumers and producers. One cannot exist without the other. Many business concerns have, therefore, been giving greater thought to the study of consumer needs and wants preliminary to their production of goods.

The study of the consumer has taken the form of analyzing all those forces that tend naturally to influence his buying. Motives, attitudes, beliefs, habits, and custom are fundamental factors. The sampling process makes it possible to study how these factors influence the buying behavior of vast numbers of people.

Consumer research has been accepted as a valuable approach to the preparation of an advertising program. It is recognized that such a program will be more effective if it harmonizes with human desires than if it attempts to alter them.

Consumer research is one answer to the perplexing problem of how to arrive at sound business decisions. It is one link in a fact-finding chain which can be used by the businessman to furnish that foundation of facts upon which a substantial business can be built. Consumer research, properly used, will link the consumer with the manufacturer in a manner which will be beneficial to both parties. It will touch the manufacturer's organization at several points. The engineering department, the production department, the sales department, and the advertising department— all will benefit by a use of data obtained through consumer research.

QUESTIONS AND PROBLEMS

1. "The consumer is king." Do you agree with this statement? If you feel that qualifications are necessary, state them.
2. What success have producers had in dictating fashions in women's apparel? Can you give any reason for this?
3. "Because consumer research is apt to be expensive, the prices of products must rise whenever it is used." Do you agree with this statement? Why?
4. Distinguish between "low-pressure buying" and "high-pressure selling." Which do you think is most effective?
5. Consumers don't really know what they want. Therefore, the job of the advertiser is to make them want what he wants them to want. Do you agree or disagree? Explain.
6. Asking consumers *why* they buy or don't buy a particular product will probably fail to bring out all significant buying motives. Explain.
7. There is seldom just one reason for buying anything. List all the motives you can think of that might lead to purchase of the following products:
   a) Cigarettes
   b) Instant coffee
   c) A man's hat
   d) Life insurance
   e) Deep-freeze cabinets for house use
8. How might a survey of consumer attitudes toward his brand benefit the advertiser?
9. Why should consumer research include a study of habits and customs?
10. "By keying their activity to human wants, businessmen are compensated for their decreased profits by their increased satisfaction in rendering such a service to society." Is this a good logical statement?
11. "With psychological *wants* becoming more significant, in total, than physiological *needs,* the importance of consumer research becomes more vital than ever." Comment on the foregoing statement.
12. The XYZ wallpaper manufacturing company developed a machine which trims wallpaper to size, evenly pasted, and ready for hanging, called the "Trim 'n Paster." It is small, portable, and sells for about $50.

In the past, the XYZ company had manufactured only wallpaper, which they sold to retailers through swatch books and catalogs. The company had done no advertising in the past, and employed only three salesmen.

The Trim 'n Paster was placed in a few selected stores in the East, but few sales resulted. Dealers reported that although homeowners were interested in this device, they did not feel that they could afford it. Professional paperhangers were not interested in it at all; many, because of union rules.

Over $150,000 had been put into the manufacture of the machines, but the inventory had increased and the machines were simply not moving.

The company's president decided that advertising might move these machines and appropriated $20,000 for advertising expenditures.

Do you believe this product will meet the needs or wants of large numbers of people? What kind of research, if any, would you recommend before undertaking specific consumer advertising?

chapter 9
CONSUMER GROUPS

ADVERTISING IS OFTEN characterized as a means of selling to the masses. This leads to the popular misconception that advertising is directed to everyone. But obviously, people of all ages, of all income levels, of all occupations, of all places, and from all walks of life do not want the same thing, do not have the same tastes, do not think the same way, and do not live by the same scale of values. Therefore, no product is consumed by everyone at the same rate and no advertisement is equally appealing to everyone. Some products have a more universal appeal than others and some advertisers have wider markets than others, but each advertisement succeeds best when it is directed to a group of consumers who can be reached on a common meeting ground.

Instead of appealing to one big heterogeneous mass, the advertiser singles out those groups of consumers who are his most promising prospects and concentrates his effort on them. He researches these groups more intensively, designs his messages to fit their way of life, and places his ads in media that reach them efficiently.

Consumers may be classified on the basis of age, sex, race, occupation, religion, income, and education. These classification factors are widely used. They have a significant bearing on consumer behavior and include information that is rather easily obtained. However, they pertain to characteristics that are interrelated such as education and occupation, occupation and income, education and income, etc. Also, their use does not assure the kind of homogeneity that may be required. Thus, one person might be in a medium-income group, have a superior education, and be a member of the legal profession. This does not mean, however, that his tastes will be the same as others who are included in any one of these groups. As a lawyer, his tastes probably will be different from those of a skilled mechanic receiving the same income. To achieve more homogeneous groupings, increased attention is now being given to composite classification systems based on the family life cycle, social class, and psychological factors.

The strategic importance of appealing to consumer groups can be readily ascertained by examining the structure of our total population and by noting the differences in buying behavior among different groups.

Age

The population of the United States can be divided into as many age groups as there are differences in ages. Such a division is unnecessary, however, since needs and wants do not change each year, nor each five years for many individuals. It is thus more valuable to classify people into those age groups which seem to differ materially in the character of needs and wants. Walter B. Pitkin classifies people into the following age groups:

1. Infancy, up to the third year
2. Childhood, from three to six
3. Prepuberty, from six to twelve
4. Adolescence, from twelve to seventeen
5. Preadulthood, from seventeen to twenty-two
6. Adulthood, from twenty-two to forty-five
7. Middle age, from forty-five to sixty-five
8. Presenility, from sixty-five to seventy
9. Senility, after seventy[1]

The desires of these nine groups are sufficiently different to warrant careful study of each. The first three present a double problem to the businessman, since most of the commodities consumed by members of those groups are purchased by their parents. It is necessary, therefore, to consider the desires of the youth and the parent. True, the age of the child will have an important bearing upon the desire of the parent; but we all know that as youngsters we played with toys which we did not like, wore clothes which we did not care for, and ate food which was not our choice. We did, however, have toys and children's furniture and

---

[1] Walter B. Pitkin, *The Consumer, His Nature, and His Changing Habits* (New York: McGraw-Hill Book Co., 1932), p. 248.

cookies and jam. Our desires were not wholly ignored. Hence, the businessman must give thought to the double influence of child and parent for persons in the first three age groups.

TABLE 9–1.   Future U.S. population projection assumes 1960–63 level of fertility (add 000)

Age	1975	1980	1990	2000
All ages	230,415	252,056	310,166	361,947
Under 5 years	27,312	30,557	35,641	43,676
5 to 9 years	24,017	27,327	33,045	39,233
10 to 14 years	21,325	24,060	30,592	35,652
15 to 19 years	20,516	21,369	27,388	33,079
20 to 24 years	19,057	20,624	24,184	30,661
25 to 29 years	17,254	19,195	21,597	27,549
30 to 34 years	13,885	17,322	20,801	24,322
35 to 39 years	11,448	13,889	19,215	21,593
40 to 44 years	11,010	11,378	17,159	20,582
45 to 49 years	11,715	10,833	13,568	18,743
50 to 54 years	11,859	11,361	10,883	16,398
55 to 59 years	10,567	11,279	10,027	12,591
60 to 64 years	9,278	9,777	10,035	9,671
65 to 69 years	7,484	8,231	9,310	8,333
70 to 74 years	5,743	6,258	7,320	7,579
75 to 79 years	3,963	4,364	5,298	6,083
80 to 84 years	2,497	2,555	3,120	3,725
85 years and over	1,485	1,678	1,983	2,479

Source: U.S. Bureau of the Census, *Current Population Reports: Population Estimates*, Series P–25, No. 286, July, 1964.

The number of people within each age group is significant as a guide to the volume of certain kinds of products that will be consumed currently and in the future. Estimated sizes of age groups at specified intervals from the year 1975 to the year 2000 appear in Table 9–1. Changes in the birth rate and a decline in the death rate bring about marked changes in the size of each group from year to year; hence, it is good business practice to keep abreast of these changes. An increase in the birth rate in 1975 would increase the number of children in the "under 5" group that year; in the 5 to 9 group five years later; and the 10 to 14 group in 1985. This would influence the sales of toys in 1977 and the sale of bicycles in 1985.

Changes in the age makeup of our population from 1970 to 1980 are graphed in Figure 9–1. As a result of the subnormal birth rates, during the late 1930's and early 1940's there will be fewer people in the 40 to 50 age group in 1980. This probably will have a depressing effect on the sales of eyeglasses. The sharp increase in the 30 to 40 age group between

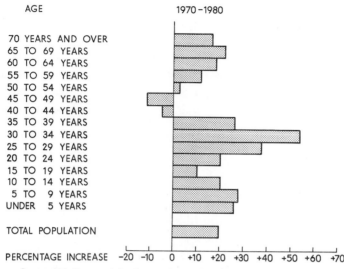

AGE   1970–1980

Source: U.S. Bureau of the Census, *Current Population Reports: Population Estimates,* Series P–25, No. 286, July, 1964.

FIGURE 9–1.   Estimated percentage increases in population by age class 1970–80

1970 and 1980 probably will boost the sales of life insurance. Also note the effect of the larger 30 to 40 age group on the size of the 5 to 14 group. Any sharp increase or decrease in the birth rate will produce a similar cyclical variation in the overall age distribution of the population at a later date.

Reflecting increased longevity and a gradual "aging" of the population, the number of people over 70 will be 18 percent greater in 1980 than in 1970. This upper age group will then include about 6 percent of the population. At the same time it is interesting to note that 49 percent or almost half of the total population will be under 25 years of age.

Of course, changes in the relative numerical importance of different age groups will not change the problems of determining the desires and habits of those within a given group. Parents will continue to have less influence on the choice of goods to be used by the child as he progresses to a higher age group. Beginning at about age 12, the youth comes into his own as a semi-independent consumer. From this age on, businessmen should direct primary attention to the needs and wants of the individual for whom production is planned.

Desires of young people are more plastic than those of older persons.

It is easier to establish new habits of consumption among these groups. This is illustrated by the quicker acceptance of new modes of dress by young people than by older persons.

The other age groups listed above will have their own peculiar needs and wants. Any study of consumer tastes must be made with a thought of measuring tastes—not of people in general, but of people in homogeneous groups. Age provides one important classification to be considered.

The family life cycle

The family life cycle refers to the progression of important stages in adult life. It breaks through the arbitrary classification of people in terms of calendar age and groups them according to more meaningful periods of their life. For example, if we assume that in family A there are two children under 6 and the parents are age 42; in family B there are two children under 6 and the parents are age 28; in family C there are no children and the married couple are age 42; we will find that for many products the buying behavior of families A and B will be more nearly alike than the buying behavior of families A and C. The presence of young children can be a more significant classification factor than calendar age.

The life cycle of a family begins with the marriage of two people and continues throughout the remaining span of their lives. It can be subdivided into stages marked by the birth of children, age level of the youngest child, the departure of children to set up their own homes, and the death of one of the spouses.

John B. Lansing and James N. Morgan in their study "Consumer Finances Over the Life Cycle" used these stages:

1. *The bachelor stage.* Single individuals living alone. They have left the home in which they were reared, but they have not founded a new home.
2. *The newly married couple* with no children.
3. *Young married with children,* youngest under 6.
4. *Young married with children,* youngest over 6.
5. *Older married (over 45)* with children.
6. *The empty nest,* the married couple after the children have left home.
7. *The solitary survivor.* In the natural course of events one of the couple dies before the other.[2]

---

[2] John B. Lansing and James N. Morgan, "Consumer Finances Over the Life Cycle," *Consumer Behavior,* Vol. II (New York: New York University Press, 1955), pp. 36–37.

			Stage					
			Young married			Older married		
Item purchased	All spending units*	Young, single	Childless	Youngest child under 6	Youngest child 6 or over	(over 45), with children	No children under 18	Older, single
House	4%	†	6%	9%	7%	4%	3%	†
New car	9	5%	11	11	20	11	9	2%
Used car	14	11	22	23	18	14	11	4
Furniture	16	10	26	23	27	16	11	5
Refrigerator	9	1	14	12	12	8	7	5
Stove	7	3	13	10	7	5	7	4
Washing machine	6	1	10	13	9	8	4	1
Television set	14	5	14	22	19	16	12	7

* A spending unit is defined as all persons living in the same dwelling and related by blood, marriage, or adoption, who pool their incomes to meet their major expenses. However, any individual who earns $15 a week or more and keeps more than half of it for his own use is treated as a separate unit. Thus, an employed bachelor son living with his parents appears as separate spending unit.

† Less than 0.5 percent.

Source: John B. Lansing and James N. Morgan, "Consumer Finances Over the Life Cycle," *Consumer Behavior*, Volume II (New York: New York University Press, 1955), p. 43.

Some comparisons of buying behavior at different stages in the life cycle are indicated in Table 9–2. For reasons obvious to parents the most washing machines are bought by young married families with children under six years of age. These families with young children also appear to be the best prospects for houses, used cars, and television sets. Purchases of furniture, refrigerators, and stoves are frequent among all married people under 45 years old, but less common in the older groups.

Families with young children are the most frequent purchasers of chest rubs, cough syrups, and packaged detergents. Newly married housewives are prime prospects for cake mixes, precooked foods, new recipes, and new labor-saving devices.

Inasmuch as the family is the important consuming unit for appliances, furniture, home furnishings, and most grocery items, the life cycle is a promising classification system for structuring consumer markets.

Sex

The question of whether the male or female is more important in the purchase of consumption goods has been debated often and long. The evidence seems to give the female of the species first place as a buyer. This place is established by reason of two facts: (1) the position of women as controllers of income and wealth, and (2) their influence as purchasers for the family.

More than 40 percent of all individual wealth in the United States is owned by women. Life insurance companies each year pay to women between one half and three fourths of a billion dollars. Sixty percent of all estates go entirely to women, only 25 percent entirely to men, the remainder being divided.

From this wealth and from their own labor, women rank high as receivers of income. Well over 18 million women earn part or all of their own living in other than family household duties. In a recent year, 54 percent of all Americans reporting incomes over $100,000 were women.

Not only is this purchasing power available to women for spending, but also much of the earnings of men are available to them. As housewives, the influence of women in determining what will be purchased is great. The woman has often been referred to as the purchasing agent for the family. The United States Department of Commerce estimates that 85 percent of all retail purchases are made by women.

There is no doubt about women doing most of the buying of consump-

FIGURE 9–2. Who determines what will be purchased?

tion goods. The more important problem of the advertiser, however, deals with the relative importance of the man and the woman in influencing the purchase. Some advertisers have admitted that women do the buying but have insisted that men really "direct" the buying. This point of view has been held by *Time* magazine and popularized in its advertising with the statement, "He who pays the fiddler calls the tune," meaning, of course, that when the man pays the bills he determines in large part what will be purchased. *Redbook* magazine has held the same philosophy and has used in its advertising the slogan, "The shadow of a man stands behind every woman who buys." But the *Ladies' Home Journal* counters with the slogan, "Never underestimate the power of a woman." See Figure 9–2.

Occupation

Human attitudes, habits, and motives are shaped or determined to some degree by the manner in which a living is made. The office man and the day laborer will select different kinds of recreation, buy different kinds of clothes, and often eat different kinds of food.

A Syracuse University survey conducted by Harry W. Hepner disclosed some interesting occupational differences. Data were obtained concerning the percentage of housewives and students operating on a definite monthly or weekly allowance. These data were segregated by occupational groups. Table 9–3 shows the wide variation in this practice between the skilled labor group and the professional group. More than twice the number of housewives in the professional group operated the household on a regular allowance than was true in the skilled labor group.

TABLE 9–3. Who gets an allowance?

Occupation of household head	Percent receiving definite allowance	
	Housewives	*Students*
Skilled laborers	30.0	38.1
Clerical and sales	54.0	53.8
Professional	62.0	61.1
Business executives or owner	56.2	54.1

Professional men and craftsmen spend much more on sports goods and equipment than other occupational groups. This was borne out in *Life* magazine's *Study of Consumer Expenditures,* as shown in Table 9–4.

TABLE 9–4.   Who buys sports equipment?

Occupation of household head	Percent of U.S. households	Percent of total U.S. expenditures
Professional, semi-professional	8	38
Proprietor, manager, official	10	8
Clerical, sales	11	9
Craftsman, foreman	17	22
Operative	21	13
Service worker	6	2
Farmer, farm laborer	9	3
Retired or not employed	18	5

Source: Adapted from *Life Study of Consumer Expenditures*, Vol. 1 (New York: Time, Inc., 1957), p. 115.

To distinguish the readers of *True Story* from readers of other magazines, McFadden Publications, Inc. focuses special attention on wage earner families. Wage earners are classified as hourly paid workers in manufacturing, mining, transportation, etc. They are distinguished not only from executive, professional, and proprietor, but from all other white-collar occupations. Including 54 percent of the United States total, wage-earner families have enjoyed rapid economic progress in recent years, and they display patterns of home life and social activities that are somewhat different from many other occupational groups, even in comparable income brackets.

Race

Eleven percent of the U.S. population is Negro. However, in the ten largest cities Negroes account for 31 percent of the population; in the 78 largest cities they account for 25 percent. Negro family income in 1970 was reported to be $8,530 in Detroit, $8,517 in Chicago, $7,140 in New York, and $8,410 in Washington, D.C.[3] This urban, growing, middle-class market has demonstrated some distinctive buying patterns.

The black household consumes 8 percent more meat of all kinds by weight than the white family, 6 percent more poultry, and 34 percent more pork. The black family consumes less coffee and tea than the white family; but consumption of soft drinks is 9 percent more. Since a greater percentage of Negro wives work, convenience foods are important. Negro

---

[3] Raymond O. Oladipupo, *How Distinct Is The Negro Market?* (New York: Ogilvy & Mather, Inc., 1970), p. 23.

families with income above $4,000 buy 26 percent more frozen vegetables than white families. In the under $2,000 income group they spend 19 percent more on canned vegetables than white families.[4]

Controversy over whether the United States is an integrated society or a dual society has extended to advertising strategy. Alternative approaches to the Negro market were categorized by D. Parke Gibson as follows:

> We have white-oriented advertising that appears in primarily white-oriented media; we have white-oriented advertising that appears in primarily black-oriented media; we have integrated advertising that appears in white-oriented and black-oriented media; we have some black-oriented advertising that appears in white-oriented media; and, of course, we have black-oriented advertising in black-oriented media.
>
> In this confusion we have reflections of social responsibility, misunderstood public relations objectives, mis-directed marketing considerations, some do-goodism and, last but certainly not least, some clear-cut marketing objectives with on-target advertising directed to specific markets.[5]

Negro-oriented media include radio stations, magazines, and newspapers. Negroes listen to radio considerably more than the average white person and are slightly less interested in TV and much less interested in print media. When the Negro does tune in his radio, he is inclined to listen to Negro-programmed stations.[6]

Different attitudes, different product preferences, and different media usage clearly indicate that there is a specific Negro market for which specific advertising strategies should be designed.

Nationality

The melting pot is supposed to have erased much of the variation normally existing between different nationalities. As yet, the melting process has not been completed in the United States; some 24 million people living in the continental United States are foreign born or had foreign-born parentage. This represented approximately one eighth of the entire population. In many ways, however, the buying habits and motives of these groups are similar to those of the native-born. This is true where the melting pot has resulted in merging the culture patterns

---

[4] *Ibid.,* pp. 30, 31.

[5] D. Parke Gibson, *Negro-Oriented Advertising—the Other Side of the 1970's* (New York: American Association of Advertising Agencies, 1969), p. 1.

[6] Raymond O. Oladipupo, *op. cit.,* pp. 48, 49.

of the foreign-born and the native population. There do exist, however, sufficient differences in product preferences and buying behavior to warrant careful analysis by the advertiser.

The advertiser desiring to reach these groups in their entirety must use the newspapers and periodicals read by them. There are many foreign-language publications, about 600 being listed by the N. W. Ayer & Son's *Directory of Newspapers and Periodicals.* There are 89 Spanish, 64 German, 45 Italian, 41 Czechoslovak, 38 Polish, 40 French, and 20 Yiddish publications listed among the total. Also, there are 25 radio stations broadcasting exclusively in Spanish. This would indicate the existence of rather large foreign groups which still maintain a considerable part of their foreign culture.

Religion

Our present age has been referred to as the "age of religious decay." Perhaps religion does not play the part in human lives that it did at an earlier date. Yet it holds a stronger grip and a deeper significance on human actions than surface observations would indicate. Even an adult may feel that the religious forces which helped to direct his childhood actions have been discarded. But nothing which has grooved itself into our life at any time can be entirely erased. To a degree, it still, consciously or unconsciously, influences our daily actions.

The things we eat and wear, the recreation in which we indulge, the character of our reading material, our marriage relationships, and our personal habits in regard to smoking and drinking have in many cases been influenced by religion. In certain parts of the United States it would be suicidal for a meat merchant to stock up with pork and beef on a Friday and fail to have plenty of fish on hand, while in some spots much Kosher meat is sold. In other sections, the druggist that kept open on Sunday would sell few products during the week, the restaurant that sold beer on Sunday would find few customers, and the promoter of a dance hall would probably be ushered out of town. There are exceptions; but to a greater degree than many advertisers realize, religious elements provide almost fixed grooves for the purchase of many products.

The seller of coffee would find returns from his advertising in Salt Lake City much less than returns from similar advertising in Cincinnati. A few years ago, when Lucky Strikes made their first appeal to women, an indirect and subtle approach was used. Eventually, however, the company became bold enough to make the appeal direct and to picture a girl actually smoking a cigarette. Such illustrations were made a part of a national outdoor poster campaign. The company found it necessary, however, to paint out the cigarette in the girl's mouth in certain sections of the country.

It would be absurd for advertisers to play the part of the crusader in attempting to break down buying habits and motives founded on a religious background. Give the religious element what it wants. If Salt Lake City people do not want coffee, then sell them postum or cocoa. The cost of selling them coffee, even though it were possible, would be prohibitive.

A study of these religious characteristics will give the advertiser an understanding which should help him in properly directing his advertising appeal. The group can usually be reached through religious publications. The advertising message carried in such publications must be in harmony with the beliefs and ideals of the readers if it is to be effective.

Income

People with money to spend make markets, and in most cases money income is the most significant factor influencing what and how much a consumer buys. The number of consumers at various levels of income is an index of potential sales. The unique tastes and desires of different income groups serve as a useful guide when selecting advertising appeals and media.

Personal income in the United States has persistently displayed two marked tendencies: the tendency to rise and the tendency to be more evenly distributed. Great numbers of consumers have been moving up into higher income groups. This fact is illustrated in Figure 9–3. In 1960, 23 percent of the spending units had incomes of $7,500 and over, while in 1966, 46 percent of the spending units had incomes of $7,500 and over. On the other hand, in 1960, 18 percent of the spending units received an income of less than $2,000. In 1966 only 11 percent of the spending units were in this lower income group. This movement upward in purchasing power by millions of people has been a fundamental factor in our expanding economy.

As consumers move up from one income group to the next, they represent substantially increased markets for goods and services. However, they do not automatically take on the same desires and standard of living of the income group into which they have moved. Habit and inertia tend

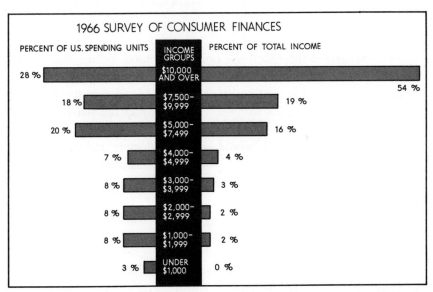

Source: From the 1960 and 1966 Surveys of Consumer Finances, Survey Research Center, University of Michigan.

FIGURE 9–3. The proportion of consumers in higher income groups has been increasing to perpetuate the earlier way of life. Stimulating their wants and spending in line with their increased income is the task and opportunity of advertising.

Even though the concentration of income in the hands of a few has been reduced, it should be noted that in 1966 about 54 percent of the income was received by the top 28 percent of the spending units. Thus, about 84 percent of the new car purchases in 1966 were in the upper half income groups.

TABLE 9–5.   Personal income distribution among selected commodity groups and savings

Year	Total personal income (billions)	Food and tobacco	Clothing	Transportation	Household operation	Savings
			Percentage distribution of income			
1957 351		22.9	8.7	10.4	11.4	6.7
1959 384		22.0	8.6	10.2	11.5	6.1
1961 416		21.4	8.3	9.7	11.4	6.2
1963 466		18.9	6.5	10.5	9.7	6.2
1965 535		18.5	6.6	10.7	9.8	6.1

Source: U.S. Department of Commerce, Office of Business Economics, *Survey of Current Business,* September, 1966, pp. S1–2.

The advertiser is interested not only in the total income but also in how it is spent. Table 9–5 shows the trends in total personal income from 1957 to 1965 and what portion of each annual total was spent for selected commodities and for savings. Accompanying the sharp increases in personal income from 1957 to 1965, the proportion spent for food and clothing steadily declined. It would appear that more and more people became so well fed and well clothed that they found other purchases such as automobiles, appliances, and recreation more attractive than more and better food and clothing.

Studies of buying habits of families in different income groups have disclosed facts that proved the fallacy of certain business practices. At one time it was generally believed that yard goods were usually purchased as a means of saving money, and hence, that advertising of such goods should be directed to families with relatively low incomes. However, a study made by R. H. Macy & Co. disclosed the fact that the best users of yard goods were women between the ages of 40 and 50 and were in the top income brackets. With *facts* concerning the desires and habits of different groups, an advertising program can be built and directed to the proper people.

Education

As a classification factor, education is interrelated with age, income, and occupation. Relatively few people in the older age groups went to college. A higher proportion of the younger men and women completed this level of education, and the percentage of high school students going on to college is steadily increasing. College educated people are more apt to be found in the higher income groups reflecting both the higher family income of their earlier years and the increased productivity made possible by their higher level of education. A college degree has long been recognized as a prerequisite for entering the professions of medicine, law, and engineering. It is becoming an almost universal requirement for top management positions in business and government.

Education probably has less effect on what people buy than on how they buy and how they are influenced by advertising. Perhaps better educated people are more discerning, more discriminating, and more rational buyers. Perhaps they are less suggestible, less susceptible to nonrational appeals, and less responsive to persuasion. If so, it would seem that advertising addressed to better educated groups should be more factual, more informative, and more reasonable. These specifications certainly should be considered, but they overlook the fact that man is a bundle of emotions regardless of the kind or degree of his education. A blending of reason and emotion can be effectively used in all persuasion. Talking the consumer's language is axiomatic. As the consuming public becomes better educated the advertiser should avoid talking beneath their notice.

Geographic location

The needs of people are materially altered by the differences in climate, topography, and general character of the section of the country in which they reside. The influence of location is distinctly heterogeneous in many respects, in that so many factors are associated with a given territory. Social customs, dress, type of recreation, racial elements, type of homes, and general energy are all fatcors that might be associated with location. The very heterogeneity occasioned by location increases the importance of study of this factor. An attempt should be made to divide these unlike elements and give each its proper weight as a factor influencing needs and wants.

Some of the obvious influences of location might be noted. Certainly the demand for lightweight suits will be much greater south of the Mason-Dixon Line than north of it. The same will be true for ice, lawn furniture, and electric fans. The demand will be less for fur coats, ice skates, sleds, furnace equipment, and skis. Only by a study of individual needs, shaped and altered by location, will the true significance of this factor to a particular producer be ascertained.

Social class

The concept of social class is especially useful in studies of consumer motivation. One's goals, attitudes, value systems, standards of taste, and behavior patterns are largely influenced by the social world in which he lives.

Social classes are determined by combining such factors as occupation, family background, education, neighborhood, and the source as well as the amount of income.

Social Research, Inc., an organization that specializes in motivation studies, uses these six social classes:

1. Upper upper— The "aristocracy" of a community, the old line families with inherited wealth who can live comfortably on income derived from investments.
2. Lower upper— Families with newly gained economic and social power.
3. Upper middle—Families in which husbands are likely to be successful business executives, or be occupied in one of the professions. Their incomes average somewhat less than the people in the upper classes and are predominantly salary and current earnings, rather than income from invested wealth.
4. Lower middle—White collar workers, tradesmen, a few skilled workers, and their families. They have accumulated little property, but are frequently homeowners.
5. Upper lower— Skilled and semiskilled workers who participate relatively little in educational and other advantages of our society.
6. Lower lower— Unskilled laborers, people on relief, unassimilated foreign groups. Many of them are poor and lack the ambition or opportunity to improve their lot.

The general distribution of our population among these groups is about 3 percent or less for the entire upper class and around 12 percent for the upper-middle class, with about 65 percent clustered in the lower-middle and upper-lower classes, and about 20 percent in the lower-lower classes. There is considerable psychological and social distance between the three top classes and the mass of people immediately below them. Although few people are able to move up the social ladder, it is likely that our rising level of incomes will produce greater similarities among all classes.

Both conformity to the standards of one's class and emulation of the classes above can be seen in consumer behavior. Where people live, their houses, furniture, home furnishings, food preferences, and entertainment tend to be the same as those of other people in their class. On the other hand, their automobiles and clothing may reflect a desire to emulate the classes above. It is not uncommon to find a member of the lower class driving a Cadillac as a means of escaping from the feeling that he has drawn a blank in this great lottery of life.

Psychological groups

Many differences in what consumers buy can only be explained in terms of their psychological makeup. We see older men with closely cropped grey hair driving flashy sports cars instead of more conservative models, thereby demonstrating that they are young-in-heart if not in years. Perhaps all men who prefer to smoke a pipe instead of cigarettes have similar personality traits regardless of their socioeconomic status. People whose taste in houses and furniture runs toward contemporary instead of traditional design may be near each other psychologically even though they are far apart economically. Sophisticated urbanites who enjoy listening to hillbilly tunes may have much in common with farm and ranch people who also like that kind of music. Such similarities of taste and preferences among people from different walks of life suggest that in many instances psychological groups are more pertinent than sociological groups.

Classifying consumers according to psychological characteristics is not easily done. A person's attitudes and personality traits are not so readily ascertained as his age and occupation. His psychological characteristics can only be inferred from how he scores on appropriately designed tests such as the more familiar I.Q. tests, aptitude tests, and attitude scales.

In a study of *Better Homes and Gardens* readers, Alfred Politz tested and classified respondents according to their venturesomeness, a characteristic which he describes as follows:

> In the course of studying the reaction of consumers to products which have been introduced, it was observed that individuals do differ with respect to venturesomeness. There are some individuals who are of the adventurous type. They are the people who are the first to buy new products and try innovations. On the other end of the scale there are people who tend to be cautious. These are the people who will buy a new product only after they have been convinced that the new product is worthwhile. While a venturesome person will tend to shift from one new product to another; a cautious person, once he has been persuaded to try a new product, will tend to be loyal to that product.[7]

As one would expect, Politz found that deep-fat fryers, electric skillets, electric rotisseries, and window air conditioners were more prevalent in households inhabited by venturesome people than in those where cautious people lived. Young people tend to be more venturesome than old. However, a large number of old people are venturesome and a large number of young people are cautious. Venturesomeness is not concentrated in any particular income group. People on the lower rungs of the income ladder are about as likely to be venturesome as those on the higher rungs.

One study of the relationship between personality traits and cigarette smoking showed that the average U.S. male smoker scored significantly higher than the average U.S. male in his expressed needs for sex, aggression, achievement, and dominance, and significantly below average in compliance, order, self-depreciation, and association.[8]

The trend toward psychological groupings is evidenced in the way some magazines are now characterizing their readers. *Sports Illustrated* describes their readers as the "enthusiastic ones." *Holiday* refers to their readers as the "spirited leaders of this more-fun-and-fine-living age."

Heavy users

A more direct approach to pinpointing market targets is to find out who are the heavy users of the product. For many product categories we find that a small proportion of the population consumes a large proportion of the product. Note in Table 9–6, that only 3.6 percent of the male pop-

---

[7] *A 12-Month's Study of Better Homes & Gardens Readers* (Des Moines, Iowa: Meredith Publishing Company, 1956), p. 147.

[8] Arthur Koponen, "Personality Characteristics of Purchasers," *Journal of Advertising Research,* September, 1960 (New York: Advertising Research Foundation), pp. 6–12.

TABLE 9–6. Percent of total product usage accounted for by the heavy users of specific products

	Heavy users	
	% of population group	% of total usage
Car rentals in past year (men)	3.6	89.6
Liquid dietary products	4.1	98.0
Air trips in past year (men)	7.8	87.3
Automatic dishwasher detergents	9.0	100.0
Hair coloring rinse or tint (women)	11.3	88.1
Scotch whiskey	12.6	98.6
Cigar smoking (men)	17.1	98.6
Rye or blended whiskey	18.4	98.5
Bourbon	18.8	98.7
Canned type dog food	19.3	99.2
Dry dog food	20.7	99.2
Canned ham	22.8	83.0
Instant coffee	26.1	80.6
Cold or allergy tablets	27.0	84.3
Cigarettes (all adults)	27.2	84.1
Hair tonic (men)	27.8	76.8
Laxatives	28.2	92.8
Rice	28.8	82.7
Peanut butter	29.6	82.4
Cake mix	34.1	84.4
R.T.E. cereal	37.2	80.2
Upset stomach remedies	37.3	89.2
Shaving cream in pressurized cans (men)	38.7	98.0
Frozen orange juice	41.0	92.1
Soft drinks	41.8	84.9
Paper napkins .:.......................	42.9	83.2
Bleach	43.7	81.6
Tomato sauce	44.9	90.7
Cleansing or facial tissues	45.2	82.9
Frozen vegetables	49.9	92.1
Regular ground coffee	50.5	92.7
H. H. laundry detergents	50.8	81.4
Headache remedies	52.6	93.1

Note: The total population group is based on total households except for those products specifically designated otherwise.

Source: "The Marketing Value of Media Audiences—How To Pinpoint Your Prime Prospects," by Norton Garfinkle. Paper presented at A.N.A. workshop, January 19, 1965.

ulation accounts for 89.6 percent of all car rentals, that only 11.3 percent of the women use 88.1 percent of all hair colorings, that 20 percent of total households use 99 percent of prepared dog food, etc. Even in the case of popular products such as soft drinks, tomato sauce, facial tissues, and frozen vegetables we find that less than one half of the population accounts for 80 to 90 percent of the usage.

Once the heavy user group is identified, their demographic characteristics can be described. Then advertising appeals most appropriate for
that group and media most efficiently reaching that group can be employed. For example, heavy users of automatic dishwasher detergents are
concentrated in the upper and upper-middle social class households, heavy
users of laxatives are concentrated in lower income households, and heavy
users of hair tonic are concentrated among men 18 to 35 years of age.
Heavy users of facial tissues tend to be in upper middle income, larger
family, and suburban households.

Even though the heavy user group is well identified, important strategy
questions remain to be answered. Should all advertisers concentrate on
the heavy users? Or, should some concentrate on other segments of the
total market? Commercial success can sometimes be achieved by building a strong brand preference among light or moderate users. Perhaps
gaining 80 percent of the moderate users can be more profitable than 10
percent of the heavy users. Chances are usually greater, however, that
those people who are responsive to a particular product category as indicated by their higher rate of purchase will be the most profitable market
to cultivate.

Summary

The study of people by groups is not valuable for its own sake, but
rather as a means of ascertaining more clearly the real needs and wants
of people as influenced by membership in given groups. It is an attempt
to determine the culture patterns of people so that advertising may be
harmonized with these patterns. It is necessary at all times to recognize
that people are members of more than one group. The advertiser must
attempt to correlate these various influences into a composite picture of
needs and wants.

John Cover has stated the problem as follows:

> The concept of an "average consumer" is fallacious, for only by the process of
> classification and reclassification is there obtained group similarity; and each crite-
> rion of income, race, nationality, creed, etc., is significant only as related to all other
> criteria. For instance, when nationality is isolated from its various neighborhood
> relationships it appears to have little weight in determining consumption habits.
> But when placed in its neighborhood environment in relation to income, prices,
> and other factors, its influence is important.[9]

---

[9] John H. Cover, *Neighborhood Distribution and Consumption of Meat in Pittsburgh*
(Chicago: University of Chicago Press, 1932), pp. 16, 17.

The study of consumers in groups is not a perfect solution to the problem of determining their needs and wants. Yet it is sufficiently valuable to encourage businessmen to intensify their efforts in such study.

QUESTIONS AND PROBLEMS

1. What differences in buying behavior would you expect to find among families in the various stages of the family life cycle with respect to: (*a*) foods, (*b*) clothing, (*c*) furniture, (*d*) life insurance, (*e*) ocean cruises?

2. Many differences in what consumers buy can only be explained in terms of their psychological make-up. Explain.

3. Of what significance to the advertiser is an increasing expenditure for education?

4. Do you believe advertisers in general take cognizance of the age-group classification made by Walter B. Pitkin? What advantages are to be derived by so doing?

5. Which sex do you believe, in view of your own experience, is the more important in the selection and purchase of consumer goods? In view of the evidence gained from tests and surveys?

6. Do you believe that religious elements still must be considered by the advertiser? Cite examples supporting your answer.

7. To what consumer groups would you direct the advertising of these products: a new hot cereal, life insurance, sterling silverware, automobile tires, a university, new homes, race horses?

8. If you were an independent retail grocer, how might your operations be influenced by the community which you serve?

9. The study of consumers in groups is not a perfect solution to the problem of determining their needs and wants. Why?

10. Of what significance to the advertiser is the trend toward increased longevity?

11. Some claim that the mother or wife is the purchasing agent for the home. How should this influence the advertiser?

12. The "Trim 'n Paster" machine described in the Questions and Problems section of the previous chapter would not have the same appeal to all groups of consumers. What group or groups do you believe would be most likely to get satisfaction from the product?

chapter 10
PRODUCT
ANALYSIS

ONE OF THE ten commandments for effective selling and advertising is "Know thy product." It is second only to the commandment, "Know thy customers' wants." Effective selling and advertising involve the correlation of these two commandments. Effective merchandising is concerned not so much with what the manufacturer puts into the product in the way of actual materials as it is with what people get out of it in the way of increased happiness, comfort, health, and other human satisfactions.

A knowledge of consumer wants should, therefore, precede the actual planning and manufacture of a product in order that real want-satisfying qualities can be built into the product. We have seen in another connection the importance of consumer research as a means of approximating direct contact between producer and consumer. Such research assists in the determination of what people want. With these wants understood, manufacturers are then in a position to work toward the development of products that will satisfy such wants.

Product analysis, therefore, might be considered as the process of subjecting goods to careful scrutiny to determine the degree to which they have been or might be molded to fit the mind of the buyer. Such an analysis should consider the class into which the product falls, all possible uses for the product, its construction and quality, the character of the present or possible package, the common unit of sale, and price.

Classification of product

A broad classification of goods might be made on the basis of their use or purpose. The terms "producers' goods" and "consumers' goods" provide such a division. The former includes those goods used in the production process such as raw materials for fabrication, and materials auxiliary to production such as machinery, factory buildings, equipment, and office supplies. Consumers' goods include all products used for their own sake. Examples would be automobiles, clothing, food, homes, and home furniture. Consumers' goods have been classified as convenience, shopping, and specialty goods. This classification is based on the buying motives and habits of consumers.[1]

The type of product will have a profound influence on the character of advertising. In the case of producers' goods, advertising should usually be directed to businessmen in their capacity as officers and executives of a business. Appeals should, in general, be directed to rational rather than emotional buyers motives.

If consumers' goods are being advertised, appeals might be directed to either rational or emotional motives. The characteristics of consumption goods chosen as the basis for an advertisement will depend to a considerable degree upon the class into which the product falls. If it is a convenience good, advertising might be used to emphasize the wide retail distribution of the product. "Get X flour at your nearest grocery store" can be used effectively only when most grocery stores carry X flour. In the case of specialty goods or those which the advertiser wishes to make a specialty good, emphasis might be placed on the qualities of the product which make it superior to competing products.

Some manufacturers have made the mistake of trying to make a specialty product out of one which was quite obviously a convenience good. While the slogan, "I'd walk a mile for a Camel," might have been an effective selling phrase, it was decidedly untrue when applied to most cigarette smokers. And the manufacturer recognized its untruth by seeing to it that Camels were made available at practically every tobacco, gro-

---

[1] Convenience goods are those which consumers wish to buy very soon after they are conscious of a desire for them. Not much effort will be expended in getting a particular brand; hence, a substitute will be accepted rather willingly. Specialty goods are those for which consumers have a strong brand preference. Effort will be expended in order to obtain the particular brand desired. Shopping goods are those for which consumers wish to compare price, quality, style, etc., before a purchase is made.

cery, and drugstore. If the manufacturer had tried to force people to walk a mile for a Camel, his efforts would have failed.

It is extremely important that the advertiser determine the classification into which his product naturally falls before undertaking an extensive advertising program. It is relatively easy to determine whether a product is a producers' or consumers' good. It is more difficult to make a correct classification of the latter into convenience, specialty, or shopping goods. The problem is one of ascertaining the buying habits of consumers with respect to the particular type of product involved.

Advertisability of product

Some products lend themselves to specific advertising effort more than others. Professor N. H. Borden has suggested five conditions which tend to influence the opportunities for effective advertising of products. These conditions are as follows:

1. A favorable primary demand trend for the product. (Is it want-satisfying in a general sense?)
2. A chance for significant product differentiation.
3. High relative importance to the consumer of hidden qualities of the product as contrasted with external qualities.
4. Opportunity to use strong emotional appeals.
5. Existence of circumstances favoring the accumulation of substantial sums to support advertising.[2]

Each of these factors should be kept in mind when analyzing the detailed characteristics of a product. Some of the detailed characteristics that might be analyzed are considered in the remainder of this chapter.

Uses

A manufacturer may think that a product has only a few uses, whereas the consumer has discovered uses other than those advertised. These other uses can be uncovered in the research laboratory and by asking consumers the uses they make of the product.

It was by accident that the makers of Listerine learned that this product was being used as a remedy for dandruff. The Johnson Wax Company discovered that its floor wax was being used on automobiles to preserve

---

[2] Neil H. Borden, *Economic Effects of Advertising* (Homewood, Ill.: Richard D. Irwin, 1942), pp. 424–28.

the finish. Consumers told the makers of Mum that men needed and used their product.

In addition to discovering the variety of uses which a product might have, it is important to determine the more popular uses. The Corning Glass Works discovered from interviewing users of Pyrex ovenware that the uses being advertised were not the ones consumers followed most. Eighty-three percent of Pyrex users limited their use to the cooking of five foods in this ovenware, while 79 percent owned only four or fewer pieces of Pyrex ware.

It is important to inquire into the degree to which the product is or may be used by different consumer groups. Are its users to be found primarily among males or females, adults or adolescents, boys or girls, high-, medium-, or low-income groups? What are its major uses?

The length of time the product has been used and the direction of the sales curve for the industry will indicate the probable future trend of industry sales. If the sales curve is upward, the advertising opportunities for individual suppliers will be enhanced.

Construction

To what degree is the product designed to meet particular consumer needs and habits? Obvious examples of products so designed would include the height of tables, location of knobs on a door, window lifts on windows, and the height of cookstoves and kitchen sinks. It took many years, however, before the switch on vacuum sweepers was placed on the top of the handle, floor lamps were connected with wall switches, and an eraser was built in the end of a pencil. We still have many examples of products being constructed without adequate coordination with consumer needs. A college fraternity house was recently constructed under the supervision of a well-known architect. Study rooms were equipped with built-in desks with four drawers on one side. The width of these drawers was 7½ inches—an inch too narrow for regular paper. The architect should have known that most students used notebook, theme, and typing paper regularly and that desk drawers afforded the most logical place to keep such paper. The architect focused his attention on the physical problems of construction and built narrow drawers because of his conception of appearance plus the fact that the bottoms of 7½-inch drawers could be made from regular 8-inch stock. Of course, such a procedure cannot produce maximum want satisfaction.

The importance and value of a different approach to the problem of construction is well expressed by H. G. Weaver of General Motors Corporation. "The designing of a car," he says, "is not merely a matter of coordinating the mechanical components. Of even greater importance is the coordination of the machine to the tastes, desires, temperaments, nerves, and physique of the driver and his passengers."[3]

The coordination in the case of General Motors has been developed in cooperation with the consumer. The results in construction have been noted in larger gas tanks, two-spoke steering wheel for a better view of instruments, a more accessible radiator drain tap, more room around pedals for foot relaxation, tire valves easy to reach, arm rest for the driver, and many other similar items. These items have been mostly listed by consumers themselves. More or less intangible suggestions made by consumers have been more difficult to follow. The desire for greater riding comfort and for better car ventilation has required the use of the research laboratory in developing appropriate construction to satisfy such desires. Independent springing, no-draft ventilation, automatic gear shift, air conditioning, and chair-height seats have resulted from efforts to meet these desires. The tangible method used to meet human desires may not succeed in its purpose. This does not invalidate the principle, but rather calls for eternal vigilance on the part of the manufacturer.

The Nashua Blanket Company discovered that the blankets it had been selling were considered too short by many consumers. Users objected to the blankets on the ground that they could not be tucked in at the bottom of the bed and leave enough blanket to cover the body. An investigation resulted in the production of longer blankets and the development of an advertising campaign around the idea.

One maker of ready-mix biscuit dough advertised the ease and quickness of making biscuits from his product. Consumers found, however, that when the dough was taken out of the icebox or refrigerator it was most difficult to prepare for baking. The manufacturer changed the ingredients so that cold would not cause this difficulty.

The makers of Johnson's wax produced a special automobile wax when they learned that their floor wax was being used for automobiles. The new wax was made so that it was easier to apply on cars than was floor wax.

Another factor in construction to be considered is color. Many modern products have been dressed up with color and, by this simple construction

---

[3] General Motors Corporation, *The Proving Ground of Public Opinion* (Detroit, 1932), p. 7.

change, have been increased in ability to meet human wants. A comparison of products today with those of a few years ago will emphasize the change in this respect. The increase in sales figures will also show the favorable response which the public has given to this introduction of color. Its application is easily noted in fountain pens, furniture, kitchenware, clocks, office equipment, and similar products.

In selecting color, care should be exercised to choose colors that are desired by actual and potential customers. It is easy to add too many colors to a line of merchandise or to add a new color that has no general appeal. Dress manufacturers a few years ago introduced a new, beet-red garment to the market and promoted it heavily, but sales were negligible. Another manufacturer had 12 different colors in his line of towels. The best selling color accounted for 17 percent of total sales, and the poorest, 2.5 percent. The firm simplified the line to seven colors after making a careful analysis of consumer desires. The reduced line not only satisfied 90 percent of all potential customers but also reduced the inventory problem of retailers. Total sales were materially increased.

Color has recently been added to machinery used in the factory. Producers' goods are supposedly purchased to perform particular production tasks. Color would seem to add nothing to their ability to perform such tasks. It has been found, however, that color will have a beneficial influence upon the person in charge of the machine. A greater pride is often manifest in such equipment, particularly in the increased attention given to keeping it clean. This adds not only to the efficiency but also to the favorable mental attitude of the attendant.

The use of color in industrial goods has often resulted in greater safety and accuracy in workmanship. Dr. Podolsky reports that when a machine-tool manufacturer "dipped rough castings in a vivid red protective coating his machinists were more accurate in the finishing of these castings. The red acted as a definite visual stimulant and made these castings stand out more clearly and distinctly."[4]

The importance of considering human desires in terms of consumer groups is well illustrated by the problem of design. Geographical location will have its influence on the style of architecture used for home building. Occupation, income, and education will influence the type of furniture demanded. Figures 10–1 and 10–2 illustrate two distinctly different types of furniture design. Neither will meet the desires of a ma-

---

[4] Edward Podolsky, *The Doctor Prescribes Color* (New York: National Library Press, 1938), p. 25.

FIGURE 10–1. Designed for those desiring modernism in furniture

FIGURE 10–2. Furniture offered to meet the desire for colonial design

Photos Courtesy American Furniture Mart.

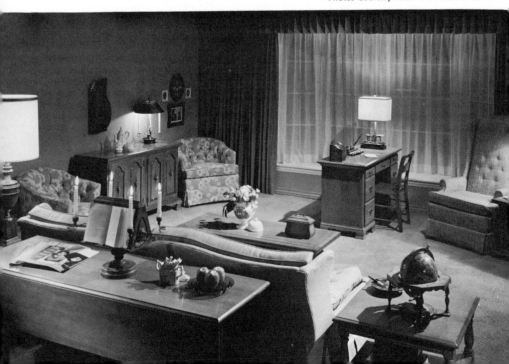

jority of consumers. Each will satisfy some people more completely than any other type of furniture. These two examples illustrate the answer of manufacturers to the desires of different consumers for colonial and modern furniture.

Quality

Some manufacturers misinterpret consumer attitude toward quality. Few men and no women want clothes that will "wear forever." Producers of clothes must recognize this and try to make garments of a quality which consumers want. An automobile could be made which would be much more economical and durable than those now offered the public; but its manufacture would be justified only if consumers want such a product and were willing to pay the price for it.

The problem of incorporating all desired qualities in a given product is beyond solution in many instances because of contradictory elements. The most economical automobile does not possess the greatest pickup and speed. The following quotation emphasizes this point:

> One of the most important characteristics of merchandise from the point of view of its evaluation arises from the fact that certain product virtues are antagonistic if not directly contradictory; if a product is "best" in one respect, it commonly follows that the product cannot be best in some other respects. The breaking strengths of textiles increase up to a point as the number of threads per inch is increased, but air premeability, on the other hand, is lowered. Those soaps and cleansers that loosen dirt most quickly and easily cannot be the gentlest in their action. The most effective insect poison may not be the safest to use under conditions in which children and pets must be considered. No one blanket can combine the virtues of maximum warmth, maximum strength, and minimum weight. Those bath towels which absorb water most rapidly are not the ones which can absorb the greatest quantity of water, nor are they the strongest. No one paint can possess the special virtues of a flat finish and an enamel finish. The sheerest silk stockings cannot give the longest wear. Doors that open to the right cannot open to the left.[5]

While these antagonistic elements are present in many instances, the manufacturer can attempt to determine the qualities most definitely desired and concentrate emphasis on those factors. This is illustrated by the practice of the American Writing Paper Company. In making each type of paper, this manufacturer analyzes the requirements of the paper user. The following questions are asked and answered in connection with each type of paper:

---

[5] Mabel T. Gragg and Neil H. Borden, *Merchandise Testing as a Guide to Consumer Buying* (Cambridge, Mass.: Harvard University Press, 1939), p. 6.

1. Must the paper be nonstretchable?
2. Is it to be water-resistant?
3. Is it to be oil-resistant?
4. Is it to be chemical-resistant?
5. Is the color to be permanent or fugitive?
6. Is it to be absorbent or nonabsorbent?
7. Is it to be dense or porous?
8. Will it have considerable handling?
9. Will it have a long life or is it only made for temporary service?[6]

By asking and answering questions of this sort before making a product, a quality in harmony with primary consumer needs can be produced. Costs are often reduced by following this procedure. Why add the cost of making a paper water-resistant when such a quality is not needed or desired?

Product differentiation

Product differentiation is the lifeblood of competitive brand advertising. To win and hold consumer preference a manufacturer seeks to incorporate desirable qualities in his product that can be clearly distinguished from his competitor's. Differentiating qualities or features may be perceivable in the product itself such as the revolving shelves in a refrigerator, or they may be imperceptible even though present in the product such as powdered eggs in a cake mix, or they may be virtually nonexistent in the product such as between some brands of cigarettes, beer, aspirin, gasoline, shortening, and instant coffee. When the product differences are imperceptible or nonexistent, the full burden of gaining consumer preference falls on pricing, packaging, advertising, and merchandising schemes.

The most effective strategy is to produce a product in which desirable and distinctive qualities are apparent to the consumer. Every effort should be exerted to do this. In competitive situations where this cannot be done differences must be found or created that can be effectively dramatized through advertising, i.e. Dial soap's "Hexachlorophene," Pepsodent toothpaste's "Irium," Shell gasoline's "TCP." The danger, of course, is that in trying to achieve product differentiation the exclusive quality may not be significant to consumers and may end up as nothing but mumbo-jumbo.

---

[6] Metropolitan Life Insurance Co., *The Use of Research in Developing Old Products and Introducing New Ones* (New York), p. 13.

Packaging

The placing of commodities in packages has been criticized by some on the ground that packaging increases the cost of the product to the consumer. From an economic viewpoint it matters not whether packaging brings about this increase; the vital element is the desire or lack of desire for packaged merchandise. Theoretical economics holds that the goal of all economic endeavor is the satisfaction of human wants whatever they may be. And practical businessmen find that, in most cases, reward is greatest by following this formula. If the consumer desires to pay more for packaged prunes, then producers and sellers of prunes should provide the packaged product.

In addition to the problem of packaging, the type of package to use is vital. Consumer needs and desires should influence the size, design, and general character of the package. Where preferences are varied many products offer the customer a choice of packaging materials, bottles or throw-away cans for soft drinks, for instance.

The size of a package should be definitely tied up with consumer buying habits. The large Bon Ami can did not prove the success hoped for, partly because the size was out of harmony with the quantity of that type of scouring powder which consumers were in the habit of buying. Size will also have an influence on the quality of the product. Certain types of breakfast food will spoil if allowed to stand any length of time. Consumers wish to purchase such items in small quantities.

Buying habits vary with changes in living conditions. The smaller family, the increase in apartment dwelling (both husband and wife often working), and the automobile have tended to encourage the purchase of many commodities—especially food—in small quantities. The 20-pound box of crackers, the gallon can of peaches, the 100-pound sack of potatoes, and the 50-pound can of lard are no longer popular with consumers.

Considerable emphasis has been placed upon the utility of packages after the contents have been used. This is a feature desired by many people. Pickles placed in jars suitable for canning, mustard in beer steins, sandwich spread in drinking glasses, and belts in cigarette boxes (Figure 10–3) are examples of the utility element. Burma Shave emphasizes this factor in the jingle, "When the jar is empty the wife begins to sing, for spices, jam, and jelly, this jar is just the thing."

An innovation in packaging might lead to the development of an entirely new product. The aerosal can led to the development of hair

FIGURE 10–3.   The utility of this belt package is quite
apparent

sprays, insect repellents, and do-it-yourself spray-on paint. An improved
polyethylene bag that withstands temperatures as high as ·250° or as low
as −100° Fahrenheit led to the development of preseasoned frozen foods
that can be cooked in the package. Lightweight, inexpensive aluminum
trays helped build the market for frozen dinners and pastries. An ingenious device for sustaining pressure in an aluminum container as its liquid
content is removed led to the development of a keg of beer that fits in
the home refrigerator. Plastic squeeze bottles hastened the entry of many
liquid detergents.

The particular needs of dealers should also be considered in the development of a package. Dealers often have limited storage space and do
not like packages that require a larger space than their actual contents
would warrant. Odd-shaped packages that will not stack well in the

warehouse, on the shelves, or in floor displays are often not desired by dealers. In the final analysis, however, the consumer is the one to choose the shape and size of the package. If he prefers an odd-shaped package, dealers will handle it.

The differentiation which a package may provide is of particular importance in the food field where a substantial part of total distribution is through self-service stores. Both the character of the container and the information printed on it are often the factors that cause the consumer to choose the product or to select one brand instead of another. In self-service outlets, all of the point-of-purchase sales burden rests with the product, its package, printed sales message, and prominence of display. It is important, therefore, to include the significant package differentiating factors in media advertising so that the association between such advertising and the displayed product will be assured.

Unit of sale

The unit of sale involves both the size of a package and the number of packages per purchase. For many years Coca-Cola found the handy carton of six 6-ounce bottles the ideal unit of sale. Recently they diversified their package line to include various combinations of 6-ounce, 12-ounce, and 16-ounce bottles of 6-, 8- and 12-unit cartons to meet the desires of people for different quantities of Coke per purchase.

There may also be a desire on the part of many consumers to purchase several packages of a product at the same time and yet be wholly satisfied with the size of the individual package. Under such conditions the size of the package should not be changed, but an attempt made to make it easy for the consumer to purchase several packages at once. Many people may run out of toothpaste or shaving cream or matches at inopportune times. This situation may be partially remedied if two units of such products were purchased at the same time. When the first one has been completely used, the other will be available for immediate use; and the consumer is prompted to replenish the supply shortly after the second unit has been opened.

A family of products may also be advantageously introduced to harmonize with consumer needs. Shaving cream, powder, and lotion may be grouped to sell as one unit. The average shaver uses all three of these items and may desire to purchase them together. Care must be taken by the producer to package each individual product in such quantities that each will be depleted at about the same time. Otherwise, after the first purchase of the combination, replacements will be made of individual items separately.

Price

The price of a commodity will be closely related to the size of package and the quality. Under some circumstances, price will be less significant than quality or size. In other instances prices will be the dominant factor and quality and/or size should be altered to fit the price. The latter is well illustrated by items sold in variety stores. Products so sold must be built to a particular price.

In the case of the Simmons innerspring mattress, quality is more vital than price. This mattress is the leader in its field even though its price is above that of many competing products. Too often manufacturers feel that price is the dominant factor in directing consumer choice. Such is not the case in many instances. No generalizations can be made, because consumer reactions will be different for individual products. The only safe procedure is to test consumer reaction to each commodity before a definite decision is made.

For some products price itself is treated as the most significant indicator of quality. One manufacturer of baby powder first put his product on the market at a price somewhat lower than the leading competitive brand. Sales lagged. Without changing the quality of his product he raised the price. Sales increased sharply. One brand of aspirin has consistently led the field at a price averaging 60 percent higher than competing brands even though all aspirin are required by law to meet U.S. Pharmacopoeia standards of quality. Apparently many people do not want to take the chance of using an inferior product when caring for the baby or their own health. They find assurance in their belief that higher price means higher quality.

Meeting changing conditions

Consumer buying motives and habits are continually changing. This fact makes it necessary for the successful businessman to keep an ever watchful eye toward changing old products or developing new ones to harmonize with changes in human desires. Producers of fashion merchandise are distinctly familiar with this fact.

The introduction and consumer acceptance of one new product will often have far-reaching effects on consumer desires. The automobile during the first decade of the 20th century made motoring togs a necessity. Goggles, coveralls, "dusters," veils for women's hats, and motoring gloves were a part of the car owner's wardrobe. When roads were improved and cars enclosed, the need for such articles was no longer felt.

The higher level of spending by people in the older age groups has made it profitable to design specifically for them. For example, the Bulova watch company started to make dials, numerals, and hands larger and the dials more contrasting on some of their watches to appeal to older people whose vision is not as good as it was when they were younger. As a result, about 5 percent of Bulova's sales are now made to that market segment.

The manufacturer can well afford to establish a product-development program to help in meeting changing conditions. Such a program should consist of three essential factors. The first is the use of consumer research to uncover new tastes, desires, and habits. This is an important part of the foundation upon which a successful new product can be built.

The second essential is the use of a research laboratory which will provide the machinery for designing and experimenting with new products or changes in old ones to harmonize with the findings of the consumer surveys. Grape-Nuts Flakes represented a new product developed through laboratory experimentation at General Foods Corporation. Jell-O was changed so that it could be prepared with warm water instead of boiling water. This latter change was largely the result of a consumer survey of cooking habits and desires. The bother of using boiling water to prepare Jell-O was great enough to encourage the General Foods laboratory to change the product so that warm water would do the job. Other companies have since come out with hot cereals specially processed so that they can be made with boiling water right in the serving dish.

The third essential to a product-development program is the use of consumer tests to determine the acceptability of the product before it is produced on a large scale. This will provide a measure of the success of the research laboratory in making a product which does harmonize with the findings from a consumer survey.

The following examples will serve to illustrate the functioning of a new product-development department. One deals with the production of a perspiration-arresting product, competitive with Odorono and Mum. This product, X, was a paste and was sold in a glass jar. The combined study of the consumer research staff and the staff of the research laboratory finally produced the product in a stick form which was easier to apply and handy to carry. The testing department discovered that consumers objected to the greasiness of the stick and did not like the appearance of the package. This resulted in further research in the laboratory. The final outcome was the production of a greaseless product put up in an attractive package. In this form it was readily accepted by the consuming public.

The method of testing used by General Foods Corporation is explained by L. W. Waters, vice president of the Corporation, as follows:

> Once we believe that a new product or a package improvement is ready for the market we choose the names of a large list of consumers. We try to make this list as nearly representative as possible of income groups, social groups and geographical groups of consumers. To this jury, we send the new product with a questionnaire and ask them to try it out in that toughest of all laboratories, the kitchen. . . .
>
> When our reports are in . . . they are gone over carefully. If they indicate that the product should be successful, we then submit it to the next test—actual marketing condition. We choose two or three markets. . . . The limits of these markets are determined by our sales territory. . . .
>
> Once a product has shown that it will be successful in the two or three markets we choose, we are then ready to spread its distribution. . . . The research and testing period is over. The product is ready to expand.[7]

In a recent year, General Food's group consumer-testers turned down three new flavors in a line of food products which had been passed by the company's own testing laboratories. As a result, none of the new flavors was introduced to the public.

Continental Can Company continually asks consumers to indicate preferences for new developments in container designs. Figure 10–4 illustrates an advertisement used to ascertain which of several types of containers were preferred.

Asking consumers what they want in a product doesn't always produce right answers. Consumer surveys have repeatedly shown a strong preference for wide-mouth catsup bottles that don't require vigorous thumping to get the catsup out. But when bottles with broad openings were placed on supermarket shelves, housewives rejected them and reached for the old narrow-mouthed bottles.

Brand image

What's in a name? Campbell's Soup, Ivory Soap, Kellogg, Listerine, Marlboro, Ford, Cadillac. These names are well known in American life, but to millions of consumers they mean much more than the mere identi-

---

[7] Lewis W. Waters, "Test—Test—Test," *Printers' Ink,* January 26, 1933, pp. 78–79.

Which is the best container for peanut butter?

one with the mar-
plus.

take familiar
ts and put them in
iliar packages—
es with a market-
us built in. Take
t butter, for ex-

mber one's a pres-
ck. It flows neatly,
n crackers. Famil-
kage number two
eally so familiar.
ear plastic that
ke glass but won't
like glass.

Number three's a
handy squeeze bottle—the
type kids love—and they
don't have to use knives.

Number four's an indi-
vidual packet for picnic or
school lunch boxes. Five's
for the big family. After

the peanut butter's gone,
you can put in cookies.

They're all part of our
experimental efforts to
give familiar products
new strength in the mar-
ketplace. At Continental
we're continually looking
for more ways like these
to make products more
attractive to buy and
easier to sell.

Which is best? We'd
like your opinion. Fill out
the coupon and we'll send
you a golden peanut tie-
tac and our thanks.

FIGURE 10–4.   How consumers help in molding the product to fit their needs or wants fication of products. Each name signifies a unique set of properties which, having been planted firmly in peoples' thoughts and feelings, combine to form a picture of the product before the "inner eye." This mental picture is referred to as the brand image. Thus, a product may be viewed as modern or old fashioned, youthful or aged, uppercrust or plebeian, feminine or masculine, distinctive or commonplace, trustworthy or questionable, etc. The image that a brand has acquired in the public mind is as important, if not more so, as any tangible attributes of the product in spelling the difference between consumer acceptance and rejection.

How is the brand image created? Through the product's design, its package, its brand name, its color, the media in which it is advertised, the television or radio shows with which it is identified, the content and style of its advertisements including pictures, layout, type faces, and art forms. These are the elements that have to be changed if the brand image has serious flaws that have been hurting sales. For example, after the makers of Marlboro cigarettes decided that the image of their product was too weak and feminine, they changed the design of their package from a nondescript white tone to a bold red and white flip-top box and embarked on a campaign featuring close-up photographs of virile he-men with tattoos on their hands. The strength of the new image was reflected in booming sales.

The ideal brand image is distinctive, one that gives a product stature in competition, one that is appropriate for the product and its market, and one that can be sustained over a period of years. A function of product analysis is to tell the advertiser how well the image of his brand meets these standards.

What to consider in consumer testing

As much care should be exercised in testing products in the consumer laboratory as in running tests in the physical, or factory, laboratory. Matilda White points out that, ideally, consumer laboratory tests should meet the following four basic criteria:

1. They should be made under conditions approximating those of normal sale and use.
2. They should focus attention on the potential market.
3. They should, wherever possible, isolate each of the many factors involved in acceptance, so that each feature of the product may be evaluated individually.
4. They should provide adequate controls, usually by testing products in pairs.[8]

---

[8] Matilda White, "Ideal Conditions for Product Testing," *Journal of Marketing* (July, 1946), p. 55.

The foregoing criteria were met by a flour mill after World War II, when all millers were forced to mill more bran into flour than previously. This higher extraction of flour from wheat produced a darker product and particularly influenced the acceptability of items like pancake flour and cake flour.

In order to determine consumer reaction to a pancake mix made from the new flour, the company supplied a carefully selected group of housewives with two packages of pancake flour, marked "A" and "B." One package contained the new flour; and the other, the former white flour. Each housewife was asked to bake an equal number of pancakes from each package and serve one of each simultaneously to each member of the family. Forms were supplied on which reactions were to be recorded for each person. Results of this test were used to guide management in deciding whether to offer the new flour under the old familiar brand name, under a new name, or not offer it at all.

It should be noted that this test was designed to measure taste preferences. Where a number of factors are to be considered—such as taste, appearance of package, size of package, and price—better results will be secured by testing each factor separately and testing the new against a package whose performance is already known.

Advertising agency and product analysis

Agencies are including in their operations an analysis of the product to be advertised. Some agencies are very thorough in their analysis, while others are superficial or make no particular study at all. The following checklist is composed of questions taken from lists in use by a number of advertising agencies. It can be used as a check against the completeness of any analysis of a product before the preparation of an advertising campaign.

1. Is the product a convenience, shopping, semispecialty, or specialty good?
2. Does classification in this respect vary in different parts of the country or in different types of cities or communities?
3. If a line, how does the variety in sizes, models, or colors compare with that offered by competing lines?
4. Is the product a familiar or an unfamiliar one? With different types of users? In different parts of the country?
5. To what wants is its appeal strongest?
   Maintain health
   Restore health

Attract opposite sex
Be great—physically, mentally, financially
Parental love
Acquisition
Construction
Protect dependents
Protect property
Save money
Superior technical performance
Play
Social success

6. Is it a utility, a luxury, or in-between? To what extent is it a utility to some people and a luxury to others?
7. If a utility, can it be given style?
8. If a luxury, how can it be brought within the reach of, or made more desirable to, a greater number of people?
9. What are major uses?
10. What are its minor uses?
11. Is the product perishable, semiperishable, or nonperishable?
12. To what extent is the product used by
Males
Females
Adults
Adolescents
Boys
Girls
Infants
13. What has been done to make the product more attractive to age or sex groups not now using it?
14. Which uses offer the greatest service to the consumer?
15. Which uses result in the most rapid consumption of the product? The slowest consumption?
16. Which uses entail the most frequent use of the product? The most infrequent?
17. Which customs, fashions, or habits help to increase consumption?
18. Which customs, fashions, or habits cause resistance to the product?
19. Are competing products quite similar to this one?
20. Are competing products chiefly trademarked or untrademarked?
21. Would minor changes open up new markets without interfering with old ones?

22. How does the product compare (for the money) with competitors' in quantity, quality, and price?
23. Can the wholesaler and retailer satisfactorily demonstrate or explain the use of the product?
24. Is the quality of the product advancing or declining?
25. Is the product advancing or declining in price?
26. Will the product resist spoilage due to wear and tear incident to demonstration, handling by clerk, exposure to light, heat, cold, dampness, or changes in climate?
27. Is the quality (or value) hidden or obvious to consumer, retailer, wholesaler?
28. Do second-class competitive goods so closely resemble these that substitution is easy?
29. Does the design suggest quality, efficiency, superiority, equality or the lack of it in comparison with competing products?
30. Is the unit of sale large enough to give the first-time purchaser an adequate demonstration of the value of the product?
31. Would a larger or smaller unit of sale open up new markets?
32. Is the product associated with innovations which failed or were removed for other reasons?
33. Has the price fluctuated to an extent that may have made consumer or trade suspicious as to quality, or fairness of price?
34. Is there any gossip or misconception about the product which operates against it?
35. To what extent do expert users favor this particular product as against competing goods?

Conclusion

From an advertising viewpoint, product analysis is valuable only to the extent that it can be of use in developing a more effective campaign or message to the consuming public. It has been pointed out that the essence of successful advertising is the interpretation of a product to the prospective buyer in terms of the ability of the commodity to satisfy the prospect's desire. A thorough knowledge of the product and its various characteristics is essential if this interpretation is to be effective.

QUESTIONS AND PROBLEMS

1. Is it economically and socially sound to redesign packages so as to make them more attractive without improving the product, and to charge and secure a higher price for the product because of such changes?

2. How might the construction of umbrellas be changed to improve their utility to, or acceptability by, the college student?

3. Do you believe that any change in men's hats would increase their use by college students? Why?

4. Why has the use of color increased the sale of many consumers' goods?

5. How might education influence the demand for various types of furniture?

6. Do you believe that consumers would readily accept an automobile that would last twice as long as those now on the market, assuming the cost to be 25 percent higher? Why?

7. Cite three cases other than those in this chapter where a change in package design has increased consumer acceptance of the product.

8. Why are most cigarettes sold in packages of 20? Cigars singly?

9. Clip representative advertisements for two competing brands in one of the following product fields: gasoline, toothpaste, toilet soap, instant coffee, beer. How have the two brands been differentiated through advertising?

10. The image that a brand has acquired in the public mind is as important as the qualities existing in the product itself. Explain and demonstrate with an example.

11. How may a firm test the selling value of the package which it now uses? How may it test the selling value of proposed packages?

12. How might the increasing popularity of frozen foods influence the advertising of canned foods?

13. It is reported that Gerber's Baby Foods were developed as a result of Mr. Gerber's having to prepare supper for the Gerber's baby daughter. The task of crushing freshly cooked peas through a strainer was not a pleasant one. As a result of this experience and subsequent observation of kitchen preparation of food for the baby, Gerber modified his puréeing machines at his cannery to strain vegetables for babies. He then introduced the famous Gerber's Baby Foods for the satisfaction of your mother and other mothers throughout the land.

Not all product developments follow this pattern, but this example does illustrate how new products can be developed, or old ones modified, to increase human satisfactions.

From your own experiences, or from current observations, suggest changes that might be made in at least two products of your own choice that would increase their want-satisfying ability.

14. Evaluate the advertisability of each of the following types of products in terms of Borden's conditions which tend to influence the opportunities for effective advertising:

a) fresh vegetables   *d*) fountain pens
b) sugar   *e*) chlorophyll toothpaste
c) women's dresses   *f*) college textbooks

chapter 11
MARKET
ANALYSIS

THE AMERICAN market is the sum total of the needs and desires of 208 million people dispersed with varying degrees of density over a mainland area measuring 1,600 miles by 2,700 miles, plus Alaska and Hawaii. It is made up of families living in a wide variety of climates, in cities, towns, and rural areas, with differing environments, tastes, and customs. It is ever growing and ever changing.

Within this vast, diverse, and changing market no product is consumed at the same rate everywhere. Therefore, every national advertiser—the one whose product is distributed throughout the country as well as the one whose product is confined to particular regions—must view his market as an aggregate of many individual market areas each of which is different from the next. Some markets are fertile and can be cultivated profitably. Others are barren and should not be cultivated at all.

The purpose of market analysis is to locate the fertile markets and estimate their sales potential. With this information the advertiser can then distribute his effort among various market areas in proportion to their relative sales potentiality and thereby maximize the return on his advertising investment.

Distribution of population and retail sales

There are some 18,000 incorporated cities and towns, and about four million farms in the United States. However, population and retail sales are highly concentrated. As shown in Table 11–1, about 40 percent of

213

the nation's population lives in 31 metropolitan areas. More than half of the population lives in the 69 "A," "B," and "C" markets where 57.3 percent of all retail sales are made.

TABLE 11–1. Distribution of population and retail sales by market size groups

		Percent of U.S. total	
Market size groups		Population	Retail sales
12	"A" Markets (populations of over 2 million)	26.7	29.5
19	"B" Markets (populations of 1 to 2 million)	12.8	14.2
38	"C" Markets (populations of 500,000–1 million)	13.4	13.6
183	"D" Markets (populations of 100,000–500,000)	19.6	19.4
Total:			
252	"A," "B," "C," and "D" markets	72.5	76.7

Source: *Sales Management, Survey of Buying Power 1969.*

The greatest population growth in recent years has been taking place in the suburbs, the areas immediately surrounding the larger cities. About one fifth of all Americans now live in the suburbs. Accompanying the rush to the suburbs are new shopping centers, changing leisure-time activities, and expanding markets for items such as power lawn mowers and patio furniture.

For identification purposes markets are referred to by the name of the central city: the Chicago market, the Los Angeles market, the Detroit market, etc. However, for market analysis purposes the county in which the central city is located or several contiguous counties are treated as an integral metropolitan area. To standardize the boundaries, standard metropolitan areas are defined by the Federal Committee on Metropolitan Areas. In general, each area is a county containing one or more central cities of 50,000 or more population, plus other contiguous counties that are economically and socially integrated with such central cities. For example, the Chicago metropolitan market area is composed of eight counties—Cook, Du Page, Kane, Lake, McHenry, and Will counties in Illinois; Lake and Porter counties in Indiana. There now are 299 such standard metropolitan areas.

Geographically, our population is concentrated in the states along our sea coasts and around the Great Lakes. The northeast section extending from the Mississippi River to the Atlantic coast includes 45 percent of total U.S. population and accounts for 47 percent of total retail sales. In fact, 44 percent of all retail sales are made in just six states: New York, California, Illinois, Pennsylvania, Ohio, and Texas.

The concentration of people and trade in relatively few areas is a boon to many national advertisers, especially those whose budgets are too small to permit blanket coverage of all areas in the nation. By concentrating their effort in the top 69 markets, they can register a telling impact where 57 percent of all retail sales are made. Of course, the same strategy would not be appropriate for advertisers of products that appeal primarily to people living in smaller towns and on farms, in which cases it may be advisable for the advertiser to avoid the big cities.

Regional differences

Climate is a basic reason for differences in regional buying preferences. Long wool underwear has a ready market along the Canadian border. Bathing suits are a year-round best seller in Florida. Antifreeze a "must" in Wisconsin, is of little importance in California. Air conditioners are more readily accepted where there are sustained periods of hot, humid weather. Bright colors are more generally preferred in the sunshine areas of Florida, New Mexico, Arizona, and Southern California. Grays, browns, and navy blue are more popular up north where there are fewer warm, sunny days.

Spring moves north each year and winter moves south, gradually stimulating purchase of seasonal items in first one and then another climate belt. Manufacturers of outdoor sports equipment have developed seasonal maps to guide their channeling of advertising effort into different regions at the most opportune time of year.

Regional likes and dislikes also stem from habit, custom, and the tendency of foreign-born groups to settle in certain areas. In New Orleans the preference for coffee with a lot of chicory in it is so strong that present-day coffee manufacturers have to prepare a special blend for that one area. Ladies in New York City use almost 30 times as much make-up as those living in Vermont. The Texan's wide brim hat contrasts sharply with the New Englander's narrow brim. Dry sausage sells best in the coastal and Great Lakes cities where immigrants from southern European countries tended to settle.

Regional differences in the consumption rates of several foods and beverages are highlighted in Table 11–2. Note how the ranking of regions differs for each product. The Northeast ranks first for bakery products but last for eggs. The South ranks first for flour, cereal, fats, and oils but last for bakery products. Some foods used in markedly larger quantities in certain regions than in others are:

TABLE 11–2.   Regional differences in the consumption of selected foods

Food group	Per person per week			
	Northeast	North Central	South	West
Fats, oils	.75 lb.	.78 lb.	.94 lb.	.77 lb.
Flour, cereal	1.08	1.20	1.95	1.31
Bakery products	2.58	2.38	2.13	2.20
Meat, poultry, fish	4.62	4.68	4.48	4.58
Sugar, sweets	.97	1.08	1.33	1.01
Potatoes, sweet potatoes	1.68	1.88	1.48	1.39
Other vegetables	3.50	3.33	3.81	3.73
Fruit	4.18	3.76	3.20	4.01
Soup, other mixtures	.68 lb.	.63 lb.	.46 lb.	.68 lb.
Milk, cream, cheese (calcium equivalent)	4.26 qt.	4.20 qt.	3.74 qt.	4.23 qt.
Eggs	.49 doz.	.55 doz.	.61 doz.	.58 doz.

Source: U.S. Department of Agriculture; *Food Consumption of Households in the U.S.*, July, 1968.

Northeast .... Fresh whole milk, butter, lamb, veal, shellfish, fresh fruit, fruit juice.

North Central ..... Fresh whole milk, cheese, butter, beef, pork, lunch meat, fresh white potatoes, commercially canned fruit, commercially frozen fruit.

South .... Evaporated milk, lard, vegetable shortening, pork, chicken, fish, sweet potatoes, rice, cornmeal, hominy grits, self-rising flour, syrup and molasses.

West .... Skim milk, cheese, beef, fresh fruit, commercially canned fruit, dried fruit.

It is not enough for a national advertiser to note that his sales are higher or lower in some regions than in others. He should seek to learn the underlying causes. If he finds that climate or other persistent environmental factors beyond his control account for these differences, he is in a better position to segregate barren from fruitful markets and to direct his advertising effort accordingly.

The farm market

The concentration of consumers in urban areas might lead one to underestimate the importance of the farm market. Even though they are widely scattered geographically, there are approximately 2,683,000 farm families in the United States. They have an average net income of $5,086 with which they are buying products much the same as those their city cousins buy.[1] In addition, farmers are a primary market for many production items such as feeds, seeds, fertilizers, tractors, combines, corn pickers, and milking machines.

The proportion of our population living on farms continues to decline. Twenty years ago one out of four persons lived on a farm. Today it is only 1 out of 18. However, this decline in numbers is more than offset by growing productivity and income. Marginal or inefficient farmers are being attracted into other industries. Their acreage is being absorbed by bigger farmers who, with greater mechanization and better farming methods, are able to produce more than enough food and raw materials for industry. As a result, today's fewer farm families represent a greater market potential for advertised products than did their more numerous predecessors.

Although they produce a substantial portion of their own food supply, farm families are good prospects for most branded food items. One study of food purchasing habits of city and farm families indicated that the average farm family spends more money on processed foods such as flour, sugar, cereals, butter, and cheese than does the average city family. More meals served at home to bigger families with bigger appetites are factors that explain the greater food consumption per farm family. The only items for which city family purchases were reported to be materially greater were meat, poultry, milk, eggs, and fresh vegetables.

The farm market, like any other, varies in purchasing power and sales potential. For example, eight midwest states (Indiana, Illinois, Wisconsin, Iowa, Minnesota, Nebraska, South Dakota and North Dakota) include one fifth of the United States farms and produce one third of the nation's agricultural income. The ranking and characteristics of other farm regions can be ascertained from the Census of Agriculture which includes data on practically all significant dimensions of farming. With this information the advertiser can single out the key farm market areas where he will be able to reap profitable sales.

Shifts in area potential

Markets are dynamic and ever changing. The Middle Atlantic and Great Lakes states have for decades represented the more fertile markets; but the last several years have seen a marked increase in the relative fertility of the Pacific, West South Central, and South Atlantic regions.

---

[1] *Statistical Abstract of the United States,* 1969.

The Pacific region continues to lead the nation in population growth with an increase of 7.2 percent between 1964 and 1968. Reflecting a rapid rate of industrial growth and retirement living, per capita income in the West South Central region increased 43.6 percent compared with an increase of 36.4 percent for the nation as a whole. The advertiser who notes such shifts in market potential will generally have a distinct advantage over his less observant competitor. Regional gains in population and per capita income are shown in Figure 11–1.

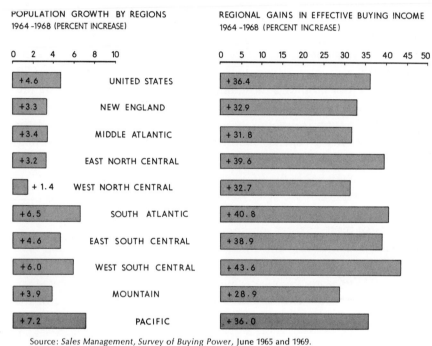

POPULATION GROWTH BY REGIONS
1964 -1968 (PERCENT INCREASE)

REGIONAL GAINS IN EFFECTIVE BUYING INCOME
1964 -1968 (PERCENT INCREASE)

+4.6 UNITED STATES	+36.4
+3.3 NEW ENGLAND	+32.9
+3.4 MIDDLE ATLANTIC	+31.8
+3.2 EAST NORTH CENTRAL	+39.6
+1.4 WEST NORTH CENTRAL	+32.7
+6.5 SOUTH ATLANTIC	+40.8
+4.6 EAST SOUTH CENTRAL	+38.9
+6.0 WEST SOUTH CENTRAL	+43.6
+3.9 MOUNTAIN	+28.9
+7.2 PACIFIC	+36.0

Source: *Sales Management, Survey of Buying Power,* June 1965 and 1969.

FIGURE 11–1.   Regional variations in market growth

Sales potentials

Sales potential is an estimate of a market's capacity to buy a given commodity. The estimate reflects economic resources of an area and indicates the scope of sales opportunity, not the actual volume of sales that will be achieved. Stated in physical units, or dollar volume, or percentages, sales potentials provide a quantitative basis for adapting advertising strategy to the different sales opportunities presented by various market areas.

Sales potentials are especially useful for allocating advertising effort and selecting media.

Allocation of advertising effort. Two fundamental questions that the planner of national advertising strategy must decide upon are: To which markets should advertising be directed? How much should be spent in each market? Decisions on both of these questions should be based on sales potentials.

By ranking markets according to their respective sales potentials and selecting in rank order the number of markets to be cultivated, the advertiser will be more certain of concentrating his effort in the most promising areas. By aligning his expenditures with sales potentials he will improve his chances of realizing a maximum sales yield on his advertising investment. To illustrate, let's assume sales potentials of $100,000 in market A and $50,000 in market B. These figures do not tell the advertiser how much to spend in each market, but they do indicate that he should spend roughly twice as much in A as in B. The practice of concentrating effort in the more productive markets and balancing expenditures against potential is now generally accepted advertising strategy.

However, sales potentials should *not* be used as the only basis for allocating advertising effort.[2] They do not allow for differences among markets with respect to competition, product distribution, and merchandising support, all of which have an appreciable influence on the sales that any one advertiser can achieve. It may be advisable to spend less than the potential would warrant in a market where a competitor is solidly entrenched, or where the product is not available in enough retail stores, or where there is a lack of aggressive merchandising by dealers and distributors. Judgment still must play an important part when deciding where to advertise and how much to spend in each place.

Media selection. To deliver the required amount of impact in target areas the advertiser selects media that circulate in line with sales potentials. If he plans to use locally distributed media such as newspapers, his decision to advertise in a given market is tantamount to selecting one or more of the mediums located there. If he plans to use nationally distributed media such as magazines, he examines the coverage each medium has in various markets and selects those mediums that cover his

---

[2] Sales potentials can be estimated for a variety of product groupings—total retail sales of all products, or industry sales *(coffee)*, or product type sales *(instant coffee)*. The last mentioned is the most common potential used—a product type narrowed down to where the next finer classification would be a *brand*. An estimate of prospective sales for a brand is generally referred to as a brand sales forecast.

target areas most effectively. For example, an advertiser of baking powder, sales of which are concentrated south of the Mason-Dixon Line, would select magazines that circulate mostly in the South.

DETERMINING SALES POTENTIALS

Firm's sales records

It would appear that a firm's sales broken down by market areas would indicate the relative sales potential of each area. If year after year a firm's sales in market X have been about 20 percent higher than in market Y, it would seem that market X has a potential about 20 percent greater than Y's. This may be so, but it would be coincidental. A firm's sales reflect the influence of many factors other than a market's capacity to consume. Competition, distribution, dealer support, personal selling, advertising, brand acceptance, and responsiveness to promotional effort—all of these factors affect sales and they differ from market to market. Their influence may be great enough to offset a difference in potentials with the result that lower sales may be registered in a market having a higher potential.

Then, too, a firm's sales represent past performance. They do not show what might be accomplished in the future with a new marketing mix. Therefore, a firm's sales are inadequate for estimating the relative potentials of various markets.

Industry sales data

In some industries the trade association compiles total industry sales data from reports submitted by its members. These data, broken down by market areas, give the composite experience of competitors and therefore are better suited for estimating potentials than are the sales of any one firm. Examples are the data reported by the Radio and Television Manufacturer's Association and the National Electrical Manufacturer's Association.

Industry data are subject to several limitations. Different firms are apt to report sales for territories of different sizes which would either produce inaccuracies in the compilation or result in a breakdown by only states and regions. Also, the data are restricted to past performance. Perhaps a total industry's performance measured up to potential better in some places than in others.

Census of retail trade

The most authoritative and extensive inventory of consumer purchases is that made by the United States Bureau of the Census. Census retail figures show total sales made by each of 11 major kinds of retail business. These 11 business groups are further broken down into 66 business classifications in terms of the kind of merchandise sold. Thus, data are presented for nine different kinds of business in the apparel group: namely, men's furnishings stores, men's clothing-furnishings stores, family clothing stores, women's ready-to-wear stores, furriers and fur shops, millinery stores, custom tailors, accessories, other apparel stores, and shoe stores. The other ten major groups are similarly broken down.

Census figures, therefore, present a rather detailed inventory of consumer purchases in broad classifications. It would, of course, be more valuable if figures were available showing, not only total sales of shoe stores, but also sales of each type of shoes—size, price, men's or women's, boys' or girls', sport or dress, etc. On the other hand, total sales by shoe stores provide the manufacturer with some measure of the total market for shoes and afford a base from which more detailed studies might be made through private initiative.

One of the outstanding values of the census material is to be found in its detailed territorial breakdown. Data for each of the 66 kinds of retail business are presented for each of the 50 states, the District of Columbia, and standard metropolitan areas. Data for the 11 major kinds of business are given by counties and towns of 2,500 population or over. Thus, the businessman can acquaint himself with the character of consumer purchases in Ohio as compared with California or the entire nation. Or he may make similar comparisons between Cleveland and Pittsburgh, Chicago and Los Angeles, Marion County and Brown County, Podunk and Riverside.

Sales management's survey of buying power

To provide up-to-date market data during the interval between censuses, *Sales Management* magazine projects census bench mark figures and publishes current estimates in their annual *Survey of Buying Power*. For every city with retail sales of $15 million or more, every county, and every metropolitan area, the *Survey of Buying Power* presents current estimates of population, effective buying income (personal income after taxes), total retail sales, and retail sales by nine store groups. Figure 11–2 shows how these estimates are published for convenient reference. To check the accuracy of their retail sales estimates *Sales Management* compared their estimates with the 1963 Census of Retail Trade and

CALIFORNIA

POPULATION— SM ESTIMATES, 12/31/69

METRO. AREA / County	Total (thou-sands)	% of U.S.A.	% White	% Male	Age Groups								House-holds (thou-sands)	Age of Household Head						Urban Pop. (thou-sands)
					0-5 Yrs.	6-11 Yrs.	12-17 Yrs.	18-24 Yrs.	25-34 Yrs.	35-49 Yrs.	50-64 Yrs.	65 & Over		Under 25 Yrs.	25-34 Yrs.	35-44 Yrs.	45-54 Yrs.	55-64 Yrs.	65 & Over	
ANAHEIM-SANTA ANA-GARDEN GROVE																				
Orange	1,374.8	.6757	98.7	49.4	15.6	13.8	12.4	11.7	10.0	19.1	11.4	6.0	415.5	13.3	16.2	23.4	21.2	14.0	11.9	1,260.9
BAKERSFIELD Kern	341.5	.1678	92.7	50.6	11.0	13.1	12.5	12.9	12.2	17.3	13.8	7.2	104.5	13.9	17.6	18.3	20.1	16.3	13.8	236.9
FRESNO Fresno	425.5	.2091	91.9	49.9	11.3	12.7	12.2	12.9	12.4	17.0	13.5	8.0	129.8	11.7	17.2	18.7	20.0	16.2	16.2	292.3
LOS ANGELES-LONG BEACH																				
Los Angeles	7,055.9	3.4676	87.5	48.6	11.0	11.9	11.0	10.8	11.3	18.9	15.5	9.6	2,474.7	9.8	15.9	19.4	20.7	17.0	17.2	6,962.2
Los Angeles Consolidated Area	*8,430.7*	*4.1433*	*89.3*	*48.7*	*11.8*	*12.2*	*11.2*	*10.9*	*11.1*	*19.0*	*14.8*	*9.0*	*2,890.2*	*10.3*	*15.9*	*20.0*	*20.8*	*16.6*	*16.4*	*8,223.1*
△MODESTO Stanislaus	196.0	.0964	98.7	49.3	11.1	11.8	11.4	12.6	11.9	16.1	14.8	10.3	62.9	11.5	16.3	17.1	17.7	17.4	20.0	111.9
OXNARD-VENTURA Ventura	370.2	.1819	96.9	51.5	15.6	13.3	11.2	11.0	12.0	17.8	12.1	7.0	105.7	9.8	19.6	23.3	20.6	14.1	12.6	216.8
SACRAMENTO	803.6	.3949	92.1	50.5	11.1	13.1	12.0	11.8	11.4	18.4	14.0	7.8	252.6	11.9	17.2	20.4	20.7	16.1	13.7	636.5
Placer	79.7	.0391	96.4	50.6	10.7	11.2	10.9	11.7	11.1	16.6	16.1	11.8	24.8	10.9	15.2	18.3	19.7	16.2	19.7	31.1
Sacramento	636.3	.3127	91.0	50.4	11.1	13.2	12.2	11.9	11.3	19.1	13.8	7.3	200.6	12.1	16.9	20.7	21.2	16.2	12.9	544.0
Yolo	87.6	.0431	96.5	51.5	11.8	13.0	11.8	11.4	12.8	17.8	13.5	7.7	27.2	11.3	20.5	20.5	17.9	15.6	14.2	61.4

CALIFORNIA   EFFECTIVE BUYING INCOME & CASH INCOME SM ESTIMATES, 1969

METRO. AREA / County	Net E.B.I. ($000)	% of U.S.A.	Per Cap-ita	Per Hsld.	Net Cash Income ($000)	Cash Income Breakdown												
						$0-2,999		$3,000-4,999		$5,000-7,999		$8,000-9,999		$10-15,000		$15-25,000		Over $25,000
						Hslds.	Inc.	Hslds.	Inc.	Hslds.	Inc.	Hslds.	Inc.	Hslds.	Inc.	Hslds.	Inc.	Hslds. Inc.
ANAHEIM-SANTA ANA-GARDEN GROVE																		
Orange	4,831,933	.7716	3,515	11,629	4,488,932	12.2	1.6	9.2	3.5	20.5	12.8	17.3	14.3	24.2	26.8	12.5	21.9	4.1 19.1
BAKERSFIELD Kern	1,007,472	.1609	2,950	9,641	936,878	17.5	2.8	12.8	5.8	23.5	17.4	16.3	16.2	18.6	24.8	8.6	18.0	2.7 15.0
FRESNO Fresno	1,143,918	.1827	2,688	8,813	1,057,650	21.4	3.8	15.2	7.5	25.1	20.2	14.4	15.7	14.5	21.2	6.8	15.6	2.6 16.0
LOS ANGELES-LONG BEACH																		
Los Angeles	27,370,534	4.3707	3,879	11,060	25,621,249	15.8	2.2	10.6	4.1	21.2	13.5	15.4	13.3	21.2	24.5	11.5	21.1	4.3 21.3
Los Angeles Consolidated Area	*32,202,467*	*5.1423*	*3,820*	*11,142*	*30,110,181*	*15.2*	*2.1*	*10.4*	*4.0*	*21.1*	*13.4*	*15.7*	*13.6*	*21.4*	*24.8*	*11.7*	*21.2*	*4.3 20.9*
△MODESTO Stanislaus	567,775	.0906	2,897	9,027	519,837	22.5	3.9	14.1	6.8	22.9	18.1	14.7	15.9	16.5	23.8	6.7	15.3	2.6 16.2
OXNARD-VENTURA Ventura	1,108,005	.1769	2,993	10,483	964,736	17.7	2.8	13.2	5.3	23.1	16.6	17.0	16.7	18.8	24.7	9.1	18.8	2.7 15.3
SACRAMENTO	2,634,827	.4209	3,279	10,431	2,418,326	14.3	2.2	10.7	4.6	24.3	16.9	17.4	16.2	20.4	25.5	10.1	19.9	2.8 14.7
Placer	235,056	.0376	2,949	9,478	206,541	16.6	2.9	12.6	6.1	28.5	22.7	17.2	18.5	16.3	23.3	7.0	15.8	1.8 10.7
Sacramento	2,141,393	.3420	3,365	10,675	1,978,163	13.8	2.0	10.1	4.2	23.5	15.9	17.5	15.8	21.3	25.9	10.8	20.7	3.0 15.5
Yolo	258,378	.0413	2,950	9,499	233,622	15.5	2.7	13.1	6.3	27.8	21.2	16.5	17.2	17.6	24.5	7.6	16.7	1.9 11.4

CALIFORNIA   RETAIL SALES— SM ESTIMATES, 1969   SALES— ADVG. INDEXES

METRO. AREA / County	Total Retail Sales ($000)	% of U.S.A.	Food		Eating & Drink. Places Total ($000)	General Merchandise		Apparel Total ($000)	Furn.- House-Appl. Total ($000)	Auto-motive Total ($000)	Gas Station Total ($000)	Lumber-Bldg.-Hdwre. Total ($000)	Drug Total ($000)	Sls. Ac-tiv-ity	Buy-ing Power	Qual-ity
			Total ($000)	Super-markets ($000)		Total ($000)	Dept. Stores ($000)									
ANAHEIM-SANTA ANA-GARDEN GROVE																
Orange	2,789,530	.8020	635,438	571,410	261,385	568,287	451,530	107,983	127,594	491,658	213,697	89,573	112,007	119	.7616	113
BAKERSFIELD Kern	595,041	.1711	127,473	97,856	48,099	87,613	61,062	21,603	24,597	109,489	59,706	40,369	22,359	102	.1654	99
FRESNO Fresno	763,838	.2196	165,548	126,953	54,584	97,025	71,963	39,755	42,335	136,384	66,278	47,041	36,588	105	.1990	95
LOS ANGELES-LONG BEACH																
Los Angeles	14,092,328	4.0518	3,001,044	2,747,181	1,315,459	2,612,843	1,893,820	777,618	681,982	2,676,385	975,818	336,353	567,716	117	4.0944	118
Los Angeles Consolidated Area	*16,881,858*	*4.8538*	*3,636,482*	*3,318,591*	*1,576,844*	*3,181,130*	*2,345,350*	*885,601*	*809,576*	*3,168,043*	*1,189,515*	*425,926*	*679,723*	*117*	*4.8560*	*117*
△MODESTO Stanislaus	402,120	.1156	79,155	64,558	23,885	56,411	34,992	16,799	19,257	72,403	31,764	30,657	19,642	120	.0993	103
OXNARD-VENTURA Ventura	618,242	.1777	162,574	139,996	45,595	98,406	64,256	24,186	117,901	52,245	26,032	28,020	98	118	.1781	98
SACRAMENTO	1,500,503	.4315	342,529	291,395	129,883	215,075	159,958	71,594	78,825	303,661	126,286	57,191	75,614	109	.4189	106
Placer	161,992	.0466	42,371	30,204	16,960	8,213	1,157	5,692	5,301	39,019	19,667	6,463	5,279	119	.0406	104
Sacramento	1,204,403	.3463	267,297	232,652	100,869	201,257	158,801	59,657	70,329	236,133	91,507	39,229	63,745	111	.3374	108
Yolo	134,108	.0386	32,861	26,739	12,054	5,605		6,245	3,195	28,454	15,112	11,499	6,590	90	.0409	95

FIGURE 11–2.   Market data available in *Sales Management's Survey of Buying Power*

found their average error to be 2 percent for regions, 2.7 percent for states, and 4 percent for metropolitan areas. These margins of error are sufficiently small to indicate that the magazine's estimates are adequate for most practical purposes. As a result, the *Survey of Buying Power* is the most widely used single source of current data for keeping abreast of rapidly changing American markets.

Sample audit of retail sales

A number of private firms operate to provide continuing information of sales of specific commodities by certain types of retail outlets. The most extensive operation in this field is that of the A. C. Nielsen Company. This organization selects a sample of food and drugstores in the United States that are reasonably representative of the total. Through field representatives, bimonthly audits of food and drug items by brand and package size are made to determine the number of packages of each item that moved out of these stores to consumers.

From such data it is easy to secure a fairly accurate picture of the total amount of coffee, ready-to-eat cereal, flour, toothpaste, and similar commodities sold during a given period. In addition, sales are classified by individual brands, which thus enables individual advertisers to determine their own as well as their competitors' position in the market. This type of analysis is illustrated in Figure 11–3.

Regular bimonthly reports of the Nielsen Retail Index are available for each of nine districts: New England, Metropolitan New York, Middle Atlantic, East Central, Metropolitan Chicago, West Central, Southeast, Southwest, and Pacific. In addition, a client may order special area breakdowns to parallel his own sales districts. Nielsen data yield ten types of information:

1. Sales to consumers.
2. Purchases by retailers.
3. Retail inventories.
4. Day's supply.
5. Distribution—number of stores carrying the brand weighted for store importance.
6. Out-of-stock—percentage of stores regularly carrying brand who do not have it in stock at time of audit.
7. Prices—wholesale and retail.
8. Special factory packs.
9. Dealer support—displays, local advertising, coupon redemptions.

10. Special observations—order size, reorders, and direct versus wholesale purchases.

With such information a manufacturer can effectively plan, control,
and evaluate his marketing and advertising effort, and at the same time
keep a watchful eye on his competitors' activities.

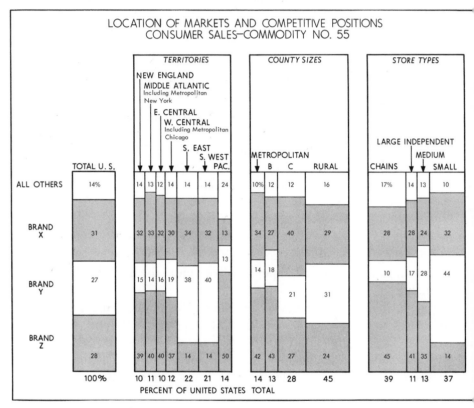

FIGURE 11–3. Market outlines of three competitive brands

Consumer panel reports

Another approach to a measure of consumer purchases is to ask consumers to report actual purchases of specified items. The more common
procedure is to select a sample of families that is reasonably representative of the market or markets to be studied. These families are asked to
serve on a continuing basis and to supply detailed information about
their purchases of various commodities. Such families are usually compensated in some manner for serving on the panel of "reporters."

Panel members are ordinarily supplied with forms or "diaries" on which all purchases are to be recorded as they are made. A copy of such a form used by one research firm is reproduced in Figure 11–4. This particular diary called for a record of purchases of only ten commodity groups. The same type of diary could be used for any number of items. Some panels provide purchase data for all groceries, household supplies, and drugs.

The organization that has perhaps done the most work with consumer panels is the Market Research Corporation of America. This company operates primarily on a national and broad regional basis and provides about the same kind of geographical breakdown of data as that provided by the A. C. Nielsen Company.

Form No. 2

Use this Form No. 2 for recording your day-to-day purchases from _March 19_ to _April 1_, inclusive. Report purchases of following products only:

1. Loaf Bread (white, rye, whole wheat, etc.)
2. Coffee and Tea
3. Cereal (hot and cold)
4. Baked Beans (pork and beans, Boston baked, etc.)
5. Macaroni, Spaghetti, and Noodles (all types--packaged and canned)
6. Flour & Flour Mixes (Regular, pastry gingerbread, biscuit, pancake, etc.)
7. Soda Crackers
8. Soft Drinks (ginger ale, colas, pop, root beer, soda water)
9. Soap (packaged, toilet, and laundry)
10. Laundry Items (starch, bluing, softeners, scouring powder, etc.)

Date of Purchase		KIND OF PRODUCT (Include cash and charge purchases from all sources; any store, mail order, home delivery, huckster, etc.)	BRAND NAME (If Any)	Do Not Write Here	Number of Units Bought	Size or Weight of Units	TOTAL PRICE PAID	WHERE PURCHASED (Name of Store)
Day of Week	Day of Month							
		USE OTHER SIDE IF NEEDED						

Signature of panel member.

Street Address.

City and State.

FIGURE 11–4. Sample diary form used by consumer panel members for reporting purchases

The consumer panel approach, however, will give a more detailed classification of the kinds of people who buy specific types of goods and the amounts purchased by each consumer group. This is made possible from detailed personal data obtained from each panel member. Personal data can include such factors as age, size of family, education, income, religion, nationality, and occupation. Markets can thus be evaluated in terms of both geography and consumer groups. In addition, the relative number of persons in any group that uses the commodity can be determined.

When members of a consumer panel are representative of the market to be studied, commodity purchase data can be projected for the entire market. This provides a means of establishing an overall potential for each area for which separate information is available, as well as a potential for individual brands. Consumer panel data can be used to modify census figures in the same manner that data from a sample audit of retail stores can be so applied.

This method is also applicable to local markets. Because of cost, there has not been wide application on a local basis. Various agencies have experimented with local consumer panels. Included in this group are the *Chicago Tribune* and the *Cleveland Press*. Perhaps the future will see much greater use of this method at the local level. Additional reference will be made to the use of local panels in connection with testing the sales effectiveness of advertising (Chapter 27).

Home inventories

Another method of gathering information about consumer purchases is the home inventory. Newspapers have been most active in utilizing this type of study. One of the early pioneers in this has been the *Milwaukee Journal*. The *Journal* method consists of mailing a confidential questionnaire to a large number of housewives whose names have been selected at random from city and suburban directories.

The questionnaire used is not a diary, but rather a form which asks such questions as: "Do you buy muffin mix? _____"; "What brand? _____"; "Do you smoke cigarettes? _____"; "What brand are you NOW smoking? _____." Sample pages of the questionnaire used by the *Milwaukee Journal* are shown in Figures 11–5 and 11–6. Questionnaires are completed and returned to the newspaper, where tabulations are made and results summarized for the use of advertisers in evaluating the local market. Summary information in general shows the relative number of families using a particular product, total number of brands in use, relative rating of brand preferences, and relative number of users by income groups.

A modification of the mail-questionnaire approach consists in using personal interviewers who call on a representative list of families and actually check, with the aid of the housewife, the pantry shelves to determine what items are stocked. In some instances, attempts are made to de-

CONFIDENTIAL QUESTIONNAIRE

For a survey relating to the needs and purchases
of Greater Milwaukee families to be compiled by

THE MILWAUKEE JOURNAL

FIRST BY MERIT

Dear Madam:

A VERY LARGE SHOPPING BAG FILLED WITH PACKAGES OF WELL KNOWN
GROCERY ITEMS IS YOURS FREE *for filling in this questionnaire.*

*In order to secure this bag of grocery products you must answer the questions herein and
have your husband or the man of the house answer those questions regarding his purchases. All replies are confidential and names are not released for any purpose.*

*You must be honest in your answers and personally bring the questionnaire to the Sur-
vey Department of The Milwaukee Journal, located on the first floor of THE JOURNAL
BUILDING, AT NORTH FOURTH AND WEST STATE STREETS, on or before the
day and date printed below.*

*This bag will be filled to overcapacity. So if you have an additional sturdy bag used for
your regular shopping, be sure to bring it along.*

*The questionnaire applies only to family groups maintaining a household, and will not
be accepted from an individual living in a boarding or rooming house who does not
maintain such separate household. Your co-operation will be appreciated.*

THE MILWAUKEE JOURNAL
SURVEY DEPARTMENT

PLEASE READ THESE

INSTRUCTIONS

1. Each major question should be answered YES or NO with an "X" or other checkmark. If
your answer to the main question is NO, do not answer any of the subquestions which follow
and which apply to main questions.
2. PLEASE do not guess in answering this questionnaire. LOOK UP THE BRAND NAME
if you don't remember it. List only brands you actually use.
3. Return your questionnaire early and get it checked quickly.
4. Do not return this questionnaire by mail.
5. Do not send children with this questionnaire.
6. *Please write plainly.* Use ink or typewriter if possible.
7. *If you use more than one brand of any product, list the brand you use most frequently unless
otherwise instructed.*

You will receive a large shopping bag of grocery products if you fill in
this questionnaire and bring it to The Journal building no later than

Name_____
(You need not sign your name, but your address is essential)

Street Address_____

City, Town or Village_____

Telephone No._____

The Survey Office Hours are 9:00 a.m. to 8:00 p.m.

FIGURE 11–5. Example of covering instructions (first page) of home inventory
questionnaire

termine the length of time items found on the shelves have been there. Such information can be summarized to show the relative number of families that stock a particular type of commodity and the relative position of individual brands carried in the householders' inventory. Since

Do you buy rye bread?	☐ YES ☐ NO	BRAND
Do you buy macaroni products?	☐ YES ☐ NO	BRAND
Do you buy regular white bread?	☐ YES ☐ NO	BRAND
Do you own a dog?	☐ YES ☐ NO	
Do you buy liver sausage?	☐ YES ☐ NO	
Do you buy prepared dog food?	☐ YES ☐ NO	
Do you ask for any certain manufacturer's brand?	☐ YES ☐ NO	BRAND
☐ Canned or loaf. Brand................ ☐ Dry. Brand..............		
Do you buy pork sausages?	☐ YES ☐ NO	
Do you buy potato chips?	☐ YES ☐ NO	BRAND
Do you ask for any certain manufacturer's brand?	☐ YES ☐ NO	BRAND
Do you buy packaged cookies?	☐ YES ☐ NO	BRAND
Do you buy wieners or frankfurters?	☐ YES ☐ NO	
Do you buy fresh milk at stores?	☐ YES ☐ NO	BRAND
(Do not include canned wieners or Vienna sausage.)		
Do you ask for a certain manufacturer's brand?	☐ YES ☐ NO	BRAND
Is fresh milk delivered to your home?	☐ YES ☐ NO	BRAND
Do you buy canned luncheon meats made of spiced ham or pork?	☐ YES ☐ NO	BRAND
Do you buy canned corned beef hash?	☐ YES ☐ NO	BRAND
(Include only 12-oz. cans.)		
Do you buy canned Chinese foods?	☐ YES ☐ NO	BRAND
Do you buy ice cream?	☐ YES ☐ NO	BRAND
Do you buy fruit cocktail?	☐ YES ☐ NO	BRAND
Where do you buy this ice cream? Please check. ☐ Grocery store ☐ Drugstore ☐ Ice cream store ☐ Confectionery store ☐ Other		

QUESTIONS ON THIS PAGE TO BE ANSWERED BY THE HOUSEWIFE
Each major question must be answered Yes or No with "X" or other checkmark. Then give brand name.

Do you buy canned whole kernel corn?	☐ YES ☐ NO	BRAND
Do you buy salad or cooking oil?	☐ YES ☐ NO	BRAND
Do you buy canned cream style corn?	☐ YES ☐ NO	BRAND
Do you buy square or oblong soda crackers in packages?	☐ YES ☐ NO	Brand, not KIND
Do you buy canned cranberries of any kind?	☐ YES ☐ NO	BRAND
Do you buy paper towels?	☐ YES ☐ NO	BRAND
Do you buy fresh cranberries?	☐ YES ☐ NO	BRAND
Do you buy soft drinks for home use?	☐ YES ☐ NO	BRAND
Were any rooms in your home wallpapered in 1951?	☐ YES ☐ NO	
Do you buy soft drinks by the case?	☐ YES ☐ NO	BRAND
Do you know what brand of wallpaper was used?	☐ YES ☐ NO	BRAND
Do you buy soft drinks by the bottle?	☐ YES ☐ NO	BRAND
Where did you purchase this wallpaper? ☐ Retail store ☐ Paperhanger ☐ Interior decorator ☐ Other		
Do you buy soft drinks in 6-bottle cartons?	☐ YES ☐ NO	BRAND
Who applied the wallpaper? ☐ Yourself or member of family ☐ Paperhanger		
At what time of the year do you prefer to have wallpapering done? ☐ Spring ☐ Fall ☐ Winter ☐ Summer		
In what type of store do you usually buy soft drinks for home use? Please check ONE: ☐ Grocery Store ☐ Delicatessen ☐ Other ☐ Drugstore ☐ Beer Depot		
Are you interested in stock and bond market quotations?	☐ YES ☐ NO	
Do you read business and financial news?	☐ YES ☐ NO	
Do you (the housewife) have a paid job outside the home?	☐ YES ☐ NO	

FIGURE 11–6. Sample page of questionnaire used in home inventory method of gathering information about consumer purchases

much can be known about the families interviewed, data can be classified by such characteristics as income, occupation, age, and size.

Home inventories are helpful in analyzing the characteristics of individual markets, but they do not have so universal an application as either retail-store audit or consumer-purchase-diary data. It is not possible to use home-inventory data to determine frequency of purchase or the total potential volume for specific commodities. Without a measure of total market potential, it is not possible to determine the dollar or quantity volume secured or expected by individual brands. This materially reduces the possibility of using such data for measuring the success of advertising effort. But even with these limitations, such studies are valuable to advertisers.

Statistical index of sales potentials

The measurement of consumer purchases helps to clarify the market picture for the advertiser. It tells what people have been buying and where. It shows that sales opportunities are greater in some markets than in others. The individual advertiser, however, wants to know not only that one market offers a greater sales opportunity than another, but also *how much greater* the opportunity is. He wants to know whether he can expect 5 percent of his total sales from territory A and 23 percent from territory B. He wants to know whether he has been obtaining from each territory all the sales volume he could logically expect. Only when he has reduced market differences to a quantitative measure can he distribute his advertising appropriation effectively.

Various statistical indexes are used to quantify market potentials. Their use is based on the idea that an unknown variable (sales potential) is so closely related to a known variable (e.g., total retail sales) that differences in the size of the unknown variable from market to market can be estimated from differences in the size of the known variable.

The usual procedure is to first establish the relationship between sales of the firm's product and the index series. This can be done subjectively by relying on one's judgment, or objectively by measuring the correlation statistically. Then the index series is reduced to a percentage distribution so that the index for each market is expressed as a percentage share of the series total (100 percent) for all markets. In this way large and cumbersome figures representing a variety of units (e.g., dollars, pounds, people, gallons) are reduced to a simple common denominator for easier comparison and projection. These percentages can then be applied to the firm's estimate of total potential sales to arrive at a potential figure for each market.

A firm's sales cannot serve as a basis for an index because it is probable that some territories have been returning more and others less than the potential would warrant. Hence, some other factor or factors must be found that either have a causal relationship to the firm's sales or fluctuate with them. To establish the relationship between an outside factor and a firm's sales it is necessary to compare variations in the two series among many market areas. If variations in the outside factor closely resemble the firm's sales pattern, then that factor could be used as an index of sales potentials. Since the firm's past sales performance is used as a criterion for selecting an index, it would seem that sales potentials for various markets would be established in the same relative amounts as past sales. This is not necessarily so because an index series that resembles the sales pattern in general may still reveal specific areas that do not match.

An index composed of one series of data is referred to as a single-factor index. If several series are used it is referred to as a multiple-factor index. Both types of indexes will be reviewed in the following pages.

Single-factor indexes

Any available series of data that are reliable, that are broken down by specific market areas, and that are related to sales of the product at hand might be used as a single-factor index. Population, income, and retail sales data meet these requirements in many cases, and therefore are widely used for index purposes.

Population. People make markets. Population size is the basic factor accounting for differences in sales potentials. For some products, such as table salt, that are low-priced staples with mass appeal, sales closely follow the distribution of population. If per capita consumption is not affected by economic, social, or climatic differences, population alone would be an adequate index. However, for most products per capita consumption is affected by socioeconomic and regional conditions, and therefore varies considerably among markets. In these latter instances some other factor that incorporates significant attributes of the population should be used.

Income. Total money income (after taxes) accruing to all the people living in an area might be an appropriate indicator of potential. Such an aggregate of disposable income represents a pool of purchasing power that is tapped by all sellers of goods and services. For relatively high-priced "luxury" items it would appear that the greater the income pool, the greater will be an area's potential. However, this fails to take into account differences in how the pool is distributed among the families living there. Two markets may have about the same total income, but in one market a higher proportion of the total may be concentrated in the upper-income families, whereas in the other market it may be more evenly distributed among all families.

If a product appeals primarily to upper-income families an index based on the number of families in that group should be used. Similarly, if it appeals to middle- or lower-income groups the number of families in these groups will be most pertinent. In any event, the income distribution will be more indicative of an area's potential than aggregate income.

Retail sales. How much people are spending for goods and services is indicated by total retail sales. Such sales data reflect not only the amount of buying power in an area, but also the people's inclination to convert that power into actual purchases.

TABLE 11–3. Illustration of use of retail sales index

Market area	Total retail sales dollars (000)	Index (percent of U.S. total retail sales)	Sales potential in dollars*
Fresno	811,316	.2406	60,150
Los Angeles–Long Beach	14,342,871	4.2528	1,063,200
Sacramento	1,407,694	.4175	104,375
San Bernardino–Riverside	1,901,790	.5639	140,975
San Diego	2,234,517	.6626	165,650
San Francisco–Oakland	6,244,544	1.8515	462,875
San Jose	1,898,797	.5630	140,750

* Based on firm's anticipated sales in United States totaling $25,000,000.
Source: *Sales Management, Survey of Buying Power,* June 10, 1969, Volume 102, No. 12.

Table 11–3 illustrates how a single-factor index based only on total retail sales can be used to estimate sales potentials in seven California metropolitan market areas. Here the index is expressed as a percent of United States total. If a company's sales were confined to a particular region, say the Pacific Coast Region, the index for each market would be expressed as a percent of total retail sales in that region. Then the percentage index for each market would be larger than those appearing in Table 11–3 because a smaller total would be the 100 percent base. However, the relationship among markets would remain the same, with Los Angeles-Long Beach still having a potential about $2\frac{1}{3}$ times the potential of San Francisco-Oakland. One's own company sales by market area could be compared against the potential for purposes of evaluating the kind of job that had been done in individual markets and to guide the allocation of advertising dollars.

Total retail sales data by market areas must be considered only as a general sales index which is composed of a heterogeneous assortment of commodities. It would be merely coincidental if a firm's sales opportunities paralleled all retail sales. Some refinement may be achieved if sales by the type of store through which the company's product is distributed were used (e.g., food-store sales as an index for cake mixes). But again sales of cake mixes would be such a small fraction of total food-store sales that an index based on these data would still provide only a rough approximation of potentials.

Corollary data. If sales of a company's product for which no detailed market data are available depend on sales of another product for which data are available, the company can construct an index of sales potentials for its product from the data on the other product. For example, sales of automobile tires in a market area depend on the number of automobiles in that area. The number of automobiles can be obtained from state licensing records. Thus, automobile registrations broken down by market areas can provide an index of tire sales potentials. Obviously, the same data would be useful as an index for gasoline, motor oil, batteries, spark plugs, and other replacement parts.

Another example of useful corollary data is the number of new dwelling units for which building permits have been issued in individual localities. These figures, which are compiled and published bimonthly by the Bureau of Labor Statistics, can be used to gauge market potentials for housing materials and equipment.

Multiple-factor indexes

The indexes thus far considered have been developed from a single series of data such as population, income, or total retail sales. However, differences in market potentials are due to many factors, and indexes that combine several factors should improve the quality of estimates. Some multiple-factor indexes are designed for general application, i.e., to estimate potentials for consumer goods in general. Others are designed specifically for a given product.

The most widely used general multiple-factor index is the *Sales Management* Buying Power Index. This index is based on the number of people in a market area, their buying habits as revealed in total retail sales, and the amount of money they have to spend. It is a weighted average of three factors: (1) percent of United States Effective Buying Income × 5; percent of United States Retail Sales × 3; and percent of United States Population × 2. These percentages are multiplied by weights as indicated, the products added together, and the total divided by 10 (the sum of the weights). Computed for each city with over $15 million of retail sales and each county in the United States, the resulting index is published annually in *Sales Management, Survey of Buying Power.*

A general-purpose index of this type is convenient to use and may be adequate for those advertisers whose sales seem to follow the pattern of general buying power. It would not be adequate if sales are affected by differences in climate, customs, racial and ethnic groups. Woolen blankets have their heavy sale in the North, as do ice skates, sleds, heavy overcoats, etc. Outboard motors sell best in the Midwest where there are many lakes. Sales of rice are greater in the South. Sales of tomato paste are greater where foreign-born populations are concentrated. In these instances a special or custom-built index is needed.

The individual advertiser constructing his own special-purpose index is confronted with two basic problems: First, he must select those factors which explain a large part of the variation in sales potentials. Second, recognizing that every factor is not of equal importance, he must assign appropriate weights to each factor entering the computation. He should start by identifying all factors that would seem to have some bearing on sales volume. This initial listing of causal factors is mainly a matter of logical reasoning. Next, he must select the factors and weights to be used in the index. Here he can depend entirely on judgment or he can apply statistical methods that measure the correlation between sales of the product and various series of market data.

To illustrate, let's assume a manufacturer of room air-conditioning units wishes to develop a multiple-factor index of sales potentials. His listing of causal factors might include: (1) number of dwelling units; (2) per capita disposable income, (3) average temperature during June, July, and August, (4) average relative humidity during these months, and (5) average number of days per year with temperatures over 85 degrees. Then he might arbitrarily combine some of these factors and assign weights according to his best judgment, or he might measure the correlation between past sales of room air conditioners and various combinations of these factors. The statistical technique referred to as multiple correlation is ideally suited for this type of measurement. Through the use of multiple correlation he can determine what part of the variance in sales among a rather large number of markets is explained by any particular combination of factors. He may find that one combination explains 60 percent, that another combination explains 70 percent, and that still another combination explains 80 percent of the variance in sales. In the same operation he can measure the relative importance or weight of each factor. With such measurements he will be more confident that the resulting index is based on the best set of factors and weights obtainable from the data at hand. Also, he will be apprised of the index's limitations and therefore be less inclined to overrate the accuracy of his estimates.

Problem of the new company

The manufacturer just starting in business or opening up a new territory will find it difficult, if not impossible, to use the correlation method in establishing an index of sales potentials. He has no previous sales with which to correlate particular outside factors. This difficulty could be overcome in part if the total sales of representative manufacturers of the commodity involved could be obtained. This figure could be used in the absence of the new manufacturer's own sales figures. The result would give a picture of the relative fertility of sales territories, but there would be no basis for determining the probable share which the newcomer might obtain. Then, too, it would be extremely difficult, if not impossible, to obtain the sales figures of competitors.

The new company can reduce the error of guesses by considering those factors that are obviously related positively or negatively to the consumption of its product. The sale of raincoats and umbrellas is closely related to frequency and amount of rainfall. The sale of safety razors is related to sex and age groups. General buying-power indexes might be used for many products to measure the ability to buy. Questionnaire studies might be employed to measure the willingness to buy. The latter might also be used to measure willingness at different price levels, although such a method must be employed with extreme care.

No method, whether it be applied to a new or an established industry or company, can measure accurately the actual total sales possibilities of an industry, an individual company, or separate territories. Much less inaccuracy will result, however, if serious and studious attention is given to the problem. One of the foregoing methods or a combination of them can usually be employed to advantage in allocating advertising effort and in checking the returns from such effort.

QUESTIONS AND PROBLEMS

1. The U.S. Department of Agriculture issues regular crop reports during the growing and maturing season in which estimates of the harvest for wheat, corn, soybeans, and other crops are given. How could these reports be of value to advertisers? Would they be more valuable to some than to other advertisers? Explain.

2. Why are population figures alone not a reliable index in comparing different geographical units?

3. A firm's sales figures broken down by market areas provide an adequate index of the sales potentials of those areas. Do you agree or disagree? Explain.

4. Distinguish between the following: (1) A general-purpose index and a special-purpose index. (2) A single-factor index and a multiple-factor index.

5. What is the primary objection to most market analyses based upon an inventory of consumer purchases?

6. Assume you are assigned the task of constructing a multiple-factor index of sales potentials for life insurance. What factors might you include?

7. What merit do you see in using statistical measures of correlation when constructing an index of sales potentials?

8. Using *Sales Management, Survey of Buying Power,* identify the top five Standard Metropolitan Areas in Ohio. Assuming that distribution of an automobile polish which retails at $2 per can is confined to those five markets, what proportion of total sales might you logically expect in each market?

9. Advertising effort should be distributed among various market areas in proportion to their sales potentiality. Do you agree or disagree? Explain.

10. To what extent might the varying interests of advertising agencies, newspapers, magazines, and independent market research agencies be inconsistent with the scientific and impartial conduct of marketing research projects?

part **III**
The advertising message

chapter 12
FACTORS
AFFECTING
RESPONSE

WITH A PENETRATING knowledge of the consumer's wants and the product's qualities the advertiser has the background to create messages that will *interpret the want-satisfying qualities of his product in terms of the consumer's wants.*

The advertising message thus becomes a connecting link between the producer with want-satisfying goods and the consumer with wants to be satisfied. Glenn Frank emphasized this concept admirably.

The nature of the advertising profession, he said, is such that the advertising man is challenged to a wide knowledge of men and of materials, if he is to be more than a peddler of epigrams. The advertising man is a liaison officer between the materials of business and the mind of the nation. He must know both well before he can serve either wisely.[1]

Knowing both the consumer and the product is fundamental. However, linking the two or succeeding as an interpreter calls for some knowledge of how advertising functions as communication, as well as how it affects and is affected by consumer behavior.

Two views of advertising communication

A traditional view of advertising communication holds that it is something the advertiser does *to* the audience. The advertisement is viewed

---

[1] Glenn Frank, "The Dignity and Duties of the Advertising Profession," *Printers' Ink,* April 14, 1927, p. 81.

as the stimulus (S) that triggers the desired response (R). The process thus becomes "a one-way flow," $S \rightarrow R$. The advertiser acts, and the audience *reacts*. Raymond Bauer labels this view "a model of exploitation of man by man" that is reflected in such popular phrases as brainwashing, hidden persuasion, and subliminal advertising.[2] Recognizing the influence of experimental psychology wherein rats are so often used as subjects, Bauer also notes:

> The model of a one-way exploitative process of communication . . . is probably further reinforced by the experimental design in which the subject is seen as *reacting* to conditions established by the experimenter. We forget the cartoon in which one rat says to another: "Boy, have I got this guy trained! Every time I push this bar he gives me a pellet of food." We all, it seems, believe that *we* train the *rats*.[3]

The traditional view overrates the power of the advertiser by underrating the power of the audience.

A more sophisticated view is that advertising is a "two-way flow," that it is an *interaction* between the audience and the message. It is not so much a matter of what the message brings to the audience, but more a matter of what the audience brings to the message. Instead of the message forcing a response, it *elicits* responses the audience was predisposed to make before the encounter. In other words, the audience's attitudes, beliefs, values, goals, etc. govern whether the message will be seen, heard, believed, remembered, or acted upon.

The concept of a powerful audience was introduced in the first edition of this book in 1937, when the senior author observed that the advertising message must be couched *"in terms of consumer needs and wants"* if it is to perform its interpreting function. This observation is substantiated by the recent findings of communication theorists and researchers.

Joseph Klapper, a leading scholar on the effects of mass communication, notes:

> The existing opinions and interests of people or more generally, their predispositions, have been shown profoundly to influence their behavior vis-a-vis mass communications and the effects which such communications are likely to have upon them. By and large, people tend to expose themselves to those mass communications which are in accord with their existing attitudes and interests. Consciously or unconsciously, they avoid communications of opposite hue. In the event of their being nevertheless exposed to unsympathetic material, they often seem not to per-

---

[2] Raymond A. Bauer, "The Obstinate Audience: The Influence Process From the Point of View of Social Communication," *American Psychologist,* Vol. 19, No. 5, May 1964, p. 319.

[3] *Ibid.,* p. 322.

ceive it, or to recast and interpret it to fit their existing views, or to forget it more readily that they forget sympathetic material. The processes involved in these self-protective exercises have become known as selective exposure (or, more classically, "self selection"), selective perception, and selective retention.[4]

Important as it is to recognize the audience's inertia, the power of advertising should not be underestimated. This kind of communication can and does influence consumer behavior. It is more likely to do so, however, when it works with and through existing audience predispositions. Also, it is more likely to modify existing attitudes slightly than to change them sharply.

Predispositions

Attitude is the predisposition of the individual to evaluate some symbol or aspect of his world in a favorable or unfavorable manner. Attitudes include both the affective, or feeling core of liking or disliking, and the cognitive elements which relate the object to prior learning. *Opinion* is the verbal expression of an attitude, but attitudes can also be expressed in nonverbal behavior.[5]

Attitudes and opinions are usually grounded in *beliefs* which are convictions derived from perceived truths. What is perceived as true and what is in reality true may be two different things. *Values* stem from beliefs about what is desirable or undesirable, justifiable or unjustifiable, right or wrong. Values do not always express what the individual desires personally, but rather what a society considers right or wrong in a particular situation. Thus, values often reflect what should or ought to ideally exist.

Personality traits are persistent characteristics of a person's reaction pattern. Traits differ from attitudes in that they are generalized tendencies to respond in a given way without having any favorable or unfavorable reference to particular objects. When we describe a person as imaginative, flexible, venturesome, enterprising, and cheerful, we are attempting to label some of his personality traits. The *self,* or self-image, is an individual's view of the kind of person he is and how he wants others to see him. Much of his behavior is a matter of trying to be

---

[4] Joseph T. Klapper, *The Effects of Mass Communication* (New York: The Free Press, 1960), p. 19.

[5] Daniel Katz, "The Functional Approach to the Study of Attitudes," *Reader in Public Opinion and Communication (2d Ed.).* Edited by Bernard Berelson and Morris Janowitz. (New York: The Free Press, 1966), p. 55.

the kind of person he thinks he is or a matter of trying to project the kind of personality traits he would like others to see in him.

Group influences include those coming from a primary group such as the family, a close circle of friends, fellow workers and neighbors, and those coming from secondary groups such as social class, occupation, race, ethnic group, and opinion leaders. The concept of group identification points to an emotional tie between the individual and the group. This can be a matter of the individual's incorporating group values to express his inner convictions, or it can result from the insecure person's attachment to the strength of the group to compensate for his own weakness. The concept of reference group implies less emotional attachment and suggests that many people turn to particular groups for their standards of judgment.

Elihu Katz and Paul Lazarsfeld postulated the role of personal influence in what they term the "two-step flow" of communication. Their theory states that the mass media directly influence opinion leaders, those people who are respected for their knowledge and competency in a particular field. The opinion leaders, in turn, exert their influence on those around them.[6]

For a well-selected and well-organized series of readings bearing on predispositions and their role in audience responses, the reader would be well advised to refer to *Consumer Behavior and the Behavioral Sciences,* edited by Steuart Henderson Britt.[7]

Responses

Various models have been offered to explain how advertising communication works. They differ in detail and terminology, but all seek to demonstrate what happens when an advertiser tries to influence the behavior of large numbers of people by placing messages in mass media that people select voluntarily. An early model viewed the process as a sequence of audience responses moving from *attention* to the message, to *interest* in the proposition, to *desire* for the product, to *conviction* the product would yield desired satisfaction, to *action* in the form of actual purchase. Later models have tried to be more precise and more consistent

---

[6] Elihu Katz and Paul F. Lazarsfeld, *Personal Influence: The Part Played by People in the Flow of Mass Communications* (New York: The Free Press, 1955), pp. 175–77.

[7] Steuart Henderson Britt (ed.), *Consumer Behavior and the Behavioral Sciences* (New York: John Wiley & Sons, Inc., 1966).

with the language of psychology. They have identified the various stages as *sensation/perception/cognition/memory/attitude change/decision*. There is a certain logic to this sequence of events. If a person is to be influenced at all by an advertisement, he must see it, understand it, remember it, accept it, and tentatively decide to buy. However, the notion that there is such a discrete series of responses obscures the importance of prior learning, which simultaneously influences all responses, particularly those labeled perception, cognition, and memory. Prior learning largely determines for each person what he will see and hear, what he will think and what he will do.

Our model, therefore, will focus on these four broad categories of response:

Exposure	The audience is within range and is capable of seeing and/or hearing the message.
Perception	The audience sees and/or hears the message and relates to prior learning the word/picture/sound symbols making up the message.
Integration	The audience accepts or rejects the message; believes or disbelieves; remembers or forgets, modifies or retains relevant attitudes and perceptions.
Action	Members of the audience buy, try, serve, repeat purchase, advocate, or openly endorse product advertised.

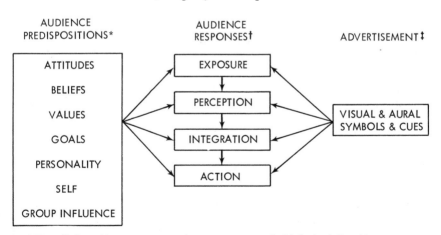

* Also called cognitive structure, neural trace patterns, acquired behavioral dispositions.
† Perception includes responses referred to as attention, cognition, comprehension, distortion meaning. Integration includes acceptance, rejection, memory; modification or reinforcement of attitudes, beliefs, and perceptions.
‡ A single advertisement or a series of advertisements (a campaign).

FIGURE 12–1. Interaction model of advertising communication

As diagrammed in Figure 12–1, all these response categories represent an interaction between the audience's predispositions and the advertising communication.

Exposure

A person is *exposed* to an advertisement when he is physically able to receive it. Thus, he is considered exposed to a television commercial when he is within range of seeing the picture and hearing the sound, when his eyes are focused on "the tube," and his ears are "tuned in." Of course, the sound and the picture must be sufficiently loud and clear to be readily heard and seen. Exposure to a radio commercial is less demanding. Sound can be heard in other rooms, in automobiles, and wherever small transistor radios are carried, which is just about everywhere. The radio audience member to be exposed need only be tuned in to a signal that is sufficiently loud and clear. Exposure to a print advertisement in magazines or newspapers occurs when the reader's eyes encounter the page carrying the ad. Exposure to outdoor advertising occurs when one's eyes are directed, however fleeting the glance, to the sign or poster.

Exposure to communications media tends to be voluntary and selective. It is voluntary in the sense that the person intentionally exposes himself to the medium. He turns the TV set on and tunes in particular programs or he purposely reads certain magazines and newspapers. It is selective in that he chooses only a fraction of all media available, and different people choose different things. The choices he makes, the programs, the magazines, the articles, the features he exposes himself to are likely to be those that gratify his expectations and that are compatible with his existing attitudes and opinions. The importance of group influence in selecting television programs is apparent in one school boy's explanation of why he watches *Batman*. "Eighth graders watch the show because it is the thing to do. When you get to school in the morning you ask your friends whether they saw *Batman* last night. Almost all of them did and a big discussion follows. Anyone who missed the show feels left out, and makes up his mind not to miss it again."

Whereas exposure to media tends to be voluntary, exposure to much advertising is involuntary, i.e., the person does not seek the advertisements. The ads "come along with" the program or editorial content and one becomes involuntarily exposed to the ads as a result of his voluntary exposure to the medium. Exceptions, of course, are exposures to classified ads, to the "yellow pages," to mail order catalogs, and to regular sources of shopping information, such as grocery store and department store ads.

From the advertiser's viewpoint the factors affecting exposure are most significant in media decisions. He should place his messages in media that are congenial to his market's predispositions. However, he also might enhance exposure to his messages if he adopts an appealing style and consistently schedules them in appropriate media. Then the audience will be inclined to keep the line of communication open when the commercial comes on or the ad page comes in view.

Perception

To *perceive* an advertisement is to be aware of it, to see and/or hear it through the senses—and more. Perception also involves an "understanding awareness," a "relating to prior experience," or "attaching meaning" to the message. Though some psychologists assign this latter part of the process to cognition rather than perception, "the two processes are so closely intertwined that it would scarcely be feasible to consider one of them in isolation from the other."[8] We communicate, write, and think in terms of signs or symbols whose very existence is dependent on meaning. As Walter Lippmann observed: "for the most part we do not first see, and then define. We define first and then see."[9]

This concept of perception also embraces a part of the communication process referred to as attention. Gaining attention of the reader, viewer, or listener is an essential function of the advertisement. To elicit any response at all the ad must be seen or heard. Insofar as some brief time might elapse between the initial sensory experience and subsequent brain activity, a case could be made for setting attention apart from perception. However, to draw such a distinction unnecessarily complicates the process and tends to emphasize technical devices for gaining attention at the expense of incorporating meaningful substance in the message. Our interaction model, therefore, combines attention and cognition in the broader context of perception.

Perception is selective. We see what we want to see. We hear what we want to hear. Gardner Murphy explains this point of view:

Needs determine how the incoming energies are to be put into structure form. Perception then is not something that is registered objectively, then "distorted,"

---

[8] Floyd H. Allport, *Theories of Perception and the Concepts of Structure* (New York: John Wiley & Sons, Inc., 1955), p. 14.

[9] Walter Lippmann, *Public Opinion* (New York: The Macmillan Company, 1922), p. 81.

. . . Needs keep ahead of percepts. The needs are always controlling; perception instead of being the lawgiver, takes orders from the need . . . It is the need pattern that plays the chief role in determining *where we shall look,* to what outer stimuli we shall attend, and what other factors shall be allowed to enter the control box (selector system).[10]

FIGURE 12–2.   Will the meaning of this headline and illustration be readily understood?

---

[10] Gardner Murphy, *Personality, A Biosocial Approach to Origins and Structure* (New York: Harper & Row, 1947), pp. 377–78.

Readership and listenership studies provide ample evidence of selective perception. New homeowners are more likely to read advertisements concerning lawn care. New car owners are more apt to read ads about their own make of car than about other makes. New parents are quick to see camera ads. Women with graying hair are more likely to see hair coloring ads. People tend to see ads portraying people like themselves.

Not only do we select the message we want to perceive, we also tend to distort message content in accordance with our different beliefs, attitudes, and values. A class experiment by Bruner and Goodman[11] found that two groups of children ages 10 to 11 overestimated the physical sizes of more valuable coins (quarters and half dollars) and underestimated the sizes of less valuable coins (pennies, nickels, and dimes). More significant was the finding that the children from poor families were more inclined to overestimate the sizes of the more valuable coins. Another study[12] showed that people who have a greater desire to own a Volkswagen see the car as physically smaller than those who are less inclined to it. Beauty is in the eyes of the beholder.

Integration

The perceiver of an advertisement may or may not believe it, remember it, or alter his attitudes as a result of his encounter with it. The likelihood of his accepting the message largely depends on how well it fits his existing beliefs and attitudes. Thus, believing, remembering, and attitude changing are selective processes, too. All these responses are affected by one's predispositions which in themselves are self-protective. Not only does one's predisposition govern which message will be let in, they also govern the extent to which they themselves will be influenced by it. This part of the response sequence, the judging, evaluating, remembering, and fitting-in with existing beliefs and attitudes we refer to as *integration*.

John C. Maloney describes integration responses as follows:

Stimuli are integrated with memories from prior learning or experience and the effects of such integration are stored in the memory structure. They remain there

[11] J. S. Bruner and C. C. Goodman, "Value and Need as Organizing Factors in Perception," *Journal of Abnormal and Social Psychology,* 1947, Vol. XLII, pp. 33–44.

[12] Samuel E. Stayton and Morton Weiner, "Value, Magnitude, and Accentuation," *Journal of Abnormal and Social Psychology,* Vol. 42 (January 1947), pp. 33–34.

until they are themselves buried (that is, forgotten) or altered by later inputs, or until they are reactivated to form a decision, a response, or a pattern of response.[13]

A person's predispositions, i.e., his attitudes, beliefs, values, and goals make up his psychological world, or what is referred to as "cognitive structure." The prevailing view among psychologists is that a person strives for stability in his cognitive structure. Dorwin Cartwright states that "everyone, after the earliest stages of infancy possesses a remarkably stable cognitive structure upon which he depends for a satisfactory adjustment to his environment."[14] When a message is inconsistent with a person's prevailing cognitive structure, it will either (*a*) be rejected, (*b*) be distorted so as to fit, or (*c*) produce changes in the cognitive structure. "Which of these outcomes will actually occur," Cartwright says, "depends upon the relative strength of the forces maintaining the cognitive structure and of those carried by the new message."

Leon Festinger, through his theory of *cognitive dissonance,* seeks to explain what happens when a person is confronted with a message that conflicts with his system of beliefs. Festinger's basic hypotheses are:

1. The existence of dissonance, being psychologically uncomfortable, will motivate the person to try to reduce the dissonance and achieve consonance.
2. When dissonance is present, in addition to trying to reduce it, the person will actively avoid situations and information which would likely increase the dissonance.[15]

Dissonance is especially likely to be experienced when a new product concept is introduced. For example, for many years housewives thought that the most effective laundry soaps or detergents were those that produced the most suds—the more suds the better the cleaning action. When the Monsanto Chemical Company introduced "All," a new low-sudsing detergent, their advertising helped housewives reduce the dissonance resulting from the conflicting concept by offering a rational explanation of low-sudsing effectiveness, showing convincing demonstrations, getting washing machine manufacturers to endorse the product, and giving away samples for home trial.

Dissonance theory also suggests that it is better strategy to advertise a product on its own merits than to disparage a competitor's product.

---

[13] John C. Maloney, "Advertising Research and an Emerging Science of Mass Persuasion," *Journalism Quarterly,* Vol. 41 (Autumn 1964), p. 526.

[14] Dorwin Cartwright, "Some Principles of Mass Persuasion," in W. Edgar Vinacke, Warner R. Wilson, and Gerald M. Meredity (Eds.), *Dimensions of Social Psychology* (Chicago: Scott Foresman and Company, 1964), p. 301.

[15] Leon Festinger, *A Theory of Cognitive Dissonance* (New York: Harper & Row, 1957).

Such disparagement is not likely to switch many customers away from the competitor's brand. Perhaps the most significant contribution of dissonance theory to advertising thought is the notion that dissonance is a motivating force causing some people to strive to reconcile new ideas to their existing cognitive structure. Therefore, advertising should be designed to enhance the reconciliation.

Action

The ultimate response is consumer *action* in the marketplace. Depending on the advertiser's objective the appropriate consumer action is manifested in different ways: trying a new or improved product, shifting from one brand to another, becoming a consistent purchaser of one brand, buying more at a time or buying more frequently. Appropriate action in response to retail advertising would be buying at a given store and becoming a regular patron. For industrial and professional advertising it would be ordering, specifying, recommending or prescribing the advertiser's product. Satisfied customers advocating the product through word-of-mouth communication would also be acting beneficially.

Action is selective, too. After the advertiser's message, or more typically his series of messages has filtered through exposure, perception, and integration, it still may fail to elicit the desired action. Those same predispositions continue to be in control. They may have let the message "in" and even let the person "think well" of the product, but still prevent his buying it. Attitudes supporting his present buying behavior may be too strongly held to permit a change. Or, to put it another way, the advertising may not be able to make a large enough dent in his cognitive structure to get him to try a new product, to change brands, or to switch patronage. The key point here is that it behooves the advertiser to carefully probe the relevant attitudes of his market to discover how strongly they are held. He might then find that there are some "immovable objects" and be reminded that advertising is not an "irresistible force."

The trite notion that national advertising gets people "to go down to the corner drug store right now and buy brand X" is far from reality. Buying action resulting from such advertising is a delayed response that typically takes places after many exposures to a series of advertisements over a period of weeks and months. This is not to suggest that each advertisement should not invite action. It simply means that it is naive to expect an immediate response. Each message should be viewed as one of many nudges toward a purchase.

When the marketing objective is to introduce a new product or accelerate sales of a going product, advertising might be used along with price deals, "cents-off" coupons, contests, premiums, and other such limited time offers to induce a more immediate response.

Most retail advertising is geared to quick action. The ads in this evening's newspaper are intended to influence tomorrow's buying. Therefore, department stores, grocery stores, and other retailers offer information that helps the consumer plan her shopping trip and make tentative choices among acceptable product alternatives on a price or service basis. Store patronage, on the other hand, is much like brand preference and comes about more slowly.

The fact that advertising seldom, if ever, is the only factor inducing buying action, and the difficulty encountered in isolating the effect of advertising on sales has led some practitioners to consider the function of advertising completed at some level of communication short of action. This level might be "awareness" of the product, "knowledge" of its selling points, "belief" in claims, or indicated "attitude change." Unfortunately, this view overlooks the pervasiveness of advertising's influence and artificially restricts its effect to responses more amenable to measurement. Reluctance to demand action responses may also be due to the small percentages of the total audience who are moved to act. Raymond Bauer reminds us that:

> . . . consistently successful commercial promotions convert only a very small percentage of people to action. No one cigarette now commands more than 14% of the cigarette market, but an increase of 1% is worth $60 million in sales. This means influencing possibly .5% of all adults and 1% of cigarette smokers. This also means that a successful commercial campaign can alienate many more than it wins, and still be profitable.[16]

Planning of the entire advertising campaign should proceed from a statement of the specific market action to be attained and every advertisement should be prepared with that action in mind.

Competition for attention

To get attention an advertisement must compete successfully against countless other attractions. If it is placed in a newspaper or a magazine, it has to compete with surrounding editorial content, with other advertisements, with whatever television or radio may be offering at the time, with conversation, and with the "other things" on a reader's mind. Competing for attention is further complicated by the great number of adver-

---

[16] Bauer, *op. cit.,* p. 322.

tisements appearing in all the various media. How large a number this might be is indicated in the following estimate as reported by Edwin W. Ebel, marketing director of General Foods Corporation:

> In the morning of this typical metropolitan family, John reads the *New York Times* on his way to his office. In the evening he reads the *New York World-Telegram & Sun* and brings that paper home with him for Mary to look at. Both John and Mary also read their local evening newspaper. On that particular day, the three papers contained 510 display ads.
>
> John took a bus to the railroad station. There were 23 car cards in the bus, and there were 40 posters in view along the way. In the railroad car there were 41 car cards. At Grand Central Terminal—along the route he took from train to subway —he passed 63 posters. Car cards in his subway train numbered 49.
>
> The radio was turned on at home from 7:30 to 8:30 A.M. and from noon to 1 P.M. During these hours, 37 commercials were spoken or sung. Mary used the car from 3:30 to 4:30 in the afternoon, turned on the radio and heard 16 more commercials. She also passed 178 outdoor advertising signs.
>
> During the day, Mary managed to squeeze in 80 minutes of magazine reading— *Life* and *Good Housekeeping*. The two magazines contained 447 ads.
>
> The children devoured two comic books during the day. These contained 50 ads.
>
> Television was turned on from 5:00 to 10:30 P.M. In that time the commercials totaled 64.
>
> Altogether, in a 15-hour day, the family was exposed to 1,518 advertisements.[17]

To get attention, any one of these 1,518 ads must not only stand out in a crowded field, but must also break through the natural indifference with which we regard anything so commonplace as advertising.

Methods of gaining attention

The corollary of *selective perception* is *selective advertising*. Just as some people are more predisposed than others to seek a product's benefits and to be influenced by certain kinds of appeals, advertising that is directed specifically to those people, that is designed to appeal to their interests, has the best chance of getting through. Therefore, gaining attention is fundamentally a matter of strategy, the strategy of singling out the group or groups of people who seem to be prime prospects and addressing them in terms of their self interest.

Appeal to prospect's wants. To appeal to everybody is to appeal to nobody. Too many advertisers fail to recognize this principle. A headline such as "Men" or "The Greatest News Ever" invites the attention of all men or anyone seeking news. Such a headline should be printed

---

[17] In a speech before a meeting of the Association of National Advertisers, May 8, 1957.

in a large type, in large space, and in color, and would be noticed by many, just as the circus barker, through noise and gymnastics, arrests the momentary notice of many passers-by. If the headline or other attention-getting device is tied up with the interest of particular individuals, attention will not only be obtained but held. If instead of "Men" the headline, "To Men Who Are Dissatisfied with Their Jobs," were used, those who were stopped by the headline would read what the advertisement had to say because of an interest in finding a solution for their own particular problem.

The advertisement illustrated in Figure 12–3 uses no special layout technique to attract attention, yet it will be read by many prospective customers because of its appeal to a fundamental human interest.

Special layout.   Attention to any object is at best momentary. The maximum time for which any object can hold the strict observance of a person is perhaps not more than ten seconds. An important characteristic of attention is, therefore, the element of fluctuation. This ebb and flow can be directed to some degree by the advertiser. The arrangement of various parts of an advertisement, the use of borders, lines drawn in certain directions, the focus of the eyes of persons illustrated in the advertisement, and the position of the product itself can all be utilized to guide the reader's eyes to particular parts of the advertisement. Figure 12–4 shows how design and mass are used to draw the attention of the reader to the product and its brand name. Care should be taken, however, to keep the special layout design from detracting from the message.

Color.   The contrasts that color affords, as well as its symbolic properties and realism can be used to gain attention. There are times, however, when color loses its attention-getting value. If the great majority of advertisements in a particular advertising medium are reproduced in color, then a black-and-white advertisement would have the advantage of contrast. Under such circumstances, color should not be used if its only function is to get increased attention.

There are, of course, other values of color. It may aid in the creation of a proper mental picture of the product if the product is one in which color is an important value factor. This will apply particularly to items like food, clothes, textiles, and furniture. Imagine how much would be added to Figure 12–5 if the lobster, shallots, tomatoes, and peppers were shown in their natural colors. To see what color adds, turn to the color advertisements in Chapter 16.

There are times when advertisers select colors that may be effective in attracting attention but actually reduce the readability of the advertisement. This may occur when a headline, or even a part of the body

Tell your bride you just guaranteed her financial security.

Watch her smile.

And why shouldn't she? You've given her peace of mind.

That's one of the nicest things about a New York Life insurance policy.

You can depend on it to protect those who depend on you.

It will protect them throughout the years your family is growing up.

Yet, that same policy can guarantee you a regular monthly income when you're ready to retire.

For a happier life

It can help you enjoy a happier life.

Why not get started on a life insurance program that fits your needs? And your wife's. She'll love you for it.

New York Life Insurance Company
51 Madison Avenue, New York, N.Y. 10010
Life, Group and Health Insurance,
Annuities, Pension Plans.
125 years of service

FIGURE 12–3. An appeal to a fundamental human interest

Born ironed.
Stays ironed.

It's Decton Perma-Iron.

Arrow Decton Perma-Iron: the shirt that defies wrinkles. It leaves the tumble-dryer with no ironing needed. Dacron® polyester and cotton blend with a rich hand. "Sanforized-Plus," of course. In white and solids, with many collar styles. $7.00.

~ARROW~

FIGURE 12–4. Layout focuses attention on product

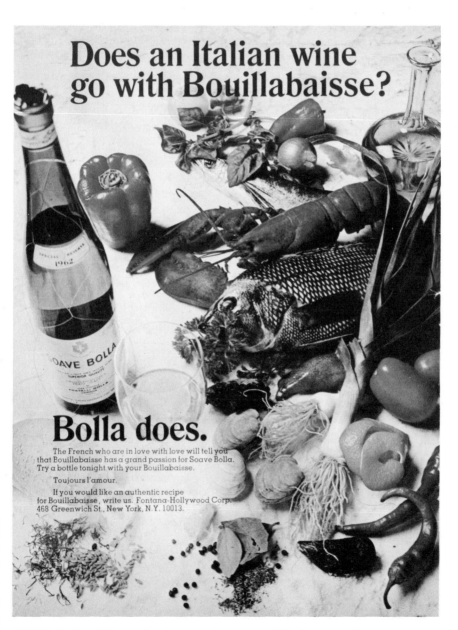

FIGURE 12–5. Without color the visual elements are difficult to recognize

copy, is printed in some pastel color, or where printed material is over-laid with color. When any reading matter is printed in color, it is usually wise to select color that is sufficiently dense in tonal quality to make read-ing easy. Generally speaking, black is best for body copy because it is what readers are used to seeing.

Size and location. The size of an advertisement will have some in-fluence. Various studies have been made in an attempt to measure the attention value of size. The results have indicated that attention value increases with increase in size, but not in the same ratio.

The location of an advertisement in a magazine will influence the number of persons seeing the advertisement. The most valuable location is the back cover. Pages near the covers are somewhat better than those in the body of the magazine. The amount of white space used in an advertisement will be a significant factor, a large proportion affording a contrast that will command increased notice.

Building the brand image

David Ogilvy, eloquent advocate of the image-building concept, says:

> Every advertisement must be considered as a contribution to the complex symbol which is the brand image—as part of the long-term investment in the reputation of the brand.
>
> What a miracle it is when a manufacturer manages to sustain a coherent image in his advertising over a period of years. . . . What guts it takes, what obstinate determination to stick to one coherent policy year after year in the face of all the pressures to "come up with something new" every six months.
>
> But what golden rewards await the advertiser who has the brains to create a favorable brand image—and to stick with it over a long period. Look at Campbell's Soup! Look at Jell-O! Look at Betty Crocker! Look at Esso! Look at Ivory Soap!
>
> The men who have been responsible for the advertising of these immortal brands have understood that every advertisement, every radio program, every TV commercial is not a one-time shot, but a long-term investment on the total person-ality of their brands.[18]

Look at the Campbell's Soup ad in Figure 12–6. The straightforward product story, the style of presentation, the label, the Campbell "kid," and the signature have been used consistently for 45 years. As a result, Campbell's stands for soup, especially tomato soup, for quality, depend-ability, wholesome nourishment, and value. So strong and clear is the image this strategy built that no competitor has been able to threaten

---

[18] David Ogilvy, "The Image and the Brand: A New Approach to Creative Operations," speech before the Central Region, American Association of Advertising Agencies, October 14, 1955.

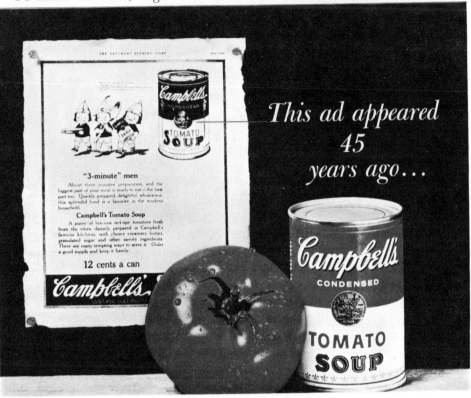

"To make the best, begin with the best—then cook with extra care."

"3-minute" men

About three minutes' preparation, and the biggest part of your meal is ready to eat—the best part too. Quickly prepared, delightful, wholesome, this splendid food is a favorite in the modern household.

Campbell's Tomato Soup

A puree of luscious red-ripe tomatoes fresh from the vines, daintily prepared in Campbell's famous kitchens, with choice creamery butter, granulated sugar and other savory ingredients. There are many tempting ways to serve it. Order a good supply and keep it handy.

12 cents a can

Campbell's

This ad appeared 45 years ago...

Have you checked the price of Campbell's Tomato Soup lately?

Anyone who goes to the store or pays the bills knows what's happened to prices over the years. That's why we thought you might be interested in this advertisement that ran for Campbell's Tomato Soup on July 2, 1921.

It shows that the price was 12¢ a can. If you have a grocery store advertisement handy —or if your memory is really good, we think you'll be mildly amazed at the price today— 45 years later—for the same size can.

The same kind of price story—though in varying degree—can be told about the other Campbell's Soups.

Of course, we can't take all the credit. The happy reason that Campbell's has been able to buck the tide of rising prices is partly you, partly the grocer and farmer, and partly us. You, because there are so many more of you these days, and because you seem to like our soups more and more as time goes on. And it's the grocer and farmer, of course, because each has become increasingly efficient...the farmer in producing, and the grocer in serving you.

As for us, we just naturally like to make soup. We like to make it as good as we can, and bring it to you for as little as we can. And we find better ways to do this as we go along.

This seems like a good time to tell you that we find this a very pleasant relationship, indeed—and we thank you.

Campbell's Quality

We blend the best with careful pains
In skillful combination,
And everything we make contains
Our business reputation.

CAMPBELL'S · SWANSON · V8
FRANCO-AMERICAN · BOUNTY
...all made by Campbell

FIGURE 12–6. One of a long series of advertisements that built a strong brand image

Campbell's leading market position. Even the chain stores have been reluctant to challenge with their own private brands.

Image-building is more often associated with national brands. However, the reputation or the persistent perception of any institution becomes a significant factor in its success. A retailer should consistently portray a desirable store personality. Similarly, an industrial advertiser should project a well-defined corporate personality. Insofar as every corporation benefits if it is highly regarded by investors, employees, civic groups, and government officials, as well as by its customers, it is desirable to use every means of communication to build a favorable image. And, of course, in politics the candidate's image is vital.

Belief

The problem of believability is especially acute in highly competitive advertising that confronts the consumer with claims and counterclaims about product superiorities, about ingredients, processes, and construction features that he cannot prove on his own because he has neither the knowledge nor technical apparatus for "running a test." And when claims concern psychological satisfaction, their authenticity can only be measured in terms of peoples' attitudes and opinions. As a result, the consumer is inclined to buy on faith. The advertisements he finds easy to believe are the ones most apt to win his purchase.

Belief is not dependent upon any one factor. If it were, there would probably be much greater uniformity in the beliefs of people on such matters as politics and religion. Poffenberger summarizes the various opinions concerning the basis of belief or conviction as follows:

1. Belief is a matter of feeling and emotion rather than of reason.
2. The truth is not a primary factor in determining belief.
3. Belief is a personal matter, a fabric of *personal* experiences.
4. Belief has also a social component to be accounted for by the need for conformity with one's fellows and especially with those in authority.
5. Belief is dependent upon desire—we believe what we want to believe.[19]

The lack of uniformity in beliefs suggests that the advertiser keep in mind the audience he wants to reach and their predisposition to believe what he wants to say. As Maloney reminds us:

Believability is not an inherent property of the advertisement itself. It is not a mystic something that some advertisements have and others do not have. Believability depends upon the *interaction* of each advertisement with the consumer's

---

[19] Albert T. Poffenberger, *Psychology in Advertising* (New York: McGraw-Hill Book Co., 1932), pp. 544–45.

attitudes and memories accumulated from proper experience. . . . Different people have different expectations about the trustworthiness of various kinds of advertising; they have developed different kinds of knowledge and different types of feelings about the products or brands being advertised. This means that an advertisement completely believable to one person may not be at all believable to another. In other words, we must specify *believable to whom* when we consider the "believability" of an advertisement.[20]

Ways of gaining belief

From what we have learned about the nature of belief it is apparent that creating a believable advertisement is more difficult than merely reporting the facts. The entire strategy and manner of presentation should be designed and executed to inspire confidence. Among the many ways of gaining belief are the following.

Start with the truth. Aside from ethical considerations it is far better to tell the truth because truthful statements are generally more believable than false ones. Misleading statements, excessive exaggeration, and false claims tend to be recognized for what they are and therefore undermine consumer confidence in the product so advertised. Yet, the truth at times is stranger than fiction, and the skill with which it is told will largely determine whether or not it will be believed.

Appeal to prospect's wants. People believe what is in line with their own wants and desires. This relationship between belief and desires has been experimentally demonstrated by F. H. Lund.[21] He took 30 propositions dealing with topics of general interest selected from the fields of religion, ethics, politics, and science and submitted them to 243 persons. They were asked to indicate their belief in the truth or falsity of each proposition. The result of this test showed a correlation between belief and desire of $+0.81$.

A somewhat similar study was made in which propositions that were not particularly desired were taken and evidence given to prove their truthfulness. People were then asked to rate their belief in the propositions. The resulting correlation between belief and evidence was only $+0.42$. This would indicate that the desire to believe is a much stronger determinant of belief than evidence supporting the truthfulness of a given proposition.

---

[20] John C. Maloney, "Is Advertising Believability Really Important?" *Journal of Marketing,* Vol. 27 (October 1963), p. 1.

[21] F. H. Lund, *Psychology* (New York: Ronald Press Co., 1933), pp. 390–95. See also F. H. Lund, "Emotional and Volitional Determinants of Belief," *Journal of Abnormal and Social Psychology,* April and July, 1925.

This fact undoubtedly accounts in large measure for the "success" of various patent-medicine advertising, fake stock-selling schemes, etc. People want to get well and they want to believe that a particular medicine will cure them. People desire to make money quickly and without effort. They, therefore, want to believe that a particular "get-rich-quick" proposition is true. This same quality can, of course, be utilized by the advertiser of goods with real want-satisfying qualities and remain completely in the realm of truth.

Substantiate with reason.   We are not apt to admit, even to ourselves, that our beliefs are founded on emotions. We tend to believe what we want to believe and then find logical reasons to justify our beliefs. Therefore, an advertisement appealing primarily to emotion is more convincing if it also gives the prospect some "reasonable" evidence with which he can rationalize his choice.

Note that logical reasoning plays a supporting role. It is difficult to convince a person by the use of reason alone. All kinds of evidence might be available to show the value of a low tariff, but such "proof" will not be sufficient to convince the high protectionist. While rejecting the arguments of the other side he is eager to grasp at any evidence that supports his stand.

Orient message to prospect's experience.   People are inclined to accept whatever conforms and to reject whatever conflicts with their previous experience.

Many readers disbelieved one advertisement that pictured a piece of luggage supporting a five-ton elephant, and another that showed a fountain pen withstanding the weight of loaded busses rolling over it, and another that claimed a phonograph reproduced the human voice so well that an audience could not distinguish the playback from the live voice.[22] These spectacular demonstrations probably scored well as attention getters, but they were not convincing. Even though true, such feats were too far removed from what people's experience would permit them to believe.

As is often the case, a newly developed product represents a wide departure from what people confidently have been using. Then the advertiser must recognize the inevitable gradualness of change and display a healthy respect for existing beliefs.

Talk prospect's language.   The plainer the talk the more understandable it is, and the more believable it is. Words much like those the prospect himself uses, pictures of "his kind of people" and of situations

---

[22] Poffenberger, *op. cit.*, 545–50.

encountered in "his kind of world" ring true. Unfamiliar words spoken by people who are out of touch with his way of life arouse suspicion and doubt.

The technical jargon of doctors and scientists fits popular conceptions of how people in these professions should talk and therefore is often used to add authority to testimonials. Such unintelligible language may be impressive. It is not convincing.

Use bona fide testimonials from recognized authorities. When we don't know what to believe, we are inclined to turn to an authority, someone who is expected to have specialized knowledge on the matter or who holds a position of high esteem in the public mind. Shifting the burden of decision to an expert makes up for the gap in our own knowledge and gives us a feeling of security. It requires little effort.

Doctors, successful businessmen, movie stars, and men of distinction are a few of the more popular authorities. Our tendency to believe what they have to say has been widely exploited by advertisers—perhaps too much so. However, if a testimonial is bona fide, realistic, pertinent, and from a qualified source, it can be an effective means of creating confidence.

Other ways. In addition to those mentioned, there are other ways of gaining belief. Tell of the product's popularity. We have faith in the consensus of large numbers of people.

Display confidence, but don't brag. Confidence is contagious. Bragging is obnoxious.

Use the specific and concrete. They are more believable than the general and abstract.

Use ordinary people in story-telling photos instead of stereotyped models in obviously studied poses. The fact that ordinary people lack the habits, polish, and experience of professionals would more than likely aid in establishing the credulity of the total impression.

Postpurchase reassurance and satisfaction

Every choice involves a sacrifice. The choice of one of several competing products involves giving up whatever the nonchosen products offer. The consumer who buys a Ford instead of a Chevrolet looks for reassurance that he made the "right" choice, that what he will gain from owning a Ford will be greater than what he gave up in a Chevrolet or in any other make of car that entered his deliberations. Research evidence has indicated that new-car purchasers are likely to read advertisements about the make of car they recently bought. The advertisements not only offer

Sitting pretty

... Dad's insured in
the New England Life

Dad, *too*, is sitting pretty. He has all of the guaranteed privileges of the New England Life contract.

If you are a Dad — or just somebody who wants to get the most for his money out of life insurance — you will do well to get the facts on this contract.

See, for example, what a wide choice you get in the way income is paid and what a generous rate of return is given.

In its all-around liberality the New England Life contract is unexcelled by any other life insurance policy.

The New England Life agent in your community will gladly explain why this contract means *a better life for you.*

A BETTER LIFE FOR YOU   **NEW ENGLAND**
Mutual **LIFE** *Insurance Company*
BOSTON, MASSACHUSETTS

THE COMPANY THAT FOUNDED MUTUAL LIFE INSURANCE IN AMERICA — 1835

FIGURE 12–7.   Keeping present owners satisfied with their purchase reassurance, they also add to the satisfaction of owning. Seeing the car portrayed to best advantage and reading about its merits not only makes the owner proud of his choice but also makes him proud of himself for having such good judgment. Also, the owner is aware of the fact that other people see the same advertisements which indirectly tells them that he made a good choice.

Instruction books and other literature accompanying new product purchases offer an apparent opportunity to reassure the buyer and inform him how to care for and get the most out of his purchase. Less apparent, but equally important is the opportunity that every advertisement offers to instill pride of ownership.

Dads who have insurance with New England Life will experience added satisfaction when they read the advertisement illustrated in Figure 12–7.

A satisfied customer is not only inclined to buy again and again, he also is likely to set in motion word-of-mouth communication that multiplies the effect of the advertising.

QUESTIONS AND PROBLEMS

1. Contrast the "stimulus-response" model and the "interaction" model of advertising communication.
2. Select three magazine advertisements that appear to recognize the principle of selective perception. Describe the audience most likely to read each advertisement and explain why they would do so.
3. Outline the various methods of gaining attention. If you were allowed to use only one method in an advertisement, which one would you pick as being the best?
4. List the various elements of an advertisement that can be drawn upon to build a brand image.
5. From current advertising select what you consider to be an outstanding image-building campaign. Why do you consider it outstanding?
6. What people believe is not always true, and what is true is not always believed. How can an advertiser increase the believability of his message?
7. Select five advertisements that you consider strong on believability and five others that you consider weak on this point. Contrast the content of the two groups.
8. We tend to believe what we want to believe and then look for logical reasons to justify our beliefs. How should this tendency affect the content of advertisements?
9. "Some have eyes and see not, ears and hear not." How might this statement apply to those who are exposed to a TV commercial, read an advertisement, or "hear" a radio commercial?

chapter 13
ADVERTISING
APPEALS

WE HAVE noted how important needs and wants are in motivating consumer behavior. What one buys, what he reads or listens to, what he believes, and what he remembers—all are largely determined by the needs he is consciously or subconsciously seeking to satisfy. Now, let us see how motivation theory can be put to work in advertising.

Classification of needs and wants

Thousands of motivational variables have been propounded in the brief history of psychology, but none has attained prolonged and universal acceptance. As Gardner Lindzey observes:

> For almost every set of motivational variables there has been a counterproposal to the effect that the last thing in the world that psychologists should be interested in is compiling lists of motives. Theorists who conceive of behavior as primarily motivated by benign and socially approved motives may be paired with theorists who see the chief impellents of behavior as primitive and unacceptable urges. For those who believe learned or socially acquired motives are of predominant importance there is opposition in the form of theorists convinced that the physiologically grounded and largely innate drives are of primary importance. Some have emphasized the abstract or logical status of motivational constructs, while others have stressed the physical reality and concrete existence of motives.[1]

Why are there so many theories of motivation? In the first place, the

---

[1] Gardner Lindzey, *Assessment of Human Motives* (New York: Grove Press, Inc., 1960), p. 4.

study of human motivation involves the difficult task of explaining *why* people behave as they do instead of merely describing *what* they do. Secondly, motives cannot be directly observed. They can only be inferred from overt acts. This injects the idiosyncrasies of the observer-inferrer. Thirdly, all social behavior involves many interactive factors rather than a single cause-effect relationship. Lastly, there are semantic difficulties in using words with different meanings to explain phenomena for which the words are not generally intended.

Among the various classifications of needs and wants one of the most highly regarded and the one that will be used for illustrative purposes here is that presented by psychologist A. H. Maslow.[2] He believes that human needs arrange themselves in hierarchies of prepotency and that the emergence of one need rests on the prior satisfaction of a more basic or more potent need. Maslow's hierarchy of needs is arranged in the following order:

1. Physiological needs (hunger, thirst)
2. Safety needs (security, health)
3. Love needs (affection, belongingness, identification)
4. Esteem needs (self-respect, prestige, social approval)
5. Self-actualization (self-fulfillment, self-expression)

Maslow suggests that a "lower" need must be adequately satisfied before the next "higher" need emerges as a determinant of behavior. A starving man has neither a safety need, nor a love need, nor any other "higher" need. It is only after his hunger is satisfied that he turns to his safety need. Once his safety is secured he then turns his attention to love, then to esteem, and finally to self-actualization. This does not mean that a lower need must be satisfied 100 percent before the next need emerges. Actually, most members of our society are partially satisfied and partially unsatisfied in all their basic needs at the same time. To illustrate the point Maslow says it is as if the average citizen is satisfied perhaps 85 percent in his physiological needs, 70 percent in his safety needs, 50 percent in his love needs, 40 percent in his self-esteem needs, and 10 percent in his self-actualization needs. In other words, in a more affluent society the self-actualization needs are more pervasive determinants of behavior than physiological needs.

Even though he suggests that his rank order of needs fits the behavior of most people, Maslow also recognizes exceptions. He points out that

---

[2] A. H. Maslow, "A Dynamic Theory of Human Motivation," *Psychological Review* (American Psychological Association, Inc.), Vol. 50, pp. 370–96.

there are some people for whom self-esteem seems to be more important than love. However, such people may actually put on a front of aggressive, confident behavior as a means of gaining love rather than self-esteem itself. There are other innately creative people in whom the drive to creativeness does not seem to follow satisfaction of more basic needs, but persists in spite of the lack of such satisfactions. In other people the level of aspiration may be permanently deadened or lowered. For example, chronic unemployment may lower one's goals to simply getting enough food. On the other hand, people who have never experienced chronic hunger might look upon food as a rather unimportant thing.

A particular need does not produce a certain kind of behavior, nor does a certain kind of behavior stem from a particular need. Most behavior is multimotivated. Eating may be partially for the sake of filling the stomach, partially for the sake of pleasurable taste sensations, partially for a satisfying routine, and partially for sociability. A student may work hard at his studies not only for self-actualization, but also for prestige, for belongingness, and for security. Likewise, the purchase of a product is seldom motivated by a single need or want. Thus, the central problem confronting the advertising strategist is to select from the many relevant needs and wants those few that are most powerful in affecting his customer's purchase behavior and that are at the same time susceptible to arousal by advertising communication. The next problem, of course, is to design advertisements that arouse or intensify the need and that clearly present the product as a desirable means of satisfying the need.

Physiological needs

The tissue needs of the body are such that food and drink are absolute essentials to life. Our hunger and thirst prompt us to strive to satisfy our appetite. Other desires are often compared with the desire to eat. Thus the expression, "I would rather do that than eat," is often used to emphasize the intensity of a desire.

Our body mechanism automatically arouses the desire to eat and drink whenever the body requires food and liquid. Hunger, therefore, is a fundamental motivating force. However, the typical well-fed American is more likely to experience hunger pains because he habitually eats at certain hours, not because his body is starving for nutrition. Apparently the body not only knows when to order food generally, but also knows what specific kinds of foods to order. This phenomenon, referred to as homeostasis, suggests that the body seeks to maintain in the blood stream a constant content of water, salt, sugar, protein, fat, calcium, oxygen, etc. If the body lacks one of these ingredients, the individual will develop a specific appetite or hunger for foods containing that particular ingredient. Some theorists have extended the homeostasis concept and suggest that all behavior is affected by the individual's automatically seeking some sort of "balance," or "consonance," or "equilibrium" in his cognitive structure as well as his diet.

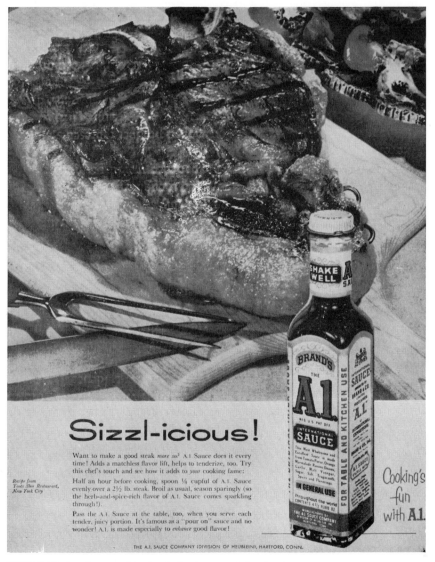

FIGURE 13–1.   An appeal to the desire for appetizing food

In addition to providing sustenance, eating and drinking are satisfying experiences in themselves. Pleasurable sensations of taste, smell, sight, touch, and even hearing can result from appetizing foods and beverages. Think of some of the foods you like most, perhaps a charcoal-broiled sirloin steak, french-fried potatoes, lettuce salad, and apple pie a la mode. Just the thought of tasty food can make the mouth water. The aroma of freshly baked bread, a turkey roasting in the oven, brewing coffee; the "eye-petizing" sight of fresh, green lettuce, ripe red tomatoes, frosty-blue blueberries; the crunch of crispy potato chips, the smoothness of ice cream; even the sound of a sizzling hamburger or the perking of a coffee percolator—all of these sensations are part of the joy of eating and drinking. And these sensations are also part of the appetites to which food and beverage advertising can appeal.

For most people the act of dining, especially "dining out," is a satisfying ritual. There is an orderliness to the sequence in which certain kinds of foods and beverages are served proceeding from the "first or appetizer course" to the "dessert course." Wouldn't it jar you to start with ice cream and finish with a shrimp cocktail? The way the table is set, the silverware, the glassware, the serving pieces—all are part of the orderly routine.

Mealtime also is a sociable time. It is the one time when all members of the family get together. It is a time for conversation, a time for companionship, a time for kinship. Having lunch with a friend or having a cup of coffee with a neighbor is a satisfying social experience that often transcends the importance of the food itself. This favorable association of sociability with dining and drinking can be effectively portrayed in food and beverage advertisements.

Safety needs

The threat of bodily harm from wild animals, criminal assault, murder, and tyranny is largely removed in our highly organized society. Fear of such attacks, while significant in the history of man, is not an active motivator in this day and age. More apparent threats to one's safety are unemployment, loss of income, loss of health, and disability. Fear of these threats is so pervasive that society has sought some protection against them through government social security programs.

Security. Security for the family, for the home, and for one's self continues to be a strong motivating force in the lives of most people. Most obvious among the institutions created to enhance one's feeling of security are the life insurance companies, the pharmaceutical industry, the medical and dental professions, the police and fire departments, and other government agencies engaged in regulating the food and drug industries, building codes, and highway construction. Less obvious, but equally important, is the institution of religion, or some kind of world philosophy, or science that seeks to organize the universe and man into

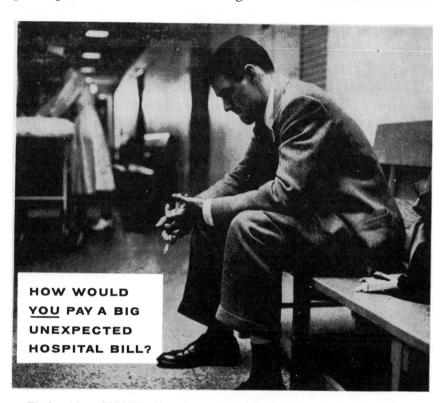

HOW WOULD YOU PAY A BIG UNEXPECTED HOSPITAL BILL?

Find out how MONY's New $50 "Deductible" Family Hospital Policy can provide economical protection for your family!

Chances are a big, unexpected hospital bill would dig into your bank account or savings bonds, perhaps wipe out years of careful planning. Now MONY's new "Deductible" Family Hospital Policy can help those who qualify meet many hospital bills that might well be ruinous to the family budget.

And this valuable protection for you and your family is budget-priced as well. That's because of the deductible feature — designed to keep the premiums down, within reach of even the young family man.

In principle, it's much the same as your deductible automobile collision insurance, wherein you pay for the dented fender and your insurance helps take care of the big smashup. By deducting the first $50 and eliminating the high cost of handling many small claims, MONY is able to provide coverage to help pay many of the bigger bills at an attractively low premium rate.

We'd like you to have our booklet which describes in more detail this modern policy and the variety of coverages it can provide. No obligation, of course.

MUTUAL OF NEW YORK

THE MUTUAL LIFE INSURANCE COMPANY OF NEW YORK, NEW YORK, N. Y

Life Insurance — Accident and Sickness — Hospitalization — Retirement Plans . . . FOR INDIVIDUALS AND EMPLOYEE GROUPS

MONY offices are located throughout the United States and in Canada.

MONY TODAY MEANS **MONEY** TOMORROW!

MAIL THIS COUPON TODAY FOR YOUR FREE COPY.

Mutual Of New York, Dept. K-27
Broadway at 55th Street, New York 19, New York

I would like a copy of your free booklet describing the $50 "Deductible" Family Hospital Policy.

Name_____

Address_____

City_____ County or Zone____ State_____

FIGURE 13–2. An appeal to the desire for security

some sort of coherent, meaningful whole. Still less obvious is the institution of advertising that makes brands, manufacturers, and retail establishments more familiar and therefore more trustworthy.

While the need for security is strong, it sometimes is difficult to transfer into action. It is difficult to get people to install fire extinguishers or burglar alarms until a fire or a theft has occurred. The adage about locking the stable after the horse has been stolen illustrates the point. Many people don't use the seat belts in their automobiles and are not inclined to always obey the speed limits. Life insurance companies have found that an appeal to providing security for the family after the breadwinner's death can be less effective than a more immediate appeal to the breadwinner's self-esteem as a good provider. Part of the problem that life insurance companies encounter is man's inclination to avoid thoughts of dying. He lives as though he will live forever. Thus, life insurance plans are tied to insured mortgage payments, annuities, and retirement plans. In this vein, one company built its advertising campaign around the idea of "living insurance."

Health. The way some people complain about their ills causes one to wonder whether the joy of complaining is not greater than the desire for health. Yet this is hardly the case. Most individuals are motivated to a greater or lesser degree by the desire for health. This is true, not only of those who are ill, but also of those who suffer no real sickness but who wish to remain in good health. Of course, the appeal to this desire is much more effective when directed to those who suffer from some ailment.

Our modern method of living is such that most people are below par in physical energy at some time during every year. This has led to the production and promotion of various products with health-giving claims. Physical-culture schools, health magazines, patent medicines, multitudinous devices, and diet fads have been offered the public as methods for gaining and keeping one's health. Many of these items possess no real value, but the desire for physical and mental health is so strong that many people will try anything if they think it has any possible merit. Such products enjoy wide sales and often much popular favor in spite of their worthlessness. Nature serves them as a powerful ally. Most people will get well in spite of medicines or devices used. Usually, however, the medicine rather than the healing power of time, receives the credit.

The sellers of many worthwhile products have found the health appeal effective in their advertising. This appeal has been used effectively in the

Eyes that trust you

...**pray you deserve their faith!** Yours to protect, to guard and to cherish— the eyes that look into yours with such serene and abiding faith. Life lies before them: beautiful or distorted, rich or impoverished, depending largely upon your forethought and devotion. Without perfect sight the world is hard to understand, difficult to cope with . . . *Don't take those precious eyes for granted.* Plan now for their consistent and constant care. Safeguarded and protected sight opens the doors of life. Neglected or abused sight raises a dark curtain before life's radiance. Yours the responsibility, yours the privilege to insure for your child the great gift of good vision . . . *Justify the faith that lies in precious eyes!* Grant them the conscientious, professional care of your Ophthalmologist or Optometrist, the skilled aid of the Ophthalmic Dispenser (Optician) . . . BETTER VISION INSTITUTE, INC., 630 Fifth Avenue, New York 20, N. Y.

Better Vision for Better Living

FIGURE 13–3. Appeal to both health and parenthood

sale of fruit juices, sporting goods, certain types of clothing, vacation tours, and home-ventilating and air-conditioning equipment. The Metropolitan Life Insurance Company uses the health appeal in its advertising for a double purpose. It attempts to educate the public in general toward developing better health habits. This not only builds up good will for the company, which results in increased sales, but also reduces the sickness and death rate by checking disease.

Closely akin to the desire for health is the desire for comfort. When people are tired, an appeal to comfort and rest is very effective. This is closely tied up with a body need and requires little effort to arouse if the effort is applied at the proper time. Many products might be advertised around this appeal. A list might include furniture, shaving equipment, automobiles, clothing, heating and air-conditioning equipment, and tobacco.

The appeal to comfort might be direct, such as the automobile advertisement which emphasized a "ride in the comfort zone" in the middle of the chassis rather than over the wheels. Good results may also be secured by a less direct approach. Indirect suggestion, through picturing a family seated in easy chairs around the fireplace or a man reclining in a lawn chair beside a pool and flowers, might be effective in arousing the desire for comfort.

Love needs

We can distinguish two kinds of love needs. First, we have the need for affectional or love relationship with other individuals. This relationship expresses itself in our society mostly between sweethearts during courtship, between husband and wife, between parents and children, and between very close friends. Secondly, we have a desire for belongingness, to have not only a close love relation with one or two or three people, but to also have a feeling of belonging to a larger group. This need is manifested in the joining of clubs, churches, unions, and political parties. It also is significant in the relationship between the individual and whatever business, professional, or organizational structure he considers himself a part.

Affection. The sex drive is exceedingly strong. It could be considered a purely physiological need. However, sexual behavior is multidetermined. It is also determined by the need for love and affection. Also, the giving of love is as important as the receiving of love.

A young girl's hair needs Gentle Care to keep it soft and shining.

Gentle Care is a truly fabulous hair conditioner. Because in just one minute, it can turn damaged hair into soft, silky, shining hair.
Hair that's bright, alive, and like satin to touch.
Hair that glows with youth, swings, glints, gleams.
Romantic hair. Fantastically fast. With Gentle Care.

WELLA **Gentle Care® instant hair conditioner**
© Wella Corp. 1968

FIGURE 13–4. Sex appeal logically used

A logical appeal to the sex need suggests that one's attractiveness to a member of the opposite sex would be enhanced if he or she used the advertised product. Such an appeal is especially appropriate for advertising cosmetics, grooming aids, jewelry, and clothing. Figure 13–4 clearly portrays sex attraction that is relevant to both the product and the message. Of course, gift items can be effectively advertised as means of expressing one's affection for someone else. A somewhat different appeal to sex interest is the use of pictures displaying a scantily clad, curvacious young female. Such pictures serve as an effective attention-compelling device—and often serve no other purpose. Figure 13–5 includes a comely eye-catcher. But will it catch the right prospect's eye and will it stimulate the kind of want that can be satisfied with a furnace?

The parents' affection for the child is manifested in the protection, care, and reassuring environment they provide. Parental concern is not entirely altruistic. The mother and father welcome the child's dependence and unquestioning affection. Some parents experience personal success for themselves in the child's achievements. Some take pictures and keep an album recording growth, special events, and other milestones in growing up—not to give to the child when grown, but to help the parents recall the happy memories of rearing their offspring. Appeals to parental affection are particularly appropriate for advertising insurance, healthful foods, encyclopedias, and safety devices. Pictures of babies, of children at play, and of underprivileged children—all appeal to parental concern. The strength of this appeal in various fund-raising campaigns demonstrates the universality of affection for all children.

Belongingness.   Beyond one's own family there is a desire to belong, to feel at home in the world, to have a place in the group. With a feeling of belonging one is apt to feel friendly, trusting, and tolerant of other people. Along with the feeling of being liked or loved or accepted goes the feeling of safety, security, and peace of mind. To achieve a feeling of belongingness the individual conforms to the social standards of the group and looks for ways of expressing himself that clearly identify him as a member of the group. Group identification can readily be demonstrated in manner of dress, in language or jargon, in positions taken on political issues, in stated values and goals, in places one frequents for sociability. Where one lives, the way he furnishes his home, the car he drives, all signal his membership in a particular group. Pride of ownership (a famous advertising theme for Cadillac) is largely a matter of pride in belonging to the group of owners.

FIGURE 13–5. Sex appeal illogically used

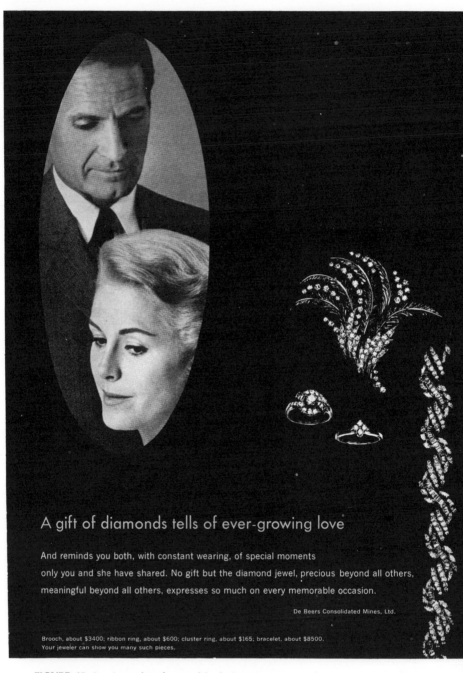

A gift of diamonds tells of ever-growing love

And reminds you both, with constant wearing, of special moments
only you and she have shared. No gift but the diamond jewel, precious beyond all others,
meaningful beyond all others, expresses so much on every memorable occasion.

De Beers Consolidated Mines, Ltd.

Brooch, about $3400; ribbon ring, about $600; cluster ring, about $165; bracelet, about $8500.
Your jeweler can show you many such pieces.

FIGURE 13–6. Appeal to the need for belongingness

Esteem needs

We all have a need to think well of ourselves and to have others think well of us, too. Self-esteem is enhanced by measuring up well against the standards set for oneself. The person seen in the mirror, his strengths, his achievements, his becoming the kind of person he wants to be and the kind of person he wants others to see—these are the bases of self-respect. The will to win, to succeed, or to compete successfully is a way of feeding one's ego. The following quotation from psychologist Donald Laird is illuminating:

Why do small men tend to buy large automobiles? Why did an unduly large proportion of leaders come from backwoods settlements? Why are most children provided opportunities far in excess of those enjoyed by their parents? Why do at least a hundred mental patients in the United States imagine they are John D. Rockefeller? Why is it almost impossible to have your voice sound natural after an evening of bad luck at cards? Why did the prospect sit up and start to show real interest when the salesman said, "Now, here is how this service will give you an advantage over other merchants."

Understand fully the answers to those questions and you are well on the road to knowing why most things other than strict necessities are bought. The unconscious *desire to be more adequate* is the hidden base from which these tendencies start.[3]

Insofar as glory is a reflected sort of thing we are constantly looking outward to other people for signals telling us that they see us as we would like to be—successful, intelligent, attractive, charitable, personable, gracious, friendly, sophisticated, informed, etc. The need for social approval is partly based on the need to belong, to belong to a group. It also is based on the need for esteem, the esteem of others. To win their esteem a person seeks ways of telling other people what kind of person he "really" is. To tell them verbally or directly would be immodest and embarrassing. So he resorts to indirect means of telling them. The clothes he wears, the automobile he drives, the brand of cigarettes he smokes, the way he decorates his home, the foods he serves, the kinds of liquid refreshment he pours—all are instruments of self-expression. As clearly as words they tell who he is, who he wants to be, and to what group he belongs. For example, the advertisement in Figure 13–8 says, "Books are born gossipers. Sitting innocently on your shelves they reveal much about your taste and your background." No doubt many handsomely bound books are purchased more for impressive display than for reading.

---

[3] Donald A. Laird, *What Makes People Buy?* (New York: McGraw-Hill Book Co., 1935), p. 35.

Put your hand over the gray half and see how much younger I look.

minor, and somewhat surprising, revolution has taken place. Today it's estimated that over 2,000,000 men from all walks of life have broken with tradition and have done something about their gray hair—bankers, farmers, longshoremen, teachers and police officers do it. Without blushing.

They all have one thing in common: they don't want to look old before their time.

No Embarrassment

Now, finally there's a product designed especially for men—a product that won't embarrass you in any way. Great Day. With Great Day a man can return his graying hair to a soft, rich natural-looking color in the privacy of his own bathroom, or have it done in any good barbershop. Without any of the worries.

We Give It To You Straight

Great Day works like a shampoo. Once every two weeks or so, you pour it on—*straight from the bottle*. (No mixing.) Lather it in, let it sit, rinse it off. No complications. Leave it on a few minutes each time, and you color the gray gradually. If you want to take the plunge all at once, just leave it on longer before rinsing.

Nobody Notices

Great Day doesn't change your natural hair color. It only works on the gray. The change is subtle. Amazingly, even though *you're* very conscious of what you've done, experience has shown that most people don't even notice the difference in color. Only the effect. "Say, Charley, you look great. Did you lose weight or something?"

Your Pillow Won't Talk

Great Day goes inside your gray hair shafts. So it can't rub off on your collar, or on the pillow. It contains no peroxide in any form. It doesn't harm your hair in any way. (Actually, it leaves your hair in better condition.) It doesn't affect the texture of your hair at all. But just by making it darker, it does make it look somewhat fuller. (Nobody will mind *that* extra benefit.)

Great Day is made by Clairol, the world's leading authority on women's haircoloring. Now, after years of laboratory work and thousands of tests on gray-haired men, Clairol can say, "Hair color so natural only his *barber* knows for sure."™ And unless your barber applied it to your hair himself, even *he* won't be absolutely certain.

Muster up your courage a little—and do something about your gray hair.

It's nice to look young.

Cover the gray hair in the photo and the years go. Cover the dark hair and the years come clumping back.

Young / old / young / old / young / old / young / old—it happens every time you shift your hand. Which goes to prove just one thing. Gray hair makes you look older. And dark hair makes you look younger.

But we suspect you've known that all along. Then how come you didn't do something about it before now?

We suspect you know the answer to that one, too.

The embarrassment.

The embarrassment of having to stand in a crowded drugstore and ask for a bottle of women's haircoloring "for-uh-your wife."

The embarrassment of having friends (and unfriends) kid you about it—"Hey, fellows, look —Charley dyed his hair."

And finally, there was the biggest embarrassment of all—the funny feeling that doing something to your gray was too flashy, too "show biz," not for a "regular fellow."

GREAT DAY® For Men

Well, let's take the last worry first. Because if we can get you over that one, we have a new product that *solves all the other problems*. (It's called "Great Day." From Clairol Research. More about it later.)

More Men Than You Think

It may have been true ten years ago that only a few actors colored their hair. But since then a

---

FIGURE 13–7. Appeal to the need for self-esteem

What do your books say about you?

Books are born gossipers. Sitting innocently on your shelves they reveal much about your taste and your background. Undoubtedly, you acquire books that speak well of you. Everyone who cares about books does. We feel, however, (and we may be prejudiced) that belonging to The Heritage Club is the most sensible way to collect books which will bring you tremendous reading pleasure and a warm pride of ownership.

FIGURE 13–8. An appeal to the desire for social approval

Through advertising it is possible to create the kind of product personality or brand image that will help people express themselves and gain social approval.

Self-actualization needs

Even though all the needs considered thus far are reasonably well satisfied, a nagging kind of discontent and restlessness might persist. Such discontent appears when one feels that he is doing less than his best, that he is not doing what he is fitted for or what his talents allow. What a man *can* be, he *must* be. Maslow calls this need self-actualization and describes it as the need for self-fulfillment, for the full flowering of one's capacities, to become actualized in what he is potentially, to become more and more what he is, to become everything he is capable of becoming. The specific form that these needs take varies from person to person. In one person it may take the form of the desire to be an ideal mother, in another it may be expressed athletically, and in still another by writing or painting. It is not necessarily a creative urge although in people who have capacities for creative work it is likely to be so expressed.

"The ultimate motivation is to make the self-concept real," says psychologist Saul Gellerman. It is:

. . . to live in a manner that is appropriate to one's preferred role, to be treated in a manner that corresponds to one's preferred rank, and to be rewarded in a manner that reflects one's estimate of his own abilities. Thus, we are all in perpetual pursuit of whatever we regard as our deserved role, trying to make our subjective ideas about ourselves into objective truths. . . . If there is one universal human characteristic, it is probably that everyone tries in his own fumbling, imperfect way to follow the advice of Polonius to his son: "This above all, to thine own self be true."[4]

Products and services that appeal to the need for self-actualization include educational programs, musical instruments and lessons, art shows, arts and crafts exhibits, home study courses, golf lessons, cook books, religious books, and "great books" study groups. Whatever the activity or the arena in which people strive for individual excellence there is an opportunity to appeal to this need.

Summary

This brief discussion of motivational forces is for illustrative purposes only. The subject is far too complex to be dealt with adequately in so

---

[4] Saul W. Gellerman, *Motivation and Productivity* (New York: American Management Association, 1963), pp. 290–91.

How to turn yourself on.

you find yourself getting off to a crawling
t each day, if you're avoiding responsibility
putting off decisions, the Dale Carnegie
rse may help you.

don't promise miracles, but we *have* helped
of people turn themselves on . . . people
went from dull jobs to creative ones . . .
following orders to giving orders.

Dale Carnegie Course taps a *real* secret—
it lies deep down inside of you. It is your
en powers, your own potential personal
ties. We simply show you how to
and use them. We help you see
easy it is to be able to

communicate effectively with other people and
be confident in every life situation. In
a matter of weeks, you will have a deeper
understanding of human motivations, get along
better with others, be more aware, more
sensitive to life and its possibilities.

Why not attend a Dale Carnegie class session
in person? It costs nothing to come as our guest.

You may find yourself "turned on" right there.

Make arrangements with your local
Dale Carnegie representative or write:

DALE CARNEGIE • FOUNDER

DALE CARNEGIE & ASSOCIATES INC.

SUITE 486T • 1475 FRANKLIN AVE. • GARDEN CITY, LONG ISLAND, N.Y. 11530

FIGURE 13–9.   Appeal to need for self-actualization

Proud symbol of integrity is the three-pointed star of Mercedes-Benz. It is the hallmark of excellence on any road in the world. You are assured that when you motor behind this distinguished insignia, you drive an automobile incorporating the most advanced engineering possible to modern technology, the most skilled craftsmanship possible to human hands, and design that is always commensurate with the best taste. You are driving the car of connoisseurs. Mercedes-Benz cars include sedans, convertibles and sports cars. Prices range from about $3,300 to $13,000. Factory-approved service available, in hundreds of locations—coast to coast. Ask your Mercedes-Benz dealer for information and a demonstration. **Mercedes-Benz Sales, Inc.** *(A Subsidiary of Studebaker-Packard Corporation)*

FIGURE 13–10. An appeal to the desire for self-expression few pages. Maslow's hierarchy of basic needs is useful in that it consistently focuses on goals of behavior—on ends rather than means. Obviously, it is not all inclusive. Curiosity, exploration, playing, tinkering, and even loafing apparently satisfy some need. Yet they don't readily fit into the system. Perhaps they come close to being ends in themselves. In any event, Maslow reminds us that motivations are only one class of determinants of behavior. While behavior is almost always motivated, it is also most always biologically, culturally, and situationally determined as well.

As demonstrated by the advertisements reproduced in this chapter the appeal should be the central idea of the message. The picture, the headline, the proposition, the style, the tone—all should clearly portray or dramatize the need to be satisfied through use of the product. You shouldn't have to read deeply into body copy to find the appeal. It shouldn't have to read deeply into body copy to find the appeal. It should be immediately apparent.

Every advertisement need not appeal to a basic need. The communication task at hand may only call for an announcement as in the "Yellow Pages," or a straight product display as in an industrial ad showing a cut-away section of a machine, or a detailed description of the product as in a mail order catalog. However, in most advertising situations the consumer needs to be sold, and the selling is done by appealing to his needs.

QUESTIONS AND PROBLEMS

1. "The experience background of the individual serves as a potent modifier of the influence of any external stimulus and conditions the character of response." Write out in some detail an example that illustrates the truth of the above statement.

2. Recently an executive of a men's clothing manufacturing firm, in a speech to an industry group, pointed out that American men were currently spending 20 percent less for clothing than they had spent two decades ago. He indicated that an important cause of the decline was the use of ineffective appeals in men's clothing advertising and urged the industry to "find the proper appeal."

   If you can find (from your library or private sources) back copies of some magazine that carries advertisements of men's clothing, examine those copies to see what appeals have been used in the past to stimulate men to buy clothing. Compare those appeals with ones used today. What appeals would you suggest as "proper" (that is, effective) for the industry?

3. What the consumer in the United States buys with most of his money is psychological satisfactions, not biological necessities. Discuss.

4. Pictures of scantily clad, curvesome young women represent an effective use

of the appeal to the desire to attract the opposite sex. Do you agree or disagree? Explain.

5. How can advertising create the kind of product personality or brand image that will help people express themselves and gain social approval?

6. What appeals would you consider most effective in advertising these products?
   a) Breakfast cereals
   b) Portable battery-powered radio
   c) Bookkeeping machine
   d) Shaving cream
   e) Correspondence school course
   f) Deep-freeze home storage cabinets
   g) Electronic grills

7. In what age groups do you believe advertising appealing to the desire for security would be most effective? To what age groups would each of the other appeals discussed in this chapter appeal most strongly?

8. Make a portfolio consisting of two advertisements appealing to each of the needs discussed in this chapter.

9. Contrast the appeals used in advertising low-priced automobiles to those used in the high-price range.

10. "There is a close relation between product analysis, consumer research, and the selection of an advertising appeal." Do you agree? Why?

chapter 14
SELECTING
THE APPEAL

UNDOUBTEDLY, the appeal or central idea of an advertisement is its most important element. Much thought and effort can well be devoted to selecting an appeal that will elicit the desired response. Generalizations regarding consumer motivation and behavior are useful in identifying alternative approaches. However, the problem of singling out the one approach that best fits the particular set of circumstances remains. And once the approach is settled upon, the problem is to verbalize, visualize, and dramatize the appeal in terms that will be meaningful to the audience. The need for esteem is basic, but John Jones thinks in terms of being promoted to a vice-presidency.

Dewey and Humber say, "When asked which motive is strongest, the answer must always be in terms of the value systems of particular persons and particular cultures. Universally, there is no *strongest* motive."[1] Therefore, it may also be said that universally there is no *strongest* appeal.

It should thus be evident that no absolute rules can be laid down concerning the selection of an appeal for advertising a given product. Again, experimentation with various approaches to the human mind must be employed in an effort to obtain the best results.

---

[1] Richard Dewey and W. J. Humber, *The Development of Human Behavior* (New York: Macmillan Co., 1951), p. 193.

Identifying alternate appeals

The appeals that might be used to advertise a given product are as numerous and varied as the motives, feelings, attitudes, and opinions that move consumers to buy. The possibilities for verbalizing or symbolizing a given appeal are infinite. Therefore, when selecting the appeal a person should not jump to a hasty conclusion, no matter how obvious the merits of a particular choice appear to be. He should first seek out and identify as many alternative approaches as he can. The more alternatives he has to choose from, the better his chances of success. Then, too, the process of identifying alternatives in itself is a powerful stimulus to creative imagination.

Identifying alternatives is most effectively achieved through a combination of creative thinking and research. A creative person's observations, introspections, hunches, and judgments, often yield successful advertising ideas. But the scope of a person's ideas are largely limited to his own experiences, his own world, and his own subjective evaluations. Consumer research, by widening the scope of the creative person's observations and sharpening his insight into consumer behavior, often uncovers alternatives that he has overlooked entirely.

Studies of consumer motivation can be particularly useful for identifying alternative appeals because they focus on the less apparent inner determinants of human behavior. Note the character of information included in the following excerpt from a study comparing the psychological meanings of instant coffee and regular coffee which was done by Social Research, Inc., and reported in Pierre Martineau's book, *Motivation in Advertising:*

Although instant coffee has made considerable progress, there is still a tremendous difference in psychological meaning between it and regular coffee.

a. Regular coffee very sharply emerges as a hearty, tasty, clear, full-bodied, hot, dark, fragrant liquid. It signifies stimulation and strength, personal comfort, vigor and activity. It is a broad symbol of sociability, universally suitable for hospitality, a gesture of friendliness and graciousness.

b. Instant coffee goes counter to virtually all these ideal qualities. In spite of its increased popularity, it is still considered an inferior substitute which can only suffer by comparison with the real thing.

When people were asked to sum up the character of coffee in three words, they said:

—Satisfying, flavorful, invigorating.

—Fresh, priceless, stimulating.

—Delicious, satisfying drink.

—Strong, hot drink.

—Rich, full flavor.

These words were almost never used in describing instant coffee. Typical comments were:

—Not very useful.

—Weak, flat taste.

—Just too sweet.

—Very poor substitute.

—Easy, no aroma, flat-tasting.

c. Instant coffee stigmatizes and typifies a certain type of housewife. The housewife can serve it on occasion, of course. But any woman who goes contrary to the ideal housewife's dedication to her home and her family is neglecting her duty. If she consistently uses a product whose main claims to fame are the time and effort they save her rather than flavor and quality, she is bound to be stigmatized. She is seen as a lazy and indifferent housekeeper, not really a devoted wife.

The women who were considered to use instant coffee the least were described thus:

—She's always baking.

—The best cook of all.

—She cooks heavy meals.

—She uses recipes all the time.

d. Nevertheless the devoted housekeeper can properly use instant coffee on occasion, for example, when she is hurried, when she only wants a cup, or when she is simply at her personal leisure and wants some refreshment. When presented with the incomplete sentence, "A good homemaker uses instant coffee to . . . ," typical answers were:

—Save time and money.

—Drink when in a rush.

—Get a fast cup of coffee.

—Make small quantities.

e. The ideal cup of instant coffee really belongs to a busy housewife having herself a cup during her morning or afternoon break. It is for the working wife getting a fast breakfast before rushing out. And it is for the young housewife who is hurried, harassed, or on a tight budget. The types who received the most votes for using instant coffee were:

(1) The working woman.

(2) The beginner.

f. But instant coffee is a social insult. Its main drawback is that it is unaccepted for sociability. Serving it to guests is somewhat insulting, because it means that the hostess doesn't care to take the trouble to prepare "the correct thing."

g. Instant coffee's advantages are mostly practical. It does serve very important functions for many, readily summed up in these three-word definitions:

—Convenient, quick substitute.

—Economical, fresh, speedy.

—Good, economical drink.

—Speedy, fast, cheaper.

—Speedy, time and money saver.

Actually, these descriptions occur more often among housewives than do derogatory words. These advantages make instant coffee especially desirable for people who want only one cup or who are under pressure of work and time. There is considerable usage among older people using only small quantities.

h. And of course the position of instant coffee is changing. Its popularity is growing, which makes people believe that the product is improved. Although it is still considered a substitute, most people feel that it is getting closer to the real thing. And it is becoming more respectable socially. It definitely has these psychological assets:

(1) It is recognized as a coming thing.

(2) It is economical when you want only a cup or two.

(3) It is time-saving and convenient.

(4) It is modern.

(5) It is suited to young people, rushing to get to work, progressive. This means that they are youthful, busy, hard-working, up to date, smart, clever enough to use modern innovations.[2]

This study concluded that "as long as instant coffee stresses purely impersonal uses of speed, economy, and convenience, which are emergency uses only, it will never acquire the rich meanings of sociability, effective activity, and stimulation that still belong to regular coffee."[3] Perhaps the principal value of studies such as this is not found in the conclusions they reach but rather in the thoughts they start.

Estimating the relative strength of alternative appeals

"Use a rifle instead of a shotgun." The advertisement that concentrates on a single dominant appeal makes a deeper impression than one that peppers the consumer with a barrage of product benefits. If the consumer's attention is thinly spread over all conceivable appeals, chances are that nothing will come through sharp and clear, nothing specific will be remembered. Therefore, once the alternatives have been identified, the next step is to select the strongest appeal around which the advertisement or campaign will be built.

This does not mean that the same appeal should dominate every advertisement. If several appeals appear to be equally strong, each may be used effectively as the major theme in different advertisements. Messages directed to different consumer groups might well use different appeals. An appeal that is strong this year may be weak next year. Essentially, however, the problem of selecting a dominant appeal for a particular ad-

---

[2] Pierre Martineau, *Motivation in Advertising* (New York: McGraw-Hill Book Co., 1957), pp. 55–57.

[3] *Ibid.*

vertisement, directed to a given consumer group, at a given time remains the same.

Again, creative thinking and research are called for. Creative thinking is required to conjure up those meaningful words, phrases, and pictures that give proper expression to any appeal. An advertiser's experience, intuition, and judgment may guide him to the best choice. But the stakes are high. The success of an entire campaign rests on his arriving at the right answer. If his copy theme centers on a nonexistent want, or on one of small importance, he is almost certain to fail. For example, a coffee campaign that extolled the joys of drinking *really clean* coffee failed because the advertiser's hunch that people wanted *clean* coffee, while probably correct, failed to take into account that people expected all brands of coffee to be clean and this was not a deciding factor when they selected a particular brand.

Research designed to measure the relative strength of alternative appeals reduces the risk of making a wrong choice. When an advertiser learns from consumers themselves the wants that are uppermost in their minds, and the motives that exert the greatest influence on their buying behavior, he is more apt to select a powerful appeal.

A number of techniques have been developed to provide help in evaluating the relative strength of specific appeals. Techniques referred to as motivation research, including depth interviewing and projective tests (the Rorschach, sentence-completion tests, thematic apperception tests, etc.), are probably more useful for uncovering and identifying hidden motives, attitudes, and feelings than for measuring their relative strength. Yet, the frequency with which a given opinion or attitude is expressed by respondents to such indirect questioning gives some idea of its importance. These techniques require lengthy interviews conducted by highly skilled interviewers. The samples are generally too small to be representative. Therefore, such research is referred to as *qualitative* instead of *quantitative*. Studies employing a questionnaire and direct questioning procedures are more appropriate for quantifying the strength of alternative appeals.

Examples of measurement

Keen competition for young college graduates, especially in science and engineering, has induced many companies to include advertising as an important part of their recruiting programs. Which appeal do you think would be most effective—starting salary or potential growth of the company? Replies by recently hired scientists and engineers to a questionnaire distributed by McGraw-Hill Book Co. are summarized in Table 14–1.

Perhaps men who are already settled in their jobs rank factors that influenced their decision differently than men who have yet to decide where they will work. But, as this evidence indicates, chances are good that a recruiting program centering on a company's growth potential and the opportunities for advancement will be more effective than one that dwells on the size of the first paycheck.

TABLE 14–1. What factors influence the job selections of young engineers and scientists?

Factors greatly influencing decision	Percent listing factor
Potential growth of company	55
Challenging opportunity	53
Company's prestige, reputation	44
Progressive research and development program	41
Geographic location	37
Permanent position	35
Starting salary	34
Educational facilities in vicinity	33
Regular salary increases	31
Chance to work on specific project, or in certain field	27
Company's facilities (laboratories, technical libraries, etc.)	25
Tuition for graduate study	25

Another example of the fruitful use of a questionnaire to help select an advertising appeal is that of a manufacturer of milking machines. This company had a superior product which was priced below its competition. Low price was the major appeal that had been used in its advertising. Because market position was not improving, the company questioned whether it had been using the right appeal.

The company employed a research firm to help in the selection of appeals for a new advertising campaign. The firm interviewed 425 dairy farmers and asked them to select from a list of qualities the four they would consider most important in their purchase or use of a milking machine. Table 14–2 shows the relative standing of each of the milking machine qualities included on the questionnaire list.

The results from this inquiry seemed to indicate that the ease of cleaning a milking machine was a factor of outstanding importance in the mind of a user or prospective buyer. The next step was to measure the attitude of dairymen toward the specific problem of keeping milking ma-

TABLE 14–2.   Relative importance of milking machine qualities to dairy farmers

Milking machine qualities	Percent checking each quality
Ease of cleaning machine	67.5
Not harmful to cow	60.6
Ease of getting repairs	60.4
Ease of operation	51.1
Reputation of manufacturer	41.4
Ease of getting service	41.0
Saving of milking time	27.5
Increased milk production	21.8
Reputation of retailer	16.3
Low initial cost	6.4

Source: Farm Research Institute, Urbana, Ill.

chines clean. This was done by submitting to farmers the statements listed in Table 14–3 and asking them to check the one or ones that indicated their attitude toward the machine-cleaning problem. Answers are shown opposite each statement.

From these studies it was concluded that an advertising campaign built around the appeal of "easy to keep clean" would be more effective than the "low-price" appeal that had been used. The brand in question was analyzed in terms of its ease of cleaning when compared with competing brands and found to be as easy to clean as any other and easier than most. It was, therefore, clear that the company could honestly use the "easy-to-clean" appeal and make that the central theme of their campaign. This they did and secured a marked increase in sales.

TABLE 14–3.   Attitudes of dairymen toward the problem of keeping milking machines clean

Statements concerning attitude toward cleaning machine	Percent answering
Saving in milking time is worth the cleaning effort	56.4
Some brands are easier to clean than others	49.0
Not much trouble to clean	30.0
Takes too long to clean	11.6
Machine too difficult to take apart	5.2

An imaginative approach to selecting a campaign theme for an industrial service was taken by Canteen Corporation, a firm that operates company cafeterias. At first glance it would seem that what Canteen Corporation offers its customers is menu planning, food purchasing, food preparation, and food serving. However, a more penetrating look would show that the customer receives benefits far beyond efficient food service. To find out what these additional benefits might be, Canteen Corporation and its advertising agency, Marsteller, Inc., conducted a series of group interviews with industrial relations and management personnel in companies using food service organizations. These interviews clearly indicated that management was not merely buying food service, but rather the improved employee morale, the means of letting their people know that management cares, the recruiting advantages, and reductions in employee turnover that better food service bring about. To verify the importance of this concept of food service as a "management tool" they conducted a mail survey among readers of *Fortune* and *Business Week*. One of the research techniques used was sentence completions. One of the sentences and the frequency of words used to complete it follows:

Please fill in the word(s) you feel best complete(s) the following sentence:

"Food service is a _____ tool."

	Mentions	
	#	%
Management	51	14
Employee relations	29	8
Necessary	21	6
Important	8	2
Employee morale	8	2
Valuable	6	2
Time saving	6	2
Beneficial	6	2
Useful	5	1
Personnel	5	1
All others*	66	19
No answer	144	41
Total	355	100

* Forty-eight other phrases received three or less mentions.

With this result and other supporting evidence, Canteen Corporation decided to concentrate their advertising on the benefits their food service offered to management. One advertisement from this series is reproduced in Figure 14–1.

It is often difficult for the advertiser to decide between the use of a positive and a negative appeal. A positive appeal dramatizes the situation

Looking for an effective way to reduce employee turnover?

We have a new idea for you. Take a look at your company cafeteria. With lunch being one of the high spots of your employees' day, an outstanding cafeteria service can make them feel pretty good about the company they work for.

Think about it. An up-graded food service is a highly-visible way to tell your employees that you're really interested in them. Sure, food service isn't the entire answer. But when you have a problem as big and as costly as high turnover, every little bit helps.

If you're having problems keeping people, take a look at your cafeteria. Better yet, let Canteen take a look. We're the one company that makes food service a management tool. The kind of tool that helps solve problems in recruiting, morale, and productivity as well as in turnover. It's all in our new booklet, "Management's Guide to Food Service." Write for it at the address below.

CANTEEN

Director of Marketing, F-7, Canteen Corporation, Merchandise Mart, Chicago, Illinois 60654.
In Canada, Canteen of Canada, Ltd., Toronto, Ontario.

FIGURE 14–1. Customer research led to this appeal

to be *gained* through use of the advertised product. A negative appeal dramatizes the situation to be *avoided* through use of the advertised product.

Note the happy state of affairs in Figure 14–2. This is the positive approach appealing to the desire to be popular, especially with the op-

The Head man is more than a skier.

He's dedicated to enjoying the best of everything. On a rally course, a wine list, a stereo system . . . or on a mountain, as above.

His skis are Heads, naturally. The Head man knows they're the world's great skis . . . always have been, since their metal first turned skiing into fun. And he knows today's Heads are even greater, the best that ever came down the *piste*.

After all, he's been a Head man for years. Skied the classic Standard, for openers . . . moved up to the Master . . . then to the hot Competition. This year he's discovered our new all-around 360, only the most versatile ski ever built.

So he has also discovered TF-8 . . . the radically new base now on *all* Head Skis (and no others). Tough and smooth-running as a permanent custom wax job.

If you're not already a Head man, become one this season. Be more than a skier. More *of* a skier, too . . . because you have more of a ski.

 SKI /HEAD 67

Head, the Skier's Ski . . . at serious ski shops the world over. Seven models, $112.50 to $148.50 . . . Poles, $24.50. For colorful new poster (new handbook free), send $1 to Head Skis, Dept. H143, Timonium, Maryland 21093, U.S.A.

FIGURE 14–2.   Use of a positive appeal

posite sex. Figure 14–3 appeals to the same basic want, but the approach is negative. It clearly portrays the sad plight of unpopularity.

There is a considerable difference of opinion as to which approach is more effective. Those favoring the positive method of expression claim that it is much better to keep the mind of the prospect focused on the real

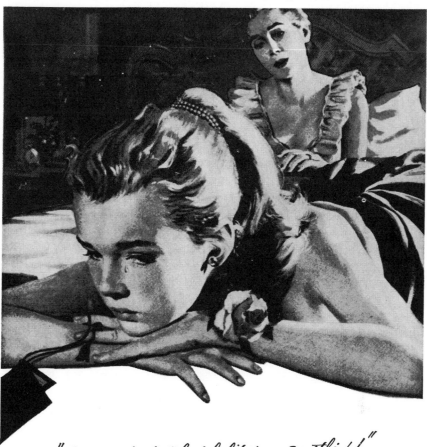

"You'd think I had halitosis or somethin'!"

Molly's remark was intended as a bitter little joke. She'd had a miserable time at the dance . . . even the boy she invited was neglectful. Molly had no way of knowing that what she blurted out in jest was actually the truth. There's no thermometer that registers when your breath offends . . . that's *why* it pays to use Listerine regularly.

The most common cause of bad breath is germs . . . Listerine kills germs by millions

Germs—which ferment the proteins always present in your mouth—are the most common cause of bad breath. The more you reduce these germs, the longer your breath stays sweeter. Listerine kills germs on contact . . . by millions.

Tooth paste can't kill germs the way Listerine does

Tooth paste can't kill germs the way Listerine does, because no tooth paste is antiseptic. Listerine IS antiseptic. That's why Listerine stops bad breath four times better than tooth paste. Gargle Listerine Antiseptic full-strength every morning, every night, before every date!

**L I S T E R I N E
ANTISEPTIC**
. . . **stops bad breath
4 times better
than tooth paste**

FIGURE 14–3. Use of a negative appeal

desire to be satisfied than to call attention to unfavorable siuations. Those holding an opposite view claim that some of the most powerful motivating forces are negative. They state that most people can be driven more effectively than they can be led. The fear motive is given to support their case. It is claimed that people are more easily driven to the purchase of products like patent medicines because of the fear of disease or death than are led to such purchase through the desire for health. They cite the fact that most people wait until they have a toothache before going to a dentist, instead of visiting their dentist regularly to maintain good teeth.

Several studies have been made in an attempt to answer the question of the relative strength of the two approaches. D. B. Lucas and C. E. Benson made a comparison of the coupon returns from 233 advertisements of both types. These were paired into 117 comparisons, each representing a positive and negative appeal. Table 14–4 gives the results of the study.

TABLE 14–4.   Relative coupon returns for positive and negative appeals

| | Coupon return comparisons | | | |
Kind of goods	Favoring positive appeals	Favoring negative appeals	Equal	Total
Tooth paste	17	13	1	31
A food drink	19	17	1	37
A breakfast food	4	9	0	13
Sanitation articles	3	4	0	7
Total for manufactured products .	43	43	2	88
Educational courses	14	14	1	29
Grand total	57	57	3	117

Source: D. B. Lucas and C. E. Benson, *Psychology for Advertisers* (New York: Harper & Row, 1930), p. 118.

These results indicate no differences in the effectiveness of one type of appeal over the other. The difference in the results of breakfast-food advertisements and of sanitation articles might be due to chance, since the sample was too small to be conclusive.

The International Correspondence School has used both types of advertising with equal success. An interesting comparison of two advertisements run by it is explained by Mr. Paul V. Barrett, its director of advertising, as follows:

Some months ago we placed two advertisements in the same issue of the same magazine. The advertisements were the same size, had the same general layout and appearance, and had occupied equally good positions. One was headed "Yes" and carried the sub-head, "It's the Happiest Moment in a Man's Life." The other was headed "No!" and had a sub-head, "You'll Never Get Anywhere in the World, Jack." In the "Yes" advertisement the girl was accepting the man's proposal of marriage. The text dwelt on the man's new responsibilities, and, the necessity of equipping himself to meet them. In the "No!" advertisement the girl was refusing the man, for the reason explained in the sub-head. The text urged the man to do something about it, by training himself for a better job.

Certainly it would be difficult to find two more clear-cut examples of the positive and negative appeal. The conditions surrounding each were as nearly identical as they could be. Which appeal was the better? Based on the business resulting from the two advertisements, and we know exactly how much business resulted from each, one appeal was just as effective as the other. Each has brought in satisfactory volume of inquiries and enrolments. The negative appeal has actually produced a few more enrolments to date, but not enough to be significant.

Later returns may increase the business attributable to either or both advertisements, but they will not change the fact that so far as we can determine from this and many other tests, it does not make any difference which appeal we use. It all depends upon how we use it. And that, I suspect, is the answer to most of the arguments about which is the better.[4]

It is interesting to note that in J. L. Watkins' compilation of *The 100 Greatest Advertisements*[5] only 29 of the 100 used the negative approach. In analyzing these and other advertisements, Mr. James D. Woolf found that the negative approach seemed to be more often used when consumers were likely to be unmindful of the need for the product. Thus, the famous Listerine advertisement, "Often a bridesmaid but never a bride," was directed to a situation usually unrecognized by the consumer. Mr. Woolf concludes: "When the promised benefit is an *unwanted* benefit—when the consumer is happily ignorant of his need for the product—when the product provides a solution of an *unrecognized* problem—then it would seem that a negative approach, possibly pitched in an emotional key, is likely to be more effective than a postive appeal."[6]

The selection of either a positive or a negative appeal might well depend upon the nature of the product, the character of the consumer need, and the degree to which the consumer is conscious of the need. Results of various tests would seem to indicate that either appeal can be made effective if properly applied. As pointed out in Figure 14–4, "the brain that works both sides of the street comes up with more selling ideas that work."

[4] Paul V. Barrett, "Coupons and Selectivity," *Printers' Ink*, May 30, 1935, pp. 54–56.
[5] J. L. Watkins, *The 100 Greatest Advertisements* (New York: Moore Publishing Co., 1949).
[6] James D. Woolf, "Positive or Negative Appeal? Are There Any Rules to Guide Us?" *Advertising Age*, October 1, 1951, p. 50.

The power of negative thinking

Every time somebody in a meeting purses his lips, shakes his head slowly, and says: "We can't do that, it's negative!" we're reminded of the old farmer's succinct description of an opinionated neighbor:

"He knows too many things that ain't so!"

As anyone who takes the trouble to think about it knows, there are times when the negative has a cutting edge that the positive lacks.

For example, contrast "Thou shalt lead a life of virtue" with the ringing, specific "Thou shalt nots" of the Ten Commandments.

Suppose Prescott had said "Commence firing when the whites of their eyes become visible" instead of "Don't fire until you see the whites of their eyes"?

John Paul Jones could have said, "I'm just getting started," but he chose to say, "I have not yet begun to fight" and his words went down in the history books along with the story of the victory won by the men those words stirred to action.

Many successful advertisements also prove the positive power of negative thinking. Two of the best, we regret to say, were not produced by this agency:

"Often a bridesmaid, but never a bride"
"Do you make these mistakes in English?"

Are we trying to say that the negative approach is better than the positive? Not at all. Our point is that the brain that works both sides of the street comes up with more selling ideas that work.

We work for the following companies: ALLSTATE INSURANCE COMPANIES · AMERICAN MINERAL SPIRITS CO. · ATCHISON, TOPEKA & SANTA FE RAILWAY CO. · BROWN SHOE COMPANY · CAMPBELL SOUP COMPANY · CHRYSLER CORPORATION · COMMONWEALTH EDISON COMPANY AND PUBLIC SERVICE COMPANY · THE CRACKER JACK CO. · THE ELECTRIC ASSOCIATION (Chicago) · GREEN GIANT COMPANY · HARRIS TRUST AND SAVINGS BANK · THE HOOVER COMPANY · KELLOGG COMPANY · THE MAYTAG COMPANY · PHILIP MORRIS INC. · MOTOROLA INC. THE PARKER PEN COMPANY · CHAS. PFIZER & CO., INC. · THE PILLSBURY COMPANY · THE PROCTER & GAMBLE COMPANY · THE PURE OIL COMPANY · THE PURE FUEL OIL COMPANY · JOS. SCHLITZ BREWING COMPANY · STAR-KIST FOODS, INC. · SUGAR INFORMATION, INC. SUNKIST GROWERS, INC. · SWIFT & COMPANY · TEA COUNCIL OF THE U. S. A., INC. · WALLACE LABORATORIES.

LEO BURNETT CO., INC.

CHICAGO, Prudential Plaza • NEW YORK • DETROIT • HOLLYWOOD • TORONTO • MONTREAL

FIGURE 14–4. Comments on the efficacy of negative appeals

Interpreting questionnaire studies

Absolute dependence must not be placed upon the results from questionnaire studies of the strength of appeals. People do not always know what appeals will influence them most in the purchase of a particular product. A considerable amount of rationalization might take place in ranking certain appeals. Many people might check economy of use as the most vital factor in the selection of an automobile and yet actually be influenced more by a desire to possess a car that is better than one owned by a neighbor. Such people may build up a belief that the more expensive car is really more economical, reasoning that it will require less repair, can be driven longer, and will have a smaller depreciation. A partial check on such rationalization can be made by analyzing the detailed information obtained from a well-constructed questionnaire.

A serious problem is presented when two more or less opposite desires are rated about equally. Thus, people might rate speed and safety as equally desirable qualities in an automobile. After reaching certain levels of speed, any further increase will usually reduce the quality of safety. Under such circumstances the manufacturer must decide to which desire he should direct his production and advertising efforts. If careful analysis discloses that the desires for speed and safety are not present to any large degree in the same people, but rather represent the desires of two distinct groups, a different product can be made to appeal to each group.

Attempts to determine the strongest appeal have led to the use of various research techniques. These include the ranking by consumers of a product's various want-satisfying qualities as well as measuring consumer responses to specifically phrased advertising themes. A further analysis of these testing methods is to be found in Chapters 24 through 27.

QUESTIONS AND PROBLEMS

1. "The advertiser may find it significant and helpful to consider the basic forces that motivate people to act, but should focus major attention on reducing these basic motives to common, everyday terms." Give three examples of advertisements where this has been done.

2. Psychologists who have rated the relative strength of various appeals have made the task of selecting an appeal much easier for the individual advertiser. Do you agree or disagree? Explain.

3. Techniques referred to as motivation research are more appropriate for iden-

tifying alternative appeals than for evaluating the relative strength of each appeal. Explain.

4. In some advertising situations a positive appeal is probably more effective. In others, a negative appeal may be best. Under what conditions would you recommend use of a negative appeal? A positive appeal? How might you determine which should be used?

5. Do you believe people are able to report accurately on their buying motives when responding to direct questions, such as, *why* do you buy X brand of gasoline?

6. A dairy company is interested in determining the most effective appeals to use in advertising milk. Make a list of all the advertising appeals you think might be appropriate. How would you proceed to evaluate the relative strength of these appeals? Prepare whatever materials (questionnaires, etc.) that are necessary to carry out the procedure you recommend.

7. Which of the following appeals do you believe is most nearly in harmony with the basic reason you are in college?

   a) To satisfy your parents.
   b) To have a good time.
   c) To stay out of the army.
   d) To increase your prospect of getting an army commission.
   e) To get a man.
   f) To increase your social prestige.
   g) To increase your future earning power.
   h) To help you serve your country better.
   i) To help you live the good life.
   j) To make you a more useful citizen.

   If you were employed as advertising director of your college, which appeal would you use to increase the enrollment at your school?

   What methods might be used to determine the stronger ones of the above appeals before you undertook your advertising campaign?

   Are there any other appeals you would want to add to the list?

8. An advertising campaign for an established television set will be launched in four months. The agency has one month more in which to perfect its advertising plan. The account executive is not sure whether a core idea featuring "clearness of reception" or one featuring "greater radius of good reception" will be most effective. He decides to make a consumer survey in selected cities to find the answer.

   What approach would you recommend that he take in trying to find out which of the two appeals might be the more effective in getting people to buy the television set? Assume that the set is, in fact, superior in both reception and radius of area effectively reached.

chapter 15
COPYWRITING

COPYWRITING is much more than the term implies. It includes the writing of advertising messages whether for print, television, or radio. But more than this it goes to the heart of the advertising business—the producing of ideas; ideas that embrace the total message, both pictures and words. Therefore, this chapter will deal with fundamental considerations bearing on the total message and the total thinking required, as well as the written components.

Fundamentally, an advertisement is an expression of an idea and the ultimate success of the advertisement depends on the strength of the idea it is intended to express. No matter how well it is executed in words and pictures, a weak selling idea is not likely to result in a strong message. Therefore, the quality of the advertisement is governed by the quality of the thinking that precedes the actual writing and designing. The "think before you write" stage is critical.

Facts about the consumer, about the product, about the market, and the strategic objectives are all essential information. But facts do not produce advertisements. Finally somebody has to think through all the facts and "get out an ad."

The creative process

The output of human creativity is spectacular, especially in the arts and sciences. Yet, there has been little systematic study in this area and little is known about how the creative process works. Even so, it is useful to view the process as taking place in stages.

The preparatory stage. A person's creativity is enhanced when he pursues knowledge of people, of their behavior, and their world; when he exposes himself to as many life experiences as he can without conscious awareness of how useful they might be. Such general knowledge and experience are most likely to be acquired if he reads widely on many fronts and deeply on some; if he has good antennae, is a perceptive observer of the social scene, and is sensitive to people's wants, fears, hopes, and dreams.

In addition to building his general store of knowledge, the creative person tackles a specific problem by saturating himself with as much pertinent information as he can. This of course points to the necessity of understanding the consumer's particular motivations and behavior with respect to the product at hand and to the necessity of a penetrating knowledge of the product as primary steps in the preparation of an advertisement. The preparatory stage is most productive when the creative person keeps an open mind—when he doesn't pigeonhole information into preconceived patterns. Perhaps the greatest barrier to creative advertising is the stereotype of an ad that restricts the initial investigation and channels thought toward a preconceived mold. It is noteworthy that even after an exhaustive investigation, the creative person seldom feels he has all the information he would like to have.

The digestive stage. Without pressing for an ultimate solution the creative person next works over the material he has gathered. He systematically sifts for relevancy, for appropriate combinations. James Webb Young, in describing this stage, says: "What you do is to take the different bits of material which you have gathered and feel them all over, as it were, with the tenacles of the mind. You take one fact, turn it this way and that, look at it in different lights, and feel for the meaning of it. You bring two facts together and see how they fit."[1] In this stage there is considerable merit in forcing oneself to produce alternative ideas or solutions to the problem without passing judgment on each alternative. In other words, let the mind range over the various possibilities. Getting the alternatives down on paper not only increases the supply of ideas at hand, but also increases the chances of reaching an optimum solution.

The incubation stage. Apparently the age-old admonition, "sleep on it," really works. In this stage the creative person turns the problem over to his unconscious mind, which seems to be capable of working

---

[1] James Webb Young, *A Technique for Producing Ideas* (Chicago: Advertising Publications, Inc., 1949), pp. 42–43.

effectively without his being aware it is doing so. Turning the problem "off" for awhile relieves the pressure of fatigue and frees the subconscious mind its miracles to perform.

The illumination stage. "Eureka, I have found it." There is something mysterious about this stage because it suggests that suddenly out of nowhere *the* idea will appear. Irving Taylor describes it as "largely an involuntary act. The experience of insight occurs when the incubated parts form a recognizable and meaningful experience. The new organization, far superior to any of the original parts or existing stereotypes, may flash into consciousness quite suddenly—the 'subliminal uprush' for which few people are prepared and many may inhibit."[2]

Intriguing as the moment of inspiration is, let the novice beware. Inspiration is no substitute for the painstaking work required in stages one and two, the importance of which is the main reason for discussing the creative process at all.

Creative people. Psychologists tell us the creative person is characterized by his high level of intelligence, his openness to experience, his freedom from restraints, his aesthetic sensitivity, his cognitive flexibility, his independence in thought and action, and his striving for solutions to the more difficult problems he constantly sets for himself.

Don Tennant, creative director of the Leo Burnett Company, spotlighted the most telling characteristic when he said:

> *Creative people are doers.* Those people we think of as "creative" are usually people who have simply learned to go ahead and do what other people simply daydream about. They are people who have learned that the key to being creative is to *act.* The so-called "creative person" stands out in a crowd not so much for what he has done, but because of what others do not do. Creativeness is simply someone's positive attitude hard at work.[3]

Creativity in action

From the abstract to the concrete—the following is a capsule case history of a highly successful creative effort as reported by William Bernbach, president of the Doyle Dane Bernbach advertising agency:

> Let me tell you about the Volkswagen campaign. When we were awarded the account the first thing we did was to spend much time in the factory in Wolfsburg,

---

[2] Irving A. Taylor, "The Nature of the Creative Process" in *Creativity,* edited by Paul Smith (New York: Hastings House, 1959), p. 64.

[3] Don Tennant, *The Creative Man in the Marketing Machinery* (New York: American Association of Advertising Agencies, 1964), p. 4.

Germany. We spent days talking to engineers, production men, executives, workers on the assembly line. We marched side by side with the molten metal that hardened into the engine, and kept going until every part was finally in its place. We watched finally as a man climbed behind the steering wheel, pumped the first life into the new-born bug and drove it off the line. We were immersed in the making of a Volkswagen and we knew what our theme had to be. We knew what distinguished this car. We knew what we had to tell the American public. We had to say: "This is an honest car."

This was our selling proposition. We had seen the quality of materials that were used. We had seen the almost incredible precautions taken to avoid mistakes. We had seen the costly system of inspection that turned back cars that would never have been turned down by the consumer. We had seen the impressive efficiency that resulted in such an unbelievably low price for such a quality product. We had seen the pride of craftsmanship in the worker that made him exceed even the high standards set for him. Yes, this was an honest car. We had found our selling proposition.

Was our job done? Was all we had to do now is tell the consumer "this is an honest car"? Well, I'm not going to stand here and tell you that it couldn't be done that way. But I am going to tell you it couldn't be done that way with the small budget we had. It is one thing to tell the truth. It is quite another to get people to listen to it and to accept it as the truth. As far as advertising budgets are concerned, the truth isn't the truth until people believe you.

I guess if we piled enough coins on top of that phrase "Volkswagen is an honest car" the sheer weight of those coins would eventually have pressed it into the public consciousness. But we had neither the time nor the money. We had to call in our ally, CREATIVITY. We had to startle people into an immediate awareness of our advantages in such a way that they would never forget it. That is the real function of creativity.[4]

How well this function has been performed has been amply demonstrated in the successful Volkswagen campaign. Commenting on one ad in this series, Figure 15-1, Mr. Bernbach said: "You know that this (Lemon) is the classic description for disappointment in a car. Yet, here it was used to prove memorably once again that here indeed was an honest car. For it was the ruthless VW inspector who considered this particular car a lemon because it had an almost invisible scratch. . . ."[5]

The various stages of thought thus far discussed should precede the actual preparation of advertising copy. After thus conditioning himself, the copywriter should be ready to define specific objectives, identify his audience, develop an outline of his message, and complete his ad.

---

[4] William Bernbach, "Selling Proposition Isn't Enough; Creativity Must Bring the Dead Truth to Life," *Advertising Age*, May 29, 1961, p. 60.

[5] *Ibid.*

Lemon.

This Volkswagen missed the boat.

The chrome strip on the glove compartment is blemished and must be replaced. Chances are you wouldn't have noticed it; Inspector Kurt Kroner did.

There are 3,389 men at our Wolfsburg factory with only one job: to inspect Volkswagens at each stage of production. (3000 Volkswagens are produced daily; there are more inspectors than cars.)

Every shock absorber is tested (spot checking won't do), every windshield is scanned. VWs have been rejected for surface scratches barely visible to the eye.

Final inspection is really something! VW inspectors run each car off the line onto the Funktionsprüfstand (car test stand), tote up 189 check points, gun ahead to the automatic brake stand, and say "no" to one VW out of fifty.

This preoccupation with detail. means the VW lasts longer and requires less maintenance, by and large, than other cars. (It also means a used VW depreciates less than any other car.)

We pluck the lemons; you get the plums.

FIGURE 15–1. A risky word boldly used

Campaign strategy

"Every advertisement should be thought of as a contribution to the complex symbol which is the *brand image*. . . . Every advertisement is *not* a one-time shot, but a long-term investment in the total personality of the brand."[6] In saying this, David Ogilvy reminds us that even though the task at hand is to make a single advertisement, the writer should view each ad as one of a series of messages being sent to the same people. It should be viewed as part of a consistent, coherent campaign. If the task is to devise a new campaign, then the writer should seek a unifying theme, a theme that can be profitably sustained over a year or longer. Occasionally, a single ad, such as the one for the Sherwin Cody School of English ("Do You Make These Mistakes in English?") or the one for Tabu perfume ("the forbidden fragrance") runs unchanged year after year and thus becomes the campaign in itself. More typically, the campaign theme—its visual and verbal and often musical expression—sets the framework and style of all subsequent advertisements in the campaign.

Campaign strategy was pioneered 77 years ago by the N. W. Ayer advertising agency. Their approach was to "keep everlastingly at it." When they were asked, "keep everlastingly at what?" they replied, "Keep your name before the public." Keeping the advertiser's name before the public still works, but introducing a new product or achieving some competitive distinction in a field of similar products requires something more. The something more offered by Albert D. Lasker, who is often referred to as the founder of modern advertising, was the notion that advertising is "salesmanship in print." The salesmanship approach is characterized as "reason-why advertising" because it gives the reader logical reasons for buying.

The importance of singling out a strong campaign theme and staying with it has been stressed by Rosser Reeves, former head of the Ted Bates advertising agency. Reeves says that each advertisement must first make a *definite proposition* to the consumer—"buy this product and you get this specific benefit." Second, the proposition must be one that a competitor cannot or does not offer. Third, the proposition must be so strong that it can pull over new customers to the brand. Finally, once you have such

---

[6] David Ogilvy, *Confessions of An Advertising Man* (New York: Atheneum. Copyright 1963 by David Ogilvy Trustee), pp. 100–101.

a *unique selling proposition* (USP), repeat and repeat and repeat it—drum it in. The multimillion dollar error, Mr. Reeves says, is to change the campaign too often. He claims that far too many campaigns are changed too soon in the quest of originality. Colgate toothpaste's "It Cleans Your Breath As It Cleans Your Teeth" is one of Mr. Reeves successful USP's.[7]

Mr. Ogilvy agrees with the strategy of repetition. He points out that "scores of good advertisements have been discarded before they lost their potency, largely because their sponsors got sick of seeing them." Recognizing the contribution of repetition to building a sharper image, Ogilvy also appreciates the dynamics of the market.

You aren't advertising to a standing army; you are advertising to a moving parade. Three million consumers get married every year. The advertisement which sold a refrigerator to those who got married last year will probably be just as successful with those who get married next year. One million, seven hundred thousand consumers die every year and 4 million new ones are born. An advertisement is like a radar sweep, constantly hunting new prospects as they come into the market.[8]

The dual challenge to the creative person in advertising is not only to come up with ads that make a refreshing contribution to an ongoing campaign, but also to come up with new campaigns.

To counter an unfavorable image, campaign strategy might be planned to gradually modify existing consumer attitudes. For example, from the early days of the mass produced Model T, Ford automobiles were widely regarded as "tin lizzies." Research undertaken to find out why this reputation persisted showed that the way a car "sounded" to the driver had much to do with his overall impression of the car. If it rattled and sounded noisy, this told the driver that the body was poorly built and that the car generally was a product of sloppy mass production. If it sounded tight and quiet, the car must be well-built. Taking its cue from these findings the Ford Motor Company spent millions of dollars to make the 1965 Ford the quietest, solidest-riding car in the industry. The advertising campaign that year compared the quietness of Ford and Rolls Royce and concentrated on the theme that a Ford was quieter than a Rolls. The "quiet" theme was continued the next year comparing Ford with other famous cars ("Quiet Man, Ford Is Even Quieter than My Jaguar"). In 1967 the campaign shifted from "quiet" to "strong" to "better built"

---

[7] Rosser Reeves, *Reality In Advertising* (New York: Alfred A. Knopf, Inc., 1961).

[8] Ogilvy, *op. cit.,* p. 99.

The man in the Hathaway shirt

At long last American men are beginning to realize that it is ridiculous to buy good suits and then spoil the whole effect by wearing a cheap, mass-produced shirt. Hence the growing popularity of Hathaway shirts, which are in a class by themselves.

To begin with, Hathaway shirts *wear* infinitely longer—a matter of years. To go on with, they make you look younger and more distinguished, because of the way Hathaway cut collars—low-sloping and 'customized'. The whole shirt is cut more generously, and is therefore more *comfortable*. The tails are longer, and stay in your trousers. The buttons are made of mother-of-pearl—very big and masculine. Even the stitching has an antebellum elegance about it.

Above all, Hathaway make their shirts of very remarkable fabrics, imported from the four corners of the earth — Viyella and Aertex from England, woolen taffeta from Auchterarder in Scotland, Sea Island cotton from the British West Indies, hand-woven silk from India, broadcloth from Manchester, linen batiste from Paris. You will get a great deal of quiet satisfaction out of wearing shirts which are in such impeccable taste.

Hathaway shirts are made by a small company of dedicated craftsmen in the little town of Waterville, Maine. They have been at it, man and boy, for one hundred and fourteen years.

If you want the name of the nearest store where you can buy a Hathaway shirt, send a card to C. F. Hathaway, Waterville, Maine.

FIGURE 15–2. An advertisement that launched a successful image-building campaign (*quieter* because they are *stronger, stronger* because they are *better built*).

Similarly, the reputation of a corporation, or a retail store, or an industry, or an institution such as a bank or an insurance company can be enhanced through carefully planned and well-executed long-term campaigns.

Defining objectives

It might be said that the objective of an advertisement or a series of advertisements is to increase sales. This is so broad as to be meaningless to the writer of an ad and, of course, it fails to state the particular role the advertising is to play along with all the other factors that influence sales. Statements of sales and profit goals with respect to particular market segments and market areas are essential in advertising planning, but they more properly are designated marketing objectives, not advertising objectives. Once the marketing objectives are set, it becomes necessary to define the communication tasks assigned to advertising. These communication tasks can be further refined in terms of media objectives (the numbers of people in particular consumer groups to be reached—where, when, and how often) and message objectives (the effects—in terms of consumer knowledge and attitudes toward the product the messages are intended to elicit). When the message objective is clearly defined, the advertisement is more likely to be prepared as a means toward an end, not as an end in itself.

The articulation of message objectives is in itself a creative operation and is not easily done. Some typical objectives and additional qualifications to make them operational are as follows:

1. Create awareness of existence of product or brand.
2. Create "brand image" or favorable emotional disposition toward the brand (What kind of image?).
3. Implant information regarding benefits and superior features of brand (What information? What benefits? What features?).
4. Combat or offset competitive claims (What claims?).
5. Correct false impressions, misinformation, and other obstacles to sales (What impressions, etc.?).
6. Build familiarity and easy recognition of package or trademark.
7. Build corporate image and favorable attitudes toward company (What kind of image? What attitudes?).
8. Establish a "reputation platform" for launching new brands or product lines (What kind of reputation?).

9. Register a unique selling proposition on the minds of consumers (What proposition?).
10. Develop sales leads for salesmen.[9]

Defining realistic and operational advertising objectives requires an intimate knowledge of the communication process, tasteful discrimination in the use of words and pictures, a sensitivity to the unique characteristics of the various media, and an empathy for the consumer.

Identify the audience

Uppermost in the writer's mind should be the people to whom he is writing. His success as an interpreter depends mainly on his ability to speak the prospects' language—not just the language of words but also the language of their needs, wants, beliefs, values, goals, etc. In fact, the whole purpose of consumer research is to identify and describe in all relevant detail that group of people to whom the advertising should be addressed. However, with all the facts at hand it still remains for the copywriter to fix clearly in his mind these distant people, to empathize with them, to put himself in their shoes. As suggested in the eight preceding chapters, he might describe them in these terms:

1. Demographic terms—age, sex, occupation, income, education, stage in life cycle.
2. Psychological terms—predispositions, attitudes, beliefs, motives, values, goals, personality traits.
3. Sociological terms—social class, status, role, reference group, life style.
4. Geographic terms—religion, climate, urban, rural, local customs.

The writer should draw on all reliable information bearing on these factors that is available. However, as often is the case, the most relevant psychological information is not available. Under such circumstances the creative writer would speculatively fill in the gaps and make assumptions. This kind of mental exploration might well yield an effective advertising idea that superficial information would only obscure. The creative person's willingness to make assumptions, to theorize, and to test ideas logically is perhaps his greatest contribution. It would be helpful if the writer could meet and talk with several members of his desired audience before starting to prepare copy for the advertisement. In the actual writing process better copy will usually be produced if one individual mem-

---

[9] See Russell H. Colley, *Defining Advertising Goals for Measured Advertising Results* (New York: Association of National Advertisers, Inc., 1961).

ber of the total consumer audience is singled out and the copy written for him. Writing would thus take on some of the warmth, directness, and meaningfulness of a personal letter. Each member of the audience who had interests similar to those of the individual the writer had in mind would also feel that the message was written specifically for him. That is an ideal situation. Note Figure 15–3 as an example of an advertisement that approaches that ideal. This advertisement was prepared especially for *Advertising Theory and Practice.*

Failure to identify the audience accurately often leads to strange and probably ineffectual copy. The headline in a hot-water heater advertisement which appeared in an issue of *Farm Journal* read, "This is the only house on the block with plenty of hot water." Another advertisement for soap in the same magazine was headlined, "She gets the *cleanest* clothes in town." Certainly the audience selected by *Farm Journal* is composed primarily of farm people. It is, therefore, somewhat incongruous to place a farm home on a "block" or to think that farm women are more interested in clothes in town than in clothes on the farm. In neither of these cases was copy written specifically to the farm audience.

The importance of directing your message to a person rather than to impersonal masses is emphasized in the advertising guide which Sears, Roebuck and Co. gives its copy staff. In that guide Sears says, "When you write Sears copy you are writing for approximately twenty-five million people. In writing for this vast audience . . . direct your message to *one* individual—not the twenty-five million."[10]

James D. Woolf expressed this same basic philosophy of advertising copy as follows: "Let us *know* those whom we would sell through the written word; let us classify our market not merely as men or women, as farmers or mechanics, but as human beings who have certain problems, feelings and emotions with respect to the product we would influence them to buy. Let us look into census figures, geographical maps, income statistics, bank clearings and such things by all means, but let us remember we will be missing half our data if we fail to look into—*people.*"[11]

Develop an outline

In the actual writing of copy an outline of what is to be included will save time and produce more effective copy. In preparing the outline the

---

[10] *Sears Advertising Guide* (Chicago: Sears, Roebuck and Co., 1942), pp. 52–53.

[11] James D. Woolf, "Salesense in Advertising," *Advertising Age,* January 10, 1955, p. 74.

Did you take notes on today's assignment?

You probably jotted down a few notes for future reference and review. And the chances are you used a pen to do it.

Funny thing about fountain pens. If they really write well, they're a boon to your thoughts. But if something goes wrong, particularly in a tight spot like an exam—real trouble!

Why take a chance? Since you do so much writing, why not invest in the world's finest writing companion—the New Parker "51" Pen. It's precision-made to give absolutely dependable performance. Each easy filling of the "51" stores many many hours of smooth, skip-free writing. You can *see* the ink supply; the hooded point protects against ink smudging. Best of all, the "51" does away with blotters. It writes *dry* with Superchrome Ink. See the beautiful new "51" Pen at your dealer's. Your choice of 8 colors, all point styles, and 2 sizes: slim regular, extra-slim *demi-size*. The Parker Pen Company, Janesville, Wisconsin.

POPULAR PARKER PENS AT ALL PRICES

NEW Parker "51"
with Lustraloy cap **$15.00**

NEW Parker "51" Special
an unusual value at **$12.50**

NEW Parker "51" Deluxe
with burnished metal cap **$7.50**

NEW Parker "21"
Octanium point **$5.00**

FIGURE 15–3. Do you feel that this copy is directed to you?

writer will be forced to set down the basic appeal to be used and the major consumer benefit to be highlighted. He will also enumerate the various product qualities that might serve to provide consumer benefits and select those to be stressed.

The sequence of ideas can be worked out in outline form before actual writing is done. It is good practice to place the most important idea first in the advertisement. Usually the most important idea will be keyed to a consumer want or benefit. Since needs and wants are the primary human motivating forces, they serve to capture attention and interest. Consumers, like all humans, are concerned most with their own welfare and care little about a manufacturer's or retailer's product except as it will add to personal satisfaction—hence, the importance of having copy start off with a consumer need or want.

Product qualities will follow consumer needs or wants in the outline. Such qualities will be developed in terms of how they will serve to bring a benefit. Notes should be included in the outline to indicate the specific qualities to be included and the amount of detail to be developed.

Use consumer viewpoint

Much has already been said about the importance of keeping the consumer uppermost in mind when preparing the advertisement, but this principle cannot be stressed too much. Kenneth Goode emphasized this principle as follows: "Hotel clerks and bank cashiers scan a signature upside down as the customer writes. A copy man requires long experience to reverse the process by writing inside out, so to speak, so that each reader unconsciously absorbs an advertisement as his *own* thought, rather than somebody else's statement to be examined and, perhaps, challenged."[12] James R. Adams, an advertising agency executive, said, "I am convinced that advertising could be greatly improved in effectiveness if it were prepared exclusively from the viewpoint of the consumer."[13]

Another way of expressing this same idea is to write with the "you" approach. Such an approach is not easy for the beginner. The personal pronoun "I" is a big word in the vocabulary of most people. This would indicate that people are interested first in themselves and, when writing, are likely to write about their own actions, ideas, products, and desires. Try leaving the word "I" completely out of the next personal letter writ-

---

[12] Kenneth Goode, *Modern Advertising* (New York: Blue Ribbon Books, 1937), p. 165.
[13] James R. Adams, "Causative Action–The Vital Element" (New York: American Association of Advertising Agencies, 1956).

ten to a friend or parent. Try, also, to think of specific interests of your friend or parent and inquire about them or pass along some new idea, an article you have read, or the experience of others you know about which would bear directly on the interests of the person to whom you are writing.

Substitution of the word "you" for "I," or the addition of "you" to a phrase or sentence, will help make copy warm and personal. Contrast "Win $100,000" with "You can win $100,000." Or compare the following pairs of sentences:

1. (*a*) We are so proud of this product and its fine quality that we guarantee it to last for 20 years.
   (*b*) You will receive an ironclad 20-year guarantee with this fine quality product.
2. (*a*) This man's knowledge will save you money and give better protection.
   (*b*) You can save money and get better protection because of this man's knowledge.
3. (*a*) Crane quality—the dependable ally against high costs.
   (*b*) You have a dependable ally against high costs in Crane quality.
4. (*a*) Ceco products make for better living.
   (*b*) You live better because of Ceco products.

The "you" approach also involves the use of consumer language. It is easy to recognize that technical product terms must be translated into words, phrases, and pictures that are understood by the prospect. It is not so easy to appreciate that, even for common words, there are often vast differences in meaning to different people. Words are merely symbols and hence stand for something. That "something" for a given person will depend upon the experiences that have been associated with the symbol. Meaning thus grows out of past experiences. The following list of common words given to any group of people will have variations in meaning for each member of the group: candy, salt, milk, bourbon, coffee, and rattlesnake meat. The word "candy" to a diabetic will recall a chain of circumstances quite different from those recalled by the obese dowager. To another it might recall that first box of chocolates which the "prince charming" brought on that first date. It is not safe for the copy man to depend upon his own word meanings—he should make every attempt to use words that stem from the consumer's frame of reference.

Headlines

In most print advertising the headline and illustration are the primary attention getters. Working together they should select from the total audience of the publication those readers who are prime prospects for the advertised product. At the same time they should promise a rewarding experience from further reading of the copy. In television and radio there are no headlines as such. However, the opening lines of the TV or radio commercial should serve a similar purpose. Without an illustration in a print ad the full burden of attracting prospects' attention and getting them to read the copy rests on the headline. In modern advertising such ads are scarce. In most cases the illustration is the dominant element and the headline serves as a caption to add meaning to the picture. In any event, picture, headline, and body text should be interrelated parts and should work together to communicate a unified message.

Self-interest is the key to successful headlines. A prospect is primarily interested in what he will get *out* of a product, not what a manufacturer put into it. Therefore, the headline that promises him a personal benefit or satisfaction is more apt to get his attention than one that proclaims the superiority of a particular product feature, or one that brags about the manufacturer's achievements. Headlines are associated with news, and news can be used to advantage in advertising. Curiosity can also be used to stimulate interest and further reading, but the risk in using curiosity headlines is that people who are merely curious may become readers while real prospects pass by.

John Caples, a veteran ad man who wrote the famous headline, "They Laughed When I Sat Down At The Piano—But When I Started To Play," suggests the following five rules for writing a good headline:

1. First and foremost, and above all else, try to get Self-Interest into every headline you write. Make your headline suggest to the reader that here is something he wants. This rule is so fundamental that it would seem obvious. Yet the rule is violated every day by scores of copy writers.
2. If you have news, such as a new product, or a new use for an old product, be sure to get that news into your headline in a big way.
3. Avoid headlines which are merely curiosity headlines. Curiosity combined with news or self-interest is an excellent aid to the pulling power of your headline. But curiosity by itself is seldom enough. This fundamental rule is violated more than any other. Every issue of every magazine and newspaper contains headlines which attempt to sell the reader through curiosity and curiosity alone.

4. Avoid, when possible, headlines which paint the gloomy or negative side of the picture. Take the cheerful, positive angle.
5. Try to suggest in your headline that here is a quick and easy way for the reader to get something he wants.[14]

By its very nature a headline is relatively brief. Depending on the idea to be communicated a headline may contain only one word or as many as 20 words. Brevity may be achieved at the expense of meaning. If it is too long it may not invite the quick reading for which it is intended. The appearance of length in a headline can be diminished by the use of sub headlines and variations in the size of type. The use of several illustrations and captions under each illustration will also aid in getting across to the glancer the central theme developed in the copy.

Provide information

What are the want-satisfying qualities of the product? Surely, the consumer would like to know and has a right to expect the advertisement to provide such information. For many items, specific information concerning size, construction, weight, color, shrinkability, price, and credit terms would be pertinent and should be included in the advertisement.

Some writers seem to think that, if certain types of information are included in copy, potential consumers would be frightened away from the product. Price is often omitted for this reason, particularly in the case of those products that are relatively high in unit cost. Those who recommend such practice suggest that the advertisement should stimulate interest in the benefit-giving qualities and let the prospect get other information at the retail store or from a salesman. The trouble is, with price information missing from the advertisement, many prospects will infer a price quite different from reality. If the inferred price is greatly lower than the actual price, the prospect will not buy when the salesman calls or when the product is examined at the retail outlet. In either case time has been wasted. If the inferred price is higher than reality, then many prospects might never seek additional information.

Information should be specific, accurate, and not misleading. The following copy was taken from an advertisement of a blanket:

These beautiful "Keep Warms" have a scientific 3-ply weave that makes use of THREE fibers instead of One—in such a way as to achieve the maximum natural advantages of ALL THREE. The Wool that accounts for half the Blanket's weight,

---

[14] John Caples, *Tested Advertising Methods* (rev. ed.; New York: Harper & Row, 1947), p. 38.

is all fine-quality, costly, IMPORTED Wool that is finer, softer, whiter, for clearer colors and greater beauty. With it is carefully blended uniformly fine viscose Rayon fibers for even greater softness, warmth and color depth. Then this fluffy, fleecy blend is ingeniously twisted around an unseen "core thread" of sturdy, long-staple Cotton that makes these NEW Blankets a full 20% *stronger*. This 3-PLY DOU-BLE WEAVE makes these NEW "Keep Warms" thicker and closer-woven, for greater warmth, added softness, longer wear!

Big six feet wide by seven feet long for cozy tuck-in against winter's coldest nights. Beautifully bound in richly shimmering Acetate SATIN that gives such amazing wear. And they're TESTED AND APPROVED by the famed American Institute of Laundering as your assurance of quality and washability.

Unfortunately, this copy tries to make an asset out of a mixture of three kinds of fibers with the possible inference that they are superior to all-wool. The qualities of being "thicker" and of "closer-weave" do not necessarily make for greater warmth. The phrase, "Big six feet wide by seven feet long," is also misleading since a 6 by 7 foot blanket is generally minimum and could hardly be classed as big.

Readership studies and other measures of consumer reactions to advertisement support the principle of including specific and full information in copy. This, in spite of the fact that such practice will usually result in longer copy. It has been demonstrated time and again that people will read long copy as long as they are getting information they seek. When a person is thinking of buying a new automobile, rug, automatic washing machine, gas range, power lawn mower, corn shredder, suit of clothes, slide rule, fountain pen, or sweater, any advertisement for the product in mind will almost surely be noticed and all copy will be read unless the reader concludes that there is no further helpful information in the advertisement. As long as advertising copy remains interesting and helpful, it will be read by the real prospects—others do not matter.

There are those who feel that superb writing has no place in advertising; that people's everyday language and only commonplace words should be used. This notion is dispatched in the advertisement shown in Figure 15–4. It is writing at its best.

Any message intended for broad dissemination merits skill and care in its composition.

Get the audience involved

Often, the casual observer suggests that all advertising should be objective, that it should just give the "cold, hard facts." This, of course, overlooks the subjective nature of human behavior, which is guided more

Henry VII, Elizabeth I and Mary Queen of Scots are buried in this chapel

Tread softly past the long, long sleep of kings

THIS IS Henry VII's chapel in Westminster Abbey. These windows have filtered the sunlight of five centuries. They have also seen the crowning of twenty-two kings. Three monarchs rest here now. Henry, Elizabeth and Mary. Such are their names in sleep. No titles. No trumpets. The banners hang battle-heavy and becalmed. But still the royal crown remains. *Honi soit qui mal y pense.*

When you go to Britain, make yourself this promise. Visit at least *one* of the thirty great cathedrals. Their famous names thunder! Durham and Armagh. Or they chime! Lincoln and Canterbury. And sometimes they *whisper.* Winchester, Norwich, Salisbury and Wells. Get a map and make your choice.

Each cathedral transcends the no·blest single work of art. It is a pinnacl of faith and an act of centuries. It is a offering of human hands as close t Abraham as it is to Bach. Listen to th soaring choirs at evensong. And, if yo can, go at Easter.

You will rejoice that you did.

FIGURE 15–4. Superb writing to achieve an advertising purpose by personal needs for security, love, esteem, and self-expression than by cold, hard facts. Therefore, the copywriter, working with the forces of motivation, should get the audience personally and subjectively involved in the message. Personal involvement can be induced in many ways. The reader who sees in an advertisement a picture of a person just like *himself* in a situation just like *his own* speaking *his kind* of language is likely to get involved. Another approach is to build a mental picture in the reader's imagination and make it so clear that he can easily project himself into the picture. Note the vivid scene created in these opening paragraphs from the advertisement illustrated in Figure 15–4.

This is Henry VII's chapel in Westminster Abbey. These windows have filtered the sunlight of five centuries. They have also seen the crowning of twenty-two kings.

Three monarchs rest here now. Henry, Elizabeth and Mary. Such are their names in sleep. No titles. No triumphs. The banners hang battleheavy and becalmed. But still the royal crown remains. *Honi soit qui mal y pense.*

Another way to get the audience member involved is to get him "in the act." Use second person singular and active verbs. Let each audience member participate in the experience of being there, of using the product, and enjoying its benefits. Note again how the copy in Figure 15–4 involves the reader.

When you go to Britain, make yourself this promise. Visit at least *one* of the thirty great cathedrals. Their famous names thunder! Durham and Armagh. Or they chime! Lincoln and Canterbury. And sometimes they *whisper.* Winchester, Norwich, Salisbury and Wells. Get a map and make your choice.

In the automobile business there is an old saying that if you can "get the customer behind the wheel" he will be well on the way to being sold. Whenever advantageous the copywriter should strive to get the audience member "behind the wheel."

Be sincere

The writer who fully believes in the merits of the product and recognizes its want-satisfying qualities is more likely to write a convincing advertisement than the writer who doubts its worth. To be sure himself he should become thoroughly informed about the product's composition, construction, performance, etc. He should digest all research reports on laboratory tests and consumer-use tests. Whenever possible he should examine the product first hand and use it himself. He might find that talking with consumers who have used it and noting their reactions as expressed in their own words will give him a sharper view of its perceived merits. Leo Burnett says there is an "inherent drama" in every product. The copywriter's job is to find that drama and stage it simply and sincerely.

Sincerity is largely a matter of respect for the other person. One is not likely to deceive one's friends. The copywriter should respect the tastes and desires of his audience even though their tastes and desires might be different from his own. Instead of writing to a mass of anonymous people he should write to an individual person, much as he would write to a friend. If he remembers that advertisements are read, heard, and/or seen by individuals, not by crowds, he might be more inclined to write as though he were writing a personal letter and as a result write more sincerely.

Consider the element of sincerity in other lines of human action, such as the host welcoming guests or bidding them goodnight; the "I do" in a mock wedding versus the same statement at the altar; the inflection of voice and facial expression of the star actor versus the amateur. Sincerity gives life and personality, as well as conviction, to the advertising message. It can be recognized in illustrations and copy alike. It may mean the difference between success and failure.

Invite action

If copy is successful, it will produce action leading to a purchase by the reader. The writer should therefore inject into copy words or phrases that will help to impel action. This may often be done by suggestion, implied or direct. Contrast the headline "El Producto Cigars" with "Smoke El Producto Cigars." The latter suggests that the reader actually smoke the advertised product. In the case of mail-order copy, the invitation to act should be direct. Action in such copy can be made easier by the use of a coupon.

The urge to action in advertising copy is not unlike the element of "closing" in personal selling. In either case, complete success has not been attained until a sale has been made. Examples of phrases that might be used to suggest action would include: "See your dealer today," "Get some this week," "Ask your dealer for a demonstration," "Send for a copy of this booklet."

Form and style

There are a number of classifications of copy that might be made. We could look at copy as either classified (want-ads) or display, retail or general, direct action or indirect action. Copy might also be classified into such forms as "reason why," emotional, news, announcements, imaginative, personal, or narrative. While copy might be so classified, such procedure often leads the writer into difficulty. Instead of focusing attention on the form of copy, consideration should be given, first, to the type of consumer to whom the message is to be directed and, then, to the preparation of the copy in terms of the characteristics and emotional make-up of that particular consumer group. True, some consumers can best be made to recognize the want-satisfying qualities of a product by reading emotional copy; others must have a logical and factual presentation of the product's qualities. Although purchases of industrial equipment will usually demand "reason-why" copy, the copywriter will obtain better results if he writes informationally to a prospective purchaser than if he follows a "reason-why" copy formula.

One successful advertising practitioner states:

> I don't . . . demand ability to write or even to recognize "Reason Why" copy. Or to differentiate "Narrative" from "News." Or "Personal" from "Poster." All this knowledge won't do you any harm. But, in practical work, it will do you astonishingly little good . . . Not once in a quarter of a century of buying advertising, selling advertising, writing copy for myself and others, have I happened to hear anybody say, "We'll run six half-pages of didactic copy." Or "Rush me up six columns of good sound colloquial." So write whatever words will clearly and forcefully deliver your message and waste no time worrying as to what type of copy it may turn out to be.[15]

The classification of copy into types also tends to encourage the writer to follow a particular type in preparing copy for a given advertisement when, in fact, many of the most successful advertisements are a mixture of types. Reasons for purchase can be and often are presented in a narrative or emotional manner. Factual copy is not necessarily entirely "reason why." Therefore, do not write copy by formula, but, rather, write sincere and simple copy, keyed to the desires of a partcular consumer group.

There is no single best style of writing for all advertising. A style that is appropriate for perfume would hardly be appropriate in an ad for motor oil. Just as the consumer's perceptions and attitudes are different with respect to different products so should the style of writing be different. If the product is utilitarian and thought of in rational, deliberate, and objective terms, the copy should be rational, detailed, and logical. If the product is viewed in personal, emotional, and subjective terms, then copy should be written in those terms.

Rudolf Flesch has focused attention on the element of readability

---

[15] Goode, *op. cit.*, pp. 142–43.

through his formula for measuring "reading ease." Flesch recommends for easy reading the use of short sentences, words with one or few syllables, and high human interest. He gets the latter through the use of personal words and sentences. Formulas such as those developed by Flesch can be helpful but should not be followed blindly. It is vital, however, to ask continually: "Will this copy be easily understood by the reader?"

How long should copy be? Again it depends on the consumers' perceptions of the product category. If the product is a chewing gum or a soft drink, consumers are not seeking much information, so the copy should be short. If, on the other hand, you are advertising an electric dishwasher or a refrigerator, give consumers the more detailed information they want. David Ogilvy makes a strong case for long copy:

> There is a universal belief in lay circles that people won't read long copy. Nothing could be farther from the truth. . . . I once wrote a page of solid text for Good Luck Margarine, with most gratifying results.
>
> Research shows that readership falls off rapidly up to fifty words of copy, but drops very little between fifty and 500 words. In my first Rolls-Royce advertisement I used 719 words—piling one fascinating fact on another. In the last paragraph I wrote, "People who feel diffident about driving a Rolls-Royce can buy a Bentley." Judging from the number of motorists who picked up the word "diffident" and bandied it about, I concluded that the advertisement was thoroughly read. In the next one I used 1400 words.[16]

If a product lends itself to objective tests, the results of such tests can often be used effectively in copy; but exact or odd, rather than round, numbers should be quoted in such cases. Thus, the statement, "19.6 miles per gallon of gasoline from a run of 100 miles at an average speed of 34.2 miles per hour," will carry greater conviction than the general statement, "about 20 miles per gallon of gasoline." Where specifications can be given in terms the consumer can easily understand, earnestness of purpose on the part of the advertiser is readily accepted by the reader.

An adroit and honest use of testimonial can often add to the feeling of sincerity impaired by copy. The forthright statement of a user of a product may well be more convincing than the same statement by the seller. That is particularly true when such statements come unsolicited and in the user's own words. This type of copy is frequently used in advertisements directed to farmers (see Figure 15–5). As O. B. Stauffer, advertising manager of the American Steel and Wire Company says, "Farmers are interested in other farmers and what they have to say. Testimonial copy has a high rate of believability with them."[17]

---

[16] Ogilvy, *op cit.*, pp. 108–9.

[17] *Rural Marketing*, January, 1952, p. 1.

Robert E. Thorp, DeWitt Co., Ill., started feeding Moor-Man's Mintrates 16 years ago. He farrows four times a year, markets 500-600 pigs, now uses MoorMan's Hog Feeding Program from breeding to market.

"My feed cost, $8.98/cwt., sows & pigs"

"MoorMan's makes me more profit than any other feed I've used, I'm certain of that," says Bob Thorp.

"I've tried a lot of other feeds since I started feeding Mintrates* but I always come back to Moor-Man's. My records from Illinois' Farm Bureau Farm Management Service back up my own judgment.

"I just don't see how anyone can farm today without accurate records.

Cash outlay for sow's feed only $1 per pig weaned

"Last year, I weaned 8.9 pigs per litter and marketed 491 pigs that averaged 213 pounds. Because I fed Sow Mintrate for the first time, I was anxious to see what it

cost me. Here's what my records show: *Total feed cost, including sow's feed*, $8.98 per 100 pounds pork produced. *Total sow feed cost*, breeding to weaning, $3.02 per pig weaned. $1 of this went for Sow Mintrate. The rest was the value of my corn, $1.03 a bushel. That's a mighty good investment, considering the size of litters it gave me.

Mintrates release pork-making power from corn

"*Birth-to-market feed cost*, $7.58 per 100 pounds of pork. These kinds of figures make me stick to MoorMan's program."

No matter how many times a year you farrow, good records like Bob Thorp's will prove you can

boost pig profits on MoorMan's, balancing corn with Mintrates.

Mintrates' powerful blend of the best proteins, vitamins, minerals and antibiotics helps pigs digest corn more completely . . . squeeze more pork-building power from it.

Your MoorMan Man can help you do it at low cost. He'll be glad to furnish you a free Personalized Hog Feeding & Management Program tailored to your feeding method.

More profit with your own grain and

MoorMan's*

MOORMAN MFG. CO. • QUINCY, ILL.

*Trademark Reg. U.S. Pat. Off.,

FIGURE 15–5. Testimonial that rings true

Qualities of effective copy

Much has been written and said about what it takes to make an effective advertisement. The articulation of these specifications in itself is a perennial challenge to advertising's creative people, most of whom apparently are more successful in making ads than in talking about how they do it. As with all true craftsmen they are guided by an instinctive feel that cannot be readily explained. However, much can be learned from a craftsman's observations on his work. An excellent list of such observations is the following, which was prepared by Leo Burnett to serve as guiding principles for his agency's creative people:

1. Every message in print or over the air must have "thought-force"—a central idea that offers an advantage to the reader or listener in an interesting and plausible manner. We have no patience with double-talk or muddy thinking.
2. The reader or listener is presumably a human being, and must be rewarded in some human manner for dwelling on your message. Much advertising, we felt, was as dull as dishwater. We decided, therefore, that we would try to make our advertising "fun to look at" or listen to. Not funny—but fun in a broad, human sense. This involves what we call the "overtones" of advertising, which are hard to describe but which make the difference between an ad that lives and one that is just so-so.
3. To plan the sale as we plan the ad—to build ads so strong in selling thought and so attractive in appearance that they would find almost automatic applications at the point of sale. We have great respect for the instinctive judgment of a good salesman regarding the advertising of his firm. If he is not enthusiastic about it, it has two strikes on it going in.
4. To observe the fitness of things in terms of all-around good taste and to keep the advertising "in character" with management thought and action.
5. To take the attitude that there is inherent drama in the product itself rather than leaning on tricks, devices or "techniques." This also involves keeping the advertising *relevant*—shunning irrelevant approaches in headlines and illustrations, no matter how clever they are.
6. Wherever possible to make important use of the advertiser's name and package rather than trying to lure people into reading our message. They know it's an ad and they like to look at good ads. Why try to fool them?
7. To keep it simple.
8. To know the rules but be willing to break them. This involves a sense of good timing—an important factor in successful advertising.
9. To have the courage to go back to the client with a better idea whenever we can find one, even if he has already ok'd the ad and is well satisfied with it. This involves a lot of wear and tear and is often expensive, but it usually pays off.
10. To keep our place free from *prima donnas;* to subordinate pride of authorship to a better overall result to which many different people may contribute.

11. To be human without being cute or smart aleck; to be sincere without being pompous.
12. To fight for what we believe in, regardless of contrary client opinion, providing our conviction is based on sound reasoning, accurate facts and inspired thought; to be intellectually honest.[18]

As guidelines, these principles can serve the copywriter well. Ultimately, of course, the experience he gains in his own pursuit of excellence will be his best teacher.

Writing for radio

Radio offers opportunities and imposes limitations not found in print advertising. Radio offers the human voice, the most persuasive instrument of all. It is personal. Even though the radio listener is part of a large audience he can be made to feel that the message is person-to-person, that it is directed to him alone. As a listener he can become personally involved. He can interact with the message and the person delivering it. The absence of a picture lets the listener create his own mental picture, a picture of his kind of dream house or his kind of social world.

The advertiser controls when the message will be received. He can select the exact time of day to best reach his best prospects, a time when they might be most receptive. The advertiser controls the speed at which the message will be received. He can have it read faster to convey excitement, news, and immediacy; or slower to convey sincerity, warmth, and friendliness. He can repeat the central idea several times to drive the point home. He can use music, songs, melodies, jingles, and sound effects to gain attention, build identity, and reinforce memory. Radio is just about everywhere. The ubiquity of small, battery-operated radios offers the opportunity to reach different audiences at all times of the day or night.

Along with the opportunities, the radio copywriter is confronted with certain limitations. The ear cannot receive as quickly as the eye, nor assimilated as much information as the eye. The radio message is fleeting; here this minute, gone the next. Whereas the reader can reread the print message at will, only the sender of the radio message can repeat it. Whatever pictures are created must be created essentially with words. The radio listener usually gives only divided attention. The housewife listens while ironing, while cleaning, while sewing, while reading.

---

[18] Leo Burnett, *Communications of an Advertising Man* (Chicago: Leo Burnett Company, Inc., 1961), pp. 254–55.

THE ZIPPO—MADE BY A TOUGH, UNRECONSTRUCTED AMERICAN CRAFTSMAN—WHO BELIEVES A LIGHTER SHOULD LAST A LIFETIME.

THE INCREDIBLE STORY OF THE ZIPPO LIGHTER

—and a man who believes a lighter should work <u>forever</u>

The man who made the first Zippo, and who still runs the show, learned his trade in his father's machine shop.

He developed manual skills. He mastered the sweet science of machinery. And he learned one thing more.

He learned to love and respect workmanship for its own sake. He became a craftsman in the 19th Century American tradition—the breed of men who made things that worked. And lasted. For a long, long time.

Today, he makes a cigarette lighter that works. The Zippo. He constructs each Zippo so carefully that he is able to offer the most sweeping guarantee in the annals of American business.

If a Zippo ever fails to work—he'll fix it free!

Some modern businessmen who make products that become obsolete on a schedule don't have much respect for the Zippo man's business sense.

But he does pretty well. And he has a rare good feeling when he goes to bed each night. The feeling that comes from making a product that *works*. Every time. Year after year. Generation after generation.

Always—or he fixes it free.

ZIPPO MANUFACTURING COMPANY, BRADFORD, PA. IN CANADA: ZIPPO MANUFACTURING COMPANY, CANADA LTD., NIAGARA FALLS, ONTARIO

FIGURE 15–6. An incredible story credibly told

Standards of broadcasting practice generally demand that the message be brief. A one-minute commercial allows about 150 words.

All the principles of planning and writing advertising copy discussed thus far also apply to radio. However, the unique characteristics of this medium call for special handling. A few points to keep in mind are:

1. *Open with an appeal to listener's self-interest.* The first words spoken must gain initial attention and promise a reward for listening further. The first few words must do what the print ad's headline and illustration do. We hear what we want to hear.

2. *Talk person-to-person.* Address your message to an individual, not a crowd. Make it like a telephone call instead of a public announcement; like a conversation instead of an exhortation.

3. *Concentrate on one theme.* It is better to develop a single idea fully and reinforce it through repetition than to touch on several ideas superficially. Keep detailed technical information to a minimum.

4. *Get the listener involved.* Describe the product, service, or experi-

---

THE ADVERTISING COUNCIL, INC.

Department of Labor -- Continue Your Education Campaign

ONE-MINUTE RADIO SPOT #2

ANNOUNCER

Read any good want ads lately? Like -- "Major corporation has opening for high school graduate"? Or -- "Trainees -- Fee Paid -- High School Graduates"? Or -- "Minimum requirement -- High School Graduate"? Those companies will get their pick of graduates, too. 7 out of 10 people applying for work have finished high school. One quarter have even been to college. Sure, there are jobs for people who quit. But not many. And if you want to make real money -- forget it. To get a good job, you need a good education. You've probably heard that a million times. But it's one of those cliches that is absolutely true. So if you're in school, stay there. If you've quit, go now to your State Employment Service or Youth Opportunity Center. They'll tell you how to get more training. And if you don't think you need all the training you can get ... better read the want ads again.

FIGURE 15–7. Straight radio commercial

ence in subjective terms, in the listener's language. Let him think along with the message as it is spoken. Make it fit readily into his world.

5. *Use the rhythm of conversation.* Use short sentences, simple structure, few qualifying clauses. Use words that are easy to pronounce, easy to hear. Read the message aloud. Does it track? Is it easy to follow, easy to understand, easy to remember?

These guidelines apply mainly to the straight commercial, the kind that is read without embellishment by one person. See Figure 15–7. Other forms include dialogue, dramatized slice-of-life, jingles, and various kinds of off-beat or humorous commercials. These other forms offer special opportunities to deliver a message in a refreshing and unobtrusive way. However, they also involve the risk of succeeding as entertainment while failing as advertising.

Writing for television

A hundred people can be involved in the production of a single television commercial, but the whole process generally begins with the copywriter. The television copywriter's contribution is his ability to think in both advertising terms and the medium's terms. He understands the marketing and communication objectives to be achieved. He develops the message idea. Then he draws on the myriad of elements of photocinematography; the visual, aural, and optical elements, to plan an effective television advertisement. He functions much as a playwright or a motion-picture script writer does. He not only writes what the characters in the play are to say, he also develops the plot, visualizes the scenes, plans the action, and writes instructions to the producers, the performers, and the technicians who are to make his ideas come alive. One view is that writing for television is easy because there is so much to work with; sight, sound, motion, and sequential development of an idea. Another view is that such writing is difficult because there are so many variables to learn how to use. Easy or not, writing for television demands specialized knowledge and skills, far too specialized to be detailed here. Thus, this brief discussion will deal only with some of the more basic basics.

The aural portion of the television commercial should embody the qualities of an effective radio commercial. It should be personal, simple, and direct. More than this, however, the aural must work *with* the visual. Let the picture do the talking too. Let the story unfold visually with the commentary playing a supporting role. Seeing is believing.

Visual elements include the setting—whether a studio set or "on location"—the visual props, the performer, his movements, gestures, and facial expressions. Of course, how the product is to be displayed or demonstrated is a vital visual consideration.

The television camera is a versatile instrument. It serves as the eyes of the viewing audience, looking where the writer wants the audience to look, seeing what he wants them to see. Inasmuch as he writes camera instructions, the writer needs to understand the language of the camera and what it can do. The basic unit of camera usage is the *shot*. A shot is as long as or as short as a single viewpoint is sustained. Some of the more commonly used camera shots are:

Establishing shot—a view of the whole set or location to establish in the viewer's mind the place, time, and situation.

LS (long shot)—taken from a distance showing a panoramic view or large sweep of background.

MS (medium shot)—a closer view concentrating on one subject head to feet.

CU (close-up)—head and shoulders or equivalent.

ECU (extreme close-up)—head alone or even closer, concentrating on one feature or detail.

Dolly in or dolly out—the camera moves slowly in toward action or slowly backs away.

Trucking shot—the camera moves along parallel to the action such as moving along side a person walking or a moving automobile.

Pan—the camera remains stationary but scans horizontally from one side to the other.

A change from one shot to another may be to change the point of view on the same action, or to change the scene. Changing the shot and/or the scene may be essential to telling the story. It also adds interest and movement to the message. Too many scene changes, however, will confuse the viewer and splinter his attention. Some typical transitions are:

Cut—an instantaneous change from one camera to another.

Dissolve—one scene fades out as another fades in. Is less abrupt than a cut and establishes a more continuous, quieter mood.

Fade to black—one scene fades out completely until screen is black and then another scene fades in. Makes a strong break between the two.

Wipe—wiping one picture off the screen as another picture appears. Many wipe patterns are available. The wipe can move from left to right, top to bottom, edges to center, center to edges, etc.

In addition, a wide variety of optical effects can be used to complicate or simplify the task of depending on one's attitude toward gadgetry. A danger, of course, is that the gadgetry might detract from the message.

The most widely used form of script presentation is the *storyboard.*

FIGURE 15-8. Storyboard for one in a series of outstanding television commercials.

FIGURE 15–8 (Continued)

14. CUT TO GIANT'S HAND STOCKING PEAS INTO CAN.
ANVCR: (VO) and cans 'em quick...to give you the sweetest taste in peas.

22. CU: HA-UP, PEAS AND 'PEAS.
SONG: Ho Ho Ho Green Giant.

10. CUT TO FIELD TO SHOW GUY PICKING PEAS. SEE GIANT'S HAND HELPING.
ANNCR: (VO) Picked at the fleeting moment of perfect flavor.

21. CUT TO GIANT STANDING IN VALLEY.
Smile from the Valley of the Jolly

18. HELPER TURNS AND SMILES.
HELPER: (IS) Hey, it's here! The sweetest moment of their little lives!

22. GIANT'S HAND REACHES IN. PICKS UP CAN.
SONG: Garden in the Valley

7. CUT TO LITTLE GUY ON BACK OF TRUCK WITH STETHOSCOPE.
ANNCR: (VO) ...Stay behind to watch over... young, tender sweet peas.

21. DISS TO HELPERS WITH A FIERELY LANTERN LEAVING CANS OF PEAS ON TRUCK.
SONG: Good things from the garden

As illustrated in Figure 15–8, a storyboard is a series of small sketches with accompanying description of action and the words to be spoken or sung. The sketches show only the major scene changes. The verbal copy is complete. The storyboard forces the copywriter to think visually as well as verbally and to coordinate the two. With the help of an artist who refines the sketches, the copywriter uses the storyboard to present his ideas to the advertiser. Once approved, the storyboard serves as a guide to the producer, director, set designer, film editor, etc.; whose interpretations are critical to the commercial's success. Because of a rather rigid division of labor along the long route from writer to eventual broadcast, it is important that the storyboard portray the writer's ideas as clearly as possible. At the same time, the writer should not be so specific that he stifles the creative contributions of the various specialists along the way.

As any television viewer knows there are many kinds of TV commercials. Without attempting to name them all, they basically are live, filmed, or taped. A live commercial is seen on the viewer's screen at the same time it is taking place before the television camera. A filmed commercial is recorded on sound motion picture film for subsequent broadcast. Filmed commercials can be either live-action or animation. A taped commercial is recorded on magnetic or "videotape." The Green Giant commercial depicted in Figure 15–8 is an example of animation with a live action long shot of a real person portraying the Green Giant in the fourth frame. To produce this scene a miniature valley was built of styrofoam hills, artificial grass, and crepe paper corn stalks. Then the real person was photographed standing in the miniature valley. He could move his arms, shoulders, and head. He could bend over to pick something up. He could smile and go "HO HO HO." But he couldn't walk.

The Green Giant advertising strategy has been eminently successful. As stated by the creative director on the account, Robert Noel of the Leo Burnett Company, the strategy is simply to "try to create a strong television personality for the brand, and sell the individual items for their specific appeals within the framework."[19]

Huntley Baldwin has developed a useful model for creating television commercials. He has organized selling ideas, basic tones or approaches, techniques of demonstration, and production techniques in a chart he

---

[19] Robert J. Noel, *The Big Idea, Nine Case Histories of Successful Advertising Campaigns Based on Big Creative Ideas* (New York: American Association of Advertising Agencies, 1966), p. 28.

refers to as "Select-A-Spot."[20] The chart and his description of various techniques of demonstration are reproduced here.

"Select-a-Spot"—A handy chart for starting commercial ideas

A.   The Selling Idea (What to Demonstrate)

1. New product concept	12. Quality
2. New product model	13. Economy
3. New product feature	
4. New form, size, package	14. "Creating" problem
5. Ingredients	15. Results of not using
6. Manufacturing process	16. Results of using
7. Company (image)	a) tangible
8. Where product is made	b) intangible
	17. Users' life style
9. Major use(s)	18. Users' dedication/loyalty
10. Versatility	19. Users' satisfaction
11. Convenience	20. Number of users

B.   Basic Tone or Approach

1. Straightforward   2. Lightly humorous   3. Wildly exaggerated

C.   Technique of Demonstration

1. *Product alone.*   The simplest way to demonstrate what a product can do is to show the product doing it. This can be done in a natural setting (shampooing a rug on the floor of a home) or in "limbo," free of background or atmosphere, where all attention is clearly focused on the product.

2. *Spokesman.*   Generally, there will be some kind of "off camera" spokesman accompanying a "product alone" demonstration, explaining what is happening on the screen. But the spokesman can take a more prominent role and appear on camera. He can be an announcer or not-really-familiar face (Avis, e.g.); he can be "real folks"; he can be a celebrity (e.g. Arthur Godfrey speaking for Axion); he can be a corporate symbol (e.g. Pillsbury's dough boy).

3. *Before-and-after.*   "See this dirty stain? . . . Watch while we add our product . . . there . . . stain's gone! *Before* women were not allowed to smoke, but then *After* (many years and the introduction of Virginia Slims) "you've got your own cigarette now, baby . . .''

4. *Torture test.*   The diver plunges from the cliffs of Acapulco and his Timex watch comes up ticking. A Bic pen is attached to the heel of an ice skater, skated around the rink, then stuck in an open flame and still "writes first time, every time." A rod attached to the wheel of a Ford truck shatters a row of light bulbs while the rod attached to the cab (insulated by Ford shock absorbers) leaves its row of bulbs untouched.

5. *Side-by-side.*   Examples have been cited. The purpose is to demonstrate the advantage of your product over its competitors.

---

[20] H. Huntley Baldwin, *How Television Commercials Are Made* (Evanston, Illinois: Department of Advertising, Northwestern University, 1970), pp. 17–22.

6. *Slice-of-life.* This is the dramatized situation in which the product saves the people from their real-life problem. "Big date tonight but about my breath"— "Don't worry, Charlie, gargle with this . . ."—(That night, at the prom) "Thanks for the tip, pal, my love life is great again." The friendly advice can come from a wife or neighbor or a continuing character who is an expert on the subject (Josephine the plumber, Madge the Manicurist, Wanda the Witch, e.g.)

7. *Vignettes.* Instead of a long look at one person's problem, try a series of short (usually amusing) looks at a lot of different people's problem—The disadvantages of Benson & Hedges, the overweight people for Diet Rite Cola ("What've you got to lose?"), the people "covering up" embarrassment for Right Guard deodorant.

8. *Testimonial.* This is a variation on the "spokesman" approach. In this case the "spokesman" may interview a satisfied user who becomes the real spokesman, such as Ed Reimers talking with satisfied Allstate policy holders. The testimonial can be "unsolicited" and "unstaged" (such as talking to airline passengers about their flight as they arrive at the airport) or it can be delivered by a known personality (sincerely or tongue in cheek).

9. *Documentary.* This approach can be used to dramatize the problem (e.g., "When there's no man around, Goodyear should be") or to document the product's performance (e.g. the Mobil Economy Run and similar events). The camera seems to be reporting on real people rather than observing a minute drama.

10. *Symbolism.* If the idea or appeal is abstract or intangible, the demonstration may have to be symbolic rather than literal. Tupperware, e.g., demonstrated "locks in freshness" by putting a combination lock on a ham, a zipper on an ear of corn, etc. Bayer Aspirin used light music and lacy-line animation to symbolize happiness and a menacing black shape to show headache pain.

11. *Fantasy.* In the world of exaggeration, almost anything is possible. Hai Karate after shave has such a passionate effect on women that the men who use it have a special training ground to learn self defense. The Green Giant and his helpers live in a world of fantasy. And did ya ever hear the one about the dove who thought he was a hand lotion . . .?

12. *Analogy.* Again, you can't actually show the effect of the product so you compare it with something you can show. "Cleans like a white tornado," "like sending your sinuses to Arizona," light up and "it's springtime."

D. Production Technique

    1. Live action   2. Animation   3. Stop motion

    4. Combinations   5. Special effects

A primary factor in selecting the kind of commercial is cost, which can vary from less than a hundred dollars for a single live commercial to a hundred thousand dollars for a spectacular production using expensive sets and expensive talent. Ultimately, however, the cost should be measured in terms of sales results, a standard of performance that always should be uppermost in the copywriter's mind.

QUESTIONS AND PROBLEMS

1. Is there any significant difference between advertising copy and a letter to your dad asking him to send you a check?
2. Why is a consumer viewpoint so important in writing copy?
3. Explain the meaning of the phrase "writing inside out."
4. Bring to class two advertisements that have ignored the consumer viewpoint.
5. Bring to class two advertisements that appear to you to be insincere.
6. Select four advertisements for the same type of product, two of which have long copy and two, short copy. Rate these advertisements in terms of which would influence you most to buy the product.
7. Many advertisers claim that both contest and premium advertising are like "shots in the arm" in that their influence soon wears off, thus necessitating further dosage. Are you in agreement with this philosophy? Explain.
8. Select an advertisement from a current newspaper or magazine and underline five words in the copy that are used to describe the product or explain its ability to satisfy a want. Take each underlined word and describe the kind of mental picture each word created for you.
9. You undoubtedly have a close friend, relative, parent, teacher, or school official whom you believe should be doing something that is not now being done. Maybe you want a friend to go camping or hiking with you, your parents to take a vacation for their own pleasure, a teacher to give fewer quizzes or examinations, or a school official to grant a longer Thanksgiving or Easter vacation. There is a possibility, too, that you might want some one of your friends or associates to recognize the logic and wisdom of your beliefs concerning a political party, a religious faith, racial tolerance, freedom of business enterprise, the beauties of music, or the fundamental values of advertising.

   In any event, select some topic or idea about which you hold strong personal beliefs. Pick out, in your own mind, some one person that you know personally and who you think would increase his or her own happiness by accepting your belief.

   Write a personal letter designed to convince him or her of the benefits that would follow the acceptance of your ideas. Let your letter be as long and as persuasive as you wish, keeping in mind always the personality of the individual to whom you are writing.
10. The advertising manager of a dairy company desires to use a contest in advertising and promoting a greater use of dairy products. You are asked to present a contest or premium program setting forth the kind of contest to be run or premium to be offered, the rules to be followed, etc. Write the copy for the first advertisement to appear in this campaign.
11. Select from current advertisements ten words whose meaning might not be clear to consumers.

12. Select a product which you have been using for some time and about which you are enthusiastic and write a letter to a specific friend telling him why he should use the product.

13. Select a copy theme for an air-conditioning plant to be sold to builders of new homes. Write the first two paragraphs of copy.

14. Do you make the best grades in courses that have an appeal to your own self-interest? Of what significance is this to the writer of advertising copy?

15. From each of the following pairs of headlines and description of illustrations select the one which you think was more effective in bringing inquiries or producing sales.

   A. Suggestions for advertising a hair-growing remedy.
   1. Illustration: Man pointing his finger at another man's bald head.
      Headline: "60 days ago they called me 'baldy'."
   2. Illustration: Man holding a check in his hand.
      Headline: "If I can't grow hair for you in 30 days you get this check."

   B. Suggestions for advertising a mail-order book entitled: "Concentration made easy."
   1. Illustration: Large picture of a grasshopper.
      Headline: "Have you a 'grasshopper' mind?"
   2. Illustration: Photograph of author of book.
      Headline: "I'll give you amazing powers of concentration or no cost."

   C. Suggestions for advertising a home-study course in business.
   1. Illustration: Picture of discouraged businessman.
      Headline: "To the man who is 35 and dissatisfied."
   2. Illustration: Picture of man reading booklet.
      Headline: "Here's proof that this training pays financially."

   D. Suggestions for advertising life insurance.
   1. Illustration: Picture of man and wife.
      Headline: "Here's one question you shouldn't ask your wife."
   2. Illustration: Miniature picture of home at other end of policy.
      Headline: "Get rid of money worries for good."

   E. Suggestions for advertising a course in piano instruction.
   1. Illustration: Pictures of man playing piano.
      Headline: "A few months ago I couldn't play a note."
   2. Illustration: Picture of group of people playing musical instruments.
      Panel showing method of instruction and displaying the words, "Easy as A B C."

   F. Suggestions for advertising a mail-order book of literary gems.
   1. Illustration: Picture of man and woman in evening dress in taxi returning from party. Woman is looking angrily at man.
      Headline: "You didn't say a word all evening."
      Copy plot: Read this book of literary gems and you will become a brilliant conversationalist.
   2. Illustration: Panel of ten test-questions on literature.
      Headline: "A test of how well-read you are."

G. Suggestions for advertising a weekly book-review magazine.
  1. Illustration: Group of men and women chatting in drawing room.
  Headline: "This fascinating literary circle now open to you."
  2. Illustration: Photograph of famous contributor to book-review magazine.
  Headline: "Can you talk about books with the rest of them?"

chapter 16
ILLUSTRATING THE ADVERTISEMENT

THE APPEARANCE of an advertisement is affected by such factors as illustration, color, art, typography, and the manner in which they are arranged. Oftentimes appearance alone will be sufficient to attract a group of interested readers. Extreme care, however, must be exercised by the advertiser to see that appearance attracts attention to the advertisement as an interpretative message rather than as a fine piece of workmanship. He should never lose sight of the fact that an advertisement is primarily an instrument to aid in interpreting the qualities or characteristics of products, services, or ideas to persons with the objective of persuading them to accept the item or idea being advertised.

Pictures

The sense of sight has always been a highly important avenue to human consciousness and understanding. Early attempts of man to transmit ideas in writing consisted of drawing pictures in the sand or scratching them on rocks. Pictures served as a common denominator of human comprehension. Today, pictures are no less effective in the transmission of ideas. The very nature of man's experience has tended to emphasize the visual until it is not surprising to find most people visual-minded. Even words used to express an idea are designed to create in the mind of the reader or listener a mental picture. The use of pictures along with words will often add tremendously to the clearness of an idea. Perhaps this helps to explain the popularity of the tabloid newspapers and the picture magazines, such as *Life* and *Look.*

Contrast the advertisements reproduced in Figures 16–1 and 16–2. Each appeals to the same audience and advertises the recreational facilities of competing states. One depends almost entirely on pictures to tell its story while the other depends on interesting type faces in a reverse cut to bring the reader's attention to its headline and to the copy that expounds the thousands of lakes, rivers, and streams, plus the mighty Mac bridge, which is one of its main attractions. The only illustration used is one of the cover of the brochure offered free to interested readers. The words in the Wisconsin advertisement, on the other hand, merely explain in more detail the sightseeing attractions and leisure-time activities that the pictures have already shown.

Factors to consider in selection of pictures

Pictures are of little value unless they assist in getting the advertiser's story across to the reader. To do this, pictures should:

1. Be keyed to the self-interest and understanding of the reader.
2. Include all or some detail of the product.
3. Be relevant to the product and copy theme.
4. Be accurate and plausible.

Keyed to self-interest and understanding of reader. This element is the very heart of all advertising. To ignore it is to invite failure. The principle of self-interest discussed in earlier chapters applies with equal force to the selection and use of illustrations. Pictures are often as valuable as headlines in stopping readers, but only the headline or picture keyed to consumer self-interest will serve adequately to attract an appreciative audience. Note the selection of pictures in Figure 16–2 and how each one tells the vacationist of the enjoyment to be found in Wisconsin.

Pictures must also be chosen in terms of the reader's background of experience if they are to be meaningful, for they can convey as little meaning to some as a foreign language. What would a geology map, a germ culture under the microscope, or an unlabeled map of the starry heavens mean to the layman? Yet some pictures used in advertisements hold as little meaning for the reader. If the product advertised is unknown, it must be explained in words and pictures that are known by the reader.

Empathy, the imaginative projection of one's own consciousness into

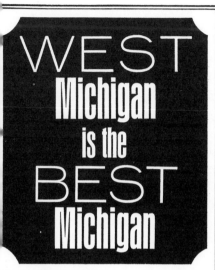

WEST Michigan is the BEST Michigan

It's a delightful playground that stretches along 400 miles of Lake Michigan coastline, from the state's southern boundary to the Straits Of Mackinac· and Mighty Mac Bridge. It's a 31-county area with thousands of inland lakes and hundreds of miles of sparkling rivers and streams — an area that abounds with clean well-kept parks, countless places of historical and scenic interest, festive summer events by the dozens. It's a vacation land that boasts excellent accommodations to fit any budget, and that offers recreational facilities to please every taste. All it really lacks is YOU!

WISCONSIN IS:
everything you expected...

and then some!

Wisconsin has scenery in such variety that it literally overflows its boundaries. There are Great Lakes seascapes, rolling dairylands, remarkable river dells, kettle moraines, the great Mississippi valley, forested highlands, huge wildlife refuges, and an unspoiled peninsula that's a ringer for New England.

The Indians called our state the "land of the gathering waters." (We have 8,700 lakes and 20,000 miles of rivers and streams.) Our lusty heritage of fur trading, lumber camps, and the circus world is still apparent in many worthwhile historical attractions.

Accommodations range from lavish resorts where creature-comforts are unsurpassed to wilderness campsites that will set your spirits soaring.

This summer, let *your* family discover Wisconsin. It's the land that was *made* for vacations!

FIGURE 16–1. West Michigan's story told in words

FIGURE 16–2. Wisconsin's story told in pictures

another human being, can be effectively used in advertising art. The reader is more apt to project himself or become emotionally involved in illustrations that depict his kind of people doing true-to-life things in familiar situations. Playing upon the advancement of women's rights, the pictures in the Virginia Slims ad, Figure 16–3, quickly dramatize the difference between "her" world "then" and "now."

Include all or some of the product. Keyed advertisements have demonstrated that a picture of the product, in whole or in part, is productive of the greatest returns. There are exceptions in the case of products that are entirely new, or in the case of services where there is nothing to reproduce. Most people wish to see what they are buying and wish sales arguments (aids to buying) built around the product. Such illustrations may be in terms of what the product will do, how it will perform, how to use and care for it, etc. But in all such cases, there seems to be value in getting the reader's attention and interest focused on the product itself. The experience of any mail-order house will bear rich testimony to the importance of accurately illustrating the product.

When the product offers an advantage as obvious as the dominant one portrayed in Figure 16–4, choice of illustration is a relatively simple matter. Showing a steam iron taking water from the tap makes a meaningful point to homemakers who know the bother and expense of using only distilled water.

Note also the manner in which the mechanism of the Accutron watch is illustrated in Figure 16–5. Understanding, and hence believability, are enhanced by providing a cross-section view of how the tuning fork operates without any balance wheel. Copy and illustration are effectively used to complement each other.

Relevant to the product and copy theme. Too often advertisers have looked upon pictures as a means of attracting attention and nothing else. Selection has often been made in terms of what would be most likely to attract a large audience rather than what would attract an audience interested in the advertised product. Pictures should support the copy theme and not detract from it.

It is assumed, of course, that the copy theme is well chosen and is worthy of support. When that is not the case, both theme and illustration might be changed with profit. Note the illustration in the GMAC advertisement in Figure 16–6. The illustration is attention compelling and that will interest him. In this connection contrast the advertisements in Figures 16–7 and 16–8 with the GMAC ad. Is there any question as to which ones do the better job of communication?

"When the after dinner cigars were passed and the political discussions began, she would rise gracefully and lead the ladies to the sitting room."

Now you can sit through dessert, coffee and long after with your own slim cigarette.

Virginia Slims.

This is the slim cigarette made just for women. Blended with the kind of flavor you'll like. Full, rich Virginia flavor. Tailored slimmer than the fat cigarettes men smoke. Extra long. In the distinctive striped pack. Regular or Menthol.

You've come a long way, baby.

FIGURE 16–3. Pictures dramatize copy theme

Accurate and plausible. Every detail of a picture should be checked to see whether it is technically accurate, plausible to the reader, and in harmony with the reader's background of experience. Women do not, as a rule, wear high-heeled shoes and silk dresses when washing, cleaning house, cooking, or performing other household duties; yet, some adver-

NEW FROM WESTINGHOUSE
NOW YOU CAN USE PLAIN TAP WATER IN A STEAM AND SPRINKLE IRON!

WESTINGHOUSE STEAM AND SPRINKLE IRON No more distilled water or demineralizers! Now you can use just ordinary tap water!

4 MORE FEATURES FOR EASIER, MORE CONVENIENT IRONING!

SPRINKLES EVEN WHILE DRY IRONING! Sprinkles on any setting—dry, steam, or wash 'n' wear. Touch a button and get a fine spray for sprinkling wrinkles away!

NEW SINGLE DIAL CONTROL! So convenient! All the iron settings are on one easy-to-read dial. No separate, hard-to-manipulate controls for steam ironing!

A FULL RANGE OF STEAM SETTINGS! 17 steam vents! Precise temperature controls for wash and wear...delicate synthetics...all the ironing you ever do!

EXTRA! IRON HOLDER! Attractive holder stores iron neatly on kitchen or closet wall, out of danger. Comes with each Westinghouse Steam and Sprinkle Iron.

You can be sure...if it's
Westinghouse (W)

PORTABLE APPLIANCE DIVISION, MANSFIELD, OHIO

FIGURE 16–4. Product advantages clearly portrayed

The Accutron slogan isn't advertising puffery. It's a law of nature.

Accutron Spaceview "G". Stainless steel See-through dial. Luminous hands and dial markers. Protected against common watch hazards. $125. Other styles from $110.

Accutron® has the only watch movement that doesn't use a balance wheel. And that's why it's so accurate. Because nature gives balance wheel watches a bad time.

Balance wheels are very sensitive to the Law of Gravity, for example. Their rate of timekeeping is constantly changing, depending upon the position the watch (that is, your arm) happens to be

in. The Accutron watch, on the other hand, has a negligible position error. Then there's the Law of Friction. Balance wheels have oiled bearings, unfortunately. As the oil deteriorates, friction builds up and the watch starts to go out of adjustment. Accutron doesn't have this problem. Its tuning fork has no bearings, so timekeeping isn't dependent upon oil.

But even if there weren't any gravity or friction to worry about, Accutron would still be a better watch. Because the tuning fork in Accutron is a more accurate timekeeper (it's physics) than the balance wheel.

Now you know why Bulova can guarantee Accutron to within a minute a month.*

We've got the Law on our side.

Accutron® by Bulova. The most accurate watch in the world.

*Timekeeping will be adjusted to this tolerance, if necessary, if purchased from an authorized Accutron dealer and returned to him within one year of date of purchase.   Bulova Watch Co.

FIGURE 16–5.   Illustration of product detail to complement copy

tisements picture them in such attire. The majority of farm folk do not attend parties in formal clothes; yet some advertisements in farm magazines picture people in formal dress. Such illustrations do not accurately portray the idea the advertising man was striving to get across to the reader.

If the picture is one of the product, care must be exercised to make it a faithful reproduction. A mail-order house had an exceptionally large number of shoes returned because the color was significantly different from that reproduced in the catalog. Nurseries selling fruit trees have lost business because the trees would not produce the kind of fruit pictured in the catalog. Pictures are more understandable than words, and exaggeration in them is more disastrous than similar exaggeration in words.

The man pictured in the Bluebonnet Beer advertisement reproduced in Figure 16–9 has two right hands. Such oversight on the part of an artist is unfortunate.

Color in pictures

The use of color in products offered the consumer has increased tremendously during the past few years. Color has come into the home and

Right decision? This one is: See the General Motors dealer who uses GMAC. He can finance your car, your car insurance, also creditor life insurance–all on terms to fit your budget.

FIGURE 16–6.   Great drama. But what is the connection?

office as well as into the fields of pleasure and recreation. This increased use of color is in harmony with fundamental human attributes. It has enabled manufacturers to increase the want-satisfying qualities of products by adding life, spirit, attractiveness, warmth, coolness, and formality to them according to the color combinations employed. Color influences the emotional behavior of individuals; hence, if properly used, it adds measurably to the value of goods offered for sale.

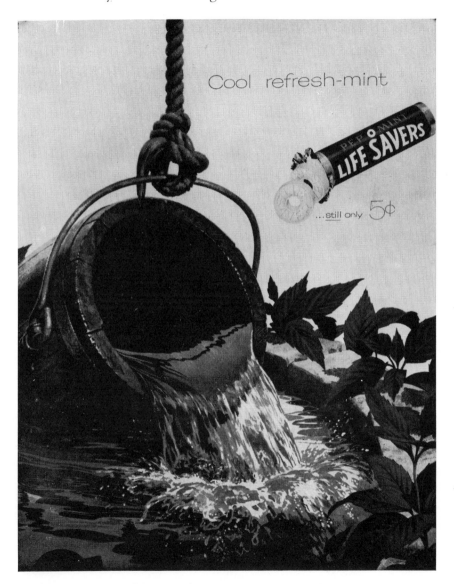

FIGURE 16–7. A powerful story in this picture

Color can be used with equal profit in advertisements. Its possible functions include: (1) attracting attention, (2) assisting in the interpretation of the product, (3) giving life to an otherwise bleak-looking advertisement, and (4) emphasizing or highlighting a distinctive trademark or symbol. Note how color is used to perform these functions in the advertisements for Roche Vitamins, Marlboro, and Green Giant.

FIGURE 16–8. A refreshing experience refreshingly portrayed

Some cold hard facts about fortifying fruit drinks.

Ever wonder what everyone wants from you?
did. So we asked.

We hired an independent research organization
conduct a nationwide survey representing some
million American consumers on what they looked
in foods and beverages.

One out of five consumers said they considered
redients listed on the label, including vitamins, as
eciding factor when selecting one brand of food
r another.

More than 25% thought fruit drinks should be
fortified. With seven out of ten saying other foods
needed vitamin-enrichment as well.

What do they want you to fortify with? Vitamin
C. More than half the respondents think it is the most
important and most needed nutrient.

And 21% said they'd be willing to pay a penny or
two more for it.

For more information on how public attitudes on
vitamin fortification of foods can help your sales increase, contact Marketing Manager, Roche Chemical
Division, Hoffmann-La Roche Inc., Nutley, N.J. 07110.

The ROCHE® food improvers

Come to where the flavor is. Come to Marlboro Count

Color enhances the mood and reinforces the image

Question, Green Giant:

"Your Niblets corn tastes just like fresh, sweet corn on the cob. Is there a trick to growing it?"

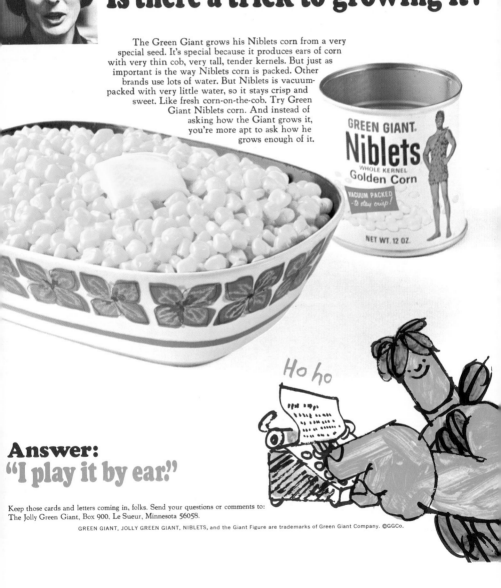

The Green Giant grows his Niblets corn from a very special seed. It's special because it produces ears of corn with very thin cob, very tall, tender kernels. But just as important is the way Niblets corn is packed. Other brands use lots of water. But Niblets is vacuum-packed with very little water, so it stays crisp and sweet. Like fresh corn-on-the-cob. Try Green Giant Niblets corn. And instead of asking how the Giant grows it, you're more apt to ask how he grows enough of it.

GREEN GIANT.
Niblets
WHOLE KERNEL
Golden Corn
VACUUM PACKED
–to stay crisp!

NET WT. 12 OZ.

Ho ho

Answer:
"I play it by ear!"

Keep those cards and letters coming in, folks. Send your questions or comments to:
The Jolly Green Giant, Box 900, Le Sueur, Minnesota 56058.

GREEN GIANT, JOLLY GREEN GIANT, NIBLETS, and the Giant Figure are trademarks of Green Giant Company. ©GGCo.

Color identifies a well known giant and a popular brand

♦ And little more than a decade later another famous
FIRST was introduced   the famous formula to which
is brewed one of the finest beers of today   extra fine
BLUEBONNET BEER   North Texas famous FIRST for
THIRST!

Smart folks favor the OLD FASHIONED FLAVOR of

☆ *Bluebonnet* ☆
EXTRA PALE BEER

NORTH TEXAS FAMOUS FIRST FOR THIRST

FIGURE 16–9.   A man with two right
hands is most unusual

Most emphasis has been placed on color as a factor in increasing the attention value of an advertisement. This, however, is perhaps the least valuable attribute of color, particularly in magazines where half or more of the advertisements are reproduced in color. We have already observed the overemphasis placed on the single problem of attracting attention to an advertisement. Attention is important only to the degree that readers interested in the product are attracted to the advertisement. The possible increase in attention value afforded by color is probably not worth the extra cost occasioned by its use, unless color gives some additional value to the advertisement.

The primary value of color in an advertisment is to aid in a more effective interpretation or translation of the want-satisfying qualities of a product. The qualities of many products cannot be adequately portrayed in black and white. Consider how much color can add to the import of illustrations of such foods as bacon and eggs, cakes, oranges, Jell-O, salads, and strawberries and cream. Add to these such items as women's dresses, men's ties, automobiles, paints, wall paper, decorations for the home, flowers, and oriental rugs, and a keener appreciation of the interpretative quality of color is afforded.

Mail-order houses have found colored advertisements to be much more effective than black and white in selling certain products. One house a few years ago issued half of its catalogs in black and white, and half with color plates for those products lending themselves to the use of color. The latter sold about 15 times as much merchandise as the former. Other advertising is not unlike that of mail-order houses. In a sense, every advertisement in a magazine or newspaper is a page in a catalog from which consumers make purchases, or are influenced to investigate the products illustrated and described.

In those cases where the product does not lend itself to the use of color, it may be placed with profit in a colorful setting, or the results of its use illustrated in color. Baking powder is white, but the cakes in which baking powder is used may be shown in color. Electric refrigerators can be illustrated with an open door and filled with foods reproduced in natural color. Certain food products, somewhat dull in appearance, can be shown in combination with more colorful food and add both to their appearance and meaning to the consumer.

In selecting colors, care should be exercised in using those that bring out the natural qualities of the product. Yellow will make an object seem larger, black on yellow will improve legibility, red possesses a maximum of attention value, and blue is preferred by most men, but all these characteristics are secondary. If a product is green, it should be so pictured, even though green has less abstract attention value than red. Under such circumstances, green will interpret the product with fidelity and perhaps attract the attention of more interested readers than would red or some other color.

Art in pictures

Untold dollars have been placed on the altar of advertising art, with little reward outside of self-satisfaction, the muffled thanks of commercial artists, and occasionally a medal or blue ribbon as a prize in some exhibition. Too often, emphasis has been placed on art for art's sake rather than on art as an aid to a more accurate and complete unfolding of the qualities of the advertised product. Annual awards given by this and that organization have helped to set up false guideposts. Awards for the best direct-mail drawing, most distinctive illustration, best black-and-white drawing, best color photograph, etc., have influenced artists to point greater effort toward winning the applause of professional judges than increasing sales of the advertised product. So successful have advertising artists been in these efforts that their works have found their way into art galleries.

No wonder, then, that many an advertising artist works primarily with the thought that his creations may win him a medal in the next exhibition. His justifiable pride in his work is not to be criticized; but from the advertiser's point of view, it is the wrong standard of achievement. In advertising, the function of art is to provide an assist in the total job of communicating a message to prospective buyers of a product, service, or idea. Fred Ludekens, famous artist and illustrator and creative director of a large advertising agency, says, "Pictures are a language. The very idea of a language is to communicate thoughts and ideas clearly. I do not believe pictures—either photography or the various art treatment—should be abstract or vague. Often . . . artists and photographers get 'carried away' and strain to be different. Many ideas are lost before they finally reach their intended audience. . . . My point is to be rational;

"Sing and dance together and be joyous, but let each one of you be alone."
KAHLIL GIBRAN

Hammond's exclusive Harmonic Drawbars put a full orchestra and thousands of tonal combinations at your fingertips.
You'll find many other exclusive

features as well, in over seventy different models . . . from $555.00 to $10,000.00.

At your Hammond Organ dealer.

HAMMONDORGAN Ⓗ
Division of Hammond Corporation.

FIGURE 16–10.   Abstract art. What does it mean?

to think out an illustrative problem in terms of people. Ask yourself, can the other fellow understand *precisely* what I am saying?"[1]

Abstract art is intended to communicate, but it is more apt to focus on what the artist intends than what the viewer understands. Figure 16–10 is a case in point. What does the illustrator mean? The mystic symbols of abstract art are less apt to influence buying behavior than a faithful interpretation of the product's merits.

Whether pictures are reproduced in black and white or color, or are drawn by the most expert artist, the factor of outstanding importance is an ability to keep the point of view of the prospective purchaser. The artist should know the fundamental purpose of the illustration and figuratively look through the eyes of the consumer in visualizing the effect desired. Consumers in general do not understand art; hence, real art is usually less effective in penetrating human understanding than pictures and drawings modeled in terms of the experience of consumers. One would not rate the crayon scratching of a youngster as art; yet the announcement, "Lemonade—1¢ a glass," scratched on a board will probably attract more customers to a child's lemonade stand than a banner with real artistic qualities. It should not be inferred from this that illustrations are not to be done well, but that the subject matter chosen be related to the level of consumer understanding.

In this connection note the subject matter chosen to illustrate the products shown in the advertisements reproduced in Figures 16–11 and 16–12. The art treatment is excellent in both cases, but the vital element is the choice of subject matter that is closely related to the level of consumer understanding. These pictures meet the admonition of artist Ludekens that "advertising pictures should be 'heard' as well as seen. Advertising pictures should be participating."[2]

IDENTIFICATION MARKS

Importance of identification marks

The advertiser has a product or service whose merits he attempts to explain to the consuming public. In order that the consumer might be able to procure the specific items whose merits have been convincingly presented, it is necessary to place a name, symbol, or other mark of identification on the product or its container. Such a mark also separates the

---

[1] Fred Ludekens, "A Plague on Art for Art's Sake," *Advertising Age,* November 11, 1957, p. 109.
[2] *Ibid.*

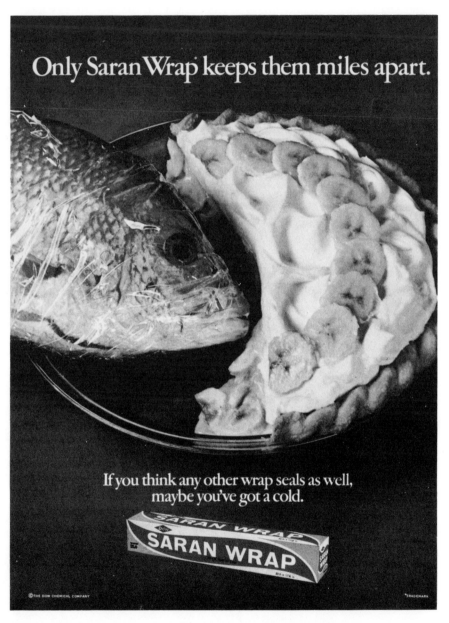

FIGURE 16–11. Illustration effectively symbolizes product benefit

product from similar items manufactured by competitors. "By this mark you shall know me and my products," must be the advertiser's motto.

Identification marks fall into one of three general groups: (1) firm or trade name; (2) brand name; and (3) trademark. From the standpoint of the manufacturer, the firm or trade name is perhaps least valu-

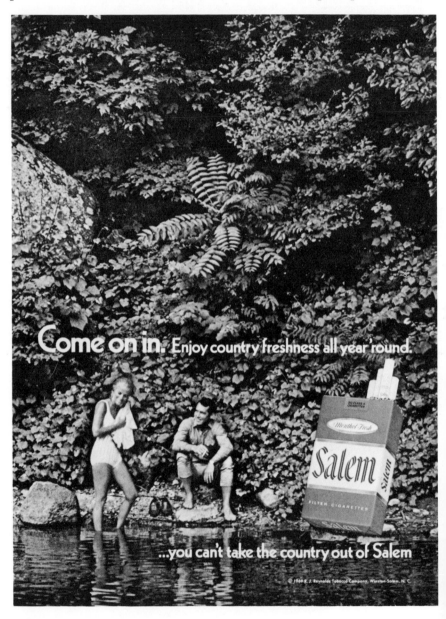

FIGURE 16–12. Sylvan setting communicates country freshness

able as a mark of identification. It is more important to identify a soap as Ivory, Camay, Cheer, etc., than merely as a product of the Procter & Gamble Company. There may be some value, however, in associating a family of products with the name of the producer, particularly if some members of the family enjoy a wide and favorable reputation. If the advertisement is designed to solicit inquiries of any kind, the firm name and address must, of course, appear in the advertisement.

The retailer, on the other hand, must consider the firm name as of paramount importance as a mark of identification. He may emphasize certain trade-marked or branded merchandise in his advertising, but his primary motive is to attract trade to his store. He usually has no merchandise of his own to offer the public, but rather a service in the way of convenient location, courteous and efficient clerks, delivery of goods, reasonable prices, quality merchandise, etc.

Brand names

This is perhaps the most common means of identifying products. Estimates of the number of brands entering the channels of modern commerce range from one half to one million. An analysis of brands offered for sale in any market area will emphasize their importance in terms of numbers. We have seen that in Milwaukee in 1970 there were 28 brands of laundry soap, 25 brands of canned peas, 19 brands of package coffee, 36 brands of women's girdles, etc. Too many writers place undue emphasis on trademarks as a means of identification, and they underemphasize brand names.

A brand name may often be registered as a trademark; but whether it is or not, its primary function remains the same. In general, a brand name serves more effectively than either a firm name or trademark in making it easy for customers to ask for a particular product. Relatively few people would recognize the Indian-head insignia as identifying the American Tobacco Company, but few would fail to recognize the name Lucky Strike.

A number of tests have been made of the degree to which potential consumers are familiar with the brand names of products in a particular generic group. The most notable of such tests were made by Professors Hotchkiss and Franken of New York University. Similar tests have been made by advertising agencies and advertising media. The technique of these studies in brand-name association consisted of submitting to a group of consumers a questionnaire with the names of such products as hosiery, watches, soap, coffee, toothpaste, cigarettes, hats, typewriters, etc., and asking the respondent to write under the name of each general commodity all the names of specific brands that could be recalled.

The Psychological Corporation has carried this type of test a step further by including in its questions to consumers the basic advertising theme along with the name of the general commodity. Thus, it will ask: "What soap advertises: 'Stop Those Runs in Stockings'?" Inclusion of the advertising theme in testing seems to be more logical. A consumer is more inclined to purchase a given brand if the brand name recalls or is associated with a selling theme.

Gene Seehafer has classified brand names as *functional* names and *fanciful* names. Under each classification he lists several types. See Figure 16–13.[2a]

Trademarks

The Lanham Trademark Act which went into effect in July, 1947, states that "the term 'trademark' includes any word, name, symbol, or device or any combination thereof adopted and used by a manufacturer or merchant to identify his goods and distinguish them from those manufactured or sold by others."[2b] Thus, a trademark is somewhat broader than a trade name and, in addition, is supported by statutory law.

A trademark under the new law need not be physically affixed to the product or its container. To be kept alive, a mark must be used, but the Lanham Act states that a mark to identify goods will be considered in use "when it is placed in a manner on goods or their containers or the displays associated therewith or on the tags or labels affixed thereto and the goods are sold or transported in commerce."[3] This would seem to indicate that the inclusion of a trademark in advertising would not be sufficient to establish use, but that the mark must be associated in some way with the physical product and not merely with a picturization of it.

The 1947 law also recognized service marks, or marks used to identify services offered by individuals and firms. The act defined a service mark as one "used in the sale or advertising of services to identify the services of one person and distinguish them from the services of others and includes without limitation the marks, names, symbols, titles, designations,

---

[2a] Gene Seehafer, "Classification of Brand Names" in *Consumer Behavior and the Behavioral Sciences* by Steuart Henderson Britt (New York: John Wiley & Sons, Inc., 1966), pp. 378–79.

[2b] Lanham Trademark Act, Sec. 45.

[3] *Ibid.*

Functional Names

a. *Promise of results*
Spic'n Span
Glo-Coat
Duz
Deepsleep
Silver Curl
Sight Savers
Beautyrest
Ditto

b. *Ease of application*
Pin It
Quick
Zippo
E-Zee-Freeze
Magic Chef
Kwikeeze
Easy-Off
Minit-On

c. *Standard of quality*
Gold Seal Glass Wax
Gold Medal Flour
Royal
Perfection
Ideal
Miracle Tuft
Old Gold
Capitol

d. *Description of product ingredient*
Wheaties
Coca-Cola
Hotpoint
Ry-Krisp
All-Bran
Almond Joy
Yello Bole
Green Mint

e. *Description of product use*
Bisquick
Sani-Flush
Py-O-My
Blim

Fanciful Names

a. *Pleasant-association names*
Breeze
Jubilee
Joy
Lux
Flying A
Prince Matchiabelli
Tide
Pet

b. *Promise of reward*
Pride
Gleem
Odorono
Breath-o-Pine
Fresh 'nd Aire
Softskin
Prom

c. *Meaningless but easily remembered*
Babo
Ajax
Drax
Kodak
B.V.D.
Tek
Vel

FIGURE 16–13. Classification of brand names

slogans, character names, and distinctive features of radio or other advertising used in commerce."[4] By this action, service firms such as hotels, accountants, advertising agencies, banks, public utilities, and research firms may secure the benefits of the trademark law.

Registration of marks

Trademarks, service marks, and certification marks (like the *Good Housekeeping* seal of approval) can be registered with the United States Patent Office. Such registration serves as: (1) constructive notice of claim of ownership, (2) prima-facie evidence of registrant's exclusive right to use the mark in commerce, and (3) conclusive evidence of registrant's exclusive right to use the mark in commerce under certain circumstances.

The incontestable right in a mark is secured after the mark has been filed with the Commissioner of Patents within the time prescribed, and providing that there are no actions pending which contest the registrant's claim of ownership. Professor Borden suggests that this "incontestability provision may possibly work hardship on small business concerns which may not be aware of the importance of registration and of vigilance in protecting their marks and thus may unwittingly lose their rights in their marks to another user."[5] On the other hand, this feature should protect valid users from "ambush" by later users.

Factors to consider in choosing an identification mark

Aside from the legal problems involved in the selection of a mark to identify a given product, there are other problems of equal or greater magnitude. The keynote of any mark should be distinctiveness. Such a quality will make it stand out and will increase its memory value. Association value can be enhanced if the symbol, word, name, or device chosen for a mark is suggestive of the product or certain of its qualities.

While a trademark should not be descriptive, it can be suggestive. Furthermore, certain explanatory words can be woven around the trademark without being a part of the legal instrument, yet enhancing its identification and association value. Note the marks reproduced in Figure 16–14.

If names are to be used, they should not only be relatively easy to pro-

---

[4] *Ibid.*

[5] Neil H. Borden, "The New Trade-Mark Law," *Harvard Business Review,* Spring Number, 1947, p. 305.

FIGURE 16–14. Some well-known marks of identification

nounce but also be pronounceable in only one way. Such words as "Pall Mall," "Gargoyle," "Clicquot," and "Unguentine" violate the above principle. They have grown into valuable marks, but the same amount of effort placed upon some other word might have produced still greater results. Certainly, in the selection of a new mark, it is not advisable to start with a handicap that is avoidable.

With the growth of giant diversified corporations and an increasing necessity for "selling" the corporation itself to various publics such as investors, government, potential employees, etc., the demand for corporate symbols has increased greatly. The corporate symbol serves as visual shorthand for the company's formal name.

Alfred Politz says that "a trademark's effectiveness rests largely on the verbalization of the words or letters used in the symbol. By creating a symbol that can be easily pronounced, or identified by a few simple words an advertiser automatically gets his product introduced to the ear as well as the eye of the consumer."[6]

The United States Trademark Association lists the following as desirable characteristics in a trademark:

> Brevity
> Easy to remember
> Easily readable and speakable
> Easily adaptable to any media
> No unpleasant connotations
> Suitable for export
> Lends itself to pictorialization
> Subtlety[7]

Caution should also be exercised in the adoption of a surname as a mark of identification. A person may have a justifiable pride in his family name and may like to see it indelibly associated with every unit of merchandise produced. Surnames, however, violate the ideal of distinctiveness and encourage imitation if the name becomes well known. Outstanding instances of such imitation are found in the names of Williams, Rogers, Dobbs, Baker, and Stetson.

The use of a surname may provide a satisfactory mark when associated with another word, a symbol, or written in a distinctive manner. The mark reproduced in Figure 16–15 illustrates all three types of association. It further illustrates how a company may alter its mark without changing

---

[6] *Advertising Age,* "Trademarks Must Sell, Not Just Identify," May 20, 1957, p. 1.

[7] United States Trademark Association, *Trademark Management* (New York, 1956), pp. 17–19.

which of these two
trademarks would YOU pick
for a big corporation ?

1. 🔺 **Thompson Products**

-this? or this?

2. 🔺 *Thompson Products*

FIGURE 16–15. Alteration of a trade-mark to symbolize progress its basic format and utilize such alteration to symbolize and call attention to the modern and progressive character of the company.

Protection afforded by identification marks

The advertiser is afforded both common and statutory law protection for identification marks that meet certain requirements and that have been used by the company in its advertising or on its products. In the case of trademarks, service marks, and some others, the law provides for registration with the U.S. Patent Office, which affords definite protection. For other marks, protection is found both in the laws dealing with unfair competition and in courts of equity for violations of common-law rights.

Important as legal protection may be, of still greater importance is the protection of favorable consumer attitudes toward the mark and a proper association between the mark and the advertised product. Emphasis must always be placed on the value of a mark as a means of helping the consumer to select the merchandise whose want-satisfying qualities have been explained and interpreted through advertising.

Protection which identification marks afford consumers should not be ignored. They provide a means whereby consumers can duplicate the purchase of products that have given satisfaction, or avoid those that have not. Thus, to the manufacturer this may prove a double-edged sword. It therefore behooves the advertiser to offer to the public merchandise that is not only good but is also uniformly good. Identification marks can thus serve as a partial guide to intelligent buying.

Clowry Chapman has summarized in admirable fashion the relationship of identification marks and advertising and their value to both the producer and consumer. His use of the term "trademark" could be broadened to include all identification marks: His statement follows:

> Trademarks will always need the help of other advertising, for at best the trademark is but a form of advertising, a very abridged or tabloid form of advertising—a word, a symbol, a phrase. Too much should not be expected of it alone, but, when helped by other advertising its service is amazing—identifying, reminding, fixing responsibility, increasing pride of production and morale, reassuring and insuring—insuring future markets for the product; reassuring customers that standards have been upheld. It inspires better morale among workers and greater pride in the product, making the manufacturer stand squarely behind the product. It reminds customers of what they know or have learned, guides and protects them in their marketing by identifying what they have set out to get and warding off the frauds that lie in the wake of confusion.[8]

---

[8] Clowry Chapman, *How Advertisements Defeat Their Own Ends* (New York: Prentice-Hall, Inc., 1931), pp. 19–20.

QUESTIONS AND PROBLEMS

1. Why are pictures so important in helping to interpret the qualities of a product?

2. What qualities or factors should be considered in selecting pictures for a specific product?

3. Why are pictures that show the product generally more effective than those that do not?

4. Bring to class four advertisements which have illustrations that are relevant to the product advertised, and four advertisements with illustrations which are not relevant to the product advertised.

5. Bring to class three advertisements with pictures that are not accurate or plausible.

6. Bring to class three advertisements that show poor use of color.

7. What is the danger of overemphasizing art in advertising? What is its proper function?

8. "Pictures are of little value in an advertisement unless they assist in getting the advertiser's story across to the reader." Analyze this statement critically.

9. How do you account for the tremendous growth in the circulation and popularity of tabloid newspapers and picture magazines? Does this growth hold any significance to the advertiser?

10. Prepare a sheet of instructions to be handed to an artist to guide him in the preparation of an illustration for an advertisement of dairy products.

11. Fred Ludekens says, "Do not put the visual message in an idiom *people* can not understand." Comment on this statement by Ludekens.

12. What protection is afforded through the registration of a trademark? What other types of protection are afforded the advertiser against infringement of trademarks, brand names, and firm names?

13. How might an advertiser's mark of identification protect the consumer?

14. Changes in consumer tastes and buying preferences often produce problems for manufacturers who have built too restricted a meaning into their product identification marks. An example of this difficulty is found in the experience of the Iron Fireman Manufacturing Co.

    This company was one of the leaders in the development and promotion of mechanical stokers for coal-burning home heating units. It achieved high popularity among consumers as a result of its quality product and its effective advertising. Its trademark consisted of an energetic, coal-shoveling robot and it adopted the trade name "Iron Fireman." In the minds of many consumers the symbol of the shoveling robot and the name Iron Fireman became synonymous with coal stokers.

    During the past several years consumer fuel preferences for home heating have undergone radical changes. There has been a rapid switch from coal to oil and gas. The Iron Fireman Company has made no attempt to influence people not to switch from coal to some other fuel. Instead, the company has kept abreast of this change by adding oil- and gas-burning heating units to its line of products. It is well equipped to meet the heating needs of the modern home regardless of the type of fuel used.

The company, however, has been faced with a serious problem in respect to its identification marks. As one official stated, "our trademark and brand name are known from coast to coast, but they are still associated in the minds of too many people with coal stokers only."

The old mark and name have been promoted for over a quarter of a century. Strong and lasting associations have been developed with these marks. Should they be kept to cover all heating equipment of the company? Should they be kept only for coal-burning equipment and new marks and names be created for oil and gas equipment? Should the company attempt to persuade consumers away from oil and gas and toward coal stokers? What recommendations would you make?

chapter 17
PREPARING THE LAYOUT

THE VISUAL composition of an advertisement, the arrangement of illustration, headline, body copy, and logotype into a unified message is referred to as the "layout." The layout serves as a means of communication among the several people involved in the creative process. As a visual representation of the finished ad it is submitted to the client for his approval. It also serves as a blueprint for the printer, comparable to the architect's blueprint furnished the builder.

The layout should be designed to provide a logical, clear, unified presentation of the advertising message. Elements that are intended to attract attention and stimulate interest should be prominent in the layout. These elements usually are the illustration and headline. The design should always be in terms of consumer reaction rather than beauty, although one may be attained without sacrificing the other. A somewhat broader view of layout preparation includes visualization of the central idea of the advertisement as well as the arrangement of elements. Therefore, the layout artist and copywriter should work closely together.

Procedure in making layouts

The layout artist should first determine the exact dimensions of the finished advertisement. The page sizes and column widths of different magazines and newspapers can be checked in *Standard Rate and Data Service*. After this has been determined, the outside dimensions of the

365

advertisement should be ruled on a piece of paper, and space indicated for border or margin of white space. The space to be occupied by each part of the advertisement is then blocked in or indicated by lines or other marks.

Most layouts follow a fairly standard pattern of headline, illustration, copy, and standing details such as identification mark, coupon, or other instructional lines. This affords a logical presentation in terms of meaning as well as structure. Nevertheless, there are sufficient variations to be considered so that the layout man can well afford to work first with thumbnail sketches. Thumbnail sketches are in the nature of thinking on paper. They afford a basis for getting one's ideas into form. As many as a dozen or more such sketches may be drawn before one feels that a satisfactory design has been developed. Even then, when the chosen sketch is worked into a rough layout, it may prove unsatisfactory.

The amount of detail included in the layout and the precision of the rendering determines whether it is a *rough layout* or a *comprehensive layout*. To the layman's eye a rough layout might appear rather smooth. It clearly shows the use of space, the form of the various elements, a sketch of the people or objects to be portrayed, hand-lettered headlines, and the logotype or other identification feature. Body copy is indicated with straight lines showing the weight of the type matter and where it will appear. Figure 17–1 is a rough layout. It is an excellent example of layout and copy theme working closely together. The visual clearly communicates the idea "He Walks Tall and Packs Two Peas." Of course, if this layout were reproduced here as it actually was rendered, the "Giant" would be "Green."

A comprehensive layout is a faithful rendering of the advertisement as it eventually would appear in print. The illustration would be precisely drawn or a print of the proposed photograph would be inserted. Lettering would be carefully done. Body copy might even be set in type and pasted in. Due to the expense and time required to turn out such a finished piece of work, comprehensive layouts are seldom used. The layout artist concentrates on making roughs and leaves the preparation of finished art to artists and photographers specializing in that kind of work.

The amount of detail going into the layout varies somewhat with the dependence placed upon the printer. Some advertising men insist that nothing be left to the discretion of the printer and, hence, include in the layout specifications of type style and size, how much leading is to be used between lines, the exact space to be occupied by copy, the extent of paragraph indentions, etc. This procedure is to be preferred when the layout

FIGURE 17–1. Layout portrays central idea

man is thoroughly familiar with type faces and sizes and can visualize how the advertisement will look when reproduced. When he is not familiar with these matters, better results will be attained if some dependence is placed on the printer, with the provision that proofs be submitted. With proofs at hand, an evaluation of the readability, appearance, and unity of the finished product is easy, and changes can be made if the printer's selection of type is not satisfactory.

Fundamental in the preparation of a layout is the idea to be visualized. Stephen Baker, a leading art director, draws a distinction between *arranging elements on a page* and *visualizing an idea.* "The former is a designer's (or layout man's) feat; his innate sense of composition, balance, color is brought fully into play. On the other hand, presenting the clearest visual interpretation requires a strong desire to communicate with the audience, a flair for the dramatic, the ability to think in pictorial terms (usually referred to as "visual sense") and, probably most significant, a firm understanding of the advertiser's goal."[1]

Qualities to be considered in layouts

No formula can be given that will assure successful layouts; but fewer failures will be recorded if the factors of balance, contrast, proportion, motion, and unity are considered.

Balance. Balance is the arrangement of elements to achieve a pleasing distribution of visual impression. The weight of visual impression is determined by size, color, shape, and density of the particular element. Generally, the bigger something is the heavier impression it makes. A dark blue square appears heavier than a light yellow square the same size. A square looks heavier than a vertical rectangle enclosing the same area. Black looks heavier than gray.

There are two kinds of balance; formal and informal. Formal balance is achieved by distributing objects of equal weight on either side of the "optical center" of the advertisement. The optical center is slightly above the mathematical center. A line drawn from top to bottom through the optical center divides the space into the equal segments. Thus, two objects of equal weight would be formally balanced when they are equidistant from the imaginary vertical line. Informal balance is attained by placing elements of different size, shape, or density at different distances from the optical center. Much like a teeter-totter, a heavier object near the center can be balanced by a lighter object farther from the center.

---

[1] Stephen Baker, *Advertising Layout and Art Direction* (New York: McGraw-Hill Book Co., 1959), p. 3.

Formal balance communicates a feeling of security, stability, dignity, dependability, and conservatism. Informal balance is more exciting, more refreshing, and more dynamic. Each, however, has its place.

Figures 17–2 and 17–3 illustrate good usage of formal and informal balance, respectively. The type of balance used in each is in harmony with

FIGURE 17–2.   Formal balance in a layout

Duke Natural!
For men who wear it like it

FIGURE 17–3. Informal balance

the products advertised. "The World's Most Honored Watch" is well displayed in a formal setting. Duke Natural, on the other hand, needs informality and casualness. The character of the layout can help in providing the feeling tone that the adviser wishes associated with his product.

Contrast. The appearance of an advertisement will be improved and its attention value and readability enhanced if its parts are arranged to provide an element of contrast. This can be attained through variations in size, shape, and color of various parts. Headlines in larger type than copy or printed in a different color provide increased emphasis. Where several illustrations are used, a pleasing contrast is afforded by varying their size and shape. The parts possessing the greatest interest to prospective buyers should stand out at first glance. See Figure 17–4.

Contrast encourages the reading of an advertisement. Copy set up as one solid mass, without paragraphs or variations in size of type, looks hard to read. The same copy set up in paragraphs, with headline and paragraph headings in different size or style of type, looks easy to read and thus attracts a greater audience. Such contrast calls attention to the various parts of an advertisement in somewhat the same manner as a collar or belt of contrasting colors calls attention to the beauty of a woman's dress. In neither case, however, should the contrast be so extreme as to offend.

Proportion. One of the more intangible qualities of good designing is proportion. Proportion involves the relationship of objects to the background in which they appear and their relationship to each other. Subconsciously things "in proportion" are more pleasing to the eye than things "out of proportion." The Greeks found that two areas held a pleasant relationship to each other when one was between one half and two thirds the area of the other. Thus, good proportions would be 3 to 5, 2 to 3, 4 to 6, 8 to 10, and so on. The eye cannot measure these ratios easily, yet they break the appearance of monotony. Having an eye for the "fitness of things" is one of the artist's more important contributions.

Gaze-motion. A harmonious arrangement of parts is desirable. Headline, illustration, copy, and identification mark, in that order, will usually provide a logical follow-through from the interest-arresting part of the advertisement to the close. It is often desirable, however, to alter this orthodox arrangement.

Some advertisers like to provide an arrangement that will tend to direct the vision of the glancer from the headline through the illustrations and to the identification mark at the close, thus to some degree eliminating copy as a barrier to a tie-up of the headline message with the name of the advertiser and his product.

The types of layouts used to obtain such results can be classified in general by letters of the alphabet, as C, S, Z, and V. To these should be added the use of arbitrary lines and the position and shape of the product itself as a means of directing the reader's attention. The C layout may use a number of pictures and illustrations, starting from the right-hand side of the advertisement, back to the left, and down the left side to the bottom. The top illustration may pull the gaze of the reader to the left by

FIGURE 17–4.   Good use of contrast in layout

After coffee...
enjoy Benedictine

Bénédictine
La Grande Liqueur Française

Nothing so flatters your guests
as serving them Benedictine.
For there is only one
Benedictine—the noble
after-dinner liqueur made
for over 400 years at
Fecamp, France—the world's
most distinguished liqueur.

LET THIS SEAL BE YOUR GUIDE TO QUALITY. 86 PROOF

FIGURE 17–5. Example of a "C" layout

having the persons in the picture looking toward the left, the product moving in that direction, or by lines drawn in the illustration for that purpose. Figure 17–5 illustrates a "C" type of layout. The eye is drawn from the headline through the curve of the illustrations to the name of the product and the text.

Another form of gaze-motion is illustrated in Figure 17–6. There the focus of the eyes of the model, the position of the product itself, the design in the model's blouse, and the position of her hands all carry the reader's eye down and through the copy. Even the choice of products and their positioning in the bottom panel of the advertisement pulls the reader's attention into, rather than away from, the center portion of the panel.

Gaze-motion is important, but it must be handled with care. Arrangement to capitalize on this force should not be so obvious as to attract attention to the technique rather than to the product or service being advertised.

Unity. The well-designed advertisement creates an impression of completeness. The qualities of balance, contrast, proportion, and gaze-motion should be employed to develop unity of thought, appearance, and design in the layout. Copy should be written and illustrations chosen to present a message in logical fashion. The layout artist should assist in maintaining and, if possible, improving a logical and unified presentation. Coupons, for example, will not be placed at the beginning of an advertisement unless the copy theme is built around the idea of clipping the coupon. If reference to the coupon is entirely secondary, unity would be destroyed by placing it at the top.

Perhaps the surest way of achieving unity is to keep the layout simple. Attesting to this principle is the overwhelming popularity of the simplest layout of all—one illustration followed by one headline, followed by one block of body copy. The greater the number of elements the greater is

FIGURE 17–6.   Good use of gaze-motion in layout

the fragmenting of attention. Another way to get visual unity is overlapping. A cut of the product overlaps into the main illustration or, if several items are displayed, one overlaps the other. Typographic unity helps tie an ad together. Generally, it is a good idea to use the same type face or style throughout the ad.

Judicious use of white space

There is no uniform conviction concerning the value of white space in advertisements. One school of thought emphasizes brief copy and a great deal of white space, holding that this procedure will secure a maximum number of readers and that the reverse will scare readers away. The opposite school of thought maintains that, unless a complete message is presented, little value will be obtained from the advertising. Its adherents claim that the kernel of the message can be presented in headlines and illustrations and the rest of the space utilized to its fullest extent in presenting details for the interested reader. They cite mail-order experience to support their belief in the value of long copy and a minimum of white space.

Stephen Baker summarizes in the following statement his attitude toward the use of white space: "Many layout men become so preoccupied with the illustration and the handling of the copy that they forget that blank space is a very significant part of the overall pattern. An overdose of it at the wrong spot can throw the composition off balance, just as an improperly placed illustration can. White space can also be considered a tool for separating the advertisement from its competition, for making an illustration more prominent."[2]

Figure 17–7 is a classic example of the effective use of white space. What better way to dramatize the idea, *Think Small?*

Use of small space in layouts

Making a layout for a small advertisement is often more difficult than making one for a full-page. The small space ad is likely to be positioned on a page along with several other ads. To gain attention the design should be simple and bold. A single idea, a single illustration, a short caption, clear display type provide the needed simplicity. Masses of black and white give the ad the boldness to stand out on the printed page. And,

---

[2] *Ibid.,* p. 47.

Think small.

Our little car isn't so much of a novelty any more.

A couple of dozen college kids don't try to squeeze inside it.

The guy at the gas station doesn't ask where the gas goes.

Nobody even stares at our shape.

In fact, some people who drive our little flivver don't even think 32 miles to the gallon is going any great guns.

Or using five pints of oil instead of five quarts.

Or never needing anti-freeze.

Or racking up 40,000 miles on a set of tires.

That's because once you get used to some of our economies, you don't even think about them any more.

Except when you squeeze into a small parking spot. Or renew your small insurance. Or pay a small repair bill. Or trade in your old VW for a new one.

Think it over.

FIGURE 17–7. Effective use of white space

PARKER-KALON *Cold-forged*

Made by a new and improved process. Neater, stronger— yet cost no more!

Compare—get prices and samples from Parker-Kalon Corp., 196 Varick St. New York

WING NUTS & THUMB SCREWS

PARKER-KALON *Cold-forged*
WING NUTS & THUMB SCREWS

Made by a new and improved process. Neater, stronger—yet cost no more! Compare—get prices and samples from Parker-Kalon Corp., 196 Varick St. New York

---

PARKER-KALON *Cold-forged*
WING NUTS & THUMB SCREWS

Made by a new and improved process. Neater, stronger— yet cost no more!

Compare—get prices and sampies from Parker-Kalon Corp., 196 Varick St. New York

---

PARKER-KALON *Cold-forged*
WING NUTS & THUMB SCREWS

Made by a new and improved process. Neater, stronger—yet cost no more! Compare—get prices and samples from Parker-Kalon Corp., 196 Varick St. New York

FIGURE 17–8. Four arrangements of a small-space advertisement of course, the limited space demands a brief message. Figure 17–8 shows a series of layouts demonstrating different uses of small space.

The large amount of black space used in these small layouts increased attention value and made the one-sixteenth page of space used do extra duty. However, since some magazines restrict the amount of black space

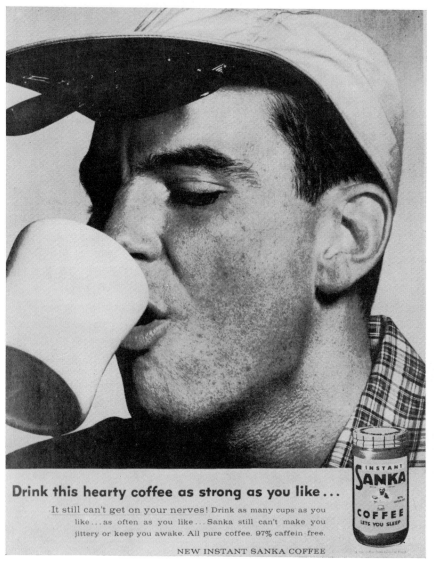

FIGURE 17–9.   Layout where picture holds dominant position

Does your bathroom pass the *Cannon Guest Test?*

Cannon towels in new Carefree colors and designs help your bathroom score with company, with the family, too!

1. **ARE YOU A MODERN HOSTESS?** You'll be one when you have these new Cannon Sun Beau towels with soft, washable luster borders. They'll prove you are up to the minute on the latest glamour style! Can you name three other modern aids to gracious entertaining? Score 10 for each

2. **ARE YOU A THOUGHTFUL HOSTESS?** Study these hospitality clues. One, the handy shelves full of Cannon fingertip terries. Another is the forget-me-not printed bath towel. Like all Cannon towels, it never wears out its welcome. It just wears well! Find 2 more clues. Score 10 each

3. **ARE YOU A FARSIGHTED HOSTESS?** If you're ready for company at the ring of the doorbell, you've got plenty of fresh, pretty Cannon towels. You stock up on new Cannons every season — try new colors, new designs. Beside towels, what two clues in this picture show how you think ahead? Score 10 for each.   See answers below.

4. **ARE YOU A CLEVER HOSTESS?** If "yes" then you know the magic that fluffy white Cannon towels work in a color scheme. And if you're clever with a needle, you can make your towels more inviting with monograms. (Write for free leaflet on unusual ways to personalize your towels.) There are three other inspired ideas here. Score 10 for each.

SCORE YOURSELF: *1.* Powder puffs, facial tissues, extra towels: 30 points • *2.* Make-up mirror, hand lotion: 20 points • *3.* Fresh flowers, hand mirror: 30 points • *4.* Bath salts, fresh soap, water pitcher and glass: 30 points

CANNON CANNON MILLS, INC., 70 Worth Street, New York 13, N.Y. • Towels • Sheets • Bedspreads • Draperies • Stockings • Terry Cloth

FIGURE 17–10. Use of picture-caption layout

in a given advertisement, *Standard Rate and Data* should be consulted for such restrictions before a layout is prepared.

Advertisements to be run in newspapers can often be drawn to such proportions that a smaller amount of space will provide greater value than the actual space used. Thus a half-page advertisement in an eight-column newspaper may be five columns wide and reach considerably above the horizontal center of the page. This will leave part of the advertisement showing, regardless of how the paper is folded, and will, in general, dominate the entire page. It will almost guarantee reading matter next to the advertisement.

Layouts where pictures dominate

The layout of an advertisement should give aid to effective communication. When the advertiser wishes to use pictures to carry the primary message, such pictures should dominate the ad. This is effectively done in the Sanka advertisement shown in Figure 17–9. The choice of illustration was excellent, but the point to emphasize here is the relationship between the picture, copy, and product. The close-up shot of a rugged sportsman drinking from a heavy mug dramatizes the "hearty coffee" theme. The jar of Sanka occupies a very small portion of the page but is positioned so that it becomes a part of the dominant picture.

Figure 17–10 also shows a layout where pictures carry the primary message, but where copy is needed to support and add meaning to them. Here the layout artist "mounted" the pictures in an "album" style and set the copy as captions under the pictures. This *picture-caption* technique provided a logical, meaningful, and easy-to-read arrangement for the total advertisement.

QUESTIONS AND PROBLEMS

1. "The main function of a layout is to enhance the ease of reading and comprehending the message." Analyze this statement critically.
2. Layouts often vary according to the medium in which they are placed. Compare layouts in the following media and write down any significant differences that you believe were influenced by the medium: newspaper, general magazine, professional journal, business or trade magazine, outdoor poster board, car card, direct mail.
3. Outline the general procedure to follow in making a layout.

4. Bring to class examples of different layouts and explain what you think to be the strong and weak points of each.

5. Construct a layout for a full-page advertisement in *Time* magazine for your favorite food product.

6. Prepare a complete layout for a one-eighth page advertisement in your local newspaper for Arrow Shirts or Pendleton girls' skirts. Prepare a similar layout for an advertisement for dairy products.

7. Bring to class examples of both good and poor layouts where pictures are used to carry the primary message.

chapter 18
REPRODUCING
THE
ADVERTISEMENT

AFTER THE typewritten text, the drawings and charts, and the layout have been prepared and the photographs and other art work secured, the advertisement must still be reproduced in sufficient numbers to reach the audience of consumers, often numbered in the millions, to which its message is directed. Aside from radio and television and a few minor forms of advertising, the message is delivered through a printed medium such as a newspaper or magazine or mailing piece. The operations by which the advertisement is put in printed form are known collectively as *mechanical production.* Involved in this process are various phases of the graphic arts.

In large organizations, one or more individuals specialize in mechanical production and are required to be familiar with all its details. The small and medium-sized advertisers and agencies, however, usually cannot afford to employ full-time specialists but must depend upon an outside organization for advice and service. Still, advertising men in such organizations will find it advantageous to understand, at least in a general way, the mechanical methods and skills used in reproducing advertisements. One need not become an expert, but a fair knowledge of production will be useful in various ways. It will facilitate the handling of the preliminary steps of copy writing, layout, and art work, and it will make possible more efficient and economical purchasing of all the elements of production.

It is true that some phases of production will not be within the control of the advertiser. Advertisements placed in such media as newspapers and magazines, unless furnished as "inserts," will automatically be printed by the same methods the media employ. But again, unless the advertiser understands something about the methods to be used in each case, he will be handicapped in supplying the advertisement in the form required.

The advertiser needs, therefore, to have a general knowledge of mechanical production. This means that he must become acquainted with these basic graphic arts processes: typography and type composition; photoengraving and platemaking; and printing. He will still need the help of the specialists, but he will be able to deal more effectively with them if he has this basic knowledge.

TYPOGRAPHY AND TYPE COMPOSITION

In one sense, typography refers to the physical composition or setting of the type; in another, it is the art of selecting and arranging for printing type faces, spacing, and decorative materials. Today, composition, in the sense of transforming original copy into a form suitable for printing or platemaking, consists of more than the setting of movable type or hot metal; it also includes cold composition—photosetting and composition by IBM or Varityper machine for reproduction by lithographic or planographic processes. We shall discuss printing methods later, but the initial problem is the selection and arrangement of type, or the effective application of the art of typography. We begin by becoming acquainted with type faces.

Type faces

A single piece of type, the unit of most type composition, has a definite anatomy. The accompanying illustration (Figure 18–1) names and illustrates the parts of a piece of handset type. Note particularly the point body and the serifs.

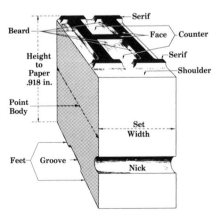

FIGURE 18–1. Anatomy of a single piece of type

All except the newest typewriters have only one kind of type face. In printing, however, there are thousands of type faces. The nomenclature and measurements of this array of types are often ambiguous, and their very abundance creates difficulties of selection. But it also offers opportunity to those who know how to use them.

Type faces vary in weight, design, and in body size (see Figure 18–2). A type *font* is a complete assortment of types of one face and size, including capitals, small capitals, lowercase letters, numbers, punctuation marks, and so on. A type *series* may run from 6 point to 72 point in uppercase and lowercase. A type *family* is made up of different series, such as roman, italic, condensed, extended, boldface, boldface italic, and so on, of the same general design of type. Many type families are amazingly versatile and complete. Among such type families are Caslon, Bodoni, Garamond, Janson, Caledonia, Baskerville, and Cheltenham.

Type faces may be classified further into groups of related faces. Some systems of classification are based on variations in historical development, often minor, rather than upon visual factors. The descendants of the earlier types, based in the beginning on manuscript writing or patterned after the first Roman alphabet, are called "Old Style." In these faces there are usually slanted serifs and the strokes flow easily from thick to thin. Examples of Old Style faces are to be found in the Garamond (in which face this book is set) and Caslon families, among others.

Transitional faces are sometimes considered a separate group. These are the faces designed in mid-18th century, such as Baskerville and Bulmer. Compared to Old Style faces, these faces have sharper contrast between thick and thin strokes and straighter serifs. The *Modern* faces carry the characteristics of the Transitional further in the direction of accentuating the contrast between thick and thin strokes. Serifs and the other square strokes become straight. Bodoni is an example of a Modern face. These type faces, although called "Modern" really are historically only slightly more recent than the Transitional, having been designed soon after them, and the distinction is often ignored, all being classified as Modern.

The trouble with the historical classifications of type is that they cut across family lines. Many type families contain faces representative of both Old Style and Modern, making classification of today's type faces on the basis of historical development rather meaningless. For the purposes of the advertiser, therefore, it is more convenient and practical to classify type, not according to historical origin but on the basis of easily

GOLD RUSH

MANDARIN

Cloister Text

LOMBARDIC

Ornamental Type

Caslon roman

Caslon italic

Caslon boldface

Caslon boldface italic

Caslon Bold Condensed

Caslon Open Face

Caslon Old Style Type Family, 18 pt. size

Garamond Italic

Deepdene Italic

Raleigh Cursive

Bernhard Cursive

Bank Script

Brush Script

Italic and Cursive Type

ABCDEFGHIJKLMNOPQRSTUVWXYZ
ABCDEFGHIJKLMNOPQRSTUVWXYZ
abcdefghijklmnopqrstuvwxyz fi ff fl ffi 1234567890
[]%†$‡¶*()$,.-;':'!?& 1234567890

aA aA aA aA aA aA aA aA aA

aA aA aA aA aA A

Caslon Old Style No. 337 Type Series, 6 pt. to 72 pt.

Univers (Sans-serif)

Stymie (Square-serifed)

Block Letter Type

Caslon Old Face (Old Style)

Baskerville (Transitional)

Bodoni (Modern)

Roman Type

ABCDEFGHIJKLMNOPQRSTUVWXYZ
abcdefghijklmnopqrstuvwxyz fi ff fl ffi ffl
[]%†$‡¶*()$,.-;':'!?& 1234567890

8 pt. Garamond Font

FIGURE 18–2. Examples of type font, series, family, and broad classifications of type recognizable visual characteristics. Such a grouping would place types into these four broad classes: roman, block letter, cursive, and ornamental.

The *roman* letter is characterized by serifs and graduated thick and thin strokes. A roman type may be either Old Style or Modern. The Modern roman letter emphasizes contrast in weight of lines and has strong level serifs. The Old Style roman has less contrast and smaller, often sloping, serifs. Roman type is adaptable to many purposes. It is possible with it to secure contrasting effects without switching to another type design. It is the easiest face to read, even in smaller sizes. Both Caslon Old Style and modern Bodoni are classified as belonging to the roman group.

The *block letter,* also called sans-serif, gothic, grotesque, and contemporary, is of two general types: (1) sans-serif, and (2) block-serifed. The sans-serif letter lacks serifs entirely. The block- or square-serifed letter has serifs, but these consist of short strokes of the same weight and thickness as the main parts of the letter, and there are no brackets. In both, the strokes forming the letters are of uniform weight throughout the letter. This uniformity and the lack of serifs make block letters harder to read than roman letters. Examples of sans-serifed type are Futura, Helvetica, and Univers; examples of square-serifed type are Beton, Karnak, or Memphis.

The basic features of *cursive* are the slanted letters and their appearance of being connected and continuous. The two main classifications of cursive types are italics and scripts. Italic is the familiar slanted form of faces in the Roman group; scripts are those faces drawn to look as if handwritten. Scripts may vary from very formal fine-line types like Bank Script to very informal brushwriting such as Brush Script or Body. These types are all harder to read than either roman or sans-serif. Used injudiciously in a headline, for example, they can conceal rather than reveal the message. Some of them offer, however, a convenient means of conveying such qualities as informality or the feminine touch.

Ornamental types are usually embellished forms of other classes of types. They are used essentially for decorative or atmospheric purposes. A common earlier form of decorative type was Black Letter or Old English, which was based on European handwriting in Medieval times. It is hard to read but is still used occasionally today to suggest antiquity or religious themes. Ornamental faces are often used to suggest the atmosphere of a particular time, place, or culture. Examples are Rustic, P. T. Barnum, Lombardic, Gold Rush, Old Bowery, and Mandarin.

Selection of type faces

When the advertiser approaches the problem of selecting specific type faces for his advertisement, he will find all of the classes of type mentioned above available in almost bewildering abundance in the type books put out by his printers. The problem is complicated by ambiguities in current nomenclature and type measurements, and by the practice of different type foundries issuing varying versions of a type face under the same name. There are, for example, numerous Caslons, Bodonis, Garamonds, and Baskervilles. San-serif faces range from the older Spartans and Futuras through the numerous Gothics to Optima, Helvetica, Venus, and Univers. Square-serifed faces go under various names from Stymie to Memphis, and like the sans-serifs, may be very condensed or quite extended. There are numerous cursives, including the special cursive designed for in the Electra family because the Electra oblique italic lacked cursive feeling. The number of ornamental faces available is abundant, indeed.

Type measurement and fitting type to space will be discussed later, but type size need not usually place restrictions on selecting type on the basis of other considerations, because most faces are available in an adequate number of sizes. To find his way through the complexities of type selection, the advertiser needs to be guided by a few simple principles, pending his development through time and experience of a competence, and perhaps a personal style, in this field. Following such guidelines he will find the problem of selection to be diminished; but in the end the advertiser, unless he turns to the specialists, will have to depend on his own good taste and sensitivity to atmosphere and appropriateness to solve his problems.

The most important principle of all is to select type faces on the basis of their *legibility*. Type is meant to communicate, and the more legible it is, the clearer and faster will be the communication. Scientific research has made contributions to understanding of the bases of legibility, but the findings are not complete or conclusive. Legibility and readability are relative terms. What is legible to one person in one situation may not be so to others. Legibility is affected by the characteristics of the type selected, the degree of familiarity of the reader with the type face, the size of the type, the length of the line, the leading or space between lines, and the use of white space in the advertisement. In selecting a type for legibility, all of these factors should be taken into account. Other considerations than legibility, important as they may be, are secondary to the ability of the type to communicate the message quickly and clearly.

In combining type faces for an advertisement, the question arises as to the relative importance to place upon *harmony* and *contrast*. Perhaps the safest procedure is to use the same type face throughout, creating close harmony, but a judicious combination of faces to employ both harmony and contrast is most effective. Variations in style and size of type help in meeting the needs of different parts of the advertisement and in making clear the relative importance of different elements. Relative importance should not be left in doubt but should be made absolutely clear by relative weights of the type chosen.

Relative weights of type will be affected not only by the size of the type but also by its style; weight; whether italic, boldface, all capitals, capitals and small capitals, or lowercase roman; and position on the page. A large type, of course, outranks a smaller one of the same style. Ornamental faces make a stronger impression than regular faces. Italic is more emphatic than roman and boldface outranks both. In the same sizes and styles, all-capital lines are stronger than those set in capitals and small capitals, and both are stronger than those set in capitals and lowercase. Position on the page also indicates the importance of a line of type.

Within the possibilities compatible with the basic requirements of legibility and emphasis, consideration should be given to type selection on the basis of feeling or atmosphere. It is usually possible to discern the differences between types in their degree of femininity and masculinity, although this and similar distinctions are subjective, and reactions may vary from person to person. Some types are felt to be rugged and masculine, others delicate and feminine. Likewise, a type may be felt to be sturdy, stable, and businesslike; warm and informal or cold and formal; elegant and aristocratic or rustic; fussy, dramatic; or just plain neutral. These qualities felt to be present in type faces may be the basis for selecting one type rather than another for a particular purpose. Occasionally an ornamental type may be chosen, as has been mentioned, to match a particular historic, geographic, or cultural atmosphere.

However, in selecting type, the advertiser should be careful to avoid trick or freak hard-to-read faces, even though such faces might attract attention because they are different. One should never lose sight of the fact that advertising space costs a great deal and the message must be read if a profitable return is to be obtained from such investment. Legibility should be kept in mind at all times; the measure of good typography is its ability to make the advertising story easy to read.

Type measurement

Printers have a system of measurement which differs from the common one of measuring in inches and fractions of an inch but which is relatively easy to understand and apply in production work. Its essential features are as follows:

Point system. The unit of measurement of type and spaces or leading between lines of type is the *point*. For all practical purposes 72 points equals 1 inch. The point measures type *height* only, not its overall dimensions, and it measures not the height of a single letter but the height of a line of the type in question measured from the bottom of the descenders, or extensions downward from the body of the type, to the top of the ascenders, or extensions upward from the body of the type. The width of a single letter depends on the style of type face—whether fat or thin, extended or condensed—and on the proportions of the letter—whether, for instance, it is a "w" or an "i."

Standard type sizes and the ones frequently used are 5, 5½, 6, 7, 8, 9, 10, 11, 12, 14, 18, 24, 30, 36, 48, and 72 point. Before specifying sizes, however, consult the printer's type book or list. Five point, 5½ point, 7 point, and even 9 and 11 point, and all of the larger sizes above 12 or 14 point may be missing from the linotype face you wish to use. The smaller size may be brought in from a matching or similar face, and the larger sizes may be found among the "display" sizes of the same type or selected from the many available display faces created especially for this purpose. Comparisons of type sizes are shown in Figure 18–3. The text of this book is set in 12 point Garamond.

The layout man may specify on the margin of his copy the size and kind of face to be used, or he may leave this to the printer. In the case of the copy shown in Figure 18–4 (pages 392–93), the agency layout man specified both the size and style of type.

Leading. Leading is also expressed in points, as for example, 12 point type leaded 1 point (also expressed as "12 on 13"). A type face 12 points high will not measure exactly 12 points since the face of the letter itself is not as high as the base on which it is mounted. This provides a small amount of white space between lines when set solid, but usually not enough for easy reading. Additional white space is provided by leading. A lead is a strip of type metal placed between lines of type. Leads come in different point sizes, so that type can be leaded to the number of points desired. The text of this book is 12 point type with 1 point leading be-

6 Point Garamond

The medieval seclusion from the concerns of the current world, which marked all but a few colleges until 1930, has happily been broken down.

8 Point Garamond

The medieval seclusion from the concerns of the current world, which marked all but a few colleges until 1930, has happily been broken down.

10 Point Garamond

The medieval seclusion from the concerns of the current world, which marked all but a few colleges until 1930, has happily been broken down.

12 Point Garamond

The medieval seclusion from the concerns of the current world, which marked all but a few colleges until 1930, has happily been broken down.

14 Point Garamond

The medieval seclusion from the concerns of the current world, which marked all but a few colleges until 1930, has happily been broken down.

18 Point Garamond

The medieval seclusion from the concerns of the current world, which marked all but a few colleges until 1930, has happily

24 Point Garamond

The medieval seclusion from the concerns of the current world, which marked all but a few col-

30 Point Garamond

The medieval seclusion from the concerns of the current world, which

FIGURE 18–3. Illustration of various sizes of type

tween lines. This gives an equivalent of 13 points in depth; thus, six lines measure 78 points or slightly more than an inch in depth.

Pica. A pica is equal to 12 points, and there are 6 picas to an inch, making it quite simple to translate picas into inches and vice versa. The pica is used to measure type horizontally, and a significant measure is the number of characters of a particular type face there are in a pica, on the average, and consequently in a line of type a certain number of picas wide. Dimensions of lines and blocks of type are given in picas and half picas, or if less than 6 picas, may be given in points. Illustrations and margins, however, are usually measured in inches, as are paper sizes.

Ems, ens, and quads. A em is a printer's unit of area measurement equal to the square space taken up by the type body of a piece of type of any particular point size. Thus, it may vary from a 6 point em up to and 18 point em or larger. "Em" is also used as an abbreviation for "pica-em" which is a 12-point em, setting six to the inch. An en is half the size of an em. Ems are frequently used to designate indentations, and ems and ens identify dashes of corresponding widths. Typesetting is usually charged for on the basis of ems—so much per 1,000 ems.

Quads or spaces are blank blocks of type metal used by the printer to space out short lines, to create spaces between letters or words, or to provide for indentations in a line or fill the space at the end of a paragraph. Quads are of several widths such as 1 em, 2 em, and 3 em quads. Spaces include not only 1 em (or em quad) but also fractions of quads, such as ½ em (en quad or nut space); ⅓ em (or thick space), and ¼ em (thin space). There is also a hair space which is about ½ point in width.

Agate line. The term "agate" was originally applied to a size of type (5½ point). The size of type to which it now refers is slightly smaller than 5½ point, measuring 14 lines to the inch. Today, its use is generally confined to measurement of space in newspapers and magazines. Practically all papers, large and small, compute their national advertising rates on the agate line basis. One agate line, one column wide, is the unit. Originally, most newspapers had a uniform column 13 picas wide, but in recent years the column has been narrowed until today we find that most large dailies have an 11½-pica column and the smaller papers a 13-pica column. The number of agate lines in a given space is the depth in inches, times the number of columns, times 14. Thus, a newspaper advertisment 6 inches deep and 3 columns wide would represent 252 agate lines (6 × 3 × 14).

Fitting copy to space

It is important to fit copy to available space because if you do not do so, and it turns out that the copy when set in type is either too long or too short to fit the layout, you will either (1) have to change to a different style of type (fatter or thinner); (2) choose a type with a larger or

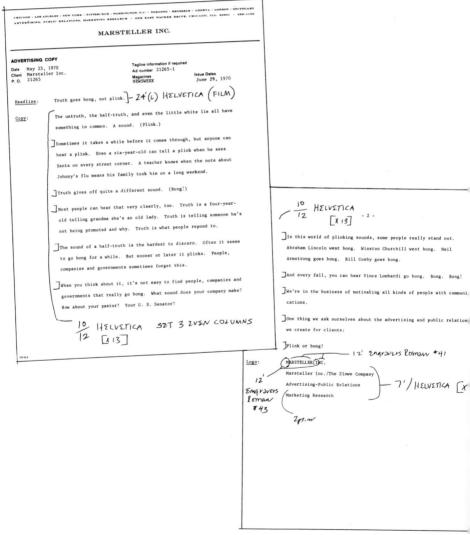

FIGURE 18–4.   Copy with type specifications for the printer

smaller point size; (3) reduce or increase the leading, or (4) arrange for a larger or smaller type area. Since all of these alternatives are inconvenient and costly, you would probably prefer to cut the copy or add to it. And this, too, is expensive after the copy is set in type: It is much better to make sure that the copy fits the layout *before* you have it set in type.

Considerations of fit will also affect to some extent the original selection of a type face, not only in point size but also in type style or design.

Truth goes bong, not plink.

The untruth, the half-truth, and even the little white lie all have something in common. A sound. (Plink.)

Sometimes it takes a while before it comes through, but anyone can hear a plink. Even a six-year-old can tell a plink when he sees Santa on every street corner. A teacher knows when the note about Johnny's flu means his family took him on a long weekend.

Truth gives off quite a different sound. (Bong!)

Most people can hear that very clearly, too. Truth is a four-year-old telling grandma she's an old lady. Truth is telling someone he's

not being promoted and why. Truth is what people respond to.

The sound of a half-truth is the hardest to discern. Often it seems to go bong for a while. But sooner or later it plinks. People, companies and governments sometimes forget this.

When you think about it, it's not easy to find people, companies and governments that really go bong. What sound does your company make? How about your pastor? Your U.S. Senator?

In this world of plinking sounds, some people really stand out. Abraham Lincoln went bong. Winston Churchill went bong.

Neil Armstrong goes bong. Bill Cosby goes bong.

And every fall, you can hear Vince Lombardi go bong. Bong. Bong!

We're in the business of motivating all kinds of people with communications.

One thing we ask ourselves about the advertising and public relations we create for clients:

Plink or bong?

MARSTELLER INC.
Marsteller Inc. / The Zlowe Company

Advertising · Public Relations
Marketing Research

Chicago · Los Angeles · New York · Pittsburgh · Washington · Brussels · Geneva · London · Paris · Stockholm · Stuttgart · Toronto

FIGURE 18–4. *(Continued)*

Different type styles of the same point size may vary considerably in width of the letters. Types may be compared in this respect by comparing their *alphabetic lengths,* a measurement of length in points of a complete lowercase alphabet, as given in type books. If you know that you are going to have difficulty securing a fit, either because the copy is long or short for the space, you can take a first step toward solving the problems by selecting a face with an appropriate alphabetic length. For example, the alphabetic length of 10 point Century Expanded is 142 points, while that of 10 point Granjon is only 117 points, as shown below:

abcdefghijklmnopqrstuvwxyz
abcdefghijklmnopqrstuvwxyz

There are two commonly used methods of determining the amount of space a given amount of copy will occupy. When only a rough approximation is required, the "square-inch" method may be used. For more accurate copy fitting, the "character-count" method is indispensable.

Square-inch method.   In this method the number of words in the copy is counted, and this number is divided by the number of words per square inch that can be set in types of particular sizes, as given in standard tables, similar to Table 18–1.

TABLE 18–1.   Estimated number of words to the square inch

	Words per square inch	
Type size	Solid	Leaded 2 points
6 point	47	34
8 point	32	23
10 point	21	16
12 point	14	11
14 point	11	9
18 point	7	6

This method will indicate roughly and in a preliminary way the number of square inches the copy will occupy in a given point size leaded a given number of points. However, it does not take into account the differences between widths of types of varying degrees of fatness or thinness, and it could be quite inaccurate if the type chosen is either very extended or very condensed. Also, the method will be inaccurate if the copy contains an unusual number of long or short words.

The character-count method.   Obviously more accurate is the character-count method, which ignores word lengths and is based on counting the number of characters (letters, spaces, and punctuation marks) in the copy and relating this to the number of lines of a given length the copy will make when set in a specific size and style of type. The basic information needed is the number of characters in the typewritten copy and the average number of characters per pica in the type chosen. In estimating the manuscript copy, it is helpful to know that copy typed in pica type will have 10 characters to the inch and copy typed in elite type will have 12. Printers, type foundries, and manufacturers of typesetting machines supply copy-fitting guides and tables that give the average number of characters per pica in the various type sizes and styles. This information is similar to that shown in Table 18–2.

TABLE 18–2. Characters per pica in different sizes and styles of type

Type size and style	Characters per pica	Type size and style	Characters per pica
Century Expanded (Lino)		Garamond (No. 3) (Lino)	
8 point	2.80	8 point	3.20
9 point	2.60	9 point	3.00
10 point	2.40	10 point	2.85
11 point	2.30	11 point	2.65
12 point	2.15	12 point	2.50
14 point	1.80	14 point	2.15
News Gothic (Lino)		Caslon Old Style (Mono)	
8 point	3.00	7 point	3.50
9 point	2.87	8 point	3.20
10 point	2.55	10 point	2.60
11 point	2.44	12 point	2.25

To illustrate copy fitting by the character-count method, let us assume that you have counted the number of characters in a typewritten block of copy which according to the layout is to occupy a space 4 inches wide (or 24 picas) by 5 inches deep (or 30 picas). You find that you have 1,500 characters, and you would like to set this copy in 12 point Garamond No. 3, leaded 1 point. The additional steps necessary to determine whether or not your copy will fit are as follows:

1. By reference to a type book or a copy-fitting guide giving information simular to that given in Table 18–2, you ascertain that 12 point Garamond No. 3 sets 2.50 characters per pica. Since your line is to be 24 picas wide, you multiply 2.50 by 24 and determine that there will be 60 characters per printed line.

2. You divide the number of characters in the copy (1,500) by 60. This gives you the number of printed lines, or 25.
3. Now, you multiply the number of lines by the point size plus leading (12 plus 1 or 13) and divide by 72 (the number of points in an inch). This will give you the vertical space required in inches, or about 4½ inches. In picas this would be a little over 27.

You are short but still fairly close to having a fit, and you could add a few lines of copy to fill or you could settle for a bit more white space in the layout.

A helpful technique is to type your copy originally the same number of characters per line as will be contained in a line of type of the same length in the size and style of type you have chosen. Bear in mind that tables giving average number of characters per pica in various type sizes and styles do not apply to display lines set in all capitals, capitals and small capitals, or ornamental faces. Here it is necessary to compare the copy letter for letter with the type face chosen.

Methods of composition

Composition—the transforming of original copy into a form suitable for printing or making printing plates—has made significant advances in recent years. There are today four principal methods in use (1) setting metal type by hand; (2) setting metal type by machine; (3) setting copy on a typewriter or typewriterlike machine such as the IBM Executive typewriter or the Vari-Typer; and (4) photocomposition. Machine composition has been made faster and more efficient by the introduction of the teletypesetter and the use of the computer to automatically "justify" lines many times faster than the operator can do this on the keyboard.

Hand setting. As its name indicates, this is strictly a hand operation in which individual characters and spaces are assembled one at a time, set in a "composing stick," and spaced out to the desired measure. Its use is limited today to display purposes and to occasional small blocks of type. Hand setting may employ any one of three kinds of type: (1) foundry, (2) Monotype, and (3) Ludlow. Foundry type, used mainly for display, is purchased ready-made from the type foundries by the compositor. Monotype consists of individual characters cast as needed in the Monotype machine. Ludlow is cast on a Ludlow machine as a slug rather than as individual characters, but it is classed as hand composition because the mats for the characters must first be assembled by hand. This method is used primarily for casting display lines.

Setting metal type by machine.   Three machines are available to-day to set metal type; Monotype, Linotype, and Intertype (see Figures 18–5 and 18–6). The Linotype and Intertype machines are virtually identical, differing mainly in the design of the type faces produced for each—and even these are interchangeable. In describing Linotype, there-fore, we shall also be describing Intertype. All three machines are essen-tially devices for pouring molten (hot) metal into small molds (mats or matrices), to form type characters in accordance with instructions fed into the machine. The instructions are given by an operator typing the copy on the keyboard of the machine or by punched tape from a teletype-

FIGURE 18–5.   Linotype machine

FIGURE 18-6. Monotype machine—*left*, keyboard; *right*, casting machine setter or computer, or in the case of Monotype, from a perforated role of paper produced by an operator on a separate keyboard machine.

In Monotype, as the perforated role is fed into the casting machine it causes the mats to be moved into place from a matrix case so that they can produce individual metal characters, which form lines of type. These lines, however, are not solid slugs but remain individual characters. They are ejected onto a galley tray. Justification of the lines is by a spaceband system, similar to that of the Linotype, which is described below. Monotype is cast of harder metal than that used for Linotype. Its main advantages, however, are greater flexibility in setting difficult material such as tables and mathematical formulas, and less difficulty and expense in making corrections.

The Linotype machine combines keyboard and caster in the same machine, linked by a magazine containing mats. When the key for a given character is pressed, the corresponding mat is released and drops into position in a rack, on which the desired length of line in picas is controlled. The mats continue to drop into their places in the line until the operator decides that when spaces are put in, it will be filled to the desired measure. Then he sends it to the casting element, where the line of mats is justified. The device that makes justification possible is the spaceband, a small, wedge-shaped piece of metal about 4 inches in length placed between words as the mats are assembled (see Figure 18–7). As the line comes into position to be cast, a bar pushed up from below tightens the line by the use of the graduated wedge in these bands and wedges out the line to full measure. Then the line is cast as a solid slug, trimmed, and ejected into a galley tray. The mats are returned automatically to the magazine for reuse.

FIGURE 18–7. Line of Linotype mats assembled with spacebands between words

Each mat can have two—and no more—characters on it. Usually this will be the roman and italic forms of the same character, but it may be roman and boldface, or even the same letter from two different type faces. Changing from one mat to another is accomplished by moving a lever which operates like the shift key on a typewriter. The limitation of being able to have only two characters on a mat is overcome by the use of a Linotype Mixer, which provides from two to four extra magazines to which access can be obtained by the operator by the shift of a lever.

Linotype and Intertype are faster, and therefore less costly, than Monotype. However, corrections are somewhat more difficult to make and cost more.

Typewriter composition. Machines similar to typewriters, such as the IBM Executive and the Varityper, may also be used to compose type which can be transformed into printing plates. They provide a typescript like an ordinary typewriter, but they have devices for spacing out lines, or justifying right-hand margins. Also, the characters vary in width like printed characters, and it is possible to secure a variety of type styles —up to 15 on the IBM Executive. Special ribbons are also available, and the typescript can be further varied by the use of art type that can be pasted in for display lines. These machines provide a sharper image than the ordinary typewriter does and give good results when the typescript is made into a printing plate by a photochemical process. This form of composition offers substantial savings, and it is used when economy is a primary consideration.

Photocomposition. Photocomposition is a machine method of setting type the development of which has been encouraged by the increased use of offset lithography. The photocomposing machine makes use of a keyboard operated either manually or from punched tape in the same way as the hot-metal machines, and it also has magazines, mats, and a system for bringing the mats into position like the hot-metal machines. However, instead of casting metal type, the photocomposing machine projects the image of the character, a negative of which is embedded in the mat, onto a photographic film. This film is developed and may be transferred directly to a lithographic or gravure plate. Photocomposing machines of this type are the Fotosetter and the newer tape-operated model, the Fotomatic.

An extremely fast machine is the Photon, which employs a continuously spinning disk on which the character negatives are embedded (see Figure 18–8). This machine also has a system for justifying lines, and it produces a positive proof that can be seen by the operator, thus making it possible to correct errors at the time of setting. A similar machine is the Phototypesetter.

FIGURE 18–8. High-speed Photon 713 Phototypsetter

Control Unit at left reads 6, 7, or 8 channel paper tapes photoelectrically at 500 characters a second. Information goes to the magnetic memory core for processing and typesetting instructions are relayed to cable-connected Photo Unit at right. Inset shows the inside of the Photo Unit where matrix drum (at right) contains 720 characters in film negative form. Xenon light flashes project characters through one of eight lenses which determine type size. A rotating mirror transfers the image onto sensitized film or paper contained in magazine at left.

Linofilm, produced by the manufacturers of the Linotype machine, and Monophoto, made by the Monotype company, are other machines in which a keyboard unit produces a punched tape, which when fed into the machine activates a photographic rather than a metal-casting process. Many of the same type faces available to the hot-metal machines are available on their photocomposing counterparts.

Advantages claimed for photocomposition are greater sharpness and clarity; greater flexibility in size of type, since size is easily adjustable in the photographic process; speed of production; and economy. As yet, however, economy has not proved to result as a matter of course through the use of photocomposition. Correction of errors has been found to be more difficult and costly and page makeup has presented problems.

Suggestive of things that lie ahead in composition is the new Video-comp, marketed by Radio Corporation of America. This is a high-speed composition system which utilizes an all-electronic method of producing characters. The machine has a computer memory which stores up to four fonts of type and generates text at the rate of 600 characters a second on the face of a cathode tube. The characters are exposed through a precision lens onto sensitized film or paper for printing by offset, gravure, or letterpress. There are no metal fonts, matrices, disks, or anything solid except the film or papers to be moved. The movable type of Gutenberg has become movable electronic dots. It is said that Videocomp can set type as fast as 100 manual linecasters, can produce 2 million characters an hour, and can set a standard newspaper page in two minutes.

PHOTOENGRAVING AND PLATE DUPLICATION

Photoengraving is a process by means of which photography can be used to create a printing surface. Its basic principle is that actinic light can change the physical properties of a light-sensitive surface, such as its solubility in water or resistance to acid, and this differentiation can be further enhanced and utilized to create either (1) a relief plate (engraving), in which the nonprinting surface is etched away or (2) its reverse, a gravure or intaglio plate in which the printing parts of the surface are etched away, or (3) a lithographic plate in which the material on the plate that is to be printed differs chemically from the nonprinting areas so that the printing areas attract the greasy ink while the nonprinting areas, when dampened, repel it.

Through the photoengraving process, art work—line charts, drawings, photographs—and paste-up of type can be transferred to a negative photochemically, and the image on the negative can be transferred to a metal plate for printing. While photoengraving is most commonly used to reproduce art work of all kinds, it can also be used to reproduce combinations of illustrations and type or even of type alone, or the products of photocomposition. We shall discuss photoengraving as it relates to (1) line plates and halftones; (2) electronic engraving, such as those made with the Fairchild Scan-A-Graver and Scan-A-Sizer; (3) combination plates and those using Ben Day and its variations; (4) color plates and color separations; and (5) duplicate plates, including electrotypes, stereotypes, and plastics. There will be additional discussion of plates in connection with the discussion of printing methods.

Line plates and halftones

The photoengravings used in reproducing art work for letterpress printing are of two kinds: line plates and halftones. Line plates are also called "zinc" etchings, although they may also be made today of magnesium or a special alloy called Micrometal. Line plates are used when the copy to be reproduced is single tone; when the copy is multitone, halftones are required, since line engravings do not show continuous tones in gradations from solid black through grays to white. The line engraving prints from solid lines or areas. Thus, a line chart of a pen-and-ink sketch can be reproduced by a line cut, but a photograph cannot.

Halftones reproduce shadings and gradations of tone by breaking up the copy into thousands of dots. This is done by photographing the copy through a glass or plastic film plate or screen on which appears a grid of fine lines. The individual size of the resulting dot is in proportion to the amount of ink to be printed in its position on the printed version. This gives the illusion of varying tones, corresponding to those of the original. Larger dots with less intervening white space produce darker tones. Smaller dots with more intervening white space produce the lighter tones. Generally speaking, a halftone consists of three tones: the very light ones, or highlights; the grays or shadows; and the dark tones or lowlights. Variations in size of dots is shown in Figure 18–9.

FIGURE 18–9. Cross-section of a halftone showing variations in the size and character of dots that serve as the printing surface (Reproduced by permission of the Colton Press and the Regensteiner Corporation)

The size and distance apart of the dots, and therefore the quality of the illusion, depends upon the fineness of the screen. This is designated as the number of lines the grid has to the inch. For example, a 65-line screen will have 65 parallel lines to the inch each way. Screens are commonly available in a range from 50 line to 150 line, though coarser and finer screens exist. Variation in fineness of screen is necessary because the paper on which the halftone is to be printed may be coarse and absorbent of ink or smooth and glossy. The paper on which newspapers are printed requires a coarser screen; slick-paper magazines will take a fine-screen halftone. Figure 18–10 shows the effect different screens have on the reproduction of a photograph. In the coarser screen, the dots can even be seen with the naked eye.

FIGURE 18–10. Halftones showing the effect of photographing the same subject through 65-line screen, 110-line screen, and 133-line screen

After the subject is photographed through a screen, and the film negative developed, it can be transferred to a sensitized metal plate which is then etched with acid to produce a raised printing surface (halftone engraving) for letterpress printing. The negative (or positive) will be handled in a different way to produce gravure or lithographic printing surfaces, and it, by itself, also bears the name "halftone."

Electronic engravings

An electronic method of producing halftones direct from copy without any intermediate steps is by means of such machines as the Fairchild

Scan-A-Graver and Scan-A-Sizer. Such machines employ a combination of precision mechanics, electronics, and optics. The resulting halftone may be used to print directly or may be matted, stereotyped, or molded for electrotyping. Engravings are made on "Scan-A-Plate," a plastic material designed to produce a clear halftone dot.

The Scan-A-Graver operates by scanning the original copy on one cylinder with a photoelectric cell which activates a stylus which cuts away portions of a blank plate on another, leaving an image of the copy in relief.

Combination plates and Ben Day

Line and halftone techniques can be used jointly to produce a combination plate. Such a plate will print varying shades of tone as does a halftone and the solid blacks as does a line cut. Although more costly than an ordinary halftone, the combination plate facilitates prior combination by the advertiser of text and illustrations in a single plate to send to magazines.

Some of the tonal effects of the halftone, and a variety of shadings and patterns, can be included in a line cut by using the Ben Day process or its variations. These are mechanical methods of applying dots, lines, stipple effects, and a wide variety of patterns, either on the art work by the artist or later by the engraver. Available to the artist are various commercial types of paste-on material consisting of shading, stippling, crosshatching, and so on which may be applied directly to the art work. The engraver has in stock numerous Ben Day screens by means of which the dots and patterns can be transferred photographically to the negative and later to an engraving. Ben Day lends itself both to black-and-white and color reproduction.

Color plates

The method of making four-color process engravings is based on the principle that all colors can be produced by combinations of three primary colors—yellow, red, and blue. Black is added to give density and detail to the reproduction. In any four-color process printing, there must be a separate impression for the black and for each of the three primary colors. In letterpress printing, separate halftone engravings are made for the black and for each of the colors. These are made by the same process as regular halftones.

The first step, however, is to produce color separations. This is done by photographing the subject four times. The copy is photographed with a special lens to secure the black, and each of the three primary colors is isolated by means of filters on the camera. The end result is four separate halftone plates, each screened at a different angle. Tiny clusters of halftone dots of the four colors in varying sizes on the printed page then give to the eye the illusion of seeing the many different colors of the original photograph or painting. For good results, four-color process printing requires that each impression be registered or aligned with precision. Otherwise the color will be blurred.

To aid the printer in matching the quality of the original as closely as possible, each color plate is proofed separately in the exact ink and on the paper to be used in the regular run of the advertisement. The printer is also furnished with a set of "progressives," proofs that show not only the individual color printings but also the color sequence in printing and the result as each additional color is added.

If the advertisement is to be printed by gravure or lithography, color-separation positives or negatives are furnished rather than plates. These are color corrected, that is improved by hand work, and transferred to the type of printing plates used in each method.

Fairchild's Scan-A-Color, and other electronic scanning devices, provide color separations, producing a set of color-corrected separations in less than an hour. These separations are on film and may be used with letterpress, lithographic, or gravure printing. Scan-A-Color has a computer that electronically relates the factors of density range, hue, brightness, and saturation for optimum results.

Besides process color printing, simple color printing may be done. This may consist of line color for printing selected lines of type or rules, borders, ornaments, and so on, or the Ben Day areas in illustrations. Or it may consist of overprinting—printing one transparent color on top of another. Halftones may also be printed in a single color or as duotones, a combination of two halftones, one black, the other in color, so treated in the photographic process that an effect of contrast and depth is secured not possible by printing a halftone over a panel or solid color. For a simple color plate, the advertiser starts with black-and-white copy—one copy for each of the colors if they overlap. If they do not overlap, a single black and white copy is used as a key and the other colors are pasted on as transparent acetate overlays.

In preparing advertising folders, catalogs, and so on, for which the entire process of production can be controlled by the advertiser, it is possible to use the paper itself to provide one color, thus securing a two-color effect with one printing impression.

Duplicate plates

Most advertisers find duplicate plates advantageous and even essential, for several reasons. If the advertisement is to appear in several periodicals simultaneously, duplicate plates are an obvious necessity. Duplicate plates can be curved to fit modern, high-speed rotary presses, and with duplicates the same material can be run at the same time on more than one press. The main types of duplicate plates are (1) electrotypes, (2) stereotypes, (3) plastic, and (4) others, including rubber, Chem-o-Type, magnesium, and Dycril.

A duplicate *electrotype* or electro is made by preparing a negative mold of the original in vinyl plastic, or the now less frequently used wax or lead, and using an electrolytic process to deposit a shell of copper or nickel on it. This, when properly backed up, becomes a duplicate printing plate. Electros are used mainly for magazine work, and for long press runs are often chrome plated for extra wear.

For newspapers, the advertisers usually supply mats. These are papier-mâché impressions made by pressing the original plate into cellulose pulp, producing a negative mold. The newspaper casts a positive plate called a *stereotype* from this mold by placing it in a casting box and pouring molten metal over it. The quality of reproduction to be secured from the stereotype is inferior to that obtainable from the electro, but the stereos are less expensive and, since the mats are light in weight, shipping costs are reduced.

Stereotyping offers an economical and rapid method of supplying multiple plates of an advertisement. When an advertiser wishes to run an advertisement in, say, 100 newspapers, it is easy and economical to supply mats and let the papers make their own casts.

Plastic plates are made by pouring a thermosetting plastic powder into a plastic mold and applying heat. The powder softens when heated, but when it cools, it hardens permanently. Plastic plates are less satisfactory for producing fine lines or dots than electros, and they are difficult to correct, but they are cheaper, lighter in weight and give satisfactory results for a wide range of uses. Plastic duplicate plates offer better quality of reproduction than do stereotypes, although they are somewhat more expensive than stereos.

Rubber plates are made by substituting rubber for plastic powder in the molds. They are best adapted for use in printing large runs on rotary letterpresses for which high quality of reproductions is not demanded. *Chem-o-Type* plates combine the qualities of rubber and plastic in a process that preserves the advantage of each. *Magnesium* plates employ lightweight and relatively inexpensive magnesium in the molds. Their principal advantage is that they can convert photocomposition products into a plate that can be used for printing by letterpress.

Perhaps the most promising of the newer types of plates are the *Dycril* and "Letterflex" plates. They are made of photopolymer, a photosensitive plastic, and also can be used with photocomposition products. An important property of photopolymer is that it is affected by exposure to light, not just on the surface but throughout its entire thickness. This simplifies the etching process so that a photopolymer plate can be produced in less than a fourth of the time it takes to make an etched metal plate. As yet, however, these plates are relatively expensive compared to molded plastic plates, and will remain so until they come into wider use.

PRINTING

There are four basic printing processes in common use today: letterpress; gravure; lithography, especially offset lithography; and screen process printing, often called silk screen.

Letterpress

The oldest, and still the most widely used, and in various ways the most satisfactory, method of printing is by letterpress. In letterpress printing, ink is applied to a raised (relief) surface and transferred to paper by direct pressing onto the paper. This may be done from lock-up metal type, but more commonly it is done from plates, in which the portions to be printed are in relief.

Although there is a distinct trend toward offset lithography, most newspapers and magazines, and much of the direct-mail advertising are printed by letterpress. The presses used in letterpress are of three types: (1) platen, (2) cylinder, and (3) rotary.

On a *platen* press there are two flat surfaces, one the bed, which holds the type form, and the other the platen, which holds the paper. These open and close much like the jaws of a clamshell. Ink is applied to the form, as the jaws open and close, by a roller which alternately passes over it and a flat ink plate behind it. At the same time a sheet of paper is fed to the platen, usually from an automatic feeder. When the jaws close, the sheet is printed, and when they open again, the printed sheet is delivered and a new sheet is fed in. Platen presses are relatively slow and are most useful in job printing and for short runs.

On *cylinder* presses the printing form is placed on a large, flat bed while a rotating cylinder applies the pressure. Ink rollers and sheets of paper carried by the cylinder alterately pass over the printing form held in the bed. There are also *perfecting* flat-bed presses which print simultaneously on both sides of the paper by means of two flat beds and two cylinders. Cylinder presses are much faster than the platen presses.

By far the fastest and most efficient of the presses for letterpress printing are the rotary presses (see Figure 18–11). On these both the printing surface and the paper are on cylinders and the plates used—generally electrotypes or stereotypes—must be curved to fit the cylinder. The printing impression is made as the two cylinders roll together. Ink rollers ink the printing surface with each revolution of the cylinder. The paper may be fed in sheets or from a continuous roll or "web" of paper. Perfecting web-fed rotary presses print both sides of the paper at the same time by means of additional cylinders. Multicolor web-fed rotary presses make possible the high-speed printing of numerous colors at the same time.

A recent development, designed to make letterpress competitive in price with offset lithography is wrap-around letterpress. In this type of printing, a one-piece shallow-relief plate of full press form size is made and wrapped around the plate cylinder like an offset plate. This adapts a plate with a relief surface to faster rotary speeds and affords a saving in make-ready and plate costs.

Gravure

The principle of gravure or intaglio printing is the reverse of that of letterpress in that the printing surface instead of being raised is etched into the plate and is depressed. Ink is laid into minute receptacles in the printing surface and transferred to paper by pressure and suction.

Gravure plates are made by a somewhat more complicated process than that for letterpress plates. The copy is photographed to produce two separate films—one for line copy and the other for halftone copy. The negatives are combined into one continuous film positive. Color separations are made in the same way as for letterpress and offset. In conven-

FIGURE 18–11. High-speed rotary press for sheet-fed letterpress printing

tional gravure, the image is transferred to a copper cylinder by the use of a sensitized medium called carbon tissue, or Du Pont's Rotofilm may be used. A method adapted especially to color reproduction is the News-Dultgen process which differs in some details from conventional gravure. A recent development is the direct transfer method, by means of which the cylinder itself is made light sensitive through the application of a coating. After processing this permits the cylinder to make a direct printing impression.

Gravure is essentially a rotary method, easily adaptable to web-fed printing. The printing cylinder revolves in a trough of ink which not only fills the wells and depressions of the printing surface but also deposits ink over the entire surface. As the cylinder emerges from the ink trough, the surface is wiped dry and free of ink by a "doctor blade," leaving the ink only in the recesses etched into the cylinder. The ink is then "lifted" out of the recesses by the paper as it is pressed against the cylinder. The inks used are quick-drying.

Rotogravure presses print long runs at high speed and are web-fed. For shorter runs sheet-fed gravure presses are also available.

Lithography

In lithography, the printing surface is on the same plane as the non-printing surface instead of being raised, as in letterpress, or depressed, as in gravure. Printing in this way is made possible by first processing the surface of the plate in such a way that the areas to be printed become grease receptive while the nonprinting surface becomes water receptive. Water and grease, of course, do not mix. When the plate is moistened with water, the water-receptive (nonprinting) areas, therefore, repel the greasy ink when it is spread over the plate, while the grease-receptive (printing) areas pick up the ink. When the plate is brought in contact with paper, a printing impression results.

The first lithographic plates were slabs of limestone, and stone remained in use until the beginning of the 20th century. The images to be printed were drawn on the stone by hand. Today lithographic plates are commonly metal and are of three main types: (1) surface, (2) deep etch, and (3) multimetal.

Surface plates are coated with a light-sensitive, ink-receptive substance so that on exposure, the light coming through a photographic negative hardens the printing area where the light hits; the nonprinting parts stay soft. When the soft parts are washed out and a coating of water-receptive substance is applied, the plate is divided into ink-receptive printing parts and ink-repellent (nonprinting) parts. Surface plates are designated, according to their materials and processing, as albumen, presensitized, and wipe-on.

Deep-etch plates are those in which the plate is processed so that the printing areas are somewhat below the surface of the nonprinting areas as in gravure. These plates are more durable than surface plate and are used for longer runs.

Multimetal plates are those that receive an extra coating of metal through an electrolytic process. Bimetal plates have an ink-receptive metal base on which a light-sensitive coating is placed. On development, the coating is removed from the nonprinting parts and these parts are given a water-receptive metal coating electrolytically. A second bath washes away the remaining light-sensitive coating, leaving bare the ink-receptive base metal (the printing area). Or the process can be reversed so that the base metal is the nonprinting area, and the plated areas are the printing parts. Trimetal plates are those in which the entire plate is metal plated. Bimetal plates are very durable, and trimetal plates are even more so. Multimetal plates are, of course, more expensive than any others described, and are used for long runs only.

The images to be printed are placed on the plates by a photochemical process similar to photoengraving. In photographing the copy, line and halftone copy are shot separately. The lithographic camera employs screens to break up tone copy into dots as in the production of any halftone. After the negatives or positives are made, line copy and tone copy are pieced together (stripped) into a single flat. Thus, the lithograph plate contains all the type matter and the illustrations, and it is not necessary to assemble individual cuts and metal type into page forms as in letterpress.

Direct lithography—printing directly from plate to paper—has largely given way to *offset lithography,* the fastest growing printing method of our day. In offset an intermediary cylinder picks up the image from the lithographic plate and transfers it to the paper. Offset presses have three printing cylinders of the same size: a plate cylinder, a blanket cylinder, and an impression cylinder. The inked and dampened plate on the first cylinder prints on the rubber-blanketed cylinder, which in turn "offsets" onto the paper held on the third or impression cylinder (see Figure 18–12). The use of rubber for the blanket makes it possible to print fine designs and photographs on fairly coarse paper, since the flexibility of rubber will adapt the printing surface to the rough paper sur-

FIGURE 18–12. An offset lithography press

face. Offset lithography is especially useful when reproducing large areas of halftone and many solid colors.

Lithography in general and offset in particular have received impetus from the development of cold-type composition, the products of which are particularly well adapted to this method of printing. Also, lithography has advantages over letterpress in that it can print type and illustrations with little more effort and cost than type alone. Until fairly recently, however, lithography produced a gray, flat tone and colors were dull and muddy, which made the result look cheap. Many improvements have been made in presses, inks, and paper so that a first-rate job can now be turned out consistently. The high-speed web offset presses of today set a hard competitive pace for any other process to match.

Screen process printing

Screen process printing, also called "silk screen," is a stencil process in which ink is forced through a mesh screen onto various kinds of printing surfaces—wood, glass, metal, plastic, fabric, and others, as well as paper. This makes the process useful for a wide variety of advertising and packaging purposes. For example, it can be used for displays, banners, and 24-sheet billboards. Today, screen process printing can also be used for longer runs than formerly, due to the introduction of faster presses. It is now one of the fastest developing processes in the printing field.

The screen used in screen process printing may be a piece of silk, nylon, Dacron, or metal mesh. The screen is stretched tightly over a wooden or metal frame and serves to hold in place the mask or stencil which has been attached to it. The stencils may be handcut from film specially designed for this purpose or may be prepared photographically from any drawing or printed design. Ink is squeezed through the screen by a squeegee (a rubber-edged bar) sliding across the surface, causing a printing impression to be made. In color printing, a separate mask or stencil is usually made for each color.

An interesting feature of screen process printing is the ink used. A heavy film of ink can be deposited by this process—even 10 times as heavy as that possible with letterpress—and the flow of the ink can be controlled in a way not possible with other methods. The ink can be built up until it looks like embossing. Formerly the ink took a long time to dry, slowing the process, but now there are new types of quick-drying inks and hot-air dryers which have speeded things up.

SELECTING GRAPHIC ARTS SUPPLIERS

In many instances the advertiser does not have control over the mechanical production of the advertising message. He sends copy, on which specifications may or may not have been marked, layout, and art work or art copy to the media, and it is processed from there on by whatever methods the media normally uses, or the advertiser may be in control up to the point of providing mats or stereos, electros, or color separations and progressives or even four-color process plates. The advertiser may or may not have full-time specialists in his employ. His art department, if he has one, will vary in the extent to which it is qualified to do finished art work. It may do the whole job, or it may be necessary to have the work done by the printer or an outside art studio.

Most advertisers do, however, on occasion, particularly in direct-mail advertising, find it necessary to select graphic arts suppliers—engravers, composition houses, binders, and complete printers, as well as art studios. In doing this, certain typical problems arise, and certain principles serve as guidelines in making selections.

The first question that arises is: To what point can we carry the job ourselves and at what stage do we turn it over to the graphic arts specialists? This question largely answers itself, but it is important that the advertiser avoid amateurish experimentation on his own and that he turn the job over to the experts at any point where such specialized skill is not available in his own company.

A second question that must be answered early is: Which is more important in this particular job—speed or production, quality, or cost? Frequently it is not possible to have all three; something of one must be sacrificed to achieve the others. An appropriate balance among these factors for the job in question should be sought.

A third consideration is: Shall we turn the job over to a printer having complete creative and production facilities or shall we deal with separate art studios, engravers, compositors, and even binders if the advertising piece is to have hard or even soft covers. Today, the graphic arts services are highly specialized, although complete printing houses are numerous. Greater economy and better quality may be possible through judicious selection of specialized suppliers. However, this takes more of the advertiser's time in securing estimates and in coordinating the work of the specialized services. It may result in a slower schedule.

A fourth consideration is: By what method shall the advertising message be produced? This choice requires relating the method appropriately to the job from the standpoints of speed, quality, and economy. It will be helpful to bear in mind the following advantages and disadvantages of the various methods.

1. *Letterpress.* This method still gives the greatest assurance of sharp detail and good quality and is the method most widely available. It does not produce as smooth a tone in illustrations as offset, and it necessitates the use of coated paper stock for fine halftones. It is more expensive than offset for small runs, but is becoming more competitive in cost for long runs on high-speed rotary presses with Dycril or wrap-around plates.

2. *Gravure.* Gravure does not produce as sharp an impression as letterpress because the entire plate is screened, and the cost of preparing gravure printing cylinders is high. But it produces excellent results at reasonable cost in runs of 100,000 or more.

3. *Offset.* This is the most economical method for extremely small runs and also is competitively at some advantage in long runs on modern web offset presses. Although improving, its quality is still below that of letterpress in reliability. Offset permits printing of halftones on a wider range of paper stocks and provides smoother tone. It makes it possible to reproduce previously printed copy and typewriter composition as well

as various kinds of art work without resetting or redrawing. It is especially well adapted to the use of the products of photocomposition. It eliminates the need for separate cuts of illustrations.

4. *Screen process printing.* The chief advantages of this method are its versatility and the effects that can be achieved through the inks used. Through the screen process, it is possible to print on a large variety of materials besides paper. The inks used give rich effects. The disadvantages are mostly in the slowness of the process relative to the speeds that can be attained by other methods.

Having made, at least tentatively, the foregoing basic decisions about the job, the advertiser should proceed systematically to secure cost estimates. Perhaps he has a printed form available for requesting estimates. In any case it is essential to cover completely what the advertiser expects the supplier to do and to provide exact specifications as to quantity, number of pages, size, number of colors, illustrations, paper stock, and so on. Unless it is possible to describe the job exactly, it will also be necessary to accompany the request for estimate with the actual copy, layout, and perhaps a dummy. A first principle in securing estimates is: Give each supplier exactly the same specifications and the same complete descriptions of what is wanted. Then make sure that the bids are exactly comparable—that is, cover precisely the same services.

In making the final choice of a graphic arts supplier, a few principles will serve as guides:

1. What is the supplier's reputation and past record—especially his past performance with the advertiser's own jobs? Has the supplier been in business long enough to have established a reputation for reliability and good work? If a new firm, are the firm's principals sufficiently experienced and well enough backed financially to inspire confidence? Few things are more frustrating than to have a supplier go broke in the middle of a job or botch the job through incompetence.

2. Will the supplier give you the kind of schedule you want and can he be relied upon to keep his promises on delivery provided you hold up your end?

3. Is his cost estimating system sound so that you can have confidence in his estimates? Does he stand by his estimates or does he come around later and beg to be rescued from a bad guess?

4. Does he have all the skills and equipment he needs to do the job? This may include creative services; all the type faces and special characters wanted—either he has them in his own type library or is willing to

secure the mats elsewhere; the right kind of presses for the job; a good composing room and proofreading services.

5. Does he have a large amount of special-priority government work or a few large customers for whom he will put your job aside if necessary?

A final word: Always insist on seeing proofs and check them carefully. The battle against errors is a never-ending one, and one frequently lost. Nothing is more embarrassing than to discover gross errors in type or illustrations after the advertisement has been printed. Errors may destroy the entire value of the advertisement or lead to costly complications, as when the price is wrong or the terms of sale are distorted. On the other hand, in proofreading, the high cost of alterations should be kept in mind and balanced against the importance of the change. The layman has little idea of the number of costly operations needed to change even a punctuation mark. To change art elements might require making an entirely new cut or plate. The advertiser can save much time and money by getting the copy and art work right in the first place.

TELEVISION PRODUCTION

The production of a typical live television commercial is relatively simple—simple, that is, if one takes the marvel of television broadcasting as a going system requiring no further explanation. The commercial is simply transmitted and reproduced electronically on the screens of millions of receiving sets in millions of homes at the very instant it is being enacted in the studio. Producing a live commercial is mainly a matter of preparing the studio set selecting whatever props are to be used and rehearsing the performance.

Production of a film commercial is considerably more complicated, too complicated to be fully described in these few pages. However, this type of commercial is so predominant in national advertising that the student should have a working knowledge of the basic steps. Also, much of the creative work on a film commercial is done in the production phases. Hooper White, Creative Manager at the Leo Burnett Company, suggests that television production is an "interpretation" rather than a mere execution of writers' and artists' ideas.

This section will outline the production phases of a live action film commercial. See Figure 18–13 for a flow chart of these phases.

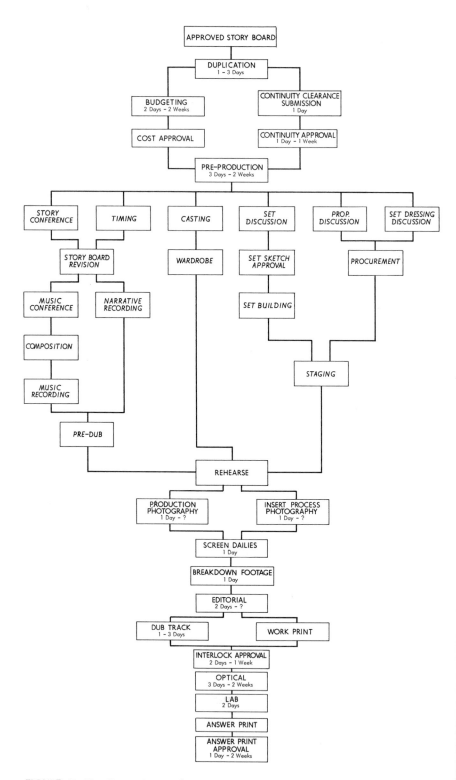

FIGURE 18–13. Live action production

Preproduction operations

Once the storyboard has been approved by the client, the advertising agency's producer sends the storyboard and accompanying production notes, such as announcer preference, set sketches, ideas for props, and music requirements to several producing studios and asks them to bid on the job. After a contract is signed with the winning studio and before the actual shooting schedule begins, the producer gets involved in:

—Casting sessions to select the actors and/or the announcer.
—Set design sessions to work out exactly how the background will look.
—Location discussions, or actual survey trips to decide where the commercial will be shot.
—Prop sessions to decide on various articles to be used such as glassware, tableware, furniture, and art objects.
—Music sessions, if music is required, with composers, singers, performing groups, etc.
—Arranging shooting schedules, recording sessions, and completion dates.
—Seeing that all of the above get done.

Filming and editing

Filming a television commercial is much the same as filming a Hollywood movie. In fact, many are done in Hollywood. The individual scenes usually are not shot in the sequence in which they will appear in the final version. Visual and sound tracks may not be recorded at the same time. Several different angles and views of each scene are taken to give the film editor a choice of best possible shots when putting the commercial together.

After the shooting begins, the film is quickly developed, often overnight, to provide *rushes* or *dailies* which are hurried prints of inferior quality. Rushes give the director an opportunity to screen the preceding day's work, to select the best shots and to decide whether any retakes are needed before the set is torn down and the cast disbanded.

From the chosen shots the film editor assembles the *work print* which is used for adjusting, cutting, and editing while the original negative is stored and protected. At this point the picture is recorded on film and the sound is recorded on a separate magnetic tape. Using a "Movieola," a device that allows him to view the film on a small screen at various speeds, fast, slow, or even frame by frame, and also gives him picture and sound separately or in synchronization, the editor locks (synchronizes) picture and sound in what is referred to as an *interlock*. At this point the interlock is shown for agency and client approval.

Next, optical effects, such as superimposed lettering, split screens, and special scene transitions are added to a fine-grain positive print of the original negative. Then, a *dubbing* session, music, sound effects, and voice are carefully balanced. Finally, the sound track and the picture positive are combined in an optical printer to produce a duplicate negative, which when printed becomes the first *answer print*. This first composite print is called an answer print because it gives the answer as to how all the components fit when put together for the first time on a single film. Several answer prints may have to be made with corrections in picture or sound quality, in synchronization or timing, before final agency and client approval is given. From storyboard to answer print, the production of a standard live action commercial takes seven to eight weeks.

After the answer print has been approved, an appropriate number of *release prints* are prepared and these are shipped to the networks and/or individual stations for broadcast.

QUESTIONS AND PROBLEMS

1. What is the fundamental difference between the following kinds of printing: letterpress, gravure, offset lithography, and screen process?
2. Type faces are classified into fonts, series, families, and groups or classes. Define each.
3. What factors should be considered in the selection of type faces?
4. Explain the different units for measuring type size.
5. What are the advantages of setting type by hand? By machine?
6. What factors should be considered in selecting a graphic arts supplier?
7. Contrast halftones and line plates in terms of the mechanics of manufacture and their usefulness in reproducing illustrations.
8. What are the principal values of electrotypes? Of stereotypes?
9. What are the differences between various types of lithograph plates?
10. As advertising manager, you have been handed a manuscript of 10,000 characters to be set in type for a direct-mail pamphlet, which will measure in page size 6 × 9 inches. This type is to be set in 10-point with 2-point leads in an area 4½ × 7¼ inches on each page.
    a) What are the minimum number of pages which are required for printing this manuscript in the design of type you prefer?
    b) Inasmuch as the economical cuts for the paper that would be used to make a booklet of this size fold into 4, 8, 16, and 32 pages, what recommendations would you make?
11. Production of a television commercial has sometimes been referred to as "creative interpretation." Why?

part IV
Advertising media

chapter 19
SELECTING THE
MEDIUM

THE ADVERTISING medium is the carrier of the advertising message. Before the days of the printing press, about the only means the advertiser had for transmitting his message were signs and town criers. Today, our vast array of printed publications, radio stations, and television stations offers the advertisers so many ways of communicating his message to the public that the problem of choosing an appropriate medium is of major importance. The principal media may be classified as follows:

1. Newspapers
2. Magazines
   - *a*) Consumer magazines
   - *b*) Business publications
   - *c*) Farm publications
   - *d*) Professional journals
3. Radio
4. Television
5. Direct mail
6. Outdoor
   - *a*) Signs
   - *b*) Posters
   - *c*) Painted bulletins
   - *d*) Electric displays
7. Transit
8. Others
   - *a*) Dealer displays
   - *b*) Packages, labels, and inserts
   - *c*) Theater-screen advertising
   - *d*) Specialties
   - *e*) Telephone directories

Estimates of total advertising expenditures in the various types of media during 1968 and 1969 are shown in Table 19–1. Expenditures for newspaper advertising are almost 30 percent of the total. Television advertising expenditures have increased dramatically in the past several years, to where this medium is now in second place. Direct mail, the importance of which is often overlooked, is third. Whereas retail or local

TABLE 19–1. Advertising expenditures in the U.S. 1968–69

	1968		1969	
Medium	Expenditure in millions	Percent of total	Expenditure in millions	Percent of total
Newspapers				
Total	$ 5,265	29.1%	$ 5,850	29.9%
National	990	5.5	1,050	5.4
Local	4,275	23.6	4,800	24.5
Magazines				
Total	1,318	7.3	1,375	7.0
Weeklies	657	3.6	660	3.4
Women's	284	1.6	310	1.6
Monthlies	342	1.9	373	1.9
Farm, national	35	0.2	32	0.1
Television				
Total	3,231	17.8	3,585	18.3
Network	1,523	8.4	1,675	8.5
Spot	1,131	6.2	1,245	6.4
Local	577	3.2	665	3.4
Radio				
Total	1,190	6.6	1,270	6.5
Network	63	0.4	65	0.3
Spot	360	2.0	370	1.9
Local	767	4.2	835	4.3
Farm publications				
(regional)	33	0.2	33	0.2
Total farm publications*	(68)	(0.4)	(65)	(0.3)
Direct mail	2,612	14.4	2,680	13.7
Business papers	714	3.9	720	3.7
Outdoor				
Total	208	1.1	206	1.0
National	137	0.7	135	0.6
Local	71	0.4	71	0.4
Miscellaneous				
Total	3,556	19.6	3,846	19.7
National	2,035	11.2	2,145	11.0
Local	1,521	8.4	1,701	8.7
Total				
National	10,883	60.0	11,460	58.6
Local	7,244	40.0	8,105	41.4
Grand total	$18,127	100.0%	$19,565	100.0%

* Included in other media totals—not to be added.
Note: Estimates include all costs—time and talent, space and production.
Source: *Marketing/Communications*, February, 1970, p. 55.

advertising is heavily concentrated in newspapers, national advertising is more widely distributed among all media.

The media-selection problem

The individual advertising situation largely determines the complexity of media selection. A retailer in a small town where there is only a weekly newspaper doesn't have much of a problem. However, a retailer in a major metropolitan area has the problem of choosing media from among newspapers, radio, television, outdoor, transit, and direct mail.

The complexity of the problem of media selection is even more discernible in the case of the national advertiser who sells to a broad nation-wide market. What types of media should he use? Magazines? Newspapers? Television? Radio? Outdoor? If magazines, what classes? General interest magazines? Women's magazines? Romance magazines? If women's magazines, which specific ones? *Ladies' Home Journal? McCall's? Good Housekeeping?* If newspapers, in which cities? If there are several newspapers in a selected city, which specific newspapers? If television, should he use a nationwide network or select stations for local coverage in individual markets? What network? What stations?

There are no rules-of-thumb or pat formulas for solving these selection problems. Each advertising situation presents its own unique set of circumstances. Each type of medium has its own character and each specific medium, in turn, differs from the next. There is no single "best" medium for all advertising situations. Each media decision must be made in light of the particular requirements of a particular situation. Even competitors selling nearly the same products to nearly the same markets employ different media strategies. As shown in Table 19–2, there are noticeable

TABLE 19–2. Distribution of advertising expenditures among media for seven petroleum companies, 1968

	Percent of advertising expenditure (by media)					
	News-papers	Magazines	Spot TV	Net TV	Radio	Outdoor
Shell Oil Co.	6.4%	15.4	42.6	26.1	9.0	.5
Gulf Oil Corp.	10.0	9.8	4.9	70.4	3.3	1.6
Standard Oil (N.J.)	9.4	31.7	13.2	17.0	22.7	6.1
Mobil	21.9	25.8	23.0	7.2	22.0	.1
Texaco	11.7	19.1	8.1	42.6	17.3	1.2
Phillips	.6	14.1	12.1	62.8	7.3	3.0
Sun Oil	3.8	13.8	21.6	22.9	36.9	1.0

Source: *Advertising Age,* August 25, 1969, p. 41.

differences in the way seven petroleum companies distribute their advertising expenditures among types of media.

A limiting factor that always must be taken into account is the budget or amount of money available for advertising. There is never enough money to fully exploit all the media opportunities available. Therefore, the advertiser must be selective. He seeks to maximize the return on his advertising investment by selecting those media that will deliver the messages most efficiently and effectively. His chances of making the right choices are greatly improved when he has carefully analyzed all available facts bearing on his marketing situation and his media alternatives. The decision-making process, however, should be creative. Characteristics of a creative media decision are described by Brown, Lessler, and Weilbacher as follows:

> A creative media decision is made when all the factors operating in a given market situation are combined with media experience and sound judgment and imagination to determine a media strategy or a media choice. To the extent that any policy factor is ignored, to the extent that the marketing realities reflected in allied marketing strategies are ignored, to the extent that applicable objective research findings are ignored or misinterpreted, a media decision is not truly creative. Furthermore, to the extent that executive judgment and imagination do not actively assimilate these factors and find a unique media solution, media decisions are not creative.[1]

A total media plan is illustrated in Figure 19–1. Principal factors to be considered when selecting the medium are (1) the market, (2) extent and character of distribution, (3) creative strategy, (4) circulations, (5) audiences, (6) costs, (7) editorial or program content, and (8) advertiser usage. Each of these factors is discussed in the following pages of this chapter.

The market—type of consumers

The first task of the advertiser in his selection of media will be a thorough and definite understanding of the market for his product. An advertising medium is a carrier of a message. The sender of the message can select the carrier with intelligence only after he knows the type or class of consumers to whom the message is to be directed. Is the message to be aimed at all types of consumers or to women, children, professional people, sport lovers, businessmen, farmers, Negroes, or some religious

---

[1] Lyndon O. Brown, Richard S. Lessler, and William M. Weilbacher, *Advertising Media* (New York: Ronald Press Co., 1957), p. 7.

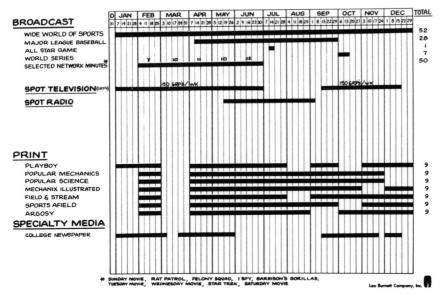

FIGURE 19–1. A total media plan

sect? If to businessmen, what kind of business—manufacturing or trading? If to the former, what particular kind of production—steel, lumber, food, automobile, glass, pottery, textile, or novelty? What kind of men in the manufacturing field are to receive the message—executives, plant superintendents, foremen, purchasing agents, or laborers?

Most of this information will have been collected in the consumer-research studies carried on by or for the advertiser. It is important that media be selected that will reach the desired group. Newspapers, magazines, radio stations, and other media are not all alike. One newspaper will have a different following from another. One will be conservative in its editorial and news policy; another liberal. One will have the laboring class as its heaviest subscribers, while another will attract the "white-collar" classes.

Magazines have a much more selective audience than newspapers. In the field of sports there are special magazines for the hunter and trapper, the golfer, the fisherman, and the tennis player. Every well-established profession has its own journal written in the language of the profession. A special group of magazines is available for those wishing to advertise to youth. There is a religious press appealing to people of each particular faith.

Radio and television stations also have their own type of audience. This is especially true of radio stations where selection is made on the basis of the character of the stations. Some stations will emphasize educational programs, in-depth news analysis, symphonic music, operas, and theatrical productions. Others will have their time predominantly filled with currently popular music and news headlines. Each kind of program attracts a different audience, the character of which can be determined by analysis. This is often done by the station, and the information made available to the advertiser.

The type of consumer to whom advertising is to be directed is often predetermined by the character of the product. Farm machinery is not sold to the public in general. It would be folly to advertise such products in a general magazine such as *Life.* Industrial goods will usually not be advertised in general consumer magazines but in those that reach a particular buyer group.

Since the real purpose of an advertising medium is that of a messenger, strong emphasis must be placed upon the necessity for knowing the direction the messenger takes. A merchant in Chicago would not think of shipping a package destined for New York City on a train going to Denver. Yet there are advertisers that put an advertisement "aboard" a particular medium not knowing whether the medium goes to the type of consumer that should logically be interested in their products. This situation can be remedied only by knowing, first, the type of prospect and, second, the ability of the medium to reach that prospect.

Extent and character of distribution

Advertising will be of little or no value in getting people to buy merchandise unless such merchandise is placed within easy reach of them. It is usually unwise to use the *Podunk Journal* as a medium if no dealers in Podunk handle the advertised goods. Likewise, it would be wasteful to use a medium covering the entire United States if there were dealer distribution in only that section east of the Mississippi River and north of the Ohio River. There are times when a local medium may be used in the absence of dealer distribution in order to bring pressure on dealers to stock the advertised product. Such procedure is rare and, when used, is only a temporary expedient.

Distribution might be classified as national, regional, or local. There are some media, like magazines and network broadcasting, that specialize in covering the national market. Other media, such as newspapers, can be applied nationally by using a sufficiently large number of them. There are a few media that serve particular regions. The *Prairie Farmer* and *Ohio Motorist* are examples. Media serving local areas are exceedingly plentiful. Every town of any size has its daily or weekly newspaper. Radio and television stations serve local and regional markets. Billboards can be rented on a local basis. Signs are distinctly local.

Even though an advertiser has national distribution, he may wish to work some territories more intensely than others. The results of a market analysis may have revealed some districts as more fertile than others, thus meriting more sales effort. In such cases, national media may be supplemented by media serving the richer areas only. New products might also be offered in a small territory to test their reception. Here, again, local media will serve best.

Dealer distribution may at times depend not so much upon the size of the advertiser as upon the character of the market. If the market is a "thin" one, dealers will logically be few in relation to total population. Under such circumstances, a medium should be selected that reaches the few, but important, prospects.

Persons in the distribution system often exert considerable influence on the national advertiser's use and choice of local media. They are inclined to want more local advertising support. Being "on the spot" they feel better qualified than the remote advertiser and agency personnel to decide which of the community's newspapers, radio or television stations do the best job. The national advertiser, of course, cannot heed all of their wishes. Yet, when making his media decisions the importance of keeping his dealers happy cannot be overlooked.

Creative strategy

In many instances the copy approach or technique of presenting the message requires a particular medium for proper expression. If top quality four-color reproduction is needed, magazines would have the edge on newspapers. Product demonstrations and personal sales deliveries are uniquely suited to television. New product introductions require the sense of urgency and newsworthiness so characteristic of newspapers, radio, and television. If creative strategy seeks to inspire confidence or dispel doubt, a medium such as *Good Housekeeping* magazine with its highly respected editorial and Seal of Approval would be appropriate.

If the advertisement is designed to build and sustain a certain brand image or product personality, it should be placed in media having personality traits that complement and reinforce the desired image. Some media—notably magazines, television programs, and radio programs—have distinct personalities that may be described in such terms as masculine or feminine, modern or old fashioned, high-brow or low-brow, homey or worldly, serious or frivolous. These media that have the kind of personality that is right for the product tend to strengthen the effectiveness of the image-building advertisement.

Copy that is to appear in a given medium should be written in terms that will be understood by readers of the publication. Thus, an advertisement appearing in *The New Yorker* might not be appropriate in *True Story* or *Physical Culture*. The readers of the former have social, cultural, and economic interests that differ from those of the readers of the latter magazines. The advertiser should talk to each audience in its own language. More important differences will, of course, be noted among the readers of magazines serving special interests. *Western Canner & Packer* attracts an audience greatly different from that attracted by the *Atlantic Monthly*.

Many advertisers believe that the same copy and illustrations can be used in all the media selected for products having an almost universal appeal, such as tobacco, furniture, automobiles, soap, and canned foods. The probabilities are that greater effectiveness will be obtained if different copy is written for each medium where differences in audience are discernible. Use the farmer's language when advertising tobacco to him through a farm magazine and he will buy more of your tobacco than he would if you used the language of *The New Yorker*.

Figure 19–2 is a reproduction of an advertisement appearing in *Farm Journal*. The creator of an advertisement to be carried in a magazine with such concentrated circulation among farm people could have been more effective in his communication to farmers than he was with the advertisement illustrated. The headline, "She gets the cleanest clothes in town," does not focus attention on the farm and the problem of getting farm clothes clean. The illustration is even worse. Surely a farm scene with farm clothing could have been used. What farm woman sends her husband off to work in a white shirt and with a dinner pail in his hand? In many respects this advertisement implies that Tide is for town women and is not to be used for overalls and other farm clothing. Surely this advertisement could not have been created with the *Farm Journal* audience in mind.

FIGURE 19–2. An advertisement which appeared in a farm magazine. Word choice and illustration not in harmony with farm setting

Circulations

The circulation of a newspaper or magazine can be clearly defined. It is the total number of copies of an average issue that are distributed to people. The unit of measurement is a *copy*. Then what is the circulation of a radio or television station, of outdoor posters or transit advertisements? The obvious answer is that these media have no circulation which is directly comparable to the circulation of a newspaper or magazine because they do not distribute *copies*. Yet, the term "circulation" has been used to describe various dimensions of all types of media and has had a different meaning for each type. To avoid the kind of fuzzy thinking associated with loose definition of terms, media analysts in recent years have restricted the circulation concept to newspapers and magazines. They measure the advertising opportunity offered by other media in terms of audiences, a concept which will be discussed later in this chapter.

Circulation figures as applied to newspapers and magazines are factual, regularly reported, and easily understood. They give the advertisers an indication of (1) how many people are reached by a publication, (2) where these people live, and (3) the degree of interest people have in the editorial content.

If magazine A circulates twice as many copies as magazine B, it is logical to assume that magazine A is reaching many more people than magazine B. However, the actual number of *readers* may not be twice as great. Magazine B may reach more readers per copy. Also, one magazine may be read more thoroughly than another with the result that the advertiser's message may be exposed to a larger share of the readers of one magazine than of another. Even though the number of copies circulated is not a direct measure of the number of people reached, circulation is generally accepted as the basic standard for estimating the advertising value of newspapers and magazines.

A geographic breakdown of circulation shows the advertiser how well a publication fits his distribution pattern. When he knows how many copies of a magazine go into the various states, counties, and metropolitan areas, he can see to what extent the magazine's circulation is concentrated in his most promising markets. When he knows how many copies of a newspaper are sold within the immediate city zone, within the surrounding trade zone, and in nearby counties and towns, he can make significant inferences about the composition of the market reached by that newspaper. City-zone circulation includes most of the copies sold to apartment dwellers, commuters, and office workers. The trading zone reaches out to suburbia where younger and larger families reside. Copies going outside of the trading zone can be expected to reach more families living on farms.

Reader interest in a publication's editorial content can be inferred from the trend of circulation and the methods used to build circulation. A consistently growing circulation may indicate greater reader interest. A declining circulation suggests less reader interest. However, circulation growth may be the result of using gimmicks instead of providing the kind of editorial content that wins readers on its own merit.

Since rates charged for space are primarily dependent upon volume of circulation, it is to the advantage of media to obtain as large a subscription list as possible. This has led to many methods of increasing the circulation figures. One method is that of offering a group of magazines at reduced subscription prices. One popular magazine is often included, and others, less popular, are taken because of the low price.

Door-to-door canvassing is a common method employed by some publishers or subscription associations. Few housewives have not heard the pleas of some young "college student" working his way through school by selling magazines. Certainly the "lady of the house" would not begrudge 4½ cents a week for such a worthy cause. Then, there is the regular subscription salesman who offers valuable premiums in the way of maps, globes, shrubbery, or books with each order of a number of periodicals. Others obtain the endorsement of the parent-teachers' associations, churches, or other local organizations to make selling easy. Often these organizations are promised a commission on all sales. Such tactics place emphasis upon factors other than the publications, and they often result in building up a list of subscribers that are not materially interested in the magazine.

Many publishers give special prices for short-term subscriptions in the hope that, when the trial period is over, the person will become a regular subscriber. Some will continue the short-term rates regularly. Bulk subscriptions are also used to increase sales. Schools are solicited for such orders where the publications can be used in classes.

There are also publishers who do not cancel a subscriber from the list when the subscription date has expired. Several months will often elapse before cancellation is effected. Some indication of the interest which a reader shows in a publication can often be obtained by checking the percentage of renewals.

Audit bureaus

The mad scramble of publishers for large circulations, together with the practice of some of falsifying their published circulation figures, led to the establishment in 1914 of the Audit Bureau of Circulations (A.B.C.). This bureau was sponsored by national and local advertisers, advertising agencies, and publishers desirous of protecting themselves against those whose statements could not be relied upon. Control of the Bureau is vested in a board of directors consisting of 27 members: 12 advertisers, 3 advertising agencies, 6 newspapers publishers and 6 magazine publishers. Note that the buyers of advertising space are in the majority.

Presently, only publications having 70 percent or more paid circulation are eligible for A.B.C. membership and audit. Paid circulation is roughly defined as those copies that people have paid for at not less than one-half the established basic prices. If the basic single-copy price is 20 cents, then only those copies for which the buyer paid 10 cents or more can be included in net paid circulation. If the basic annual subscription price is $7.00, then only those subscriptions for which $3.50 or more was paid can be included in net paid. The A.B.C. treats the payment of money as substantial evidence that the buyer is sufficiently interested in the publication to read it.

The A.B.C. performs three important functions: (1) audits the circulation figures of member publishers and certifies to the accuracy of publishers' statements, (2) establishes standards for reporting the quantity, quality, and distribution of circulation, and (3) serves as a clearing house, gathering statements from member publishers and disseminating circulation reports to advertisers and agencies. Figure 19–3 shows a publisher's statement to the A.B.C.

Not all publishers are members of the A.B.C. The Bureau has had its influence on them, however, since many advertisers are skeptical of figures not certified by some recognized agency. Nonmembers often make sworn statements of their circulation. If most copies are mailed out, such statements can be checked with the post office for accuracy. The work of the A.B.C. has made advertisers more conscious of the importance of accurate figures and has thus greatly reduced the number of false statements by nonmembers.

Publications that confine their distribution to special groups on a free basis are not now eligible to have their circulation figures audited by the

AUDIT BUREAU OF CIRCULATIONS
123 NORTH WACKER DRIVE · CHICAGO 6, ILLINOIS
[This statement is subject to audit by the Audit Bureau of Circulations. For Audit Report refer to latest white paper form.]

Publisher's Statement — Newspaper
6 months ending March 31, (year)

Chicago (Cook County), Illinois
The Chronicle (Evening)
See Par. 9

8. Average net paid circulation: | Evening | See Par. 9

CITY ZONE	
Carrier Delivery by independent carriers filing lists Par. 28(a)..........	21,742
Dealers & Carriers not filing lists.....	3,283
Street Vendors	21,266
Publisher's Counter Sales..............	9
Mail Subscriptions....................	
Total City Zone Population 1950 Census 3,684,491	46,300
RETAIL TRADING ZONE	
Carrier Delivery by independent carriers filing lists	5,115
Dealers & Carriers not filing lists.....	24,821
Mail Subscriptions....................	1,497
Total Retail Trading Zone Population 1950 Census 1,816,168	31,433
Total City & Retail Trading Population 1950 Census 5,500,659	77,733
ALL OTHER	
Dealers & Carriers....................	11,862
Mail Subscriptions....................	9,600
Total "All Other"	21,462
Subscriptions to Armed Forces (orders for 11 or more only)..............	
TOTAL NET PAID excl. Bulk (For bulk sales, see Par. 10)	(a)99,195
AVERAGES BY QUARTERS:	
October 1 to December 31, (year)	96,365
January 1 to March 31, (year)	102,025

(a) Includes predate edition, see Pars. 9 & 28(b).

9. Net Press Run & time of editions: Evening Issue for Thursday, March 18, (year)

Edition	Press Time	Date Printed	Issue Dated	Net Press Run	Sales Release See Note	Approx. Distribution City Zone	Retail Zone	All Other
1st	9:00 AM	3|18	3|18	3,000	A–C	56%	12%	32%
2nd	11:00 AM	3|18	3|18	3,740	A–C	60%	29%	11%
3rd	1:30 PM	3|18	3|18	16,250	A–C	83%	16%	1%
4th	3:30 PM	3|18	3|18	75,000	A–C	42%	41%	17%
Predate	6:00 PM	3|18	3|19	9,000	C	6%	10%	90%

For explanation see Par. 28(b).

Note: A Immediate sales release in City.
C Sales release on arrival at destination in Retail Zone and All Other.

10. Average bulk sales in all zones: 123.

11. Average unpaid distribution: | Evening |

Arrears Over Three Months...................	
Short Term Subscriptions in Arrears........	
Credit Subscriptions in Arrears................	
Total Arrears	
Service Copies, Local Advs., Employes, etc.....	893
Advg. Agencies, Complimentary, Samples, etc.	1,380
Other Not Qualifying as Paid	1,963
Total Arrears, Service Copies, etc.	4,236

12. (a) & (b): See reverse side.

13. (a) Basic | By Mail in Retail Trading Zone | By Carrier in City Zone | Single

Prices:	1 Yr.	6 Mos.	3 Mos.	1 Mo.	1 Yr.	6 Mos.	3 Mos.	1 Mo.	1 Wk.	Copy
E. only	$9.00	$5.00	$2.75	$1.00	$15.60	$7.80	$3.90	$1.30	30c	5c

(b) Basic price by mail in city zone: None.
(c) Basic price by mail in all other zone: Same as by mail in Par. 13(a).
(d) Basic price to R. F. D. subscribers in retail trading zone: Same as by mail in Par. 13(a).
(e) Basic price to R. F. D. subscribers in all other zone: Same as by mail in Par. 13(a).
(f) Basic price by carrier in retail trading zone: Same as by carrier in Par. 13(a).
(g) Basic price by carrier in all other zone: Same as by carrier in Par. 13(a).
(h) Basic price to motor route subscribers in retail trading zone: Same as by carrier in Par. 13(a).
(i) Basic price to motor route subscribers in all other zone: Same as by carrier in Par. 13(a).
(j) Special reduced prices: By mail, during January (year), 1 year $6.00.
13 (k) & (l): For prices higher than basic and prices lower than basic see Audit Report.
14. (a) Were returns accepted?
Dealers and street vendors in city zone were allowed 15% return privilege and dealers in retail trading zone and all other were allowed 10% return privilege.
(b) Were these deducted, so that only net paid is shown in Par. 8? Yes.

FIGURE 19–3. An Audit Bureau of Circulations form for reporting circulation figures

A.B.C. Such papers may be audited by the Business Publications Audit of Circulations, Inc. (B.P.A.). A Business Publications Audit report is reproduced in Figure 19–4. The term "controlled circulation" refers to the number of copies that are sent to those groups of business or professional people who are most apt to be interested in the publication's editorial content. Note, from the data presented for *Mass Transportation,* the extent to which circulation is limited to persons engaged in mass transportation.

Audiences

An audience is defined as those people whose minds are reached by the medium carrying the advertiser's message. Whereas circulation is measured in numbers of *copies,* an audience is measured in numbers of

MASS TRANSPORTATION

Controlled Circulation
is Qualified Circulation

BPA

FORM A

PUBLISHER'S STATEMENT
Subject to Audit
BUSINESS PUBLICATIONS AUDIT OF CIRCULATION, INC.
420 Lexington Avenue   New York 17, N. Y.
Formerly Controlled Circulation Audit, Inc.

No. 12351P

---

1. MASS TRANSPORTATION
   Name of Publication

2. Hitchcock Publishing Company
   Publishing Company

3. 222 E, Willow Avenue   Wheaton, Illinois
   Address

4. 1904
   Established

5. Monthly
   Frequency

6. FIELD SERVED AND DEFINITION OF RECIPIENT QUALIFICATION

MASS TRANSPORTATION serves the field of public passenger transportation.

Those eligible to receive MASS TRANSPORTATION are persons on the executive or supervisory level in companies operating:

1) City and suburban transit service - using buses, trolley coaches and/or street cars.
2) Intercity bus service.
3) School bus service.
4) Charter bus service.
5) Sight-seeing bus service.
6) Airport limousine and bus service.
7) Passenger air line service.
8) Passenger railroad service.

Also eligible are men in allied occupations serving the companies operating the above services, such as manufacturers and suppliers of equipment and supplies used by these companies, government officials, investment and financial houses, transportation consultants and research organizations.

7. AVERAGE TOTAL CONTROLLED AND NON-CONTROLLED FOR PERIOD

Average Controlled Circulation — single copies (Mailed in separate wrappers or otherwise separately addressed)	11,612	Advertisers, Agencies, Advertising Prospects	740	
		Samples	810	
Average Controlled Circulation—bulk	48	All other	264	
		Average Total Non-Controlled	1,814	
AVERAGE TOTAL CONTROLLED	11,660	AVERAGE TOTAL CONTROLLED AND NON-CONTROLLED	13,474	

MASS TRANSPORTATION
DECEMBER 19--

FIGURE 19–4. First page of form used for reporting distribution of a controlled circulation magazine *people.*[2] Whereas circulation figures are *indirect* evidence of how many and what kinds of people a medium reaches, audience data are *direct* evidence obtained from sample surveys of the people themselves. As one would expect, the total number of people reached by a magazine or a newspaper is greater than the number of copies circulated. This difference is clearly indicated in the comparison of circulation and audience figures shown in Table 19–3.

TABLE 19–3. Comparison of circulation and total audience of selected magazines

Magazine	Average paid circulation 2d six months 1968	Total audience 18 years of age and older
Newsweek	2,307,921	11,993,000
Time	3,904,462	17,541,000
Life	7,802,820	35,293,000
Look	7,797,521	32,847,000
Reader's Digest	17,602,526	41,977,000
Better Homes & Gardens	7,571,606	20,776,000
McCall's	8,532,497	19,140,000
Playboy	5,379,003	15,183,000

Sources: SRDS; Consumer Magazine and Farm Publication Rates and Data, June 27, 1969, and Brand Rating Index, 1969.

Composition of a medium's audience is often more important than its size. If an advertiser's market is concentrated in particular consumer groups, he wants to know to what extent a medium's audience is concentrated in those groups. For example, an advertiser considering *Good Housekeeping* and *McCall's* as possible choices is in a better position to determine how efficiently these magazines reach his best prospects when he has the kind of information included in Table 19–4. He could infer from the editorial content of these two magazines that their readers are predominantly women, but any assumptions he might make about their readers' ages, incomes, and education levels are likely to be erroneous if he doesn't have factual evidence reflecting such characteristics. Having the data that are included in Table 19–4, he can determine with reasonable accuracy that the readers of these magazines are mostly women under

---

[2] Audiences are also measured in numbers of households (groups of people) and numbers of television or radio sets tuned to a station or network (assumes people are viewing or listening).

TABLE 19–4. Audience composition of two women's magazines

Adult audience classification	Good Housekeeping	McCall's
Age		
10–17 years	13.3%	15.5%
18–24	16.5	14.1
25–34	19.0	14.1
35–44	16.5	17.2
45–49	8.4	8.5
50–54	8.1	8.7
55 & older	18.2	21.9
Education		
Grade school or less	8.0	8.0
Some high school	13.3	14.5
Graduated high school	49.0	45.8
Some college	18.6	19.4
College graduate	11.1	12.3
Marital status		
Married	88.6	88.0
Race		
White	94.6	96.0
Nonwhite	5.4	4.0
Annual household income		
Under $3,000	5.6	6.3
$3,000–4,999	9.8	10.0
$5,000–7,999	28.6	25.8
$8,000–9,999	16.8	17.7
$10,000 and over	39.2	40.2

Source: Daniel Starch, 1967 Consumer Market and Magazine Report.

50 years of age, who have not gone to college, and whose annual household incomes are less than $10,000.

The similarity in the composition of these two audiences suggests that either the readers of *Good Housekeeping* are much the same as the readers of *McCall's,* or the readers are different but the classification factors used here are inadequate for highlighting the differences. The latter circumstance is probably true and this points to a current frontier in audience research. Studies have shown that sociopsychological factors reveal significant audience differences that do not appear when the traditional socioeconomic factors (age, income, education, occupation, etc.) are used. For example, one study classified readers according to their economic venturesomeness and found that 15.5 percent of all the people who are venturesome in willingness to try new products read an average issue of *Better Homes and Gardens.*[3] Another magazine, *House Beautiful,* refers

---

[3] *A 12-Month Study of Better Homes & Gardens Readers,* conducted for *Better Homes & Gardens* by Afred Politz Research, Inc. (Des Moines, Iowa: Meredith Publishing Co., 1956).

to its readers as "the beautiful families" who do things—parties, vacations, gardens, interiors—beautifully.

Lack of standards in audience measurement

In practice, there is no single definition of an audience that is appropriate for all types of media. Communication channels differ. People *read* newspapers and magazines. They *listen* to radio. They *view* or *watch-while-listening* to television. Readers, listeners, and viewers are all people, but they are people receiving different forms of communication under different circumstances. If a magazine's audience is defined as all those people who report reading at least one item in a given issue how should a radio station's audience be defined? Should it include all those people who listen to the station at least once a week, or only those who listen once a day? Whereas reading of one item in a magazine implies exposure to all items, listening to one of the programs broadcast by a radio station by no means indicates exposure to all of its programs. Without laboring over these differences, the point is that exposure to a tangible, space-organized, printed publication has no direct counterpart in exposure to a time-organized broadcast medium.

Audiences exposed to outdoor and transit media are defined in terms of traffic: those people who during a given period of time were in a position to see the outdoor sign transit advertisement. For outdoor advertising, automobile and pedestrian traffic passing by places where signs are located reflects the size of audience. In the case of transit advertising placed in subways, busses, or street cars, the audience is defined in terms of the number of passengers using the vehicles over a period of time.

Thus, each channel of communication functions in a different way, and the audience each reaches must be defined in different terms.

Even when measuring audiences of the same medium various research techniques employ various criteria for qualifying a person as a member of an audience. One technique uses *recognition* as a criterion for determining whether or not a person read a particular issue of a magazine: "readers" are those who, when shown the cover, claim they saw or read part of that issue; if they aren't sure, they are permitted to look inside. Another technique uses *aided recall:* "readers" are those who are able to describe an item in the magazine after being shown only the cover. As one would expect, the more rigorous criterion, recall, produces a smaller audience than the less rigorous criterion, recognition. One study that measured the size of audience (age 18 and up) reached by an issue of *Life* using both criteria found 12,241,000 readers when aided recall was used and 18,785,000 readers when recognition was used.[4]

Depending on the research technique used, radio- and television-station audiences are variously defined as those people who respond to a mail questionnaire, or those who report in a personal interview, or those who reply when telephoned, or those who record in a diary, or those in whose homes an electronic device automatically records that they received a station's broadcast. Each technique gathers *different* information in *different* ways from *different* samples of *different* populations. There-fore, even though they set out to measure the same audiences, no two techniques yield the same results. Radio and television audience measure-ment methods currently used will be discussed in greater detail in Chapter 21.

Confronted with such a variety of definitions and measurement stan-dards, the media analyst must be cautious when he uses audience data. He is on safer ground when he compares audiences reached by media of the same type (two or more magazines, two or more television stations, etc.) and uses data arrived at through the same research procedure. He is on weaker ground when he compares audiences of different media types (magazine versus television, etc.) or uses data arrived at through differ-ent research procedures.

For planning purposes the advertiser is interested not only in the size and character of audiences reached by individual media vehicles, but also in the audiences reached by combinations of media. Alfred Politz Media Studies has recently launched its *Politz Media Service* (PMS)—a semi-annual national survey of population exposure to major consumer maga-zines and national network television programs. The service is designed to provide detailed analyses of the performance of individual magazines and individual television programs in terms of reach, frequency, and se-lectivity. Magazine audiences are profiled, for some 12 magazines, in terms of the numbers and kinds of people who read an average issue of a particular magazine. Readers are described according to demographic characteristics (see, for example, Table 19–4), of more than 100 specific product and service categories. The television report provides comparable data for the viewers of individual network programs.[5]

[4] *Printed Advertising Rating Methods Study,* Advertising Research Foundation, Inc. (New York, 1956).

[5] *Media/scope,* Vol. 9 (November, 1965), p. 76.

Media costs

The common expression, "You get what you pay for," is as true in the purchase of space or time in advertising media as in buying commodities. It is therefore important to compare costs with the ability of the medium to render the kind of service desired. Since the advertiser is interested in using a carrier that will deliver his message to his prospects with a minimum of waste, the first task of selection is that of measuring such abilities. A number of media may qualify as possibilities. Then, when appraising this select group the advertiser must deal with two basic questions: How much will I have to pay for the space or time? What do I get for what I pay?

Most newspapers quote their rates in terms of a standard unit of space referred to as a *line*. A line (short for *agate line*) is one fourteenth of an inch deep and one column wide. A comparison of line rates tells the advertiser how much more he will have to pay for space in one paper than in another, but does not reveal the differences in advertising value he will receive. To illustrate this point, in St. Louis there are two daily newspapers each of which also publishes a weekend or Sunday edition. Recent line rates were as follows:

Newspaper	Line rate
Globe-Democrat, morning	$ .95
Globe-Democrat, weekend	.95
Post-Dispatch, evening	1.20
Post-Dispatch, Sunday	1.35

On the basis of line rates alone, the Sunday *Post-Dispatch* is the highest-priced medium. This comparison, however, does not take into account the number of people reached by each paper. A family would expect to pay more rent for an eight-room house than for a four-room house, other things being equal. A trucker would be willing to pay a higher rental for a two-ton truck than for a one-ton truck. Likewise, an advertiser would be willing to pay a higher price for space in a newspaper circulating 100,000 copies than for space in one circulating 50,000 copies. A glance at the circulation figures of the papers mentioned above will give a picture of their value as carriers of advertising messages. Recent circulation figures for these papers as certified by the A.B.C. were as follows:

Newspaper	Circulation
Globe-Democrat, morning	306,586
Globe-Democrat, weekend	342,001
Post-Dispatch, evening	345,675
Post-Dispatch, Sunday	581,591

In the light of these circulation figures, the rate of $1.35 per line for the Sunday *Post-Dispatch* does not appear so unfavorable.

The usual procedure for comparing prices of different quantities is to reduce the prices to a common denominator of one unit, the price per unit. However, the rate per line per copy circulated is an unwieldly fraction of a cent ($0.000003 for the first of the papers listed). Multiplying this small fraction by one million moves the decimal six places to the right and thereby produces a dollars and cents figure. Thus, we arrive at the most widely used yardstick for comparing newspaper rates, the "milline rate." The formula for figuring the milline rate is:

$$\frac{\text{Line rate} \times 1,000,000}{\text{Circulation}} = \text{Milline rate}$$

This converts the rate charged by each paper to a common standard—the rate per line per one million circulation.

Milline rates for the St. Louis newspapers turn out to be:

Newspaper	Milline rate
Globe-Democrat, morning	$3.09
Globe-Democrat, weekend	2.78
Post-Dispatch, evening	3.47
Post-Dispatch, Sunday	2.32

As a rule, the greater the circulation of a newspaper the lower is its milline rate; the smaller the circulation the higher is its milline rate.

If the advertiser were interested in reaching only those people living within the city and trading zones, he might omit the circulation going outside of this area when comparing rates. The city and trading zone circulation of the St. Louis papers varies from 73 percent of the total for the weekend *Globe-Democrat* to 86 percent for the evening *Post-Dispatch*. When the standard rate of comparison is based on this part of total circulation, it is referred to as the "truline rate."

The same general problems involved in comparing space costs in newspapers are present in magazine cost comparisons. The common unit of space for which magazine rates are quoted is a page or fraction of a page rather than the agate line, although the latter is often included on the rate card. The most widely used standard for comparing magazine rates is the cost-per-page-per-thousand circulation, or as it is more simply called, "cost-per-thousand" (often written as C.P.M.). The formula is:

$$\frac{\text{Page rate} \times 1,000}{\text{Circulation}} = \text{Cost-per-thousand (C.P.M.)}$$

In recent years, the availability of a greater number of studies reporting size of magazine audiences has permitted advertisers to compare rates on the basis of people reached as well as copies circulated. To figure a magazine's cost-per-thousand readers, its total audience would be used in the above formula instead of its circulation. In effect, as demonstrated in Table 19–5, this modifies a rate comparison based on circulation by allowing for differences in the number of readers per copy.

TABLE 19–5. Comparison of cost-per-page-per-thousand based on circulation and total audience

Magazine	Rate per 4-color page	Cost per thousand	
		Circulation	Total audience
Newsweek	$20,745	$8.98	$1.73
Time	33,000	8.45	1.88
Life	64,200	8.22	1.82
Look	55,500	7.12	1.69
Reader's Digest	58,275	3.30	1.39
Better Homes & Gardens	38,775	5.12	1.87
McCall's	45,900	5.38	2.40
Playboy	35,780	6.65	2.36

Source: SRDS; Consumer Magazine and Farm Publication Rates and Data, June 27, 1969 Brand Rating Index, 1969

If the advertiser is primarily interested in reaching a particular group of readers, say men between the ages of 30 and 45, he might compare rates on the basis of the number of such readers in each magazine's audience. This more nearly approaches the ideal standard for comparing media costs—the cost of reaching a thousand real prospects.

Media analysts in a leading advertising agency have evaluated farm publications in terms of cost-per-thousand hogs on farms reached by various publications. They have evaluated television stations in terms of cost-per-thousand dairy cows within station coverage areas. They have evaluated magazines in terms of cost-per-thousand cake bakers and cost-per-thousand cakes baked per month.

Television and radio rates are quoted for units of time—a half hour, a quarter hour, one minute, etc. To compare rates charged by different stations or networks, an appropriate standard is the cost-per-commercial-minute-per-thousand viewers or listeners. However, at the present time, use of such a standard is mainly limited to comparing rates of a few stations in major cities and of the nationwide networks, audiences of which are regularly and rather well measured. Reliable and standard audience measurements are not currently available for most individual stations. Therefore, when buying time on most stations rate comparison is mainly a matter of subjective evaluation.

Space or time should never be purchased solely on a price basis. Other factors are also important. It may happen that the publication with a relatively high cost-per-thousand should be the first choice because it provides a better climate, more favorable reader attitudes, or better advertising associations. However, when a number of specific media possess about equal merit in everything but price, the advertiser would probably depend on cost comparison to indicate the most economical medium.

Standard Rate and Data Service

The one source of information most often referred to by media buyers is *Standard Rate and Data Service*. Published monthly, *SRDS* lists current rates, circulations, mechanical requirements, issuance and closing dates, contract and copy regulations, sales offices, and pertinent market data for media grouped as follows:

1. Newspapers (all U.S. daily and Sunday newspapers including ABC foreign language papers)
2. Consumer magazines and farm publications (650 consumer magazines and 300 farm publications)
3. Radio stations (approximately 3,000 AM and FM stations)
4. Television stations (all U.S. television stations)
5. Radio and television networks
6. Business publications (2,450 business papers in 159 market classifications)
7. Transit advertising (450 transportation advertising facilities)

Obviously, with all this information available for handy reference, the planning of media strategy and the buying of space and time for national advertising is greatly expedited.[6]

---

[6] Rates published in *SRDS* for newspapers, radio stations, and television stations are those charged national advertisers and are generally higher than those charged retail advertisers. Retailers generally obtain rate information and other data direct from representatives of the media serving their local community.

Editorial or program content

Less susceptible to measurement, but no less important than other dimensions of a medium, is the quality of its editorial or program content. It is logical to assume that the environment in which an advertiser's message appears has an appreciable influence on the effectiveness of the advertisement itself. A magazine's editorial content may center on subject matter into which the advertiser's product readily fits, thereby conditioning readers to be more receptive to his message. (This is particularly true of business publications such as *Rock Products, Railway Age,* etc.) Or, the editorial content may provide a backdrop of prestige and authority that "rubs off" on the advertiser's product. Or, the magazine's articles and stories may be the kind with which readers identify themselves and get personally involved, thereby becoming more responsive to an advertisement reaching them when they are in such a mood. These are but a few of the many possible relationships between a medium and its audience that can work in the advertiser's favor. Therefore, it behooves the advertiser to carefully appraise the editorial content of newspapers and magazines, and the programing of television and radio stations before making a selection.

Evaluating content is mainly a matter of judgment. However, a few studies employing the techniques of motivation research have sought to analyze media content as reflected in the attitudes and feelings of readers, viewers, and listeners. One such study was conducted by Social Research, Inc. for *Good Housekeeping.* Some of the findings of this study are illustrated in Figure 19–5.

Television or radio program content and station programing practices are often the basis for selecting a broadcast medium. Without detailed audience data the advertiser can only infer from the program itself how well it attracts this type of customers. This can be risky business as evidenced by the popular but erroneous assumptions that classical music appeals primarily to upper-income groups and that "westerns" appeal only to youngsters.

Advertiser usage

The extent to which other advertisers use a given medium is often used as an indicator of its effectiveness. A medium that consistently carries a greater total volume of advertising is presumed to be the one that advertisers generally consider more effective. However, the total volume car-

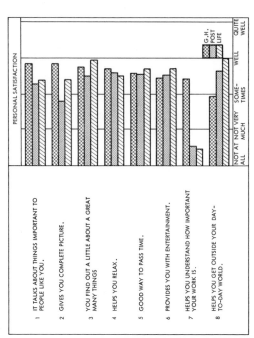

PERSONAL SATISFACTION

1 IT TALKS ABOUT THINGS IMPORTANT TO PEOPLE LIKE YOU.

2 GIVES YOU COMPLETE PICTURE.

3 YOU FIND OUT A LITTLE ABOUT A GREAT MANY THINGS

4 HELPS YOU RELAX.

5 GOOD WAY TO PASS TIME.

6 PROVIDES YOU WITH ENTERTAINMENT.

7 HELPS YOU UNDERSTAND HOW IMPORTANT YOUR WORK IS.

8 HELPS YOU GET OUTSIDE YOUR DAY-TO-DAY WORLD.

NOT AT ALL — NOT VERY MUCH — SOME-TIMES — WELL — QUITE WELL

G.H. / POST / LIFE

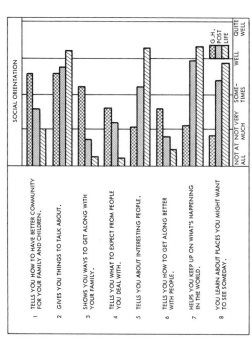

SOCIAL ORIENTATION

1 TELLS YOU HOW TO HAVE BETTER COMMUNITY FOR YOUR FAMILY AND CHILDREN.

2 GIVES YOU THINGS TO TALK ABOUT.

3 SHOWS YOU WAYS TO GET ALONG WITH YOUR FAMILY.

4 TELLS YOU WHAT TO EXPECT FROM PEOPLE YOU DEAL WITH.

5 TELLS YOU ABOUT INTERESTING PEOPLE.

6 TELLS YOU HOW TO GET ALONG BETTER WITH PEOPLE.

7 HELPS YOU KEEP UP ON WHAT'S HAPPENING IN THE WORLD.

8 YOU LEARN ABOUT PLACES YOU MIGHT WANT TO SEE SOMEDAY.

NOT AT ALL — NOT VERY MUCH — SOME-TIMES — WELL — QUITE WELL

G.H. / POST / LIFE

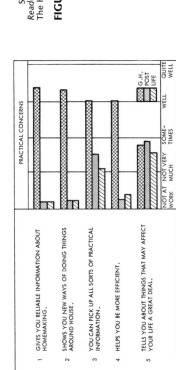

PRACTICAL CONCERNS

1 GIVES YOU RELIABLE INFORMATION ABOUT HOMEMAKING.

2 SHOWS YOU NEW WAYS OF DOING THINGS AROUND HOUSE.

3 YOU CAN PICK UP ALL SORTS OF PRACTICAL INFORMATION.

4 HELPS YOU BE MORE EFFICIENT.

5 TELLS YOU ABOUT THINGS THAT MAY AFFECT YOUR LIFE A GREAT DEAL.

NOT AT WORK — NOT VERY MUCH — SOME-TIMES — WELL — QUITE WELL

G.H. / POST / LIFE

Source: *The Meaning of Good Housekeeping and Its Advertising to Its Readers*, prepared by Social Research, Inc. for *Good Housekeeping* (New York: The Hearst Corporation, 1956).

FIGURE 19–5. Comparison of satisfactions received from three magazines ried is less significant to an individual advertiser than is the amount of advertising for his type of product. A food advertiser, for example, is most interested in the volume of food advertising carried.

When selecting local media such as newspapers, national advertisers are inclined to favor those preferred by their local retail dealers. For example, in Los Angeles the *Los Angeles Times* consistently carries about 75 percent of all the advertising placed by women's shoe stores in the major metropolitan papers. This indicates that women's shoe retailers in Los Angeles, who are in a position to observe sales resulting from their advertising day by day, generally favor the *Times*. Chances are, therefore, that most national advertisers of women's shoes would also choose to place the major portion of their Los Angeles newspaper space in the *Times*. A further refinement of this type of evidence would be the records of media usage by individual retailers.

An advertiser's selection of media should not be governed by his competitor's choices, but where and how competitors place their advertising should be considered. A competitor's marketing strategy and tactics can be rather well determined from records showing the extent to which he uses specific media.

Media Records, Inc. measures and reports the advertising linage carried by 386 daily and Sunday newspapers in 138 cities. A Media Records Report gives each newspaper's linage broken down by various classifications. Retail classifications include department stores (by departments), clothing stores (men's, women's), drugstores, grocery stores, etc. National classifications include passenger cars, gasolines and oils, grocery products, sporting goods, etc. From these figures an advertiser can quickly see how newspapers in a given city rank as carriers of different kinds of advertising. A Media Records Report also gives the linage used by individual national advertisers in each newspaper. These figures enable an advertiser to check the linage of his competitors.

Publishers Information Bureau, Inc. (P.I.B.) reports expenditures in national magazines, national farm publications, and newspaper supplements by industry classifications, by individual companies, and by brands. In addition to expenditure data, P.I.B. also reports detailed schedule information such as space sizes and insertion dates in each publication.

Broadcast Advertising Reports, Inc. (BAR) reports advertising expenditures and scheduling activity on the three national television networks and the three national radio networks, ABC, NBC, and CBS. It provides gross time costs by advertisers and individual brands.

BAR-Local Market Report supplies similar information on spot television usage by national brands in the top 75 spot markets.

Rome Report gives advertising expenditures for a limited number of business publications.

Summary

To select media that will carry his messages most efficiently to the people comprising his market, the advertiser should carefully analyze all available facts bearing on his marketing situation and media alternatives.

Who are the people who buy the product, who influence the purchase, where do they live, where and how is the product distributed—all of the questions that pinpoint the marketing task must be answered, and they must be answered in terms of the particular product in question.

The creative strategy to be employed, the mood or product-image the advertising is designed to emphasize, the need for color, for demonstration, for news, for authority—all are essential considerations.

Audited circulations and available audience data indicate how many and what classes of people a medium reaches.

How much does the space or time cost? What do you get for what you pay? The "milline rate" and "cost-per-thousand" are widely used standards for comparing the cost efficiency of alternative media.

Editorial or program content reflect the kind of environment in which the advertiser's message will appear. The volume and types of advertising a medium carries reflect how other advertisers view its worth.

But facts and figures are not enough. Sound judgment and imagination are required to exploit the unique advertising opportunities offered by any medium.

QUESTIONS AND PROBLEMS

1. The fact that more money is spent for newspaper advertising than for advertising in any other medium is substantial evidence that newspapers are the most effective medium. Do you agree or disagree? Explain.
2. Selection of advertising media should be preceded by an analysis of all factors involved in the total marketing situation. What factors would you consider in such an analysis?
3. Message content or the creative strategy deemed necessary in a particular advertising situation has a direct bearing on choice media. Explain.
4. Would it be good policy for a company to run identical advertisements in the *Ladies Home Journal*, *Time* and *Successful Farming?*

5. Distinguish between *circulation* and *audience* as measures of media values.
6. The growth of newspaper and magazine advertising is partially due to the work of the Audit Bureau of Circulations. Do you agree or disagree? Explain.
7. Why should the advertiser be interested in how the circulation of a medium has been built up?
8. Composition of a medium's audience is often more important than its size. Why?
9. The readers of one magazine may be psychologically different from the readers of another magazine. Explain.
10. Which of the following newspapers is more reasonably priced?

NEWSPAPER	LINE RATE	CIRCULATION
a	.06	16,000
b	.05	12,500

11. A comparison of magazine rates in terms of cost-per-thousand circulation doesn't mean very much if the magazines being compared reach different types of audiences. Do you agree or disagree? Explain.

chapter 20
NEWSPAPERS AND MAGAZINES

A NUMBER OF FACTORS of importance in selecting media were discussed in the preceding chapter. A more detailed discussion of the characteristics of the various media available to advertisers will be considered in this and following chapters.

NEWSPAPERS

There are several kinds of newspapers available to advertisers in the United States. To simplify the evaluation of their character, they can be roughly divided into five groups: (1) daily, (2) Sunday, (3) weekly or community, (4) shopping news, and (5) special interest.

Daily and Sunday newspapers make up the great majority of the total circulation of all newspapers. About 1,534 English-language daily newspapers with a combined circulation of 60,381,142 are published in the United States. There are 556 English-language Sunday papers circulating a total of 49,230,987 copies. Of the total number of dailies, about nine out of ten are evening papers.

The weekly or community newspaper is a product of the small, rather homogeneous, community. There are approximately 8,200 of them in the United States. They probably have a total circulation of between 20 million and 25 million. The average circulation is, therefore, not more than about 3,000 copies per issue. Publishers of such papers often depend heavily on sources of revenue other than subscriptions and advertising space, else many could not operate profitably.

Community papers generally have an interested local following, perhaps born from the closeness of the community served. Relationship studies that have been made for such papers show substantially higher readership than for metropolitan dailies.

The shopping-news type of newspaper is unlike either the regular metropolitan daily or the community weekly in that it carries little or no news and is distributed free. Its space is often wholly devoted to advertisements. The term "news" is associated with it on the grounds that advertisements are news of a vital type desired by many people. That this claim is true can hardly be denied in light of readership figures for advertisements in orthodox papers which show many advertisements read by vastly more people than many of the regular news items in the paper. The shopping newspaper is distributed free, and thus its circulation can be controlled by the publisher. It can, and often is, distributed only to certain sections of a town or to selected types of households.

Special-interest newspapers may be dailies or weeklies, but they deserve a separate classification because of their selection of an audience. Such newspapers serve groups that have common ties in the realm of religion, labor, race, language, trade, finance, and production. These papers often take on many of the characteristics of magazines but follow the format and publishing policy of newspapers.

Community acceptance

The newspaper has become an integral part of the life of almost every community. It takes its place alongside the church, school, bank, and department store as a necessary adjunct to living. The newspaper at the breakfast table and on the bus to and from work is a familiar part of the American scene. In the few instances when communities have been temporarily without newspapers because of strikes, the intensity of feeling toward such loss has been observed and partially measured.

The daily papers in Detroit were strikbound for 134 days in the fall of 1964. A study made by the MacManus, John & Adams advertising agency showed that "there still is no adequate substitute for the printed word as an informational vehicle."[1] The study, conducted among a sample of Detroit newspaper readers, found that 69 percent said they "missed their papers a lot," whereas 31 percent said their sense of loss was "little or not at all." When asked what substitutes they were finding for their newspapers, respondents replied:

---

[1] "Detroiters Find TV a Poor Substitute," *Editor and Publisher,* October 31, 1964, p. 16.

	Men	*Women*
Television	61%	59%
Other papers	60%	42%
Radio	53%	45%

However, 74 percent of the men and 66 percent of the women stated that these substitutes were "not satisfactory."

During a printers' strike that shut down nine New York City newspapers in December, 1962, New Yorkers bought less, landed fewer jobs, rented fewer apartments, attended fewer funerals, cut theater going, and scrambled for substitute reading matter. They also, in the opinion of one psychiatrist, failed to develop Christmas spirit to the full. "People are used to being stimulated by newspapers, especially advertising, just before Christmas," he said.[2]

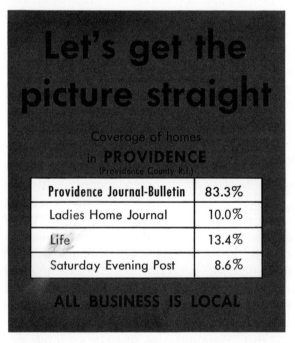

FIGURE 20–1. Newspaper circulation contrasted with that of magazines

Another measure of community acceptance is the percentage of the residents who subscribe to a local paper. That percentage is exceedingly high, ranging from 70 to 95 percent for the great majority of papers.

---

[2] *The Wall Street Journal,* December 14, 1962, p. 1.

Figure 20–1 reproduces an advertisement of the Providence *Journal-Bulletin* which dramatizes this high-acceptance factor and contrasts it with local acceptance of leading magazines.

A motivational study analyzing the role the newspaper plays in the daily lives of its readers reported these observations:

1. People identify themselves with the community through newspapers.
2. The newspaper helps a person guard against feeling isolated, . . . against being shut out from the world and from the local community.
3. The authority of the newspaper is reinforced by a belief that, to a much greater extent than media which use the perishable spoken word, the newspaper is somehow accountable for what it prints.
4. Newspaper advertising is familiar . . . has a strong connotation of immediacy. The image that is firmly entrenched is that newspaper advertising is practical for immediate use.
5. Dependence on the newspaper as a shopping guide is indicated by a housewife's statement: "I go over the ads every day. It's part of reading the paper. I like to keep well up on prices, and I'm always on the lookout for clothes buys, what with three children."[3]

Customer selectivity

The newspaper serves a local and highly concentrated market. Any area that can support a daily newspaper must have a rather high degree of centrality and fairly active trade. The map reproduced in Figure 20–2 shows the counties in the United States in which daily newspapers are published. They represent only one third of all counties in the country; yet they correspond closely to population concentration, income-tax returns, retail sales, and other factors indicative of the more fertile markets.

Newspapers, however, do not generally select their readers to the same degree as many magazines. In Chicago, newspaper readers must choose from four general papers. This means that the subscribers of a particular paper will usually be a heterogeneous group. The newspaper-reading population of Chicago will subscribe to scores of magazines, according to the particular interest served by a magazine. A newspaper advertisement must, therefore, appeal primarily to a mass audience. It would be extremely wasteful to use newspapers to reach a small specialized group. Appeals directed only to doctors, lawyers, musicians, or carpenters should, in general, find no place in newspapers. Selection of the better territorial markets is admirably done by newspapers, but they do not select particular consumer groups for the advertiser wishing to appeal to

---

[3] *People Speak Their Inner Minds about Newspapers* (New York: Bureau of Advertising, American Newspaper Publishers Association, Inc., 1956).

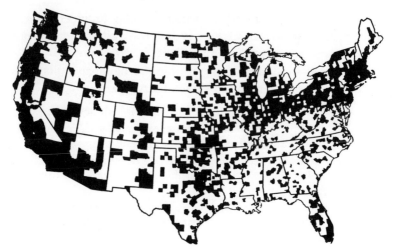

FIGURE 20–2.   Counties in the United States in which daily newspapers
are published

such groups except in the case of the relatively few special-interest newspapers.

Since newspapers do reach a heterogeneous group, attempts are made
to produce a paper which will meet varied interests; and material success
has been achieved in performing this difficult task. The paper is divided
into sections of news, sports, homemaking, comics, etc. An increased circulation among satisfied subscribers has resulted. But some buy a given
paper because of its comic strip; others, because of its sports news. Advertisements appearing in other sections of the paper will have little
chance of even being seen by some individuals.

Use by retailers

The newspaper serves both local and national advertisers, but local
retailers take by far the greater amount of newspaper space and account
for a much larger share of total expenditures. It is estimated that total
advertising expenditures in newspapers in 1969 was $5,850,000,000. Of
that total, retailers accounted for $4,800,000,000, and national adver-
tisers accounted for $1,050,000,000. Thus, about 82 percent of total
newspaper advertising expenditures are made by retailers.

The newspaper is an ideal medium for most retailers. Its circulation
area generally conforms to their trading areas. Even retailers located in
the suburban shopping centers of major cities usually have access to a
suburban community newspaper. In addition, many major metropolitan

daily newspapers offer "zoned editions," whereby a paper's circulation is split into geographic areas or zones. In this way, a retailer serving only a part of the metropolitan area can beam his advertising into this area.

Daily publication readily fits into the day-to-day selling and quick action promotions that characterize most retailing. A print medium effectively carries pictures of the merchandise, product specifications, and prices. Consumers have a habit of turning to their newspapers for shopping information. The wide range of space sizes and insertion schedules that can be bought gives small as well as large retailers an opportunity to advertise profitably. It's no wonder that the newspaper is the only mass medium used by many retailers.

Department stores are the largest single users of newspaper space and account for about one third of all local advertising linage.

Use by national advertisers

National advertisers in 1969 allotted about 10 percent of their total national advertising investment to newspapers. Until 1941, newspapers received a greater share of the national advertiser's budget than was received by any other medium. From 1941 to 1951 the lead fluctuated between general magazines and newspapers. But now television holds the lead. These figures are based on direct expenditures of national advertisers; however, they do not include the substantial sums contributed by national advertisers to retailers for cooperative advertising.

Whether newspapers or some other medium stands first does not matter. The significant fact is that national advertisers find newspapers, which are essentially a local medium, of value as a means of reaching specific markets and use them extensively for that purpose. Newspapers emphasize that all markets are local. Advertisers can achieve national coverage by using many newspapers. However, the cost is considerable. To place a one-page, black-and-white ad in the top paper in each of the top one hundred markets costs $165,800. This amounts to about $6 per thousand circulation. These markets include only 60 percent of all U.S. households and the top paper averages about 45 percent coverage in each city.

Territorial flexibility

The newspaper offers great flexibility in the territorial distribution of advertising. Although most communities that support a daily newspaper are better markets than those that do not, there is a great difference even among those communities having a newspaper. Advertisers who wish to concentrate their sales efforts on the better markets will find newspapers an adaptable medium.

Professor Borden emphasizes this element of flexibility when he says: "Newspapers as a basic coverage medium are particularly suitable for those companies which for one reason or another need to adjust their advertising and promotion from market to market in order to avoid waste in effort and gain greatest effectiveness."[4]

Some markets are good today and bad tomorrow. Local business depressions are often occasioned by drought, labor troubles, recession in an industry which dominates a community, or other factors that do not spread to other regions. The newspaper advertiser can avoid such markets. If he has been working such a territory, he can cancel it from his total budget and transfer his efforts to other sections. This can be done on short notice. In the case of magazine advertising, cancellation orders must often be given months in advance.

FIGURE 20–3. Newspaper advertising can be concentrated where desired

Figure 20–3 illustrates the territorial flexibility afforded by newspapers. A northern market can thus be covered by an advertiser of winter merchandise without waste on southern circulation. Efforts can be fo-

---

[4] Neil H. Borden and Others, *National Advertising in Newspapers* (Cambridge, Mass.: Harvard University Press, 1946), p. 185.

cused on Detroit when the automobile business is good and reduced in San Francisco during a strike.

When new advertising ideas are to be tried out on a small scale or when new products are to be introduced, newspapers will generally be used. This procedure reduces the investment in experimentation. It also provides a means whereby those advertisements with greater effectiveness can be discovered prior to their use on a larger scale. Closer supervision can also be given such trial efforts.

Newsvertising

The time flexibility of newspapers is demonstrated in the opportunities which they give the advertiser to tie his advertising message in with the national or local news of the moment. An advertisement for a newspaper needs to be presented for publication only a few hours before press time. Thus, it can be almost as fresh as the news printed in the same paper. This characteristic of newspapers allows the advertiser to adapt his advertisement to outstanding happenings of the day if such incidents are relevant to the product being advertised. The seller of rain apparel can place his advertising more or less in harmony with the weather. If a disaster like a flood, fire, or tornado hits a particular city or community, it might serve as the theme for advertising copy. Such advertisements can appear a few hours after the disaster. The same thing is applicable to national news. Newspapers call this quality of their medium "newsvertising." It permits the advertiser to capitalize on current events.

The advertisement for Borden's milk reproduced in Figure 20–4 illustrates how effectively that company used "newsvertising." Inserted in the copy was the following statement: "Yesterday in the worst storm in years our service was 97.7 percent normal." The interest of people in the influence of the storm naturally added to the effectiveness of the advertisement.

Life of a newspaper

Newspapers have a very short life. They are usually read as soon as they are received and then thrown away. Some are kept for more than a day, but this is not the common case. Because of this short life, newspaper advertisements are not exposed to the readers for any length of time. If an advertisement is not seen during the time of the first reading of the paper, it probably will not be seen at all, since the first reading is usually

FIGURE 20–4. An effective use of "newsvertising"

the last reading. Magazine publishers are quick to point to this weakness of newspapers. Newspaper publishers claim that the characteristic is valuable, pointing out that newspapers offer a *daily* opportunity to reach the entire reading public. A fresh message is provided every day instead of one that presumably lasts a week or a month. Most national advertisers, however, do not use the newspaper every day. This means that the old advertisement does not last until the new one appears.

Services for advertisers

Newspapers provide a number of services for retail advertisers. Most small retailers, and many larger ones, have either no advertising department or an inadequate one. Most daily newspapers have facilities to help such retailers create individual advertisements or plan complete campaigns. This service will include writing copy, preparing layouts, and minor art work.

For the national advertiser, newspapers will often provide merchandising service to support national advertisements. This may involve getting retailers to display the products advertised by the manufacturer, encouraging retailers to time their own advertising with the manufacturer, or helping the manufacturer secure adequate distribution for his product locally.

Research studies are made by many newspapers which have value to both the local and national advertiser. Such studies include a measure of consumer buying habits, consumer patronage of different types of retail outlets, the flow of goods (by brands) from the retail stores or into consumer homes, and linage data for difficult kinds of advertising. There are studies to show the quality and character of the market served by the newspaper. These include the assemblage of population and economic data pertinent to the market, and circulation figures to show the degree of newspaper penetration of the market. Figure 20–5 shows the emphasis that one paper placed on such data in an advertisement designed to influence national advertisers to purchase space. Professor McClure has pointed out that most newspaper research is designed to "fulfill one or more of three functions: (1) to serve as a basis for improving the content of a newspaper; (2) to accumulate information about the market, consumers, and media for use by business firms in planning their merchandising programs; and (3) to develop information that the sales department can use in selling space in the newspaper."[5]

Various organizations are employed or sponsored by individual newspapers to facilitate the purchase of space by national advertisers or their agencies. The newspaper representative is a general salesman who maintains offices in the major cities where advertisers and agencies are found. He will represent a number of newspapers and has the power to contract with advertisers for space in the papers he represents.

Space in weekly and college newspapers can be purchased through the specialized press associations supported by those papers. This is of material value to an advertiser who wishes to reach the nonurban or college markets but does not wish to contract for space directly with each of the hundreds or thousands of papers involved.

---

[5] Leslie W. McClure, *Newspaper Advertising and Promotion* (New York: Macmillan Co., 1950), pp. 174–75.

FIGURE 20–5.   Newspaper use of market data to attract advertisers

Rates

You'll see the terms *flat* and *open* used in newspaper rate cards. If a newspaper quotes a *flat rate*, the advertiser is charged the same rate per line regardless of the quantity of space he buys. Whether he buys 50,000 lines a year or only 100 lines the advertiser is charged the same rate.

Open rate signifies that the newspaper is offering discounts to advertisers for buying greater quantities of space or for advertising more frequently. The open rate is the maximum price charged. As the number of lines purchased increase, the rate gradually steps down. The following is a typical example of such a sliding-scale rate structure:

Lines per year	Line rate
Open	$ .43
1,000 lines	.42
2,500 lines	.41
5,000 lines	.40
10,000 lines	.39
20,000 lines	.38
30,000 lines	.37
50,000 lines	.36

The quantities involved in most sliding-scale plans pertain to the linage used in a year's time. The advertiser signs a contract for the volume of space he expects to use, and each month he pays for the space he actually uses at the contract rate. If at the end of the year he has used less space than he contracted for, he will receive a *short-rate* bill from the newspaper for the difference between the contract rate that he paid and the higher rate that he actually earned.

For example, using the above sliding-scale plan, assume that an advertiser contracted for 20,000 lines but by the end of the year he has used only 15,000 lines. In accordance with the contract, he paid $5,700 (15,000 lines × 38¢). For the quantity of space used he should have paid $5,850 (15,000 lines × 39¢). Thus, he will receive a *short-rate* bill for $150.

If, under the same contract, this advertiser had used 30,000 lines, he would receive a *rebate* of $300 for the difference of one cent per line that he paid (38¢) and the rate he earned (37¢).

Some newspapers avoid the problems of short rating and rebating by eliminating contracts and billing the advertiser according to the rate he earns each month.

Rate differentials

Newspapers do not operate on a strict one-price policy. A majority of newspapers charge the national advertiser substantially more than the local or retail advertiser. This differential will average from 35 to 50 percent. In a number of instances the national rate will be as much as double the retail rate. Whereas retailers are offered liberal sliding-scale plans, national advertisers are generally charged a flat rate.

Newspapers justify this higher rate for general or national advertising on the grounds that high commissions or brokerage fees are entailed in the sale of such space. A 15 percent commission is allowed the advertising agency; and, when space is sold through a publisher's representative or a press association, an additional 15 percent is paid. Thus, many newspapers receive only 70 percent of the rate quoted to national advertisers.

The variance between local and national rates has caused advertising agencies and national advertisers, not only to use methods to take advantage of the lower local rates, but also to urge a reduction of the discrepancy. National advertisers have increased their practice of having newspaper advertising placed by their dealers so that the lower local rate might be obtained. An official of the American Association of Advertising Agencies recently stated that, within a six-year period, the amount of general advertising in newspapers placed at retail rates increased 10 percent. Such practices have caused some newspapers to revise their rate policy and place general advertising in a less unfavorable position. Most recently, there has been a slight trend for some newspapers to offer the same rate to both local and national advertisers; it is still too early to determine how extensively this "one-rate" policy will develop.

Newspapers also maintain rate differentials for different types of advertising. A given amount of space used for advertising amusements would not cost the same as the same space used for a political announcement or a financial advertisement.

Rate variations are made also for space purchased by retailers. These differences are in the form of discounts for quantity of space used and for frequency of insertion. Such discounts are often substantial.

Space and color selection

Most advertising in newspapers is placed ROP (run of paper). It is possible, however, to buy a special position in some papers, although such position will not always be guaranteed. A particular section of the paper may be requested by the advertiser, with fair assurance of obtaining a position in that section. Most daily papers have such sections as automobile, resorts and travel, real estate, boys and girls, finance, sports, comics, foods etc. Many Sunday papers also have a magazine section. Consideration might well be given to the purchase of space in such specialized sections.

The development of comic-strip advertising is most impressive. A majority of all daily newspapers accept comic-strip advertising for regular issues, and most Sunday papers accept color advertising in their comic sections. In many instances, space in such sections can be purchased through one sales agency for a group of newspapers.

The use of ROP color in daily papers has also had a rapid development in recent years. As of January, 1970 some 1,335 daily papers would accept "spot color" (ROP in black and one or two colors), while 919 would accept four-color ROP.[6] The extra cost of such advertising is illustrated in Table 20–1.

TABLE 20–1. How color adds to advertising cost (average % R.O.P. color premium over B/W costs)

Circulation group	Full-page ads		1,000-line ads	
	1 extra color	3 extra colors	1 extra color	3 extra colors
Under 25,000	22	47	41	92
25,000–100,000	19	36	37	70
100,000 plus	18	29	34	62
All daily papers	19	34	37	70

Source: Bureau of Advertising, ANPA as cited in *Advertising Age,* April 20, 1970, p. 197.

In addition to ROP color, some newspapers accept "preprint" color advertising, whereby the printing of the color advertisement is done away from the newspaper plant and shipped to the newspaper. There are three types of such preprints: (1) roll-fed ("hi-fi"), (2) in-register ("Spectacolor"), and (3) multipage inserts. Hi-fi color is printed on one side of a newsprint roll; the color side is of a high-quality paper, and the net result is a color advertisement of "magazine quality." The newspaper uses the unprinted side, which is of regular newsprint quality, for regular copy. Because of the varying "stretch" of newsprint, the layout for hi-fi is done in a "wallpaper" design.

SpectaColor is the same as hi-fi except that the wallpaper format is eliminated by using an electric-eye system to automatically cut the advertising page at the proper point.

Multiple inserts are tabloid-size pages which, likewise, are printed in color away from the newspapers and shipped to the newspaper plant where they are inserted into the regular paper.

Information as to which papers accept color preprints, costs, mechanical requirements, closing dates, etc. is available in a special section of Standard Rate & Data Service, Inc.'s *Newspaper Rates and Data.*

[6] *Advertising Age* (April 20, 1970), p. 196.

Color certainly adds to the attention value of an advertisement. This is particularly true in newspapers, where relatively few advertisers use it. The extra cost, however, can be justified only on the grounds of increased sales; hence, tests should be run to determine the influence on sales. In a recent experiment designed to measure the effectiveness of color versus black and white advertisements, the *Milwaukee Journal* found that the addition of color increased readership 77 percent among men and 55 percent among women. Retention was 125 percent greater for men and 67 percent greater for women.

A comparison of the cost of ROP color with the cost of black-and-white rates is given in Table 20–1.

The rotogravure section of Sunday newspapers should not be ignored. For certain types of products, this space provides an excellent medium. This space, like comic-strip space, can be purchased by newspaper groups if desired. Rates are much higher than for other sections of the paper.

Reading habits

Newspapers are read hastily. Various investigations have shown that the average length of time a person spends in reading a newspaper is about 20 minutes. This does not give much time for reading the advertisements, especially since most of the time is spent reading the front-page news or certain special sections, such as sports or financial news. Newspaper copy is usually prepared to conform with these hasty reading habits. The result is a minimum of copy for the amount of space used.

There is a difference in the amount of time spent in reading a morning, evening, or Sunday edition of a paper. The morning paper gets less time than either of the others. It comes at a time when most men are in a hurry to get to work. Time is often divided between the paper and breakfast. Not much turning of pages will take place under such circumstances. People have more time to read an evening paper and are usually more relaxed and read more slowly. Those who publish only morning papers claim that such relaxation militates against the advertiser because people are not in a buying mood. The argument is perhaps not very sound. Sunday papers receive much more time from readers. They are often read thoroughly by several members of the family. From the point of view of attention given to the paper, the Sunday edition provides an excellent medium.

The continuing study of newspaper reading conducted by the Advertising Research Foundation has provided excellent data on reading habits. Those studies show that readership of some advertisements in a specific issue of a paper is high, that local advertisements get more readers than national advertisements, and that readership is influenced by the character of the product advertised and the appeal used. Readership of individual advertisements seems to range from a low of about 1 percent to around 65 percent.

MAGAZINES

In his book, *Magazines in the Twentieth Century,* Theodore Peterson says: "One can fairly well trace the economic fortunes of the United States in the amounts spent on national advertising in magazines from 1915 through 1955." Magazine advertising expenditure climbed from less than $100 million in 1933 to $379 million in 1946—and to an all-time high of almost $1.4 billion in 1969.[7] Circulation of consumer magazines has increased in the past 20 years from 141,000,000 an issue to 237,101,000 an issue, a gain of 68 percent. A growing population, a growing economy, greater personal income, more education, and more leisure time are all factors contributing to the rapid growth of magazine circulation.

Magazine buying related to family income and education levels is graphically illustrated in Figure 20–6.

Reader interest

Magazine reading provides a wide variety of satisfaction. Women read women's service magazines, such as *Good Housekeeping, McCall's,* and *Ladies' Home Journal,* for practical information concerning cooking, home decorating, child care, entertaining, gardening, and home management; for social orientation, such as how to handle guests, the kinds of food appropriate for specific occasions, how to meet and deal with lawyers, doctors, school teachers, and how to get along with one's husband and family; for the personal satisfaction of daydreaming, escaping from routine, relaxing, identifying one's self, and finding means of self-expression.[8]

Along with the entertainment they provide, our modern large-circulation magazines are opening up new worlds of knowledge and ideas to their readers. Well-known, authoritative articles on science, economics,

---

[7] Theodore Peterson, *Magazines in the Twentieth Century* (Urbana, Ill.: University of Illinois Press, 1956), p. 23.

[8] *Women and Advertising, A Motivation Study of the Attitudes of Women Toward Eight Magazines* (New York: Good Housekeeping Magazines, 1954).

philosophy, and art—the kind of article found only in small, specialized journals in the past—are now regular fare in general interest magazines. Stanley High, a senior editor of *Reader's Digest,* reports: "As recently as 1930 the average large-circulation magazine was 70 percent fiction. Today it's 70 percent *non*-fiction."

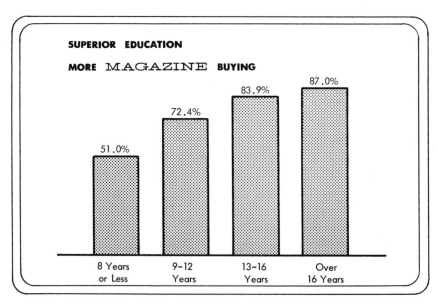

FIGURE 20–6. People with higher incomes and more education buy more magazines

Most any person can find a magazine that appeals to his own special interest—whether it be hot rods or beekeeping, boating or business management.

Classification of magazines

Standard Rate and Data Service divides magazines into three groups: consumer magazines, farm publications, and business publications. These are then divided into more detailed classifications. Figure 20–7 shows a detailed classification of consumer magazines and farm publications.

The detailed classification for business magazines is not given here because *SRDS* lists 159 classes for the some 2,400 magazines of this type. These numbers should, in themselves, indicate the high degree of specialized interests served by such magazines. Practically every industry, trade and profession is included.

These classifications help to show the wide variety of magazines in all fields available to advertisers. A specific advertiser, however, will have to analyze the individual magazine and the character of its market penetration.

Customer selectivity

The detailed classification of magazines listed in the preceding section should help emphasize the very high degree of selectivity of audience which magazines provide. In the case of advertisers wishing to reach the farm market, magazines are available that will offer a general farm audience, or a highly specialized one in terms of specific farm interests (dairying, bee-raising, vegetable-growing) or, in some cases, restricted geographic areas. If it is the total farm market that is to be cultivated, then some general farm magazine like *Successful Farming* or the *Farm Journal* might be selected. If a more narrow or "thin" market is to be reached, a wide range of possibilities is presented. As shown in the previous section, there are 11 general divisions of the farm market, each served by specialized magazines. In each field, from 2 to 50 or more magazines are available. A manufacturer of poultry supplies may select the *Poultry Press* or the *Turkey World,* according to the specialized character of the product.

Selectivity on a geographical basis is provided to a lesser degree. A number of the farm papers concentrate their circulation in a given state or region; but such territorial selectivity is much less pronounced than in the case of newspapers, billboards, radio, direct mail, etc. *Standard Rate and Data Service* provides state or regional circulation figures for maga-

Consumer Magazines Classified

Airline, Motel, and Other
    Distributed Magazines
Almanacs and directories
Alumni and College
Art and antiques
Automotive
Aviation
Babies
Boating and yachting
Brides
Business and finance
Children's
Civic (Male)
Comics and comic technique
Crafts, hobbies, and models
Dancing
Detective
Dogs and pets
Dressmaking and needlework
Editorialized and classified advertising
Education and teacher
Entertainment guides and programs
Epicurean
Ethnic
Exposure-type
Family service
Fashions
Finance
Fishing and hunting
Fraternal, professional groups, service clubs, and associations

Gardening
General editorial
Health
Home service and home
Horses, riding and breeding
Labor-trade union
Literature and Writing Techniques
Mechanics and science
Men's
Metropolitan
Military and naval
Mobile Homes—Trailers
Motion picture and TV Personalities
Music
Mystery and Adventure
Nature
News
Newspaper comic supplements
Newspaper distributed magazines
Photography
Political and social topics
Professional
Religious and denominational
Romance
Society
Sports
Travel and touring
TV and radio
Veterans
Women's
Women's fashions
Youth

Farm Publications Classified

Dairy and dairy breeds
Diversified farming and farm home
Farm education and vocations
Farm electrification
Farm organizations and cooperatives
Field crops and soil management

Fruits, nuts, vegetables, and special
    products
Land use and conservation
Livestock and breed
Newspaper distributed farm publications
Poultry

FIGURE 20–7.

zines that are members of the Audit Bureaus of Circulations. Such figures can be used to determine the territories in which a message will be carried. These data can be compared with the distributive outlets of the advertiser to check possible waste circulation. The *Ohio Farmer* had an average net paid circulation of 102,184 for the period ending June, 1969. Of this total, 100,120 subscribers were in Ohio. The remainder were divided among the bordering states of Pennsylvania, Indiana, Michigan, West Virginia, New York, and Kentucky. *Hoard's Dairyman* does not appeal to a special group confined to one territory but, rather, to all dairymen, wherever located. It had a net paid circulation of 345,519 as of June 30, 1969. There were subscribers in every state. Twelve percent of the circulation, however, was in the dairy state of Wisconsin. Other states with 10,000 or more subscribers were New York, Ohio, Michigan, Indiana, Illinois, Minnesota, Missouri, Pennsylvania, and Iowa. These ten states accounted for two thirds of the total circulation. These same states accounted for about 60 percent of the milk and butter produced in the United States. The coverage of the magazine, therefore, parallels the dairy industry which it is designed to serve. Similar comparisons could be made of other magazines serving different groups.

Business magazines are equally selective. Some go so far as to refuse subscriptions from persons not closely associated with the field served by the magazine. Controlled-circulation (free distribution) papers are designed to ferret out business and industrial groups with common specialized interests and limit their distribution to such persons. Obviously, in the case of business papers, there is little or no emphasis placed on territorial selection. Trades and professions are not generally confined to a particular area; but, in the few cases where such is true, the occupation rather than the address of the reader is of primary importance. Figure 20–8 illustrates an advertisement emphasizing the specialized audience reached through a business magazine.

General magazines select their audience more on the basis of general social and cultural interests than in terms of occupation. Mass-circulation magazines, such as *Life* and *Look,* emphasize general circulation throughout the United States, but circulation that varies, area by area, with variations in purchasing power of consumers. Thus, these magazines claim to pick out of each community those families that provide the richest opportunities for cultivation by advertisers. Magazines like *Fortune* and *Newsweek* claim to offer the "cream of the mass market" to advertisers.

A survey of males who read *Playboy* showed that 24.3 percent were college graduates, 60.7 percent were 18 to 34 years of age, and 34.8 percent were single.

FIGURE 20–8. High audience selectivity offered by a business magazine

As one might expect, 73 percent of the readers of *Seventeen* are high-school girls.

The Macfadden publications, particularly the "true story" women's group, emphasize sociological as well as economic factors in detailing the character of audience. Emphasis is placed on its high concentration among wage-earner families and women under middle age.

Time restrictions

Magazine advertising cannot be tied to day-by-day events. Occasionally this is tried, but the news element is stale by the time it reaches the reader. Generally, magazine advertising which does capitalize on recent events, such as the winner of the Indianapolis "500," serves merely as a testimonial.

The nature of magazine publication militates against the early appearance of an advertisement after it has been submitted for printing. Many magazines are published in great quantities, requiring days to complete the run. The preparation of the forms takes a great deal of time. The use of color prolongs the completion of printing. The widespread distribution of the magazine requires time to get it from the publisher to distant points. This period is lengthened still further when magazines are shipped in bulk in carload lots to central points and then distributed to dealers. When a publication is to appear on the newsstands simultaneously all over the country, the areas near the printing plant must wait until the distant areas are supplied before distribution is made available to prospective buyers of the magazine. All this means that an advertisement must be in the hands of the publisher weeks before it is received by prospective customers. *Life* magazine requires that all copy, plates, etc., for a four-color advertisement be in its hands seven weeks before publication date.

Regional editions

The flexibility of consumer magazines has been greatly increased through regional editions which enable advertisers to place ads in copies circulated in particular market areas. *Look* pioneered regional editions in 1959 with its Magazone plan that then divided total circulation into eight marketing zones, each of which was available individually or in any combination. The *Saturday Evening Post* followed a year later with its Select-A-Market plan that covered four regions and a variety of geographical split-runs.

Presently, *Look* offers a "MagaMarket Plan," which permits regional advertising in 25 "MagaCities," and 50 "MagaStates." The advertiser must buy a *minimum* circulation of 300,000; but even with this circulation requirement, he could run his advertising *solely* in New York City, or Los Angeles, or Chicago, or Philadelphia, since each city has a *Look* circulation of more than 300,000. *Life* magazine also offers a number of regional plans, the most recent of which is "Spot Life," as illustrated in Figure 20–9.

Regional editions enable smaller advertisers whose distribution is confined to part of the country to benefit from the prestige of national publications. Large national advertisers benefit too in that they can promote products whose popularity is restricted to one section of the country. Regionals are also finding favor among makers of items whose markets are determined by climate, as well as proving useful for test marketing and advertising experimentation.

Regional advertising is likely to continue its substantial growth rate, as more and more magazines begin to offer regional breakouts. Sixty-eight consumer magazines were offering regional editions as of January, 1966. At that time some 24 brands were each using over $500,000 annually for regional magazine advertising. Ford Motor Company alone spent $2,722,143 in 1965. The total investment in regional advertising for all magazines represented 15 percent of total dollar volume. For nine magazines with the greatest regional dollar volume, the figure is 21 percent, as noted in Table 20–2.[9]

A further refinement of regional editions is "demographic advertising." To give advertisers an opportunity to reach certain income and/or occupation groups, some magazines offer a separate edition that is delivered only to subscribers in those particular demographic classifications. *Time* magazine, for example, seeks to attract more business-oriented advertising with a special edition that goes to 1.4 million readers who reported on a questionnaire that they are business men. *Reader's Digest, McCall's,* and *Better Homes and Gardens* also offer demographic editions aimed at their more affluent readers.[10]

Mechanical and quality characteristics

Magazines are usually printed on good paper that will allow for excellent reproductions of art and color work. Halftones can be used effec-

---

[9] *Media/scope,* Vol. 9 (March, 1965), p. 31.
[10] *The Wall Street Journal* (March 17, 1970), p. 1.

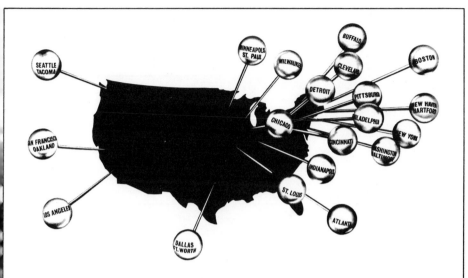

SPOT LIFE

lets you buy LIFE the way you buy spot TV.

Now you can buy LIFE in your choice of these top television markets. You'll reach more people than you can with a weekly television show—and at a more efficient cost per thousand.

Pick any combination of markets, so long as the insertion totals at least 750,000 circulation. Circulation is based on credited TV coverage in each market.

Use SPOT LIFE with TV. When you add SPOT LIFE to your network TV, you get better numbers than with a prime-time spot, heavying up among light television viewers.

Use SPOT LIFE alone. LIFE's coverage in these 20 markets exceeds LIFE's national reach of 34% of all homes. In 6 of the top markets, for example, a single insertion reaches 44% of homes. And LIFE delivers better homes, too: 45% of LIFE adults live in households with incomes over $8,000.

Use SPOT LIFE like a newspaper. Now you can change copy, city by city. National advertisers can use specific stories in specific markets.

SPOT LIFE has a seven-week closing for black and white and four-color ads. Ask your LIFE salesman to show you how SPOT LIFE can work for you.

FIGURE 20–9. How *LIFE* emphasizes its market segmentation

TABLE 20–2.   Comparison of regional or split runs to total advertising
expenditures in leading publications

Magazine	Advertising sold (in millions of dollars)		Percent of total used in regional or split runs
	Total	Regional or split run	
Life	158.7	33.4	21
Look	75.6	14.1	19
TV Guide	26.5	12.5	47
Time	69.7	11.5	17
McCall's	46.6	8.1	17
Sunset	8.4	8.0	95
Reader's Digest	57.9	7.7	13
Better Homes & Gardens	26.6	5.4	20
Farm Journal	12.2	4.3	35
Total 10 magazines $482.2		$105.0	21

tively for either black-and-white or color illustrations. Some magazines
are even prepared to print advertisements in metallic ink in different
colors. To achieve the maximum use of page area, a magazine ad may
often be designed to bleed off the page on one or more sides. An example of this is shown in Figure 20–10 where the picture is carried to the
very edge of the paper at top and sides. To accomplish this, the original
illustration had to exceed the page dimension so that some of it was
actually cut off when the page was trimmed, hence the use of the term
bleed or bleed edge.

The life of a magazine is an important quality. An old issue is often
kept some time after a new issue has been received. This gives to an
advertisement a greater opportunity of being seen and read. The reading
habits of magazine subscribers are also favorable to an advertisement.
Most magazines are not read at one sitting but are picked up and read
at various intervals between issues. A research study estimated the average number of days that a reader reads an issue of the following
magazines one or more times.[11]

Magazine	Average reading days
Reader's Digest	5.3
Good Housekeeping	4.1
Life	1.3
Look	1.5
McCall's	4.9
This Week	1.0

[11] *A Study of Seven Publications,* conducted by Alfred Politz Research, Inc. for *Reader's Digest* (Pleasantville, New York: Reader's Digest Association, Inc., 1956).

She's just completed the analysis
of 131 electronics companies
and selected two for inclusion in her portfolio.

She does it the easy way—by having Bank of America's experienced professional managers take care of all her investments. These men work full-time researching, analyzing and selecting stocks, bonds, real estate and other investments. They can tailor an individual portfolio for maximum performance in growth, income or tax-free holdings.

This Investment Management Service—which takes care of all details and paperwork—is available for you and your family today. Just see the manager at your local Bank of America branch or stop in soon at any of our District Trust Offices.

BANK OF AMERICA

NATIONAL TRUST AND SAVINGS ASSOCIATION • MEMBER FEDERAL DEPOSIT INSURANCE CORPORATION

FIGURE 20–10. Magazine production quality not feasible in newspapers

As one might expect, an issue of a monthly or a reading-type publication is read more often than an issue of a weekly or a picture-type publication.

Rates

Magazine space is generally sold in units of a full page or a fraction of a page. For example, *Look* quotes rates for one page, half-page, quarter-page, and eighth-page, with the requirement that all nonstandard units of less than one eighth page be multiples of 14 agate lines. Fractional-page units vary according to the number of columns on a page. A magazine with a three-column page quotes rates for full, two-thirds, and one-third pages. *Reader's Digest* does not accept ads measuring less than one-half page.

The variation in page sizes among magazines might be considered important. However, a full page in a magazine with a small format will possess the same relatively dominance as a full page in a magazine of larger size. Page size is probably more significant as a factor influencing the design of the advertisement than as a factor affecting the value of the space.

Most magazines make an additional charge for certain preferred positions. The cover pages are highly desirable because of their greater attention-getting value. *Life* charges the same for the second and third cover pages as for a regular four-color page ad, which was $64,200 in January, 1970. The fourth cover (back cover) carries an additional cost of 31 percent over other color pages, and thus costs $84,100. A full-page ad in black and white costs $42,500, almost one-half of the charge for the back cover. Those magazines that accept orders for bleed pages generally charge extra.

Many magazines offer discounts based on the quantity of space used and the frequency of insertions within a year. For example *The New Yorker* quotes the following bulk space discounts:

Pages per year	Discount
13 pages or more	7%
26 pages or more	12
39 pages or more	16
52 pages or more	20

and the following frequency discounts:

Frequency	Discount
13 times	5%
26 times	10
39 times	12
52 times	16

If the advertiser's schedule earns both space and frequency discounts, he is entitled to the larger of the two.

As demonstrated in the preceding chapter, magazine rates are usually compared on the basis of cost-per-thousand circulation. The following cost comparisons indicate some significant characteristics of magazine rates:

	Rate per page B/W	Circulation	CPM
Look	$37,000	7,797,521	$ 4.75
New Yorker	4,300	478,781	$ 8.98
Fortune	8,120	504,904	$16.08
Marketing Communications	1,415	77,588	$18.24

The wide range of costs-per-thousand among these four magazines indicates differing degrees of selectivity, differing buying power per audience member, and differing influence per audience member on business purchases. *The New Yorker's* circulation is more concentrated among higher-income families than is the circulation of *Look*. *Fortune* and *Printers' Ink* reach businessmen whose decisions influence large-scale business buying. Generally speaking, the greater the selectivity, or the greater the buying potential per person reached, the higher is the cost-per-thousand.

Copy and contract requirements

Advertisements are, in general, accepted subject to the approval of the publisher. Thus, no guarantees are given to print any copy that is submitted. Many magazine publishers assist the advertiser by setting up specific standards to which copy must conform.

The majority of publishers specify certain contract requirements. Those dealing with ethics are reproduced here:

24. All advertisements are accepted and published by the publisher on the representation that the advertising and/or advertising agency are properly authorized to publish the entire contents and subject matter thereof. When advertisements containing the names, pictures and/or testimonials of living persons are submitted for publication, the order or request for the publication thereof shall be deemed to be a representation by the advertiser and/or advertising agency that they have obtained the written consent of the use in the advertisement of the name, picture and/or testimonial of any living person which is contained therein. It is understood that the advertiser and/or advertising agency will indemnify and save the publisher harmless from and

against any loss, expense or other liability resulting from any claims or suits for libel, violation of rights of privacy, plagarism, copyright infringement and any other claims or suits that may arise out of the publication of such advertisement. All copy, text and illustrations are subject to the publisher's approval before execution of the order; and the right is reserved to reject or exclude copy which is unethical, misleading, extravagant, challenging, questionable in character, in bad taste, detrimental to public health or interest otherwise inappropriate or incompatible with the character of the publication, or that does not meet with the approval of the Federal Trade Commission; whether or not the same has already been accepted and/or published. In the event of such cancellation or rejection by the publisher, the advertising already run shall be paid for or billed at the rate provided for in the order.

25. Acceptance of advertising for any product or service is subject to investigation of the product or service, and of the claims made for it upon its package, labels and accompanying material, and in the advertisement submitted for publication.[12]

QUESTIONS AND PROBLEMS

1. Why do some newspapers charge more for national than for local advertising?

2. In preparing a newspaper schedule, what factors would influence your selection of morning, evening, or Sunday newspapers?

3. If given an appropriation to be spent in *Life*, either (1) in a series of four black-and-white, full-page advertisements, or (2) in two, four-color cover advertisements, which would you choose? Why? How much would each series of ads cost?

4. The specialized business or trade magazine assembles for the advertiser a number of people with similar business or trade interests. This provides a high degree of homogeneity, at least in respect to certain interests. Does this high degree of homogeneity make this type of magazine a highly desirable medium for advertisers? Would it be more desirable for some than for other advertisers? Explain.

5. Newspapers emphasize that "all markets are local." Magazines place emphasis on the quality aspects of markets, in terms of kinds of people reached rather than their territorial location. Is it safe to generalize on the relative values of those two claims? What is your evaluation of these claims? Be specific and give examples supporting your observations.

6. The satisfactions people get out of reading their daily newspapers are different from the satisfactions they receive from reading magazines. Do you agree or disagree? Explain.

7. Compare the "milline" rates of the following newspapers: *Cincinnati Enquirer, Cincinnati Times-Star, Chicago Tribune,* and *Chicago Daily News.*

---

[12] "Contract and Copy Regulations," *Consumer Magazine Section, Standard Rate and Data Service,* January 27, 1966, p. 22.

8. Why are milline rates generally higher for small circulation papers than for large circulation papers?

9. Compare the cost-per-black-and-white-page-per-thousand circulation of the following magazines: *Time, Newsweek, Advertising Age,* and *Sales Management.* What factors probably account for these cost differences?

10. Compare the editorial content of any two magazines in a particular classification. What qualitative differences do you observe that you think might have some bearing on the value of each magazine as an advertising medium?

11. Magazines cover so many specialized fields that their use makes it possible to reach markets profitably in a manner not possible by the use of newspapers. Do you agree? Why?

12. You have been asked to buy some space in the daily newspaper which you read (or believe you should read) regularly. You are to buy space equivalent to 4 columns by 12 inches. This space is to be used by a national advertiser. How much will this space cost if you were to use the same amount of space once a week for 52 weeks?

Is there a possibility that this space would cost less if it were to be used by a local retailer? How could you find out whether that is true?

chapter 21
TELEVISION AND
RADIO

As CHANNELS of communication, television and radio are fundamentally different. One combines sight, motion, and sound. The other depends entirely on sound.

Yet, these media also have much in common. Both use the airwaves to broadcast messages which are received instantaneously in the home. Both depend on the public's voluntary investment in receiving sets to complete the communication channel. Both are regulated private enterprises and are licensed to operate by the same government agency, the Federal Communications Commission. Both are time-organized. They schedule programs and commercials by the hour of the day and sell units of time to advertisers. Both provide nationwide networks of stations for simultaneous broadcasting in all parts of the country. Both use the same methods of audience measurement. Both belong to the same trade association, the National Association of Broadcasters.

Whether he is buying television time or radio time, the advertiser is dealing with media that are organized, operated, and sold in much the same way. Therefore, these two media are treated together in this chapter.

Advertising volume

Television is the fastest-growing medium. In the short span of 23 years, expenditures for television advertising grew from zero to about $3.5 billion dollars annually. With national advertisers spending about

$3 billion in 1969, television is the leading national advertising medium.

Radio, in the wake of television's impact, declined from a volume of $624 million in 1952 to $545 million in 1955. However, from the mid-1950's radio advertising expenditures have had a consistent upward trend, with 1969 volume estimated at $1,270 million.

Network television, which provides simultaneous coverage of a nationwide market, accounted for 47 percent of total television advertising expenditures in 1969. *National spot* television, which involves national advertiser's selecting individual stations to reach individual markets ("spots" on the map), accounted for 35 percent of the total. *Local* television, the use of local stations by retailers, accounted for 18 percent. These relationships are illustrated in Figure 21–1.

Radio advertising expenditures in 1969 were 66 percent *local,* 29 percent *national spot,* and 5 percent *network.* Thus, radio today is primarily a local medium with strong support coming from national spot. This has not always been so. Before the advent of television, network advertising accounted for the major share of radio advertising expenditures. However, as more and more people began watching network television programs during prime evening hours, the value of network radio as an advertising medium declined.

Facilities available

Advertisers are naturally interested in knowing what facilities a medium can offer for reaching prospective customers. Physical facilities offered by television and radio are represented by the number of stations, networks, and receiving sets.

Number of stations. On April 1, 1970, there were 689 commercial television stations on the air. Of these stations, 509 were VHF (very-high-frequency—channels 2 through 13) and 180 were UHF (ultra-high-frequency—channels 14 through 83).[1]

Further expansion of television broadcast facilities largely depends on the number of new stations that will be added in the UHF range, where most of the unassigned channels are available. However, several factors have limited the growth of UHF facilities. During the first five years of commercial television all the stations on the air were VHF and all the

---

[1] The VHF range is from 54 to 216 megacycles. UHF range is from 470 to 890 megacycles. Each channel assigned for television broadcasting is 6 megacycles wide. Twelve of the VHF channels are allocated for commercial broadcasting and the others are for use by military and other services.

receiving sets sold were equipped to receive only VHF broadcasts. Most of these early stations were located in the densely populated metropolitan markets. Thus, by 1952, when the Federal Communications Commission began licensing UHF stations, the system of television broadcasting had been fairly well established in the VHF channels. As a result, there was

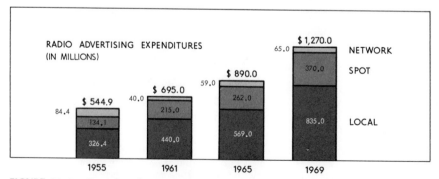

FIGURE 21–1.   Growth and composition of television and radio advertising

little or no incentive to construct UHF stations in the major markets where practically all the receiving sets received only VHF. In smaller markets where both V's and the U's went on the air about the same time, the networks and national advertisers favored the V's, thereby making the operation of a UHF station unprofitable. Obviously, would-be UHF broadcasters have not been eager to seek a license to lose money. Now, however, as a result of a Congressional law passed in 1964, all television sets shipped in interstate commerce must be able to receive both UHF and VHF channels. Presently, about 49 percent of U.S. television households are equipped for all-channel reception.

In 1970, almost all commercial stations were equipped to carry some form of color programming. Color set penetration in TV households is presently about 35 percent and this is expected to grow substantially in the next few years.

There were 6,391 radio stations on the air in 1970. Of this number, 4,280 were AM stations, 2,111 were FM.[2] The majority of these stations are low-power local outlets and are located in the smaller markets. Radio blankets the United States. Anyone with a receiving set, regardless of where he might be, can be assured of radio service. In the vast majority of localities, listeners can choose from a half dozen or more stations at will.[3]

Networks. There are three national television networks and four national radio networks. Columbia Broadcasting System (CBS), National Broadcasting Company (NBC), and American Broadcasting Company (ABC) operate both television and radio networks. The Mutual Broadcasting System operates a radio network only. The total number of interconnected stations offered by each network in 1970 was as follows:[4]

Network	TV stations	Radio stations
CBS	192	252
NBC	214	222
ABC	157	321
Mutual		578

---

[2] The AM broadcast band ranges from 535 to 1,605 kilocycles and consists of 107 channels, each 10 kilocycles wide. The FM band ranges from 88 to 108 megacycles (1,000 kilocycles) and consists of 100 channels, each 0.2 megacycle wide.

[3] Radio stations are generally classified as *local, regional, or clear channel*. Local stations operate with power not in excess of 250 watts and have an average daytime range of 15 to 20 miles. *Regional* stations operate with power not in excess of 5,000 watts and have an average daytime range of 40 to 65 miles. *Clear channel* stations operate at 50,000 watts and have an average daytime range of 100 to 125 miles.

[4] Standard Rate & Data Service, Inc., *Network Rate and Data,* January 10, 1966.

The networks perform several important functions: (1) they assemble the network by negotiating station affiliation agreements and arranging for American Telephone and Telegraph facilities (coaxial cables and microwave relays) by which affiliated stations are interconnected for simultaneous broadcasts, (2) they provide physical facilities, such as studios, cameras, microphones, scenery, sets, etc., for originating network programs, (3) they produce programs, and (4) they sell network time periods and programs to advertising agencies and advertisers.

Networks offer advertisers the opportunity to reach nationwide audiences during specific time periods at a low cost-per-thousand figure. By making it possible to distribute talent and program production costs over many markets, the networks enable advertisers to benefit from the popularity, prestige, and publicity of high-priced talent and expensive shows.

Even though the number of television stations has increased greatly since the infant stage of the industry, the number of television networks decreased from four to three. Claims that network practices were stifling competition and preventing the formation of new networks led the Federal Communications Commission to undertake a special study of television networks. In the report of the FCC's network study group, which was issued in 1957, it was noted: "The high concentration of control exercised by networks, the barriers to new network entry, the strong bargaining position of the networks in their relations with stations in many markets, and the limited opportunity for nonnetwork groups to compete represent in combination a serious problem for the realization of the objectives of the commission."[5]

Until the existing structure of television broadcasting is considerably modified it would appear that there is little prospect for more networks. In fact, with the growth of communications satellites like "Early Bird," it is difficult to assess the future of network television. Not only will television become more international as a result of satellite relay, but the entire method of beaming network programs into the home through local stations is subject to change.

Community Antenna Television (*CATV*) uses a master antenna to receive signals from distant TV stations and then distributes the signals to subscriber homes by cable. CATV has become a $200 million industry with 2,300 operating systems and 3,700,000 subscribers.

Even though CATV is used in all areas of the United States, it con-

---

[5] *Report of the Network Study Staff to the Network Study Commission,* Federal Communications Commission, 1957.

tinues to be used primarily in rural and mountainous regions where regular television reception is poor and channel availabilities are minimal. The greatest concentrations of systems and subscribers are in the East along the Appalachians, in the Northwest in Washington, Oregon, and Idaho, and in the Southwest in California, Arizona, and Texas.

Number of receiving sets. An analysis of the number and location of stations provides a picture of the facilities for getting messages into the airwaves. Such an analysis must be combined with a message of the number of receiving sets capable of reproducing those messages for consumers.

In 1970, there were 58 million U.S. homes equipped with one or more TV sets. This included 95 percent of all homes. Geographically, penetration varies somewhat, with the highest percentage figures, 96 percent, in the New England, Middle Atlantic, and East Central regions. Next are the West Central region, 95 percent; Pacific, 93 percent; Southwest, 91 percent; and Southeast, 92 percent.[6]

The expression "radio is everywhere" is close to the truth. In 1966 there were an estimated 60 million radio homes, 98.6 percent of all homes in the United States. And over 90 percent of the automobiles are so equipped. The ubiquity of radio was dramatically increased with the development of battery-powered, transistorized, pocket-sized, portable receiving sets. Now radio goes wherever people go.

There are totally about 25 million homes presently receiving FM broadcasts. However, ownership varies not only with FM station concentration but also with the character and quality of programs offered by such stations. There are areas with a high percentage of homes owning FM receivers and others where ownership is very low. Advertisers using this medium would probably wish to collect data on set ownership for each area used.

Audiences

In the course of a week about 50 million U.S. families make some use of their TV sets. Their viewing averages 6 hours and 41 minutes per day.[7]

Television audiences are big. For example, the Emmy Awards program in May, 1969 was viewed by almost 16 million homes; "Bonanza," a consistently top ranked program in recent years, often reaches an audi-

---

[6] *Broadcasting,* January, 1970.

[7] *1969 Broadcasting Yearbook.*

ence of 12 to 15 million homes and 35 to 40 million persons. The largest audiences are assembled when all three television networks cover the same event. Neil Armstrong and "Buzz" Aldrin's moon walk was viewed by over 44 million homes.[8]

Obviously, television viewing is influenced by time of day. Changes in the hour by hour activities of various members of the family influence the number of viewers per home and the composition of the audience by age and sex. School, job, and household routines are reflected in the TV audience. As illustrated in Figure 21–2, through the early daytime hours

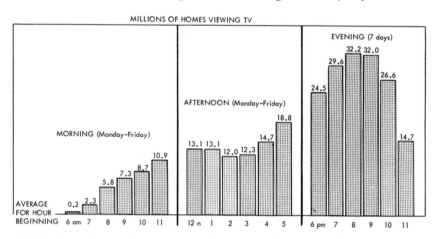

FIGURE 21–2. Hour by hour pattern of television viewing

the number of families viewing television increases steadily to a high immediately after noon. After a slight dip in mid-afternoon the viewing audience again increases hour by hour to reach its peak for the entire day at mid-evening.

Composition of the television audience at different hours of the day is shown in Figure 21–3. Children are the biggest viewing group during the early morning and late afternoon hours. Women are the biggest group watching in the early afternoon and in the evening. Teen-agers consistently comprise a relatively small segment of the TV audience. It should be noted, however, that these figures are national averages. Composition of audiences reached by specific programs may differ greatly from the average.

---

[8] *Nielsen Television Index, Program Ratings Summary Report, 1969.*

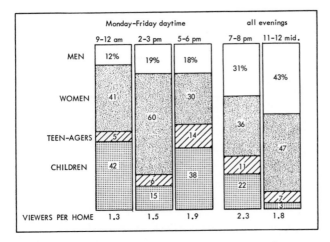

FIGURE 21–3.   Composition of national television audience
by time of day

The pattern of viewing changes with the season of the year. The evening audience is 66 percent greater in winter than in summer. Viewing is influenced day by day, by holidays, news stories, sports contests, and special events.

The omnipresence of radio receiving sets makes it more difficult to measure the radio listening audience. In a typical week, radio sets are used in more than 60 million homes at an average rate of more than 14 hours per family, or 2 hours per day per family.[9] This level of in-home listening is exclusive of auto radio use and battery-only portable set use.

The hour by hour pattern of in-home and auto radio listening is shown in Figure 21–4. In-home listening reaches its peak for the entire day at 8–9 A.M. when it averages 7.6 million homes. Auto radio usage is substantial through most of the day, and in the late afternoon accounts for over one third of all radio listening.

Whereas teen-agers are relatively light users of television, they are among the heavy users of radio. And children, of course, do not have much time left over from television to listen to radio. Again, reflecting the mobility of receiving sets, total radio listening remains fairly constant in both summer and winter.

[9] Radio Advertising Bureau, *Radio Facts Pocket Piece,* 1967.

FIGURE 21–4. Hour by hour pattern of home and auto radio listening

Measuring size of specific audiences

Advertisers, of course, are interested, not only in the pattern of total listening and viewing, but more particularly in the number and type of people tuned to a particular program. Just as some magazines and newspapers have high and low readership, so do similar differences exist among radio and TV programs. Since such differences are so important to advertisers, much attention is given to measuring the size of specific program audiences.

There are a number of methods employed to measure audience size and character. The *Nielsen Audimeter* is an electronic device about the size of an automobile battery which is installed somewhere out of sight in the home. It makes a minute-by-minute record on photographic film —24 hours a day, all year—of the set tuning of all television and radio receivers in the home. It thus provides a continuous record of the time periods when a set is turned on, the specific stations to which the set is turned, the dialing from one station to another, and the length of time spent with each station. The film cartridges are sent in every two weeks by panel members to the Nielsen organization where the data are tabulated and matched against the program schedules of the television and radio stations involved. While the Audimeter provides a precise record of set tuning, it does not show how many people were viewing or listening, nor does it show which members of the family were doing so.

The *coincidental telephone* method consists of telephoning homes and asking whether a radio or television set is turned on and, if so, to what station or program. This method is used extensively in local market areas. It is relatively inexpensive.

The *roster-recall* method is used in a number of the larger metropolitan areas. It consists of having personal interviewers present to people a roster of all stations and programs readily available in the area and asking people to check those programs or stations which they recall having heard or seen. People are generally asked to recall a time period of only a few hours. The method is especially valuable for use among non-telephone homes and where there are significant ethnic differences in the population.

A somewhat more qualitative picture of listening or viewing can be secured from use of the *diary* method. This consists of placing either a family diary or individual diaries in the hands of a sample of people and asking them to record listening and viewing in the diary at the time such activity occurs. This method can supply data related to different age, sex, and occupational groups as well as nonhome listening and viewing. This latter factor is especially important with the great growth in the number of automobile and portable radios and the significant amount of nonhome viewing of television.

To combine the advantages of the Audimeter and diary methods the A. C. Nielsen Company supplements its Audimeter homes with a matched sample of homes in which family members keep a diary, known as an *Audilog*, of their program viewing. To verify the accuracy and completeness of Audilog entries, Nielsen installs a *Recordimeter* which automatically records the total minutes of set usage daily.

Commonly used measurements of television and radio audiences are: (1) program rating, (2) sets-in-use, (3) share-of-audience, (4) projected audience, and (5) audience composition.

Sets-in-use is the percentage of all homes in the sample where a receiving set was turned on.

Program rating is the percentage of all homes in the sample tuned to the program.

Share-of-audience is the percentage of homes with a set turned on that was tuned to each program. (If sets-in-use were 60.0 and program rating were 15.0, then the program's share-of-audience would be 25.0.)

Projected audience is the number of homes reached by the program. (If there were 300,000 homes in the area sampled and the program rating were 15.0, then the projected audience would be 45,000 homes).

Audience composition is the percentage distribution of the total num-

ber of people viewing or listening by sex, age, education, or other classification factors.

Program ratings are the most widely publicized measurement of television and radio audiences, but a comparison of programs on the basis
of rating alone does not take into account differences in the number of
viewers per set and difference in the composition of audience. For example, a program rated at 20.0 with three viewers per set has a larger
audience than a program rated at 25.0 with only two viewers per set.
Similarly, a program rated at 10.0 may reach many more *adult* viewers
than a program rated at 15.0 which has a greater appeal to children.
Thus, the total number of people viewing a program and the composition
of the audience are more meaningful measures to an advertiser than the
program rating.

Why then, are program ratings, which reflect the number of *homes*
tuned to programs instead of the number of *people* viewing or listening,
so widely used? The answer lies in the prevailing research methods for
measuring television and radio audiences. Users of the coincidental telephone and roster-recall methods generally obtain information from only
one member of the family. This person functions as a reporter for the
home. The A. C. Nielsen Company, a leading firm in the audience measurement field, primarily uses the Audimeter which measures set usage in
the home, not individual viewing or listening. Users of the diary method
do measure individual viewing and listening, but they are in the minority.
Since the majority of firms in this field provide program ratings based on
samples of *homes* instead of *people,* they have, in effect, set the standards
for the entire broadcast industry.

Nationwide network audiences have been measured extensively for
many years. The A. C. Nielsen Company, the American Research Bureau,
Pulse, Inc., and Videodex all report on the performance of network programs. A page from a National Nielsen Television Report is reproduced
in Figure 21–5. Since the Audimeter, which is used to gather these data,
keeps a continuous minute-by-minute record, it is possible to determine
the total number of homes tuned to each program sometime during the
broadcast. The number of such homes is referred to in this report as
total audience and is somewhat larger than the *average audience,* which
is the number of homes tuned in during an average minute of the program.

Network audience measurements do not reflect differences in program
performance in individual markets. A given network program may go
over great in New York but not so well in San Francisco. Furthermore,

NATIONAL *Nielsen* TV AUDIENCE ESTIMATES

EVE. · SUN. FEBRUARY 12, 1967

TIME	7:00	7:15	7:30	7:45	8:00	8:15	8:30	8:45	9:00	9:15	9:30	9:45	10:00	10:15	10:30	10:45	11:00

ABC TV

TOTAL AUDIENCE (Households (000) & %)
- 7:00: 11,030 / 20.1
- 8:00: 14,820 / 27.0
- 9:00: 18,010 / 32.8

Programs: ← Voyage to the Bottom of the Sea → (Co-sponsor) [7:00–8:00] · The F.B.I. (Ford) [8:00–9:00] · Sunday Night Movies "THE SHEEPMAN" (9:00–10:50PM) (Co-sponsor) [9:00–11:00]

AVERAGE AUDIENCE (Households (000) & %): 7,960 (7:00) · 12,020 (8:00) · 14,110 (9:00)

	7:00	7:15	7:45	8:00	8:15	8:45	9:00	9:15	10:00	10:30
SHARE OF AUDIENCE %	14.5	13.7*	15.2*	21.9	20.7*	23.2*	25.7	24.1*	25.5*	27.9*
	23.8	23.1*	24.2*	33.0	31.5*	34.6*	40.3	35.3*	37.7*	45.7*

AVG. AUD. BY 1/4 HR. %: 13.2 · 14.2 · 14.8 · 15.7 · 20.1 · 21.3 · 23.2 · 23.4 · 24.7 · 25.2 · 25.8 · 28.0 · 27.7 · 26.9 · 19.0

CBS TV

TOTAL AUDIENCE (Households (000) & %)
- Wizard of Oz: 15,430 / 28.1
- Ed Sullivan Show: 16,910 / 30.8
- Smothers Brothers Comedy Hour: 14,710 / 26.8
- Candid Camera: 9,610 / 17.5
- What's My Line: 9,390 / 17.1

Programs: Wizard of Oz ® (6:00–8:00PM) (P&G) · ← Ed Sullivan Show → (Co-sponsor) · ← Smothers Brothers Comedy Hour → (Co-sponsor) · Candid Camera (Co-sponsor) · What's My Line (Co-sponsor)

AVERAGE AUDIENCE (Households (000) & %): 13,340 · 15,430 · 12,240 · 8,620 · 7,910

SHARE OF AUDIENCE %	31.3*	31.5*	24.3	28.1	22.3	22.7*	21.9*	15.7	14.4
	52.9*	50.2*	37.0	41.9	32.8	33.3*	32.3*	25.7	26.8

AVG. AUD. BY 1/4 HR. %: 31.2 · 31.5 · 31.6 · 31.4 · 24.2 · 24.5 · 27.4 · 28.8 · 22.6 · 22.7 · 22.4 · 21.3 · 16.1 · 13.0 · 15.3 · 15.8

NBC TV

TOTAL AUDIENCE (Households (000) & %)
- Walt Disney's World Of Color: 15,590 / 28.4
- Hey Landlord!: 8,840 / 16.1
- Bonanza: 14,000 / 25.5
- Andy Williams Show: 11,970 / 21.8

Programs: ← Bell Telephone Hour → (6:30–7:30PM) (Bell Telephone System) · ← Walt Disney's World Of Color → "THE COYOTE'S LAMENT" ® (R.C.A.) · ← Hey Landlord! → (P&G) · ← Bonanza → (Chevrolet) · ← Andy Williams Show → (Co-sponsor)

AVERAGE AUDIENCE (Households (000) & %): 9,500 · 7,960 · 12,130 · 8,780

SHARE OF AUDIENCE %	7.4*	12.5*	14.2*	20.4*	14.5	22.1	22.2*	22.1*	22.1*	16.0*	16.4*	15.7*
			22.6*	31.1*	21.6	32.5	32.6*	32.2*	32.6*	27.9	26.9*	29.2*

AVG. AUD. BY 1/4 HR. %: 7.3 · 7.6 · 13.5 · 14.9 · 20.1 · 20.7 · 14.7 · 14.4 · 22.0 · 22.3 · 22.4 · 21.7 · 16.7 · 16.1 · 15.7

HOUSEHOLDS USING TV (See Def. 1)

EVE. · SUN. FEBRUARY 19, 1967

	7:15	7:30	7:45	8:00	8:15	8:30	8:45	9:00	9:15	9:30	9:45	10:00	10:15	10:30	10:45	11:00
WK 1	58.2	60.3	62.0	63.7	65.1	66.3	66.4	67.5	68.2	68.3	68.1	67.2	61.9	60.0	56.7	50.7
WK 2	54.8	56.9	59.7	62.3	64.9	66.3	65.7	67.0	68.2	69.1	68.5	67.1	61.8	59.3	55.3	51.3

U.S. TV Households: 54,900,000
(OP) Other Programs; See Pages 70-73
® Originated in Black & White

† For Sponsorship Detail, See Program Index.
® Repeat. See page 4.

(1) FOR RATINGS, SEE PAGE 68
(2) "INDONESIA, THE TROUBLED VICTORY".

*Half-hour ratings (for immediately preceding and subject quarter-hours).

FIGURE 21-5. Excerpt of a page from the National Nielsen Television Report national spot advertisers and retail advertisers are concerned with the audiences reached by individual stations, not network audiences. To bridge this gap in audience measurement the A. C. Nielsen Company offers another service, the *Nielsen Station Index,* which reports periodically on the audiences reached by individual stations in 220 markets. The American Research Bureau offers a similar service in the form of their *ARB Local Market Reports.*

Radio and television programs

Both radio and television stations operate under license from the Federal Communications Commission. Licensees agree to operate in the public interest. Programs represent the very heart of radio and television so far as the public is concerned. Those who have any responsibility in the development of programs should never lose sight of the public interest factor.

This is of special concern to advertisers who use radio or television, since many stations and networks have permitted advertisers either to build their own programs for sponsorship or to exercise substantial influence over the character of programs developed by others. There is no fundamental reason why public interest cannot be served with programs that also offer specific values to advertisers.

The basic function of a program from the point of view of the advertiser is to provide an audience that will be receptive to a commercial message hitched to, or sandwiched in with, the program. Either the size or the character of the audience, or both, might be important to the advertiser. If the product or service to be advertised is one of broad universal use, the size of the audience might be more important than character or quality, since practically all people would be prospective customers. If the item has a specialized market (farm tractors, dog food, fishing tackle), then the character of the audience should rate above size in importance.

Specialized audiences can be selected by the type of program used. Opportunities along this line are almost unlimited. Examples of program types that will attract people with special-product interests would include classical music, sports, science, religion, labor news, foreign-language broadcasts, book reviews, and farming.

The history of broadcasting indicates that advertisers have tended to place heavy emphasis on reaching a mass rather than a class audience.

Programs have been built with such an objective in mind. Variety shows, popular music, light drama, general news, and popular sports have tended to dominate the scene. Audience-measurement services have been keyed to that emphasis. The size of the program rating (percentage of families listening) has often been the factor guiding program selection and promotion.

Television is having a significant influence on changing the emphasis of radio on mass appeal for most of its programs. Television has adopted the mass-appeal approach and is successfully pulling a high percentage of entertainment seekers to it and from radio. As a result, radio has become a much more selective medium. In time, the growth of UHF-TV will also likely make TV a more selective medium.

Building the audience

Radio and television programs can be promoted the same as any other service. There is no reason to believe that all interested people will be aware of new programs soon after they are introduced or even old programs that have been on the air for some time. The promotion or advertising of both new and old programs can acquaint people with such programs, where and when they can be found, and give enough detail about them so that people can estimate their possible want-satisfying qualities.

The promotion of programs that are designed for some specialized group (farmers, sports fans, etc.) can often increase materially the number of listeners. The cost of such promotion then becomes an investment and not an expense. Once new people have been attracted to a program, many will continue as regular or semiregular members of the audience if the program lives up to its claims. This larger audience is then available to the advertiser for his commercial messages at no greater time cost than for the original smaller audience.

Too many advertisers and station managers have believed that special-interest programs cannot draw an audience sufficiently large to warrant either sponsorship or promotion. There is now a considerable amount of evidence which indicates that significant numbers of people can be drawn to specialized programs. An experiment at the University of Illinois shed some light on this question. That experiment consisted of promoting four specialized educational-type programs in a one-county area. The four programs were (1) a homemaker's half-hour, (2) chamber music,

(3) semiclassical "pops" music, and (4) a university classroom literature hour.

These programs were promoted over a short period of time (two months). Careful measurements were made of audience size before, during, and after the periods of promotion. Results showed more than a threefold increase in audience size during and immediately after promotion. Thirteen months after promotion was stopped the audience was still more than twice the size of the original. Each of the four programs attained a "rating" comparable to the vast number of standard radio programs.[10]

Television and radio rates

Television and radio rates are quoted for various units of time: one minute or less, five minutes, ten minutes, quarter-hour, half-hour, and one hour. Units of one minute or less are referred to as *announcements.* They are placed between programs or within *participating programs,* such as disk-jockey shows, that carry announcements of several noncompeting advertisers. Participating programs function much as magazines and newspapers in that advertisers have no direct control over the program's content. *Station breaks* are announcements of 20 seconds or less that are broadcast by network-affiliated stations between network programs.

Program time units may be sold for *exclusive, alternate,* or *shared sponsorship.* Through exclusive sponsorship, a single advertiser gains the full benefit of being identified with the program, but he also must bear the full cost. To provide some of the advantages of sponsorship without requiring an advertiser to bear the full burden of a costly program, especially a network television program, alternate and shared sponsorship arrangements have been developed. Through alternate sponsorship, two advertisers sponsor alternate broadcasts of a regularly scheduled program. Through shared sponsorship, two or more advertisers buy particular segments of a program.

In an attempt to adjust their rates to reflect the differences in audience size at different times of the day, television and radio stations classify various time periods as AA, A, B, C, and D. Classes of time are based

---

[10] C. H. Sandage, *Building Audiences for Educational Radio Programs* (Urbana, Ill.: Institute of Communications Research, 1951).

primarily on total sets-in-use. Thus, Class AA television time includes those evening hours when the maximum number of TV sets are turned on. A typical television station in the Eastern Time Zone lists the following classes of time and quarter-hour rates:

Class AA $600.00
    7:30 p.m. to 10:30 p.m. daily
Class A $400.00
    10:30 p.m. to 11 p.m. daily
    6:30 p.m. to 7:30 p.m. Saturday
Class B $300.00
    6:00 p.m. to 7:30 p.m. Sunday through Friday
    6:00 p.m. to 6:30 p.m. Saturday
Class C $200.00
    9:00 a.m. to 6:00 p.m. daily
    11:00 p.m. to midnight daily
Class D $140.00
    Midnight to 9:00 a.m. daily

A glance at Figure 21–2 on page 486 will show the logic behind these time classes. Class AA represents the evening peak. Classes A and B represent time periods when the audience is building-up-to and dropping-off-from the peak. Class C includes the daytime hours.

All stations do not classify their time the same way. For example, small market stations have fewer time classes than big city stations.

Reflecting the influence of television many radio stations now quote the same rate for all hours of the day. Some radio stations are charging more for daytime hours than for evening hours. For example, the highest priced times on WGN (Chicago) are the periods from 6:00 A.M. to 9:30 A.M. Monday through Friday and 7:00 to 9:00 A.M. Saturday. These, of course, are the hours when the audience listening to automobile radios is at its peak.

An ideal rate structure might be one in which rates varied directly with the actual audience reached by a station or network during each specific time period. This would more nearly approach charging for what is actually delivered, but it would require continuous audience measurement and would complicate pricing and billing practices. The idea of a "guaranteed audience," which involves giving a rebate to the advertiser if the audience reached was smaller than that on which the rate was based, has been proposed, but it has gained little support.

Television and radio rates are subject to a wide variety of discounts. The usual practice, however, is to charge a lower rate per minute for longer time segments and for greater frequency of broadcasts. For example, if a radio station quotes a rate of $100 for one hour, it is likely to charge the following rates for other segments.

One hour	$100
Half-hour	60
Quarter-hour	40
Five minutes	30
One minute or less	20

An advertiser who buys program time is limited as to the amount of that time that can be devoted to actual commercial messages. Generally, he can use approximately three minutes for commercials out of a 15-minute program.[11] Therefore, rates charged for different lengths of time should be considered in terms of the cost-per-commercial-minute.

Frequency discounts are usually quoted for cycles of 13, such as 13 times, 26 times, 52 times, 104 times, etc., and rates charged usually decrease by 5 percent as frequency of broadcasts purchased increases to the next higher cycle.

Network rates are essentially a composite of the rates charged by the individual stations making up the network. Discounts depend on the number of stations the advertiser uses, the number of consecutive weeks he uses the network, weekly billings for time, and annual volume of business done with the network. Negotiation plays a more important role when buying network time than when buying station time.

The cost of using television and radio includes not only time costs, but also talent and program production costs. These latter costs reach staggering heights in some instances. It is not uncommon for a big network television show to cost $100,000 per broadcast for talent only. However, when such shows attract the big audiences for whom they are intended, the cost-per-thousand viewers is rather reasonable.

With network operations, the cost of talent can be spread over many stations or markets; but that cannot be done so readily by retailers. *Cooperative programs* which originate with a network but are available for sponsorship in local markets give some retailers and regional advertisers an opportunity to benefit from the popularity of high-priced talent. Use can also be made of filmed or transcribed programs offered by organizations that specialize in program production.

---

[11] NAB standards for length of commercial copy in sponsored programs are:

One hour ....7:00 minutes		Ten minutes ....2:10 minutes
Half hour ....4:15 minutes		Five minutes ....1:15 minutes
Quarter hour ....3:00 minutes		

Budgets

Radio and television are major advertising media and budgets should be planned in such terms. Advertisers can probably secure maximum benefits from any major medium only when a substantial percentage of the total advertising is allocated to the medium.

Some evidence to support the above recommendation came from an intensive study of the use of radio by retailers. Their budgeting practices were correlated with their success from radio. From that analysis it was concluded that retail "firms with annual advertising expenditures of $50,000 or more generally should expect to spend at least 15 percent of their total budget on radio if they wish high success, and that smaller firms should expect to spend as much as 20 percent of the total advertising budget on radio for high success."[12] It would seem logical to apply this same reasoning to national advertisers and also to the use of major media other than radio.

Users of television and radio

Producers of mass-consumption items have been the largest users of television and radio. The 50 leading network television advertisers in 1969 were manufacturers of food products, automobiles, toiletries, drug items, soap products, and cigarettes. These same product categories accounted for the major share of national spot television, national spot radio, and network radio advertising. Procter & Gamble, a firm that produces a broad line of soap products, toiletries, and food products, has consistently been the leading user of television.

Although newspapers continue to be their primary medium, retailers spent about $835 million for radio advertising in 1969. This was more than double the amount they spent in 1960. Much of this increase resulted from the construction of many new stations during this period. Also, much radio broadcast time formerly used by network advertisers became available for local advertisers. With more radio time available at suitable hours and at relatively low rates, it is likely that retailers will continue to increase their use of radio.

High cost and scarcity of broadcast time has deterred many retailers

---

[12] C. H. Sandage, *Radio Advertising for Retailers* (Cambridge, Mass.: Harvard University Press, 1945), p. 13.

from using television. However, with local advertising expenditures totaling $665 million in 1969, it is apparent that some retailers have been finding television a profitable medium.

Advertising values of radio and television

Each of the mass media communications offers advertisers effective opportunities to present specific commercial messages. Maximum effectiveness can be obtained from utilizing the particular strengths of each medium.

Radio and television provide timeliness to an even greater extent than do newspapers. This can be of particular value in the case of very sudden changes in conditions. During rain or snow storms, floods, outstanding news happenings, or sudden changes in temperature, the radio commercial can be given almost simultaneously with the event. A department store planned its outstanding promotion of the year to celebrate its 25th anniversary. The evening newspapers on the night before the "big day" carried pages of advertising by the store. Morning papers duplicated the previous evening emphasis. Unfortunately, the morning was shrouded in the worst rainstorm in the history of the city and the weather report offered no hope for relief. To meet this situation the store purchased all radio time available to talk with local residents about the storm and what the store was offering in its big sale that day. Special inducements in respect to transportation and lunch were offered, too. As a result of this timeliness, the store had a tremendously successful day.

"Tennessee Ernie" Ford, when he was a radio announcer in Bristol, Tennessee, "had all the fires sold." Whenever there was a fire, the station would cut in with an announcement telling where the fire was, advising listeners not to foul up the traffic trying to get there, and then follow up with a one-minute commercial for a fire insurance company.

Radio and television are, or can be, more personal than any other medium. They provide the warmth of the human voice and come closer than any other medium in matching personal selling. In the case of television, the ability to demonstrate visually the advertised items is added to the personal factor.

Radio is highly flexible territorially. Television is, too, up to the limit of the number of markets served and the number of stations in each market. Both TV and radio provide, through networks, combined market coverage on a simultaneous basis. Both media provide local market selectivity. A national advertiser can use spot TV or spot radio for seasonal promotions, for saturation campaigns, for bolstering weak markets, for launching new products, for localizing appeals, for pretesting messages, and for complementing network advertising.

The opportunity to reach selective audiences is offered by both TV and radio through choice of program and time of broadcast.

Limitations

All advertising media have some limitations. The life of a radio or television advertisement is no longer than the time it takes for presentation. If an announcement is broadcast at a time when few prospects are listening, it is lost forever so far as most prospects are concerned, unless word-of-mouth publicity occasioned by listeners or viewers is developed. An advertisement in a magazine has a chance of being seen and read as long as the magazine remains in the home. In addition to the fleeting nature of the radio message, two out of every three listeners to the radio engage in some other activity while the radio is on. This might consist of reading, performing household tasks, playing cards, dancing, or carrying on a conversation with guests. Such activity reduces the effectiveness of the advertising message. Forced attention demanded by television limits the long-range daily and weekly audience.

A serious limitation is the fact that there are only 24 hours in a day, some of which must be spent in sleep. And people cannot listen to more than one program at a time. Thus, television advertising on a large scale cannot be employed by a great number of advertisers. One national network could accommodate only 64 advertisers for 15 minutes each, if every 15-minute period between 8 A.M. and midnight were taken. When a number of networks are organized to carry the message of other advertisers, the audience of each network is diminished.

Of course these limitations do not necessarily impair the effectiveness of individual radio and television advertisements, but, rather, indicate limitations of facilities to meet all possible advertising demands.

QUESTIONS AND PROBLEMS

1. The tremendous popularity of television in its early development caused many to predict that it would greatly diminish the effectiveness of radio as an advertising medium. What is your estimate of the future trends of radio and television as competition for the consumer's time? Will radio be relatively stronger or weaker in the future than in the past?

2. G. Maxwell Ule, formerly research vice-president of Kenyon & Eckhardt adver-

tising agency, reported on research done on how to increase the sales effectiveness of television commercials. Some of the do's and don'ts reported by Mr. Ule were: "Show more and talk less; stress the familiar and known; be helpful and informative to the viewer; space the commercial so as to interrupt the program the least obtrusively; don't throw too much at the viewer at once; don't attack consumer's present habits or ways of doing things."

Comment on Mr. Ule's observations. Would you agree with all of them? Are they in harmony with or do they contradict any of the advertising fundamentals already developed in this course?

3. Television and radio can be used to reach particular consumer groups efficiently. How would you use these media to reach (1) teen-agers, (2) homemakers, (3) office workers, (4) farmers?

4. The total number of people viewing a television program and the composition of the audience are more meaningful measures to the advertiser than the program rating. Explain.

5. Each of the various methods of measuring television and radio audiences employs a different channel of communication to gather a different kind of information from a sample of a different population. Explain.

6. Distinguish between the following: exclusive sponsorship, shared sponsorship, alternate sponsorship, cooperative program, participating program, and station-break announcements. What advantages and disadvantages do you see in each of these buys?

7. Within a given time classification the size of audience reached by specified programs may vary considerably, yet advertisers are charged the same rate for any time they buy during the hours included in that time class. Wouldn't it be more appropriate to base rates on program ratings instead of time classifications? Support whatever position you take on this question.

8. Compare the cost of 52 one-minute announcements to be broadcast at 10:30 A.M. on Tuesdays, Wednesdays, Thursdays, and Fridays over a 13-week period on the following television stations: WLW-T and WKRC-TV in Cincinnati; WGN-TV and WBBM-TV in Chicago.

Compare the costs of the same schedule on the following radio stations: WLW and WKRC in Cincinnati; WGN and WBBM in Chicago.

chapter 22
DIRECT MAIL

ADVERTISING media previously described offer space or time on a contract basis to manufacturers, retailers, and other advertisers who wish to have their message distributed on a mass basis. Those mass media have already selected the groups to whom they will deliver the advertiser's message, and the advertiser has no control over that selection.

In the case of direct mail, the advertising message is carried directly from the advertiser to individuals selected by him. The Direct Mail Advertising Association defines such advertising as "a vehicle for transmitting an advertiser's message in permanent written, printed, or processed form, by controlled distribution, direct to selected individuals."[1]

Because it employs the principle of *selected* rather than *mass* distribution of the advertisement, direct-mail advertising has often been described as the "rifle," in contrast to the "shotgun," method of conveying a sales message. Edward N. Mayer, Jr., president of James Gray, Inc., New York, has called direct-advertising messages "the paratroopers of advertising" since they can be concentrated on a specific objective with great effectiveness.[2]

Scope of direct mail

The term "direct mail" does not adequately cover all of the advertising usually included under that name. While this term is used here because

---

[1] Direct Mail Advertising Association, 230 Park Avenue, New York 10017.

[2] Edward N. Mayer, Jr., *How to Make More Money with Your Direct Mail* (New York: Funk & Wagnalls Co., 1950), p. 5.

of its long acceptance, a more accurate designation would be "direct advertising." This latter term would include *direct-mail* and *nonmailed-direct* advertising. Most direct advertising is distributed by mail, but a substantial and increasing amount is passed from door to door or to pedestrians in a limited area, placed in parked automobiles, handed to customers in retail stores, inserted in packages or bundles, presented by salesmen or messengers, or in some other way conveyed directly to the intended recipient. Giveaway novelties, if they bear an advertiser's message, also belong in the category of direct advertising, provided they reach the prospect by one of the above methods, mailed or nonmailed.

Closely associated with *direct-mail advertising,* and therefore often confused with it, is *mail-order selling.* This latter term is properly used to describe that type of merchandising operation which depends upon orders coming through the mail, without aid of personal salesmanship. In seeking orders and advertising its goods, the mail-order firm need not, and, indeed, scarcely ever does, depend entirely upon direct mail to carry the sales message. One expert pleads, "Let's recognize mail order as merely a way of doing business, in regard to *how* orders come back— regardless of what type of advertising was used to persuade people to send in the orders."[3] Mail-order selling by letter, folders, catalogs, and order forms is employing direct-mail advertising; mail-order selling by means of space advertisements and television or radio commercials is not.

Expenditures for direct mail

In compiling data on the expenditures of direct mail, the statistician's task is obviously complicated by the widespread local use of this form of advertising, especially by small enterprisers. Unlike other major media, direct-mail's advertising volume is neither measured nor reported regularly. Estimates of the total volume are generally arrived at by determining direct-mail's share of total postal volume and by adding an amount to cover costs of producing the pieces mailed.

Marketing/Communications estimated the volume of direct-mail advertising in 1969 to be $2.6 billion. This represented 13.7 percent of the total for all media. Among all media, then, direct mail was third, following newspapers with 29.9 percent, and television with 18.3 percent.[4]

---

[3] Harrie A. Bell, "Should *Mail* Be Dropped from Direct Mail Advertising?" *The Reporter of Direct Mail Advertising,* March, 1948, p. 2.

[4] *Marketing/Communications,* February, 1970.

Characteristics

The factors of selectivity of audience and flexibility of territorial coverage, which every advertiser looks for in choosing a medium, are the basic characteristics of direct advertising. The Direct Mail Advertising Association, the Mail Advertising Service Association, and other advocates of direct advertising as an effective sales-promotion medium, have long emphasized these qualities of selectivity and flexibility. The D.M.A.A. lists the following ten points as the advantages of direct advertising:

1. Direct advertising can be directed to specific individuals or markets with greater control than any other medium.
2. Direct advertising can be made personal to the point of being absolutely confidential.
3. Direct advertising is a single advertiser's individual message and is not in competition with other advertising and/or editorial.
4. Direct advertising does not have the limitations on space and format as do other mediums of advertising.
5. Direct advertising permits greater flexibility in materials and processes of production than any other medium of advertising.
6. Direct advertising provides a means for introducing novelty and realism into the interpretation of the advertiser's story.
7. Direct advertising can be produced according to the needs of the advertiser's own immediate schedule.
8. Direct advertising can be controlled for specific jobs of research, reaching small groups, testing ideas, appeals, reactions.
9. Direct advertising can be dispatched for accurate and in some cases exact timing, both as to departure of the pieces as well as to their receipt.
10. Direct advertising provides more thorough means for the reader to act or buy through action devices not possible of employment by other media.[5]

The ultimate clue as to whether direct-mail advertising is suited to the advertiser's needs lies in the fact that it is the most personal, the most intimate of all forms of advertising. Edward N. Mayer, Jr., past president of D.M.A.A., says: "You address your customer or prospect individually by the most important word he knows—his name. Basically, you seek to create the impression that you know who he is and what he is like. In most direct-mail copy you talk to him as you would if you were face to face. Therefore, direct-mail advertising is best suited to situations where

---

[5] Direct Mail Advertising Association, Manual File #1201.

it is logical and likely that you should so approach your prospects."[6]

The high degree of selectivity and adaptation to individuals and to groups which is inherent in this medium is realized as an asset, however, only when the advertiser is sure the right people have been reached. The relatively high per-contact cost of direct advertising is justified only when the advertiser knows his message has reached the hands of those for whom it was written. A brochure costing nearly $2 each, for instance, sent to approximately a thousand steel and foundry executives to sell a furnace installation costing $750,000, was not considered an out-of-line expense when the mailing brought in $7 million worth of orders.

Functions and uses

Media/scope magazine, in their "Check List For Direct Mail Advertising," lists the following circumstances as to when to use direct mail:

1. When sampling would be both practical and desirable.
2. When the advertising message is too complicated or too detailed to be conveyed efficiently in other media.
3. When a specific, selected market is desired and other media can provide it only at the cost of waste circulation.
4. When personal, personalized, or confidential communication is desired.
5. When the format or color that an advertiser's marketing strategy requires can't be carried in other media.
6. When a specific market area needs to be covered with a minimum of slop-over into adjacent areas.
7. When specific timing or frequency of contact is desired.
8. When couponing is desirable.
9. When controlled research is called for (e.g.: measuring of effectiveness within certain markets; ascertaining prospect profiles; or testing price, packaging, or logical users for new products).
10. When a controlled mailing is desirable (mailings will go only to certain income groups, owners of certain makes of cars, boat owners, etc.).
11. When mail order (sale of the product directly to the prospect, without retailers, dealers or other media) is desirable.
12. When you want to accomplish the following jobs in the marketing process:
    A. Obtain responses indicating interest (as in "securing leads")—
       a. to be followed up by more direct mail.
       b. to be followed up by salesmen.
    B. Put the prospect into position for personal selling (as in "traffic building")—
       a. in a retail outlet or showroom.

[6] Edward N. Mayer, Jr., "Direct Mail Advertising," *Harvard Business Review,* July, 1951, p. 48.

   b. in front of an exhibit of products—particularly those which salesmen cannot take to the prospect for demonstration.

C. Create a receptive atmosphere for salesmen—
   a. through cordial-contact mailings which build an "image."
   b. through institutional types of direct mail (for example, mailings such as the paper and printing companies use to illustrate the product features or the company's abilities).
   c. through the "impact" created by any type of mailing sent out. Any mailing will create some kind of impression. Well-executed mailings will identify the advertiser favorably.

D. Influence selected groups to action—
   a. building salesman incentive.
   b. obtaining credits and collections.
   c. building mailing lists.
   d. developing political campaigns.

E. Make more effective the impact of advertising in other media—
   a. by gaining the cooperation and building the enthusiasm of all persons involved with your advertising efforts, through keeping them properly motivated and informed.
   b. by helping to convert impressions created by other advertising media into sales through—
     (1) bringing the prospect and product together at the point of sale.
     (2) following up inquiries developed by other media.
     (3) using ads from newspapers or magazines as a mailing piece or part of a mailing unit to precede or follow up the issue of the magazine or newspaper in which the ad appears.[7]

To carry out these functions of direct advertising, a myriad of styles and forms are at the disposal of the advertiser. Let us look at some of them.

Forms of direct mail

In style of copy, direct advertising parallels the other media. The principles of language choice, psychological patterns, emotional appeals, and layout discussed elsewhere, therefore, need not be discussed in detail here. In personalized letters and postal cards, of course, the forms acceptable in business correspondence prevail. In "circular" letters and in all other types of pieces, the headline and body-copy style of presentation is usually followed. The same semantic theories and readability principles hold for the copy of this medium. The copy appeals are slanted to the same basic buying motives employed successfully in other copy.

While this similarity of copy style holds for direct advertising, the

---

[7] *Media/scope*, Vol. 10 (June, 1966).

physical forms which it may take are innumerable. Size, shape, typography, color, and illustrations are not nearly so predetermined here as in other media; therefore, the design they take is determined by the advertiser's needs for each separate occasion. He can use any kind of paper or ink, die cut a piece to resemble the shape of his product, emboss to simulate the feel, or perfume to imitate the odor.

The following list has been presented by Mayer as representing the most commonly used forms or types of direct advertising:

Letters	Programs
Folders	Sales, research, and informative
Broadsides	bulletins
Booklets	Charts
Brochures	Posters
Self-mailers	Blow-ups
Postal cards	Coupons
Mailing cards	Calendars
Catalogues	Reprints
House magazines	Memorandums
Blotters	Printed novelties
Price lists	Business cards
Sales and informative manuals	Order forms
Invitations	Reply cards and envelopes[8]

Figures 22–1 and 22–2 illustrate two of the more widely used types of mailing pieces. Figure 22–1 is a mailing card, 5¼ by 8 inches, with self-contained postage-prepaid reply form. Figure 22–2 is a typical non-personalized letter with the "FREE" headline taking the place of salutation.

Securing and maintaining the mailing list

The keystone in the arch of direct-advertising effectiveness is the list. If the advertiser is going to reach prospects rather than mere suspects, and thereby hold mailing waste to a minimum, he must start with a carefully built list. As Mayer says: "Your copy can sparkle, your layout and format be an art director's joy, your printing good enough to win a Graphic Arts top award, and your postage can be the newest and hardest-to-get commemorative stamp, but if your mailing piece is directed to people who are not prospects and cannot buy the product, your entire effort will be an expensive bust."[9]

---

[8] Mayer, *How to Make More Money with Your Direct Mail*, p. 29.
[9] *Ibid.*, p. 189.

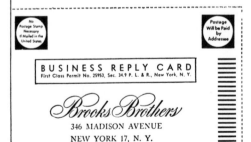
FIGURE 22–1. Front and back of a common type of mailing card

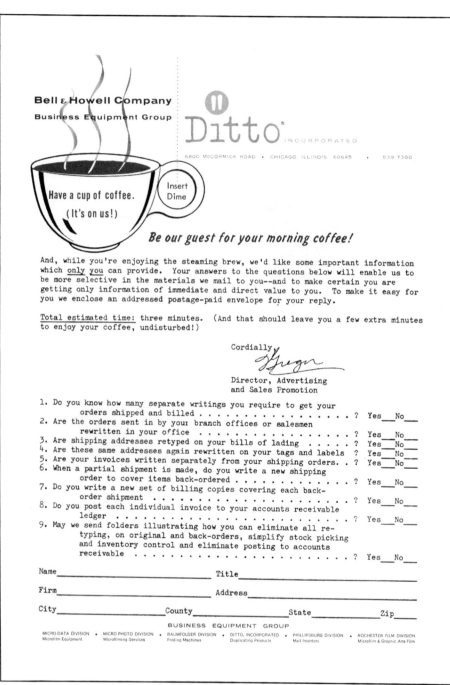

Bell & Howell Company
Business Equipment Group

Ditto®
INCORPORATED

6800 McCORMICK ROAD • CHICAGO, ILLINOIS 60645 • 539-7300

Have a cup of coffee.
(It's on us!)

Insert Dime

Be our guest for your morning coffee!

And, while you're enjoying the steaming brew, we'd like some important information which only you can provide. Your answers to the questions below will enable us to be more selective in the materials we mail to you--and to make certain you are getting only information of immediate and direct value to you. To make it easy for you we enclose an addressed postage-paid envelope for your reply.

Total estimated time: three minutes. (And that should leave you a few extra minutes to enjoy your coffee, undisturbed!)

Cordially,

Gregn

Director, Advertising
and Sales Promotion

1. Do you know how many separate writings you require to get your orders shipped and billed . . . . ? Yes___No___
2. Are the orders sent in by your branch offices or salesmen rewritten in your office . . . . ? Yes___No___
3. Are shipping addresses retyped on your bills of lading . . . . . ? Yes___No___
4. Are these same addresses again rewritten on your tags and labels ? Yes___No___
5. Are your invoices written separately from your shipping orders. . ? Yes___No___
6. When a partial shipment is made, do you write a new shipping order to cover items back-ordered . . . . ? Yes___No___
7. Do you write a new set of billing copies covering each back-order shipment . . . . ? Yes___No___
8. Do you post each individual invoice to your accounts receivable ledger . . . . ? Yes___No___
9. May we send folders illustrating how you can eliminate all re-typing, on original and back-orders, simplify stock picking and inventory control and eliminate posting to accounts receivable . . . . ? Yes___No___

Name_____ Title_____

Firm_____ Address_____

City_____County_____State_____Zip____

BUSINESS EQUIPMENT GROUP

MICRO-DATA DIVISION • MICRO PHOTO DIVISION • BAUMFOLDER DIVISION • DITTO, INCORPORATED • PHILLIPSBURG DIVISION • ROCHESTER FILM DIVISION
Microfilm Equipment   Microfilming Services   Folding Machines   Duplicating Products   Mail Inserters   Microfilm & Graphic Arts Film

FIGURE 22–2. Nonpersonalized direct-mail letter

Mailing lists are composed of the names of people who are prospective customers for the good or service the advertiser has to offer. Once the advertiser has defined the group he wishes to reach, the sources of a mailing list of such persons are practically unlimited. As a rule, lists are obtained by one of the following methods:

1. Build your own.
2. Trade or exchange with others.
3. Rent from a broker.
4. Buy from a list house.
5. Arrange to use expiration list of a periodical.

Figure 22–3 represents many specific and detailed sources of lists available to the direct mail user.

Building one's own list is indeed a job to be performed with extreme care. A well-trained person is needed to use directories discriminately so that they yield only the kinds of prospects being sought. The lowest cost and often the most profitable names available are those to be had in the present list of customers, from inquiries, and from reports of salesmen's daily calls. The standard sources for mailing lists are telephone and city directories; trade directories; trade reports; commercial rating books; tax lists; club-membership lists; and the records of state, county, and city officials. More limited in usefulness, but frequently used, are press clippings, court proceedings, real estate sales records, stock-ownership records, credit-agency reports, social registers, and lists of charity contributors. It must be borne in mind that the cost of a list of names varies with the amount of labor involved in compiling and checking them.

Today businessmen lean heavily on professionally compiled lists. These may be purchased either through a broker or direct from a list-compiling firm. The list-broker concentrates on knowing where to obtain lists which the advertiser might wish. When the broker receives a request for a particular kind of list, he obtains one from the best source he can, adds a brokerage fee, and delivers it to his client.

The list company is a far more complicated operation. In its files are contained the names and addresses of business executives, shoeshops in the Bronx, wealthy widows, Hudson Bay trappers, and millions of other persons and establishments. The more popular lists are ready-made and ready for immediate delivery. Specialized lists have to be made on order.

A list is supplied to the buyer in one of several ways. It may consist merely of names and addresses typed on sheets of paper. The list house may, however, address envelopes or gummed labels furnished by the

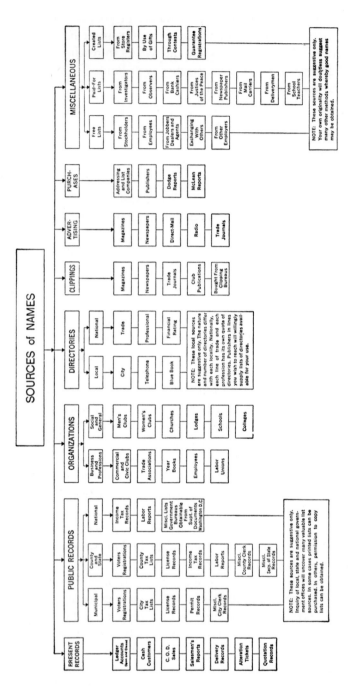

FIGURE 22-3. Sources of names as suggested by the Addressograph-Multigraph Corporation

buyer. One of the largest list companies is R. L. Polk & Company of Detroit, specializing in lists of automobile owners, but also furnishing many other types of lists gleaned from the many city directories it publishes. In New York, W. S. Ponton, Inc., publishes a large *List o' Trades,* which is an alphabetical catalog of the lists the company is prepared to furnish. The leading list-sellers in Chicago include Buckley-Dement Company, Reuben H. Donnelly Corporation, and the Trade Circular Addressing Company.

The maintenance of lists is costly, painstaking, and continuously necessary. People are constantly moving, getting married, divorced, having children, dying. Business firms fail, merge, change name, or move. In the United States during normal times an estimated 4,000 to 5,000 firms daily go out of business or otherwise move, requiring change of address. The whole task of minimizing wastage in direct-mail advertising hinges upon keeping the list constantly up to date. Commercial list houses and private list-users alike must continually be on the alert for changes. Checking of returned mailing pieces against the most recently issued address information is a most important phase of maintenance activity. First-class mail is automatically returned to sender with directory notations provided by the post office. Third-class mail, since it travels at a lower rate, is not entitled to this service unless the sender imprints on each mailing piece "Form 3547 Requested" then the sender pays for each form returned bearing the most recent post office directory information. Where lists are used frequently, one or the other of these methods must be employed periodically to assure accuracy of the list. Mailers may also use a questionnaire-type postal card from time to time to see whether the name and address being used is correct.

Direct-mail costs

The factors of cost which the direct advertiser must consider are those of the mailing list, production and handling, and distribution.

Rental fees for mailing lists are normally quoted on a "cost-per-thousand names" basis, and the costs vary greatly according to the specialized nature of the lists. General-type lists usually average around $20 per thousand. Special lists, requiring extensive research to compile, can cost as much as 50 cents a name. Most lists are guaranteed to reach a certain percentage of the names on them, usually varying from 90 to 100 percent. The company refunds postage on all undelivered mail below the percentage guarantee.

Very little can be said here about production and handling costs such as printing, folding, assembling, and envelope stuffing. These vary with the form of the mailing, quality of printing and paper, quantity produced, and facilities for handling distribution. Estimates of production costs for each direct-mail undertaking should be secured from a printer before it is undertaken. The printer can often make suggestions for reducing costs.

Since postal rates and regulations change frequently, no attempt is made to quote them specifically. The user of direct mail should always consult his postmaster before undertaking any mailing, no matter how large or small. Usually the advertiser finds third-class more advantageous than first-class because of the favorable bulk rates for mailings in excess of 200 identical pieces (or 20 pounds). There are times, of course, when the first-class letter or postal-card rates are paid because the added prestige and attention value of this kind of postage are desired.

Since costs in direct advertising are extremely flexible, they must be judged entirely in relation to results. Accordingly, it is often wise to judge the effectiveness of a direct advertising effort on a "cost-per-order" basis. The cost of the mailing is divided by the number of orders received so as to obtain a cost-per-order figure. Where traceable sales results are an objective of the direct advertising campaign, the cost-per-order figures can be used to measure the relative efficiency of the advertising.

QUESTIONS AND PROBLEMS

1. A dealer in medium-price automobiles, contemplating a direct-mail campaign, has two possible sources for his mailing list. One is the city directory, giving names and addresses of people by sections of the city, so that people living in the better sections of the city could be selected. The other is a company which tabulates automobile registrations by make of car owned, and which will furnish lists of owners of any make of car in any territory for $0.02 per name. The dealer reasoned that since he had free access to a city directory, it would be to his advantage to use it. Do you agree? Why?

2. It is often said that direct mail provides advertisers with the most selective medium of all. Do you agree with that point of view? Support your stand with examples.

3. Assume that after you graduate you set yourself up in a direct-mail advertising service business. You offer to plan and execute direct-mail advertising campaigns for retailers, local clubs, hospitals, community chests, and other local institutions. At lunch one day a local businessman told you that he thought most of the money spent in direct mail was wasted. He pointed out that most of that type of mail which came to him was immediately thrown in the wastebasket.

He was confident that the same practice was followed by the great majority of people. If that were true, he reasoned, then it would be foolish to spend much, if any, money in direct mail. He advised you to close up your business and get into something else.

How would you answer your luncheon partner?

4. Many of you will be looking for a job when you graduate. When that day approaches you will have an opportunity to develop your first real advertising campaign. You will have the problem of "interpreting your own personal qualities to a prospective employer in terms of his needs or desires."

You are asked to prepare such a campaign now, depending completely on direct mail as your medium. As a part of this assignment, bring to class the following:

a) A statement of specific sources you would use in compiling a mailing list.

b) A detailed listing of the kinds of information, if any, you would want to obtain about each name on your mailing list before preparing a specific advertising letter or folder.

c) How you would proceed to secure the desired information. Name specific sources of information.

d) A detailed outline of your campaign procedure, including such things as what kind of material you would mail, in what form, to how many people, at what time, and whether follow-up mailings would be made if there was no response from your first mailing.

e) A one-page "sales" letter designed to (1) show how the prospective employer could benefit from having you on his payroll, and (2) to secure a personal interview for you.

f) A statement of the estimated cost of your campaign, broken down into (1) money to be spent (2) number of hours of your time required to plan and execute the entire campaign.

chapter 23
OTHER MEDIA

IN PREVIOUS CHAPTERS, consideration was given to the types of media that claim the major portion of the advertiser's dollar. Other media available to the advertiser will be treated in the following pages.

OUTDOOR

The use of outdoor advertising is one of the oldest methods employed by advertisers to get their message before the public. Outdoor advertising, as used in this chapter, consists of the following types: (1) signs, (2) posters, (3) painted bulletins, and (4) electric displays. The most pervasive of these is the outdoor poster which accounts for over three fourths of the volume in this medium.

Outdoor advertising provides a medium to reach people when they are out of doors or traveling, rather than when they are in the home or office. The copy requirements of outdoor are different from those of magazines, newspapers, direct mail, or radio. In the former, the message must be presented so that pedestrians and motorists can get its meaning in a very short space of time. Brevity is a necessity in copy, and pictures are highly important in gaining attention. Because of these limitations, outdoor advertising can be used effectively for only those products or services whose sales message can be told in pictures and brief copy. It can be used to remind people of the merits of known products and where they can be secured. This principle is illustrated by the policy of the California Fruit Growers' Exchange. This organization allocated only between 2 and 3 percent of its advertising appropriation to outdoor advertising in its early years, concentrating most of its effort on acquainting the public with the merits of oranges and other citrus fruits. Later, however, it was felt that the merits of these products were well established in the minds of consumers and that therefore brief reminder copy on poster boards would produce effective results. Consequently, the exchange revised its advertising budget, allocating from 20 to 25 percent of the total to outdoor advertising.

Store signs

The purpose of store signs is to identify a place of business. For most stores, such signs should emphasize the kind of merchandise sold or service rendered rather than the name of the proprietor or company. Passers-by are more interested in locating a place where food, drugs, or clothing can be purchased than where John Smith operates a store. But department stores are somewhat of an exception, since reputation is a factor in patronage and the vast window-display space provides a method for informing the public concerning the kind of merchandise sold.

Store signs are either on the building itself or on boards or metal overhanging the street. They may be painted or electric. Electric signs have increased in popularity with the introduction of the neon sign. This has permitted a wide range of attention-getting techniques.

Outdoor posters

Posters lining our streets and highways are one of the most common forms of outdoor advertising. They appear in various sizes, but the most common size is the 24-sheet poster which has a copy area of 8' 8" by 19' 6". Three-sheet posters have a printing surface 82 inches high and 48 inches wide. They are most often used near the point of sale as last-minute reminders. Popular places for such signs are grocery, tobacco, and drugstores located at street intersections. A more recent innovation is the 30-sheet poster. It has the same size frame as the 24-sheet, but the copy area is larger by 25 percent, thus permitting a greater visual impact.

The use of large outdoor posters along streets and highways developed with the growth of automobile traffic. Any medium that will provide an economical means for reaching the vast numbers of automobile drivers will be of value to the advertiser of many types of products. The potential value of poster boards is therefore measured in terms of the number of persons passing during a given interval of time. To provide an authentic measure of such traffic, the Traffic Audit Bureau has been established to do for outdoor advertising what the Audit Bureau of Circulations does for newspapers and magazines.

Buying poster space. Poster-board advertising space can be purchased in some 15,000 city and town trading areas. National coverage can be attained by combining many local areas, or coverage can be spotted in those areas where added advertising emphasis is desired. In fact, space on a single board can often be purchased by a local advertiser who wishes to reach a very limited area.

The principal item of cost is the rental of space. Such costs vary a great deal according to the volume and character of traffic past the board. Illuminated posters, of course, cost more than other boards under similar traffic conditions. The use of fluorescent ink does not increase the space cost but does increase the hours of visibility and thus increases the advertising value of such posters.

Space is usually purchased in terms of relative coverage, designated by numbers 50, 75, 100, 150, etc. A No. 100 coverage is the accepted standard of full coverage of a market. If an advertiser buys No. 100 coverage in a given market, his message will appear on that number of boards considered necessary to reach the entire mobile population within a 30-day period. Thus, the number of boards required for No. 100 coverage varies from market to market and depends on the market's population and number of traffic arteries. In most markets about 80 to 90 percent of the traffic moves over 10 to 20 percent of the streets. Accordingly, plant operations build most of their panels along these arteries. An example of such concentration can be observed in Figure 23–1. No. 50 coverage consists of half as many boards as No. 100; No. 75 is three fourths as many, and so forth.

Rates for various coverages are quoted on a monthly basis. The data in Table 23–1 reflect the cost of outdoor advertising in a few selected cities.

National advertisers generally place their outdoor campaigns through advertising agencies. The agencies, in turn, are likely to use the services of the National Outdoor Advertising Bureau, Inc. (NOAB), an organization which is cooperatively owned and maintained by advertising agencies. Functioning as a middleman between the agencies and the widely scattered plant operators, the NOAB assembles cost estimates for outdoor space, draws up contracts, bills the agencies, handles payment to plant operators, and provides field inspection services.

FIGURE 23–1. Location of boards within a city

Local advertisers or other small users of outdoor space place their orders directly with the plant operators.

TABLE 23–1. Cost of outdoor advertising in selected metropolitan areas

City	Population	No. of poster boards in a No. 100 coverage		Monthly cost/mkt.
		Nonilluminated	Illuminated	
Chicago, Ill.	6,870,400	132	182	$30,628
Seattle, Wash.	1,247,100	38	49	$ 7,675
Sacramento, Cal.	790,300	29	26	$ 5,236
Greenville, S.C.	288,300	34	16	$ 2,512
Champaign-Urbana, Ill.	151,300	27	5	$ 1,626

Source: NOAB 1969 Poster Advertising Rate Card.

Regardless of the channel through which purchase is made, the plant operators assume responsibility for posting the advertisements and keeping them in repair for the full 30 days before the advertisement is changed and new sheets provided. If a portion of the advertisement is torn or marred during the 30-day period, the local plant is responsible for repairing the damage if the advertiser has furnished extra sheets.

Printing is also an important item of cost in the use of posters. Printing is done by the lithographic process and will average around $4 per board, although for large runs the cost may be somewhat lower. Costs of printing can often be reduced by a careful arrangement of color in illustrations, so that a minimum of color sheets needs to be run. While large posters are referred to as "24-sheet posters" (because that was at

FIGURE 23–2. Possible layout arrangement of sheets for 24-sheet poster one time the number of sheets printed for each board), larger sheets are printed today. The usual number is 10, but these can be cut so as to be arranged in 12 or 15 pieces for more economical and practical manufacturing. Three suggested layouts are given in Figure 23–2. Other arrangements are possible according to the design of the poster, subject to the one restriction that the sheets must be so cut as to necessitate no more than five separate sections lengthwise of the board, and these sections must run from top to bottom in vertical lines.

Since the same design remains on a board for 30 days, it is important that colors be used that will not fade readily when exposed to sunlight. Pinks, purples, and certain types of blues and greens should be used sparingly because of their tendency to fade.

Advantages of poster advertising. Poster boards constitute a primary advertising medium. The enterprise is well organized, making it easy for the advertiser to avail himself of its facilities. Although this form of advertising is limited in its application for the reasons already set forth, its advantages for certain products and services are numerous. According to "Essentials of Outdoor Advertising," published by the Association of National Advertisers, outdoor is bought because:

1. It can deliver a message simultaneously across the country, giving the medium the characteristic of national magazine, network radio and tv.
2. Outdoor can be used to cover individual markets and can be bought market-by-market.
3. While used on a national scale, it also can be tailored in frequency and coverage to meet special sales problems in individual markets.
4. A truly mass medium, it is exposed to all economic and social groups, delivering messages to people on their way to work, to play, to shop.
5. Outdoor is unique in that other media deliver primarily during a period of indoor activity.
6. Outdoor must speak quickly, memorably and repeatedly.
7. Its low cost enables it to be used as an impulse-trigger, for it delivers at the time the prospect is apt to recognize his need for the product.[1]

National advertisers account for two thirds of total outdoor advertising expenditures. Advertisers of automobiles, gasoline, oil, tires, soft drinks, and beer are the principal users of this medium. A listing of the top 25 outdoor advertisers and their expenditures can be noted in Table 23–2.

---

[1] *Advertising Age,* "The World of Advertising," January 15, 1963, p. 131.

TABLE 23–2. Top outdoor advertisers—1969

Advertisers	Expenditures
1. General Motors	$7,417,500
2. Distillers Corp.-Seagrams	7,261,100
3. Rapid-American Corp.	4,315,100
4. Ford Motor	4,279,300
5. National Distillers & Chemical	2,911,600
6. Heublin	2,080,100
7. Hiram Walker-Gooderham & Worts	1,944,800
8. General Motors (dealers)	1,566,900
9. Bankamerica Corp.	1,527,600
10. Standard Oil Co. (N.J.)	1,502,100
11. Coca-Cola	1,432,000
12. Volkswagen of America	1,349,600
13. Chrysler Corp.	1,284,300
14. Ford Motor Co. (dealer assns.)	1,270,300
15. Carbonated Beverage Can Makers	1,204,700
16. Liggett & Myers	1,168,600
17. Crown Zellerbach	1,126,200
18. American Airlines	1,025,600
19. Atlantic Richfield	1,020,300
20. Norton-Simon	1,015,400
21. Standard Brands	1,006,200
22. Seven-Up Co.	967,100
23. AT&T	963,600
24. Brown-Forman Distillers	931,700
25. Pepsi-Co.	878,400

Source: *Advertising Age*, April 13, 1970, p. 112.

Painted and electric displays

The same general principles that apply to poster boards apply to painted displays, for the two are comparable in matters of circulation and copy requirements. Painted displays appear on buildings, bulletin boards, and wall panels. Farm buildings often afford a site for a painted display. Wall panels are comparable to the 3-sheet poster, and painted bulletins to 24-sheet and 30-sheet posters, except that bulletins are usually larger than poster boards and may be built in special shapes and designs.

Copy remains without change for a longer period of time on painted displays than on posters, the period varying from four months to one year, according to type of display and location. The most common period is six months. Location and the presence or absence of illumination are the principal factors influencing cost.

To give advertisers the impact of a big painted display plus wider coverage of a market than would be possible with one or a few fixed position displays, outdoor plants in several cities now offer a *rotary plan.* Under the rotary plan one or several movable display units are rotated every 30, 60, or 90 days on a series of choice locations.

The most imposing of all outdoor-advertising media are the large electric displays erected at heavy traffic centers in our larger cities. In the daytime they compete with other street signs, but at night they have the field more or less to themselves. Their cost is enormous, owing to the scarcity of choice locations and the expense of operation and maintenance. World-famous electric displays are located in New York's Times Square area, where monthly rental costs alone often run $25,000.

TRANSIT

As a medium for reaching the millions of people who depend on streetcars, subways, or buses to take them shopping or to work and bring them home again, transit advertising is unequaled. The medium actually consists of three types: (1) *car cards,* found on the inside of public transportation vehicles, (2) *outside displays,* located on the fronts, backs, and sides of vehicles, and (3) *station posters,* placed in and around vehicle stations (as a subway station).

Car-card space is generally sold on the basis of full or partial service. Full service provides one card in every unit of transportation service. Purchase is usually made for a full, half, or quarter service, although an occasional advertiser will buy a double service which provides two cards in each vehicle. Purchase can be made in one of three ways: (1) direct from the local franchise holder, (2) through an advertising agency, or (3) from a national representative of local operators.

Statistics concerning ridership and readership are supplied for various cities from studies made by the National Association of Transportation Advertising. These show that in the larger cities, other than Los Angeles, from two thirds to three fourths of all men and from 75 to 90 percent of all women use the public transportation facilities. The average length of ride is from 25 to 30 minutes.

A study of outside displays on buses in Philadelphia revealed that a full showing reached 17 million people in a 30-day period. The audience consisted primarily of pedestrian traffic (92 percent), with only 8 percent viewing from vehicles. The heaviest exposure occurred later in the day, between 3:30 P.M. and 8:30 P.M.

Readership of car cards averages higher than for newspapers but does not show the extremes found in the latter. It is doubtful whether any car cards would ever have as low a readership as 1 percent, which is common for some newspaper advertisements. An average readership of around 25 percent is common for car cards. This is not surprising, in view of the average length of time each rider spends in a vehicle and the fact that cards remain in the car for 30 days before they are changed. With car cards, as with other printed media, readership is influenced by the interest people have in the product advertised, character of the card, size, and location in the car.

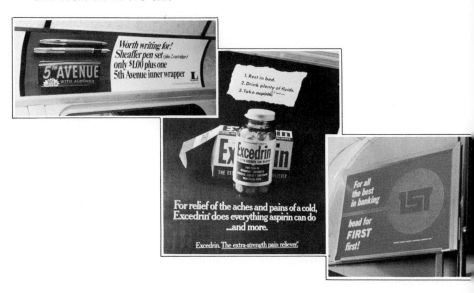

FIGURE 23–3. Typical car cards

Rates for car-card advertising vary with the number of riders but will average from 4 to 5 cents per thousand monthly rides. Space can be purchased for one month but usually not for a shorter time. The more common practice is to contract for space for one year. Discounts are generally provided if space is used for three months within one year. The production cost of cards is not a part of the space cost. The cost of cards varies materially with the quality of stock and printing. Rates, number of monthly rides, size requirements, and other valuable information relative to all types of transit advertising are found in SRDS's *Transit Advertising Rates and Data.*

The most common size for car cards is 11 inches high by 28 inches long. Two other lengths (42 and 56 inches) are also considered standard, but these latter two are in the distinct minority in use. Figure 23–4 shows some examples of outside displays.

FIGURE 23–4.   Examples of outside displays

Car-card advertising is flexible. Its use can be confined to one city or expanded to include almost any combination of markets desired. It cannot, of course, reach the farm and village market; but for metropolitan areas intense coverage is provided.

The audience delivered is a large one and includes all economic groups. Mr. Lackey summarizes the character of the transit audience as follows:

> Probably the primary characteristic of transportation advertising is that it provides a vast audience which in the aggregate runs into many billions of riders each year. Moreover, this audience can be and is made available to advertisers apparently at low cost. Inasmuch as the advertising is a by-product of the transit industry, the audience is in a sense ready-made. Thus many of the basic production and distribution costs of other media are not applicable to transportation advertising and the minimum supply price consequently tends to be lower.
>
> Not only is this audience a vast one, it is also a desirable one from an advertiser's standpoint. It is composed largely of wage earners and shoppers of all economic levels. In the case of shoppers, transportation advertising offers an advantage of

timeliness in that it may be the last contact a shopper has with advertising before buying; it is therefore the next thing to point-of-purchase advertising.[2]

SPECIALTIES[3]

According to early records, the specialty advertising industry began in the United States in 1845. It was then that an anonymous insurance salesman placed calendar pads on his advertising signs. Calendars and other simple promotional items characterized the early history of the medium. By 1900 specialty advertising encompassed such things as horse blankets, wagon umbrellas, and wooden gasoline measuring sticks. Some early items, as yardsticks and pencils, are still extensively used today.

Specialty advertising is an advertising medium employing useful articles, known as advertising specialties, that are imprinted with the advertiser's name, address, and/or sales message. Specialties are utilized to reach a preselected audience and are given without cost or obligation, thus serving as items of good will and reminder values. The specialty advertising industry consists of approximately 2,500 manufacturers, distributors, and direct selling houses. Volume is estimated to be around $500 million annually.

Advertising specialties are generally divided into three main categories: calendars, imprinted specialties or novelties, and business or executive gifts.

Calendars account for about one third of the total business done by the advertising specialty industry. They are used by virtually any business, ranging from the small retailer to the giants of American industry. For example, the Ford Motor Company distributed over three million Norman Rockwell-illustrated calendars during their 50th Anniversary celebration. Surveys have shown that 75 percent of all calendars produced and distributed are kept by the recipients. Some examples are shown in Figure 23-5.

There are more than 10,000 different types of imprinted specialties, including such typical items as ash trays, cigarette lighters, thermometers, key chains, ballpoint pens, memo pads, paperweights, rulers, and bal-

---

[2] James B. Lackey, Jr., *Transportation Advertising* (Boston: Harvard University, 1950), pp. 46–47.

[3] Information in this section comes largely from the Specialty Advertising Association, 740 N. Rush Street, Chicago, Illinois 60611, and especially a pamphlet, *Specialty Advertising*, by Walter A. Gaw.

FIGURE 23-5. Examples of imprinted calendars

loons. Several examples are shown in Figure 23–6. Often such novelties are used to tie-in with a campaign theme carried in other media.

Business or executive gifts are primarily distinguished from other specialties by price. It is usually a more prestigious item given personally on a selective basis. It may be imprinted or personalized, but usually is not. Business gifts range in price and variety, including such things as attache cases, luggage, and desk sets. Changes in the tax law have a bearing on what can properly be placed in this category. Presently, business gifts that cost more than $4 or which are not imprinted are fully deductible for the first $25 per recipient.

Advertising specialties, as all other media, are characterized by both advantages and limitations. Probably the greatest limitation of the medium is the limited amount of space available for a sales message. Often,

FIGURE 23-6. Some examples of imprinted specialties

the imprint consists of no more than the advertiser's name and address. Also to be taken into consideration when using specialties is the limited circulation generally affordable. Cost of the specialty and distribution expenses normally preclude the building of large audiences which are obtainable in some media.

The specialty advertising industry recognizes the fact that a specialty has certain intrinsic value as merchandise, but they prefer to emphasize their *advertising* value. Accordingly, the following advantages are generally credited to the medium.

1. *Ad specialties are useful items of value given without obligation.* The recipient is actually getting a useful item in return for being exposed to the advertiser's message.
2. *Ad specialties are received with appreciation and are usually kept and used frequently.* They have lasting value and, most importantly, repeat advertising exposure and impact without repeat cost.
3. *Ad specialties zero in on their target.* The market can be completely controlled by the advertiser because specialties can be created to reach a preselected audience at a specifically selected time. The advertising message is told directly to the target audience.
4. *Ad specialties can achieve preferred position.* They can be placed permanently in places such as purses, pockets, office walls, inside or on top of desks, in the home, and even in the boudoir, where no other advertising medium normally reaches.
5. *Ad specialties are welcomed by their recipients and received gratefully,* creating an atmosphere of goodwill and appreciation.
6. *Ad specialties, in addition to getting the advertising message read on initial impact, provide multiple impressions as the gift is kept and used as well as shown and exposed to others.*
7. *Ad specialties are inexpensive* whether created for a selected or mass market and because they are not competitive with other media, can be integrated into campaigns which use a variety of media.
8. *Ad specialties aid and complement other advertising and promotional methods,* and they provide the vital element of direct and personal impact.

DEALER DISPLAYS

The retailer's display space is probably worth more than many other types of advertising he might use. The National Association of Retail

Druggists considers that window space alone is worth from one fourth to one half the rent of an entire store building. Imagine, if possible, a retail store without windows and its chances of competing with an adjoining store with ample window-display space.

While windows and other display space provide the retailer with his most valuable advertising medium, he must advertise in that space either his own products or the products of a wholesaler or manufacturer. Since retailers have few products under their own brand name, display space is available to wholesalers and manufacturers. For a given manufacturer or wholesaler, the problem is one of getting his display material and his products featured by the retailer in windows and on counter, floors, and walls within the store.

In the sale of most consumer goods, the retailer is the last link in the chain of distribution from manufacturer or producer to consumer. He therefore holds an exceptionally strategic position at the point of sale. Manufacturers that can get their merchandise on display at the point of sale, where it may be seen by consumers in a buying mood, will usually be rewarded by a generous increase in sales.

Traffic

The traffic exposed to dealer-display material consists of the number of people, within a given period of time, who pass and who have an opportunity to see the display. In general, only pedestrians passing on the near side of the street would be included in traffic figures for window displays; and only those coming into the store, for interior displays. The traffic for a given store will vary according to the size of town and location in the town.

Both the volume and character of traffic are vital items in determining advertising value. In measuring character or quality of traffic, consideration should be given to sex, age, and income groups passing the displays and the reasons for their walking past the store (going to or from work, train, theater, or on a buying trip). Certain types of stores located near a railroad station will have a volume of pedestrian traffic far out of proportion to its quality as measured in terms of potential customers of that store. Furthermore, people going to and from trains are generally not in a receptive mood to buy merchandise. The same is true of people going to work.

A number of years ago some work in measuring and verifying window-display traffic was done by the Advertising Research Foundation. An intensive analysis of traffic movements was made in 19 cities chosen as representative of trading centers in the United States. In these cities more than 21,000 retail outlets were recorded, 16,578 windows of retail outlets were subjected to detailed analysis, and some 49,000,000 personal movements observed.[4] On the basis of this study, the Research Foundation concluded that there were 1.9 display windows per retail outlet.

The outstanding value of the analysis made by the Foundation was the establishment of a basis for measuring the amount of traffic and the number of windows required by an advertiser to obtain reasonable coverage of particular markets. In answering this question, markets were divided into the following four districts:

1. The central business district
2. The secondary business district or districts
3. The neighborhood business districts
4. The outlying district or districts (the remainder of the market)[5]

An advertiser wishing minimum intensity of distribution in drugstores would need one window out of every ten in each business district. This would provide a daily traffic of 25 percent of the population. The Foundation developed formulas for determining the number of windows required for greater degrees of intensity. Four types of coverage were designated: (1) minimum, (2) normal, (3) second degree, and (4) third degree. Normal distribution would provide a traffic of 50 percent of the population; second intensity, 75 percent; and third intensity, about 100 percent. The general philosophy underlying the measurement of window-display traffic is similar to that used in measuring outdoor-poster traffic.

One shortcoming of traffic figures is the heavy weighting by men pedestrians. The Foundation found that, in central business districts, traffic consisted of 51 percent men, 43 percent women, and 6 percent children. In neighborhood business districts, the proportions were 50.6 percent men, 36.6 percent women, and 12.8 percent children. Since women do most of the family buying, the effectiveness of total traffic might be somewhat diminished by the greater percentage of men pedestrians.

Kinds of dealer displays

Dealer displays can be classified into two general groups—window displays and inside displays. A wide variety of material is regularly sent

---

[4] Advertising Research Foundation, *Window Display Circulation and Market Coverage* (New York, 1937).

[5] *Ibid.*, p. 7.

to the dealer for use both in the windows and inside the store. Many display pieces can be used in either place; hence, a careful distinction between the two major groups is unnecessary.

Often the most valuable of all display material is the product itself. As has been emphasized, pictures of the product in magazine and newspaper advertisements produce better results than almost any other kind of picture. In the case of dealer-display space, the product itself, rather than merely a picture, can be shown—and shown at the point of sale. Around the product can be placed various kinds of lithographed cards, posters, and cutouts, to explain various features of the product, how it can be used, what it will do, and its price. In addition to material built around the product itself, other material stating the kind and brand of merchandise sold and containing a brief sales message may be used.

Cutouts. These consist of lithographed cardboard displays in various sizes and shapes usually constructed so they will stand without support. In their construction, dies are used to cut and crease the boards. The large displays often consist of three panels that can be used as a background for a complete window display. Since the windows of most small retail stores are open in the back, such displays are popular, although they should be sufficiently low to allow passers-by to see into the store. The background display can serve to create an atmosphere for one of the featured products as well as for related products. For example, a background for shotguns may serve for a window of hunters' equipment and supplies.

Cutouts usually have high attention-value; and if they are designed so that, not only the particular product advertised, but also related products, can be displayed, their life as useful display pieces will be lengthened. In designing and using this type of display, primary consideration should be given to displaying the merchandise itself, using the printed panel to increase the general attractiveness of the window and to help in a logical arrangement of merchandise.

Display cards. These are usually plain-shaped, medium- or small-size cards that can be used in the window or on a counter or wall. They may be reproductions of magazine or newspaper advertisements, to be used as a means of point-of-sale tie-up with other advertising efforts, or they may merely feature a brief selling message, a special offer, or a special price. If they are too large, the retailer will not use them because of space requirements. The advertiser will also find that more of them will be used if printed on both sides. Those printed on one side only provide good cardboard on which the retailer can paint his own message.

Comparable to display cards are name plates designed to be hung on walls. Of such plates, the ones most used are those that tie in with the needs of the retailer. A plate for a proprietary product may carry the term "Prescription Department" above the advertised product and thus encourage the druggist to use the plate to call attention to the location of that department. One should never lose sight of the fact that the retailer is the final judge as to what display material is to be used, and one must remember that he has much more material available than he can use.

Counter displays. While display cards may be used on counters, the usual counter display has greater utility than a card. It usually provides a method for displaying the merchandise itself. It is particularly valuable for so-called "impulse goods," where purchase is often made on sight. Quite often the package itself is designed to serve as a counter display. Examples include candy, gum, cigarettes, cigars, and cheese. Usually, only merchandise with a high turnover will rate a counter position, although occasionally long-profit items will be accorded such a place.

Cabinets and racks. Serving the same function as counter displays, but designed for more permanent use, are fine metal, wood, and glass cabinets and racks. Some are designed for use on the counter and some for use on the floor. These displays are expensive but perhaps provide as great or greater return to the advertiser as any other form. Their very costliness emphasizes their value to both the retailer and the advertiser. Consequently, the latter is careful in his distribution of such material, often requiring a certain volume of business from the retailer before providing him with a permanent cabinet or rack. The retailer, in turn, thus impressed by the value of the material, will usually give it a preferred position. Examples of products displayed in permanent racks and cabinets include electric-light bulbs, motor oil, certain types of men's clothing accessories, crackers and cookies, jewelry, and fountain pens.

Window strips. These are perhaps the least expensive of all dealer display material but often are quite productive when the retailer can be induced to use them. They consist of strips of paper of various sizes to be stuck on the windowpane. They are usually gummed on the edges to facilitate sticking. They should, of course, be designed so their use will not obstruct the view of products displayed in the window. Smaller stores are the most common users of this kind of material.

The decalcomania window sticker provides a more permanent and attractive strip. Dealers are naturally reluctant to allow many such signs to be placed on their windows, limiting them to signs for products that are popular or that carry a large profit margin. Among the types of products advertised by this kind of sign are tobacco, soft drinks, hardware items, and paint. Their principal value is to tell the public where the particular brand of goods in question can be purchased.

Getting display material used

The advertising value of space in retail stores and windows is well recognized by most retailers and manufacturers. So great, however, is the competition for such space that more material is supplied than can possibly be used. This, together with the kind of material supplied and the method used to distribute it, often reduces the percentage of material used from any given manufacturer to a small part of the total. Some studies indicate that, when no particular effort is exerted by the manufacturer to get his material displayed, only from 1 to 20 percent of it is used, but with emphasis on how, when, and why to use it, plus help in installation, as much as 80 percent will be used.

Naturally, some products will get more display space and attention than others. Sugar, flour, and similar grocery staples will not be displayed as much as fresh fruits and vegetables. The producer should study the practices of retailers in this respect before preparing his displays. For those products that do lend themselves to display, a number of methods might be employed to increase the use of display material. Manufacturers may promote window-display contests, offering monthly prizes for the best window. This method has been successful in the drug, tobacco, and grocery fields. Helps may be given the dealer in checking the results in terms of actual sales of different display material. Once the retailer can see values in terms of dollar sales and increased profits, he will be ready to give greater attention to display material.

Methods of distributing material. In the final analysis, the extent to which material is used depends largely on the methods employed in placing it in the hands of retailers. Possible distributive agencies and methods would include: (1) manufacturers' salesmen; (2) packed with merchandise itself; (3) mail; (4) wholsalers or jobbers; and (5) display crews, either in the direct employ of the advertiser, or of a regular professional display-service organization.

Of the various methods listed, the first, and particularly the last, will give better results. Many retailers are not expert in the art of dressing windows or arranging inside displays and, hence, welcome expert assistance. If such assistance results in a noticeable increase in the sales of displayed items, the advertiser will continue to receive valuable display space. The salesman or professional display man should provide the retailer with a well-rounded display, not insisting that all space be devoted to the particular product in question.

There are organizations available to the advertiser through which window-display coverage in any number of cities can be secured for given periods of time. These organizations work through local display-service groups, which contact retailers to secure the space and to install the display. The cost of such service will vary from $2.50 to $5.00 per window. Agencies will usually be granted their 15 percent commission on orders for such space.

The cost of providing professional display crews may appear to be great, but it is much better to spend money in getting material used than in preparing material for the wastebasket. Cost should be measured in terms of results; and if advertisers will check on the results obtained from various methods, the basis for a sound procedure would be established. Some advertisers have gone so far as to install display material for a dealer and, in addition, to pay him a sum for the use of space. When dealers become conscious of the real value of their window, counter, and floor space, they may insist on payment for its use in the same way that a magazine or newspaper charges for advertising space. Such development may, in fact, react to the benefit of the advertiser, for it would force him to give greater attention to the quality of material prepared and to the manner in which it is used.

Further suggestions concerning dealer displays

In developing any display, attention should be given to the character of the goods and the type of consumer to whom they might appeal. In general, goods that are popular and attractive are best for display purposes, since they will stop a greater number of passers-by. Thought should also be given to the particular buying mood of consumers. This is difficult to ascertain, but certain days and seasons give an indication of probable buying attitudes. Rainy days should encourage displays of umbrellas, raincoats, rubbers, and perhaps magazines, scrapbooks for youngsters, games, and other items for inside use. Particular kinds of commodities are associated with Easter, Thanksgiving, the opening of school, etc., and should be emphasized at those times.

The type of commodities to display, however, is not the only factor making for effectiveness. The manner of arrangement, the number of items included, and color combinations are factors of importance. There is as much value in testing the sales effectiveness of window and inside displays as in testing the effectiveness of newspaper, magazine, and other forms of advertising. What a normally good window display should do is explained by Kenneth Goode as follows:

> If your window doesn't stop passers-by, you might as well not bother with it. Take count some day. Normally a window should attract a glance from about one man in ten. And one woman in seven. So, if your window doesn't cause five out of every 100 to turn around and glance perceptibly, it isn't a display at all. And it should cause at least 2½ percent of those who glance to stop. That is to say, a window doing average should stop about 1 out of each 270 who pass. See if yours will stop one out of 250.[6]

In addition to checking on the number of people stopped by a display, changes in sales volume can be measured with a reasonable degree of accuracy. Methods discussed in later chapters should prove of value.

PACKAGES, LABELS, AND INSERTS

The problems of package design were discussed in Chapter 10, where emphasis was placed upon presenting products to the public in a form to meet consumer desires. People prefer packaged merchandise and, consequently, they get it. But packages are more than safe and attractive containers for goods—they are also a medium for carrying an advertising message.

The audiences reached by packages as a whole, when duplication and repetition is not considered, run into untold millions. The primary audience of the packages of a given manufacturer can easily be determined. Furthermore, this audience includes consumers that have demonstrated, through purchase, a definite interest in the product.

Advertising copy on packages must be brief and pictorial. It should usually be limited to the brand name, perhaps a picture of the product itself or in use, and a statement concerning its qualities, variety of uses, and methods of use. Packages are often examined and copy on them read by potential buyers before a final choice of brand is made. It is therefore highly advisable to include a brief message to help consumers judge the want-satisfying qualities of a product in their effort to make a choice. This is particularly true today when self-service is the rule in many lines of retailing.

Some items are distributed in two packages, particularly liquid and

---

[6] Kenneth Goode, *Modern Advertising* (New York: Blue Ribbon Books, 1937), p. 346.

other products put up in glass containers. In such cases, the label on the inside container should carry an advertising message similar to that on the cardboard box. These items will be of value to the purchaser and, in addition, may attract the attention and interest of nonusers who may be introduced to the product through satisfied customers. Packages thus have a secondary circulation value that should not be ignored.

Package inserts. The package insert has practically as great a circulation as the package itself and, in addition, affords a means of presenting a different kind of advertising message. There is no less costly method of carrying a piece of direct advertising to consumers. Furthermore, the audience is a very selective one because the purchase of the product itself indicates the character of its interest. The potentialities of the insert as a means of reaching a preferred list of consumers has probably not been adequately appreciated.

The package insert has been very poorly handled by many advertisers. It has too often been used as a piece of paper in which to wrap a bottle being placed in a cardboard container. Too little thought has been given to the appearance, readability, and simplicity of the insert. If the insert were keyed to the self-interest of consumers, it would have a larger audience. The great majority of users of the insert try to put a long sales story on a minimum amount of paper; they fold it in a difficult manner; and then they expect to get effective results. The same insert is included in every package, month in and month out, without thought of changing it to give repeat customers a different sales message.

Inserts could be made more profitable by—

1. Printing in legible type.
2. Emphasizing one copy theme.
3. Changing the sales message occasionally. (Shredded Wheat obtains variety by changing inserts regularly and obtains interest and continuity by encouraging consumers to look for the recurring inserts and use them in a scrapbook.)
4. Making greater use of pictures and briefer copy.
5. Judicious folding. (Fold them so that an interest-arresting picture or headline appears on the front and so that the unfolding process will be easy and logical.)
6. Printing on substantial paper and, if possible, in a form that encourages keeping (blotters, recipes on cards that can be filed, etc.).

As to the kind of information that might be included in package inserts, Paul Hillery many years ago suggested that the advertiser consider:

1. How best to use the product. (If this is a long story, as in the case of recipes, follow the plan of changing the package insert frequently. Make it a serial story, even though the customer may miss some of the installments: that's better than having her miss the entire message.)
2. How to correct troubles that may develop when using the product—service tips
3. How other items in your line will also serve to increase her happiness
4. How to fit your product in with other items with which it is naturally related
5. About new, novel, unusual uses for the product
6. About special offers which you may be making, such as premiums
7. How to make the product last longer or last better
8. How to use package leftovers
9. Use the insert as a reminder to order a new package—put the insert toward the bottom of the package[7]

These suggestions are still valid today.

SAMPLING

Sampling is based on the idea that a product will sell itself if once used. To get people to use the product, a small- or regular-size package is distributed to potential consumers. Naturally, this form of advertising is limited to merchandise of relatively low cost, with a large amount of repeat business. It is most effective in introducing a new product or in building distribution in a new territory. Breakfast food, candy, gum, and toilet articles lend themselves to sampling.

There are four general methods of sampling: (1) direct delivery to consumer or home, (2) direct distribution of coupons that can be redeemed at local retail store, (3) demonstrations in retail store, and (4) sampling in connection with other forms of advertising.

Direct delivery is usually accomplished through the use of regular crews that go from house to house, handing out small packages of the product. Better results are usually obtained if the package is handed direct to the housewife with a statement of the purpose of the sampling as well as a brief statement concerning the merits of the product. An alternative method is to distribute coupons, having the distributor give a brief sales talk concerning the product and explaining that the coupon can be redeemed at the local store. This method obtains the cooperation of the dealer, which is usually quite important.

Certain types of products can best be distributed in the store itself. This is particularly true where some sort of preparation is necessary before

---

[7] Paul Hillery, "The Neglected Package Insert," *Advertising and Selling*, October 8, 1936, p. 34.

using the product. Soup can be heated and served to customers; cookies, crackers, sandwich spreads, and preserves can be served with tea or some other drink; Instant Postum and coffee can be made before the customer. In this way, the product is sampled in its proper form and the advertiser is sure the product has reached the consumer.

A great deal of sampling is done in connection with other forms of advertising. Many newspaper and magazine advertisements carry coupons which, if sent direct to the advertiser or presented to the dealer, will bring the consumer a sample of the product. Television advertising directed to children has employed sampling to a high degree. Much of this kind of sampling is not free but, instead, requires the consumer to send money to "cover costs of packing and mailing." It has previously been pointed out that contest and premium advertising may be a form of sampling where such advertising requires the submission of proof of purchase before qualifying in a contest or receiving a premium.

Sampling is also accomplished through car-card advertising by attaching a package of coupons or "take-ones" to the card. Riders are thus invited to help themselves to the "take-one" literature and send in the coupon for a sample of merchandise.

FILMS

Advertisers have long recognized the inherent value of sound motion pictures as a means of selling ideas and goods. This medium combines sight with sound and motion. In addition, and of extreme value, motion pictures obtain the undivided attention of the audience. The major problem associated with this medium is that of obtaining an audience. Recent years have witnessed great strides in meeting this problem.

Methods of distributing films

There are two major methods of distributing advertising films: (1) theatrical, and (2) nontheatrical. The first method gives the advertiser a large audience without much effort on his part. Such an audience, however, is interested in entertainment rather than advertising. This dictates extreme care in the preparation of the advertising film. It must, in general, follow the television technique.

Two types of advertising films are in general use. One type is comparable to a movie short consisting of one reel of film. This type must be entertaining or educational in nature if it is to be accepted by the audience.

The "commercial" must be short as in broadcast advertising. The second type of theatrical film is the minute, or trailer, movie. This is comparable to the advertising of "coming attractions" regularly shown in most movie houses. Such trailers take from 45 to 90 seconds to run. They are spliced on the end of some part of the regular movie program. There is no attempt to disguise the fact that they are pure advertisements.

About 80 percent of the 10,000 or so movie theaters accept theater-screen advertising. Virtually all of an additional 4,000 drive-ins accept screen advertising. In a special study of this medium and its audience, the J. Walter Thompson Company found that during a sample week in the summer, over 56 million people saw advertising on the screens of theaters and drive-ins. For many products in this country theater-screen advertising is the lowest cost advertising available. In many foreign countries it is virtually the *only* mass sight and sound medium available.

Nontheatrical distribution has the problem of building an audience for the film. Audiences are solicited through schools, clubs, lodges, women's organizations, churches, conventions, etc. Longer films are usually used and a pure entertainment movie often run in connection with the advertiser's film.

This type of distribution may be developed through: (1) film-distributing agencies, (2) film libraries, or (3) the advertiser's own organization.

Film-distributing agencies take the responsibility of finding the audience and showing the picture. An advertiser may contract with such agencies for a certain volume of distribution. Regular reports will be furnished the advertiser.

Film libraries provide a means whereby organizations having their own projection equipment may borrow films to show to their own group. Schools and clubs make extensive use of these facilities. Advertisers can deposit prints of their films with these libraries and have them included in the library's listing.

OTHER MEDIA

Other methods of getting an advertising message or the name of the product to the public include stunts, skywriting, match covers, programs, and directories.

Of these, perhaps the use of directories has the widest application. Various industrial and trade directories provide a valuable means of advertising certain products and services. Classical sections of telephone directories are particularly valuable.

For example, a study done for the National Yellow Pages Service revealed that 83.5 million adult Americans use the Yellow Pages. The average number of references per user was 44 in a year, and 93 percent of such references were followed up with action—phoning, visiting, or writing the advertiser.

QUESTIONS AND PROBLEMS

1. What is the principal function of store signs?
2. What measurement is used to estimate the size of the potential audience exposed to outdoor poster boards?
3. How would you rate outdoor advertising as a medium for reaching particular consumer groups?
4. Outdoor advertising is essentially a medium for building and reinforcing a brand image. Do you agree or disagree? Explain.
5. What factors determine the number of poster boards needed for No. 100 coverage? For No. 50 coverage?
6. It has been urged that billboards along the roadside be eliminated because they mar the natural beauty of the country and constitute a driving hazard. What argument would you offer in defense of billboard advertising?
7. Discuss the question of waste in dealer displays and suggest methods for reducing this waste.
8. Discuss the place of sampling in advertising.
9. Some people have urged that homogeneous retail groups organize and offer window space to advertisers for a price, in much the same manner as newspaper and magazine space is sold. What suggestions would you make for developing such a group organization? What advantages would such a program give to the advertiser?
10. The Tom Sawyer company, a small producer of potato chips in a metropolitan area, sought to find a way to compete with large producers who could spend as much as thousands of dollars weekly for television and other media. The Tom Sawyer company was on a limited budget of about $2,000 a month.

    The agency hired by the company undertook extensive research. Three members of the agency spent several days in the factory observing the process of making potato chips. In fact, it was during one of these tours that a basic idea for the campaign took shape.

    It was observed that white clouds were rising from the potatoes during the preparatory process; these clouds were starch being washed out of the potatoes. In planning conferences later, "Starch Reduced" became the selling theme and the keynote of the campaign.

    Agency representatives also spent a day with each of the salesmen on trucks to get market and grocer reaction to the products, observe merchandise displays and note the type of selling being done by competition at point of purchase.

Observation of consumer purchases disclosed that 67 percent of the potato chip purchases were being made on impulse. The company then thought it logical to place major stress on a point-of-purchase campaign with a distinct attempt made at dramatizing the Tom Sawyer packages replete with the "Starch Reduced" slogan and laid out on special fluorescent displays.

After the new packages and displays had been in markets for two weeks, sales records showed a 37 percent increase over sales before the point-of-purchase campaign started.

Evaluate the use of point-of-purchase advertising for this and other types of goods. Is such advertising more valuable for impulse goods than for other types? How would you compare the relative value of the appeal "starch reduced" with that of the advertising medium used as causes for major increases in sales?

part V

Testing
advertising
effectiveness

chapter 24
THE RATIONALE
OF TESTING

RESEARCHING THE CONSUMER, the product, and the market, as discussed in earlier chapters, enlarges the advertiser's knowledge about what consumers want and why, about the want-satisfying qualities inherent in the product, about who and where his prime prospects are. Such research is useful in planning advertising strategy, in deciding what should be said to whom through what types of media to accomplish what objectives. Another kind of research generally referred to as testing is used to measure the performance of specific elements of an advertising program or of the entire program itself.

Why test?

The effectiveness of advertising depends primarily on the knowledge, skill, and experience of the people preparing it. Their ability, call it what you will—disciplined intuition, experienced judgment, skilled craftsmanship, feel, taste, sensitivity, insight, or creativity—is the thing that more often than not makes the difference between advertising that makes the cash registers ring and advertising that goes unnoticed into oblivion. However, the most widely acclaimed experts come up with a dud now and then. They, too, when confronted with several promising approaches wonder which would be best. And, of course, they don't always agree among themselves. And how did they become experts? Chances are they learned by trial and error, by recording in their minds what worked well and what didn't. These conditions point up the principal reasons for testing: *to avoid mistakes, to select the best from apparently equal alternatives, to resolve differences of opinion, and to add to the store of knowledge bearing on advertising efficiency.*

There is no precise way to determine the cost of a mistake. A single advertisement scheduled for national media typically requires an expenditure of $125,000. A single idea destined to become a campaign theme often calls for an expenditure of millions of dollars. In terms of out-of-pocket cost alone it is obvious that the prudent business man would want every assurance available that he will get maximum results. But the cost of running inferior advertising is greater than the out-of-pocket cost. The additional sales that would have been generated by superior advertising would be lost. A competitive advantage would be lost. Time would be lost. And ultimately, some profits would be lost. The loss of opportunity to do the job better must be reckoned as part of the cost of advertising that is less than the best attainable. In other words, it pays to test not only because advertising costs money, but because it makes money.

The preparation of advertising is seldom a one-man show. In the chain of events leading from the conceptualization of an ad, writers, artists, media specialists, plans board members, client executives, and occasionally clients' wives all get in the act. As it so often happens, different people with different ideas resolve their differences in different ways— arguing it out, majority rule, turning to higher authority. A reasonable approach and often an expedient one is to marshal as much evidence as possible on the relative merit of each alternative. Such evidence, if it is obtained through sound testing procedures, may not be decisive, but it should give the best alternative a better chance to prevail.

Some creative people view testing as a threat to their particular role. Some feel that it stifles creative venturesomeness. Others treat it as unwarranted interference. In the quest for certainty where perhaps there is no certainty it is conceivable that testing might be overdone. Leo Burnett refers to excessive research on the creative product as "a banana peel in the path of advertising" and clarifies his positions as follows:

> I am one who believes in going the limit in research in trying to find out what people want and why, and how best to serve them. But I believe that in its creative aspects a lot of advertising today is being analyzed, engineered, researched and nitpicked within an inch of its life.
>
> The guiding principle in many quarters today, both among advertisers and agencies, seems to be, "Play It Safe."
>
> The search for the unique selling proposition, or whatever you want to call it, has become so intense and so scientific that the same tense, tightened-up type of

thinking tends to carry over to the words and pictures. The result is a lot of very expensive advertising that is irrefutably rational but hopelessly dull.[1]

Hopes were high in the 1930's that testing techniques would be developed and put into regular practice which would establish standard performance ratings for various advertising strategies. It was assumed that an ever-expanding library of recorded test results could then be drawn upon to increase advertising efficiency. Now, more than 30 years later, no such store of knowledge has materialized. Research has not made great strides in this direction. As Norman Heller observed:

> Rarely is an attempt made to conduct the study within a conceptual framework, to extend the data beyond the immediate problem, to inter-relate it with other studies, to theory-build, or to understand beyond the immediate boundaries of the study. Our copy tests tell us which of two or three specific ads look most promising; our motivation studies tell us which themes to develop for brand X—but when the next research request comes through, the only benefit derived from these previous studies is perhaps an improvement or refinement in some research technique. To put it another way, our studies, for the most part, provide us with islands of isolated data, which live short lives.[2]

But hope springs eternal. Peter Langhoff, research director of Young & Rubicam, Inc., expressed it well when he said:

> Tests must be employed to aid in the development of increased communications efficiency. We need to know more about the symbolic power of words, colors, and pictures—why one phrase catches on, becomes part of our folklore, while another apparently no less clever, dies on the printed page. Copy tests, as part of an orderly copy research program, can teach us how to write and talk more effectively to consumers.
> This is by way of saying that copy development and copy testing should work as an organic unit. Measurement makes possible the collection, storage and use of past experience. It should build a body of usable experience which is banked in the library and in the creative blood stream rather than starting afresh at every decision point.[3]

As evidenced by extensive testing programs now underway at major corporations, such as the Du Pont Company,[4] the Ford Motor Company,

---

[1] Leo Burnett, *Communications of an Advertising Man* (Chicago: Leo Burnett Co., Inc., 1961), p. 11.

[2] Norman Heller, "The Next Development in Copy Research," speech before the Copy Research Council, New York, March 19, 1958.

[3] Peter Langhoff, "Should the Agency Test Copy?" Speech before the Eastern Annual Conference of the American Association of Advertising Agencies, November 3, 1960.

[4] *The Management and Control of the Visual Efficiency of Advertisements* (New York: The Advertising Research Foundation, Inc., 1962).

and the Scott Paper Company to name a few, and publications of the Association of National Advertisers[5] and the National Industrial Conference Board,[6] there is a resurgence of research effort to enrich the store of knowledge about advertising performance.

What to test

Theoretically, any variable subject to the advertiser's control might appropriately be tested. In practice, several factors tend to restrict testing to a small fraction of its potential. These limiting factors are: the role assigned to this kind of research, time, cost, and the efficacy of known testing techniques.

When the assigned role is to provide a quality control check of finished or nearly finished advertisements before they are scheduled for publication or broadcast in costly media, individual messages are tested rather quickly at relatively low cost per test. Such measurements are limited to visual characteristics and text matter that can be handled in assembly line laboratory checks or in speedy field trials. When the assigned role is to develop generalizations to guide strategic planning, then many variables inherent in media choices, scheduling, and budgeting, as well as in the message, are tested. Such basic research requires considerable time, much money, and elaborate experiments. In practice, peripheral quality control checks have prevailed over basic research.

Message variables. Deciding which variables to test in the advertising message depends on the way the message itself is viewed. If it is treated as a composite made up of several parts with the strength of the completed structure being no greater than the total strength of the parts, then the variables to be tested in a typical print advertisement would be the headline, the illustration, the body text, the layout, and the typography. This is a mechanistic view that fails to take into account the way the reader, who is not an ad maker, sees the advertisement. The reader is apt to see it as a single entity apart from its technical components.

If the message is treated as a dichotomy with a distinction being made between "what it says" and "how well it says it," then the variables to be tested would be the selling ideas, the information, and symbolic content

---

[5] Russell H. Colley, *Defining Advertising Goals for Measured Advertising Results* (New York: Association of National Advertisers, Inc., 1961).

[6] Harry Deane Wolfe, James K. Brown, and G. Clark Thompson, *Measuring Advertising Results* (New York: National Industrial Conference Board, Inc., 1962); Harry Deane Wolfe, James K. Brown, Stephen H. Greenberg, and G. Clark Thompson, *Pretesting Advertising* (New York: National Industrial Conference Board, Inc., 1963).

on the one hand and the various verbal and visual devices used to impart the content on the other. This, of course, is a fictitious distinction, because ideas cannot be considered apart from the means used to communicate them. A given proposition presented as a single sentence on a 3-inch by 5-inch card can hardly be considered the same as when it is presented in the context of a finished advertisement.

If the message is treated as a gestalt or a totality greater than the sum of its parts, then the variables to be tested would always be presented in the context of an entire advertisement. Time and cost factors in pretest situations, especially for television commercials, might prohibit the preparation of finished ads, but the nearer the finished form the better. Then, any of the variables—appeals, themes, propositions, rhetorical style, symbolic content, visual devices, format, typography, illustration technique, etc.—would be manipulated to measure performance differences in the total message environment.

Media variables. The alternatives encountered at four levels of media decisions mark the wide range of media testing opportunities.

First, the advertiser must decide which among broad classes of media (newspapers, television, magazines, radio, outdoor, direct mail, etc.) he is to use.

Second, he must decide on the sub-classes of media. What kind of newspapers: Daily? Sunday? Evening? Morning? What kind of television or radio: Spot? Network? Regional? What kind of magazines: Women's? Shelter? General? Farm?

Third, he must select specific media vehicles: Which newspapers in Chicago? Which television stations in St. Louis? Magazine A, B, or C? Or all three? What combination of vehicles is to be used?

Fourth, he must specify space units: Full page? Half-page? Spread? And broadcast time units: Thirty seconds? Twenty seconds? Sixty seconds? And position: Back cover? Front of book? Sports section? ROP? And television program environment: In what program, if sponsored show? Between what programs, if not?

Considerable data bearing on these alternatives are available in the form of circulation reports and audience measurements. Such data are useful, but they do not fully explain differences in media performance. The so-called "qualitative factors" are significant too. Short of testing, the advertiser can only infer the effect of these factors by examining editorial and program content.

Obviously, advertising has to be placed in media to test media alternatives. This can be costly. The cost can be kept down, however, by experimenting in local markets and in regional editions of national magazines. If seemingly sound alternatives are tested, there should be some advertising value received for the space and time costs incurred.

Scheduling variables.   Important, but seldom researched variables are timing, frequency, and continuity. Consumer behavior is largely influenced by time—season of the year, week of the month, day of the week, and hour of the day. Seasonal influence is obvious in the case of Christmas gift items, Easter bonnets, antifreeze, and swim suits. And good judgment would suggest that advertising of these items be heaviest in the peak buying seasons. But how far ahead should the season be anticipated? We've seen Christmas selling moved ahead to the first part of November. For some gift items perhaps year-round advertising would be more effective than a concentrated schedule in only the gift buying seasons. Not so many years ago grocery advertising in newspapers was heaviest on Friday, the day before the biggest sales day of the week. Now such advertising is heaviest on Thursdays. In other words, traditional assumptions that have guided the timing of advertising are not necessarily valid.

Should the schedule be concentrated in an intensive burst or should it be spread out over a longer period? Should continuity be sacrificed for frequency or vice versa? For the same expenditure should a smaller number of consumers be exposed to the advertising many times or should a larger number be exposed fewer times? The strategic importance of these variables and the paucity of research on them makes scheduling a promising area for testing in the future.

Budgeting variables.   How much should be spent for advertising? How should the total be allocated to markets, to media, to sales territories, and to specific items in the product line? These are the most complicated questions of all, not only because the budget affects all other advertising variables but also because all other variables affect the budget. The economizing advertiser recognizes that there can be as much waste in spending too little as in spending too much. But how much is too little and how much is too much? Without some measure of the various yields from various increments of advertising, budget decisions are mere speculations.

In a report on *Measuring Advertising Results* prepared by the National Industrial Conference Board it was observed that "most companies have no idea of how much they really should be spending on advertising or what they should expect to receive in return. Prudently managed companies that would never think of appropriating funds for new plants or equipment without first carefully studying the purpose, the cost, and the expected yield readily appropriate similar amounts for advertising with only a vague idea of what will be accomplished."[7]

Operations research has produced some interesting models or theoretical statements of the relationship between budgeting variables and profit yields. Individual advertisers, however, must actually measure these relationships through testing or experimentation before they can be of much use in making budget decisions.

When to test

Testing is appropriate at any stage of the advertising process. In the planning stage it may be used to test the efficacy of alternative appeals or themes. In the execution stage it may be a matter of testing alternative means of presentation. In the quality control stage advertisements may be tested to see that they meet predetermined standards of performance. In retrospect, campaigns may be tested after they have run to determine what results were achieved.

Pretesting and posttesting are popular terms to distinguish between testing done prior to publication or broadcast and testing done afterwards. Since the variable inherent in selecting media, scheduling, and budgeting cannot be tested without actually running the advertising, the terms pretesting and posttesting apply only to the measurement of messages. Pretesting increases the likelihood of preparing the most effective messages before media costs are incurred and before profitable business is lost by failure to run the best advertisements available. Pretesting should be to advertising what the proving ground is to the automobile manufacturer. It should eliminate weaknesses before consumers force such elimination either by indifference or by negative response to inferior advertisements.

Posttesting requires a greater expenditure of money and time, but it permits testing of advertisements under actual running conditions and overcomes the artificiality of pretest situations. Some of the advantages of both posttesting and pretesting can be enjoyed when advertisements are run on a small scale in a few test markets before embarking on a full-scale national campaign.

When the stakes are high—when millions of dollars are invested in an advertising program or in a single theme, when thousands of dollars are

---

[7] Wolfe, Brown, and Thompson, *op. cit.,* p. 4.

spent to run a single advertisement, when advertising is the only or the dominant selling force in the marketing mix—these are times when testing would seem to be most appropriate. Yet, it would behoove the small-scale advertiser to test, too. Efficiency is a relative concept. The dollar amount may not be as great in small business, but the importance of efficiency may be even greater. As we shall see in subsequent chapters, simple, inexpensive tests can be tailor made for the small advertiser, just as more elaborate ones can be designed to meet the more complex problems of the big spenders.

Testing may be done sporadically or continuously depending on the role assigned to it—sporadically, if only called upon when the experts disagree or when the client demands; continuously, if used for quality control or as an approach to seeking optimum solutions to advertising problems.

How to test

There is no single best way to test. Different techniques have been developed to test different advertising variables in terms of different aspects of effectiveness. We have seen, for example, that pretesting techniques are well suited to measuring message variables, but are not appropriate for measuring media, scheduling, and budgeting variables. Also, it is apparent that television and radio messages call for techniques different from those used in testing magazine advertisements. Since the ultimate purpose of most advertising is to increase sales profitably, it would seem that a test which would tell us how sales would be affected by alternative strategies would be the "best" test. This would be true if there were enough time, enough money, enough importance attached to the problem, and enough confidence in the experimental design to undertake a sales results test. These conditions are prerequisite to such a test because there is no quick and easy way to control all the many factors influencing sales of a product. Seldom do these conditions exist. Usually, the advertiser wants quick answers to immediate problems whose solution he does not consider important enough to warrant the investment of a large sum of money.

Since direct measures of sales effectiveness are so seldom practical, researchers have turned to "intermediate criteria" of effectiveness. Reasoning that advertising must function as communication before it can influence a sale, they have designed various tests to measure communication performance in terms of getting attention, arousing interest, transmitting information, building an image, being understood, inspiring confidence, engendering favorable attitudes, registering selling points, portraying benefits, and making a lasting impression. Assuming that persuasion is a gradual process and that the function of advertising is to *predispose* people toward buying, researchers have designed still other tests to measure awareness of the advertised product, knowledge of what it has to offer, attitudes toward it, preference for it, and willingness to buy it.

As evidenced by a recent publication of the Association of National Advertisers, advertising managers are becoming more concerned with what people think of the *product* as a result of advertising, not merely with what people think of the *advertising* itself:

> The purpose of an advertisement is not just to get itself seen. It is not just to get itself heard or read. The purpose of an advertisement is to convey information and attitudes about a product (service, company, cause) in such a way that the consumer will be more favorably disposed toward its purchase.
>
> . . . Obviously, an ad must be seen before it is read. Obviously a viewer must physically be present to receive a television announcement. *Traffic counts* of the number of people who are exposed to ads, who stop, look and read or listen, are necessary and helpful. But they do not go far enough. In addition we need to know—
>
> . . . How many *more* people are *more acutely aware* of our brand or company name after being exposed to our advertising?
>
> . . . How many more people comprehend the features, advantages and benefits of the product because of the advertising?
>
> . . . How many more people are favorably disposed (rationally or emotionally) toward the purchase of the product?
>
> . . . How many more people have gone the whole route—taken action by asking for, or reaching for, the product?[8]

In a sense, every test is an experiment to measure the relationship between advertising variables on the stimulus side and changes in perception, knowledge, attitudes, predispositions, and other relevant behavior on the response side. In the ideal experiment the research works on the stimulus side with one variable at a time or with several variables the interactions of which he precisely controls, and on the response side with measures that clearly isolate the effects of the stimulus variable. Such ideal experimental conditions seldom, if ever, are obtained in advertising where causation is multiple, complex, and simultaneous—where each stimulus variable produces many effects and each effect is the result of many causes. The researcher, therefore, must exercise considerable judgment in deciding which measure of response is to be used.

---

[8] Colley, *op. cit.,* pp. 35–36.

If he tries to measure too many aspects of advertising performance at once he will end up in a state of confusion. If he measures only one or two peripheral aspects of advertising effectiveness very neatly, his results will seem too sterile and unrealistic to those who must use the test results for decision making. If he uncritically equates recall with impact or attitude change with sale in the mind he may often be making wholly unwarranted leaps of faith.[9]

Sound sampling procedures should be used in testing as in all forms of advertising research. Test results can only be generalized to real life if the people on whom the test is conducted are representative of the advertiser's market. When pretesting messages that are designed to reach a particular market segment through a particular medium, the sample should be made up of people in that segment who are likely to be exposed to that medium. When experimenting in test market areas, the areas selected should be representative of the broader market which the advertising eventually will reach. Size of the sample should be governed by the purpose of the test. For quality control purposes—to avoid mistakes, to check on comprehension of specific phrases, to check on believability of claims—relatively small samples may be adequate. If 25 out of the first 30 respondents get a wrong impression from a proposed advertisement, it should not be necessary to complete 100 interviews to discover that something is wrong with the ad. On the other hand, the testing of alternative themes for a major campaign may require a relatively large sample to assure selection of the strongest theme. In posttesting, a large number of interviews may be necessary to reach an adequate subsample of respondents who were exposed to the advertising in question.

Where is the test to be administered: In a laboratory or in the field? How are the advertising variables to be exposed to respondents: Artificially or naturally? How are responses to be obtained: Forced or voluntary?

In laboratory testing, consumers are brought individually or in a group into a studio or auditorium where they are confronted with some form of advertising—print, television, or radio. Print ads are handed to them separately, or bound in a dummy magazine, or projected on a screen, or shown through some kind of apparatus to vary the illumination, distance, exposure time, or visual field. Television commercials are projected on a large screen or transmitted via closed-circuit to a regular television set. Taped radio commercials are piped through a studio sound system or through standard receiving sets. Responses to the material presented are

---

[9] Leo Burnett Co., Inc., Research Department. Unpublished report on advertising pretests.

obtained in various ways—through direct questioning, written question-naires, rating scales, preexposure to postexposure changes in attitudes and brand preferences, or through various kinds of laboratory apparatus, such as opinion-voting machines, eye cameras, the psychogalvanograph, the tachistoscope, and binocular rivalry test equipment.

Laboratory testing offers the advantages of speed, low cost, and a high degree of control. The researcher can be sure that the respondents saw, read, or heard the material in question. He can control the way they were exposed. He can measure responses immediately, before confusion and forgetting intervene. He can use technical apparatus for presenting the material and measuring response. He can pretest some material, tele-vision commercials for example, that could not be as readily presented in the field. However, the validity of laboratory findings is questionable. Forced exposure in such a setting does not square with "real life." The people who agree to serve as subjects for such tests may not be represent-ative of the advertiser's market.

Testing in the field does not necessarily overcome the obstacles of the laboratory. If a respondent in her home is shown some advertisements, or is asked to look through a magazine, or to watch a commercial, the exposure is forced and artificial. Some researchers have sought to reduce artificiality by inserting test ads in a dummy magazine or in a limited number of copies of a regular magazine and by leaving these magazines in the home for normal reading. On the response side, whether a re-spondent is questioned in the laboratory or in the home, his or her reac-tion to the advertisement is likely to be different than it would be in the normal course of events. However sophisticated the measuring device, it "always represents a less than perfect means of *inferring* something about the respondent's reaction to the advertisement. The research has no *direct* way of observing whether or not the correspondent is more or less aware of, interested in, or apt to buy the product. This automatically means that any reaction obtained to the advertisement includes reactions to both the advertisement *and* the test."[10]

Controlled experiments, in which the advertising is actually published or broadcast and the voluntary responses of consumers are objectively observed, offers the most promise for testing under "real" conditions. Such experiments are designed so that one sample of consumers is ex-posed to the advertising variable and another sample is not. If a signifi-cant difference in the active response of the two samples is observed, the

---

[10] *Ibid.*

difference is attributed to the advertising variable. The exposed and non-exposed samples can be achieved in advance by using split run or by selecting several local market areas, some of which will get the advertising and the others won't. Or, the two samples can be isolated through audience tracing techniques after the advertising has run. Differences in the overt responses of the two groups are registered in the form of inquiries, mail orders, or product purchases. Controlled experiments will be discussed further in Chapter 27.

Considering all the various combinations of exposure techniques and response measures, it is no wonder that such a wide variety of tests are used. For classification purposes the response side has dominated. Thus, tests are generally classified as those based on opinion and attitudes, those based on recognition and recall, those based on inquiries, and those based on sales results.

Criteria for testing the test

We have noted that instead of a single test there are many different techniques to test different variables in terms of different aspects of effectiveness. It is apparent, therefore, that testing itself poses challenging problems in decision making, the very process it is intended to serve. The skilled researcher should be called upon to design and execute most tests, especially the more complicated ones. However, the decision maker, whatever his particular role in advertising, should be well enough informed to evaluate test results in terms of their validity, reliability, and relevance.

Validity. The most important question that needs to be raised regarding any test concerns its validity—does the test actually measure what it purports to measure? The question is not intended to cast doubt on the researcher's integrity, although this might be appropriate at times, but rather to challenge the test itself. The determination of validity requires some criterion of the performance the test is designed to predict. For example, if a pretest is designed to predict the sales effectiveness of alternative themes, some criterion of ultimate sales effectiveness would be required to validate the test. But sales resulting from an advertising theme are exceedingly difficult to trace. Consequently, tests usually resort to compromise measures (attention, comprehension, believability, memorability, etc.) and are formulated in terms of *inferred* psychological functions for which no objective verification is available. The tests are validated "logically," but not "empirically."

Empirical validation would involve the comparison of two sets of data, test scores, and criterion measures, on the same advertising variable. A high correlation between test scores and criterion measures would indicate a high degree of validity for the test. For example, to validate a consumer opinion test to be used by a mail order advertiser in selecting selling themes, ultimate mail order sales would be the criterion. Test scores would be obtained for several different themes. Then all the themes would be used in a split run and records would be kept on the volume of mail orders produced by each theme. A high correlation between test scores and mail orders would signify that the themes which scored high on the test had been relatively successful in producing mail orders, while those scoring low on the test had been inferior producers of orders. A low correlation would indicate little correspondence between test scores and criterion measures, and hence poor validity for the test.

Reliability. The reliability of a test refers to the consistency of results obtained when the same advertising variable is tested again and again. If the results varied sharply from one application to the next, the testing technique would be in doubt. In its broadest sense, test reliability indicates the extent to which differences in test results are attributable to errors of measurement or to factors not controlled in the test. Thus, when the researcher tries to maintain uniform testing conditions by controlling the sample, the testing environment, the instructions to respondents, the wording of questions, the recording of responses, time limits, and other such factors, he is seeking to make the test results more reliable. The most obvious method for determining reliability is to repeat the same test of the same advertising variable on successive matched samples of respondents. The higher the correlation from application to application the greater is the test's reliability.

Relevance. Since it is not practical to test every aspect of advertising performance every time, careful attention must be given to the relevance of the variables and response measures selected. Whenever possible the test should go to the heart of the most important decisions. It should not dwell on peripheral matters that might be neatly measured but which contribute little to overall efficiency. Perhaps too much testing time has been devoted to mechanical details such as the logotype, the typography, the layout, the size, position, color versus black and white, and not enough to the underlying proposition, the symbolic content, and the meaningfulness of the message. Media costs represent the biggest outlay of funds, but relatively few substantial tests of media variables have been done. It may well be that the more important the matter, the more difficult it is to test. But if difficulty is permitted to overrule importance there can be little progress.

Before undertaking a test the objectives to be served by the advertising should be clearly defined. As Lucas and Britt caution:

> Without clear-cut objectives for the advertising, there can be no clear-cut objectives for the advertising research. The research can be done in dozens of different ways, and there is no single *best* way to test advertising effectiveness. But the choice of methods can be narrowed down effectively if the research practitioner can get a statement of advertising objectives more specific (and thus less whimsical) than "Which of these campaigns will sell the most goods?" or "Which ad will do the best job?"[11]

The task, then, of initially establishing advertising objectives in order to properly research advertising effectiveness is a function of management.

For research to be able to measure advertising effectiveness, management must be willing to commit the effort and the discipline to clearly and concisely state exactly what it is that management expects advertising to do in terms that are not only measurable but realistic.

Programs to measure advertising effectiveness must be initiated by management; must be constructed upon management's concept of how it believes advertising works; must be designed to meet management's expressed needs and interests.

So, when we talk about a company's advertising effectiveness program, we are really describing the basic operating concepts under which its management conducts its advertising—the convictions upon which advertising budgets are based.[12]

The test should be relevant to the particular advertising objectives at hand. If the objective is to launch a new product or a new improvement in an established product, the test should focus on the news value, excitement, and brand identification in the advertising. If the objective is to obtain new users of the product, the test should focus on attitude change among nonusers. If the objective is to offset competitive claims, the test should focus on the strength of the appeal and believability. If the objective is to build an image, that is what the test should measure. In other words, tests should be designed to fit the problem, problems should not be cut to fit existing testing techniques.

QUESTIONS AND PROBLEMS

1. Since advertisers themselves are the primary beneficiaries of testing work, why do they not insist that all their advertising be tested?

---

[11] Darrell Blaine Lucas and Steuart Henderson Britt, *Measuring Advertising Effectiveness* (New York: McGraw-Hill Book Co., 1963), p. 8.

[12] Stanley J. Pokempner, Vice President, Audits and Surveys, in a speech before the New York chapter of the American Marketing Association as quoted in *Media/scope,* Vol. 10 (June, 1966), p. 23.

2. Do you believe that testing advertising effectiveness will eventually make past experiences and human judgments unnecessary?

3. Will a widespread use of testing reduce the need for highly trained copywriters, artists, media buyers, etc.? Discuss.

4. If you were a publisher or an executive in an advertising agency, what would be your attitude toward testing?

5. "Because testing is not a recognized scientific substitute for human judgment and experiences, the business executive should not place much faith in testing advertising effectiveness." Do you agree? Why?

6. The direct cost of running advertisement A in magazine X is the same as that of running advertisement B in magazine X. Is the actual cost of each of these advertisements therefore the same? Why?

7. The director of research in one of the leading advertising agencies uses the term "copy research" instead of the term "copy testing" when referring to the agency's work in attempting to predict the relative effectiveness of alternative copy approaches. Which of these two terms do you think would be more acceptable to copywriters?

8. Would it be better to test a whole advertisement or the headline, copy, and illustration separately? Discuss.

9. Why are direct measures of sales effectiveness seldom practical?

10. What value has a measure of communication when the real objective is to sell the product?

11. It has been said that if the researcher "measures only one or two peripheral aspects of advertising effectiveness very neatly, his results will seem too sterile and unrealistic to those who must use the test results for decision making. . . ." How can the researcher solve this problem?

12. How might it be possible to find out if advertising test measures themselves are really impartial and accurate?

13. Do you think people behave differently when they are being asked questions about their behavior than they would normally? Why? How could this affect test results?

14. Would it be better to measure the consumer's attitude toward the advertisement or the consumer's attitude toward the product after seeing the advertisement? Why?

15. It is said that "any reaction obtained to the advertisement includes reactions to both the advertisement *and* the test." Is there some way to separate these reactions for measurement? What would it be?

chapter 25
OPINION AND
ATTITUDE TESTS

THE CONSUMER is king. Let's ask the king. This, in a few words, expresses the logic of various tests that go directly to the consumer and seek his opinions, attitudes, or other reactions to the advertising in question. The basic assumption of such tests is that the people to be influenced can be helpful in selecting the most influential advertising ideas. This is not to say that consumers should be the final arbiters of which messages to run, but rather that their reactions to the alternatives at hand can be a useful guide to the advertiser's judgment.

The principal methods for obtaining consumer reactions are (1) those that ask for opinions through direct questioning, (2) those that measure attitudes through the use of rating scales, and (3) those that probe for underlying reactions through indirect questioning or projective techniques.

Opinion ratings

The most direct approach is to show a few proposed advertisements to a number of consumers and ask them which one they think would be most effective. In the early days of testing this is what was done. The method was called the "consumer-jury test," reflecting the role of consumers as jurors rendering a verdict. The idea of going to the consumer has prevailed, but some refinements have been made in the criteria for judging effectiveness and in the rating techniques employed.

Selecting the test group

In selecting a test group of consumers, as in selecting any sample, the first question to be answered is: What large group of consumers is the relatively small test group intended to represent? Or, in other words, what universe is to be sampled? A partial answer might be that the test group should represent the consumers to whom the advertising is addressed. But to *what* consumers is the advertising addressed? To present buyers or prospective buyers or both? To narrow, well-defined market segment or a broad anonymous public? To consumers who are regular users of the medium which will carry the message or to consumers who seldom, if ever, are exposed to the medium? It would seem that the target audience, and therefore the universe, should be composed of prime prospects whose characteristics are well defined and who are regular users of the scheduled medium. However, for many products such prime prospects are not clearly identified, and even if they were, the individual members of such a universe could not be readily isolated for testing purposes. As a result, test groups of respondents are apt to be selected by judgment sampling instead of probability sampling methods.

Selecting respondents for personal interviews is relatively simple when the advertiser's market is highly concentrated geographically or when it is so widespread that a high percentage of the general public can be considered prospects. Selection is most difficult when the advertiser has a thin national market. If the test is to be conducted by mail, which is especially appropriate for industrial advertisers, the difficulty of selection depends on the quality of available mailing lists.

The problem of sample bias or lack of representativeness is ever present when selecting test groups. Some consumers are more available and more willing to serve as respondents than others. Women generally are more available than men. People who have a high regard for their own opinions are more apt to serve than those who are not so sure of things. On the assumption that it does not significantly affect validity of the test some researchers are willing to tolerate a biased sample. However, the possibility that selected respondents do not reflect the opinions of all prospects should not be overlooked.

Size of the sample often is governed by the responses registered in successive interviews. If a high degree of consistency is noted in the early opinions expressed, a relatively small sample, perhaps 30 to 40, is likely to be considered adequate. If opinions are more evenly divided, a larger sample is used. However, consistency alone should not be the determinant of sample size. Early interviews might be concentrated among a narrow segment of prospects whose similar reactions do not reflect the wider differences of opinion that would be expressed by segments not yet reached. Sample size should be determined by balancing factors such as the heterogeneity of the advertiser's market, the variance in anticipated responses, the probable error to be tolerated, the time available, and the funds provided for the test.

Criteria for judging

A critical factor in opinion testing is the criterion against which respondents are asked to judge. As indicated in the following questions different criteria might be used:

1. Which advertisement do you *like* best?
2. Which advertisement do you find most *interesting?*
3. Which advertisement *convinces* you most of the superiority of the product?
4. If you were looking through a magazine, which advertisement would you most likely *notice* first?
5. Which advertisement would you most likely *read* first?
6. Which advertisement would most likely cause you to *buy* (name of product)?

Each of these questions employs a different criterion. The first three involve immediate reactions—*liking, interesting, convincing.* The last three questions are hypothetical and require the respondent to speculate what his behavior would be if he were exposed to the advertisements in the normal course of events sometime in the future. The first three are likely to yield more valid results, but are not as relevant to ultimate buying behavior. The last question is the most relevant, but the least likely to produce valid results. Researchers tend to favor the immediate, nonhypothetical, nonspeculative criteria. They question the ability of people to predict ultimate responses to advertisements encountered in artificial test situations.

Dissatisfaction with a single criterion has led some researchers to seek opinions on several bases—interest, comprehension, believability, personal pertinence, etc. For example, each respondent might be asked to rate the advertisements on the basis of three or four of the above listed questions. However, once he has registered his opinion on the first criterion, chances are he will rank the ads in the same order on subsequent criteria. He is apt to rate the best-liked ad highest in all respects. Psychologists call this the "halo effect."

Whatever criterion is specified, there is no assurance that it will be interpreted by respondents as the researcher intends, or that it will be used at all in reaching an opinion. Asking consumers to rate ads on the basis of believability in no way guarantees that their choices will be made on the basis of believability. Some kind of undefinable feeling may be the controlling factor. Also, respondents tend to vote against negative appeals and hard selling copy, yet such approaches often are effective in advertising.

Rating techniques

When more than two advertisements are opinion tested, it is desirable to have the respondent select not only the best, but also the second best, the third best, and so on. Two methods used to facilitate comparison and ranking are: (1) order-of-merit, and (2) paired comparisons.

Order-of-merit method. In the order-of-merit method the respondent is handed the several proposed advertisements and asked to arrange them in rank order. Score sheets indicating the rankings by each respondent are compiled to obtain a composite picture of the rankings by the entire test group. Table 25–1 illustrates the composite score sheet from a test involving 8 advertisements and 25 respondents. By averaging the scores the relative standing of each advertisement can be observed. Thus, ad F in first place with an average score of 2.52 fared considerably better than ad H with an average score of 6.04.

When asked to rank more than six or seven advertisements, several of which appear to have nearly equal merit, the respondent finds that the task is rather difficult. The paired comparisons method, to be described next, makes the task somewhat easier.

Paired comparisons method. This method consists of comparing each advertisement with every other advertisement in the group. At any one time, only two advertisements are being judged. As each comparison is made, the winner of the pair is listed. Then another pair is compared and the winner listed. This procedure is continued until each advertisement has been paired with each of the others. The number of comparisons necessary increases rapidly as the number of advertisements increases. The number of comparisons is equal to

$$\frac{n\,(n-1)}{2}$$

where n equals the number of advertisements. Thus, where 8 advertisements are to be ranked, 28 comparisons will be necessary. This is about the upper limit for number of advertisements. If the number is any larger, the procedure becomes too burdensome.

TABLE 25–1. Opinions of 25 respondents concerning the relative merit of eight advertisements

Respondents	Advertisements							
	A	B	C	D	E	F	G	H
1	1	5	7	8	3	4	2	6
2	4	7	6	3	2	1	5	8
3	1	8	5	3	4	2	7	6
4	6	4	2	1	5	3	8	7
5	2	7	4	6	3	5	1	8
6	5	8	3	2	4	1	7	6
7	2	7	6	5	4	1	8	3
8	7	6	5	4	1	2	3	8
9	2	5	7	8	6	1	4	3
10	4	6	8	5	1	2	3	7
11	3	2	1	4	7	5	6	8
12	5	7	6	2	4	3	1	8
13	3	8	7	1	6	2	5	4
14	4	7	8	5	3	2	6	1
15	2	4	8	6	3	1	5	7
16	4	3	6	1	8	7	2	5
17	1	3	7	6	4	2	5	8
18	1	2	8	3	6	4	7	5
19	6	7	2	5	1	3	4	8
20	5	8	7	2	6	1	3	4
21	4	1	2	7	8	5	3	6
22	1	6	3	5	7	2	8	4
23	5	7	3	4	2	1	6	8
24	5	2	7	4	3	1	6	8
25	4	8	6	1	7	2	3	5
Total	84	138	134	101	108	63	118	151
Average	3.36	5.52	5.36	4.04	4.32	2.52	4.72	6.04
Rank	2	7	6	3	4	1	5	8

Table 25–2 shows how a score card would look after a respondent had completed the comparisons for eight advertisements. A letter representing each ad is listed along the top and at the side of the card. Ad A compared with B and the winner of these two is listed in the square opposite

TABLE 25–2.   Individual score card in paired comparison test

	A	B	C	D	E	F	G	H
A	—							
B	A	—						
C	C	C	—					
D	A	B	C	—				
E	E	E	C	E	—			
F	A	B	C	D	E	—		
G	G	G	C	G	G	G	—	
H	A	B	C	D	E	H	G	—

B. Then A is compared with C and the winner listed opposite C. After A has been compared with all others, B is compared with the remaining six, then C with the remaining five, and so on. A single count of the number of times each ad won would determine the ranking. For the score card in Table 25–2 the ranking is as follows:

	A	B	C	D	E	F	G	H
Number of times a winner	4	3	7	2	5	0	6	1
Rank	4	5	1	6	3	8	2	7

To reduce the "halo effect" in the paired comparison method an advertisement from one pair would not be used in the next succeeding pair. When comparing five or more ads it is possible to arrange a sequence of different pairs—AB, CD, AE, BD, AC, DE, BC, etc. The sequence should be rotated through successive interviews. Another refinement would be to alternate each ad between left-hand and right-hand position as it is presented to the respondent. This would reduce position bias.

The rankings compiled in any opinion test should be subjected to appropriate statistical tests of significance to determine whether or not the differences among scores are due to respondent opinions or to chance.

Evaluation

Opinion ratings are open to question on several counts. Do respondents report their own reactions or do they turn "expert" and try to estimate other people's reactions? Are the reactions reported in an interview situation apt to be the same as those occurring in normal exposure? Are the criteria used by respondents relevant to advertising effectiveness? Are opinion tests discriminating enough to establish significant rankings between advertisements of similar quality?

Chances are that many respondents do assume the role of "expert" or "critic," a role they are not qualified to fill. Their opinions are of little importance if they set themselves up as critical, artistic, and perceptive judges of questions they have never asked themselves and have no reason to ask themselves. There is a strong possibility that respondents employ irrelevant criteria, such as "cleverness" or "cuteness," and seek to make favorable impressions on the interviewer by ranking rational, pleasant, neutral advertisements ahead of emotional, negative, intrusive ones. The few attempts that have been made to check the validity of opinion tests have indicated that such tests are successful in discriminating between extremely good and extremely bad advertisements, a distinction the advertiser himself generally has little difficulty in making. However, they are not as successful in differentiating ads of similar quality, the kind of task the advertiser is most likely to assign to testing. In other words, opinion tests function well when least needed, and not so well when most needed.

Consumer opinions can serve a useful purpose, however, and they still are sought, but more often for checking on particular strengths or weaknesses in individual advertisements, than for ranking alternative ads.

ATTITUDE MEASUREMENT[1]

In an attempt to get at more specific consumer reactions than gross opinion and to measure intensity as well as direction of the reactions, researchers have turned to various attitude scaling techniques. Whereas opinion ratings force the respondent to generalize, to conceal points of weakness in higher rated advertisements as well as points of strength in lower rated ones, and to conceal "how much" higher he rates the superior ad, attitude scales seek to remove the burden of generalization, to reveal specific strengths or weaknesses, and to quantify reactions.

An attitude is often defined as a predisposition to react in an evaluative way—to like or not like, to feel "it's for me" or "it's not for me"—toward a designated class of stimuli. As such, attitudes cannot be directly ob-

---

[1] For a more detailed discussion of attitude measurement, see Irving Crespi, *Attitude Research* (Chicago: American Marketing Association, 1965).

served, but must be inferred from overt behavior, both verbal and nonverbal. Attitude scales in general use are designed to provide a measure of a person's relative position along a continuum from favorable to unfavorable concerning a particular issue or object. The respondent is confronted with a number of statements which are relevant to the behavior in question and asked to indicate his position on the scale. Positions on the scale are numbered or assigned numbers in scoring. Statement scores can be combined to get a group score. Attitude information also is obtained through nonscaling methods such as depth interviewing and projective techniques.

On the assumption that advertising should engender favorable attitudes toward itself as well as the product, some form of attitude measurement is incorporated in many test designs. Some tests deal with attitudes toward components—themes, messages, media, etc. Others deal with attitudes toward the overall advertising effort. Still others deal with attitudes toward the thing advertised—the product, the brand, the corporation. Researchers who feel compelled to stop short of measuring sales results are inclined to treat attitude change as an appropriate measure of advertising effectiveness.

A recent survey of research directors of the 50 largest advertising agencies revealed that attitude tests are highly valued as a research tool. Attitude was the highest rated criterion for determining *campaign* effectiveness, and was considered to have "high" value for testing single advertisements.[2]

Rating scales

A popular scaling device is the *semantic differential,* which requires respondents to make repeated judgments against a series of bipolar-adjectival scales. To see how this works, look at the picture of the man in Figure 25–1. Is he sad or is he cheerful? Is he worried or unworried? The advertiser knew what kind of mood he wanted this picture to project, but would consumers see it that way? To find out, he ran a test using the semantic differential. Respondents were shown the picture and rating scale and asked to "rate where this man fits on these scales."

The majority of respondents rated the man in the mood that was

---

[2] Lee Adler, Allan Greenberg, and Darrell B. Lucas, "What Big Agency Men Think of Copy Testing Methods," *Journal of Marketing Research,* Vol. 2 (November, 1965), pp. 339–45.

Average

Rich	(——)	(——)	(——)	(——)	(——)	(——)	(——)	Poor
Short	(——)	(——)	(——)	(——)	(——)	(——)	(——)	Tall
Healthy	(——)	(——)	(——)	(——)	(——)	(——)	(——)	Unhealthy
Worried	(——)	(——)	(——)	(——)	(——)	(——)	(——)	Unworried
Likeable	(——)	(——)	(——)	(——)	(——)	(——)	(——)	Unlikeable
Cheerful	(——)	(——)	(——)	(——)	(——)	(——)	(——)	Sad

FIGURE 25–1. Is he sad or is he cheerful? Is he worried or unworried?

intended and the picture was used with the headline, "Peaceful Outlook Pictured Here."[3]

The principal advantage of the semantic differential is its simplicity. Also, when administered quickly, it might elicit the kind of spontaneous responses that reveal underlying attitudes more clearly than would lengthy deliberation. In its simplicity, however, lies its weaknesses. Some attitudes cannot be verbalized. The adjectives used may not reveal the most important attributes of the thing judged. Words have different meanings and the intervals on the scales are perceived differently by different people.

Another scaling technique, sometimes referred to as a *three-dimensional* or *trivariant* test, is especially appropriate for evaluating a relatively large number of possible advertising themes. Each theme is typed on a 3 x 5 card. The cards are shuffled and handed to the respondent one at a time. The respondent is asked to rate each theme on a scale according to a particular criterion, such as *desirability* of the claimed feature or benefit. Then the cards are shuffled again and the respondent goes through the deck again rating each theme according to another criterion, *exclusivity* or *uniqueness*. The same procedure is followed to obtain ratings in terms of a third criterion, *believability*. Those themes that score high on all counts are then considered to be most promising.[4]

A trivariant test of eight themes for advertising coffee yielded results as graphed in Figure 25–2.[5] Those themes appearing in the upper right-hand part of the graph were rated best on the two dimensions of desirability and exclusivity. The numbers in parentheses indicate the believability scores. The proposed theme, the subject of the test, was number 23: "The Delicious Accent of Hawaiian Coffee Makes This Coffee Richer Yet Smoother." It ranked among the top three themes in terms of exclusivity, but it ranked lowest on desirability and believability. It should be noted, however, that the top four themes had been heavily advertised over a considerable period of time prior to the test. The high ranking of these themes might have resulted from successful advertising, as well

---

[3] Perham C. Nahl, "Speedy, Inexpensive Pretests of Ads–Capsule Case Histories," Proceedings, Fourth Annual Conference, Advertising Research Foundation (New York: October 2, 1958), p. 55.

[4] Dik Warren Twedt, "New 3-Way Measure of Ad Effectiveness," *Printers' Ink*, September 6, 1957, pp. 22–23.

[5] William A. Mindak, "Selecting Copy Themes or Appeals Via the Use of Trivariant Analysis." Unpublished paper delivered to Association for Education in Journalism annual convention, August 29, 1961.

as any merit in the themes themselves. Perhaps with equally heavy advertising the proposed theme would have scored among the leaders on all counts. This, of course, is one of the imponderables encountered when testing an unadvertised, unfamiliar idea against those that have become well known through successful advertising. Also, it should not be assumed that desirability, exclusivity, and believability are equally important in every advertising situation.

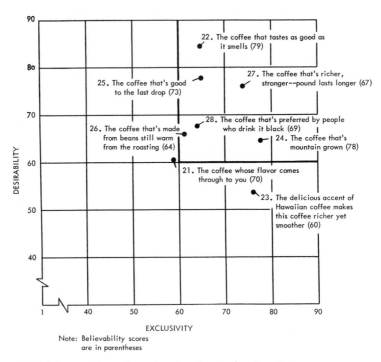

FIGURE 25–2. Three-dimensional evaluation—coffee claims

Changing, building, or maintaining the image that consumers have of a product, a brand, or a company is an important function of advertising. Inasmuch as the image is a composite of attitudes, feelings, and perceptions, scaling techniques are used to delineate images and to measure changes resulting from advertising exposure. For example, the Curtis Publishing Company's research department sought to measure what influence the first two advertisements in a Pontiac campaign would have on the Pontiac image. They developed a list of 51 phrases about automobiles and asked respondents to rate Pontiac on each of the phrases.

Then the respondents were shown a magazine containing articles, fiction, and the two advertisements. After exposure to the advertisements, respondents again were asked to rate Pontiac on the same list of phrases. As shown in Figure 25–3, the image profile changed most on the phrases "a world-of-tomorrow car," "revolutionary improvements," "changing from conservative to modern," "a bold new car." These also were the main ideas stressed in the two advertisements which were headlined "A New Kind of Car Is Born" and "Bold New Pontiac." Thus, it was concluded that the two advertisements succeeded in changing the Pontiac image in the desired direction. One might question whether these results indicated attitude changes, or merely that there had been some learning and recall of the advertised themes. Most conjectures on attitude formation suggest that attitudes are not changed so expeditiously.

Brand preferences

Brand preferences, expressed in some manner short of actual purchase, represent another form of attitude measurement. Respondents are asked to rank competing brands prior to exposure to alternative advertising presentations and again after exposure. The presentation that results in the greatest shift of preferences to the advertised brand is presumed to be most effective.

The Schwerin Research Corporation has developed a unique procedure for testing television commercials on the basis of brand preference changes. About 350 people are invited to a theater to see some filmed television shows and commercials. Upon entering the theater each person is handed a ticket, the stub of which is torn off and deposited in a box for subsequent drawing in a lottery. Before any testing starts each person is asked to indicate on a checklist which brand of a particular product, instant coffee, for example, he wishes to receive a year's supply of if he is the winner in the drawing. Next, the audience is shown the commercial for the brand in question, either in the advertiser's own show or in a special program. Following the viewing of the program and the commercial, the audience is told that, as an added gesture of appreciation, a second drawing will be made, and the participants are asked to indicate their choice for the second draw. In this way the difference in the percentage of people choosing the advertised brand before and after exposure to the commercial is observed. Different commercials are tested in separate sessions with different audiences which are intended to be matched samples.

The commercial producing the greatest increase in percentage of respondents preferring the advertised brand is assumed to be most effective. In addition to brand preference changes, the Schwerin technique requires respondnts to record whatever they remember having seen or heard in the commercials.

ITEMS SHOWING SIGNIFICANT CHANGE ON PONTIAC BEFORE - AFTER ADVERTISING

FIGURE 25–3. Attitude changes after exposure to Pontiac advertisements

The chance of winning a year's supply of a brand places some monetary value on the choice decision and presumably encourages more careful deliberation than a simple no-cost, no-reward statement of preference. However, choices made in a lottery can hardly be considered equivalent to choices made in the market place. Artificiality of the test situation and the assumption that a single exposure can significantly alter established brand preferences are other weaknesses in the Schwerin technique.

PROJECTIVE TECHNIQUES

We have noted that direct questioning of consumers about the efficacy of alternative advertising ideas forces them to assume the role of expert, to judge on the basis of inadequate criteria, to restrict their responses to the relatively few that can be verbalized, to conceal some of their reactions, and to deal with advertising in a way entirely different from the way they encounter it in everyday life where it influences people without their being particularly aware of it, without their making it the object of a critical analysis. To overcome some of these limitations, depth interviewing and projective techniques are used. Among the more common applications of these techniques in testing are the following: (1) to find out if the proposed advertising conveys the intended image, (2) to determine the emotional impact of the message or the degree to which it stimulates self-reference ("it's for me"), (3) to ascertain the connotations of words and phrases (do they mean what they are intended to mean?), and (4) to see if particular themes or illustrations induce positive or negative reactions.

In a depth interview the respondent is shown the advertising material in question and encouraged to talk freely about it. Instead of seeking specific answers to specific questions, the interviewer stimulates discussion by improvising leading questions as the interview progresses and lets the respondent determine what features of the advertisement are worthy of comment or elaboration. If the respondent is kept talking, it is assumed that eventually traces of his unconscious underlying reactions will come to the surface to be perceived by the interviewer. Such interviews are time consuming and expensive. And so much depends on the competence of the interviewer that lack of competence is a constant threat to reliability. "In fact, the findings of depth interviews are so dependent upon the interpretive abilities of the analyst that some wonder whether the interviews are not merely used as a vehicle for expression of the opinions the analyst has already formed from his accumulated knowledge of human behavior."[6] Yet, when competently done, depth interviewing can provide important insights that are not obtainable through direct questioning and attitude scaling.

On the assumption that people talk more freely in a group and react to the stimulus of comments by others, some researchers use group inter-

---

[6] Harry Deane Wolfe, James K. Brown, and G. Clark Thompson, *Measuring Advertising Results* (New York: National Industrial Conference Board, Inc., 1962), p. 151.

viewing for test purposes. Advocates of this technique suggest that respondents enjoy greater security in a group situation and therefore are more apt to express their private views. On the other side it is argued that they may become even more secretive about their true reactions because they would be exposing their inner selves to a number of people rather than to a single interviewer. And there is some likelihood that group discussions are dominated by people who like to hear the sound of their own voices. Here again, however, the skill of the interviewer or psychologist-leader is the critical factor.

Many variations of the projective techniques used in clinical psychology have been applied to the testing of advertising, especially in the developmental stages. Such techniques include word associations, sentence completions, role playing, and perhaps most dramatic of all the thematic apperception test (T.A.T.). In the standard thematic apperception test respondents are shown a patented set of pictures of people in an ambiguous form of action, and are asked to tell the story of each picture. The idea is that the respondent will project his own true, and perhaps deeply hidden, feelings into the story he tells about the characters in the pictures.

A simple derivation of the T.A.T. is to show respondents a proposed illustration for an advertisement and ask them to tell a story about it. The purpose here, of course, is not to analyze the respondent but rather to test the illustration for self-reference or person pertinence. Is the illustration one in which the respondent readily identifies himself and his kind of people? Does it induce the kinds of reactions the advertiser intended?

Another derivation of T.A.T. is the cartoon technique as demonstrated in Figure 25–4. The Granite City Steel Company prepared these cartoon pictures of two farmers talking to each other, with a question in the balloon over one farmer's head and a blank balloon over the other's head. Respondents were asked to imagine what the second farmer would say and give the first answer that came to their minds. It was hoped that the respondent would project his own thoughts into the words he concocted for the second farmer. Using this technique the company learned that their advertising had been effective in informing farmers about the advantages of not accepting substitutes for steel.[7]

Evaluation of any test employing projective techniques must necessarily turn to the qualifications of the researcher. In the hands of skilled, insightful, and professionally trained psychologists such techniques have produced meaningful results. There is ample evidence that they serve

---

[7] *Ibid.*, pp. 54–57.

FIGURE 25–4.   Cartoon test used by Granite City Steel Company

the objective of obtaining unguarded responses revealing hidden or subtle reactions. However, the results are difficult to quantify, the tests are not readily duplicated, and the samples are remarkably small. Lucas and Britt comment on reliability and validity as follows:

The values of projective techniques in forecasting human behavior can best be understood by admitting that reliability is likely to be low, and that validity is unknown. Even in the clinical applications, for which these methods were invented, projective analysis is not the most precise predictor of subsequent behavior.[8]

But, then, no opinion or attitude test in popular use is noted for its validity. The various techniques for seeking consumer reactions would seem to substitute one kind of uncertainty for another—the uncertainty in testing for the uncertainty in advertising decision making. Again it must be remembered that testing is an aid to, not a substitute for, judgment. The test of reasonableness must be applied to all test results. Insofar as opinion and attitude tests reduce the chances of making costly mistakes and insofar as they give the advertiser greater confidence in the decisions he makes, they serve a useful purpose. Advertising is still an inexact speculation. Testing cannot make it otherwise, only less so.

QUESTIONS AND PROBLEMS

1. Why is it necessary in the selection of opinon test subjects to pick only those people who have a distinct interest in the type of product to be advertised?
2. If you were to select test subjects to pass on advertisements of a new type of dentist's drill, where would you look for subjects? How big a group would you deem necessary?
3. What is the advantage of testing the separate elements of an advertisement over testing only for general effectiveness of an advertisement?
4. What advantages, if any, do you see in the use of attitude scales and depth interviewing instead of direct questions calling for such generalized answers as "like" or "dislike" when conducting an opinion test?
5. From a recent issue of *Life,* select all the advertisements for a particular product, such as an electric razor, automobile, soap, or refrigerator, and rank them by the paired-comparison method.
6. What advantages does the trivariant test have?
7. Discuss some ways of reducing or compensating for the halo effect.
8. Which is more important—to find out if people like an advertisement, or to find out how people's attitudes toward the product have been changed as a result of an advertisement?
9. Is it better to find out what a respondent thinks, what he thinks he should think, or what he thinks other people think? Which responses are most likely to be obtained in opinion testing?

---

[8] Darrell B. Lucas and Steuart Henderson Britt, *Measuring Advertising Effectiveness* (New York: McGraw-Hill Book Co., 1963), p. 152.

10. Is it possible that a person might be influenced emotionally toward buying a product without realizing this himself? How can the researcher measure such subconscious changes in attitude?

11. How are the research techniques of psychology used in advertising research? Discuss.

12. *Use of an opinion test by a milk company:*

A large New England milk company, with branches in small towns, was meeting sales resistance because it was looked upon as being an "outside" firm. To counteract this negative attitude, the company decided to run an institutional campaign featuring pictures of a different routeman each week and emphasizing the fact that he was a local resident and an active citizen of the town.

A series of 11 ads, spaced one week apart, was to be run in one small town as a test campaign. Each ad with a news story format would also contain quotes concerning the quality of the company's products. If the campaign in this one town produced the desired results, the company planned to expand its use to the other branches. Therefore, it was necessary to find some way of measuring the impact of these advertisements on the townspeople.

Management felt that door-to-door interviewing would prove of little value in measuring effectiveness, and so the group opinion test was chosen.

Procedure:

A group of 26 women, members of a local Women's Club of the town, was selected. The only inducements offered were an opportunity to be of service in furthering basic advertising research and reimbursement for the cost of refreshments served at their weekly meetings.

The actual testing was performed under the name of the advertising agency handling the account, in order to avoid any bias that might be created by revealing the company's name.

The advertisement for the milk company, plus one similar advertisement from each of three competing milk companies were mounted on cardboard. Each woman was asked to rate the ads on readership, sincerity, believability, general feelings, and objective of the company's campaign.

After the rating sheets were filled, discussions with two groups, one rating the campaign "high," the other "low," were led by trained interviewers. A recording was made of the reactions of the respondents as they justified their ratings.

Conclusions:

An analysis of the data revealed: (1) the milk company's ad had comparatively good readership; (2) the purpose of the campaign was identified correctly; and (3) the milk company ad's was rated as less sincere, less truthful, less reasonable, and less friendly than the ads of competitors.

Comments of respondents revolved around a feeling: (*a*) of being tricked by news story format; (*b*) that routemen were not a voluntary part of the advertising campaign; (*c*) of "corny," crude, simple, undignified, highly emotional appeals; (*d*) of general negative reaction toward photographs and general tenor of campaign.

As a result of these findings, management decided not to use this type of advertising in other small towns. They also agreed that the ads had failed principally because attempts to create good will and sell products in the same advertisement apparently created suspicion and antagonism with many people.

Problem:

1. Do you agree with the decision of the management? Why?
2. Do you think the evidence disclosed by the opinion test was sufficient?
3. Was the consumer-jury test a good one to use in this instance?
4. Was interviewing the jury as a group rather than on an individual basis satisfactory?
5. Evaluate the opinion test in this case for validity and reliability.

chapter 26
RECOGNITION
AND RECALL

WHATEVER ITS PURPOSE an advertisement must first get itself seen, read, or heard. In the competition for attention one ad might get 80 percent of a magazine's readers to stop, look, and read while another might attract less than 5 percent. Such differences in readership were documented by George Gallup in 1931 in his *Survey of Reader Interest*. Since that time advertisers have been interested in finding out how many people read their ads.

Purchase of the advertised product typically is a delayed response. To bridge the time-lapse between perception of the ad or a series of ads and purchase of the product, lasting impressions must be made, impressions that will be retained long enough to influence behavior at the point of sale. Looking at it another way, advertising is intended to bring about learning, and learning is inseparable from memory.[1] Therefore, the memorability of an ad has long been considered an appropriate index of its effectiveness.

This chapter deals with recognition and recall as measures of ad readership and remembrance.

THE RECOGNITION METHOD

Recognition is simply a matter of identifying something as having been seen before. The aid to memory is the thing to be remembered. To

---

[1] For a discussion of the implications of memory in advertising see James Playsted Wood, *Advertising and the Soul's Belly* (Athens, Ga.: University of Georgia Press, 1961).

determine whether or not a person saw or read a given advertisement he is shown the ad and asked if he had previously seen or read any part of it. If the answer is "yes," it may be assumed that a previous encounter actually occurred. Yet, as we shall see, such an assumption is open to question.

The staunchest advocate and principal user of the recognition method is Daniel Starch and Staff, who established a syndicated Advertisement Readership Service in 1932. In the course of 35 years of surveys of most leading magazines, Starch ratings have had a considerable influence on copy and layout techniques. The method as practiced by the Daniel Starch organization is as follows:

Personal interviews are conducted with a national quota sample of 100 to 200 readers per sex of each magazine included in the service. To give respondents time to obtain and read their copy, interviewing begins three days after the on-sale date for weekly and biweekly magazines and two weeks after the on-sale date for monthly magazines.

The first step in the interview is to determine if the respondent qualifies as a reader of the issue. He is shown the cover and asked if he has seen or read any part of that particular issue. If he is not sure, he is allowed to look through it to establish whether or not he read it.

After qualifying as a reader of the issue, the respondent goes through it, page by page with the interviewer, and is questioned about each advertisement one-half page or larger in size. Starting points are randomized to equalize the fatigue element in long interviews. The respondent is asked, "Did you see or read any part of this advertisement?" If yes, he is asked to indicate what was seen or read. All data resulting from the interviews are recorded on standardized questionnaires and made available to Starch subscribers in final tabulations as illustrated in Figure 26–1. Results are expressed for three levels of readership: *Noted* is the percent of issue readers who reported they had seen the advertisement. *Seen-Associated* is the percent of issue readers who reported they had seen or read any part of the ad containing the name of the product or advertiser. *Read Most* is the percentage of issue readers who reported they had read 50 percent or more of the reading matter.

When comparing advertisements of different sizes (full page versus half page), or that use a different number of colors (four colors versus black and white), or that appear in different media, allowance should be made for the difference in cost. Starch uses the common denominator "readers per dollar," which indicates the number of primary readers attracted by the ad for each dollar invested in space cost. This is calculated

FIGURE 26–1. Section from a Starch readership report on *Life*

by projecting the "noted" score (the percent of issue-readers who reported having seen the advertisement) to the total primary readers and dividing by the space cost.

$$\frac{\text{Percent noted} \times \text{Magazine's primary readers}}{\text{Space cost}} = \text{Readers per dollar}$$

For example, if full-page advertisement A had a noted score of 25 percent, and half-page B had a noted score of 17 percent; if ad A cost $20,000, and ad B cost $11,000; and if both ads were run in the same magazine which reached 8 million primary readers; the half-page ad would have been most efficient, having attracted 124 readers per dollar as compared to the 100 readers per dollar attracted by ad A.

For quick comparison of ad ratings against par for the issue Starch includes *cost ratios* which express the relationship between readers-per-dollar for each ad and the median average readers-per-dollar for all half-page or larger advertisements. A cost ratio of 175 would mean that the ad scored 75 points above par.

In addition to the information described above, Starch also provides his clients with a copy of the magazine tested and in which each tested advertisement is "tabbed" showing the scores of various *components of the ad*. Thus, the percent of readers (men and women) seeing the *illustration* is given, as well as other components such as the *headline* and *signature*. These "tabs" can be noted in Figure 26–2.

Usefulness of readership scores

More ingenious than the method itself are the many ways that readership data have been used. Without attempting to catalog all the possible analyses here, the following questions are the principal ones that the Starch organization suggest their data be used to answer: To what extent is my advertisement seen and read? Are my present advertisements better read than previous ones? Are my advertisements better read than those of my competitors? Is the reading of my current campaign increasing or decreasing? How can I tell my ad story so that it will be better read?

Most widely used of the Starch data are the "noted" scores. This perhaps reflects many advertisers' preoccupation with getting attention as well as their uncertainty about the meaning of other measures. In any event, "noted" scores are likely to be affected by a number of factors other than the content of the advertisement itself. Some of these factors are: (1) the proportion of the publication's readers who have an interest in the product—readership of an automobile ad placed in *Life* generally would be higher than readership of a cash register ad placed in the same magazine; (2) the number of advertisements in the issue—the greater the number of ads, the lower the average score, such a decrease resulting from respondent fatigue or boredom in the interview situation as well as from the greater competition for attention in the reading situation; (3) degree of reader-interest generated by issue's editorial content; (4) time spent reading each issue; (5) position of advertisement in the book; (6) degree of interest in adjacent pages; and (7) exposure to same or similar advertisements in other media. Therefore, when comparing readership scores of different advertisements every attempt should be made to control such outside variables.

Insofar as possible comparisons should be limited to advertisements for the same type of product appearing in the same medium. Also, determining an advertisement's performance readership-wise is much like establishing a golfer's handicap. Both require an average of many scores.

The typical Starch survey does not classify readers beyond the groupings of men and women. This impairs the usefulness of the data for ad-

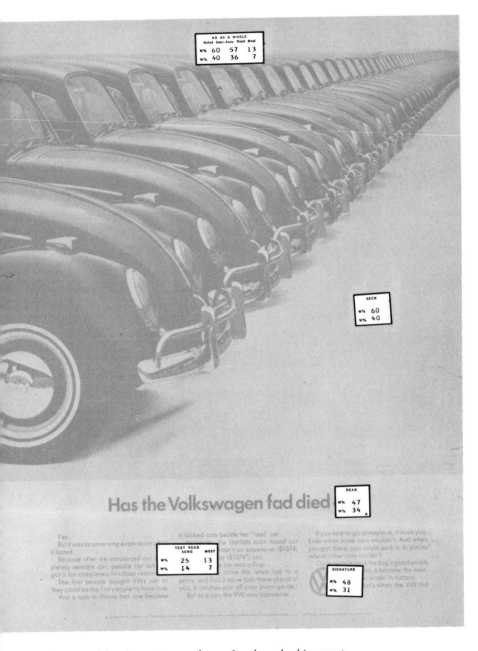

FIGURE 26–2. Advertisement scores from a Starch readership report

vertisers who wish to reach a particular market segment. Such advertisers are interested in finding out how many prospective buyers read their ad, not how many men or how many women. It might be assumed that the higher the "noted" score the greater the number of prospects included in the noting group. But this is not necessarily so. Donald R. Murphy demonstrates that it isn't in his book, *What Farmers Read and Like.*[2] Reporting on 20 years of readership research done by two farm papers, *Wallaces' Farmer* and *Wisconsin Agriculturist,* Murphy shows that some ads are more successful than others in attracting likely prospects even though overall "noted" scores indicate otherwise. For instance, two hog feed ads in *Wallaces' Farmer* were noted by about the same number of men readers. But when the readers were classified by ownership of spring pigs, the record for the ads was as follows:

	Total nothing	Readers with no pigs	Readers with 1–74 pigs	Readers with 75 pigs or more
Ad X	65	21	14	30
Ad Y	67	6	21	40

It is evident that Ad Y attracted considerably more prospects than Ad X.

Evaluation

The primary virtue of the recognition method is its simplicity. Available on a syndicated basis, readership data are current, continuous, and inexpensive, costing each subscriber to the Starch service only $25 to $50 per report. The method focuses on pertinent aspects of advertisement performance. The fact that it has been used for so long a time suggests it is serving a useful purpose. Yet, it is a perennial target of much criticism.

Controversy over this and other methods of measuring advertisement reading and remembrance led the Advertising Research Foundation to undertake an elaborate field experiment to test the methods. The ARF's *Study of Printed Advertising Rating Methods,*[3] popularly known as the PARM study, found that the Starch method was reproducible, that sampling procedures were adequate, that it was not overly sensitive to

---

[2] Donald R. Murphy, *What Farmers Read and Like* (Ames, Iowa: Iowa State University Press, 1962).

[3] Advertising Research Foundation, *A Study of Printed Advertising Rating Methods* (New York: Advertising Research Foundation, 1956).

interviewer skill, and that noted scores were not significantly affected by elapsed time since reading, by time spent reading, by age, education, and socioeconomic level of respondents. These findings would seem to represent an endorsement of the method. But to some researchers they were an indictment. Shouldn't "noted" scores decline with the passage of time?[4] Shouldn't they be affected by differences in interviewer skill and by differences in the education level of respondents? If they aren't so affected, are "noted" scores truly a measure of recognition?

The Starch organization agreed that scores should drop with the passage of time and stated that their own studies showed this to be the case, thus casting doubt on the PARM study.[5] Resuming the attack based on PARM data, two researchers, Appel and Blum, reasoned that "since conventional ad recognition methods do not conform to what might be expected either on the basis of learning theory or common sense there was reason to believe that a substantial portion of the variance among advertisements of such recognition measures is attributable to factors other than exposure of a particular ad in a particular magazine issue."[6] They subjected this hypothesis to experimental test and reached the following conclusions:

1. The noted score is not an uncontaminated measure of ad recognition. Only part of the noted score variance is attributable to ad recognition *per se*. The remaining variance is attributable to such factors as consumer interest in the product advertised, nearness to purchase of the brand advertised, etc.
2. There are certain consumers who have a higher tendency to note ads and there are other consumers who have a lesser tendency toward ad noting, regardless of whether they were actually exposed to the ad.
3. This noting set, or tendency to note ads, is related to multimagazine readership. Multimagazine readers are more likely to note ads falsely than non-multimagazine readers.[7]

It frequently has been demonstrated that some respondents claim to have seen advertisements they could not possibly have seen. The usual procedure for detecting false claiming is to insert bogus ads among those that actually appeared in the copy of the magazine shown the respondent. Some of the more commonly accepted causes for false claiming are: genuine confusion with other advertising, guessing when uncertain,

---

[4] Darrell B. Lucas, "The ABC's of ARF's PARM," *Journal of Marketing*, Vol. 25 (July, 1960), pp. 9–20.

[5] D. Morgan Neu, "Measuring Advertisement Recognition," *Journal of Advertising Research*, Vol. 1 (December, 1961), p. 21.

[6] Valentine Appel and Milton L. Blum, "Ad Recognition and Respondent Set," *Journal of Advertising Research*, Vol. 1 (June, 1961), p. 13.

[7] *Ibid.*, p. 14.

deliberate exaggeration, deduction that advertisement was seen based on recognition of surrounding material, deduction of likely noting based on memory or knowledge of one's own reading habits, eagerness to please interviewer, hesitation to appear ignorant, misunderstanding of instruction given by interviewer.[8] To these causes might be added the respondent's desire to make a favorable impression on the interviewer. Thus some housewives might be less inclined to report they read a beer advertisement and more inclined to report they read a baby-food ad.

What all this adds up to is considerable confusion about the meaning of readership scores. Yet, the surveys continue to be made and the scores continue to be used. No doubt the users assume that such data reflect something about the attention-getting power of advertisements and therefore can be used to isolate those elements that get more people to stop, look, and read. It was on the basis of readership data that the picture-caption layout and the cartoon technique became widely adopted in advertising. One large food advertiser switched to cartoons and watched readership figures soar, only to find that sales figures did not develop in the same fashion. The company substituted a straight appetite appeal. Readership fell, but sales did well.

It is difficult to assess the long-range utilization of the recognition method as a test of advertising effectiveness. Research directors of the 50 leading advertising agencies were queried relative to their feelings about current testing methods. Although their reactions were varied, there was considerable agreement that "recognition ratings and those methods requiring consumers to judge the effectiveness of copy have only minor value."[9] Thus, this method may give way to other measuring techniques.

LABORATORY TESTS OF RECOGNITION

Recognition has long been used by experimental psychologists to measure perception, learning, and memory. Perhaps the most sophisticated recognition tests of advertisements in a laboratory setting were conducted by HRB-Singer Inc. for the Du Pont Company and the Advertising Research Foundation.[10] The purpose of these tests was to measure the visual efficiency of advertisements having different physical char-

---

[8] Darrel B. Lucas and Steuart Henderson Britt, *Measuring Advertising Effectiveness* (New York: McGraw-Hill Book Co., 1963), p. 60.

[9] Lee Adler, Allan Greenberg, and Darrell B. Lucas, "What Big Agency Men Think of Copy Testing Methods," *Journal of Marketing Research* Vol. 2 (November, 1965), p. 344.

[10] *The Measurement and Control of the Visual Efficiency of Advertisements* (New York: Advertising Research Foundation, 1962).

FIGURE 26–3. "It may not sell your product, but think of the readership!"

acteristics—different layouts, designs, colors, and typographic treatments. Visual efficiency was measured in terms of how near, how brightly, and how long the ad must be exposed to be subsequently recognized. A fourth measurement was how well the ad competed against other ads for readers' attention.

An apparatus, illustrated in Figure 26–4, was devised to carry out all

FIGURE 26–4. Apparatus for testing visual efficiency of advertisements

four visual tests. Apparent distance between subject and ad was controlled by two zoomar lenses. Illumination was controlled by neutral density filters. Exposure time depended on the shutters, which were synchronized and controlled by a solenoid. Binocular rivalry was achieved by presenting two advertisements simultaneously through separate lens systems.

The tests were given to 24 students with normal vision from the Pennsylvania State University. In the distance test, each student viewed 36 different ads in random order under three different settings of apparent distance. The greatest distance was used first, and the shortest last. The three settings were selected so that most ads would not be recognized at the greatest distance. Illumination and exposure time were held constant.

The illumination test was similar to the distance test, except that three levels of illumination, rather than distance, were used. Time and distance were held constant.

The time test was also similar, except that the three presentations varied in length while illumination and distance were held constant. Exposure times used were a fiftieth, a tenth, and a fifth of a second.

In the binoculor rivalry test, each presentation consisted of flashing two ads simultaneously, one to each eye. Under these conditions a subject usually sees first one of the ads, then the other. Then the first reappears and the second vanishes, and so on. A problem that had to be considered in this test was that of eye dominance. Almost everyone has one eye that sees better than the other, and this could have biased the results. To control this effect, each subject was presented all possible comparisons a second time. On the second presentation of each pair, the ads were switched so that the one formerly presented to the right eye was then presented to the left. Each ad was given a score on this test equal to the number of times it was recognized in preference to the competing ad.

The response required from each subject in each of these tests was simply recognition. After each presentation the subject scanned a large card showing reproductions of the 36 ads plus 6 dummies. The subject then identified the ad he thought he had seen.

Results of these tests indicated that an advertisement to be easily recognized should:

1. Contain a small number of perceptual units for its area
2. Have a dark illustration
3. Have an illustration no more than two or three times as large as its copy area

4. State its headline message directly
5. Have its largest single color darker than the rest of the ad.

These results were no great revelation to experienced advertising men who know the importance of simplicity, contrast, dominance, color, etc. in layout and design. However, by confirming some well-established principles, the laboratory apparatus and procedures developed in these tests should continue to be useful for predicting visual performance of alternative advertisements. The fact that visual performance is only part of the communications spectrum within which advertising functions should never be overlooked.

RECALL TESTS

As a test of memory, recall is more demanding than recognition. Recall involves questioning the respondent about what he has seen or read without having the ad in front of him while he is answering.

Various recall tests differ in the subject matter they deal with and the aid to memory they supply. Some deal with messages that have circulated in either print or broadcast media: How many people recall seeing or hearing the ad? How much and what do they remember about it? Some deal with campaign themes and slogans: How fast and how widely is the theme registering? Some are designed to pretest advertisements prior to circulation: How well are test ads recalled after controlled exposure in a dummy magazine or in a portfolio of ads? Others are designed to find out what people have learned about the product, the company, or the service advertised. The aid to memory of the amount of help given the respondent ranges from merely limiting the field of inquiry to supplying successive cues until little remains to be remembered.

Principal methods currently used are (1) Gallup & Robinson's Impact Post-test, (2) dummy magazine test, (3) portfolio tests, (4) television recall tests, (5) association tests, and (6) knowledge or awareness tests.

Gallup & Robinson's Impact Post-test

Gallup & Robinson's Impact data are gathered through personal interviews which probe magazine readers' ability to describe the ads they have seen and to play back the ideas that the advertiser tried to register.

The respondent is shown the magazine cover and asked if he has read that particular issue. If he reports that he has, he is asked to describe something in it he remembers having seen. If he correctly describes at least one item, he qualifies as an issue-reader.

With the magazine remaining closed, the respondent is then handed a deck of cards bearing names of brands and advertisers included in the issue, and is asked to state which ads he remembers having seen. When this stage of the interview is completed, the respondent is asked to "play back" everything he can remember about each of the ads he mentioned. What did the ad look like? What did it say? Did it increase interest in buying the product? Interviewers are instructed to probe in a neutral fashion, in order to obtain complete information about each ad recalled.

Next, the interviewer opens the magazine to the ads mentioned and asks if these were the ads the respondent was thinking of. The percentage of all qualified issue-readers who successfully associated the brand or advertiser with some specific feature or sales point of the advertisement is referred to as "Proved Name Registration" (PNR).

A unique feature of this method is getting readers to "play back" the main ideas of advertisements. These playbacks provide material for detailed analyses of the ads' strengths and weaknesses.

As one might expect, the PNR's produced by Gallup & Robinson's aided-recall technique are much lower than the "noted" scores produced by Starch's recognition method. How great the difference is was demonstrated in the Advertising Research Foundation's *Study of Printed Advertising Rating Methods*.[11] The average PNR's and noting scores for the same group of ads were:

Proved Name Registration 3.0%
Noting 21.7%

Perhaps the most significant conclusion drawn from the data provided by this study is that the recognition method is more expedient for gathering *quantitative* evidence of advertisement readership, but aided recall with playback gathers more *qualitative* information from the relatively few people who can supply it.

Dummy magazine tests

Dummy magazines are used to pretest advertisements under conditions approximating normal exposure. Gallup and Robinson also pio-

---

[11] Advertising Research Foundation, *op. cit.*

neered this type of research, and the organization bearing their names conducts regularly scheduled tests in its *IMPACT—The World Today.* This is a dummy magazine containing standard editorial material in which are inserted ads to be pretested as well as a number of control ads which already have been tested in a regular issue of one of the consumer magazines. Interviewers distribute copies of *IMPACT* to a sample of households and ask the recipients to read it some time that day as they ordinarily would read any magazine. The next day the interviewer returns and conducts an aided-recall test as described above.

To test its client's ads, Young and Rubicam advertising agency publishes its own magazine, *New Canadian World,* and follows much the same procedure as Gallup & Robinson. To save the cost of producing a dummy magazine some agencies obtain advance copies of a real magazine and bind test ads in these copies before distributing them to respondents.

Dummy or altered magazines, in addition to assuring a quasi-natural exposure of test ads, make it possible to control the sample, the number and location of ads in the issue, the editorial environment, and the time interval between exposure and response. Under these circumstances alternative ads for a given product can be inserted in the same page position of alternate copies and tested among matched samples of respondents. Against these advantages must be weighed the fact that exposure is somewhat forced, with the result that recall scores are likely to be higher than they would if obtained after normal exposure.

Portfolio tests

The portfolio test makes no pretense of duplicating normal exposure. This method places the test ad in a folder which also contains a number of control ads. The respondent is handed the folder of ads, asked to look through it and to read just what interests him. When he has finished, the folder is closed and returned to the interviewer. Beginning with a question such as, "What brands and products do you remember seeing ads for?" the interviewer establishes which ads are recalled. Due to the absence of cues this part of the interview is referred to as *unaided recall.* Additional questions, narrowing the inquiry to specific products and brands, are asked to verify recall and to find out what the respondent got out of the ads. Such recall measures typically are expressed as a percentage of respondents who can remember the brand advertised, the principal selling points, or the pictorial and copy elements.

The relative merit of alternative ads can be measured by changing only the test ads in successive interviews. A comparison of recall scores for test and control ads gives some indication of the test ad's performance. Validity of such comparisons, however, depends on the neutrality or consistency of scores for the control ads. Finding that recall scores for control ads varied more than recall scores for test ads in several experiments, one researcher concluded that variations in recall scores "result from the fact that people are most likely to notice and least likely to forget ads for those brands and products in which they are most interested or which they know the most about."[12] This suggests that the portfolio should include only advertisements for the same type of product. However, the similarity of advertisements of competing brands might further contaminate the recall scores. These are problems that could be met by using larger samples than those ordinarily used in portfolio testing.

Television recall tests

Recall is used to test television commercials that were actually broadcast and received under normal viewing conditions. Burke Marketing Service offers advertisers the opportunity to test television commercials in any of 25 cities. The day after the test commercial is broadcast telephone interviews are conducted with a sample of housewives or other pertinent group to determine (1) whether or not they viewed the program in which the test commercial appeared, (2) what products they recall seeing advertised on the program, (3) what they recall about the commercial's content, and (4) what they thought of the commercial. It is assumed that the numbers of respondents who remembered seeing the commercial, and remembered its content, and were favorably impressed are indicators of its effectiveness.

Gallup & Robinson's Total Prime Time Television Research measures all television commercials appearing in both program and station-break positions between the hours of 7:30 and 11:30 P.M. on 28 nights in the Philadelphia metropolitan area. Personal interviews are made with the aid of a program roster. Respondents are asked to plot their TV viewing pattern during the previous evening for any half-hour segment in which they were actively watching all or nearly all of the time. Then, using a roster of all the commercials identified by brand name that appeared in those segments the previous evening, respondents indicate

---

[12] John C. Maloney, "Portfolio Tests—Are They Here to Stay?" *Journal of Marketing,* Vol. 25 (July, 1961), pp. 32–37.

which commercials they recall seeing. For each commercial recalled, open-end questions are asked to determine if the respondent can prove recall and to measure levels of idea communication, attitudinal reactions, and persuasiveness.

Association tests

Association, the connecting of one fact or experience with another, is implicit in learning and remembering. Getting consumers to associate a satisfaction with a brand name is a fundamental function of advertising, and the extent to which consumers make the intended association is sometimes used as a measure of advertising effectiveness.

The *triple-associates* test, as developed by Henry C. Link, consists of asking respondents this type of question: "What brand of watch is advertised as 'The World's Most Honored Watch'?" Such a question gives the respondent two associates, (1) the generic product (watch), (2) the theme or slogan ("The World's Most Honored Watch"), and asks for the third element, (3) the brand name, which in this case is Longines. The percentage of respondents who correctly identify the brand provides a measure of how effective the advertising has been in registering the theme and brand association in consumers' thinking. Typically, a triple-associates test includes themes for several products and brands, thus permitting a comparison of competitive standings. To estimate the rate at which a new theme is registering on consumers, the test is given at successive intervals during the introductory campaign.

Being a test of themes, selling propositions, or slogans, the triple-associates test has limited value. It measures only a little bit of learning and is useful only in those advertising situations that depend heavily on such abbreviated messages. Such brevity is prevalent in the advertising of cigarettes, soaps, dentifrices, and beverages. Again, it must be remembered there is no assurance that completion of the desired association will result in favorable action. The respondent might disbelieve the claim or react negatively to it.

Awareness and knowledge tests

The extent to which people have become aware of a product's existence and the knowledge they have of its want-satisfying properties are often considered appropriate measures of advertising performance. Obviously, creating awareness is most important when introducing a new product and when opening a new market for an established product. Getting more prospects to be more knowledgeable about a product's attributes is a more universal concern.

The variety of questions asked to test consumers' knowledge of advertised products and services is as great as the variety of quizzes encountered by the college student. Open-end questions, multiple choice, true-false, fill-in-blanks, and check lists are just a few of the questioning techniques used. For example, the Sun Oil Company tested consumer knowledge of its new gasoline blending system by asking these questions:

1. Have you ever heard of a gasoline pump that dispenses more than one grade of gasoline through the same hose?
2. What gasoline company uses that kind of pump?
3. How many different grades of gasoline does that pump dispense?
4. Have you ever heard of "custom blended" gasoline?
5. What gasoline company sells "custom blended" gasoline?[13]

If advertising were the only means of communications used, the amount of knowledge people have of the company and its products could readily be attributed to advertising. But this seldom is the case. Typically, many kinds of communication—personal selling, packaging, labelling, and store display—are employed. To isolate advertising's contribution to consumer knowledge, an appropriate experimental design must be used. To serve any diagnostic purpose, knowledge tests would have to be conducted for alternative advertising strategies.

As criteria of advertising effectiveness, recognition, recall, awareness, association, and knowledge have one thing in common. All are indicators that some degree of communication was achieved. Until there is much more experimental evidence of the relationship between such intermediate effects and buying behavior, the ultimate influence on sales can only be inferred from the nature of the communication itself.

QUESTIONS AND PROBLEMS

1. Do you believe the correlation between recognition and the ability of an advertisement to stimulate purchase is high enough to warrant extensive use of the recognition test?

   Summarize the strong and weak points of the recognition test. What variables must be considered?

---

[13] Henry Deane Wolfe, James K. Brown, and G. Clark Thompson, *Measuring Advertising Results* (New York: National Industrial Conference Board, Inc., 1962), pp. 15–16.

3. Contrast the recognition test with the aided-recall test with respect to qualifying issue-readers and determining advertisement readership.

4. The recognition method is more expedient for gathering *quantitative* evidence of advertisement performance, but aided-recall with playback gathers more *qualitative* information from the relatively few people who can supply it. Explain.

5. What is the value of measuring the extent to which advertising has made a positive impression upon the mind of the reader?

6. Do you think that a test of "belief of advertising claims" is worth while to the advertiser? Why?

7. When comparing the scores of individual advertisements appearing in different issues of a given magazine each score should be related to the average score of all ads in the issue. Why?

8. Prepare a triple-associates test for six advertisements appearing in current magazines or newspapers. (Sample: What cigarette advertises "Tastes Good Like a Cigarette Should"?)

9. It is probably good practice for any creator of a "purposeful" communication message to examine the message critically before approving it for publication. Such critical examination would probably involve a check against the objective of the message and an appraisal of the extent to which its form followed principles of persuasive or purposeful writing.

   Prepare a check list that you believe would be helpful to any writer of advertising messages in the critical evaluation of the worth of the message.

chapter 27
CONTROLLED
EXPERIMENTS
IN THE FIELD

ALL OF THE TESTS discussed thus far involve some degree of artificiality. Whenever people are forced to examine advertisements in an interview situation or in a laboratory setting, whenever they are forced to respond to questions bearing on some aspect of communication, the conditions are different from those under which advertising works in real life, where people select media and messages voluntarily, where they form opinions and attitudes without submitting to interrogation, where they respond in the marketplace without giving much thought to how their buying behavior was influenced. Also, the aforementioned tests focus primarily on the message. They do not deal with the many important variables inherent in media selection, scheduling, budgeting, and spending strategies.

To approximate reality a test should be conducted in the field. The experimental variable should be introduced in a natural setting; that is, the advertising should actually be placed in the media so that it will reach people during their normal reading, viewing, or listening. Exposure should be voluntary. Response in the form of overt behavior should be objectively observed. Under these conditions there can be little doubt that test results would be sustained in actual practice. Under these conditions it is possible to test media, schedules, and budgets, as well as messages.

Testing under conditions of reality, however, poses a real problem. How can the effect of advertising variables be isolated from the effect of all other variables that influence consumer behavior? This can be done through controlled experiments. In the simplest of such experiments one group of people is exposed to the advertising variable and a comparable group is not exposed. If the response, say purchase of the advertised product, is significantly greater among the exposed group than among the nonexposed group, it can logically be inferred that the advertising variable was the causal factor. More complicated experimental designs permit the simultaneous testing of several variables and several applications of each variable, for example, different media and different levels of expenditure in each medium. Some of the designs that are particularly appropriate for advertising experiments are discussed here.[1]

INQUIRY TESTS

The mail order advertiser who distributes his ads by mail is in an ideal situation to experiment. If he wishes to test advertisement A against advertisement B, he can send ad A to every other name on the mailing list and ad B to the intervening names. Such a distribution assures him that each ad will reach a similar group of prospects. By keying each ad, perhaps with a different address for replying, he can keep a record of the number of orders each produced. He can be assured not only that the observed difference in response is due to differences in the advertisements, but also that the better performing ad in the test is also the better producer of sales. A similar opportunity to experiment is available when using direct mail designed to secure leads for company and distributor salesmen.

Advertising which is intended to produce mail orders, or requests for a sample, a booklet, or a premium, but which is placed in published media, does not offer the same degree of controlled exposure as in direct mail. However, the inquiries may be an important element in the company's sales promotion program and may be considered an appropriate measure of an advertisement's performance.

In more typical situations, the purpose of advertising is to influence consumer purchases in retail stores, not to produce inquiries. Therefore, a critical factor in inquiry tests of such advertising is the relationship between an advertisement's ability to generate inquiries and its ability to exert a favorable influence on retail sales. The validity of inquiry tests

---

[1] The reader who desires a more detailed investigation of experiments may wish to refer to Seymour Banks, *Experimentation in Marketing* (New York: McGraw-Hill Book Co., 1965).

in these situations rests heavily on the relevance of motives underlying requests for the offer to motives prompting purchase of the product.

External variables affecting inquiries

Several factors outside of the advertisement itself affect the number of inquiries received. They are seasonal differences, media differences, and differences in the nature and presentation of the offer.

Seasonal differences reflect the greater amount of time people spend reading magazines and newspapers during the winter months and their greater inclination to "send in" for things when outdoor leisure time activities are curtailed. The number of inquiries generally is highest in February and March and lowest in June and July. One exception to the winter-summer pattern of difference is December, which with its busy holiday season yields fewer inquiries.

FIGURE 27–1.

In his *Analysis of 12 Million Inquiries,*[2] Daniel Starch found that the highest inquiry producing month, February, stood 20 percent above the average; that the lowest months, June and December, stood 20 percent below average. This seasonal variation is portrayed in Figure 27–1. Dr. Starch's data represent the combined experience of many companies who tabulated inquiries resulting from many of their advertisements over a period of many years. Such a generalized seasonal pattern may not fit the

---

[2] Daniel Starch, *An Analysis of 12 Million Inquiries* (Evanston, Ill.: Standard Rate & Data Service, Inc., 1959).

experience of individual companies, especially industrial advertisers, for whose products there may be peak buying interest during the summer months. For example, the Republic Steel Company found that their advertisements in architectural magazines produced the most inquiries during May, June, and July.

Regardless of the pattern of variation, it is important to recognize that the seasonal factor affects inquiries and therefore must be controlled if any valid results are to be obtained through inquiry testing.

Media differences include differences in size and character of audiences, differences in editorial content, and differences in positioning of advertisements. A large number of inquiries should be expected from a test advertisement placed in a magazine with a larger audience, with a larger proportion of prospects, and with more attention-compelling editorial content. Positioning the ad toward the front or the back of the book may or may not affect the number of inquiries, but it can be assumed that an ad positioned adjacent to a high-traffic editorial page will fare better than one buried in a low-traffic section. These observations suggest that whenever test advertisements are placed in different publications, or in different issues of the same publication, or in different positions, there can be no assurance that a difference in the number of inquiries was due to a difference in the ads.

Nature and presentation of the offer have a material effect on the number of inquiries. Frequently the offer is a sample of the product, or a booklet providing more detailed information about the product, or a premium that prospects are likely to want. Whatever is offered, the number of requests will depend on how appealing the offer is and how well it is presented. To increase the number of requests, John Caples recommends: (1) offer the sample or booklet free, instead of for 10¢; (2) set a value on the offer, such as "regular 35¢ size"; (3) describe the offer attractively by listing its good features; and (4) sweeten the offer by adding a free gift.[3]

As an example of sweetening the offer, Mr. Caples reports on a test of advertisements for airplane trips to Bermuda:

We found that a hidden offer of a booklet pulled less than 100 replies. This was not considered sufficient.

We sweetened the offer by including the offer of a free pair of sunglasses and a free map of Bermuda, in addition to the free booklet. We called the offer a *"Free*

---

[3] "How to Get More Replies from Hidden Offers," by John Caples, *Printers' Ink,* October 11, 1957, p. 27.

Bermuda Vacation Kit." This offer brought more than enough replies for a copy test, namely over 400 replies per ad.[4]

A coupon generally produces more inquiries than an offer buried in the copy. An industrial advertiser compared inquiry returns from three methods of offering a booklet to those who would write the company. The relative pulling power of the method used was as follows:

```
Offer buried in copy ....................................  26
Word "free" and paragraph describing booklet added ...... 100
Coupon added ........................................... 185
```

Obviously, inquiries can be boosted if the advertisement is designed to achieve that objective; if the headline, illustration, and body text focus on the offer; if the coupon is given dominant display and placed at an outer corner of the page for easy clipping. The response to such an ad, however, would merely demonstrate its power to generate requests for the item offered. Devices that succeed in motivating people to get something "free" have little or no bearing on the kind of message needed to get people to buy a product at the usual price through the usual channels.

For testing purposes the offer should be related, but incidental, to the objective of the advertisement. A recipe book, for example, is generally accepted as an appropriate offer for a food advertisement. Dominance of the offer should depend on the purpose of the test. If the purpose is to test attention-getting power, a clearly displayed, but nonintrusive, coupon is appropriate. If the purpose is to test thoroughness of readership, a buried offer is called for. These are matters requiring the exercise of good judgment. It is apparent, however, that the offer and its presentation should be the same in all advertisements involved in an inquiry test.

Split run

Split run is a technique that makes it possible to test two or more advertisements in the same position, in the same issue of the same publication with assurance that each ad will reach comparable groups of readers.

Alternate-copy or "50-50" split runs involve a mechanical technique whereby every other copy off the press carries advertisement A, and each copy in between carries advertisement B. Since the two test ads alternate throughout the press run, each reader of the publication has a 50-50

---

[4] *Ibid.*

chance of receiving a copy carrying either of the two ads. Thus, readers of copies carrying advertisement A should have the same general characteristics as readers of copies carrying advertisement B. Appearing in the same position in the same issue, each advertisement is subjected to the same editorial environment and reaches both groups of readers at the same time. Under such controlled conditions it can be inferred that differences in the number of inquiries are due solely to differences in the advertisements themselves.

Some publications which cannot provide an every-other-copy or "true" split can arrange a change of advertisements midway in the press run. This has the disadvantage of concentrating distribution of the ad appearing in the first half of the run in geographic areas farthest from the place where the publication is printed. Most national magazines now offer a geographical split which permits the advertiser to insert different advertisements in different regional parts of the total circulation. This type of split, however, is more appropriate for matching advertising coverage to a firm's product distribution than for testing purposes.

Service charges for split-run insertions vary. For alternate-copy split runs the *Reader's Digest* charges $200 for black-and-white ads, $300 for two-color ads, and $500 for four-color ads.

As a technique for controlled experimentation, split run is objective, reliable, and inexpensive.

Keying the advertisement

To keep a record of the number of inquiries produced by each advertisement it is necessary to adopt some method of identifying which inquiries came from which ad. Where coupons are inserted in the advertisements, this problem is easily solved. A key number or some other identification mark placed on each coupon will allow a proper sorting. There are numerous keying devices. The address given for reply might be varied for each advertisement. Thus, one address might be 1215 Prospect Place, while another might be 1217 Prospect Place. There might be included in one address, Department C, and in another, Department D. Arrangements can be made with the Post Office for varying addresses. Where booklets are offered, the name or number of the booklet can be varied in each ad and thus serve as a key. Figure 27–2 reproduces a number of pairs of coupons keyed in different ways. Can you detect the keys?

FIGURE 27–2. Pairs of coupons illustrating methods of keying advertisements

Media tests

Inquiries may be used to measure the relative effectiveness of different media. In such tests the message and, insofar as possible, the time factor should be controlled. For example, to determine the relative pulling power of different magazines, the same advertisement would be placed in each magazine and a record kept of the inquiries received. To control whatever effect different seasons, months, or weeks might have on response, the ads would run at the same or approximately the same time.

The magazine with a higher circulation might be expected to produce more inquiries. To equalize circulation differences the inquiry count would be related to some standard unit of circulation, say 100,000 circulation. If magazine A with a circulation of 200,000 produced 240 inquiries and magazine B with 130,000 circulation produced 195 inquiries, magazine A scored 120 and B scored 150 per 100,000 circulation.

A more meaningful standard of comparison would take into account the difference in space cost. Thus, if cost of the space used in magazine A above were $720, and the cost in B were $480, the cost-per-inquiry would be $3.00 for A, and $2.46 for B. In this comparison the magazine producing the fewer inquiries was the more efficient.

Evaluation

Inquiry testing offers several advantages. The advertisements actually run in published media and reach people in the course of their normal reading. Therefore, exposure is voluntary and takes place in a natural setting. The response is a voluntary act, which at the very least indicates the person saw the ad and was motivated to take a positive action. If the offer is buried in body text, a reply is substantial evidence of thorough readership. If the offer requires sending a coin for a sample of the product or for a premium, there is further evidence that the person was motivated to spend something for the item offered.

Split run is ideal for controlled experiments. The experimental variable in the advertisements can be manipulated with assurance that all other variables are adequately controlled. Such experiments are easy to conduct. They can provide quick results at relatively low cost. No interviewing or elaborate laboratory apparatus is required. It is simply a matter of counting replies and applying statistical tests of significance to the data. Cost is limited mainly to the cost of the offer, its handling and mailing, and the extra charge for the split run, which we have noted is minimal. Assuming that only advertisements of recognized merit would be included in the test, some advertising value is received for the production costs and space costs incurred. These costs, therefore, should not be charged against the experiment. Also, if the offer has value as a sales promotion device, such as a cook book that includes recipes calling for use of the advertised product, the cost of the offer should not be borne entirely by the experiment. In the final analysis, split run is the least expensive technique for controlled experiments in the field.

On the negative side, critics of inquiry tests say that respondents are apt to be bargain hunters looking for anything free, or chronic coupon-clippers who are not typical of prospects for the advertised product. No doubt many such people do respond, but when split run is used they are equally divided between the two groups exposed to each ad and therefore do not affect the difference in response. In this connection it should be remembered that the number of inquiries provides a comparative measure of each ad's performance, one versus the other, not an absolute measure of effectiveness. The purpose is to test one treatment against another and to infer from the difference in inquiries which one worked the better. Through systematic and consistent experimentation much can be learned about the efficacy of alternative message strategies.

The most serious limitation of inquiry testing concerns the relationship between motives leading to requests for the offer and motives leading to purchases of the advertised product. When these motives are highly related, test results can be projected with confidence to regular advertising practice. Otherwise, the results would merely indicate that one ad scored better than another in achieving some kind of communication and in prompting some kind of response that may or may not be effective in promoting sales of the product. Therefore, the usefulness of inquiry testing is limited to those situations in which the advertising is intended to produce mail orders, sales leads, or requests for additional information and to those situations in which a relevant premium or sample offer is feasible.

SALES TESTING

Ideally, the advertiser would like to know which among alternative strategies and tactics would most influence sales and profit. He may attach significance to measures of communication efficiency, to how well his advertising performs in gaining attention, in transmitting information, in modifying perceptions, in creating brand awareness, in changing attitudes, etc., but he is constantly reminded that the payoff is sales. The fundamental question remains: How many dollars does he get for the dollars he spends?

Paradoxically, little research has been done on the fundamental question. It would seem that researchers have been overawed by the task of isolating the advertising effect from the effect of all other variables operating in the marketplace. They have been quick to point out that sales are the result of many factors: the product, the package, price, distribution, display at the point of purchase, personal selling, all the elements in the marketing mix that are subject to the advertiser's control. In addition, there are the activities of competitors, dealer support, economic conditions, the capriciousness of consumer behavior, the weather, and all the environmental factors over which the advertiser has no control. To these complicating circumstances are added the further observations that the effects of advertising are delayed and cumulative, that a change in advertising today does not produce a change in sales tomorrow, that even a continuing change in advertising may not produce a perceptible change in sales because the passage of time multiplies the effect of other variables as well. Yet, impossible as it may seem, the task is not hopeless.

Some researchers are facing up to the challenge. Their views are typified in the following statement by Paul Gerhold, formerly research director of Foote, Cone and Belding:

> The question of measuring dollar returns from dollar advertising expenditures is a problem that can be solved if any substantial portion of the industry's brain power can be diverted from preparing rationalizations on why the problem cannot be solved to active work toward its solution. Those who argue that dollar returns from dollar investments are unmeasurable would, I suspect, also have us believe:
>
> —that we cannot measure the effect of the moon on tides, because the moon is far away and uncontrollable, and because the level of the water is influenced by the action of the winds and passing ships and similar uncontrollable variables.
> —that we cannot determine the effect of spark plugs on the performance of an automobile, because spark plugs, after all, are only a small part of the complex system that moves a car.
> —that we cannot evaluate what soil enrichment does for agriculture because the enrichment takes place at one time, and the crops come along a lot later.[5]

A recent survey of large-agency research directors asked the question, "Can sales be the criterion of campaign effectiveness?" Adler, Greenberg, and Lucas report that:

---

[5] Paul E. J. Gerhold, from his part in a panel discussion on "Measuring What We Pay For," presented at the 1962 American Association of Advertising Agencies Annual Meeting.

The answers to whether sales effects of campaigns are obtainable were emphatic, in that 27 of the 37 committed responses indicated they are obtainable. Statements by the majority point out that sales effects have been measured, that case histories are available, that controlled experiments have continually proven their potential, and that it is merely a question of enough time and money to do accountability studies properly. In other words, it appears that suitable sales data may not be generally available, but that such data can presently be obtained.[6]

The control problem is not unique to advertising. The social scientist is faced with a host of highly variable social, economic, and psychological factors that he cannot change at will. The agricultural experimenter must contend with variability in weather conditions and soil characteristics. The presence of factors not readily manipulated by the researcher does not rule out the possibility of isolating the influence of test factors. The presence of side variables simply calls for the use of a well-designed and carefully executed experiment.

Single-variable experimental design

Let us assume that a national advertiser is planning to add spot television to his present media line-up. He wants to know if spot TV is going to increase sales enough to warrant the additional cost. To test this medium using a simple experimental design he would select several market areas totally isolated from one another. For a period of time, say two months, during which advertising proceeded as usual without spot TV he would record retail sales of his product in all the selected markets. Then, during the next two months he would add spot TV advertising in half of the markets while at the same time continuing his regular media schedule without spot TV in the other half. During this second period he would continue recording sales in all markets. Then, he would compare the change in sales volume from the first period to the second period in the *test* markets, those where spot TV was added, with the change in sales volume registered in the *control* markets, those where spot TV was not added. This single-variable experimental design is diagrammed in Table 27–1.

In such an experiment it is assumed that "all other" variables exerted a similar influence in all markets. Therefore, if there is a significant difference in sales changes between the test and control markets, the difference would be attributed to the spot TV advertising. A simple comparison

---

[6] Lee Adler, Allan Greenberg, and Darrell B. Lucas, "What Big Agency Men Think of Copy Testing Methods," *Journal of Marketing Research,* Vol. 2 (November, 1965), p. 343.

of sales changes in test and control markets is illustrated in Table 27–2. In this hypothetical case the sales increase of 5 percent in the control markets indicates that sales in the test markets would have increased about $37,500 without spot television advertising. However, sales increased 8 percent in the test markets, suggesting that the difference of 3 percent, or $22,500 in sales, was due to the effect of spot TV. If we further assume that an appropriate statistical test of significance showed that this difference of 3 percent would be expected on a chance basis less than five times in a hundred, the advertiser could be reasonably certain that spot TV did increase sales. But was the increase enough to justify the expenditure? If, in this case, a 3 percent increase in sales returns a profit of $10,000, and the cost of spot TV was $8,500, it can be said that this advertising returned $1,500 in profit.

TABLE 27–1.   Single-variable experimental design

	First period	Second period
Test markets	No spot TV	Spot TV
Control markets	No spot TV	No spot TV

Conceivably, sales in the test markets might decline. Insofar as such a decline resulted from a seasonal drop, from competive activity, from weakening economic conditions, or from other extraneous factors, the depressing effect of these factors would also be registered in the control markets. If sales declined less in test markets than in control markets, the difference would reflect a positive effect from the experimental variable. To illustrate, let's change the figures around in the hypothetical test of spot TV. Let's say that instead of increases we found a 5 percent decrease in sales in the test markets and an 8 percent decrease in the control markets. Here again, spot TV would have been effective, for it prevented sales from going down an additional 3 percent. Again, assuming

TABLE 27–2.   Comparison of test and control markets

	Sales before spot TV	Sales during spot TV	Percent change	Sales change attributed to other factors	Sales change attributed to spot TV
Test markets	$750,000	$810,000	+8%	$37,500	$22,500
Control markets ..	$600,000	$630,000	+5%		

the same profit relationship, the use of spot TV prevented a loss of an additional $10,000 in profit.

To measure the delayed response or cumulative effect of advertising, the experiment might be continued for another period of time during which the experimental variable would be withdrawn from the test markets. However, posttest data lead to conflicting interpretations. If sales continued at or near the level attained during the test period, it might be assumed that this demonstrated the cumulative effect of the advertising variable. On the other hand, if sales declined when the advertising was stopped, was the decline due to a lack of cumulative effect or a lack of continuity?

A single-variable experiment, as the name implies, involves the testing of one variable at a time. In the above hypothetical case the variable was the medium, spot television, not alternative uses of the medium. To control scheduling variables the medium should be used "normally" or as it eventually would be used in the firm's overall advertising program. To do otherwise, to hypo sales through overuse of the medium, or to subject it to an acid test through curtailed use, would make it impossible to project test results to future operations. The number of stations, the timing, and frequency of broadcasts scheduled in test markets should parallel the kind of schedule the advertiser would be likely to sustain on a broader scale. It is advisable, therefore, to plan the ultimate use of the medium before planning the test schedule.

To test alternative schedules, such as concentrated frequency versus longer continuity, one schedule would be used in one group of markets, the other schedule would be used in another group of markets. Insofar as all other factors were operating similarly in both groups the difference in sales observed would be attributed to the scheduling difference. In like fashion, different budgets, different spending strategies, and different campaign themes can be tested in single-variable experiments. Ordinarily, different message components—headlines, illustrations, and copy treatments—are not apt to produce significant differences in sales and, therefore, are more appropriately tested through techniques discussed earlier.

Selection of test and control markets

The selection of market areas for sales testing is essentially a sampling problem. The relatively few local markets selected should be representative of the advertiser's total market. Ordinarily, the number of markets included in the experiment is not great enough to permit the use of random selection procedures. Therefore, purposive selection, the selection of markets that best conform to predetermined criteria, is generally employed. Size, location, population characteristics, social customs, economic structure, distribution patterns, competition, and media availabilities, all are factors that must be taken into account in the selection process. And all of these factors must be considered in light of the purpose of the particular experiment.

Number and size of markets.   There is no standard number of markets to be used. The greater the number used in the experiment, the greater the chance they will adequately represent the advertiser's total market and the greater the confidence that can be placed in the findings. However, if too many markets are used the purpose of experimentation, which is to discover on a small scale what is likely to happen on a large scale, is defeated. In view of the relatively small amounts of money advertisers have been willing to invest in this kind of research, it would seem there is greater danger in using too few instead of too many markets. Clearly, one test and one control are too few. There is little or no likelihood of finding one market that is representative of the whole. And there is too much risk in "putting all your eggs in one basket." If anything went wrong in one market all would be lost. While there may not be any particular magic in the number "three," it would seem that the minimum number of markets should be three test and three control. Four or five of each would be more appropriate in most cases. Of course, if the value placed on test results and the level of confidence required were high enough, the number of test and control markets might well be 20.

Each market should be large enough to provide a diversity of economic activity, a well-developed retail trade, and a variety of advertising media. Yet, it should not be so large that media costs and the costs of measuring sales would be unnecessarily high. The right size markets for experimental purposes are most likely to be found among those with populations ranging from 100,000 to 200,000. Each and every market selected need not meet the criteria of representativeness. It is the combined characteristics of each group, test and control, that should approximate the characteristics of the advertiser's total market.

Location factors.   To prevent any spill-over of the experimental variable into control areas and to relate sales results to a known advertising input, all markets should be isolated geographically one from another. Each should be a discrete trading area, neither a suburb of nor a satellite to a major metropolitan area. Otherwise there could be no assurance that recorded sales were not subject to outside promotional effort or that sales resulting from the experimental variable were not registered elsewhere.

Test and control markets should be spotted in different regions to match the regional distribution of the advertiser's product and to include regional differences in climate, styles of life, and consumer preferences.

Social and economic factors. Local habits and customs stemming from different climates, different ethnic backgrounds and religious beliefs produce marked differences in sales of many products. For example, Salt Lake City would not be satisfactory for testing coffee or Postum. It has an antipathy for the former and an affinity for the latter. The experiment should not be loaded with test markets where people are unusually receptive to the advertiser's product unless, of course, these are the only places in which he sells. Nor should the experiment be treated as an acid test including only those markets where exceptional opposition is encountered. Both types of situations should be represented or a happy medium should be struck between the two.

Markets having a diversity of industry should be sought. Such markets enhance the representativeness of the sample and reduce the risk of invalidity in the experiment because of a local industrial disturbance. The one-industry town, such as a mining town, a railroad town, or a steel town should be avoided. A variety of occupations—factory workers, office workers, tradesmen, professional people, etc.—should be represented.

Distribution factors. Only markets in which the advertiser has adequate distribution should be selected. Obviously, his product should be readily available in the types of retail stores through which he regularly distributes. Inventories and prices should be maintained at normal levels. Dealers and salesmen should not be informed about the test. If they knew about it they might feel compelled to give the product more prominent display or to sell harder than usual to make a good showing. "Business as usual" should prevail. If dealers departed from usual practice by cutting prices or running special promotions, there would be no way to determine whether changes in sales volume were due to the national advertiser's experimental variable or to the dealer's promotional activity. Markets in which such unusual activity occurred during the test would have to be discarded when compiling the final results.

Competitive factors. The advertiser's competitive position in test and control markets should approximate his position nationally. Markets where his share of market is unusually high or unusually low should be avoided. Where his share is high he might be benefiting from exceptionally weak competition. Where his share is low he might be up against exceptionally strong competition. In either situation, sales gains registered during a test are apt to be atypical.

The activity of competitors should be carefully observed during the test. If a competitor cuts prices or runs a special promotion in some of the test or control markets, sales of the product involved in the test are likely to be depressed in those areas. If a competitor notes the entrance of another firm's test advertising in a particular market, he might counter with increased advertising of his own. This, of course, would impair the usefulness of test results.

Media factors. When the purpose of the experiment is to test strategies involving the use of local media—newspapers, spot television, spot radio, outdoor—it is not particularly difficult to find markets in which these facilities are available. The problem becomes more complicated when the purpose is to test strategies for ultimate use in national media, such as network television or national magazines. If network television is involved, test markets should have three television stations in order to reproduce network competition. If national magazines are involved, test markets should have a local roto supplement that offers magazine-type format and color. The availability of regional editions of national magazines makes it possible to select markets for actual magazine coverage at reasonable cost. The soundest approach to translating a national media plan into local media is to equalize delivered impressions. This requires the scheduling of sufficient broadcasts or insertions in the test markets to match the reach and frequency that probably would be achieved by the anticipated national media schedule.

Measuring sales

Ordinarily, a manufacturer's sales records do not reveal week-to-week or even month-to-month retail sales in individual markets. His records indicate shipments to distributors, but do not show the extent to which inventories at the wholesale or retail level are being built up or depleted over short periods of time. Therefore, some means must be employed to provide a standardized audit of retail sales in test and control markets.

Retailers should not be counted on to furnish a record of their own sales. Some could not give accurate information on a particular item's sales and others would not do so. If they knew their store was being used in a test, some retailers would be tempted to create the impression that they were superior outlets for the product in question. They might devote greater than usual effort to the item or they might overstate its sales.

The local media, especially newspapers, often are willing and able to check sales. They also should not be counted on, for they might be tempted to make their medium look good in the test. Similarly, the company's own sales force might work overenthusiastically if they knew a test was on in their territory. Therefore, they also should not be asked to check sales.

Generally, the most efficient way to get current retail sales data is to buy such information from an independent research firm specializing in this service. Best known of these firms is the A. C. Nielsen Company, which regularly audits retail sales of food and drug items in various markets and sells standardized reports of these data on a syndicated basis. If the markets selected for an experiment are not included among those regularly audited, the Nielsen Company is prepared to send their investigators into the selected areas to gather the necessary sales data. Cost of the Nielsen service is apt to be less than what it would cost the advertiser to hire and train investigators to obtain the information on his own.

An acceptable procedure for auditing sales and the one used by the Nielsen Company is as follows: A sample of the types and sizes of stores carrying the advertised product is selected for audit. At the start of the experiment investigators check the quantity of the product each store has on hand. At regular intervals, preferably every other week, the investigators return to each store, check the invoices showing the quantity of the product purchased since the last visit, and check the stock on hand again. With this information each store's sales during each period of time between visits can be readily calculated.

$$(\text{Beginning inventory} + \text{Purchases}) - \text{Ending inventory} = \text{Sales}$$

A cumulative record of product sales in the sample of stores in test and control markets prior to introduction of the experimental variable establishes the benchmark figures. Totals for the test period during which the experimental variable is operating are arrived at similarly. With these data the before-after comparison can be made and sales resulting from the experimental variable can be inferred.

Instead of checking the flow of his product out of retail stores, the advertiser may prefer to measure the flow into the homes of consumers. This can be done by using consumer panels and product purchase diaries as explained in Chapter 11.

Retail audits do not tell the advertiser whether his product is being purchased infrequently by a large segment of consumers or frequently by a small segment. Nor do such audits tell him what kinds of people are responding to the test advertising. When data are gathered through consumer-purchase diaries, the advertiser can classify his customers according to age, family size, income, occupation, or some other relevant factor. If he finds that increases in sales result from purchases made largely by a particular consumer group, he can exploit the marketing opportunity such prime prospects represent or he can modify his advertising program to more effectively cultivate other segments.

Multivariable experimental design

More sophisticated experimental designs, in which several variables are tested simultaneously, are now being used in advertising research. Such designs not only make it possible to measure the sales effect of each variable, but also take into account the *interaction* between variables. The interaction may produce a combined effect that is greater than the algebraic sum of the separate effects. For example, a given expenditure on television and radio together may yield greater sales than the same expenditure on either one of the media separately. Multivariable experimental designs offer the most promise for testing alternative advertising strategies under conditions of reality.

A design used by the Ford Motor Company to test various combinations of four media in sixteen market areas is illustrated in Table 27–3.

TABLE 27–3. Sixteen-area multimedia experimental design

	No newspapers				Newspapers			
	No radio		Radio		No radio		Radio	
	No TV	TV	No TV	TV	No TV	TV	No TV	TV
No outdoor	1	2	3	4	5	6	7	8
Outdoor	9	10	11	12	13	14	15	16

George H. Brown, Ford's director of marketing research, commented on this experiment as follows:

A brief study of this design will show that for any single medium, eight geographic areas have been exposed and eight have not been exposed. Thus it is possible to execute the basic test-control, before-after analysis inherent in an elementary design. It is also possible to observe how each medium behaves alone and in all possible combinations with other media. (See Table 27–4.)

If identical dollar expenditures (at national rates) are established for each medium, area No. 1 will receive no advertising expenditures, areas 2, 3, 5, and 9 will receive advertising at the same dollar rates; areas 4, 6, 7, 10, 11 and 13 will receive advertising at twice this dollar rate; areas 8, 12, 14, and 15 at three times

TABLE 27–4. Media combinations contained in sixteen cell design

Combination	Area number
No media	1
TV only	2
Radio only	3
Newspaper only	5
Outdoor only	9
TV—radio	4
TV—newspaper	6
Newspaper—radio	7
Outdoor—TV	10
Outdoor—radio	11
Outdoor—newspaper	13
TV—radio—newspaper	8
Outdoor—radio—TV	12
Outdoor—TV—newspaper	14
Outdoor—radio—newspaper	15
Outdoor—TV—radio—newspaper	16

as much dollar advertising, and area 16 at four times this dollar expenditure. The information-producing potential of such a design is obviously quite great.[7]

Whereas dollar expenditures in each medium were held constant in the Ford experiment, the factorial design illustrated in Table 27–5 permits the testing of three levels of expenditure.

In this design each of nine markets receives a different mixture of radio and television advertising. A single experiment of this type provides useful results. Predictability, however, can be considerably improved by rotating the combinations among the same nine markets or by reproduc-

TABLE 27–5. Factorial design for testing two media at three levels of expenditure

I	II	III
$5M Radio	$10M Radio	$15M Radio
$5M Television	$5M Television	$5M Television
IV	V	VI
$5M Radio	$10M Radio	$15M Radio
$10M Television	$10M Television	$10M Television
VII	VIII	IX
$5M Radio	$10M Radio	$15M Radio
$15M Television	$15M Television	$15M Television

[7] George H. Brown, "Measuring the Sales Effectiveness of Alternative Media," *Proceedings: 7th Annual Conference, Advertising Research Foundation* (New York: Advertising Research Foundation, Inc., 1961), pp. 43–47.

ing the experiment in different sets of markets. Insofar as such experimentation enables the advertiser to predict sales returns from alternative spending strategies, it increases the likelihood of his maximizing profit on the media investment. Similarly, the same type of experiment could be used to evaluate alternative scheduling patterns with respect to frequency, continuity, and space and time units.

The design and analysis of complex experiments is a branch of applied mathematics and will not be dealt with further here. The above examples are intended to demonstrate the logic of such experiments and to indicate that techniques are available for measuring the particular effect of advertising variables on dollars and cents sales.

Matched samples of exposed and nonexposed groups

Instead of isolating test and control groups prior to introducing the advertising variable, audience-tracing techniques may be used to isolate exposed and nonexposed groups after the advertising has run. The logic of such ex post facto experiments is simply that some people will voluntarily expose themselves to the media carrying the advertising in question and others will not. Some will see a given television program, others won't; some will read a given magazine, others won't; some will listen to radio at a given time, others won't. Once viewers and nonviewers, or readers and nonreaders, or listeners and nonlisteners are identified, the difference in their purchases of the advertised product is observed, and the part of the difference attributed to the advertising is determined.

The consumer panel technique best serves the dual purpose of identifying exposed and nonexposed groups and recording purchase behavior of each group. To illustrate, let's assume the sales effectiveness of radio or a particular use of this medium is under test. Panel members would keep one diary of their radio listening and another diary of their product purchases. From the listening diaries it can be determined which panel members regularly listen at the time the test advertising is broadcast and which panel members do not. If the purchase diaries indicate that listeners are buying more of the advertised product than nonlisteners it might seem reasonable to credit the difference to the radio advertising. However, the listening group can be much different from the nonlistening group, as evidenced by the fact that one group chose to listen to the program while the other group did not. The program itself tends to select a particular kind of audience. The difference in purchases may be due to inherent differences between listeners and nonlisteners, and not due to the radio advertising. Therefore, it is necessary to adjust the composition of each group so that they will be matched in all observable respects. They should, in other words, be *matched samples.*

The key factor in the success of this method is the adequacy with which the two groups, the exposed and nonexposed groups, can be matched. If the exposed group includes a higher proportion of low-income members than the nonexposed group, this factor may account for part of any observed difference in their respective purchase patterns. Therefore, the two groups should be matched, either through a random pruning which leaves each group with the same proportion of members within various income levels, age groups, family size groups, occupational classes, education levels, etc., or through the application of statistical weighting procedures. It should be recognized, however, that two groups of human beings may be matched in terms of observable characteristics, but still be different in terms of underlying personality traits. This is the principal weakness of the matched sample technique.

Whatever method is used, sales testing is expensive and time consuming. It requires technical skills that are not in plentiful supply. Such experiments are most appropriate when the product is purchased at frequent intervals, when the likelihood of quick response to advertising is high, and when advertising is the dominant selling force in the marketing mix. These also happen to be the conditions when the advertising investment is likely to be high. The greater the investment the more prudent it is to employ testing procedures that measure the return in dollars and cents.

QUESTIONS AND PROBLEMS

1. Reviewing the previous chapters on advertising testing techniques, where do you think the exposures to the ads and the responses to them differ from real life?
2. An inquiry test merely measures the ability of an advertisement to produce inquiries. It doesn't measure the advertisement's ability to produce sales. Do you agree or disagree? Explain.
3. Describe a split run. What variables that might influence the results of an inquiry test are controlled by a split run?
4. How would you design an inquiry test to measure the relative effectiveness of two different magazines?
5. The value of sales-results tests is generally recognized. Why, then, have they been infrequently used?
6. What is the difference between conducting a sales-results test and starting an advertising campaign on a small scale?

7. What are test cities and control cities? Why are three or more of each considered necessary to the testing process?

8. The sales in test city T were 680 units in the period before the advertising was run and 1,240 units after it was run. In the control city, sales were 920 units for the first period and 966 for the second. What increase in sales was logically attributable to advertising?

9. One of the problems involved in a sales-results type of test is that of measuring changes in sales volume before, during, and after the test period. There are several ways such sales volume can be measured. Describe in detail two methods of doing this. Which of the two would you recommend? Why?

10. The sales-results test of advertising effectiveness is best suited for products which are purchased by consumers at frequent intervals. Do you agree or disagree? Explain.

part VI
The advertising
organization

chapter 28
THE ADVERTISING AGENCY

THE ADVERTISING AGENCY has evolved to provide the specialized knowledge, skills, and experience needed to produce effective advertising campaigns. It provides a quality and range of service greater than any single advertiser could afford or would need to employ for himself.

Operating outside the advertiser's own organization, the agency is in a position to draw on the broad experience it gains while handling the diverse problems of different clients. Also, as an outsider it can approach the advertiser's problems with an objective point of view.

The agency functions mainly in the "national" field, handling the advertising campaigns of manufacturers who distribute nationally or regionally, rather than in the local field of retail advertising.

The agency has come to represent the core of the advertising profession, and "Madison Avenue," an area in New York where several large agencies are located, has become a symbol of advertising to the nonadvertising world.

History

The development of the advertising agency can be divided roughly into four periods:

1. Period of early growth: 1841–65
2. Wholesaling period: 1865–80
3. Semiservice period: 1880–1917
4. Service period: 1917–present

Period of early growth.   The first advertising agency on record in the United States was Volney B. Palmer. In 1841, Palmer organized a newspaper advertising and subscription agency. By 1849 he had established offices in the cities of New York, Boston, Baltimore, and Philadelphia.

At this early date, there were no directories of newspapers and no published rates for space to be sold to advertisers. Palmer acted as an informatory agent in these matters to prospective advertisers. In essence, he served as a salesman of space for publishers; and they, in turn, gave him a commission of 25 percent of such sales. The publishers found this method of selling more effective than trying to sell direct, and advertisers wishing to reach more than one territory found value in such service.

Palmer seems to have been the only agent for advertising space until 1848, when one of his employees left him and started a similar business for himself. Competition increased, and the usual price cutting occurred. Success seemed to depend upon one's ability to bargain with the publisher and the advertiser. The natural result of this policy was a general reduction in profits to the agency; this led to a search for new competitive tools which would return a profit.

Wholesaling period.   The new competitive tool was supplied by George P. Rowell, who opened an agency in 1865. Rowell contracted with one hundred newspapers to sell him a column of space each week for a year. By contracting for such large amounts of space for a period of time, Rowell was able to obtain a greatly reduced price from the publishers. In addition to the lower price obtained from buying space in quantity, he also received the 25 percent agency commission. He resold space to advertisers in 1-inch units. The price he charged was not necessarily a uniform one; nor was it the price which he paid the publisher, less his 25 percent. His plan was successful, the main element of success being the principle of buying in wholesale lots and reselling to small buyers.

Throughout the wholesaling period, the agent continued as a seller of space for publishers. This took on different forms, one of which was the exclusive right to sell space in certain publications. Thus, one agency developed a controlled list of religious papers, another a "List of Thirty" household magazines. Any advertiser wishing to buy space in any of the controlled publications was forced to buy through the exclusive wholesaler for that paper.

Semiservice period.   The wholesaling phase of agency work was checked when publishers began to establish their own sales departments for selling space. Some of these departments sold direct to the advertiser;

others, to the general advertising agency. Thus, the agency was forced to turn its attention somewhat away from the particular function of selling or peddling space for a publisher and toward the function of buying space for the advertiser.

This about-face at least changed the surface character of the agency business. It tended to make it a semiservant of the advertiser. Emphasis was placed upon the value of obtaining space in the proper publications, and the agency represented itself as being capable of choosing the proper publications.

Early in the semiservice period, agencies offered to write the copy for the advertiser, thus giving added weight to their claim of being servants of the advertiser. This concept of service was slow to develop; but in the early part of the 20th century, agencies began to emphasize strongly this "free" service. One agency in 1905 advertised that it paid $28,000 a year for a copywriter. These methods increased the agency business and forced most space sales to be made through them.

Service period.   By 1917 the idea of service had grown until not only was copywriting done for the advertiser but many other things as well. During the service period, many agencies have grown to the position of advertising and marketing counselors for advertisers. Market research, media testing, merchandising service, layout construction, art work, the supervision of engraving, etc., now constitute regular agency service.

The service element has solidified the position of agencies to such a degree that magazine publishers have come to depend upon them as the primary channel through which space is sold. Publishers claim to have had an important part in the encouragement of agencies to provide extra service to the advertiser. By providing advertisers with the kind of assistance that will improve the effectiveness of advertising, more space naturally will be sold.

Functions of a modern agency

The modern advertising agency ranges in size from a one-man agency to a large organization employing hundreds of people to carry on its work. The functions performed by these agencies vary to a considerable degree. Some concentrate major attention on the preparation and placing of advertisements. Many, however, have organized themselves to perform the broad functions of marketing and advertising counselors. To perform such functions well requires a keen understanding of the complete marketing and merchandising problems of the advertiser, as well as a knowledge of markets, media, and consumer psychology. The older service functions of writing copy and designing the form of a finished advertisement are thus only a part of the total work of most modern agencies.

The American Association of Advertising Agencies emphasizes the service function its members perform for clients and points out that such service consists primarily of interpreting to a specific public or publics the advantages or want-satisfying characteristics of a product, service, or idea. The Association offers the following seven-point program as necessary for an adequate job of interpretation:

1. A study of the client's *product or service* in order to determine the advantages and disadvantages inherent in the product itself, and in its relation to competition
2. An analysis of the *present and potential* market for which the product or service is adapted
   a) As to location
   b) As to extent of possible sale
   c) As to season
   d) As to trade and economic conditions
   e) As to nature and amount of competition
3. A knowledge of the factors of *distribution and sales* and their methods of operation
4. A knowledge of all the available *media* and means which can profitably be used to carry the interpretation of the product or service to consumer, wholesaler, dealer, contractor or other factor. This knowledge covers:
   a) Character
   b) Influence
   c) Circulation
      Quantity
      Quality
      Location
   d) Physical Requirements
   e) Costs
5. *Formulation of a definite plan* and presentation of the plan to the client
6. *Execution of plan:*
   a) Writing, designing, illustrating of advertisements, or other appropriate forms of the message
   b) Contracting for the space or other means of advertising
   c) The proper incorporation of the message in mechanical form and forwarding it with proper instruction for the fulfillment of the contract
   d) Checking and verifying insertions, display or other means used
   e) The auditing, billing and paying for the service, space and preparation
7. Cooperation with the client's sales work, to insure the greatest effect from advertising

In addition to strictly advertising service, there is a willingness among many agencies to assist the client with other distribution activities. They do special work for clients in such fields as package designing, sales research, sales training, preparation of sales and service literature, designing of merchandising displays, public relations and publicity.[1]

Some perspective on the breadth of agency services beyond the traditional functions of planning, creating, and placing advertising can be gained from the following list of "extra" services now provided by advertising agencies:

Marketing
Pricing policies
Distribution policies
Sales policies
Sampling

Merchandising Pieces
Wall banners
Package inserts
Counter, floor, and window displays
Shelf tape
Talking displays
Counter giveaways
Sampling cards
Dispensers

Trade Promotion
Dealer promotions
Dealer contacts
Convention exhibits
Catalogs
Sales literature
Bulletins
Broadsides

Public Relations
Employee-employer relations
Consumer relations

Publicity
News stories
Product promotion
General

Research
Consumer panels
Audience and readership analysis
Market research
Copy research

Sales Training
Sales meetings
Sales portfolios
Visual sales aids
Slide films
Demonstrations

Product Analysis
New product development
Product design and styling
Brand name development
Trademark design
Labeling
Packaging
Pretesting
Motivational studies
Recipe testing

Direct Mail
Letters
Folders
Booklets
Envelope stuffers
Return cards
Brochures
Couponing and sampling

---

[1] Frederic R. Gamble, *What Advertising Agencies Are—What They Do and How They Do It* (New York: American Association of Advertising Agencies, Inc., 1963), pp. 6 and 7.

Miscellaneous
 Annual reports
 Testimonials
 Contests
 Recipes

Reminders—calendars, desk gifts, etc.
Instruction booklets
House organs
Premiums
Cookbooks[2]

Any organization performing all these services might properly be called a "marketing agency" instead of an advertising agency.

Agency organization

In harmony with the expansions of service, agencies have generally developed an internal organization based upon functions performed. The scope and character of organization vary according to the size of agency. A typical advertising agency organization chart is illustrated in Figure 28–1.

Research. The research department gathers, analyzes, and interprets facts concerning the *consumer*—his motivations, opinions, attitudes, and buying behavior, the *product*—its want-satisfying qualities and competitive selling points, the *market*—its location, composition, and potentiality, the *competition*—their positions and marketing practices, and the *effectiveness of alternative advertising strategies.* The work of this department is more fully explained in Parts II and V of this book.

Media. The choice of media is very important. Should magazines, newspapers, radio, television, direct mail, or some other medium be used to carry the advertising message to the consumer? If magazines, what kind of magazines—women's, general, trade, or professional?

It is the function of the media department to answer these and many other questions. A close harmony should exist between this and the research department. A satisfactory answer to the above questions can come only from a knowledge of the location of prospective customers, their tastes, and their living and buying habits. The extent of dealer representation for the advertised product must also be considered.

The media department will be charged with the responsibility of knowing, not only all the available media and means which can be used to carry the message of the advertiser, but also the cost and probable effectiveness of each. After a selection has been made, a detailed media schedule should be drawn up, including the names of the media to be used, the exact dates the advertisements are to appear, and the exact size

---

[2] "Growth of Advertising Agency Services," *Printers' Ink,* January 27, 1956, pp. 21–30.

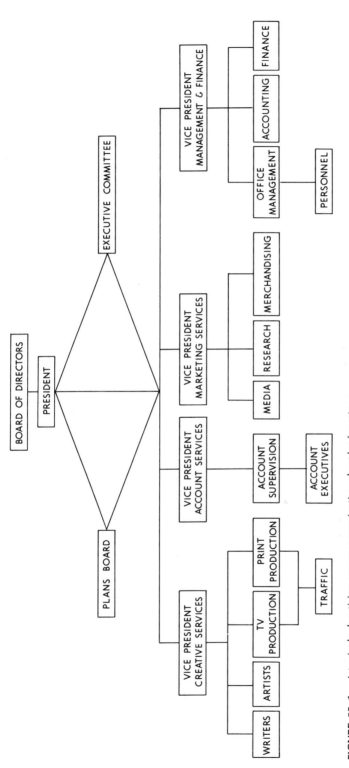

FIGURE 28–1. A typical advertising agency organization chart by functions

of the advertisements (if to be printed) or length of time to be used (if broadcast). This schedule will serve as a blueprint to be followed in the preparation and insertion of advertisements. Figures 28–2, 28–3, and 28–4 illustrate media schedules for newspapers, spot television, and spot radio.

LEO BURNETT COMPANY · INC. ADVERTISING PRUDENTIAL PLAZA · CHICAGO, ILL. 60601 TELEPHONE CEntral 6-5959						**SCHEDULE OF ADVERTISING** NEWSPAPER			
CLIENT	SCHEDULE NUMBER	REV	SCHEDULE NAME			MARKETING AREA		DATE	PAGE
GREEN GIANT	69-20B-0210-0541		F 69/70 ROTO FROZEN NIBLETS C/S					09/17/69	2
ED C S	INSERTION DATES	PROD CODE	SPACE	RATE	ADDITIONAL CHARGE	COST PER INSERTION	C D	FOOT NOTES	SPECIAL INFORMATION

INSERTION DATES		SPACE		COST PER INSERTION	FOOT NOTES
PHOENIX REPUBLIC GAZET	12/14	ARZ 3/5 PG 4/C	163,381	859.32 *	
L A TIMES	12/14	CAL 3/5 PG 4/C	845,150	4,144.00 *	2%
SAN FRAN CHRON & EXAMN	12/14	CAL 3/5 PG 4/C	486,330	2,584.00 *	
SAN JOSE MERCURY NEWS	12/14	CAL 3/5 PG 4/C	112,371	816.54 *	
HARTFORD COURANT	12/14	CON 3/5 PG 4/C	141,780	754.23 *	2%
NEW HAVEN REGISTR JRNL	12/14	CON 3/5 PG 4/C	29,977	558.00 *	2%
WASHINGTON POST	12/14	D C 3/5 PG 4/C	438,741	1,776.30 *	
ST PETERSBRG TIMES IND	12/14	FLA 3/5 PG 4/C	121,654	692.85 *	
ATLANTA JOURNAL CONST	11/16	GA 3/5 PG 4/C	200,165	1,488.00 *	2%
CHICAGO SUN TIMES	12/14	ILL 3/5 PG 4/C	534,298	2,071.11 *	
INDIANAPOLIS STAR NEWS	12/14	IND 3/5 PG 4/C	221,489	1,124.12 *	
NEW ORLEAN TMS-PIC S&I	11/16	LA 3/5 PG 4/C	196,302	1,113.21 *	

THESE FIGURES ARE ESTIMATED COST BASED ON LATEST QUOTATIONS AND SUBJECT TO CHANGE.
FORM 6-02 PRINTED IN U.S.A. 3-69

SCHEDULE APPROVED BY_____ DATE_____

FIGURE 28–2. Newspaper schedule

After media have been selected, checking on their relative effectiveness in doing the job is coming to be an important function of the agency. This, again, requires a close working arrangement between the research and media departments. Reference should be made to Part IV of this book for more detailed material dealing with media.

Creative activities. Included in creative activities are copy, art, TV and radio production, and mechanical production. There are those who consider the copy department the most important part of an agency. It is, insofar as it interprets to prospective buyers the product or service being advertised in terms of its want-satisfying ability. The copywriter is usually supplied with the results of research to determine the strength of particular appeals, the medium in which the copy is to appear, and the

FIGURE 28–3.   Spot television schedule

amount of copy to write. He is governed, also, by the advertising plan that has been established by the client and the agency's account men. An effort is then made to develop copy that will assist in the effective execution of the planned program.

It is being recognized more and more that such qualities as beauty of expression, snappy slogans, and clever phrases in copy should not be the goal of the copywriter. He should attempt, instead, to ascertain the fundamental characteristics of the consumer and to determine the most effective avenues of approach to his consciousness. It is not copy for copy's sake, but copy that will sell goods. Results from tests of copy effectiveness are being used more and more as a guide to the copywriter. Some copywriting principles and techniques of testing copy effectiveness were given in Parts III and V.

Art in advertising is valuable in dramatizing the product and its want-satisfying qualities. This consists of not only determining the type of illustrations to use in an advertisement but also the development of a plan of physical arrangement for the entire advertisement. Thus, this department is responsible primarily for developing more or less rough sketches

JOS. SCHLITZ BREWING COMPANY

CURRENT ANNOUNCEMENT SCHEDULE - SPOT RADIO

SCHEDULE DATES: 4/19–5/9/70
5/24–7/4/70
7/12–8/8/70
8/16–9/5/70
- - - - - -
9/6–9/12/70*

Brand	Schlitz Beer
Station & Kc.	WLS – 890 kc
City of Origin	Chicago
Station Format	Top 40
Male GRP Goal	150/180

A.I. #	5631
MCA:	Chicago
Division	Illinois
Rating Data Source	Apr/May '70 ARB
Actual Male GRP	51

Day of the Week S M T W T F S	Time	Comm'l Length	Avg. Male Metro RTG	Total Area Men (000)	Total Area Men 18-34 (000)	Class	Plan or Freq.	Cost Per Spot ($)
1 1 1 2 2	Art Roberts 6–10 am	60"	2.1	76.9	62.6	AA	30X	128.25
1 1 2 2 2	Larry LuJack 3–7 pm	60"	1.9	69.0	59.6	AA	30X	128.25
2 1 2 2 2 2 2	Chuck Buell 7–10pm; Kris Stevens 10–12pm 7–12 pm	60"	.9	32.7	28.5	A	30X	85.50
3	12Mn–6 pm	60"	1.5	62.2	49.0	AA	30X	128.25
3	12Mn–3 pm	60"	1.6	54.3	46.7	B	30X	71.25
	Station Totals:		50.9	1,864.9	1,572.6			$3,633.75
	34 spots (All :60s)							

* Make good spots for 1969 schedule – same schedule as above – no charge

AK/cb 6/24 Rev. #2: to update ratings

Rate card #10 less 5% discount for 26 consecutive weeks
Rate Card No./date _____ Net_____ Gross____ x

6-07 – 4/70

FIGURE 28–4. Spot radio schedule

of layouts and illustrations. The finished art work is usually done by an outside artist. Layouts sufficiently clear to guide the printer are all that will be necessary, unless a more comprehensive one is needed to show the client a close approximation of what the finished advertisement will be like. The important function is the effective coordination of all parts of an advertisement into a complete and unified selling message. The employees in this department should be consumer conscious as well as art conscious. It is their function to arrange a selling message in effective form rather than to produce great art.

The production of television and radio commercials requires different talents and procedures than are required for producing print advertisements. Therefore, agencies doing much television and radio work have separate creative departments for these media.

The mechanical production department is responsible for converting art work and copy into the printing plates, typography, and mats used to reproduce the finished advertisement in print media.

Account management. After a new account has been obtained, a contact man or account representative is assigned to serve as the liaison between agency and client. It is usually through the contact man that the various services of the agency are made available to the advertiser. It is his responsibility to obtain the client's acceptance and approval of the agency's campaign plan, individual advertisements, selection of media, etc. The account representative may take part in the research and marketing activities of the advertiser. In fact, he is supposed to be thoroughly familiar with all of the marketing and advertising problems of the client and capable of presenting suggested solutions to these problems in such a way that they will be accepted by the advertiser.

Merchandising activities include developing favorable dealer relations, providing dealer aids, keying the advertising program to other promotional activities of the advertiser, planning retail promotions, etc.

Internal services.   As in most business enterprises, an advertising agency requires financial control, personnel management, office management, secretarial work, and clerical help.

Business-getting.   The agency, like the advertiser, has something to sell. If the agency is to give the service expected, a volume of business compatible with its facilities for service must be maintained. It is, therefore, quite logical to set up a department charged with the responsibility of getting new business to replace accounts that have been lost, to balance declines in the business of present clients, and to secure new accounts where an increased volume of business is desired.

The agency has an opportunity, through the work of this department, to demonstrate its ability to do an advertising and selling job. No "client" is present to veto a proposed program. The sales problem is strictly an individual one. All the merchandising, research, copy, and art facilities of the agency are available for the development of an effective sales program. A challenge should be laid down to do for itself the kind of selling job it claims to be able to do for a client.

Methods followed in obtaining new business are determined by the individual agency. Competition for new business is based largely upon service, rather than price, because of the rather intangible nature of that which is being sold.

Coordination of complete campaign

The advertising agency may be referred to as a collection of specialized business brains. The functional organization of the agency is designed to facilitate the work of these specialists. It is vital, however, that the work of each person be directed toward one common goal—the successful planning, development, and execution of the complete campaign.

The basic plan underlying a given campaign will usually be determined by the account executive serving as contact man with the client, other key executives, and certain members of important departments. Upon the work of this committee or plans board will depend much of the success of the campaign. In many respects, this is the very heart of the agency's operation—the creative application of its specialized knowledge and experience to build a successful advertising *plan* for the product. Molding the work of specialists in research, copy, art, media selection, and production into a harmonious and coordinated program is the particular task of agency management.

It is important that the work of various departments or functionaries be scheduled in a manner that will make possible the completion of an advertisement in ample time to meet media deadlines. Here, again, the coordination efforts of management are vital. Production schedules somewhat comparable to assembly-line techniques are often necessary. Plates cannot be made until art work is finished, the printer must wait for finished copy, insertion orders cannot be placed until media have been selected and approved by the client, etc. Delays in one department must thus be made up in another if the advertisement is to be in the hands of the publisher before the closing of forms. Good management will see that there is a minimum of delays and conflicts.

Protection of ideas

Ideas and the ability to make them articulate and alive constitute the primary properties of the advertising agency. The character of ideas used in advertising often encourages persons to submit suggestions to agencies for possible use with the hope of monetary reward. Likewise, the agency will at times submit ideas to a prospective client in the process of soliciting new business. The agency thus has the dual problem of protecting itself against the use of ideas belonging to others and protecting its own ideas from being appropriated.

In the past, and to a considerable degree today, primary protection is afforded by the integrity of those involved in the commerce of ideas. In 1935, however, two cases were tried in United States courts in which theft of advertising ideas formed the basis of the litigation. One of these cases was *Ryan and Associates* v. *Century Brewing Association,* tried in the Superior Court of King County, Washington and affirmed by the Supreme Court of Washington.[3] The plaintiff, How. J. Ryan & Associates, Inc., had previously solicited the account of the Century Brewing Association. They had outlined various advertising suggestions in the one and one-half hour presentation made to the company. These suggestions included the slogan, "The Beer of the Century." An agency other than How. J. Ryan & Associates obtained the account. Some time later, however, when the advertising of the Century Brewing Association appeared, the slogan, "The Beer of the Century," formed a prominent part.

The plaintiff brought action against the brewing company. During the trial they were required to establish three points: (1) that the slogan was first conceived by the plaintiff, (2) that it is customary in advertising agency practice for the agency to receive compensation for its ideas if used by the advertiser, and (3) that the Century Brewing Association received value from the use of the slogan in question. The verdict was in favor of the plaintiff. A sum of $7,500 was granted them by the court. The legal basis for the decision was the common law doctrine of unjust enrichment.

The other case decided in 1935 was somewhat different. It was brought by a man who had written a letter to Liggett & Myers Tobacco Company in which he suggested a certain advertising theme for billboard advertising and asked for compensation for the idea. The tobacco company did not acknowledge the letter in any way. Some two years after receipt of the letter, Liggett & Myers used advertising which was similar, but not identical, to the suggestion sent in by the plaintiff.

Court action was brought, and a verdict in favor of the plaintiff was handed down. A judgment of $9,000 was awarded. The decision in this case was based upon an implied contract rather than unjust enrichment. An offer was made by the plaintiff when he mailed the letter. He had at no time withdrawn the offer, and the company had not rejected it. The use of the idea by the company, even though some two years later, was construed as an acceptance of the offer.[4]

The problem of protecting ideas is a delicate one and is difficult to handle. Many agencies and advertisers have adopted the policy of refusing to receive ideas from anyone until a clear understanding of possible liability has been established.

---

[3] *Ryan and Associates* v. *Century Brewing Association,* Washington Reports, Vol. 185, p. 600.

[4] *Meyer* v. *Liggett & Myers Tobacco Co.,* 194 N.E. 206.

Methods of paying the agency

The methods by which the agency receives compensation for work performed have been the subject of much discussion. It is therefore pertinent to inquire into both method and philosophy.

Commission plan. The most common method by which the advertising agency receives compensation for its services is the so-called "commission plan." It is, in essence, a discount from list price given the agency by the medium in which space is purchased. In other words, the medium —newspaper, magazine, radio, etc.—pays the agency.

An example will illustrate the general procedure. Company A contracts with Agency X to have X engineer an advertising campaign for the company. A total of $500,000 has been appropriated for this campaign. X will perform a part or all of the functions set forth above. Let us assume that space amounting to $450,000 is contracted for in magazines and newspapers. These media will bill X for the $450,000, less the regular discount allowed agencies, usually amounting to 15 percent. This leaves a net bill of $382,500, which X will pay the various media. X will bill the advertiser for the full $450,000.

Commissions from advertising media provide some 65 percent of agency income, on the average. The larger the agency the higher is the proportion of income accounted for by commissions. But even among the largest agencies between 10 percent and 25 percent of their income comes from other methods of payment.[5]

Other methods of payment. In addition to the commissions received from media, agencies also receive direct payment from advertisers for materials and services, such as engravings, finished art, comprehensive layouts, TV storyboards, producer's services for TV commercials, research, and publicity. Various methods of charging advertisers are used. For some materials and services the advertiser is charged the *cost* to the agency. For others the charge is *cost plus 15 percent,* to compensate the agency for service in connection with specifying, controlling, and consummating the purchase. For still others a *flat fee* is charged.

There is no standard practice to determine what services are performed in consideration of commissions received from media and what services are charged for separately. It seems obvious, however, that a fixed percentage commission will cover the cost of more services for an advertiser

---

[5] Ira W. Rubel, "Rubel Spells Out Agency Operating Facts to Dispel Visions of High Profits, Easy Living," *Advertising Age,* December 9, 1957, p. 85.

spending $1 million a year than for one spending only $50,000. In many respects, it is as costly to produce an advertisement to be placed in a small circulation magazine as it is to produce an ad to be placed in a large circulation magazine; yet, the former provides a much smaller commission than the latter. Thus, the smaller the agency and the smaller the account, the greater is the dependence on fees and service charges as sources of income.

In cases of direct mail, dealer display, and some business publication advertising, the fee basis is often most advisable. Certainly, the commission plan cannot be depended upon for direct mail and dealer-display work, since these media are noncommissionable.

Charging the advertiser an annual retainer—or "professional fee" is another method used by some agencies. Under this method, commissions granted by the media are usually credited against these fees, although some agencies work for a minimum annual retainer and add commissions from media to this. This works well where the bulk of the advertising is done through noncommissionable media.

An agency's work on a campaign to introduce a new product can become a losing proposition if the product fails. To protect the agency from this kind of loss, one client, the Lever Brothers Company, pays a fee "for a large portion—but not all—of the direct cost of new product work; with these fees recoverable from subsequent agreed levels of billing if the product succeeds, and retained by the agency if it does not."[6]

The relative importance of various methods of compensating agencies for different types of service is indicated in Table 28–1.

Qualifications for agency commission

Allowance of commissions to advertising agencies is the method developed over the years by advertising media to promote the sale and more effective use of their space and time. In effect, the 15 percent commission operates as a *functional discount* granted to agencies for performing functions that benefit media. Agencies promote advertising as a marketing instrument. They develop new business. They increase the productivity of advertising. They centralize the servicing of many accounts. They reduce the publisher's cost in the mechanical preparation of advertising. They reduce credit risk.

To qualify for the commission an agency has to meet certain require-

---

[6] Milton C. Mumford, *The Advertising Agency As A Business Institution* (New York: American Association of Advertising Agencies, 1966), p. 4.

TABLE 28–1. Principal methods of compensating agencies

Type of service	Percent advertisers using different compensation methods						
	Method 1, media com- mission only	Method 2, fee, plus media com- mission	Method 3, fee, media com- mission credited	Method 4, flat fee	Method 5, at cost to agency	Method 6, cost to agency plus per- centage	Total
Copy (magazines, newspapers)	66.6	17.6	4.3	3.7	2.1	5.7	100
Copy (direct mail, display)	21.5	15.1	3.9	23.9	9.6	26.0	100
Finished art	9.1	17.1	1.0	13.9	12.4	46.5	100
Marketing research	9.1	9.1	.6	41.5	19.6	20.1	100
Publicity	8.2	8.9	1.1	40.5	23.8	17.5	100
Engravings, typography	10.5	13.2	1.1	8.3	13.0	53.9	100

Source: "Frey Report On Agency Services and Compensation," *Advertising Age,* November 4, 1957, p. 132.

ments. Prior to 1956, media granted commissions only to "recognized" agencies. Recognition was a function performed by individual media owners and their trade associations, such as the American Newspaper Publishers Association, Publishers Association of New York City, Associated Business Publications, Periodical Publishers Association, and Agricultural Publishers Association. To secure recognition an agency had to meet the following requirements:

1. Be a *bona fide* agency—i.e., free from control by an advertiser, in order that it may not be prejudiced or restricted in its service to all clients; free from control by a medium owner, in order that it may give unbiased advice to advertisers in the selection of media.
2. *Keep all commissions* (i.e., not rebate any) received from media owners, in order to maintain their rate cards and to devote the commissions to such service and development of advertising as the individual media owners desire.
3. Possess *adequate personnel* of experience and ability to serve general advertisers.
4. Have the *financial capacity* to meet the obligations it incurs to the media owners.

On May 12, 1955, the Department of Justice filed a civil antitrust suit against the American Association of Advertising Agencies and the five media associations listed above. In the complaint it was alleged that the defendants in violation of the Sherman Act, engaged in "unlawful combinations, conspiracies, understandings, and agreements" with particular reference to the uniform standards for recognition of advertising agencies, the withholding of commissions from agencies not recognized, the charging of gross rates to direct advertisers, and the fixing of the commission at 15 percent of the gross rate.

On February 1, 1956, a consent decree was entered in the U.S. District Court in New York City enjoining and restraining the A.A.A.A. from engaging in the alleged practices. Similar consent decrees were entered later for the defendant media associations involved in the suit. It should be noted, however, that this suit dealt entirely with acts by the associations and did not relate to individual arrangements between an agency and a medium or between an agency and its clients.

Considerable speculation followed the settlement of this suit. Did it spell the end of the 15 percent commission as a standard of agency compensation? Would there now be many house agencies? Would there be widespread rebating? Would advertisers be able to buy at net rates? As of 15 years later, no major changes along these lines have taken place. The traditional recognition procedure, especially the role played by the associations, has been abandoned, but individual media continue to grant the 15 percent commission much as they have in the past. The associations continue to furnish "credit ratings" of advertising agencies to their members. In the case of A.N.P.A., an agency applying for credit rating may be required to demonstrate that it:

1. Itself assumes sole liability for the full performance of its contracts with newspapers;
2. Makes prompt payments;
3. Is morally responsible;
4. Is engaged in the business of developing, servicing, and placing national advertising in newspapers; and
5. Maintains a minimum of 25 percent of its average monthly billing in liquid capital and surplus.

Perhaps the most significant development growing out of this antitrust action has been a renewed attack on the commission system.

Appraisal of the commission system

The commission system has been the subject of controversy for many years. Major criticism has hinged around the unique client-agency-medium relationship. The agency, instead of being a vendor for the publisher as it once was, is now a "close-working partner" of the advertiser, but the compensation system has not been changed to meet these new conditions. There is strong feeling among advertisers that they, the agency's "clients"—not the various media—should be the ones to pay the agency for its services. They suggest that media should sell to the advertiser at net rates so that the advertiser can negotiate with the agency to arrive at a mutually satisfactory compensation.

Principal objections to the commission system concern (1) the fixed percentage of media cost, and (2) the client's lack of control over services paid for through the commission.

A fixed percentage of the cost of space and time provides the agency with compensation that may or may not be related to the cost of services performed. The agency's cost of producing an advertisement to appear in space costing $40,000 would probably not be ten times the cost of producing an ad to appear in space costing $4,000. Yet, the agency's compensation would be ten times greater for the former than for the latter. Also, on a fixed percentage basis, the more the client spends the more the agency makes. This creates the suspicion that the agency has no incentive to hold down the cost of advertising.

Lacking control over the services covered by the commission, the advertiser is compelled to negotiate for these so-called "free services." Is he getting all of the services to which he is entitled? Is he being forced to pay for services that he would not order if he controlled the amount and kind of work done on his account? Are the fees that he pays over and above the commission justified? Many advertisers feel that they do not have a large enough part in planning what the agency is to do for the commission it receives.

Supporters of the commission system claim that it is a means of rewarding agencies in direct proportion to the use that is made of their creative work. This is a "box office" approach to determining the value of an agency's service. It assumes that the value of an advertisement depends on the size of audience it reaches, not on the cost of producing it. However, most agencies would be quick to point out that they allocate more time and higher-salaried creative people to producing advertisements for big audiences than for small audiences, thereby also adapting the cost of production to the size of audience to be reached. To further reduce possible inequities arising from a fixed commission on media expenditures, agencies generally include more "free services" on big billings than on small billings.

Other arguments in favor of the commission system are that it places agency competition on a creative service basis instead of a price basis, that it has worked satisfactorily though imperfectly through the years, and that it will have to do until a better system comes along.

Both the Association of National Advertisers and the American Association of Advertising Agencies have made studies of the merits and shortcomings of the commission system. The former has, in general, questioned the wisdom of the method, while the latter has considered it superior to any other as a basic method of compensation. The latest study of agency services and compensation was commissioned by the ANA and was conducted by Professors Albert Frey and Kenneth Davis. This study indicated that a majority of all advertising managers, agencies, and media found the commission system satisfactory, but about one third of the advertising managers believed that a system involving net rates, no commissions, and fees fixed by negotiation between agency and client would be a better system.[7]

Specialized agencies

As in many other fields, there has been a tendency toward specialization in the advertising agency field. The general advertising agency centers major attention on serving those companies selling goods for general human consumption, which bulk heavy in the total volume of agency work. General agencies serve companies making such products as automobiles, refrigerators, medicines, personal items, foods, clothing, etc.

There are agencies concentrating in the field of industrial goods. The problems of selling here differ somewhat from those found in selling consumption goods; the techniques of presentation and the types of appeal to prospective buyers call for a different kind of advertising, and this encourages the specialized agency.

The same factors have caused a development of specialized agencies serving financial houses, sellers of service, and companies doing a large export business. The same fundamental principles of organization and operation hold for these agencies as for the general agency.

Future of the advertising agency

The future of the advertising agency can be exceedingly bright. Its substantial growth and success in the past have resulted in large measure from the increased degree to which it has turned from a mere peddler of

---

[7] Albert W. Frey and Kenneth R. Davis, *The Advertising Industry; Agency Services, Working Relationships, Compensation Methods* (New York: Association of National Advertisers, Inc., 1958), pp. 298, 299.

space to a true servant of the advertiser. Today, the opportunity awaits the agency to broaden its scope of service. It does now, in a number of instances, and can in the future in many more instances, serve as an efficient marketing and advertising counselor to business.

There were 4,800 advertising agencies in the United States in 1970. However, total agency billings, a measure of the business done by agencies for their clients, are highly concentrated in relatively few agencies. *Advertising Age* estimated that 66 agencies, each billing over $25 million a year, accounted for total billings of $7.5 billion in 1969. These 66 agencies accounted for 75 percent of all agency billings. The top ten agencies, each billing over $200 million, billed a combined $3.85 billion or 39 percent of the total. These agencies and their estimated billings, including international business for some, are listed here:[8]

1969 Rank	Agency	1969 Billings (in millions)
1	J. Walter Thompson Co.	$736.0
2	Young & Rubicam	522.9
3	McCann-Erickson	511.1
4	Ted Bates & Co.	375.1
5	Batten, Barton, Durstine & Osborn	356.2
6	Leo Burnett Co.	355.9
7	Doyle Dane Bernbach	269.9
8	Foote, Cone & Belding	265.5
9	Ogilvy & Mather International	229.8
10	Grey Advertising	228.1
11	Compton Advertising	180.0
12	Benton & Bowles	175.9
13	William Esty Co.	169.0
14	Dancer-Fitzgerald-Sample	163.0
15	N. W. Ayer & Son	148.6
16	Kenyon & Eckhardt Advertising	140.0
17	Norman, Craig & Kummel	140.0
18	MacManus, John & Adams	125.8
19	Campbell-Ewald Co.	123.8
20	Lennen & Newell	122.5
21	SSC&B Inc.	115.9
22	Needham, Harper & Steers	115.6
23	D'Arcy Advertising Co.	102.0
24	Ketchum, MacLeod & Grove	95.2
25	Wells, Rich, Greene	80.2
26	Campbell-Mithun	76.1
27	Cunningham & Walsh	75.3
28	Marsteller Inc.	74.1
29	Erwin Wasey Inc.	72.0
30	Tatham-Laird & Kudner	62.5
31	Marschalk Co.	60.6
32	Clinton E. Frank Inc.	59.0
33	Gardner Advertising Co.	58.3
34	LaRoche, McCaffrey & McCall	52.9
35	Post-Keyes-Gardner	50.0

---

[8] *Advertising Age,* February 23, 1970, p. 40.

1969 Rank	Agency	1969 Billings (in millions)
36	Grant Advertising	49.8
37	Fuller & Smith & Ross	49.7
38	Rumrill-Hoyt	49.4
39	Doremus & Co.	43.8
40	Griswold-Eshleman Co.	43.4
41	Ross Roy Inc.	38.1
42	Warwick & Legler	38.0
43	Albert Frank-Guenther Law	36.0
44	Lake-Spiro-Shurman	34.0
45	Bozell & Jacobs	33.1
46	Reach, McClinton & Co.	31.9
47	North Advertising	30.8
48	Carson/Roberts	30.5
49	Wunderman, Ricotta & Kline	30.4
50	Carl Ally Inc.	30.0
50	Geyer-Oswald	30.0
50	Sudler & Hennessey	30.0
53	Parkson Advertising Agency	29.6
54	Daniel & Charles	29.2
55	Coordinated Communications Inc.	29.1
56	L. W. Frohlich & Co./Intercon Int'l	28.5
57	Jack Tinker & Partners	28.3
58	DKG Inc.	28.0
59	Honig-Cooper & Harrington	27.7
60	Edward H. Weiss & Co.	27.0
61	Tracy-Locke Inc.	26.2
62	Al Paul Lefton Co.	26.0
62	Lois Holland Callaway	26.0
62	John F. Murray Advertising	26.0
65	William Douglas McAdams Inc.	25.1
66	Clyne Maxon Inc.	25.0

The small agency will, of course, find it difficult to provide the same breadth of service as that afforded by the large integrated agency. On the other hand, the large agency seldom makes its services available to the small advertiser, and hence the latter is deprived of that outside counsel unless the small agency is accepted. Recent developments in the form of agency networks have given the small agency some of the values of integration afforded by the large agency. A network consists of the grouping of many small agencies in all parts of the country for purposes of exchanging ideas, pooling research undertakings, trading operational data, and exchanging pertinent information in respect to successful campaigns. This development holds much promise for the small agency as well as the small advertiser.

QUESTIONS AND PROBLEMS

1. The commission method of compensating advertising agencies has often been questioned. What are some of the reasons for questioning the method? What do you recommend as a method of payment? Why?

2. "The research department of the advertising agency should provide the advertiser with valuable information and suggestions concerning the entire selling program." Do you agree? Why?

3. What is meant by the term "wholesaling" in connection with advertising agencies?

4. Outline the organization of a modern advertising agency by departments. What effect does the size of the agency have upon its functions?

5. What protection does the creator of ideas have when such ideas are offered to an advertising agency? Why is this so important to the agency?

6. A close harmony should exist between the media department and the research department of the advertising agency. Why?

7. What differences do you see in the *recognition* procedure as practiced by media trade associations prior to 1956 and the furnishing of *credit ratings* such as those provided by the A.N.P.A. after 1956?

8. In effect, the 15 percent commission granted to agencies by advertising media is a *functional discount* to compensate agencies for performing certain functions that benefit media. What are these functions?

9. The advertising agency has increased its functions over the years until it is now a potent factor in developing merchandising and selling ideas for the advertiser. What changes in agency practice would you recommend as a means of increasing still further the services rendered the advertiser?

10. "When we are ill, we call in a doctor. When we have legal difficulties, we call in a lawyer." Is it therefore logical that, when we have product promotional problems, we call in an advertising agency? Should we place the same faith in the agency that we place in the doctor or the lawyer? Explain in detail.

11. After 10 years with a nationally known advertising agency, Bob Peterson has finally been able to return to his first love—his own agency in his own home town in Indiana. The town is small, a little under 50,000 population, but Peterson knows every retail establishment there.

   In fact, he hopes to serve retailers primarily. In his town these include 2 "department" stores, about 15 specialty shops, 6 supermarkets, and a number of stores of other types.

   Peterson knows how to write copy, make layouts, and has worked in the media department in an agency. He has been able to get two other men, both able to perform most of the services offered by larger advertising agencies, although not on the same scale and perhaps not as expertly.

   Peterson is aware that most agencies avoid retail clients as much as possible because of their unique merchandising situations, but he thinks that by having as many noncompeting retailers as possible he can make a go of his business.

   Many policy-making problems present themselves. One problem is the selection of a method of compensation that is satisfactory to the retail stores and to himself. He bears in mind that his is the first agency of its kind in this area and that he has to prove himself.

   Recently, there has been a great deal of talk about an "agency network," a cooperative organization of small agencies who band together for legal, accounting, and research advice. Individually a small agency could not undertake these services, but spread over a number of them the cost would be relatively small. Peterson has been approached by a representative of such a network and must make a decision.

What sort of advice would you give Peterson concerning his problems? If you were offered an opportunity to join his agency, would you take it? Why?

chapter 29

THE ADVERTISING DEPARTMENT

AT ONE TIME the advertising policies and all advertising work carried on directly by the advertiser were the responsibility of the sales department or the president's office. More recently, most large-scale advertisers and many of those operating on a smaller plane have established a separate department in which all advertising problems are centered. In a number of instances the head of this department will be a vice president of the organization. Advertising has thus taken its place alongside production and sales in the organization structure of many companies.

Organization of advertising department

To promote more effective integration of advertising management functions within corporate organizations, the Association of National Advertisers has studied the methods of a number of representative firms. Although A.N.A. studies produced no single best organization plan, perhaps the most significant conclusion reached was the following:

The advertising manager today in more and more companies is recognized as a part of management. The old thinking resulted in such phrases as "making a presentation *to* management" or, "if only we could get *management* to take this course of action." The new and growing school of thought is that the chief advertising executive starts with the company point of view. He knows company policies and is conversant with all phases of the company's marketing activities. He recommends the kind of advertising organization and advertising policies that will serve the best overall interests of the company.

This kind of *advertising executive* is a far cry from the man of the past who used to content himself with the job of getting out ads. It is the kind of advertising manager demanded by today's conditions in which integrated marketing is required for growth and for competitive survival.

The way the advertising function is organized, and the kind of responsibilities and decision-making authorities delegated to the advertising manager lie at the core of almost every other necessary step toward making advertising more productive. It is therefore incumbent upon the advertising manager to search out all the facts and logic on how advertising should be organized and operated in his company, and to communicate this thinking to the policy-making group in his company.[1]

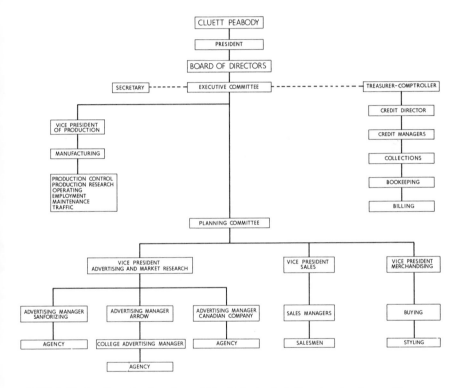

FIGURE 29–1.   Organization chart of Cluett, Peabody & Co., showing the position of the advertising department

The organization chart of Cluett, Peabody and Company, Inc., as reproduced in Figure 29–1, shows both the manner in which the advertising department of that company is organized and its relation to other departments.

---

[1] Association of National Advertisers, Inc., *Practical Guides and Modern Practices for Better Advertising Management,* Vol. II (New York: Association of National Advertisers, Inc., 1957), pp. 6 and 7.

It is clear from the chart that Cluett, Peabody places advertising on the same level with sales and merchandising and that the work of all three is coordinated by a planning committee.

A more detailed organization chart for an advertising department is that of General Mills, Inc., as reproduced in Figure 29–2.

FIGURE 29–2. Chart showing the organization of the advertising department of General Mills

It should be noted that General Mills operates its advertising department on both a commodity and a functional basis. Thus, the grocery-products division has its own advertising organization, which is responsible for (1) administering the grocery-products advertising budget; (2) providing the agency with factual data, such as nutritional value of products, manufacturing processes, markets to be covered, reactions to product, and other material that might serve as a part of final advertising copy; and (3) censorship and final approval of copy before it is placed.

On the functional side, the advertising department of General Mills has separate divisions for market analysis, home service, radio program, and accounts. These specialized divisions provide service for each of the commodity divisions when called on to do so.

Relations with other departments

The fact that a separate department has been established for advertising should not imply that advertising is to be operated independently of all other departments. Departmentalization usually signifies that the particular field has become sufficiently large and important to demand the full time and attention of one or a number of individuals. Such size allows for specialization of labor but, at the same time, calls for greater thought in coordinating the work of all the specialists.

Sales department. The advertising department will need to work with the sales department more than with any other. It must always be remembered that advertising is one type of selling. True, it is of such importance that it often needs to be separated from the direct supervision of the sales manager. However, the same fundamental principles that govern one should govern the other. There are certain kinds of data that each department will want collected, although the use made of such data may differ. The measurement of sales possibilities, both in total and by territories, will be of value to both departments. Both will be interested in determining an effective appeal or appeals in presenting the sales message to prospective customers by personal salesmen, by radio or television, or by the printed word. The basic appeal should be used by all sales agencies.

Those data and ideas that are used cooperatively might be collected cooperatively. A few companies have established a research department to perform these common tasks. In the absence of such a separation of function, common supervision of such work by those interested in the results may be advisable.

There are other matters in which the degree of success attained from the work of one department is dependent upon the work of the other. Thus, the effectiveness of an advertising campaign can often be increased materially by getting dealers to time the use of counter and window displays with magazine, newspaper, television, and/or radio advertising. The sales or merchandising department is usually in the best position to solicit this cooperation from dealers. In turn, the advertising department might be called upon to prepare trade-paper or direct-mail advertising to pave the way for personal solicitation by salesmen.

These mutual problems necessitate close and harmonious relations between the sales and advertising departments. In some companies, the advertising manager or his assistants spend part of their time traveling with the salesmen or visiting dealers to know selling problems at first-hand. Conversely, a few concerns include in their training of new sales-men a period of work in the advertising department.

Production department.   There is also a close relationship between the advertising and production departments. The advertiser might like to have the product restyled, changed in color, standardized as to size, improved in its operation, or packaged differently. The sales and adver-tising departments together should be charged with the responsibility of finding out what people want and the extent to which the products they have to sell meet these consumer wants. Their findings must be reported to the production department if any changes are desired, and conferences held to determine whether such changes are technically possible and eco-nomically feasible.

Executive department.   The executive department usually passes on all matters of policy before work is undertaken on a project or program. This department also acts as the coordinator of all functional divisions of the company. The advertising department, therefore, must clear all major problems with the executive offices.

The advertising department will initiate ideas, draw up proposed ad-vertising campaigns and strategy, outline the kind of research that might be carried on, figure the monetary needs in carrying out a given program, and suggest the methods by which such proposals might be accomplished. The use of an advertising agency might be recommended. All such mat-ters will be taken to the executive department for final approval. Thus, a selling job within the organization must be performed before real work is started. This task is not to be underestimated. Advertising is a field in which problems must be scientifically handled if satisfactory results are to be obtained. It is also a field in which everyone thinks that he knows what should be done and, hence, gives advice and criticism freely. Those in the executive offices are often of this type. It therefore requires tact, as well as much objective evidence, to obtain the executive's stamp of ap-proval on a proposed program. Changes which an executive may feel to be minor may often prove disastrous if made. Thus, the relationship between the advertising and executive departments is both a difficult and vital one.

Other departments.   There are other divisions with which the adver-tising department will have dealings from time to time. The purchasing department may be called upon to buy supplies of various kinds. If no advertising agency is employed, the volume of supplies to be purchased will be increased. Specific instructions as to the kind and quality of material desired must accompany any requisition.

If engravings or dealer-display materials are to be sent out, the advice of the shipping department should be sought. The same should be done when a new package is designed. The shipping department can often offer suggestions concerning the shape of a new package which will reduce the packing and shipping costs, although such suggestions should not be accepted if they would force a change in design out of harmony with probable human desires. Quite often, however, both needs can be met if the needs are recognized before the package is designed.

The accounting department might be called upon to keep the record of advertising expenditures in a particular way, especially when detailed cost figures are desired. A running record may be desired for expenditures by type of medium, for mechanical costs, overhead, research, etc. Such record will usually be of value, particularly where careful budgeting is done or where careful checks are made on the monetary value of particular media or advertisements.

The legal department is often a very important ally of the advertising division. A competitor may attempt to copy the company trademark, or a suit might be brought against the company for trademark infringement. The recent court decisions granting judgments against advertisers for using ideas of others without compensation might tend to multiply such suits in the future. Under such conditions the legal department will be called upon to defend the company. This department may also be called upon to render an opinion upon the legality of proposed new trademarks, package designs, etc. If any advertisements are copyrighted, the responsibility for having this done usually comes under the jurisdiction of the legal department.

Functions of the advertising department

The relationship between the advertising department and other departments as outlined here might lead the reader to believe that the other departments do all the advertising work—that the advertising department merely gets ideas and orders others to execute them. Such, however, is not the case. There is plenty of work for the advertising department to do.

If the services of an advertising agency are utilized, the advertising department will be relieved of much of the work of planning and executing product advertising in mass media. The functions performed or activities engaged in, aside from product advertising, are many. The management-consulting firm of McKinsey & Company obtained from 202 companies, who were members of the Association of National Advertisers, an accounting of the various activities, other than product advertising, engaged in by the advertising department. These firms reported 33 separate activities for which the advertising department was wholly responsible or in which it assisted other departments. That list of activities is given in Table 29–1 together with figures showing for each activity the percentage of firms where the advertising department (1) had full responsibility or (2) assisted other departments.

From a review of the activities listed in Table 29–1, it should be obvious that the advertising department of a large advertiser is concerned with many aspects of the company operation. It should be expert in the art of communications and thus serve as the informational and interpretative arm of the firm.

TABLE 29–1. Activities engaged in by advertising department

Activity	Percentage reporting advertising department	
	Fully responsible	Assisting others
Handle institutional advertising	86.6	6.4
Prepare displays for dealers or distributors	85.6	4.9
Prepare exhibits and other material for shows, conventions, etc.	79.7	19.3
Handle publicity releases	73.2	11.9
Develop visual sales material, such as easels and portfolios	72.3	16.3
Prepare catalogues	68.8	8.4
Prepare motion pictures or sound slides for use in sales departments	56.9	14.8
Prepare easels, slides, etc., for speeches by others	55.4	18.8
Edit house magazines for dealers	52.0	3.9
Edit consumer house organs	49.5	14.5
Handle dealer cooperative advertising	48.5	6.9
Do package design work	47.5	26.7
Do market research	47.5	31.2
Prepare motion pictures or sound slides for use in strengthening public relations	47.0	11.4
Edit employee publications	42.1	12.3
Hold consumer meetings or schools	36.6	8.4
Handle ceremonies such as "E" awards, etc.	35.6	26.7
Prepare internal posters for employee morale building	35.2	26.7
Provide facilities for public functions	32.6	20.3
Prepare material for interpreting company policies to employees	32.2	25.7
Advertise company's products and/or policies direct to stockholders	31.2	14.8
Hold dealer meetings	31.2	28.7
Do sales analysis work	28.2	27.7
Handle pretesting of products	27.2	28.8
Prepare speeches for others	26.7	42.1
Prepare motion pictures or sound slides for use in strengthening employee relations	23.3	17.8

TABLE 29–1 *(Continued)*

| | Percentage reporting advertising department | |
Activity	Fully responsible	Assisting others
Prepare releases and bulletins to stockholders	22.7	23.3
Handle company drives, such as bond and community fund ..	21.8	39.6
Arrange employee affairs, such as athletics, parties, etc.	15.8	24.2
Prepare annual report	15.3	40.1
Advertise for new employees	14.8	58.4
Prepare material for use in dealing with the government	13.3	27.2
Prepare material for stockholders' meetings	7.4	18.3

Source: Paul B. West, "How the Advertising Department Is Organized and What It Does," *Advertising Handbook,* Roger Barton (ed.) (New York: Prentice-Hall, Inc., 1950), p. 815.

Of course the major and primary job of advertising for most companies is to sell or help to sell products or services. Generally, either the advertising department itself is responsible for planning and executing the entire product advertising program, or it is responsible for selecting an agency to serve the company. Most large advertisers use an advertising agency and have the advertising department work with the agency to present company policy and coordinate agency operations with those company activities that relate to product advertising.

Choosing the agency

The results of an advertising program may depend to a considerable degree upon the care with which an agency is chosen to carry out the details of the program. Before a choice is made, the definite purpose that advertising is to accomplish should be recognized. A selection should be made on the basis of the probable ability of an agency to help carry out a program that will bring the results desired. This may occasion the choice of two or more agencies, each equipped to render a particular, although different, service.

While the selection of an agency cannot be reduced to scientific rules, the advertiser will benefit by weeding out all agencies unsuited to his needs. He should first draw up a preliminary list of likely agencies. Then he should set up yardsticks based on what he desires from the agencies. The agencies then usually prepare presentations for the solicitation and call on the advertiser's executives to make their presentations. From these the advertiser can decide where to award his account.

The General Electric Company uses the following check list and rating scale when selecting an agency:

Criteria	Rating points
Agency history	
1. Growth	1
2. Experience	5
3. Account history	5
4. Man power	7
5. Marketing concept	2
Total	20
Marketing services	
6. Campaign planning	10
7. Creative	11
8. Media	5
9. Sales promotion	7
10. Research	7
11. Merchandising	7
12. Product publicity	5
13. Production	3
Total	55
Handling of our account	
14. Personnel	15
15. Technique	5
16. Contact	5
Total	25

Under each of these criteria, General Electric Company executives look for such things as:

1. *Growth.* Have growth and billings been sound and consistent or have billings been up one year and down the next? Why?
2. *Experience.* In what fields of industry do its accounts lie? Has it demonstrated extreme versatility in all product areas or does it have particular strength in an individual product classification area?
3. *Account History.* What is its average age of service to its clients; what has been its account turnover?
4. *Man Power.* Here we look at the depth of experience and the number of people on second and third levels as well as the top level; here, too, we look at turnover.
5. *Marketing Concept.* Here we ask for the agency's philosophy of business operation. Is it progressive or conservative? Does it treat each problem individually or does it stick pretty close to a rigid formula? Does it reveal a keen appreciation of the place of business in its economic, social and political environment?
6. *Campaign Planning.* Here we judge the ability of the agency to secure, analyze and interpret all the facts and conditions affecting the marketing problem and their ability to develop advertising objectives and competitive strategy that form the essence of the campaign.
7. *Creative.* This is the judgment of the agency's ability to create essentially good ideas—applying imagination to the problem and developing sound ideas of unique value with great competitive impact.
8. *Media.* Here we are judging the evidence of thoroughness and soundness

in media research, the preliminary media recommendations, relative cost compared to budget, and so on.

9. *Sales Promotion.*   As used in this appraisal, this is that part of the campaign plan designed to stimulate, persuade and inform all people who sell the product; department salesmen, wholesalers and their salesmen, retailers and their salesmen.

10. *Research.*   This means primarily evaluating the resources to collect and interpret facts for a campaign plan that will help determine and achieve the sales and advertising objectives. Here we evaluate the abilities of the agency in the many forms of research such as copy research, motivation research, product planning research, package research, and others.

11. *Merchandising.*   This is an evaluation of the ideas devised and materials that an agency can provide to make all forms of selling pay off at the point of purchase.

12. *Product Publicity.*   This service need not necessarily be performed by *any* agency, especially if other means for clearing news of Company operations is maintained.

13. *Production.*   This is an evaluation of the agency's resources to produce or supervise production of all types of advertising, promotional and merchandising material. This will include slide films, motion pictures, radio and television programs and commercials, if they should be an essential part of the advertising campaign.

14. *Personnel.*   This is the number and quality of the people who will be assigned full time to the account—the most important factor in agency service. In a sense, we want to regard these people as being a part of our organization and thus their personalities and attitudes, as well as their planning and creative abilities, should be of a nature that will work well in harness with our people.

15. *Technique.*   Here we evaluate the mechanics of getting a job done. Who does what, when and how, must be planned, controlled and communicated to all who are affected both within the client's organization and that of the agency.

16. *Contact.*   This means the availability of agency personnel for personal contact with the frequency desired; the convenience and speed of contact for both regular and emergency purposes.[2]

Working with the agency

It takes more than an agency to conduct a successful campaign. There must be close cooperation between the agency and advertiser. The advertiser must be willing to furnish the agency with records, tests run on the product, quality characteristics of the product, and other information which is available and desired by the agency.

---

[2] C. J. Coward, "Effective Methods for the Selection of An Advertising Agency," *New Understanding in the Agency-Client Relationship,* Bureau of Business and Economic Research, Marquette University, 1957.

A most important element in modern advertising is product, market, and consumer analysis. Often, such research projects are carried out through the cooperation of the agency and the advertising department of the advertiser. The agency might draw up the form for questionnaires and send them out, while the advertiser takes over the responsibility of tabulating and summarizing the results.

In some instances the advertiser chooses to do a major portion of all research work. Thus, General Motors Corporation maintains its own research organization as a part of its advertising department. It is there that the General Motors consumer studies have been made; but once these studies are completed, the results are given to the advertising agency to be used as seen fit in the conduct of a campaign.

The agency should have the primary responsibility for an effective presentation of the advertising message, but it is the advertiser who should assume the primary responsibility for determining what that message should be. In arriving at his decision the advertiser should consider and respect his agency's opinion, but he should make the decision.

Checking on work of agency

When an agency is selected to do a particular job, confidence is usually placed in its ability to perform the task satisfactorily. Under such circumstances it would appear unnecessary to check or supervise its work in any way. Some draw an analogy between the work of a lawyer or a physician and an advertising agency. A patient usually would not advise the doctor; nor would a lawyer's client attempt to direct his plan of procedure.

In both these cases, however, the parties paying the bills would want to check the results obtained. They might even observe the degree to which the lawyer or the physician seemed to place the client's or patient's interests and welfare ahead of all else. To an even greater degree might the advertiser check the sincerity of the agency.

As has already been pointed out, the advertising agency often receives its pay, not from its client, but from various media. This might lead to advising a greater appropriation than might be necessary. It might result in the choice of media not suited to the advertiser's needs, purely because such media carried the 15 percent discount; effective media might be left out of consideration because of the absence of a commission. Likewise, since the agency often receives no extra remuneration for the research work done, such work might be done in a very superficial manner. But these things do not necessarily happen. Undoubtedly, most agencies work earnestly and effectively for the advertiser. They may even sacrifice a possible increased income in order to increase the profits of their client. But to avoid the continued use of an agency of the other type, it behooves the advertising director of the manufacturer to keep a continual check on the work of the agency. Of course, this should be a constructive check rather than one designed to pry into the affairs of others. The advertiser does not wish to catch the agency betraying the trust placed in it but, rather wishes to keep it conscious of the advertiser's interests.

The advertising department will usually check all detailed work of the agency and approve it for release. Sometimes suggestions for changes will be made in the choice of media as well as in the finished advertisement itself. In general, however, matters pertaining to the construction of an advertisement are left to the judgment of the agency because they are technical in character, and the technician will usually be better qualified to pass judgment than a layman. This is not true of the results of research, the basic appeal used in an advertisement, the use of certain media, or the methods employed to measure advertising effectiveness.

TABLE 29–2. Documentation required from agency

Client classification	Marketing strategy	Creative strategy	Research results
All types	50%	75%	40%
Industrial	45	70	35
Package goods	50	90	60
Durables and services	50	75	30
Small	40	60	25
Medium	55	80	35
Large	50	85	60

In a study of the creative approval process the Association of National Advertisers found that 50 percent of the clients surveyed re-require a marketing strategy statement, 75 percent require a creative strategy statement, and 40 percent require research documentation when the agency submits creative work for approval. As shown in Table 29–2, package goods advertisers and large advertisers are more inclined to require creative strategy statements and research documentation.[3]

---

[3] Association of National Advertisers, *The Creative Approval Process* (New York: Association of National Advertisers, Inc., 1966), p. 3.

Control of advertising expenditures

The problems incident to determining the amount of money to spend for advertising and the ways in which it will be spent are of vital importance. Chapter 31 is devoted to a consideration of this subject.

After the budget has been established, it becomes the duty of the advertising department to direct the expenditure of all sums thus provided. Effective supervision will involve a careful breakdown of expenditures into classes representing the character of services purchased. These classes may represent media by types, overhead expense, mechanical costs, etc. True, the budget will carry a total figure for each of these items for the entire year. It becomes the duty of the advertising department, however, to follow these expenditures by the week or month. This may be done graphically on a chart or by noting the total figures. The value of such a continual check is found in its currentness. Without it, the total allotment might be spent long before the end of the year.

The breakdown and charting of expenditures are not so important for amounts spent on major advertising schedules in magazines, newspapers, etc., because these are easily determined accurately in advance or are controllable at any time. The opposite is true for the expenses of window display, sampling material, and certain types of direct mail. The number of coupons received cannot be predetermined, and most coupon returns necessitate the sending of some type of material. It is this kind of expenditure that necessitates constant checking and charting in order to keep within the overall advertising budget.

In addition to charting expenditures for each type of advertising used, a record should also be kept of expenditures by territories. As changes in sales possibilities occur, owing to weather conditions, strikes, floods, changes in general business activity, activities of competitors, etc., changes in the amount of advertising money allotted to such territories should be made to harmonize with changed conditions. This function is discussed further in Chapter 31.

Getting new ideas

Every progressive manufacturer is looking for new ideas which will improve his product or make his selling or advertising appeal more effective. The advertising department is usually the contact point between the manufacturer and those having new ideas to give.

One company saved $50,000 a year, merely by changing the name on the shipping boxes; thus, the product fell in a different freight classification, calling for a lower rate. The idea came from outside. Another company adopted a new name, suggested by an outsider, for a golf ball. This name was passed on to the agency serving the company, and a successful campaign was built around it.

Changes in package design have often resulted through suggestions made from outside sources. If contests are conducted for the express purpose of getting new ideas, it is the advertising department that will receive and study their possibilities. The work involved in supervising a contest and digesting the returns is often very great, and the value of contests depends to a considerable degree upon the manner in which the returns are handled.

The court decisions granting a judgment against an advertiser for using ideas without compensation increases the burden upon the advertising department. Extreme care must be taken to protect the company against unreasonable claims from those offering new ideas. Too much encouragement to get the layman to send in ideas without proper safeguards to both the advertiser and the layman might be disastrous.

QUESTIONS AND PROBLEMS

1. Why is it difficult to establish a "best" type of organization for the advertising department of the manufacturer?

2. In choosing the agency, why would the advertising department consider the experience of the agency more important than its size? Compare the relative importance of the other factors in agency selection.

3. What advantages accrue from a long-term contract with an advertising agency?

4. Why do agencies usually let the advertiser himself do part of the work on research projects?

5. If sufficient care is taken in selecting an agency, is there any need for checking the agency's work?

6. In what way does the breakdown and charting of expenditures for magazine and newspaper advertising differ from that for window-display and poster advertising?

7. Why can a company not accept new ideas for the betterment of its product indiscriminately from the general public?

8. "By subordinating the advertising department to the sales department, a greater degree of departmental cooperation would be secured." Do you agree? Support your stand.

9. "Because of the greater degree of specialization attained in the advertising agency, more powers are delegated to it, thereby decreasing the need for the

advertising department in the business organization." Do you agree? Why?

10. Do you think it a good policy to select more than one advertising agency as a means of increasing the degree of specialization in functions performed? Why?

11. A large cosmetic producer has developed a new nail polish remover for which it makes the following claims:

   a) Since it contains lanolin it does not dry out the nails and thus keeps them from becoming brittle and easy to break.

   b) It is guaranteed to remove polish on the first application.

   c) It is packaged in a self-sealing tube and therefore does not evaporate as quickly as other polish removers.

   d) Because of the self-sealing feature of the tube, the remover will last twice as long as competing brands.

   While this new product is apparently much superior to competing brands, the cost of production is such as to require a price approximately three times that of competitors' products.

   The product is new and hence unknown to the public. The company is small and has only a moderate amount of capital. It is not sure what the public reaction would be to the new product, especially with the premium price that is necessary.

   The company questions whether it should undertake to do its own advertising through its advertising department or to solicit the services of an agency. It also wonders whether any consumer research should be undertaken before launching an advertising campaign, and if research is done, whether it should be done by its own advertising department.

   What advice would you give the company? Support your recommendations.

chapter 30
RETAIL
ADVERTISING

THE IMPORTANCE of retail advertising is often underestimated. It does not present the glamour of network television and magazine advertising; it does not get the criticism that is often leveled against the advertisements of certain branded and trademarked articles. Few general agencies bother with such small-scale advertising. And yet, retail advertising accounts for almost 40 percent of the total annual advertising bill.

Extent and character of retail advertising

Retail advertising is distinctly local in character. It can, therefore, tie the products being advertised directly to the store handling them. In this respect, it is a focused type of advertising. Direct action can be emphasized much more than in national advertising. "Buy the XYZ radio at your nearest retailer," does not possess the same tone or carry the same weight as "Buy your XYZ radio from the John Jones Radio Store, Sixth and Walnut Streets." This directness allows for greater ease in checking the results of retail advertisements. Many retailers keep a record of the sales of specific products before, during, and after the time they have been featured in the advertising.

The retailer must, in general, initiate his own advertising program and follow it through to completion. The large retail organizations like department stores and chain stores can afford a well-rounded advertising department. Such a department will be capable of accomplishing for the retailer what the general agency and the advertising department do for the manufacturer. The work will include development of the basic research program preliminary to advertising, selection of media, writing copy, getting art work done, putting the advertisement together, taking care of the mechanical problems incident to reproduction, checking on the effectiveness of advertisements already run and to be run, etc.

The small retailer cannot make use of specialization, and no separate department can be established for advertising. Dependence must, therefore, be placed upon the general ability of the manager and the use of certain specialized agencies that stand ready to serve the small retailers.

Working with other departments

If the retailer is large enough to justify a separate advertising department, this department's work must be coordinated with the other departments of the store, just as described in connection with manufacturing concerns. In the larger stores, the advertising department is likely to have these chief functions: preparing and planning of advertising, displaying goods within the store, preparing signs, doing advertising research, and obtaining favorable publicity about the store and its featured selling events. Its association will be particularly close with the various merchandising departments, which perform the buying and selling functions.

The advertising department must learn all it can about the features of the merchandise it is promoting, and the buyers in the various merchandising departments should see that full information is provided. The advertising and merchandising executives together must determine the space to be devoted to each department and the items to be featured. The advertising staff should give valuable assistance by originating promotional ideas and by providing the customer's viewpoint. Teamwork in the store is essential for, although advertising may draw shoppers to the store, sales will be made only if sales efforts within the store support the advertising. Edwards and Howard have indicated that "the failure of stores to support external advertising with adequate inside-the-store promotion is undoubtedly one of the most serious shortcomings of present-day retail sales promotion."[1]

Relations with advertising agencies

The retail advertiser, in general, has not used the advertising agency to plan and execute an advertising program. Several factors have helped

---

[1] C. M. Edwards and W. H. Howard, *Retail Advertising and Sales Promotion* (rev. ed.; New York: Prentice-Hall, Inc., 1950), p. 18.

to produce this situation. The time element is one factor. The advertising strategy to be employed by the retailer may be planned well in advance of the appearance of any advertising, but the actual advertisements are often written "against time." An advertisement may be scheduled for a given edition of the local newspaper, and yet preparation may not be started on it until a few hours before press time. This delay is often necessary in order that full advantage can be taken of such factors as weather, competitors' activities, trend of consumer demand, etc. If an agency is to serve the retailer well, either a branch should be established in the city served by the retailer, or an agency representative should be stationed there. A close acquaintanceship with the problems of the retailer is necessary if an effective advertising job is to be done. The large retailer, therefore, has usually preferred to depend upon his own advertising department for all such work. The small retailer spends such a small amount on advertising that no general agency finds it profitable to solicit his business.

The differential existing between local and national newspaper and radio rates also militates against the use of the general agency. We have seen how newspapers, for example, grant to local advertisers a special rate that is much lower than that granted national advertisers. Usually, no agency discount is allowed on the local rate. The retailer who would like to use an agency must, therefore, pay directly for such services. The apparent additional cost often encourages the retailer to plan and execute his own advertising program without the help of the general agency.

While several factors have tended to keep the general agency out of the retail field, there are certainly no unsurmountable obstacles to the entrance of the agency into this field. In fact, there has been some tendency for large stores to utilize agencies' services. This was indicated in one survey among retailers which showed that 40 percent of all retailers with annual sales of $5 million or more used an advertising agency, but only 5 percent of those with sales under $100,000 used an agency.[2] Another study reported that "one important New York advertising agency now has 140 store accounts."[3]

What has been said of the general agency does not apply to certain specialized agencies. The retailer should be as vitally interested in certain types of research as the manufacturer. Certainly, the effectiveness of an advertising program for the retailer will depend upon the degree to which it is keyed to consumer desires. The location of those consumers

---

[2] C. H. Sandage, *Radio Advertising for Retailers* (Cambridge, Mass.: Harvard University Press, 1945), p. 231.

[3] *Advertising Age,* March 10, 1947, p. 60.

whose needs and wants can be satisfied by the products carried for sale should be ascertained. Media should be chosen in terms of their ability to reach such consumers. Some means of checking the effectiveness of advertisements should be devised. The retailer, particularly the small one, is often not in a position to perform all these tasks. There are specialized agencies that stand ready to perform such services, and the cost is usually not excessive. When measured in terms of values received, the expenditure is certainly not an expense but a wise investment.

Media used

The retail advertiser can use practically any medium except magazines, which are ruled out because they cover a much wider area than that served by the retailer. Even magazines, however, can be used by some of the larger chain-store organizations. The following media are suggested as being of value to retail stores:

Newspaper advertising
  a) Daily newspapers
  b) Weekly newspapers
  c) Shopping news

Direct-mail advertising
  a) Letters
  b) Postal cards
  c) Circulars, booklets, leaflets, etc.

Radio and television advertising
  a) Spot announcements
  b) Sponsored programs

Outdoor advertising
  a) Billboards
  b) Illuminated store signs
  c) Signs on delivery trucks

Streetcar advertising
  a) Streetcar cards
  b) Bus cards
  c) Suburban train cards

Motion-picture theater advertising
  a) Colored slides
  b) Commercial trailers

Advertising by personal distribution
  a) Handbills
  b) Dodgers

Classified advertising
  a) In newspapers
  b) In telephone directories
  c) In buyers' directories

Advertising confined to store itself
  a) Window displays
  b) Counter and floor displays
  c) Elevator bulletins

Transit radio
  a) Program sponsorship
  b) Special announcement

Doorstep advertising is used by a number of both large and small retailers. *Retail Ledger* recently conducted a survey to determine the attitude of consumers toward this type of advertising. More than 500 customers, representing various social and economic groups, replied to the questionnaire. Some of the results secured are presented in Table 30–1. Only about one third of those people answering the questionnaire resented the use of doorstep advertising. More than half of them, however, stated that less confidence was placed in such advertising than in newspaper or certain other forms of advertising. The inclusion of news would seem to add to the effectiveness of doorstep handbills, dodgers, and shopping news.

TABLE 30–1. Results of doorstep-advertising study (ratios by sex)

Query	Women and men (526 replies)		Women (352 replies)		Men (168 replies)	
	Yes	No	Yes	No	Yes	No
Usually pick up and look at	62%	38%	65%	35%	56%	44%
Resent such use of doorstep	34	66	34	66	34	66
Less confidence in such advertising	59	41	55	45	54	46
Influenced by name of firm	65	35	61	39	66	34
More attention to regularly distributed ..	63	37	66	34	51	49
More likely to read that with news, etc. .	65	35	65	35	66	34

The retailer will find that advertising within the store itself, such as counter and window displays, will prove of great profit if properly used. Good windows, attractively decorated and carrying out one central idea, will prove effective. Displays should be changed often. Suggestions for displays can be obtained from manufacturers whose goods are handled and from companies that sell decorative materials.

In terms of the amount of money spent, newspapers are by far the most important medium for retailers. Perhaps as much as 75 percent of the total retail advertising budget is spent in newspapers. Radio advertising, however, is growing in importance for certain types of retailing; and television is being used by an increasing number of firms.

Regardless of what media are used, it is important that all efforts be carefully coordinated. This will increase the effectiveness of each.

Budgeting expenditures

The general problems of budgeting are considered in Chapter 31. Retailers will find their budgeting problems somewhat simpler than those of some companies covering a large territory. The retailer need not divide his appropriation on the basis of sales territories. He must, however, consider the basis upon which he shall arrive at the total amount to be spent and the distribution of this amount to various media and products.

Measured in terms of sales, the expenditures for retail advertising averages from nothing at all for some types of stores to 8 or 9 percent for others. Flower and beauty shops will have an average advertising expenditure amounting to about 5½ percent of sales. Department stores will set aside from 2 to 5 percent of sales, according to the size of the store. The percentage, in general, varies directly with the volume of sales except for those stores doing more than $10 million business, in which cases the percentage declines. Grocery stores will, in general, appropriate 1 percent or less of their sales for advertising.

These are average figures and have all the shortcomings of averages. But they do serve as a rough guide to what is done. Naturally, many stores spend less and many spend more for advertising than the average figures quoted. It should be recognized that the percentage of sales is not the best guide to the establishment of the advertising appropriation. A better method consists of correlating the appropriation to the task to be performed (see Chapter 31).

Retailers' advertising expenditures tend to vary in relation to other characteristics also. A detailed study has shown that stores selling appliances and luxuries tend to spend the highest percentage of sales for advertising.[4] Size of the town also seems to influence relative expenditures. Mr. Mitchell indicated that places of from 20,000 to 100,000 population spent relatively more for advertising than stores in either smaller or larger places. This was attributed to the lack of local advertising media in small places and to the many neighborhood stores in larger places that could not afford to use citywide media.

After the appropriation has been established, it should be divided according to the media to be used and the products to be advertised. In relating expenditures to products, thought must be given to the general popularity of the product, the season of the year, unit price, gross margin, and similar factors. It is not wise to place much advertising behind slow-moving items. The fact that they do move slowly is probably an indication that consumers do not care for them. Push those items for which there is a potent demand, and better results will be obtained. It is extremely costly to change human desires; it is much better to harmonize advertising efforts with existing desires. Thus, by placing the major portion of the appropriation behind those items most desired, a greater percentage of total area sales will probably be received.

Special days, weeks, and seasons will, of course, have a direct influence

---

[4] W. L. Mitchell, Jr., "How Retail Advertising Expenditures Vary with Sales Volume and Size of City," *Dun's Review,* January, 1941, pp. 13–20.

on the desires of customers for given products. These periods can be anticipated and provision made in advance for extra promotional and advertising effort. Of course, such days as Christmas, New Year's Day, Independence Day, and Thanksgiving will not be forgotten. But what of Flag Day, Army Day, Candy Week, Baseball Week, Education Week, Golf Week, etc.?

The following list of special weeks and days indicates the great variety

Alphabetical Index of Special Weeks and Days

American Education Week
American Legion Convention
American Toy Fair in New York
Apple Week, National
Armistice Day
Ash Wednesday (beginning of Lent)
Baseball Week, National
Better Homes Week, National
Boy Scout Anniversary Week
Business Women's Week
Candy Week, National
Cheese Week, National
Cherry Week, National
Children's Day (Commercial)
Children's Week, National
Coffee Week, Iced
Columbus Day
Constitution Week
Cotton Week, National
Decoration Day (Memorial Day)
Defense Week, National
Dog Week, National
Easter Sunday
Egg Week, National
Election Day
Father's Day
Father and Son Week
Fire-Prevention Week

First-Aid Week, National
Fisherman's Week, National
Flag Day
Flower Shut-In Day, National
Foot Health Week, National
Foreign Trade Week
Garden Week, National
Girl Scout Week
Golf Week, National
Good Friday
Grocers' Week, National Retail
Halloween
Hobby Week, National
Immaculate Conception, Feast of
Labor Day
Lent
Lincoln's Birthday
May Day
Mother's Day
Music Week, National
Navy Day
Palm Sunday
Picture Week, National
Poppy Week
Red Cross Roll Call
Restaurant Week, National
St. Patrick's Day

of occasions when advertising and promotion efforts might be coordinated with national, regional, or local celebrations. Naturally, many of these days or weeks are of significance to a limited number of retail institutions; but where they do apply, an extra amount might be appropriated for advertising during such periods.

Items with a high price and large gross margin can usually sustain a larger amount of advertising than the lower-price items. Here again attention must be given to general consumer attitudes before much is spent.

Brand policy

Most advertising carried on by a manufacturer is built around the promotion of an identified product. In fact, were it not for the existence of branded merchandise, national advertising would be very different and perhaps very much diminished. This does not hold for retail advertising because the retailer has no monopoly or control of branded merchandise unless he has his own private brands or an exclusive agency contract for a manufacturer's brand. Hence, retail advertising should not be built around the promotion of branded merchandise as such.

The true position of the retailer is that of a buyer for the community rather than a seller of goods for the manufacturer. A multiplicity of brands is available to the retailer. Retail advertising emphasis should therefore be placed upon the general character of goods made available to the community and the type of service rendered. Such factors as style, quality, price, delivery, credit, location, honesty, and variety of merchandise are the things in which the retailer deals. The factors provided by a particular retailer should be emphasized and associated with his name. Branded merchandise might be advertised as a means of portraying the idea of quality or style; but, in any event, such factors must be associated with the name of the retailer. Note the contrast in national and retail advertising in this respect. In the latter the name of the merchant is prominently displayed, while in the former it is the brand name of the product.

Working with the manufacturer

The retailer has no particular interest in the products of any one manufacturer. His interest is that of stocking and selling merchandise that his customers want. The product advertising problem becomes one of informing the public of the qualities of such products, how these qualities will meet consumer desires, and where the products can be purchased.

Too many retailers have felt that the qualities of a product need not be advertised in specific terms; that such terms as "superb quality," "outstanding value," and "bargain of the century" are adequate to draw in the buyers. This philosophy is apparently on the decline. Consumers are demanding more detailed information about the products offered for sale.

The retailer can obtain this detail from the manufacturer and should insist upon it. Quite often, much value will be received by having a representative of the advertising department visit the manufacturer in order that a more thorough understanding of the qualities of a product might be obtained before copy is written. The manufacturer also should have an interest in this procedure. If the retailer does not or cannot contact the manufacturer, the latter might send a representative to the larger retail establishments or, by mail, explain in detail the qualities possessed by products offered for sale.

A different kind of cooperation between the retailer and manufacturer is that in which the latter offers advertising allowances to retailers to pay part or all of the cost incurred in advertising a specific item on a local basis. By having the local store contract for space in the local papers, the manufacturer may receive the advantage of local rates. Such cooperation on the part of the manufacturer also places the prestige of a local establishment behind his brand and encourages the retailer to give extra promotion to specific brands. The retailer gains by receiving some compensation for his efforts in this promotion and by being able to purchase more advertising space, thus getting better quantity discounts from media. However, the retailer must not permit this inducement to detour him from his fundamental job of stocking and promoting those goods that are most desired by his customers. The manufacturer, on the other hand, should be sure that allowances granted are used for advertising purposes and, also, be wary lest such allowances constitute discrimination between dealers which would violate the Robinson-Patman Act.

Intraindustry cooperation

The small independent retailer is, in many ways, unable to compete with the larger concerns in the use of advertising. He cannot employ specialists, and his advertising volume is not sufficiently large to give him sizable quantity discounts from newspapers. Neither can he utilize the large circulation of newspapers or audiences of broadcasting stations, whose readers or listeners largely are outside the area from which he draws trade. The large downtown retailer, and particularly the chain organizations, can obtain the services of specialists, get the more favorable rate discounts, and utilize media with citywide circulation.

When independent retailers work together in group advertising, they largely can offset these disadvantages. With stores spread throughout the community, they waste little of the circulation of newspapers. By dividing the cost among many, they can afford competent talent, can buy large enough space to be effective, and can obtain quantity rate discounts. Some of the same advantages apply to use of other media, such as handbills, direct mail, and window displays.

Retailers may organize themselves into cooperatives for advertising and other mutual benefits, or they may join groups sponsored by wholesale concerns known as "voluntary" chains. The usual procedure in such organizations is for each member to contribute a certain sum periodically for advertising purposes. This common fund supplies sufficient money to employ efficient technicians to prepare circulars, handbills, newspaper advertisements, and other material to be used by members individually or jointly.

Special mat and other services

The small retailer wishing to "run an ad" in the local paper often hesitates because he does not know how to prepare an advertisement. This lack of knowledge need not keep him from having a relatively good advertisement. He can subscribe for a regular advertising service, or he can obtain from his local publisher examples of advertisements from which he can choose.

The Metro Associated Services, Inc. and Stamps-Conhaim Senior Newspaper Advertising Service are two of the forty firms preparing regular catalogs or "proof books," as they are called, of illustrations and sample advertisements. The retailer can select illustrations or complete advertisements from these books. Each illustration in the proof book is accompanied by a matrix from which the advertisement can be set up for printing. The publisher will add the retailer's name, the prices of the products advertised, and any minor items desired.

This service is usually provided by newspaper publishers at little or no cost to the advertiser; the publishers receive their income from the sale of space. The service does provide the small merchant with advertisements which are prepared by specialists and are usually better than the ones which he might prepare himself. In addition, he saves the cost of hiring specialists to write individual advertisements.

A similar service is given by many manufacturers. The makers of laundry machinery, radios, electric refrigerators, automobiles, etc., are interested in having their retail outlets advertise their products. To encourage such advertising and to make sure that it will be of a relatively high standard, the manufacturer furnishes retailers with sample advertisements. The retailer can select a particular advertisement, order the matrix from the manufacturer, and turn it over to the local newspaper for publication. Reproductions of suggested advertisements available in mat form from the manufacturer are given in Figures 30–1 and 30–2. These mats can often be ordered by number, as noted at the bottom of Figure 30–1.

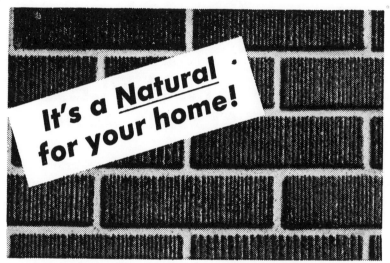

You get that solid "NATURAL BRICK" look with this Flintkote Insulated Siding with a Natural Color Mortar Joint. This remarkable siding not only beautifies your home, but will keep your house much warmer in winter and cooler in summer and, what's more, you'll save money on your fuel bills and house painting costs.

See for yourself how clearly this siding duplicates actual brick in color, texture and overall appearance. Let us show you this amazing Insulated Siding and give you a free estimate.

574

DEALER'S NAME
ADDRESS AND PHONE NUMBER

FIGURE 30–1. Mat available from manufacturer

specially made for ROLLERS

New

Dutch Boy® NALPLEX
LATEX FLAT WALL PAINT

NEW NALPLEX is specially blended for perfect roller application. Virtually eliminates roller marks, splatter or spray. NEW NALPLEX also has the BUILT IN SECOND COAT so high in hiding, so smooth in leveling one coat looks like two. Quick drying. Truly washable. No mess either— brushes and rollers clean-up with soap and water. Try it.

more years to the gallon

DEALER NAME

FIGURE 30–2. Manufacturer's mat with blank space for retail price and store name

Wholesalers and trade associations often provide mat services. Thus, the National Retail Hardware Association provides such a service to hardware dealers. Each month in the *Hardware Retailer* are shown proofs of the mats obtainable for the following month's use. Any such illustration can be obtained at small cost in either electro or mat form.

In addition to mat services, manufacturers and wholesalers may provide the retailer with definite help in conducting a direct-mail campaign, obtaining outdoor-poster advertising at low cost, and in making attractive window displays. The American Laundry Machinery Company has prepared a complete direct-mail campaign which can be used by the local operator of a steam laundry. This material can be obtained in quantities, with the name of the local operator printed or stamped at the bottom. The cost to the local operator is much less than it would be if the printing were done individually. Bundle inserts are obtainable in the same way.

The Morey Mercantile Company of Denver includes in its regular bulletins to Morey grocers the photographic reproductions of actual windows set up in the most approved manner. Detailed diagrams are provided, showing exactly how many cans of this and that article to place in each window and just how to arrange them.

The small retailer in particular can well afford to acquaint himself with these aids to more effective advertising. While his advertising appropriation will be small, results obtained from his expenditures can be increased by making use of the many free or inexpensive aids available.

Retailers who use wholesalers as sources of supply will often be able to obtain helpful assistance from such suppliers in planning advertising programs. This may be of particular value in securing point-of-purchase display material and in getting the personal assistance of the wholesaler in developing window and store displays.

The importance of advertising displays at point of purchase has become most evident with the development of self-service retailing. Manufacturers, wholesalers, and retailers are involved in the problem of getting specific brands of merchandise forcefully and dynamically brought to the attention of consumers during their self-selection of merchandise inside the store. Manufacturers and private-brand wholesalers strive to get their brands displayed in favorable spots in the retail store, and the retailer wishes to secure and maintain strong consumer patronage. The retailer can still select the specific brands of merchandise to promote actively; but, once that is done, advertising and merchandising helps should be solicited from the manufacturer or supplier of those brands.

Truth in retail advertising

Recent federal legislation has increased the powers of the Federal Trade Commission over interstate advertising. In general, however, the authority of the Commission does not reach the retail advertiser. Perhaps the most potent forces in promoting truthful retail advertising are the Better Business bureaus and censorship by local media.

Retailers should recognize the wisdom of using a type of advertising that carries conviction to the reader. False and exaggerated statements militate against this. It is important to keep truthful, not only one's own advertising, but also that of other retailers. Cooperation with the local Better Business bureau will help in both cases. The publication, *A Guide for Retail Advertising and Selling,* published by National Better Business Bureau, Inc., should be in the hands of every retail advertiser. The *Guide* provides the retailer with specific standards and definitions of terms often used in retailing, which enable him to keep his advertising truthful. It gives 314 rules on such items of general interest as comparative prices, "bait" advertising, and other factors. By following the recommendations of the Bureau, retailers will have greater assurance of maintaining the confidence of customers.

QUESTIONS AND PROBLEMS

1. A new and profitable development in the organization of advertising agencies might be the local agency that meets the requirements of the small independent retailers. Do you agree? Why?
2. Why is the budgeting of the retail advertiser's appropriation less complicated than that of a general advertiser?
3. Who takes the place of the general advertising agency in the preparation and placing of a retail advertisement?
4. The retail advertiser cannot depend upon the general advertising agency to plan and execute an advertising program. Why?
5. Contrast the advertising carried on by the retailer with that carried on by the manufacturer.
6. Does cooperative advertising between the retailer and manufacturer benefit both organizations? Explain.
7. In your role as a consumer, what is your attitude toward retail advertising in general?
8. In what respects is retail advertising a "buyer's-guide" type?
9. Bring to class three retail advertisements that do and three that do not appear

to you to be beneficial aids to the consumer. Point out the reasons for your appraisal.

10. G. Lynn Sumner, vice president of Abbott Kimball & Company, recently wrote in *Printers' Ink:*

". . . Why shouldn't any outstandingly good advertisement be repeated? It is one of the mysterious inconsistencies of advertising practice that repeating a proved-successful advertisement is considered the soundest kind of gospel in the mail-order business and rank heresy in the field of general advertising. Why? If the best possible piece of mail-order copy repeated, say, three times during a year in the same publication will bring greater response than three new and untried advertisements, why won't the best possible piece of merchandising copy repeated three times send more people into the stores than three new and untried advertisements?"

How would you answer Sumner's question?

chapter 31
THE ADVERTISING BUDGET

ADVERTISING management is essentially a matter of setting objectives, planning operations to achieve the objectives, putting the plans into action, and controlling operations. The principal instrument used in performing these functions is the advertising budget. In a sense, the entire administrative process—reviewing past operations, controlling on-going operations, and planning ahead—centers on the budget. Budgeting encourages more precise planning. It enhances a most profitable allocation of resources. It helps keep expenditures within predetermined limits.

An advertising budget encompasses two areas of decision: (1) the total number of dollars to be spent for advertising, often referred to as the appropriation; and (2) how these dollars will be spent.

SIZE OF THE BUDGET

The amount of money to be spent in advertising is of vital concern to the company and to the agency chosen to serve the company. To both, it serves to establish a limit to the advertising to be done during a given period. It provides the cloth from which the advertising campaign is to be cut; the size of this cloth should be considered carefully before the campaign is planned and started.

The following factors are significant in determining the size of the budget: (1) the procedure for arriving at the total number of dollars to be spent, (2) the role of advertising in the marketing plan, and (3) the items to be charged to advertising.

Procedures for determining size of the budget

The procedure used to determine the size of the budget should not only arrive at the number of dollars to be spent. It should also provide justification for the expenditure. The more common procedures in use include the following: (1) percentage of past sales, (2) percentage of anticipated future sales, (3) percentage based on both past and anticipated sales, and (4) objective-and-task method.

Percentage of past sales. Both this method and the one based on future sales justify themselves by assuming the existence of a definite relationship between the volume of sales and the volume of advertising necessary to produce those sales. Of course, they presuppose a proper coordination of advertising and all other sales activities. It is in the establishment of this proper coordination that the advertising percentage is set.

Let us assume that a given product sells for $1. Of this dollar, 20 percent goes for all selling costs. These costs include salesmen's salaries, office expense, billing and shipping expense, advertising, etc. What combination of these factors will provide the best results? Should 12 percent go for expenses of personal selling, 5 percent for advertising, and 3 percent for other selling costs? When these ratios have been worked out, the relative importance of advertising in the selling program has been established in terms of a percentage of total sales. This figure can then be applied to total sales of the previous year to get the total appropriation.

The percentage finally arrived at will differ materially for different industries and for different companies within an industry.

A study of 2,325 "advertising companies" showed that advertising expenditures as a percent of sales ranged from an average of four tenths of 1 percent for insurance companies to an average of 16.47 percent for makers of cosmetic and beauty aids. Among individual companies the range was wide. A total of 328 companies reported they spent less than one half of 1 percent of sales for advertising. At the other extreme, 21 companies reported spending more than 40 percent of sales for advertising.[1]

As indicated in Table 31–1, within a given industry the percentage of sales spent for advertising tends to be higher for the smaller companies.

The percentage-of-past-sales method has certain distinct weaknesses.

---

[1] C. H. Sandage and S. B. Bernstein, *Study of Advertising As a Per Cent of Sales, 1954* (Chicago: Advertising Publications, Inc., 1956).

TABLE 31–1. Variation of advertising investment by selected industries according to size of business

	Advertising percent of sales (medium figure) by size of business (in millions)										Number in sample
	Less than 1	1–2½	2½–5	5–10	10–25	25–50	50–100	Over 100	No size given	All sizes	
Insurance	*	*	*	0.44%	0.78%	0.41%	0.30%	0.28%	0.13%	0.40%	45
Industrial materials and supplies	2.64%	1.95%	1.85%	1.62	1.28	0.82	0.56	0.24	1.15	1.27	243
Miscellaneous	4.00	3.27	1.29	1.87	1.47	1.00	*	0.84	1.20	2.00	152
Women's ready-to-wear	2.96	1.91	2.86	1.54	3.50	*	*	*	*	2.00	44
Building materials	3.35	3.06	2.04	1.62	1.75	1.50	*	1.00	1.00	2.01	93
Office equipment	6.00	2.50	1.69	2.45	2.30	1.48	*	*	*	2.02	58
Furniture	3.78	1.50	1.80	1.52	2.65	*	*	*	2.89	2.09	45
Home equipment, fixtures, etc.	3.00	2.55	2.60	1.90	2.00	2.00	*	*	1.50		134
Farm machinery and equipment	3.85	1.46	2.46	1.67	*	*	*	*	*	2.20	61
Shoes	3.40	2.02	1.95	2.79	3.20	1.90	*	*	*	2.45	52
Auto accessories	8.00	5.22	1.93	1.92	1.12	1.00	*	*	4.00	2.73	47
Publishing and media	5.80	2.92	3.00	3.20	1.40	*	*	*	*	3.00	53
Sporting goods and toys	5.00	2.74	2.77	2.75	*	5.00	*	*	3.44	3.62	80
Gardening supplies	4.50	4.55	*	*	*	*	*	*	*	3.89	44
Canned and packaged foods	4.75	4.15	4.00	3.50	1.10	3.28	*	7.00	*	3.95	80
Major home appliances	3.20	3.71	4.49	4.15	4.05	4.30	*	6.00	2.80	4.18	50
Paint, varnish, wallpaper	7.10	4.34	4.60	5.00	3.95	*	*	*	3.00	5.00	45
Personal hygiene and health	14.60	2.22	*	*	*	*	*	*	28.00	13.85	32
Medicines and proprietaries	16.25	25.60	18.59	13.15	12.50	12.00	*	18.65	19.43	15.65	78
Cosmetics, beauty aids	17.18	13.00	*	*	*	*	*	*	*	16.47	27
Three preceding lines combined	16.25	16.00	13.37	11.65	13.00	12.00	*	18.65	15.00	15.00	137
All categories	5.00	3.00	2.25	2.00	2.00	1.40	1.00	1.00	2.72	2.50	2,325

* Fewer than three in sample.
Source: C. H. Sandage and S. R. Bernstein, *Study of Advertising As a Percent of Sales, 1954* (Chicago: Advertising Publications, Inc., 1956).

It makes no allowance for the trend of individual sales or cyclical fluctuations of business. It is based on the seeming assumption that advertising is to follow sales, rather than precede sales, in spite of the theoretical assumption that this is not the case. The amount to be spent can be increased or decreased by increasing or decreasing the percentage figure. The general principle underlying this approach is that a certain relationship exists between total sales and the advertising cost of obtaining those sales. The percentage figure finally applied to sales will determine the total sum to be spent. This will be discussed later in this chapter. The method would not be particularly weak if sales were relatively stable from year to year. It does not meet the problem of altering the appropriation to harmonize with cyclical changes in business activity.

Percentage of anticipated future sales. This method involves looking forward into the future and estimating the sales volume expected for the following year. It is similar to the use of a percentage of past sales, in that it is predicated on the philsophy that a certain relationship exists between sales and advertising cost in obtaining such sales. It differs, in that avertising is applied against the sales volume which advertising is supposed to help bring in. In this respect, it tends to correct some of the weaknesses of the method just reviewed. Its strength lies in the fact that advertising is tied to the future rather than to the past; it assumes that advertising precedes, rather than follows, sales. A company that opens up a new territory with the expectation of increasing its sales volume could not logically base the advertising appropriation on past sales. The expected future sales, however, could be used as a basis for making the appropriation.

Where this method is used, the advertising budget should be revised at least every three months. This revision will result from changes in the forecast of sales. Only by chance will a given forecast be accurate. As the year for which a forecast is made progresses, the error in the forecast for the remainder of the year can be reduced.

Combination percentage method. This method attempts to bring together the strong points of the past-sales and the future-sales methods and to eliminate most of their weaknesses. Just how much emphasis is to be placed on past sales and how much on future sales will be a problem for the budget committee. In practice, the relative importance of these two factors will vary from year to year. Past-sales records can be used to provide a picture of sales stability or instability. They can give some help in directing future actions. Often, the sales records of the past five years or so are averaged in with the forecast made for future sales, in order to give a percentage base. This practice has worked well for some of those companies selling products which have a relatively inelastic demand.

Objective-and-task method. The outstanding weakness of any sales-percentage basis for setting advertising appropriations lies in the fact that sales volume does not fluctuate regularly with the ease or difficulty of the selling task. A given amount of selling effort in one year will produce a certain sales volume. Increased activity of a competitor in one territory will force either a decrease in the company's sales or an increase in the selling effort applied to that territory. The sales-percentage method will not allow for this difference in difficulty of selling except by altering the percentage figure to be applied to sales.

The objective-and-task method offers perhaps the best basis for determining the size of an advertising budget. It focuses attention on the objectives to be reached and on the role to be played by advertising. It treats advertising as a cause of sales instead of a result of sales.

The first step when using this method is to define objectives, such as the volume of sales and profits to be attained, the share of market to be won, the consumer groups and market areas to be cultivated, and the nature of the consumer responses sought. Next, the tasks—or advertising strategy and tactics—deemed necessary to attain the objectives are planned. Then, the estimated cost of the required advertising program becomes the basis for setting the size of the budget.

"Marketing thinking dominates in setting up the objectives, in outlining the tasks, in estimating the costs, and finally, and most important, in reaching the critical decisions as to whether the objectives are realistic in view of the monetary outlay which is required to achieve them."[2]

This method, too, requires a periodic revision of the budget. If the advertising campaign results in greater returns than were expected, then expenditures can be reduced. Increases might be made where results are less than expected. Consider the example of advertising in which coupon returns are solicited; here, the cost per inquiry can be measured. The objective may be the receipt of 50,000 coupons during a year. The cost per inquiry may be estimated at $2. This would call for an appropriation of $100,000. If the first three months of advertising bring in inquiries at a cost of $1.50 each, then the budget can be reduced, since the object established can be reached for less than $100,000. This same procedure can be followed where the objective is an increase in total sales, or in the

[2] L. O. Brown, R. S. Lessler, W. M. Weilbacher, *Advertising Media* (New York: Ronald Press Company, 1957), p. 272.

number of customers, regardless of sales volume, or in the unit of purchase.

Advertisers are giving more and more attention to this procedure in setting advertising appropriations. The effectiveness of the method is more easily demonstrated in cases where particular advertisements or advertising campaigns can be measured for their ability to accomplish the end desired. The advance in the techniques of measuring advertising results has increased the use of the objective method.

Role of advertising in the marketing plan

Advertising is only one part of the total marketing process. The marketing process includes product design, pricing, distribution, personal selling, merchandising, sales management, etc. All of these functions are interrelated. Should any one of them break down, the danger to the business would be great. It is advisable for a company to determine, as accurately as possible, the most profitable combination of these various marketing elements. Decisions on this point will influence the size of the advertising budget.

Some companies require advertising to carry the full burden of generating sales. Other companies depend almost entirely on personal selling. Other things being equal, the greater the selling burden placed on advertising, the larger the budget tends to be.

New or established product.   The introduction of a new product generally requires a heavier advertising budget than is required to sustain an established product. The cost of launching a new product in a highly competitive field may very well wipe out any gross profit for the first year. A spectacular example of this was Procter & Gamble's launching of *Gleem* toothpaste. The product and copy were tested in local markets for almost a year; and when it went into national distribution the first-year budget was around $15 million. Yet, other products, *Dial* soap for example, achieved success with saturation campaigns in a few key local markets before going national. When a company's financial resources are inadequate for a heavy introductory campaign on a nationwide scale, a market-by-market campaign is often the best strategy.

Product differentiation.   If the product possesses distinct qualities which the buyer can readily observe, the amount of advertising needed would probably be less than that required for a product not so easily differentiated. When there are no apparent differences among competing brands, the budget should allow for a kind of "investment spending" that is designed to build a long-term capital asset referred to as the "brand image."

Profit margin per unit and volume of purchases. Profit margin and volume of purchases are inseparable considerations. If the profit margin is substantial, even though volume is relatively light there is considerable leeway in establishing the size of budget. We see this demonstrated in the case of automobiles. Car makers spent an average of $31.22 in measured media in 1965 to sell one car. Advertising cost for selling each Lincoln that year was $70.56.

On the other hand, a small profit margin per unit may be more than made up for by a large volume. Because volume of purchase is so high, cigarettes, soap, and detergent products can afford to spend a large amount on advertising. With sales of 68.1 billion Winston cigarettes in 1964, the Reynolds Tobacco Company was able to spend almost $19 million to advertise Winstons that year. Yet, this amounted to an advertising cost of only 5.4¢ per carton.

Extent of the market. Obviously, more money should be budgeted to advertise to a mass market on a national scale than to advertise to a class market that is geographically concentrated. The problem is to scale the size of the budget to the size of the market to be reached.

Advertising of competitors. Strangely enough, many companies follow the lead of the larger advertisers in their field, a situation which to some degree results from that more or less blind faith in advertising which so many possess. Apparently the reasoning is that, if the leaders advertise a great deal, they must be leaders because of their advertising; therefore, if one also wishes to become big or to be recognized as a leader, he must advertise extensively. This is fallacious reasoning, but common, nevertheless.

A more valid viewpoint would be that of considering advertising effectiveness in terms of sales rather than in terms of the amount of advertising done. In that sense a competitor's advertising might profitably be studied in terms of its ability to sell goods and not in terms of its size alone.

Cigarette advertising appears to have been built to some degree upon the policy of the leader. When an advertising-minded president of one of the large companies increased advertising appropriations and obtained the largest sales volume of any cigarette manufacturer, the easy conclusion as to the cause was found in advertising volume. This led to increases in appropriations by other companies.

Trend of business.   Paul G. Hoffman has commented on the question of advertising and business fluctuations in the following manner:

> In the past American concerns have kept their sales and advertising budgets high when business was good and easy to get. . . . When business was slow and sales tough to get, sales and advertising were pared to a minimum. This is neither good business nor good sense. If we are to have a stabilized market demand, selling pressures should be maintained—perhaps increased—at the first sign of a decline in business. We must avoid spending sprees when business is good, so that reserves will be available when extra pressure is needed. I know of no single way business managers can do more to help stabilize market demand than through greater stabilization of sales and advertising expenditures.[3]

The words of Mr. Hoffman apply to both periods of recession and inflation. It is perhaps easier to get advertisers to maintain or increase advertising efforts in periods of recession than to curtail appropriations during "spending sprees" by consumers. Yet, if restraint were practiced during business peaks, recessions might be modified. Concerted efforts along these lines might be necessary for adequate results.

A number of persons and agencies in the advertising field have made recommendations designed to encourage business to curtail advertising expenditures during periods of prosperity and to establish reserves during such periods to be used in recession years. Some government men recommended a tax on advertising in order to reduce its amount and thus relieve some inflationary pressures in the market.

S. R. Bernstein in an editorial in *Advertising Age*[4] proposed a plan which would encourage business not only to reduce advertising expenditures during boom times, but also to increase expenditures in periods of slow business. His proposal would have the United States Treasury allow individual business firms to divide advertising appropriations into two parts: (1) money to be spent during the current year and (2) a contingency for future years. Both parts of the appropriation would be treated as a deductible expense for the year when appropriated. This would encourage businesses to add monies to the advertising contingency or reserve fund when selling was relatively easy (consumer demand high) and have such funds available for use when consumers need strong urging to buy. Such a program would seem to have some promise for modifying extremes of a business cycle.

Size of the company.   The size of the company will influence materially the total amount spent for advertising. Not only will the small

---

[3] "The Advertising Appropriation," *Tide,* January 17, 1947, pp. 17–18.

[4] April 16, 1951, p. 12.

company have less money to spend, but it will have a smaller selling job to do. Consideration must also be given to the production capacity of the company. There is no value in advertising for the sake of advertising. Neither is there value in advertising to increase sales when such increase can neither be readily produced nor handled properly. Perhaps some individual business concerns would be better off if more emphasis were placed on reducing selling costs and stabilizing sales than in using all possible selling tools to increase sales.

Twenty-one companies marketing food and grocery products spent a total of $690 million on advertising in 1965. Twenty-three companies marketing drugs and cosmetics spent $630 million. Five companies in soaps and cleansers spent $465 million. Five automobile manufacturers spent $409 million. These 54 companies alone accounted for 25 percent of all national advertising expenditures. The top ten national advertisers in 1969 were:[5]

1.	Procter & Gamble	$275,000,000
2.	General Motors	171,500,000
3.	General Foods	151,000,000
4.	Sears, Roebuck & Co.	125,000,000
5.	Colgate-Palmolive	121,000,000
6.	Bristol-Myers	115,800,000
7.	Ford Motor Company	112,132,000
8.	American Home Products	97,000,000
9.	Warner-Lambert	92,000,000
10.	American Tel. & Tel.	85,808,000

Character of items to be charged to advertising

The size of an appropriation will depend somewhat on the items to be charged to the advertising account, and practice in this respect differs. Some companies include as advertising any sales-promotion expenditure which cannot conveniently be placed in other recognized accounts. Where, for example, should contributions to the community chest, the firemen's ball, Christmas presents to employees, liquor for parties, sales-convention expense, and similar expenditures be placed? The phrase, "Charge them to advertising," has become all too common. The advertising account, however, can be divided into these four major divisions: (1) media costs; (2) advertising production, or mechanical costs; (3) administrative overhead; and (4) research.

---

[5] *Advertising Age,* August 24, 1970.

Figure 31–1 shows the recommendations of *Printers' Ink* in respect to the items to be charged to advertising. Too often, items included in *Printers' Ink's* black list are charged to advertising.

Media costs represent the largest part of the advertising dollar. They include the cost of space purchased in magazines and newspapers, radio and television time, outdoor posters, car cards, electrical spectaculars, handbills, and direct mail. Production costs include those costs incurred in preparing an advertisement for mechanical reproduction. The major elements involved are art work, photographs, drawings, engravings, electrotypes, and matrices. These costs will claim from 3 to 10 percent of the total appropriation. Administrative overhead expenses can include anything the company auditor wishes to place there. Major items found in this classification are salaries of those working in the advertising department; office expense, such as stationery and postage but not direct-mail costs; rent of the department; telephone and telegraph expense; and traveling and entertainment expenses of the advertising department. These expenses will run from 5 to 10 percent of the advertising dollar. Research is a relative newcomer to advertising, but it is destined to be given greater consideration and to receive a greater part of the advertising dollar.

Naturally, budget committees must consider all the foregoing items when the budget is being drawn up. The media space costs by no means represent the total cost of advertising.

The McGraw-Hill Publishing Company in a study of industrial advertisers to determine what type of expense was charged to the advertising account found that practices differed considerably. See Table 31–2.

ALLOCATION OF ADVERTISING DOLLARS

The second major problem to be met by the budget is the allocation of advertising dollars. The principal allocations to be made are these: (1) to advertising functions, (2) to sales territories, (3) to media, and (4) to products.

Allocation to advertising functions

The items included in advertising have already been classified under the headings of media, general administrative overhead, costs of mechanical production, and research. The advertising budget should include the amounts allocated to each of these major functions. If a budget is

What charges belong in the advertising account?

- Printers' Ink guide to allocation of the advertising appropriation
- Charges that do not belong in the advertising account: black list
- Charges that belong in the advertising account: white list
- Charges that are borderline: gray list

WHITE LIST

(These charges belong in the advertising account)

SPACE:
(Paid advertising in all recognized mediums, including:)
Newspapers
Magazines
Business papers
Farm papers
Class journals
Car cards
Theater programs
Outdoor
Point of purchase
Novelties
Booklets
Directories
Direct advertising
Cartons and labels (for advertising purposes, such as in window displays)
Catalogs
Package inserts (when used

as advertising and not just as direction sheets)
House magazines to dealers or consumers
Motion pictures (including talking pictures) when used for advertising
Slides
Export advertising
Dealer helps
Reprints of advertisements used in mail or for display
Radio
Television
All other printed and lithographed material used directly for advertising purposes
ADMINISTRATION:
Salaries of advertising de-

partment executives and employees
Office supplies and fixtures used solely by advertising department
Commissions and fees to advertising agencies, special writers or advisers
Expenses incurred by salesmen when on work for advertising department
Traveling expenses of department employees engaged in departmental business
(Note: In some companies these go into special "Administration" account)
MECHANICAL:
Art work

Typography
Engraving
Mats
Electros
Photographs
Radio & TV production
Package design (advertising aspects only)
Etc.

MISCELLANEOUS:
Transportation of advertising material (to include postage and other carrying charges)
Fees to window display installation services
Other miscellaneous expenses connected with items on the White List

BLACK LIST

(These charges do not belong in the advertising account although too frequently they are put there:)

Free goods
Picnic and bazaar programs
Charitable, religious and fraternal donations
Other expenses for good-will purposes
Cartons
Labels
Instruction sheets
Package manufacture
Press agentry
Stationery used outside advertising department
Price lists
Salesmen's calling cards
Motion pictures for sales use only
House magazines going to factory employees
Bonuses to trade
Special rebates

Membership in trade associations
Entertaining customers or prospects
Annual reports
Showrooms
Demonstration stores
Sales convention expenses
Salesmen's samples (including photographs used in lieu of samples)
Welfare activities among employees
Such recreational activities as baseball teams, etc.
Sales expenses at conventions
Cost of salesmen's automobiles
Special editions which approach advertisers on good-will basis

GRAY LIST

(These are borderline charges, sometimes belonging in the advertising accounts and sometimes in other accounts, depending on circumstances:)

Samples
Demonstrations
Fairs
Canvassing
Rent
Light
Heat
Depreciation of equipment used by advertising department
Telephone and other overhead expenses, apportioned to advertising department
House magazines going to salesmen
Advertising automobiles
Premiums

Membership in associations or other organizations devoted to advertising
Testing bureaus
Advertising portfolios for salesmen
Contributions to special advertising funds of trade associations
Display signs on the factory or office building
Salesmen's catalogs
Research and market investigations
Advertising allowances to trade for co-operative effort

This chart is based on the principle that there are three types of expenses that generally are charged against the advertising appropriation.

The first charge is made up of expenses that are always justifiable under any scheme of accounting practice. These have been included in the white list of charges that belong in the advertising account.

A second type consists of those charges which cannot and should not under any system of accounting be justified as advertising expenses. These have been placed on the black list.

There is a third type of expense which can sometimes be justified under advertising and sometimes not. Frequently the justification for the charge depends upon the method used in carrying on a certain activity. These charges have been placed in a borderline gray list.

The chart is the result of the collaboration of the editors of PRINTERS' INK and several hundred advertisers. It has been revised for a third time for publication in this Annual, with the aid of advertising and accounting men. It may be considered, therefore, to represent sound, standard practice.

FIGURE 31–1. *Printers' Ink* white, black, and gray lists of charges to the advertising account

TABLE 31–2. Type of expenses charged to advertising by industrial advertisers

Expense item	Number reporting expense	Percentage charging to advertising
1. Direct mail	124	100
2. Mechanical costs for ads—artwork, engraving, etc.	145	100
3. Television advertising	12	100
4. Publication advertising	144	99
5. Commissions and fees to advertising agencies	128	98
6. Catalogue advertising	120	97
7. Dealer helps	87	97
8. Radio advertising	19	95
9. Directory advertising	128	95
10. Counter and window displays	62	95
11. Reprints of advertisements	134	94
12. Posters	34	94
13. Booklets	111	91
14. Company catalogues	127	90
15. House organs going to dealers or consumers	49	88
16. Car cards	6	83
17. Publicity	107	82
18. Novelties	72	79
19. Outdoor advertising	13	77
20. Maintenance of mailing lists	116	72
21. Display racks	42	71
22. Advertising portfolios for salesmen	73	70
23. Visual sales presentation	46	70
24. Films	45	69
25. Demonstrations and fairs	91	68
26. Premiums	17	65
27. Traveling expenses of advertising department personnel	114	64
28. Advertising department salaries	136	60
29. Public relations	89	51
30. Advertising department office supplies	127	47
31. Price lists	125	46
32. Market research	59	37
33. Free goods	37	35
34. Showrooms	35	34
35. Association membership	134	32
36. Telephone and other overhead expenses	126	31
37. Rent, light, heat for the advertising department	110	27
38. Sales convention costs	102	26
39. Display signs on factory or office building	71	24
40. House magazines for company employees	63	24
41. Salesmen's samples	92	21
42. Charitable, religious and fraternal donations	124	20
43. Cartons and labels	127	19
44. Testing bureaus	37	19
45. Entertaining customers and prospects	128	16
46. Salesmen's calling cards	133	16
47. Annual reports	78	13
48. Company recreational programs	92	3
49. Employee welfare activity	107	2

Source: A. R. Venezian, "How Much Water in Your Ad Budget?" *Printers' Ink,* May 16, 1952, p. 38.

to be a guide and a control, then it should be altered only for good reasons.

Amounts allocated to media will normally take from 70 to 90 percent of the total advertising budget. Administrative overhead will vary from 5 to 20 percent of the total, and production costs should average about 5 percent. Research may range from nothing to 15 percent of the total. The relative amounts distributed to each will depend to some extent on whether the company plans and executes its own advertising or depends on an agency to do much of the work. This element will influence particularly the relative amounts going to overhead and research.

The expenditures for research have often been charged to administrative overhead or to the sales department. Occasionally a separate research department having its own budget is maintained. This particular item has been, for the most part, relatively small; hence, its place in the budget has not been of particular consequence. This situation has been unfortunate because of the fundamental value of research in charting the way for an effective advertising and selling campaign. A more detailed treatment of this factor has already been presented in previous chapters.

Allocation to sales territories

The sales department and the advertising department must work together in allocating the total advertising expenditure by territories. Various factors will determine this distribution. These would include the number of dealer outlets in a given territory, the population, the number of salesmen, the sales potentialities, and the character of the media reaching the district.

The most valid test of distribution is that of sales potentialities. The number of dealer outlets is not in itself significant. The volume of dealer sales would be more valuable in so far as this would give some indication of the sales possibilities of the territory. Population figures are not of outstanding importance. One territory with a population of 100,000 might easily produce more sales than one having twice the number of people. It is therefore important to consider the purchasing power, buying habits, desires, and general character of the population rather than numbers alone.

Once a figure representing sales potentials has been obtained, the character of the media reaching the given territory and the dealer representation must be considered. In a large area with a scattered population, newspaper advertising might be inadvisable. Where a company does not have dealer representation nationally, the use of national advertising will usually be wasteful. Under such conditions, a relatively larger proportion of the total selling effort may have to be done through personal selling. These factors will limit a strict observance of sales potentials in allocating advertising to different territories.

Allocation to media

By far the largest part of the budget is allocated to media. The distribution of planned expenditures among the various media to be used largely determines the scope and character of the entire advertising program. The number and kinds of people to be reached, the number of messages to be delivered, when the messages are to be delivered—these are basic dimensions of any advertising program and should be carefully planned.

Reach is a term used to designate the number of different homes or individuals reached by a given medium or combination of media over a period of time. Reach is expressed as a percent of all the homes or individuals comprising the market involved. When two or more issues of the same media vehicle or when two or more vehicles are used, there is likely to be some "duplication," i.e., some homes or individuals will be reached by both issues or by both vehicles. For example, the reach of a single issue of *Life* is 34 percent of all U.S. homes. With three issues, *Life's* reach extends to 46 percent of U.S. homes, half of which receive all three issues. For television, the term *reach* generally is used to designate the number of different homes (expressed as a percent of total homes) reached over a four-week period. A major network television program, Red Skelton for example, reaches 50 percent of U.S. homes with four telecasts. Even though reach deals with an unduplicated audience, duplication need not and generally cannot be avoided. Repetition can be a good thing. However, the advertiser's first objective should be to seek that combination of media that will maximize the reach among his prime prospects.

Frequency refers to the average number of times different households or individuals are reached by a particular media schedule within a period of time. For example, the frequency attained with three issues of *Life* is 2.2 times. In other words, in the 46 percent of U.S. homes reached by at least one of the three issues of *Life* an average of 2.2 issues are read. Frequency of impressions is depended upon to reinforce the image, to remind, and to sustain a share of the customer's mind. The greater the frequency, the greater the probability that the message will make a deep and lasting impression.

Continuity refers to the overall pattern of message deliveries over a period of time. Insertions and/or broadcasts may be scheduled at about the same frequency the year around, or they may be concentrated in particular seasons. Continuity may also pertain to the way a specific medium is used. A continuous schedule in the same medium provides repeated impressions on the same audience. Shifting from one medium to another tends to sacrifice continuity in favor of wider coverage.

Size of the message, measured in space units for print media and time units for broadcast media, affects the strength of each impression. It is generally assumed that a two-page spread makes a stronger impression than a single page; that a full page makes a stronger impression than a half page; that a one-minute commercial makes a stronger impression than a thirty-second commercial, etc. Color generally strengthens the message, and also increases the cost. Therefore, the extent to which color is to be used should be allowed for in the budget.

Interrelation of reach, frequency, continuity, and size

When planning media expenditures the advertiser must deal with reach, frequency, continuity, and size as interrelated and interdependent elements that can be combined to form many different message delivery patterns. The interdependence of these elements and the variety of possible combinations are indicated in the following alternatives:

1. Greater reach at the expense of frequency, and/or continuity, and/or message size.
2. Greater frequency at the expense of reach, and/or continuity, and/or message size.
3. Greater continuity at the expense of reach, and/or frequency, and/or message size.
4. Larger message size at the expense of reach, and/or frequency, and/or continuity.

It should be apparent that there is no single combination of these elements that is ideally suited to every advertising situation. Each advertiser, within the limitations of his budget, must develop the pattern of reach, frequency, continuity, and message sizes that he deems best to achieve his own objectives. If he does not deliver messages broadly enough, or in sufficient number, or with sufficient regularity, his advertising dollars will be largely wasted.

Allocation to products to be advertised

It is generally good policy to concentrate advertising effort on those products and price lines readily accepted by the public. When the public has indicated its preference for a particular product, common sense would seem to dictate the policy of catering to this public desire. It is not necessarily the line of least resistance but, rather, the line of good business judgment to generally place most emphasis on major volume items.

The advertising budget should list the articles to be advertised and the amounts to be spent on each. This will provide the control over policies carefully worked out in advance.

Many companies make products whose heavy sales come at different times of the year. Postum and prepared breakfast foods are examples. The seasonal factor must be considered in distributing the advertising appropriation for these products. Seasonal variation is especially important to the department store advertiser. The situation seems to have discouraged many such advertisers to the extent that they do not draw up a systematic advertising budget. The more obvious seasonal goods are advertised during the period in which they are in great demand, but the less obvious ones are often advertised out of their natural season unless a budget has been drawn up in harmony with sales figures.

Some retail advertisers have focused undue attention on allocating funds to specific products in terms of what competitors are promoting rather than on the basis of what items seem to be in greatest demand at the moment. One national service firm measures the amount of newspaper advertising space devoted to specific types of products by price lines and recommends that such figures be a guide to individual store allocation of funds.

ADMINISTRATION AND CONTROL OF THE BUDGET

A successful budget system requires a constant and careful check on all expenditures. Care must be taken to see that advertising practice does not run counter to the plans worked out carefully and systematically and incorporated into the budget. This will require a periodic checking of expenditures, especially for such items as window displays, special sampling campaigns, convention expenses, and similar items that are not subject to specific contracts.

Complete and systematic records should be kept if proper administration and control are to be accomplished. Such records should consist of the total amount appropriated for advertising and the complete and detailed listing of how this is to be expended. Not only the amounts for the major advertising expenditures, but also the anticipated expenditures for each item within each major group, should be included. If possible, distribution should be made to specific media. Certain amounts might be set aside for (1) paying the space cost of 13 advertisements in *Better Homes and Gardens*, (2) printing and distributing 50,000 handbills, (3) preparing 1,000 window displays, or (4) paying the cost of fifty-two 15-minute radio programs. The same detail should be provided for production costs, research, and administrative expenses.

Not all of the appropriation should be allocated to specific purposes. A certain amount should be set aside as a reserve to meet unforeseen conditions. Research during the year might uncover territories in which additional advertising should be placed; some might need extra promotion. Costs of advertising might rise unexpectedly, and business conditions might change a great deal within the year. A reserve will allow a rearrangement of expenditures to harmonize the advertising program with present conditions.

Proper control will involve the checking of sales results by products and by sales territories. On the basis of these checks, the budget can be changed to harmonize with the philosophy which directed its creation. A budget is, of necessity, made for the future. When sales of a given product or sales in a particular territory differ materially from the figures established in the budget, the budget should be changed to harmonize with the facts.

QUESTIONS AND PROBLEMS

1. There is no standard formula for determining the size of the advertising budget because no two advertising situations are alike and there is no way of readily measuring the results achieved from a given advertising investment. Discuss.
2. The advertising budget expressed as a percent of sales tends to be lower for industrial goods than for consumer goods. Do you agree or disagree? Explain.
3. Advertising dollars represent both an expenditure and an investment. Explain.
4. The objective-and-task method for determining the size of the advertising

budget focuses attention on the job to be done and treats advertising as a cause of sales instead of a result of sales. Discuss.

5. Reach, frequency, continuity, and message size are elements of an advertising campaign that must be simultaneously determined. Explain.

6. What relation should exist between the sales potentials for the various market areas as determined by market research and the size of the advertising appropriations for those areas?

7. Do you believe that using the amount of advertising done by competitors as a guide in formulating a plan is advisable? Why?

8. In what ways might cyclical fluctuations in business affect the advertising budget?

9. If you were a beginner in national advertising, what factors would you consider in deciding whether to start out on a large scale or to develop slowly?

10. The Modern Maid Manufacturing Company manufactures a line of incinerators comprising three distinct classes: those for private homes, those for apartment buildings, and those for hotels or institutions. The budget submitted called for an expenditure of $200,000 for the new year. The method of presentation follows. Criticize this in view of the suggestions given in this chapter.

Productions and overhead expenses		$ 10,000
Media costs:		
Magazines	$75,000	
Newspapers	40,000	
Radio	10,000	
Dealer helps	65,000	190,000
		$200,000

11. "It is generally a good policy to concentrate advertising effort on those products and price lines most readily accepted by the public." Do you agree? Why?

Index

INDEX

693

This book has been set in 12 and 10 point Garmond Oldstyle, leaded 1 point. Part numbers and titles and chapter numbers and titles are in Optima and Optima Semibold. The size of the type page is 27 by 45 picas.